Christianity

Christianity

An Introduction

Second Edition

Alister E. McGrath

Blackwell Publishing

BLACKWELL PUBLISHING

350 Main Street, Malden, MA 02148-5020, USA
9600 Garsington Road, Oxford OX4 2DQ, UK
550 Swanston Street, Carlton, Victoria 3053, Australia

First edition published 1997 as *An Introduction to Christianity*
Second edition published 2006 by Blackwell Publishing Ltd

1   2006

Library of Congress Cataloging-in-Publication Data

McGrath, Alister E., 1953–
Christianity : an introduction / Alister E. McGrath.—2nd ed.
p. cm.
Includes bibliographical references and index.
ISBN-13: 978-1-4051-0901-7 (alk. paper)
ISBN-10: 1-4051-0901-7 (alk. paper)
ISBN-13: 978-1-4051-0899-7 (pbk. : alk. paper)
ISBN-10: 1-4051-0899-1 (pbk. : alk. paper)
1. Christianity. I. Title.

BR121.3.M33 2006
230—dc22
2005012639

A catalogue record for this title is available from the British Library.

Set in 10.5 on 12.5pt PhotinaMT
by SPI Publishers Services Pvt Ltd., Pondicherry
Printed and bound in the United Kingdom
by TJ International Ltd,
Padstow, Cornwall.

The publisher's policy is to use permanent paper from mills that operate a
sustainable forestry policy, and which has been manufactured from pulp
processed using acid-free and elementary chlorine-free practices. Furthermore,
the publisher ensures that the text paper and cover board used have met
acceptable environmental accreditation standards.

For further information on
Blackwell Publishing, visit our website:
www.blackwellpublishing.com

Brief Table of Contents

Contents

Plates

Figures and Maps

Preface

A nyone interested in understanding the modern world, or the process by which it came into existence, needs to understand something about the Christian faith. Christianity is by far the largest religion in the world, with somewhere between 1,250 and 1,750 million adherents, depending on the criteria employed. To understand the modern world, it is important to appreciate why Christianity continues to be such an important presence in, for example, the United States, and a growing presence in China. A basic understanding of the beliefs of Christianity is therefore essential to a person's basic education, particularly in western cultures whose traditions and values have been deeply shaped by Christianity.

There is also a fascination with Christianity, particularly the person of Jesus, on the part of many who would not consider themselves to be Christians. In April 1996, the American evangelist Billy Graham spoke for an hour on the subject of the Christian gospel and its relevance for today. The talk was relayed by video and other links to a worldwide audience now known to have been in the region of 2.5 *billion* people. In western culture, a decline in church attendance has often been understood to imply a loss of interest in religion in general, or Christianity in particular. However, this represents a serious misreading of a complex situation. There has been a growing drift away from traditional institutions – whether these are social, political, or religious – in the west, as people have opted for more individual-orientated activities. Christianity, which offers personal spiritual consolation as well as a community-based ethos, continues to have a considerable appeal, which it is important to understand.

This book sets out to introduce Christianity to its readers. It is an introduction in the proper sense of the term, as it assumes that those using it know little about Christianity, and would welcome an introduction to its ideas, history, development, and distinctive ethos. The present work aims to meet this need by providing an entry-level introduction to Christianity, understood both as a system of beliefs and as a social reality. Every idea and development is introduced and explained; wherever possible, the reader is given information about suitable access points for further study of all the themes dealt with in this volume. Every effort has been made to keep the language and style of this book as simple as possible.

Introduction

At some point around the year 60, the Roman authorities woke up to the fact that there seemed to be a new secret society in the heart of their city, which was rapidly gaining recruits. They had not the slightest idea what it was all about, although it was clearly due to some agitator. The reports that filtered back spoke of some mysterious and dark figure called "Chrestus" or "Christus" being the cause of all the trouble. His origins lay in one of the more obscure and backward parts of the Roman empire. But who was he? And what was this new religion all about? Was it something they should be worried about, or could they safely ignore it?

It soon became clear that this new religion might have the potential to cause real trouble. The great fire which swept through Rome at the time of the emperor Nero in 64 was conveniently blamed on this new religious group. Nobody liked them much, and they were an obvious scapegoat for the failings of the Roman authorities to deal with the fire and its aftermath. The Roman historian Cornelius Tacitus gave a full account of this event some fifty years later. He identified this new religious group as "the Christians," a group who took their name from someone called "Christus," who had been executed by Pontius Pilate back in the reign of Tiberius. This "pernicious superstition" had found its way to Rome, where it had gained a huge following. It is clear that Tacitus understands the word "Christian" to be a term of abuse.

Yet, muddled and confused though the official Roman accounts of this movement may be, they were clear that it centered, in some way, on the figure of "Christus." It was not regarded as being of any permanent significance, but was rather seen as something of a minor irritation. At worst, it was a threat to the cult of emperor worship. Yet less than three hundred years later, this new religion had become the official religion of the Roman empire. Where once Roman historians dated events from the founding of the city of Rome, those events would now be dated from the coming of Jesus Christ.

So what was this new religion? What did it teach? Where did it come from? Why was it so attractive? How did it come to be so influential in its first few centuries? What happened after it had achieved such success at Rome? And how has it shaped the lives of individuals and the history of the human race? It is these questions which this book will attempt to begin to answer. The study of Christianity is one of the most fascinating, stimulating, and intellectually and spiritually rewarding undertakings available to anyone. This little book aims to lay the foundations for such a study, opening doors to discovering more about the world's leading religion. It can only hope to whet its readers' appetites, and lead them to explore Christianity in much greater detail.

Encountering Christianity: Some Gateways

Christianity is a way of life, not simply a set of ideas. As a result, it can be encountered in many different ways. So what are the gateways to the Christian faith? And how can these act as portals to a deeper understanding of the movement? In what follows, we shall explore the most common ways of encountering Christianity, and explain how this may help illuminate its distinctive nature.

Texts

Most religions – though not all – have some texts that they regard as having special significance. In the case of Christianity, the most important such text is known as "the Bible." In most parts of the world – though not in some more repressive Islamic countries – it can be bought openly in public bookstores. It is regularly read in church services and private devotions. Many parts of it have been set to music. One of the best known of these works is the *Messiah*, by George Frederick Handel (1685–1759), the libretto of which is a series of biblical passages dealing with the coming of Christ. We shall consider the nature and contents of the Bible in chapters 2–4 of this work.

Services

For many, the Christian faith is encountered through attending church services. For those who are not themselves Christians, this experience is most likely to take the form of attending the wedding or funeral of Christian friends or relatives. The text of these services – often referred to as the "liturgy" – gives some important indications of the core beliefs and values of Christianity. We shall explore the structure of Christian worship in chapter 9, and explain how experiencing such worship can help deepen your understanding of Christianity. We shall also be exploring the different forms of worship that are associated with various forms of Christianity, and how these cast light on their respective visions of the Christian faith.

Buildings

The buildings of Christian churches are themselves important gateways to the Christian faith. Whether you attend a church as a tourist or a worshipper, its physical structure alone can act as a portal to an understanding of Christianity. Older Christian churches – such as the great cathedrals of medieval Europe – were often designed to communicate aspects of the Christian faith to a largely illiterate culture. Many cathedrals are cross-shaped, to remind believers of the central place of the cross in Christian life, thought, and worship. A baptismal font was often placed near the main door of the church, to symbolize the idea that baptism was the means by which entry to the church took place. Stained glass windows acted as windows into the mysteries of faith. The walls of churches were often painted with scenes from the gospels, to remind worshippers of the basic events on which their faith was based. To put it succinctly: church buildings embody Christian belief. In this book, we shall explore some of the ways in which church buildings can be "read" in this way.

Music

The Christian emphasis on the public worship of God led to a new interest in developing music to accompany it. The vast assortment of music designed to accompany worship ranges from the simplicity of monastic plainsong to the complex musical structures of Verdi's *Requiem* or Beethoven's *Missa Solemnis*. A huge variety of Christian texts have been set to music. These are regularly performed, both as part of Christian worship and as a celebration of human cultural activity in general. Once more, music can act as a portal to the core values and ideas of Christianity. We shall explore this point later in chapter 9.

Art

Finally, we come to the importance of Christian art. From the outset, Christians realized the value of the visual arts in communicating their faith. Sculpture and paintings were both used to depict key scenes from the gospels. Some of the best-known images in history derive from this genre – for example, Michelangelo's *Creation of Adam* and Leonardo da Vinci's *Last Supper*. The crucifixion came to be of especial significance, on account of its central place in Christian thought and devotion. We shall explore some aspects of Christian art in chapter 9, and indicate how art illuminates key themes of the gospel.

From what has been said, it will be clear that Christianity is far more than just a set of ideas. This has an important implication: Christianity can never be understood or appreciated properly by reading a book about it. It is often difficult to understand or appreciate the inner dynamics of Christianity if you are looking in from the outside. At times, it is like looking into a lighted room from outside, being able to see people moving and talking, yet not understanding what is being said or done. This book will be of some use to you, just as a guide book to Rome or New Zealand will help prepare you for a visit to those places. But neither this introduction nor those guide books can be a substitute for encountering the real thing.

This book will certainly provide you with invaluable information about what Christians believe, and why. But it cannot hope to do justice to Christianity as a way of living. For this reason, you will find it helpful to get to know some Christians, and ask them to take you to their meetings, or talk about their faith. A book can never convey adequately the full richness and diversity of the Christian faith. This introductory work will be useful as an introduction to the beliefs of Christians, and help you to understand the central themes of the Christian faith. Yet being a Christian is not just about beliefs and values; it is about a definite way of living which involves everyday life being affected in certain ways by faith. At its most obvious, this is reflected in going to a church or other form of Christian community which meets for prayer and worship.

While this book will attempt to describe at least some aspects of Christian living, you need to be aware that the best way of understanding Christianity at this point is to get involved in a local Christian church or community. There are enormous variations in the ways in which Christianity expresses itself, reflecting differences of climate, geography, culture, tradition, and theology.

So where do we start? What is the most helpful entry point to a study of Christianity? Looking at Christian beliefs? Exploring the history of the church? Surveying Christian art? In the end, the best place to begin is the historical event that got all of these under way. It is impossible to think or talk about any aspect of the Christian faith without talking about Jesus Christ. He is the center from which every aspect of the Christian faith radiates outward. We therefore turn immediately to begin our exploration of Jesus, and his significance for Christianity.

1

Jesus of Nazareth

It is entirely proper to begin an account of Christianity by engaging with the central figure of the movement – Jesus of Nazareth. The commonsense view of Jesus is that he is one of many religious teachers competing for attention in the spiritual marketplace. His significance lies in the excellence – or otherwise – of what he taught, and how he behaved.

Christians have always appreciated the importance of both the teaching and example of Jesus of Nazareth. However, it soon becomes clear that Christians do not see Jesus simply as a teacher or role model. To describe Jesus as the Christian's rabbi or guru – to borrow categories from other religious cultures – is to misunderstand the very distinctive Christian belief that Jesus is God incarnate, the son of God who died on the cross and was raised again in order to deliver humanity from its sins. Jesus simply cannot be assimilated to the categories of "teacher" or "role model." He is both; yet he transcends both.

These are difficult yet important ideas, which we will examine at several points in this work, especially in chapter 6. The first chapter of this book will lay the foundations for the Christian understanding of Jesus. To begin with, we shall try to identify some of the fundamental elements of the Christian understanding of Jesus.

The Centrality of Jesus to the Christian Faith

The figure of Jesus Christ is central to Christianity. Indeed, there is a sense in which Christianity *is* Jesus Christ. Christianity is not a set of self-contained and freestanding ideas; it represents a sustained response to the questions raised by the life, death, and resurrection of Jesus Christ. Christianity is a historical religion, which came into being in response to a specific set of events, which center upon Jesus Christ, and to which Christian theology is obliged to return in the course of its speculation and reflection.

Yet the importance of Jesus far exceeds his historical significance. For Christians, Jesus is more than the founder of their faith: he is the one who makes God known, who makes salvation possible, and who models the new life with God that results from faith. To set this out more formally:

1 Jesus tells us and shows us what God is like.
2 Jesus makes a new relationship with God possible.

3 Jesus himself lives out a God-focused life, which Christians are encouraged to imitate.

In what follows, we shall explore each of these ideas briefly.

First, Jesus reveals God. The New Testament sets out the immensely important idea that God, who is invisible, is in some way made known or made visible through Jesus. Jesus does not simply tell us what God is like, or teach us what God expects of us. He enables us to see God. Christianity holds that Jesus reveals both the *will* and the *face* of God. One of the dominant themes in the Old Testament is that nobody has ever seen God. A number of factors lie behind this assertion, including the belief that human nature is simply not capable of grasping or coping with the full wonder of God, and the related belief that human sinfulness prevents a clear apprehension of God.

Two passages from the New Testament letters bring this point out with particular clarity. Colossians 1:15 affirms that Jesus "is the image of the invisible God." The Greek word here translated as "image" (*eikon*) has a number of senses, conveying the basic idea of correspondence between the image and the reality which it depicts. It is used elsewhere in the New Testament to refer to the image of the emperor on Roman coinage. The same theme emerges as important at Hebrews 1:3, which refers to Jesus as "the exact representation of [God's] being." The Greek word here translated as "exact representation" (*charakter*) is also used to refer to the imprint on coins, perhaps with the sense of the exact reproduction of a likeness. The word occasionally seems to have the sense of "a copy." Both these passages express the idea that Jesus in some way makes God known in a way which would otherwise not be possible.

"Anyone who has seen me has seen the Father" (John 14:9). These remarkable words, so characteristic of John's gospel, emphasize that God the Father speaks and acts in the Son. God is revealed through, in, and by Jesus. The Christian claim that God is most fully and authentically revealed in the face of Jesus Christ is simply a summary statement of the kaleidoscope of New Testament descriptions of the intimate relation between the Father and the Son, between God and Jesus. To have seen Jesus is to have seen the Father. Martin Luther makes this point as follows. For Luther, Islam has the Qur'an and Judaism the Torah; yet for Christians, "God does not want to be known except through Christ; nor can he be known in any other way."

To put this another way: God chooses to be revealed definitively in this form and in this way – that is, in Jesus of Nazareth. This point is stated clearly by the Swiss theologian Karl Barth (1886–1968), widely regarded as one of the greatest theological writers of the twentieth century. For Barth, Jesus is the key to an understanding of the nature of God:

> When Holy Scripture speaks of God, it does not permit us to let our attention or thoughts wander at random ... When Holy Scripture speaks of God, it concentrates our attention and thoughts upon one single point and what is to be known at that point ... If we ask further concerning the one point upon which, according to Scripture, our attention and thoughts should and must be concentrated, then from first to last the Bible directs us to the name of Jesus Christ.

This point is developed further in the doctrine of the incarnation (see pp. 139–141) – the characteristically Christian idea that God entered into the world of time and space in the person of Jesus Christ. The doctrine of the incarnation provides a basis for the distinctively Christian belief that Jesus provides a "window into God." It also underlies the practice, especially associated with the Orthodox church, of using icons in worship and personal devotion.

In the second place, Jesus is understood to be the ground of salvation. One of the more significant titles used in the New Testament to refer to Jesus is "Savior." Jesus is the "Savior, who is Christ the Lord" (Luke 2:11). One of the earliest symbols of faith used by Christians was a fish. The use of this symbol may partly reflect the fact that the first disciples were fishermen. But the real reason is that the five Greek letters spelling out "fish" in Greek (I-CH-TH-U-S) are an acronym of the Christian slogan "Jesus Christ, Son of God, Savior." According to the New Testament, Jesus saves his people from their sins (Matthew 1:21); in his name alone is there salvation (Acts 4:12); he is the "author of their salvation" (Hebrews 2:10).

Finally, Jesus is the model of the redeemed life. The Christian is called to "imitate Christ." To understand the importance of this point, we shall consider a passage in the New Testament in which Paul asks his readers to "be imitators of God" (Ephesians 5:1). But if Christians are to be "imitators of God," they need to know what God is like. The doctrine of the incarnation affirms that Jesus Christ tells us in his words, and shows us in his actions, what God is like. He fleshes out what God is like. Or, to put it another way, Christians declare that God is Christlike.

To give an example of the application of this point. Christians are urged to "love one another" (1 John 4:7–11). But what does this word "love" mean? The doctrine of the incarnation allows us to flesh out what we mean by the "love of God." Throughout his ministry, we notice Jesus Christ accepting individuals, being prepared to associate with those who were regarded as socially acceptable as much as those who were regarded as social outcasts. The good news of the kingdom was for all, without distinction. That same pattern of divine acceptance should be ours as well. To recognize that Jesus Christ is God incarnate is to recognize that he maps out patterns of behavior that ought to be characteristic of Chris-

tians. Yet many Christian writers would want to add a theological footnote at this point. We are not saved by imitating Christ; it is by being saved that we are moved to be conformed to his likeness, as we seek to be imitators of God through him.

Jesus of Nazareth, then, is of central importance to the Christian faith. But what do we know about him? What are the sources for our knowledge of him? To begin to answer this question, we may turn to consider the four gospels of the New Testament.

The Gospels and Jesus

The gospel of Mark, widely regarded as the first of the gospels to be committed to writing, opens with the following words: "The beginning of the gospel of Jesus Christ, the Son of God" (Mark 1:1). It is all too easy to assume that the word "gospel" refers to the book which Mark wrote. Yet Mark is not referring to his book with these words. He is declaring that the "gospel" – that is, the "good news" – *is* Jesus Christ. After two thousand years or so, people have got used to referring to the first four books of the New Testament as "gospels." Yet the reason that the books are called "gospels" is that they deal with the central figure of the Christian gospel – Jesus Christ, or, to use a title often encountered in the gospels and the Acts of the Apostles, Jesus of Nazareth.

So what does this important word "gospel" mean? As we have seen, it has come to refer to one particular type of writing – a book which deals with the life of Jesus. Its real meaning, however, is "good news." The New Testament was written in the everyday Greek of the first century (a particular form of Greek which is often referred to as *koine*, meaning "common" or "everyday"). The Greek word which is translated as "gospel" is *evangelion*, which comes from two Greek roots meaning "good" and "news" or "message." The term refers to something having happened with positive implications for its hearers. The gospels are thus books which relate "the good news of Jesus Christ."

If Christianity has a center, it is Jesus Christ. It is impossible for the Christian to talk about God, salvation, or worship without bringing Jesus into the discussion, whether explicitly or implicitly. For New Testament writers, Jesus is a window into the nature, character, and purposes of God. Jesus is the ground of salvation. Since the time of the New Testament onwards, Christians have worshipped Jesus as the risen Lord and Savior of the world.

It is interesting to compare the Christian understanding of the role of Jesus Christ with the Islamic understanding of the role of Mohammed. For Islam, Mohammed himself is not of fundamental importance, except in that he is the bearer of revelation from Allah. Allah is unknown and unknowable. Through Mohammed, Allah's will for humanity is made known. Islam therefore tends to center on principles revealed through Mohammed by Allah. Yet Christianity focuses on the person of Jesus. Islam speaks of a revelation *from* God, where Christianity speaks of a revelation *of* God, seeing that revelation being concentrated and focused on the person of Jesus.

The name "Jesus Christ" needs some explanation. The word "Jesus" (Hebrew *Yeshua*) literally means "God saves." The word "Christ" is actually a title; the name "Jesus Christ" is perhaps better written as "Jesus the Christ." The word "Christ" is the Greek version of the Hebrew term "Messiah," referring to an individual singled out or raised up by God for some special purpose. There seems to have been a general consensus that the Messiah would be like a new King David, opening up a new era in Israel's history. While Israel looked forward to the coming of a messianic age, different groups understood this in different ways. The Jewish desert community at Qumran thought of the Messiah in priestly terms, whereas others had more political expectations. Yet despite these differences, the hope of the coming of a "messianic age" seems to have been widespread. It can certainly be detected in the gospel accounts of the ministry of Jesus.

During the first phase of its existence, Christianity existed alongside (or even within) Judaism. Christians insisted that the God who was known and encountered by the great heroes of faith of Israel – such as Abraham, Isaac, Jacob, and Moses – was the same God who was more fully and clearly revealed in Jesus. It was therefore of importance to the early Christians to demonstrate that Jesus of Nazareth, the central figure of the Christian faith, brought the great messianic hopes of Judaism to fulfillment. As the question of the relationship of Christianity to Judaism became of less pressing importance, there is some evidence that the original meaning of the term "Christ" became lost. It seems to have become simply a name, whose implications were not fully understood.

In any case, Jesus was referred to in other ways. In the gospels and Acts of the Apostles (an early compilation of accounts of the expansion of the church in the 40s and 50s), Jesus is often referred to simply as "Jesus of Nazareth." This seems to have been something like a term of contempt. Nazareth was a village about 100 kilometers north of Jerusalem, in the region of Galilee. For historical reasons, Jews from the region of Judaea (which includes the city of Jerusalem) tended to look down on Jews from Galilee, seeing them as less Jewish and less cultured than themselves. This sense of religious and cultural superiority underlies one incident reported in the New Testament, in which Jews from Jerusalem refused to take seriously the idea that the Messiah could come from Galilee (John 7:41). From another

1.1 The Sea of Galilee. AKG-Images/Erich Lessing.

incident, it is clear that the distinctive accent of Galilean Jews marked them out as strangers in Jerusalem (Matthew 26:73).

Our primary sources for the life of Jesus are the four gospels of the New Testament – Matthew, Mark, Luke, and John. Roman historians provide relatively little helpful information concerning Jesus, although they are important sources for our understanding of the way in which Jesus was understood within early Christianity. For this reason, we shall focus on the portrayal of the history of Jesus in the gospels. We shall consider their general features, as well as the distinctive characteristics of each of the four gospels, in chapter 4. The first three of these are usually referred to as "synoptic gospels." This term derives from the Greek word *synopsis*, meaning "summary" or "list." It points to the way in which each of these gospels presents related, though distinct, accounts of the ministry of Jesus. Matthew's gospel, for example, brings out the importance of Jesus for the Jewish people, and is particu-

larly concerned to explore the way in which Jesus brings the expectations of Israel to their proper fulfillment. Mark's gospel takes the form of a rapidly paced narrative, often leaving readers breathless, as they are led from one event to another. Luke's gospel has a particular interest in bringing out the importance of Jesus for non-Jewish readers. John's gospel is more reflective in its approach, characterized by a distinctive emphasis on the way in which the coming of Jesus brings eternal life to those who believe in him.

The gospels cannot really be thought of as biographies of Jesus, in the modern sense of the term, although they unquestionably provide us with much helpful biographical information. For example, they do not present us with a full account of the life of Jesus. Mark's gospel, for instance, focuses on a few years of Jesus' life, characterized by his intensive public ministry and ending in his crucifixion and resurrection. Matthew and Luke both relate brief accounts of the birth and childhood of

Jesus, before resuming their narratives with the public ministry of Jesus. It is clear that the gospels draw on and bring together several sources to build up their overall portrayal of the identity and significance of Jesus. Thus Mark's gospel draws on material which is traditionally attributed to Peter, the leading disciple of Jesus. Furthermore, the gospels are more concerned with bringing out the significance of the life of Jesus than with documenting it in full detail. Nevertheless, the gospels present us with a portrait of Jesus which mingles history and theology to tell us who Jesus is – not simply in terms of his historical identity, but in terms of his continuing importance for the world.

Jesus and Roman Historians

There are few references to Jesus in the writings of Roman historians, who had relatively little time for events which took place in the backwaters of their empire. Their histories focused on Rome itself, and the leading figures and events which shaped its destiny. Their interest in Christianity therefore concentrated on its impact at Rome itself. They had little interest in tracing its historical origins, although they were aware that it could be traced back to events in the Roman province of Judaea at a time when it was governed by Pontius Pilate.

Three Roman historians make reference to Jesus in their writings: Pliny the Younger, writing around AD 111 to Trajan about the rapid spread of Christianity in Asia Minor; Tacitus, who wrote in approximately AD 115 concerning the events of AD 64, in which Nero made Christians the scapegoats for the burning of Rome; and Suetonius, writing around AD 120 concerning certain events in the reign of the emperor Claudius. Suetonius refers to a certain "Chrestus" who was behind rioting at Rome. "Christus" was still an unfamiliar name to Romans at this stage, whereas "Chrestus" was a common name for slaves (meaning "someone who is useful"). Even in the third and fourth centuries, Christian writers were still complaining about people who misspelled "Christus" as "Chrestus." The following points emerge from the brief comments of these historians.

1 Christ had been condemned to death by Pontius Pilate, procurator of Judaea, during the reign of the Roman emperor Tiberius (Tacitus). Pilate was procurator of Judaea from AD 26 to 36, while Tiberius reigned from AD 14 to 37. The traditional date for the crucifixion is some point around AD 30–33.
2 By the time of Nero, Christ had attracted sufficient followers in Rome to make them a suitable scapegoat for the burning of the city. These followers were named "Christians" after him (Tacitus).
3 "Chrestus" was the founder of a distinctive group within Judaism (Suetonius).
4 In AD 112, Christians worshipped Jesus "as if he were a god," abandoning the worship of the Roman emperor to do so (Pliny).

We continue our reflections by considering the background against which the gospels set the coming of Jesus – the history of Israel, as the people of God.

Jesus and Israel

The coming of Jesus did not take place in a vacuum. It is vitally important to appreciate that Jesus was born into Israel, the people of God. Christians stress that the God who was proclaimed and revealed by Jesus is the same

God who was known and worshipped by the great saints of Israel, such as Abraham and Moses. From a Christian perspective, the history of Israel is seen as a preparation for the new phase of God's dealings with humanity. The theme of the continuity of God's revelation, initially through Israel, and subsequently through Jesus Christ, is of major importance to Christian writers. This can be seen at point after point in the New Testament, part of the body of writings known as the Bible, and regarded as normative by Christians (see pp. 36–50).

The continuity between Judaism and Christianity is expressed in a number of ways. Judaism placed particular emphasis on the law, through which the will of God was made known in the form of commands, and the prophets, who made known the will of God in certain definite historical situations. Jesus himself stressed that he had "not come to abolish the Law or the Prophets, but to fulfill them" (Matthew 5:17). The same point is made by Paul, who refers to Jesus as "the goal of the Law" (Romans 10:4, using the Greek word *telos*, which means "end" or "objective"). Paul also stresses the continuity between the faith of Abraham and that of Christians (Romans 4:1–25), while the Letter to the Hebrews points out the continuity of the relationship both between Moses and Jesus (Hebrews 3:1–6) and between Christians and the great figures of faith of Israel (Hebrews 11:1–12:2).

Throughout the New Testament, the same theme recurs: Christianity is continuous with Judaism, and brings to completion what Judaism was pointing towards. This has several major consequences, of which the following are the most important. First, both Christians and Jews regard more or less the same collection of books as having authority. The body of writings which Jews refer to as "Law, Prophets, and Writings" is referred to by Christians as "the Old Testament." Although there

have always been more radical thinkers within Christianity who would like to break the link with Israel, the majority opinion has always been that it is important to affirm and value the historical link with Israel. A body of writings which Jews regard as complete in itself is seen by Christians as pointing forward to something which will bring it to completion. We shall explore the implications of the term "Old Testament" later in this book (p. 57).

Second, New Testament writers often stress the manner in which Old Testament prophecies are fulfilled or realized in the life and death of Jesus Christ. By doing this, they drew attention to two important principles – that Christianity is continuous with Judaism, and that Christianity brings Judaism to its true fulfillment. This is particularly important for early Christian writers who have a particular concern to demonstrate the importance of Christianity for Jews, such as Paul and Matthew. Thus at twelve points, Matthew points out how events in the life of Jesus can be seen as fulfilling Old Testament prophecy (Matthew 1:22; 2:15, 23; 3:15; 4:14; 5:17; 8:17; 12:17; 13:14, 35; 21:4; 27:9). In view of the importance of this matter, we shall look at two Old Testament passages, and the way in which New Testament writers saw them as being fulfilled in the life of Christ.

Psalm 22 is of particular significance to Christians. Jesus cited its opening words as he was dying on the cross (Matthew 27:46). The psalm speaks of the torment of a righteous sufferer, in response to the attacks of enemies who at present are gaining the upper hand. The "righteous sufferer" awaits deliverance from the Lord – yet at present there is no sign of any such deliverance. While the original situation addressed by this psalm is almost certainly linked with the personal difficulties of David, the psalm is of especial importance in casting light on the crucifixion of Christ as the righteous suffering servant of God. Even though the psalm relates well to events of the tenth century before Christ, it seems to Christians to be fulfilled especially in the death of Jesus. The psalm clearly relates to the events of David's lifetime; it is also prophetic, pointing ahead to events which would only be fulfilled in the coming of Jesus Christ.

Thus the psalm speaks of the "righteous sufferer" being scorned and despised, surrounded by those who mocked him (22:6–7) – a description in anticipation of the scene around the cross (Matthew 27:41). The psalmist speaks of people taunting him: "he trusted in the Lord; let the Lord rescue him" (22:8). The same words were used by the scoffing crowd who surrounded the dying Christ (Matthew 27:43). The description of the sufferer's anguish (22:12–16) corresponds well to the pain experienced by Christ on the cross. The piercing of Christ's hands and feet at crucifixion are prophesied here (22:16; see John 20:25), as is the casting of lots for his clothes (22:18; see Matthew 27:35; Luke 23:34).

A second Old Testament passage is also of especial importance to Christians. This is one of the "servant songs" found in the prophecy of Isaiah (Isaiah 52:13–53:12), which is generally regarded as one of the most important pieces of Old Testament prophecy concerning Jesus Christ. The passage, which dates from the sixth century before Christ, seems to speak of the suffering of God's servant Israel on behalf of other nations. Yet for Christians, the passage can be seen to have been fulfilled in Jesus Christ. Thus it speaks of the "servant" as being despised and rejected by others, yet at the same time suffering for them and bearing their iniquities. Although the servant was righteous, he was nevertheless "numbered with the transgressors." Jesus was crucified between two criminals (Luke 22:37; 23:32–33). The servant prayed for those who sinned; just as Jesus prayed for those who were cruci-

fying him as he died upon the cross (Luke 23:34). Other New Testament writers pick up this theme of the fulfillment of this prophecy in the suffering of Jesus (most notably at 1 Peter 2:21–25, which explicitly relates this prophecy to Jesus).

In seeing great passages such as these as being fulfilled in the life and death of Jesus, Christians are in no way denying that they had real relevance and application to the situations faced by Jews at the time they were written. They are simply pointing out that their *full* significance was not appreciated at the time. They possessed a deeper – perhaps a more mysterious – meaning, which only became clearer in the fullness of time.

Jesus and Jewish Groups

As has just been stressed, Jesus must be set in the context of Judaism. At the time of Jesus, Judaism was an enormously complex phenomenon. It embraced both Jews who were resident in the region of Judaea itself (often referred to as "Palestinian Judaism"), and the various Jewish communities dispersed throughout the civilized world of the time. Jewish communities, of various sizes, were scattered throughout the region of the Mediterranean and beyond. Jews in this category were often referred to as the "Diaspora" (from a Greek word meaning "dispersion" or "scattering"). This raises the question of how Jesus relates to the various groups which existed within Palestinian Judaism of the period. The five most important such groups are the Samaritans, Pharisees, Sadducees, Zealots, and Essenes. In what follows, we shall explore what is known of these groups, and the manner in which Jesus related to them.

The *Samaritans* were a people living in close proximity to Judaea, sharing some of the key beliefs of Judaism, yet regarded with intense suspicion and hostility by the Jews. The traditional Jewish account of the origins of the Samaritans lies in the events surrounding the Assyrian overthrow of the northern kingdom of Israel, and the forcible settlement of peoples from elsewhere within the Assyrian empire in the region (described in 2 Kings 17). These peoples mingled their own religious beliefs and practices with those of the Jews who remained in the region, leading to a form of syncretism. However, this view is regarded with some misgivings by historians. Furthermore, there seems to be no Old Testament text which specifically and explicitly refers to "the Samaritans." The Jewish historian Josephus dates the emergence of the Samaritans as a distinctive grouping to the Hellenistic period, rather than the period of the exile. The New Testament represents the Samaritans as a generally conservative religious grouping within Judaism, which recognized Shechem and Mount Gerizim (rather than Jerusalem and Mount Zion) as their place of worship.

Whatever their origins may have been, the Samaritans were regarded as outsiders by Jews. It is this factor which gives the Parable of the Good Samaritan (Luke 10:25–37) and the account of the meeting between Jesus and the Samaritan woman (John 4:4–42) their particular significance within the New Testament.

The origins of the *Pharisees* and *Sadducees* are generally traced back to the Maccabean revolt. This revolt had its origins in 168 BC, in response to the threat posed to Judaism by the political imposition of Greek forms of religion in the region. During the period 333–332 BC, Palestine was conquered by Alexander the Great. This development opened the period in Jewish history often referred to as "the Hellenistic period," in which the Greek language and Greek forms of religion came to play an increasingly prominent role in the region of Palestine. Initially, Judaea was controlled by the Ptolemies; later, by the

Seleucids. One particularly explosive development took place in 167 BC, and led directly to the Jewish revolt. Antiochus Epiphanes IV, a Seleucid ruler, dismantled the walls of Jerusalem, and massacred those Jews who resisted him. He then forcibly rededicated the Jewish temple (which was the political and cultic center of the Jewish religion) to the Greek god Zeus. This act of profanation, linked with various local incidents, sparked off the Maccabean revolt (the word "Maccabee" is a nickname, meaning "hammerer"). By 164 BC, the revolt had achieved its objectives. Jewish worship was formally reestablished, and the temple rededicated to the God of Israel (an event which continues to be celebrated at the Jewish festival of Hanukkah). This vigorous reassertion of Jewish national and religious identity caused tensions within Judaism, particularly over the role of the Jewish law or Torah. It is against this background that the emergence of the Pharisees and Sadducees as distinct religious groupings is to be seen.

The Sadducees argued for the priority of the written law, as found in the five books of the law (also known as the Pentateuch: see p. 60). Nothing other than the teachings found in these writings was to be regarded as authoritative. While the Sadducees had their own traditions, these were regarded as subordinate to the law. The Sadducees were particularly hostile to any forms of innovation, such as the adaptation of the law to the new situations which emerged in the late Hellenistic period. Equally, they regarded the prophets and other writings of the Old Testament (see pp. 60–73) as not having the same status as the law. For the Sadducees, only the five books of the law were of binding authority. This point underlies the response of Jesus to the Sadducees' question concerning whether there is a resurrection (see Matthew 22:23–33). In responding affirmatively to this question, Jesus cites Exodus 3:6, where a modern reader might have expected a more explicit citation from the book of Isaiah (where the theme of "resurrection" seems to be clearly stated at several points). Yet the Sadducees would not have regarded a citation from Isaiah as having any weight whatsoever. Jesus therefore cites from the Pentateuch, appealing to an authority which he knew would be taken seriously by his questioners.

In contrast to the Sadducees (who, as we have seen, admitted no doctrinal or religious innovations), the Pharisees regarded the law as evolving rather than static. The issue at stake was therefore to adapt the law to the new situations faced by Judaism. In addition, they permitted doctrinal developments, in that they accepted doctrines which were not explicitly stated in the law yet seemed consistent with its general thrust – such as the ideas of the resurrection of the dead (denied by the Sadducees: see Acts 23:8). The program adopted by the Pharisees could be summed up in the slogan "Torah and tradition," meaning "fidelity to the law as interpreted by the scribes." (The "scribes" were the official teachers of the Torah, many of whom were sympathetic to the Pharisees.) For the Pharisees, the interpretation and application of the law by the scribes were to be given as much weight as the law itself. The written law (the Torah) was thus to be supplemented by the oral law ("the tradition of the elders"), which represented an interpretation and application of the Torah. Both written and oral law were to be regarded as having equal authority. In contrast, the Sadducees refused to acknowledge any concept of a binding tradition or authoritative oral law.

The Pharisees were of considerable importance in early first-century Palestinian Judaism, which explains why they are referred to so often in the gospels. The Jewish historian Josephus suggests that there were six thousand Pharisees at the time. It must be stressed that the gospels do not portray the Pharisees as hypocrites, as so many mistakenly assume; indeed, it is clear that the program outlined by Jesus has many points of similarity with that of the Pharisees, most notably their agreement on the summary of the entire law in terms of loving God and neighbor. Yet there are points of difference between Jesus and the Pharisees, of which the following are of particular importance. For example, Jesus argued that, at points, the oral law was simply mistaken (a point particularly clear in his teaching on ritual cleanliness: Mark 7:1–23). Of specific importance, however, is the idea of "separation," which needs detailed comment.

The word "Pharisee" is often thought to derive from the Hebrew word *parush* ("separated"). Unlike the Essenes, who chose to separate themselves physically from their contaminated fellow Jews by retreating into the wilderness, the Pharisees remained within Jewish life, while distancing themselves from those of its aspects they regarded as unacceptable. There is no doubt that the Pharisees' emphasis on ritual purity led them to "separate" from other Jews with laxer religious and moral standards. Jesus, however, chose to associate with sinners, particularly those whom the Pharisees regarded as unclean or impure, such as prostitutes (e.g., see Matthew 9:9–13). Jesus clearly regarded his mission as reaching out to the lost, whereas the Pharisees seemed content to shun them, while criticizing them from a safe distance.

Two other groups of importance may be noted. During the period of Jesus' ministry, Palestine was occupied and administered by Rome. The *Zealots* were probably a group of more politically radical Jews, concerned to overthrow the Roman occupation of their native land. Although the term is used primarily to refer to the revolutionaries of AD 66, in which the Jews revolted against the Roman occupying forces, there are reasons for suspecting that the term was used earlier than this, perhaps dating back to the census of AD 6. There was fierce nationalist feeling at the time, fueled by intense resentment at the presence of a foreign occupying power. This is of importance in relation to the overtones of one of the New Testament titles for Jesus – that of "Messiah" or "Christ" (see pp. 29–30). The Roman occupation of Palestine appears to have given a new force to the traditional expectation of the coming of the Messiah. For many, the Messiah would be the deliverer who expelled the Romans from Israel and restored the line of David. The gospels indicate that Jesus refused to see himself as Messiah in this sense. At no point in his ministry do we find any violence against Rome suggested or condoned, nor even an explicit attack on the Roman administration. Jesus' attacks are directed primarily against his own people. Thus after his triumphal entry into Jerusalem (Matthew 21:8–11), which gives every indication of being a deliberate messianic demonstration or gesture, Jesus immediately evicts the merchants from the temple (Matthew 21:12–13).

The final group to be considered is the *Essenes*. This group, like the Pharisees, placed considerable emphasis on religious purity. Unlike the Pharisees, however, the Essenes chose to withdraw from everyday Jewish life, forming dedicated communities in the wilderness. The Dead Sea scrolls (discovered over the period 1947–1960) give crucial insights into the beliefs and practices of the Essenes, although the precise interpretation of these documents is difficult, due to uncertainties over their origins. The scrolls can all be dated to the last two centuries of the Second Temple; it is entirely possible that some date from the lifetime of Jesus. The scrolls are of particular interest in relation to understanding Jewish messianic expectations around the time of Jesus. It has also been suggested that John the Baptist may have been an Essene, or had links with Essene communities. However, there are no grounds for the suggestion, occasionally encountered in

sensationalizing media reports, that the Dead Sea scrolls discredit the gospel narratives, or force a total revision of our understanding of the origins of Christianity.

Having explored this important issue, we may now turn to explore the life of Jesus, as we find it in the gospels.

The Birth of Jesus

Matthew and Luke provide complementary accounts of the birth of Jesus, on which traditional Christmas cards and carols are based. Matthew's account is related from

1.2 The birth of Christ, as depicted by Fra Angelico in a mural in the monastery of San Marco, Florence, between 1437 and 1445. AKG-Images/ Rabatti-Domingie.

the standpoint of Joseph, and Luke's from that of Mary. Neither the day nor the year of Jesus' birth is known for certain. Non-Christians often assume that Christians believe that Jesus was born on December 25. In fact, Christians have chosen to celebrate the birth of Jesus on Christmas Day. December 25 is the date fixed for the celebration of the birth of Jesus, not the date of the birth itself. Early Christian writers suggested a variety of dates for the celebration of Jesus' birth – for example, Clement of Alexandria (ca. 150–ca. 215) advocated May 20. By the fourth century, the date of December 25 had been chosen, possibly to take advantage of a traditional Roman holiday associated with this date. For Christians, the precise date of the birth of Jesus is actually something of a non-issue. What really matters is that he was born as a human being, and entered into human history.

The traditional Christmas story has become somewhat stylized over the years. For example, most traditional versions of the story tell of the "three wise men" and of Jesus "being born in a stable." In fact, the New Testament relates that the wise men brought three gifts to Jesus; many have simply assumed that, as there were three gifts, there must have been three wise men. Similarly, we are told that Jesus was born in a manger; many have assumed that, since mangers are kept in stables, Jesus must have been born in a stable.

A point of particular importance concerns the identity of the birthplace of Jesus. Bethlehem was a minor town in the region of Judaea, not far from Jerusalem. Its significance lies in its associations with King David, given particular emphasis in one of the writings of a prophet of Israel. Micah, writing in the eighth century before Christ, made reference to the future emergence of a ruler of Israel from Bethlehem (Micah 5:2). This expectation is noted in Matthew's gospel (Matthew 2:5–6), where it is seen as one of many indications that the birth

and ministry of Jesus are in direct fulfillment of Israelite prophecies and hopes.

Luke stresses the humility and lowliness of the circumstances of the birth of Jesus. For example, he notes that Jesus was placed in a manger (normally used for feeding animals), and that the first people to visit him were shepherds. Although the force of the point is easily lost, it needs to be remembered that shepherds were widely regarded as socially and religiously inferior people by Jewish society, on account of their nomadic lifestyle.

Both Matthew and Luke stress the importance of Mary, the mother of Jesus. In later Christian thought, Mary would become a focus for personal devotion, on account of her obedience and humility. She often had a particular appeal to women, who felt marginalized by the strongly masculine ethos of Christianity during, for example, the Middle Ages. The hymn *Stabat Mater* (the Latin title of which means "The mother stood [by the cross]"), which was written during the thirteenth century, describes the deep feeling of sorrow experienced by Mary at the death of her son on the cross. This hymn, which was subsequently set to music by several major composers, had a deep impact on the spirituality of the Middle Ages and beyond. At the time of the Reformation, devotion to Mary was often criticized. It was suggested that this devotion could threaten the central place of Jesus Christ in Christian prayer and worship. Nevertheless, most Christians regard Mary as an excellent example of several central Christian virtues, especially obedience to and trust in God.

The place of Joseph in the gospel accounts of Jesus should also be noted. At no point is Joseph described as the "father of Jesus," despite the numerous references here and elsewhere to Mary as the "mother of Jesus." Matthew shows how Joseph was legally related to David (Matthew 1:1–17), with the result that Jesus possessed the legal status of being descended from David. Yet Joseph is not understood to be the physical father of Jesus. For Matthew and Luke, the conception of Jesus is divine in its origins.

The Beginning of the Public Ministry of Jesus

The gospels all locate the beginning of the public ministry of Jesus in the countryside of Judaea, by the River Jordan. It is specifically linked with the activity of John the Baptist, who attracted widespread attention with his calls to repentance. It is clear that John's ministry takes place at a moment of some significance in the history of Israel. Perhaps there were those who felt that God had abandoned Israel; perhaps there were those who felt that the great acts of divine deliverance and encouragement in the past would never be repeated. Israel was under Roman occupation, and seemed to have lost her identity as the people of God. We shall probably never fully understand the complex web of expectations, fears, and hopes which focused on the appearance of John the Baptist.

The New Testament picks up two themes which may help us understand why John the Baptist attracted such enormous interest at the time. The final work of Jewish prophecy – the book of Malachi, probably dating from the fifth century before Christ – spoke of God sending a messenger, to prepare the way for the coming of God (Malachi 3:1–2). It also hinted at the return of Elijah, one of the great figures of faith in Israel, before this event. When John the Baptist appeared, he wore the same simple clothes of camel's hair as Elijah had before him. Malachi spoke of the need for corporate repentance. The whole people of God needed to repent of their sins, before national restoration to divine favor was possible. John the Baptist spoke of this same need for repent-

ance, and offered baptism as a symbol of an individual's willingness to repent. (The word "baptism" comes from the Greek word meaning "to wash" or "to bathe.")

The implications of these developments would have been clear to anyone steeped in a knowledge of the Jewish prophets, and alert to the signs of the times. The coming of John the Baptist pointed to the coming of God. John himself made this point, declaring that someone who was greater than him would follow him – someone whose sandals he was not worthy to untie (Mark 1:8). And at that moment, Jesus appeared. It is impossible to read Mark's vivid and racy account of this encounter without realizing that Mark clearly wants us to understand that it is Jesus to whom John was referring. John is the forerunner of Jesus, pointing the way to his coming.

After Jesus was baptized by John, he slipped away into a solitary place for forty days and nights. This period of Jesus' ministry – usually referred to as "the temptation of Christ" – involved his being confronted with all the temptations which he would encounter during his ministry. Although Mark only hints at this (Mark 1:12), Matthew and Luke provide fuller details (e.g., Luke 4:1–13), allowing us to see how Jesus was confronted with the temptation to personal power and glory. The New Testament writers subsequently stress the importance of Jesus' obedience to the will of God. The period of Lent, immediately before Easter, marks the time of year when Christians are encouraged to examine themselves in this way, following the example of Christ.

A theme which now develops is that of the rejection of Jesus by his own people. This theme culminates in the crucifixion, in which Jesus is publicly repudiated by a crowd in Jerusalem, and taken off to be crucified by the Roman authorities. The theme also appears at earlier points in the ministry of Jesus, and is particularly linked with the severely hostile criticism of Jesus by the Pharisees and the teachers of the Jewish law. For the New Testament writers, the paradox is that those who were most deeply committed to and familiar with the Jewish law failed to recognize its fulfillment when this took place.

Nevertheless, the theme of "rejection" can be seen much earlier than this. One incident in particular illustrates this point: the rejection of Jesus in his home town of Nazareth. Luke's gospel relates how Jesus attended synagogue regularly on the sabbath. On one occasion, he was asked to read a section from the prophecy of Isaiah, which included the following words (Luke 4:18–19):

> The Spirit of the Lord is on me, because he has anointed me to preach good news to the poor. He has sent me to proclaim freedom for the prisoners and recovery of sight for the blind, to release the oppressed, to proclaim the year of the Lord's favor.

Jesus declared that these words were fulfilled in himself, and that his ministry would prove more acceptable to Gentiles than to Israel. The synagogue congregation were outraged, and

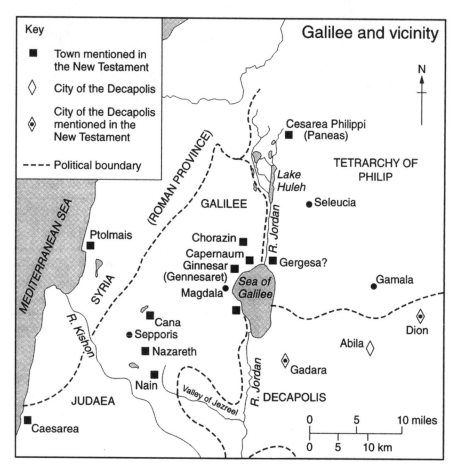

Map 1.1   The Galilean ministry of Jesus.

1.3   The calling of Peter and Andrew by the Sea of Galilee (1481), fresco by Domenico Ghirlandaio. Vatican Museums and Galleries, Vatican City, Italy/www.bridgeman.co.uk.

threw him out of their town, even trying to push him over the edge of a nearby hill. After this, Jesus ministered in the region of Capernaum, on the northwest shore of Lake Galilee.

Jesus then gathered around himself a small group of disciples, who would accompany him as he traveled, and subsequently form the core of the early church. The group of twelve apostles (often referred to simply as "the twelve") were drawn from a variety of backgrounds, mostly from jobs in the rural economy of the region. Two pairs of brothers – Peter and Andrew, and James and John – were called to leave their fishing business behind them, and follow Jesus. At a late stage, possibly a year or so into his ministry, Jesus divided the twelve into two groups of six, sending them out into the countryside to preach the kingdom of God.

Jesus then began his ministry of teaching and healing, initially in the region around Galilee, and subsequently in Judaea. On the basis of the accounts provided in the gospels, it may be estimated that this period lasted roughly three years. Important though both the teaching and healing are in their own rights, their true importance lies partly in what they demonstrate about Jesus. This becomes clear from a question posed later by John the Baptist. By this stage, John had been imprisoned by Herod Antipas, ruler (or, more precisely, "tetrarch") of the region of Galilee. Still uncertain as to the true identity of Jesus, John asked him this question: "Are you the one who was to come, or should we expect someone else?" The implications of the question are enormous. Is Jesus the Messiah? Has the messianic age arrived?

Jesus (who never directly claimed to be the Messiah during his ministry) answers indirectly, by pointing to what has happened in his ministry: "The blind receive sight, the lame walk, those who have leprosy are cured, the deaf hear, the dead are raised, and the good news is preached to the poor" (Matthew 11:6). In other words, the expected signs of the messianic age were evident in his ministry. Jesus does not directly answer the question of whether he is the Messiah. The inference, however, is clear. The healing miracles are to be seen as signs, pointing to a right understanding of the identity and significance of Jesus.

John's gospel is also of importance in allowing us to understand the significance of the healings and other works accompanying Jesus' ministry. For example, John notes the constant demand from Jesus' critics to "show a sign" in order to prove his authority to speak on behalf of God (e.g., John 2:18). He also points out the distinct role of these "signs," noting that they both revealed Jesus' glory and allowed his disciples to put their faith in him (John 2:11). The synoptic gospels also allow us to follow the growth of faith in the disciples themselves, as they hear him teach and see the signs which he performed. We shall return to this point presently. Our attention now turns to Jesus' attitude to one social grouping which was marginalized at the time: women.

Jesus and Women

It is clear from the gospel accounts of the ministry of Jesus that women were an integral part of the group of people who gathered round him. They were affirmed by him, often to the dismay of the Pharisees and other religious traditionalists. Not only were women witnesses to the crucifixion; they were also the first witnesses to the resurrection. The only Easter event to be explicitly related in detail by all four of the gospel writers is the visit of the women to the tomb of Jesus. Yet Judaism dismissed the value of the testimony or witness of women, regarding only men as having significant legal status in this respect. Interestingly, Mark tells us the names of these women witnesses – Mary Magdalene, Mary the mother of James, and Salome – *three times* (Mark 15:40, 47; 16:1), but never mentions the names of any male disciples who were present on this occasion.

It is also of importance to note that the gospels frequently portray women as being much more spiritually perceptive than men. For example, Mark portrays the male disciples as having little faith (Mark 4:40; 6:52), while commending women – a woman is praised for her faith (Mark 5:25–34), a foreign women for responding to Jesus (Mark 7:24–30), and a widow being singled out as an example to follow (Mark 12:41–4). Further, Jesus treated women as human subjects, rather than simply as objects or possessions. Throughout his ministry, Jesus can be seen engaging with and affirming women – often women who were treated as outcasts by contemporary Jewish society on account of their origins (e.g., Syro-Phoenicia or Samaria) or their lifestyle (e.g., prostitutes).

Jesus refused to make women scapegoats in sexual matters – for example, adultery. The patriarchal assumption that men are corrupted by fallen women is conspicuously absent from his teaching and attitudes, most notably towards prostitutes and the woman taken in adultery. The Talmud – an important source of Jewish law and teaching – declared that its readers (who are assumed to be men) should "not converse much with women, as this will eventually lead you to unchastity." This was studiously ignored by Jesus, who made a point of talking to women (the conversation with the Samaritan woman, related in

John 4, being an especially celebrated instance). In much the same way, the traditional view that a woman was "unclean" during her period of menstruation was dismissed by Jesus, who made it clear that it is only moral impurity which defiles a person (Mark 7:1–23).

Luke's gospel is of particular interest in relation to understanding Jesus' attitude to women. Luke brings out clearly how women are among the "oppressed" who are liberated by the coming of Jesus. Luke also sets out his material in a parallel manner, to emphasize that both men and women are involved in and benefit from the ministry of Jesus. For example, the following passages demonstrate this parallelism especially clearly:

Luke 1:11–20, 26–38	Zacharias and Mary
Luke 2:25–38	Simeon and Anna
Luke 7:1–17	A centurion and a widow
Luke 13:18–21	A man with mustard seed and a woman with yeast
Luke 15:4–10	A man with sheep and a woman with coins

By this arrangement of material, Luke expresses the fact that men and women stand together side by side before God. They are equal in honor and grace; they are endowed with the same gifts and have the same responsibilities.

Luke also draws our attention to the significant role of women in the spreading of the gospel. For example, Luke 8:2–3 indicates that "many women" were involved in early evangelistic endeavors, referring to the twelve being accompanied by "some women who had been cured of evil spirits and diseases: Mary (called Magdalene) from whom seven demons had come out; Joanna the wife of Cuza, the manager of Herod's household; Susanna; and many others." The inclusion of women in such a significant role would have seemed incomprehensible to the male-dominated society of contemporary Palestine.

It is probably difficult for western readers, who are used to thinking of women as having equal rights and status as men, to appreciate how novel and radical these attitudes were at the time. Possibly the most radical aspect of Jesus' approach to women is that he associated freely with them and treated them as responsible human beings, indulging in theological conversation with them, encouraging and expecting a response. It is hardly surprising that early Christianity proved to have a deep appeal for women.

It is entirely possible that Jesus' teachings attracted women partly on account of the new roles and status they were granted in the Christian community. There were many cults in Greece and Rome that limited their membership to men only or which allowed women to participate only in very limited ways. We shall explore later developments in Christian attitudes towards women in chapter 7 (see pp. 175–178).

The Teaching of Jesus: The Parables of the Kingdom

The theme of the "kingdom of God" (or, in the case of Matthew's gospel, "the kingdom of heaven") is widely agreed to be central to the preaching of Jesus. The public ministry of Jesus begins with his declaration that the kingdom of God has "drawn near," and that "the time is fulfilled" (Mark 1:15). The Greek word *basileia*, traditionally translated as "kingdom," does not so much express the idea of a definite political region over which a king rules as the idea of "rule" itself. In other words, the Greek word refers to the idea of "kingship" rather than a "kingdom." The "Sermon on the Mount" (the block of teaching contained in Matthew 5:1–7:29) is widely regarded as setting a remarkably high standard for conduct before other people and God, and is often referred to as setting out the "ethics of the kingdom of God." In other words, the acknowledgment of the rule of God leads to a certain pattern of behavior, which is embodied in the life and ministry of Jesus, and echoed in his teaching. The basic theme of Jesus' preaching can thus be thought of in terms of the coming of the kingly rule of God. This theme is expressed in the prayer which Jesus instructed his followers to imitate, and which is widely known as "the Lord's Prayer."

Jesus' preaching about the kingdom is best understood in terms of "inauguration." Something has happened which sets in motion a series of events which has yet to reach its fulfillment. A series of parables expresses the idea that the kingdom is something which progresses from a seemingly insignificant starting point to something which is much greater. The Parable of the Mustard Seed (Matthew 13:31–32) is a particularly good example in this respect, as it illustrates the idea of growth and development. The Parable of the Vineyard (Matthew 21:33–41) makes the point that those who are entitled to be tenants of the vineyard are those who produce its fruit, a clear indication of the need for those who claim to be within the kingdom to conform to its ethics. The kingly rule of God carries obligations.

So important are the parables in relation to Jesus' teaching about the kingdom that we must consider them in more detail. Parables are often defined as "earthly stories with heavenly meanings." This is a useful way of beginning to understand the importance of parables within the ministry of Jesus. The word "parable" reflects a number of ideas, including that of "illustration" and that of "mystery" or "riddle." A parable illustrates a spiritual truth – but the meaning may not be clear, and may therefore require illustration. Some of the parables are based on shrewd observation of everyday life in rural Palestine. Just as a pearl of great value is worth selling lesser possessions in order to own it, so the kingdom of God is worth giving up everything for (Matthew 13:45–46). Just as a small amount of yeast can raise a large amount of dough, so the kingdom of God can exercise its influence throughout the world (Matthew 13:33). Just as a shepherd will go out and look for a sheep that has got lost, so God will seek out those who have wandered away (Luke 15:4–6).

Sometimes, the parables are more complex. The Parable of the Prodigal Son (Luke 15:11–32) is an example of this kind of parable. It tells of a son who decides to leave his father's home and seek his fortune in a distant land. Yet life away from his father turns out not to be as rosy as the prodigal son had expected. He falls on hard times. The prodigal son comes to long to return home to his father. However, he is convinced that his father will have disowned him and will no longer wish to acknowledge him as his son. The remarkable feature of the parable is the picture of God which it gives us. The father sees the returning son long before the son notices him, and rushes out to meet him, and celebrate the return of the son he had given up for lost.

The parable is clearly intended to be interpreted along the following lines. The father represents God; the son represents those who have sinned, or turned their backs on God. The message of the parable is therefore simple: just as the father was overjoyed at the return of his son, so God will be overjoyed at the return of sinners.

The teaching of Jesus concerning the kingdom of God is an important element in the Christian faith. However, Christianity is not only about what Jesus taught. It is also about the person of Jesus himself. Who is he? And what is his importance? For the New Testament, the death and resurrection of Jesus are of central importance. We shall turn to consider these in what follows.

The Crucifixion

The theme of the crucifixion of Jesus Christ is deeply embedded in the New Testament. The Latin word "crucifixion" literally means "being placed on a cross." The tradition of the crucifixion of Jesus Christ is deeply embedded in the New Testament witness to him at every level. One of the earliest literary witnesses to the central importance of the crucifixion is Paul's first letter to the Christian church at Corinth, which probably dates from the early months of 55. In the first chapter of this letter, Paul lays considerable emphasis upon the fact that Christ was crucified. The subject of his preaching was "Christ crucified" (1:23); the power lying behind the gospel proclamation is "the cross of Christ" (1:17); the entire gospel can even be summarized as "the message of the cross" (1:18). The idea of a crucified savior was immediately seized upon by the opponents of the early church as an absurdity, demonstrating the ridiculous nature of Christian claims. Justin Martyr, attempting to defend Christianity against its more sophisticated critics in the second century, conceded that the Christian proclamation of a crucified Christ appeared to be madness: "[The opponents of Christianity] say that our madness lies in the fact that we put a crucified man in second place to the unchangeable and eternal God, the creator of the world."

The background to this within Judaism is of importance. For a Jew, anyone hanged upon a tree was to be regarded as cursed by God (Deuteronomy 21:23), which would hardly commend the Christian claim that Jesus was indeed the long-awaited Messiah. Indeed, one of the Dead Sea scrolls suggests that crucifixion was regarded as the proper form of execution for a Jew suspected of high treason. Yet the first Christians regarded the preaching of the gospel to Jews as one of their top priorities. Why would they include an idea which would have been so deeply offensive to a Jewish audience? The answer is quite simple: they had to. It was a historical fact, known to all, which had to be acknowledged and preached, even if it could lead to the alienation of many potential Jewish converts.

It is clear from contemporary evidence that crucifixion was a widespread form of execution within the Roman empire, and that there was an astonishing variety of manners in which this execution might be carried out. The victim was generally flogged or tortured beforehand, and then might be tied or nailed to the cross in practically any position. This form of punishment appears to have been employed ruthlessly to suppress rebellions in the Roman provinces, such as the revolt of the Cantabrians in northern Spain, as well as those of the Jews. Josephus' accounts of the crucifixion of the many Jewish fugitives who attempted to escape from besieged Jerusalem at the time of its final destruction by the Roman armies in 70 make horrifying reading. In the view of most Roman jurists, notorious criminals should be crucified on the exact location of their crime, so that "the sight may deter others from such crimes." Perhaps for this reason, the Roman emperor Quintilian crucified criminals on the busiest thoroughfares, in order that the maximum deterrent effect might be achieved.

It is therefore little wonder that the sophisticated pagan world of the first century reacted with disbelief and disgust to the Christians' suggestion that they should take seriously "an evil man and his cross" (*homo noxius et crux eius*) to the point of worshipping him. Crucifixion was a punishment reserved for the lowest criminals, clearly implying that Jesus belonged to this category of people. Yet the gospels, in common with the remainder of the New Testament, insist that this was the fate which Jesus endured.

The background to the crucifixion is the triumphal entry of Jesus into Jerusalem mounted on a donkey, in fulfillment of a great messianic prophecy of the Old Testament (Zechariah 9:9). Jesus enters Jerusalem as its king, an event especially celebrated by Christians on Palm Sunday. Yet this final week in the life of Jesus is marked by increasing controversy, culminating in his betrayal, arrest, and execution. Luke relates Jesus and his disciples gather together "in an upper room" to celebrate the Passover (Luke 22:14–23). With great solemnity, Jesus tells the gathered disciples that he will never celebrate Passover again "until it finds fulfillment in the Kingdom of God." The Passover is seen as something which points beyond itself, to something greater which is yet to find its fulfillment. The implication of these words is that the true meaning of the Passover is about to find its fulfillment in and through him. In view of the importance of this idea, we may consider it in more detail.

The Jewish feast of Passover celebrates the events leading up to the Exodus and the establishment of the people of Israel. The Passover lamb, slaughtered shortly before, and eaten at the feast, symbolizes this great act of divine redemption. It is thus very significant that the last supper and the crucifixion of Jesus took place at the feast of Passover. The synoptic gospels clearly treat the last supper as a Passover meal, with Jesus initiating a new version of the meal. While Jews celebrated their deliverance by God from Egypt by eating a lamb, Christians would henceforth celebrate their deliverance by God from sin by eating bread and drinking wine. Passover celebrates the great act of God by which the people of Israel came into being; the Lord's Supper celebrates the great saving act of God by which the Christian church came into being, and to which she owes her life and her existence.

John's gospel suggests that Jesus is crucified at exactly the same moment as the slaughter of the Passover lambs, indicating even more forcefully that Jesus is the true Passover lamb, who died for the sins of the world. The real Passover lamb is not being slaughtered in the temple precincts, but on the cross. In the light of this, the full meaning of the words of John the Baptist can be appreciated: "Behold the Lamb of God, who takes away the sin of the world" (John 1:29). The death of Christ takes away our sins, and cleanses us from its guilt and stain.

The coincidence of the last supper and the crucifixion with the Passover feast makes it clear that there is a vitally close connection between the Exodus and the death of Christ. Both are to be seen as acts of divine deliverance from oppression. However, while Moses led Israel from a specific captivity in Egypt, Christ is seen as delivering his people from a universal bondage to sin and death. While there are parallels between the Exodus and the cross, there are also differences. Perhaps the most important difference relates to the New Testament affirmation of the universality of the redemption accomplished by Christ. For the New Testament, the work of Christ benefits all who put their trust in him, irrespective of their ethnic identity, or historical or geographical location.

The "last supper" is of particular importance to Christians, in that it is remembered in Christian worship. Note the explicit command to the disciples to repeat this action in remembrance of Jesus. The use of bread and wine as a remembrance of Jesus – which focuses on the sacrament or ordinance usually referred to as "holy communion," "the Lord's Supper," "the eucharist," or "the mass" – has its origins here. We shall return to consider this in more detail later.

This is followed by an account of the betrayal of Jesus to the Jewish authorities for thirty pieces of silver. The betrayal of Jesus by Judas for thirty pieces of silver (Matthew 27:1–10) is seen as the fulfillment of Old

Testament prophecy (the prophecy in question seems to bring together both Jeremiah 19:1–13 and Zechariah 11:12–13).

After a theological interrogation, Jesus is handed over to the Roman authorities. The sections of the gospels which relate the betrayal, trial, and execution of Jesus are usually known as "the passion narratives," on account of their focusing on the sufferings (Latin: *passiones*) of Jesus. Why should Jesus have been handed over to the Roman authorities? Jesus was accused of blasphemy, specifically in relation to his admission that he was "the Christ, the Son of God." Under Jewish law, the penalty for blasphemy was death. However, with one exception, the Romans had deprived the Sanhedrin (that is, the seventy-one-member supreme Jewish court, consisting of the chief priests, elders, and teachers of the law) of the right to sentence anyone to death. This was now a matter for the Roman authorities.

Jesus is therefore brought before Pontius Pilate, who was the Roman governor of Judaea from AD 26 to 36. Pilate's inclination would probably have been to order some token punishment, but take things no further. However, the crowd demands that Jesus be crucified. Washing his hands of the whole affair, Pilate sends Jesus off to be flogged and crucified. Jesus is then humiliated by the Roman soldiers, who dress him up in a caricature of royal costume, including a crown of thorns.

The floggings administered by the Romans were vicious; they had been known to cause the death of victims before they were crucified. Under Jewish law, victims were only allowed to be flogged with forty strokes; this was invariably reduced to thirty-nine, as an act of leniency. But under Roman law, there were no limits to the extent of the suffering to be inflicted. The whips used for this purpose generally consisted of several strands of leather with small pieces of metal or broken bones at the end; these tore apart the skin of those being whipped, with the result that many did not survive the ordeal.

Jesus was clearly severely weakened by his beating, and proves unable to carry his own cross. Simon of Cyrene was forced to carry it for him. Finally, they reached Golgotha, the place of execution (Matthew 27:32–43). This place is also often referred to as "Calvary," from the Latin word *Calvaria* meaning "the skull" – the literal meaning of "Golgotha." As Jesus hangs on the cross, he is mocked by those watching him die, while the Roman soldiers cast lots for his clothes. These events can be seen as a fulfillment of the Old Testament prophecy of the fate of the righteous sufferer of Psalm 22 (see Psalm 22:7–8, 18). The identity of Jesus with this sufferer is confirmed by his cry of despair from the cross – "My God, my God, why have you forsaken me?" (Matthew 27:46) – which draws upon the opening verse of this psalm (Psalm 22:1). It is here that Jesus experiences a sense of the absence of God. Finally, Jesus dies.

The period of three hours on Good Friday is often commemorated in Christian churches. A common pattern of worship is known as the "three hours of the cross," which typically takes the form of meditations on the passion narratives, prayers, and periods of silence. A particularly common form of meditation is known as "the seven words from the cross," which focus on the words uttered by Jesus during his crucifixion, and which form a framework for the exposition of some of the leading themes of the Christian gospel. Musically, the passion narratives are particularly associated with Johann Sebastian Bach, whose Matthew Passion and John Passion can be regarded as the passion narratives of Matthew and John set to music.

The disciples, we now discover, are nowhere to be found. Matthew carefully identifies some witnesses of the death of Jesus. Not a single disciple is mentioned; it seems that they, like sheep without a shepherd, have scattered – just as Jesus had predicted. The witnesses who are identified are the Roman centurion, who declared that Jesus was the "Son of God" (Matthew 27:54) – a critically important testimony, coming from a Gentile, given that the Jewish high priest, here representing his own people, had refused to accept that Jesus was the Son of God. Yet here we can see the acceptance of this fact among the Gentiles, anticipating both the mission to the Gentiles and the enormous appeal which the gospel would prove to have to those outside Judaism. The other witnesses are women. Notice how Matthew names them (Matthew 27:55–56), so that they will not be forgotten. Finally, Jesus is buried in a borrowed tomb (Matthew 27:57–61). That is not, however, the end of the story, according to the New Testament.

The Resurrection

The gospels now turn to narrate a series of events which are of vital importance to the Christian faith. The term "the resurrection" is used to refer to the series of events that took place. In general terms, "the resurrection" refers to a cluster of related happenings, focusing on what happened to Jesus after his death. We may summarize them as follows.

1   The tomb in which the corpse of Jesus was laid late on the Friday afternoon was discovered to be empty on the Sunday morning. Those who discovered the empty tomb were frightened by what they found; their reports were not taken seriously by many of those in Jesus' close circle of friends.
2   The disciples reported personal appearances of Jesus, and experienced him as someone living.
3   The disciples began to preach Jesus as the living Lord, rather than as a past teacher.

The "empty tomb" tradition is of considerable importance here. It is a major element in each of the four gospels (Matthew 28:1–10; Mark 16:1–8; Luke 24:1–11; John 20:1–10) that it must be considered to have a basis in historical fact. The story is told from different aspects in each of the gospels, and includes the divergence on minor points of detail which is so characteristic of eye-witness reports. Interestingly, all four gospels attribute the discovery of the empty tomb to women. The only Easter event to be explicitly related in detail by all four of the gospel writers is the visit of the women to the tomb of Jesus. Yet Judaism

1.4   Piero della Francesca's depiction of the resurrection of Christ, ca. 1460–1464. Sansepolcro, Pinacoteca Comunale, AKG-images/Rabatti-Domingie.

dismissed the value of the testimony or witness of women, regarding only men as having significant legal status in this respect. Mark's gospel even names each of them three times: Mary Magdalene, Mary the mother of James, and Salome (Mark 15:40, 47; 16:1), but fails to mention the names of any male disciples who were around at the time. It is perhaps too easy for modern western readers, accustomed to a firm belief in the equality of men and women, to overlook the significance of this point. At the time, in the intensely patriarchal Jewish culture of that period, the testimony of a woman was virtually worthless. In first-century Palestine, this would have been sufficient to discredit the accounts altogether. If the reports of the empty tomb were invented, as some have suggested, it is difficult to understand why their inventors should have embellished their accounts of the "discovery" with something virtually guaranteed to discredit them in the eyes of their audiences. Why not attribute this discovery to men, if the story was an invention?

A further point of interest here concerns the practice of "tomb veneration" – that is, returning to the tomb of a prophet as a place of worship. This is known to have been common in New Testament times, and is probably hinted at in Matthew 23:29–30. The tomb of David in Jerusalem is still venerated by many Jews to this day. But there is no record whatsoever of any such veneration of the tomb of Jesus by his disciples. This would have been unthinkable, unless there was a very good reason for it. That reason appears to be the simple fact that Jesus' body was quite simply absent from its tomb.

It is quite clear that the resurrection of Jesus came as a surprise to the disciples. It must be pointed out that there was no precedent in Jewish thinking for a resurrection of this kind. After two thousand years of preaching the resurrection, Christians have become used to the idea of Jesus being raised from the dead. Overfamiliarity has dulled our minds to its astonishing novelty, by the standards of its age. The idea of a resurrection in human history, at a specific moment, and at a specific place, is actually very strange. Far from fitting into popular Jewish expectations of the resurrection of the dead, what happened to Jesus actually contradicted it. The sheer novelty of the Christian position at the time has been obscured by two thousand years' experience of the Christian understanding of the resurrection. At the time, however, it was highly unorthodox and radical. Most Jews at this time seem to have believed in the resurrection of the dead. Yet the general belief of the period concerned the future resurrection of the dead, at the end of time itself. Nobody believed in a resurrection before the end of history. The Pharisees may be regarded as typical in this respect: they believed in a future resurrection, and held that men and women would be rewarded or punished after death, according to their actions. The Sadducees, however, insisted that there was no resurrection of any kind. No future existence awaited men and women after death. (Paul was able to exploit the differences between the Pharisees and Sadducees on this point: see Acts 26:6–8.)

The Christian claim of the resurrection of Christ in history – rather than at the *end* of history – thus does not fit any known Jewish pattern at all. The resurrection of Jesus is not declared to be a future event, but something which had already happened in the world of time and space, in front of witnesses. What the Jews thought could only happen at the end of the world was recognized to have happened in human history, before the end of time, and to have been seen and witnessed by many. There was something quite distinct and unusual about the Christian claim that Jesus had been raised from the dead, which makes it rather difficult to account for.

To put this question pointedly: why should the first Christians have believed something which was so strange by the standards of their time, unless something had happened which forced them to this conclusion – something unexpected and shattering, which called their existing ideas into question? The simplest answer is that they were confronted with the resurrection of Jesus, and had to rethink their entire conceptual world as a result. For Paul, the resurrection was a public event, open to challenge and verification by the five hundred or so who had witnessed it (1 Corinthians 15:3–8).

Luke records one incident which brings out the unexpected nature of the resurrection of Jesus. This is usually referred to as the "road to Emmaus" (Luke 24:13–35). In this narrative, Luke tells of two disciples, one of whom is named Cleopas, who are discussing the day's bewildering events as they walk along the road from Jerusalem to Emmaus (24:13–17). As they talk, they are joined by a stranger. It is only when he breaks bread with them (an important allusion to the last supper) that they realize who he is.

But what are the implications of the resurrection? We shall discuss these in more detail in chapter 6. In this chapter, we have been documenting the history of Jesus, including the crucifixion and resurrection. But what is the *meaning* of that history? What does the resurrection mean? What does the crucifixion tell us about Jesus? To answer such questions, we need to explore what the New Testament has to say about the identity and the significance of Jesus.

In addition to reporting the basic events which underlie the Christian gospel, the New Testament includes extensive reflection on the identity and significance of Jesus. The present chapter provides an analysis of the main lines of reflection we find within the New Testament, as well as exploring how Jesus has been understood as a result of the church's

long reflections on how best to represent and describe Jesus. This process of reflection and development is often likened to the process of the growth of a plant.

But before we can begin to explore Christian understandings of the meaning of Jesus, we need to consider the all-important distinction between events and meanings. In what way can something that happened in history be said to possess a meaning, over and above the event itself?

Events and Meanings

In thinking about the significance of Jesus, we need to explore the relation between the events of his life and their meaning. Christianity is not just about the recitation of the history of Jesus; it deals with the meanings of the events in that history, particularly his death on the cross (usually referred to as "the crucifixion"). The Christian faith certainly presupposes that Jesus existed as a real historical figure, and that he was crucified. Christianity is, however not simply about the mere facts that Jesus existed and was crucified. Some words of Paul, probably written fifteen years after the resurrection, will help make this point clear.

> Now, brothers, I want to remind you of the gospel I preached to you, which you received and on which you have taken your stand. By this gospel you are saved...For what I received I passed on to you as of first importance: that Christ died for our sins according to the Scriptures, that he was buried, that he was raised on the third day according to the Scriptures, and that he appeared to Peter, and then to the Twelve [Apostles]. (1 Corinthians 15:1–5)

The use of the words "passed on" is of particular interest. These words are taken from the technical Jewish language of tradition, of "handing down" or "handing over," and point to the fact that Paul is passing on to his readers something that had earlier been passed on to him. In other words, Paul was not the first to summarize the Christian faith in terms of the two essential components of Christ's crucifixion and resurrection. He had learned this from others. Paul is not here relying on his own memory at this point, but on the collective memory of a much larger group of people.

It is widely believed that Paul is here reciting a formula, a form of words, which was in general use in the early church, and which he had received not just in general terms, but in almost exactly the form which he passes down to the Corinthian Christians. He is not relying on his own memory, but on that of the Christian church in the earliest period of its existence. Earlier in this letter, Paul had made clear that the content of his preaching to the Corinthian Christians, upon which their faith was based, was "Christ crucified" (1 Corinthians 1:17–18; 2:2).

Paul here makes a clear distinction between the *event* of the death of Christ, and the *significance* of this event. That Christ died is a simple matter of history; that Christ died *for our sins* is an insight which lies right at the heart of the gospel itself. This all-important distinction between an *event* and its *meaning* can be illustrated from an event which took place in 49 BC, when the great Roman commander Julius Caesar crossed a small river with a legion of soldiers. The name of the river was the Rubicon, and it marked an important frontier within the Roman empire. It was the boundary between Italy and Cisalpine Gaul, a colonized region to the northwest of Italy, in modern-day France.

Considered simply as an event, it was not especially important. The Rubicon was not an especially impressive river, and there was no particular difficulty about crossing it. People have crossed wider and deeper rivers before and since. As a simple event, it was not remarkable. But that is not why the crossing of that river was important. It is the meaning of the event that guarantees its place in the history books, for the political significance of that event was enormous. Crossing this national frontier with an army was a deliberate act of rebellion against Rome. It marked a declaration of war on the part of Caesar against Pompey and the Roman senate. The *event* was the crossing of a river; the *meaning* of that event was a declaration of war.

In many ways, the death of Christ may be said to parallel Caesar's crossing of the Rubicon. The event itself appears unexceptional, except to those who know its significance. On the basis of contemporary records, we know that an incalculable number of people died in this way at that time. Jesus would not have been alone in being executed by crucifixion. Indeed, the gospel accounts of the crucifixion make it absolutely clear that two other criminals were crucified with Jesus on that day, one on either side of him. As an event, the crucifixion hardly seems important or noteworthy. It is a witness to the cruel and repressive measures used by the Romans to enforce conformity throughout their empire. But is it more than this?

The New Testament makes it clear that those who were aware of the meaning of an event saw behind the mere external event itself – to what it *signified*, to the reason that it was *important*. Pompey and the Roman senate were not especially interested in the mechanics of how Julius Caesar crossed the Rubicon: for them, the bottom line was crystal clear – it meant war. Similarly, Paul was not particularly interested in the details of the crucifixion of Jesus. For him, it meant salvation, forgiveness, and victory over death. Thus the "message of the cross" was about far more than the simple historical fact that Jesus was crucified. It is about the significance of this event for humanity: Jesus died, in order that we might live. Jesus was numbered among sinners, so that sinners might be forgiven.

Another example of the link between an event and its meaning can be seen from an incident linked with the death of Jesus on the cross. Matthew's account of the death of Jesus notes one event which happened around this point, which has particular theological significance. The "curtain of the temple" was torn from top to bottom (Matthew 27:51). We are not told how; for Matthew, it is the event that is significant. But what does it mean? The "curtain of the temple" was an especially important feature of the Old Testament tabernacle (Exodus 26:31–35). It was included in order to provide a means of restricting access to the "most holy place," the region of the tabernacle which was regarded as sacrosanct. Although the curtain served an important practical function in relation to the worship of Israel, it came to have a deeper significance. The fact that the curtain prevented ordinary worshippers from entering the "most holy place" came to be seen as pointing to a much deeper separation between God and sinful humanity. The curtain thus came to be a symbol of the barrier placed between God and humanity by human sinfulness.

The tearing of this curtain at the crucifixion can be seen as a symbol of one of the chief benefits Christianity understands to have been brought about by the death of Christ. The barrier between God and humanity caused by sin has been torn down, so that there is now free access for believers to God on account of Christ's death. This theme is explored further by Paul at Romans 5:1–2.

Thus far, we have focused on the distinction between "event" and "meaning." Once the importance of this has been appreciated, we are in a position to move on, and look at some of the interpretations of Jesus that we find in the New Testament.

The New Testament Understandings of Jesus

Who is Jesus? What does he *mean?* One of the easiest ways to begin to reflect on these questions is to look at the terms used to refer to Jesus within the New Testament, especially the gospels. These are often referred to as the "Christological titles" of the New Testament. Each of them must be considered as the outcome of a process of reflection on what Jesus said and did, and the impact that he had upon people. In what follows, we shall explore several of these titles, and consider their implications for the Christian understanding of the identity of Jesus.

Messiah

It is very easy for a modern western reader to assume that "Christ" was Jesus' surname, and to fail to appreciate that it is actually a title – "Jesus the Christ." The word "Christ" is the Greek form of the Hebrew title "the Messiah," which literally means "the anointed one" – someone who has been anointed with oil. This Old Testament practice indicated that the person anointed in this way was regarded as having been singled out by God as having special powers and functions; thus 1 Samuel 24:6 refers to the king as "the Lord's anointed." The basic sense of the word could be said to be "the divinely appointed King of Israel." As time passed, the term gradually came to refer to a deliverer, himself a descendant of David, who would restore Israel to the golden age she enjoyed under the rule of David.

During the period of Jesus' ministry, Palestine was occupied and administered by Rome. There was fierce nationalist feeling at the time, fueled by intense resentment at the presence of a foreign occupying power, and this appears to have given a new force to the traditional expectation of the coming of the Messiah. For many, the Messiah would be the deliverer who expelled the Romans from Israel and restored the line of the greatest king of Israel, David.

It is important to note that Jesus was not prepared to accept the title "Messiah" in the course of his ministry. Mark's gospel should be read carefully to note this point. When Peter acclaims Jesus as Messiah – "You are the Christ!" – Jesus immediately tells him to keep quiet about it (Mark 8:29–30). It is not clear what the full significance of the "messianic secret" is. Why should Mark emphasize that Jesus did not make an explicit claim to be the Messiah, when he was so clearly regarded as such by so many?

Perhaps the answer may be found later in Mark's gospel, when he recounts the only point at which Jesus explicitly acknowledges his identity as the Messiah. When Jesus is led, as a prisoner, before the high priest, he admits to being the Messiah (Mark 14:61–62). Once violent or political action of any sort is no longer possible, Jesus reveals his identity. He was indeed the deliverer of the people of God – but not, it would seem, in any political sense of the term. The misunderstandings associated with the term, particularly in Zealot circles, appear to have caused Jesus to play down the messianic side of his mission.

Lord

A second significant title is "Lord." The word is used in two main senses in the New Testament. It is used as a polite title of respect, particularly when addressing someone. When Martha addresses Jesus as "Lord" (John 11:21), she is probably, although not necessarily, merely treating Jesus with proper respect. However, the word is also used in another sense.

The confession that "Jesus is Lord" (Romans 10:9; 1 Corinthians 12:3) was clearly regarded by Paul as a statement of the essential feature of the gospel. Christians are those who "call upon the name of the Lord" (Romans 10:13; 1 Corinthians 1:2). But what is implied by this? It is clear that there was a tendency in first-century Palestinianism to use the word "Lord" (Greek: *kyrios*; Aramaic: *mare*) to designate a divine being, or at the very least a figure who is decidedly more than just human, in addition to its function as a polite or honorific title. But of particular importance is the use of this Greek word *kyrios* to translate the cipher of four letters used to refer to God in the Old Testament (often referred to as the "Tetragrammaton": see p. 77).

When the Old Testament was translated from Hebrew into Greek, the word *kyrios* was generally used to translate the sacred name of God. Of the 6,823 times that this name is used in the Hebrew, the Greek word *kyrios* ("Lord") is used to translate it on 6,156 occasions. This Greek word thus came to be an accepted way of referring directly and specifically to the God who had revealed himself to Israel at Sinai, and who had entered into a covenant with his people on that occasion. Jews would not use this term to refer to anyone or anything else. To do so would be to imply that this person or thing was of divine status. The historian Josephus tells us that the Jews refused to call the Roman emperor *kyrios*, because they regarded this name as reserved for God alone.

The writers of the New Testament had no hesitation in using this sacred name to refer to Jesus, with all that this implied. A name which was used exclusively to refer to God was regarded as referring equally to Jesus. This was not some error made by ill-informed writers, ignorant of the Jewish background to the name. After all, the first disciples were Jews. Those New Testament writers, such as Paul, who make most use of the term "Lord" to refer to Jesus were perfectly well aware of its implications. Yet they regarded the evidence concerning Jesus, especially his resurrection from the dead, as compelling them to make this statement concerning his identity. It was a deliberate, considered, informed, and justified decision, which is entirely appropriate in the light of the history of Jesus. He has been raised to glory and majesty, and sits at the right hand of God. He therefore shares the same status as God and is to be addressed accordingly.

On occasion, the New Testament takes an Old Testament text which refers to "the Lord" (in other words, "the Lord God"), and deliberately applies or transfers this to "the Lord Jesus." Perhaps the most striking example of this tendency may be seen by comparing Joel 2:32 with Acts 2:21. The passage in Joel refers to a coming period in the history of the people of God, in which the Spirit of God will be poured out upon all people (Joel 2:28). On this "great and dreadful day of the Lord" (that is, God) "everyone who calls upon the name of the Lord will be saved" (Joel 2:31–32) – in other words, all who call upon the name of *God* will be saved.

This prophecy is alluded to in Peter's great sermon on the Day of Pentecost (Acts 2:17–21), which ends with the declaration that "everyone who calls upon the name of the Lord shall be saved" (Acts 2:21). It is then made clear, in what follows, that the "Lord" in question is none other than "Jesus of Nazareth," whom God has made "both Lord and Christ" (Acts 2:36). Peter declares that the resurrection has established that the same Jesus who was crucified has now been publicly declared by God to be the Messiah and Lord, with the right to equal status with God.

A further interesting example may be found in the use made of Isaiah 45:23 in Philippians 2:10–11. Isaiah speaks prophetically of a day in which "the Lord" (that is, "the Lord God") declares that "every knee shall bow" to him, and "every tongue confess him." It is a powerful passage, in which the uniqueness of the God of Israel, and especially his universal claims to authority and sovereignty, are firmly stated (Isaiah 45:22–25).

This practice of transferring from one Lord ("the Lord God") to another ("the Lord Jesus") is known to have infuriated Jews at the time. In the second-century dialogue between Trypho the Jew and Justin Martyr, Trypho complains that Christians have "hijacked" passages referring to God, in order to refer them to Christ. There was, of course, no suggestion that there were two "Lords" (in other words, two Gods), simply that Jesus had to be regarded as having a status at least equal to that of God, which demanded that he be addressed and worshipped as such. The use of the term "Lord" to refer to Jesus may therefore be seen as a recognition of his exalted status, arising from his resurrection.

Savior

For New Testament writers, Jesus is the "Savior, who is Christ the Lord" (Luke 2:11). This theme is echoed throughout the New Testament: Jesus saves his people from their sins (Matthew 1:21); in his name alone is there salvation (Acts 4:12); he is the "captain of salvation" (Hebrews 2:10). And in these affirmations, and countless others, Jesus is understood to function as God, doing something which, properly speaking, only God can do. In the Old Testament, Israel was regularly reminded that she cannot save herself, nor can she be saved by the idols of the nations round about her. It is the Lord, and the Lord alone, who will save. This point is made with special force in some of the prophetic writings, such as Isaiah 45:21–22:

> Who declared it of old? Was it not I, the Lord?
> And there is no other god apart from me, a righteous God and a Savior.
> There is none apart from me.
> Turn to me and be saved, all the ends of the earth!

This theme is also reflected in the gospel accounts of how Jesus healed a paralytic (Mark 2:1–12). Jesus tells the paralytic that his sins are forgiven, to the outrage and astonishment of the Jewish teachers of the law watching him. Their reaction was one of disbelief: "He is blaspheming! Who can forgive sins but God alone!" (Mark 2:7). Underlying this objection was a fundamental belief of the Old Testament: only God can forgive sin. Unless Jesus was God, he had no authority whatsoever to speak those words. He was deluded, or blaspheming. Yet Jesus declares that he does have such authority to forgive, and proceeds to heal the man (Mark 2:10–11). The resurrection of Jesus demonstrated that Jesus had the right to act in this way, retrospectively validating his claims to authority on earth.

God alone forgives sins; yet Jesus forgives sin. God alone saves; yet Jesus also saves. So what does this say about the identity of Jesus? In the full knowledge that it was the Lord God alone who was Savior, and that none other than God could save, the first Christians affirmed that Jesus was Savior – that *Jesus* could save. This was no misunderstanding on the part of people ignorant of the Old Testament tradition. It was a confident statement of who Jesus had to be, in the light of what he achieved through his saving death and resurrection.

The New Testament's use of the title "savior" to refer to Jesus thus has important implications for an understanding of Jesus' function and identity. In terms of Jesus' function, the title affirms that he is able to bring the salvation that God promised to his people. Salvation is something that Jesus both proclaims and effects. He makes possible what he promises. In terms of Jesus' identity, the title points to the need to think of Jesus in terms that make clear his unique status. If Jesus is able to achieve something that God alone is able to achieve, our understanding of his identity must be brought into line with this insight. Tradition-

ally, Christian theology sees Jesus' role as savior as important confirmation of his entitlement to be spoken and thought of as both divine and human.

Son of God

A further title used by the New Testament to refer to Jesus is "Son of God." In the Old Testament, the term is occasionally used to refer to angelic or supernatural persons (see Job 38:7; Daniel 3:25). Messianic texts in the Old Testament refer to the coming Messiah as the "Son of God" (2 Samuel 7:12–14; Psalm 2:7). The New Testament use of the term seems to mark a development of its Old Testament meaning, with an increased emphasis upon its exclusiveness.

At one level, the realization that Jesus was the "Son of God" can be seen as a result of reflection on the resurrection. One outcome of this rumination was a realization of the unique status of Jesus himself. Paul opens his letter to the Christians at Rome by making a crucially important statement concerning Jesus Christ. Jesus "was descended from David at the human level, and was designated as the Son of God . . . by his resurrection from the dead" (Romans 1:3–4). This brief statement picks out two reasons why Jesus is to be regarded as the Son of God. First, on the physical level, he was a descendant of David, the great king of Israel to whom God had promised a future successor as king. A similar point is made by Matthew, as he opens his gospel (Matthew 1:1). Second, Jesus' resurrection established his identity as the Son of God. We see here an appeal to the resurrection as clinching the argument as to the true identity of Jesus as the "Son of God."

Although all people are children of God in some sense of the word, Jesus is *the* Son of God. Paul distinguishes between Jesus as the natural Son of God, and believers as adopted sons. Their relation to God is quite different from

Jesus' relationship to him, even though both may be referred to as "sons of God." We shall explore this point further when we consider the idea of "adoption" as a way of thinking about the benefits which Christ obtained for us on the cross. Similarly, in the first letter of John, Jesus is referred to as "the Son," while believers are designated as "children." There is something quite distinct about Jesus' relation to God, as expressed in the title "Son of God."

The New Testament understanding of Jesus' relationship to God, expressed in the Father–Son relationship, takes a number of forms. First, we note that Jesus directly addresses God as "Father," with the very intimate Aramaic word "Abba" being used (Mark 14:36: see also Matthew 6:9; 11:25–26; 26:42; Luke 23:34, 46).

Secondly, it is clear from a number of passages that the evangelists regard Jesus as the Son of God, or that Jesus treats God as his father, even if this is not stated explicitly (Mark 1:11; 9:7; 12:6; 13:32; 14:61–62; 15:39).

Thirdly, John's gospel is permeated with the Father–Son relationship (note especially passages such as John 5:16–27; 17:1–26), with a remarkable emphasis upon the identity of will and purpose of the Father and Son, indicating how close the relationship between Jesus and God was understood to be by the first Christians. At every level in the New Testament – in the words of Jesus himself, or in the impression which was created among the first Christians – Jesus is clearly understood to have a unique and intimate relationship to God, which the resurrection demonstrated publicly (Romans 1:3–4).

In recent years, increasing attention has been paid to Islamic critiques of the divinity of Jesus. It must be stressed that the Christian doctrine of Jesus as the "Son of God" is not to be understood as God physically fathering Jesus. Muslims generally regard referring to Jesus as the "Son of God" as an instance of the heresy of *ittakhadha*, by which Jesus is ac-

knowledged to be the physical Son of God. This is not a correct perception. The point being made by this title for Jesus is fundamentally relational – that is to say, it is an affirmation of the unique status of Jesus in relation to God, and hence the unique role of Jesus within the Christian tradition as a bearer of divine revelation and the agent of divine salvation.

Where Islam holds that one may know the will of God but not the face of God, Christianity holds that both have been fully and definitively revealed in Jesus Christ. Mohammed is seen as one who wrote down the revelation entrusted to him by the angel Gabriel; Jesus is one who was himself the definitive revelation of God. As God incarnate, Jesus reveals God and makes restoration to him possible through his saving death and resurrection. Underlying the Islamic criticism of the doctrine of the Trinity is a more fundamental concern about the identity of Jesus Christ himself. For Islam, Jesus is a prophet – and not God incarnate.

Son of Man

For many Christians, the term "Son of Man" stands as a natural counterpart to "Son of God." It is an affirmation of the humanity of Christ, just as the latter term is a complementary affirmation of his divinity. However, it is not quite as simple as this. The term "Son of Man" (Hebrew: *ben-adam* or Aramaic *bar nasha*) is used in three main contexts in the Old Testament:

1 as a specific form of address to the prophet Ezekiel.
2 to refer to a future eschatological figure (Daniel 7:13–14), whose coming signals the end of history and the coming of divine judgment.
3 to emphasize the contrast between the lowliness and frailty of human nature and the elevated status or permanence of

God and the angels (Numbers 23:19; Psalm 8:14).

The third of these meanings relates naturally to the humanity of Jesus, and may underlie at least some of its references in the synoptic gospels, especially those stressing the humility of Jesus and his willingness to suffer alongside others.

However, the sense of the term which has attracted most attention is that of a coming figure of judgment. This is certainly the sense which the term bears in the vision of Daniel in the Old Testament. In one of his visions of a future judgment, Daniel sees someone who he refers to as "a son of man" coming to judge the world. The term "Son of Man" is also used in the gospels to refer to a future judge, who will come in glory at the end of time. This way of referring to Jesus would thus stress the continuity between the humble figure of Jesus during the time of his ministry and the future judge, who will come at the end of time. The Nicene Creed refers to Jesus as the one "who will come again in glory to judge the living and the dead"; this affirmation echoes the New Testament understanding of Jesus as the coming judge. It also emphasizes the authority of Jesus as one with the divine right to judge. This is further consolidated by the final New Testament title for Jesus which we shall consider – that of "God."

God

Finally, we must note a group of texts which explicitly refer to Jesus as God. All the other material we have considered in this chapter can be seen as pointing to this conclusion. The affirmation that Jesus is divine is the climax of the New Testament witness to the person of Jesus Christ. At least ten texts in the New Testament seem to speak explicitly of Jesus in this way (such as John 1:1; 1:18; 20:28; Romans 9:5; Titus 2:13; Hebrews 1:8–9; 2 Peter 1:1; 1 John 5:20). Others point in this direction, implying the same conclusion (such as Matthew 1:23; John 17:3; Galatians 2:20; Ephesians 5:5; Colossians 2:2; 2 Thessalonians 1:12; 1 Timothy 3:16). We shall consider some of these verses in what follows.

One of the most remarkable passages in the New Testament describes how the doubts of Thomas concerning the resurrection of Jesus are dispelled (John 20:24–29). Thomas doubted that Jesus really had been raised. However, those doubts give way to faith when the risen Jesus is able to show him the wounds inflicted upon him at the crucifixion. Thomas responds with a declaration of faith in Christ, addressing him with the following words: "My Lord and my God!" (John 20:28). These remarkable words are totally consistent with the witness to the identity of Jesus Christ which is provided by this gospel. We have already noted how the term "Lord" could be used as a way of referring to God. However, Thomas explicitly addresses Jesus not merely as "Lord" but as "God," making explicit what might otherwise only be implicit.

The second letter of Peter is one of the later writings in the New Testament. The letter is addressed to "those who through the righteousness of our God and Savior Jesus Christ have received a faith as precious as ours" (2 Peter 1:1). A similar phrase is found in Paul's letter to Titus, which refers to Jesus Christ as "God our Savior" (Titus 1:3). The Greek form of both these statements makes it clear that they cannot be translated as if "God" and "Savior" were different persons. Both titles refer to one and the same person, Jesus Christ.

In the present chapter, we have begun to explore something of the significance of Jesus, as set out within the New Testament. Christians have seen it as an issue of major importance to ensure that the significance of Jesus for humanity is articulated as accurately and adequately as possible. As a result, the Christian tradition has developed a number of ways of explaining and defending the identity and relevance of Jesus, several of which have become classic.

In what follows, we shall be exploring some classic approaches to the identity of Jesus – a general area of Christian thought dealing with the identity of Jesus often referred to as "Christology." Yet although Christianity is strongly Jesus-centered and Jesus-focused, it affirms other ideas as well. In a later chapter, we shall explore some more of the basic ideas of the Christian faith. Our attention now turns to the Bible, the central text of the Christian faith.

2

Introducing the Bible

Anyone beginning to study Christianity soon realizes that the Bible plays a very important role in Christian life and thought. If you attend a Christian service of worship, you will hear the Bible read publicly as an integral part of that worship. You will probably hear a sermon preached on one of the biblical passages read during the service. If you join a small group of Christians meeting for study and prayer, you may well find that "Bible Study" – that is, reflection on the meaning and relevance of a short passage from the Bible – is an important part of their time together. Millions of Christians begin the day with a personal study of a short biblical passage. Countless commentaries on the Bible as a whole, or individual books of the Bible, are available in bookstores, and are part of the staple intellectual and devotional diet of many active Christians.

So what is the Bible? And why is it so important? In this part of this introduction, we shall begin to explore what the Christian Bible is, and the role it plays for Christians.

The Bible: The Origin of the Term

The term "the Bible" is used to refer to the collection of writings regarded as authori-tative by Christians. Other ways of referring to this collection of texts are also used: for example, the terms "Sacred Scripture" or "Holy Scripture" will be encountered regularly in Christian writings. However, the term "Bible" is widely regarded as the most acceptable way to refer to this collection of writings. The unusual word "Bible" needs explanation. Like many words in modern English, it derives from a Greek original. The Greek phrase which has been rendered into English is *ta biblia* – literally, "the books." The Greek phrase is plural, and refers to the collection of books, or writings, regarded as authoritative by Christians.

The Bible is divided into two major sections, traditionally referred to as the *Old Testament* and the *New Testament*. A brief overview of the contents of each of these testaments will be provided below; a more detailed analysis is provided in chapters 3 and 4. The Old Testament consists of thirty-nine books, beginning with Genesis and ending with Malachi. It is almost entirely written in Hebrew, the language of Israel; however, some short sections are written in Aramaic, an international language widely used in the diplomacy of the ancient near east. The Old Testament itself includes a number of different kinds of writings, of which the most important are the following.

1 The *five books of the law* are sometimes also referred to as *the five books of Moses*, reflecting a traditional belief that they were largely written by Moses. In more scholarly works, they are sometimes referred to as *the Pentateuch*, from the Greek words for "five" and "scrolls." These are: Genesis, Exodus, Leviticus, Numbers, and Deuteronomy. These deal with the creation of the world, the calling of Israel as a people, and its early history, including the Exodus from Egypt. The story they tell ends with the people of Israel being about to cross over the Jordan and enter the promised land. One of the most important themes of these books is the giving of the law to Moses, and its implications for the life of Israel.

2 The *historical books*: Joshua, Judges, Ruth, 1 and 2 Samuel, 1 and 2 Kings, 1 and 2 Chronicles, Ezra, Nehemiah, and Esther. These books deal with various aspects of the history of the people of God from their entry into the promised land of Canaan to the return of the people of Jerusalem from exile in the city of Babylon. It includes detailed accounts of the conquest of Canaan, the establishment of a monarchy in Israel, the great reigns of kings David and Solomon, the breakup of the single nation of Israel into two parts (the northern kingdom of Israel and the southern kingdom of Judah), the destruction of Israel by the Assyrians, the defeat of Judah and exile of her people by the Babylonians, and the final return from exile and the rebuilding of the temple. The books are arranged in historical order.

3 The *prophets*. This major section of the Old Testament contains the writings of a group of individuals, inspired by the Holy Spirit, who sought to make the will of God known to their people over a period of time. There are sixteen prophetic writings in the Old Testament, which are usually divided into two categories. First, there are the four *major prophets*: Isaiah, Jeremiah, Ezekiel, and Daniel. These are followed by the twelve *minor prophets*: Hosea, Joel, Amos, Obadiah, Jonah, Micah, Nahum, Habakkuk, Zephaniah, Haggai, Zechariah, and Malachi. The use of the words "major" and "minor" does not imply any judgment about the relative importance of the prophets. It refers simply to the length of the books in question. The prophetic writings are arranged roughly in historical order.

Other types of book can be noted, including the *wisdom writings*: Job, Proverbs, Ecclesiastes. These works deal with the question of how true wisdom may be found, and often provide some practical examples of wisdom. Another category of writings which lies outside the Old Testament should also be noted – the *Apocrypha*. This small collection of seven books (which is roughly 15 percent of the length of the Old Testament) is also sometimes referred to as the "deuterocanonical writings." It includes a number of later writings from Old Testament times which, although informative, have not been regarded as of binding importance by Christians. Some Bibles include this section of writings; others do not (see pp. 42–45).

The *New Testament* is of particular importance to Christians, as it sets out the basic events and beliefs of the Christian gospel. The New Testament, which consists of twenty-seven books, is considerably shorter than the Old Testament. It is entirely written in Greek. It is strongly recommended that new readers of the Bible begin by reading one of the four *gospels*: Matthew, Mark, Luke, and John. The word "gospel" basically means "good news." Each of the four gospel writers – or "evangelists," as they are sometimes known – sets out the basic events lying behind the good news.

Referring to Passages in the Bible

How do you identify the biblical passage you want to study or talk about? To make this as easy as possible, a kind of shorthand way of referring to biblical passages has evolved over the years. To locate a verse in the Bible, you need to identify three things: the *book* of the Bible, the *chapter* of that book, and the *verse* of that chapter. To make sure you understand this, turn to the Acts of the Apostles, chapter 27, verse 1. What is the name of the centurion mentioned in this verse? If your answer is not "Julius," check your reference again. Now try turning to Paul's letter to the Romans, chapter 16, verse 5. Who was the first convert to Christ in Asia? If your answer is not "Epenetus," check it again.

The above system is potentially quite cumbersome. Writing out everything – as in Paul's letter to the Romans, chapter 16, verse 5 – takes up too much space. So it is abbreviated, as follows: Rom 16:5. This is the standard form of reference, with the following features:

1   An abbreviation of the book of the Bible being referred to, usually two or three letters in length (such as 1 Ki for "1 Kings," Mt for "Matthew," and 1 Co for "1 Corinthians").

2   The number of the chapter of that book, usually followed by a colon (:).

3   The number of the verse in that chapter.

A full list of the books of the Bible, and their standard abbreviations, may be found on p. 39. There is no need to identify the writer of the book (such as Paul), or state whether it is found in the Old or New Testament. All that is needed are these three parameters.

Having got used to referring to individual verses, we now need to explore how to refer to a passage of more than one verse. This is very simple. The reference "Mt 3:13–17" is to the passage which begins at Mt 3:13 and ends at Mt 3:17. To indicate a passage within a single chapter of a biblical book, you need only identify the opening and closing verse in this way. Sometimes the passage will include material from two or more chapters. The following reference is of this kind: 1 Th 4:13–5:11. This refers to a passage which begins at 1 Th 4:13 and ends at 1 Th 5:11.

Now that you are familiar with the basic aspects of this system, there are some minor points that need qualifying. First, some biblical books are so brief that they consist only of one chapter (Obadiah; Philemon; 2 John; 3 John; Jude). In this case, only the verse number is cited. Thus Phm 2 is a reference to the second verse of Philemon. Second, individual psalms are treated as chapters of the Psalter. Thus a reference to Ps 23:1 is a reference to the first verse of the twenty-third psalm.

Finally, in older books, you will find that this system is not always followed. Roman numerals, superscript numbers, and all kinds of punctuation may be used. To give you an idea of the variety, the following are all ways of referring to Paul's second letter to the Corinthians, chapter 13, verse 14.

2Co 13:14	II Cor. xiii.14	2 Cor 13.14	*II Cor* 13.14

These four books describe the life of Jesus Christ, which reaches its climax in his resurrection, as well as presenting his teachings.

The four gospels have distinctive characteristics (see chapter 4) – for example, Matthew is concerned to present Jesus' teaching, whereas

The Books of the Bible and Their Abbreviations

Old Testament		New Testament	
Genesis	Ge	Matthew	Mt
Exodus	Ex	Mark	Mk
Leviticus	Lev	Luke	Lk
Numbers	Nu	John	Jn
Deuteronomy	Dt	Acts	Ac
Joshua	Jos	Romans	Rom
Judges	Jdg	1 Corinthians	1 Co
Ruth	Ru	2 Corinthians	2 Co
1 Samuel	1 Sa	Galatians	Gal
2 Samuel	2 Sa	Ephesians	Eph
1 Kings	1 Ki	Philippians	Php
2 Kings	2 Ki	Colossians	Col
1 Chronicles	1 Ch	1 Thessalonians	1 Th
2 Chronicles	2 Ch	2 Thessalonians	2 Th
Ezra	Ezr	1 Timothy	1 Ti
Nehemiah	Ne	2 Timothy	2 Ti
Esther	Est	Titus	Tit
Job	Job	Philemon	Phm
Psalms	Ps	Hebrews	Heb
Proverbs	Pr	James	Jas
Ecclesiastes	Ecc	1 Peter	1 Pe
Song of Songs	SS	2 Peter	2 Pe
Isaiah	Isa	1 John	1 Jn
Jeremiah	Jer	2 John	2 Jn
Lamentations	La	3 John	3 Jn
Ezekiel	Eze	Jude	Jude
Daniel	Da	Revelation	Rev
Hosea	Hos		
Joel	Joel		
Amos	Am		
Obadiah	Ob		
Jonah	Jnh		
Micah	Mic		
Nahum	Na		
Habakkuk	Hab		
Zephaniah	Zep		
Haggai	Hag		
Zechariah	Zec		
Malachi	Mal		

Common Terms Used in Relation to the Bible

Pentateuch	The first five books of the Old Testament (Genesis, Exodus, Leviticus, Numbers, and Deuteronomy)
Five books of the Law	The first five books of the Old Testament (Genesis, Exodus, Leviticus, Numbers, and Deuteronomy)
Major prophets	The first four prophetic writings of the Old Testament (Isaiah, Jeremiah, Ezekiel, and Daniel)
Minor prophets	The twelve remaining prophetic writings of the Old Testament (Hosea, Joel, Amos, Obadiah, Jonah, Micah, Nahum, Habakkuk, Zephaniah, Haggai, Zechariah, and Malachi)
Synoptic gospels	The first three gospels (Matthew, Mark, and Luke)
Pastoral epistles (or letters)	A way of referring collectively to 1 Timothy, 2 Timothy, and Titus, which takes note of their particular concern for pastoral matters and church order
Catholic epistles (or letters)	Those New Testament letters which are not explicitly addressed to individuals (James, 1 Peter, 2 Peter, 1 John, 2 John, 3 John, Jude). In older works, sometimes referred to as "epistles general"

Mark is more interested in focusing on the last week of his earthly life. Taken together, all four build up to give a comprehensive account of the life, death, and resurrection of Jesus Christ. They provide the main building blocks of the Christian faith, allowing readers to understand why Christians have believed that Jesus Christ is indeed the Lord and Savior of the world. The term *synoptic gospels* is often used to refer to the first three gospels (Matthew, Mark, and Luke). This term refers to their similar literary structure.

This is followed by an account of the expansion of Christianity. How were events described in the gospels received at the time? How did the gospel spread from Palestine to Europe? These questions are addressed in the fifth work to be found in the New Testament, the full title of which is "the Acts of the Apostles," but which is more usually referred to simply as "Acts." The gospel of Luke and Acts are widely agreed to have been written by the same person – Luke.

The next major section of material in the New Testament is the *letters*, sometimes still referred to by the older English word *epistles*. These letters provide teaching concerning both Christian beliefs and behavior, as important today as they were when they were first written. Some of the false teachings which arose in the early period of the church's history are in circulation once more, and these letters provide important resources for defending the integrity of the Christian faith today.

Most of the letters were written by Paul, whose conversion to the Christian faith led him to undertake a major program of evangelism and church planting. Many of his letters were written to churches he had planted, giving them advice. Other letter writers include the apostles Peter and John. Often, the letters describe the hardship being faced for the gospel, or the joy which it brings to the writer and those to whom he is writing. This reminds us that Christianity is not just about beliefs; it is about changed lives. The letters should not be thought of primarily as doctrinal textbooks, but living testimonies to every aspect of the Christian faith, which include doctrinal teaching along with moral guidance and spiritual encouragement. The term *pastoral letters* is sometimes used to refer to the two letters addressed to Timothy and his letter to Titus, which deal particularly with issues of pastoral importance.

The New Testament then ends with the book of Revelation, which stands in a class of its own. It represents a vision of the end of history, in which the writer is allowed to see into heaven, and gain a glimpse of the new Jerusalem which is prepared for believers.

The Continuity between Old and New Testaments

The Christian terms "Old Testament" and "New Testament" are strongly theological in nature. These Christian terms rest upon the belief that the contents of the Old Testament belong to a period of God's dealings with the world which has in some way been superseded or relativized by the coming of Christ in the New Testament. Roughly the same collection of texts is referred to by Jewish writers as "the law, prophets, and writings" and by Christian writers as "the Old Testament." There is thus no particular reason why someone who is not a Christian should feel obliged to refer to this collection of books as the "Old Testament," apart from custom of use.

The Christian theological framework which leads to this distinction is that of "covenants" or "dispensations." The basic Christian belief that the coming of Christ inaugurates something new expresses itself in a distinctive attitude towards the Old Testament, which could basically be summarized thus: religious principles and ideas (such as the notion of a sovereign God who is active in human history) are appropriated; religious practices (such as dietary laws and sacrificial routines) are not.

How, then, are the Old and New Testaments related to one another, according to Christian theology? One option was to treat the Old Testament as the writings of a religion which had nothing to do with Christianity. This approach is especially associated with the second-century writer Marcion, who was excommunicated in the year 144. According to Marcion, Christianity was a religion of love, which had no place whatsoever for law. The Old Testament relates to a different God than the New; the Old Testament God, who merely created the world, was obsessed with the idea of law. The New Testament God, however, redeemed the world, and was concerned with love. According to Marcion, the purpose of Christ was to depose the Old Testament God (who bears a considerable resemblance to the Gnostic "demiurge," a semi-divine figure responsible for fashioning the world), and usher in the worship of the true God of grace. A similar teaching was associated with the Manicheans, who had a significant influence on the leading Christian writer Augustine of Hippo during his younger period. In refuting the Manichean view of the Old Testament as an irrelevance, Augustine argued that it was necessary to see the Old Testament in the light of the New to appreciate its full significance and importance for Christians. Augustine's views are conveniently summarized in his famous dictum: "The New Testament lies hidden in the Old, and the Old Testament is unveiled in the New."

The majority position within Christian theology has on the one hand emphasized the continuity between the two testaments, while at the same time noted the distinction between them. This seems to be the approach found within the New Testament itself. Thus New

Testament writers clearly saw themselves as continuing the great history of salvation, narrated in the Old Testament. Matthew's gospel, for example, brings out the continuity between Jesus and Moses, the gospel and the law, and the church and Israel. Paul's letters often focus on the continuity between the faith of Christians and that of Abraham. The letter to the Hebrews provides what is virtually a point by point comparison between Christianity and Judaism, stressing both the continuity between them and the way in which Christianity brings to perfection the themes of the Old Testament. Several strands can be seen in the New Testament affirmation of continuity with the Old Testament; we shall consider two of particular interest.

In the first place, there is a continuity of divine action, purpose, and identity between the testaments. The New Testament writers stress the fact that the God to whom the New Testament bears witness is the same God who is present and active in the history of Israel, and who may be read about in the Old Testament.

In the second place, there is a continuity of institutions between the testaments. This is a more complex idea, and requires a little explanation. In the sixteenth century, what is usually referred to as the "threefold office of Christ" became of major importance within Protestant circles as a means of highlighting the continuity between the Old and New Testaments. Later in this work, we shall explore the importance of three major institutions in the Old Testament: prophecy, the priesthood, and the monarchy. Jesus' identity and relevance can be summed up in the threefold formula "prophet, priest, and king." The prophetic aspects of Jesus' identity relate to his teaching and his miracles; the priestly aspects of his identity concern his offering made for the sin of humanity upon the cross, and the continued intercession of the risen Christ for his people;

the kingly aspects of his identity concern the rule of the risen Christ over his people.

These three categories were seen as a convenient summary of all that Jesus Christ had achieved in order to redeem his people. Jesus is prophet (Matthew 21:11; Luke 7:16), priest (Hebrews 2:17; 3:1), and king (Matthew 21:5; 27:11), bringing together in his one person the three great offices of the Old Testament. Jesus is the prophet who, like Moses, would see God face to face (Deuteronomy 17:15); he is the priest who will cleanse God's people from their sins; he is the king who, like David, will establish and reign over the people of God (2 Samuel 7:12–16). Thus the three gifts brought to Jesus by the Magi (or wise men: Matthew 2:1–12) were seen as reflecting these three functions.

The Contents of the Bible

The Christian Bible is a collection of sixty-six books, of which thirty-nine are found in the Old Testament and twenty-seven in the New Testament. But how were the contents of the Bible decided? By what process were the sixty-six books of the Bible selected? At a fairly early stage in its history, the Christian church had to make some important decisions as to what the term "Scripture" actually designated. The patristic period witnessed a process of decision-making, in which limits were laid down to the New Testament – a process usually known as "the fixing of the canon."

The word "canon" derives from the Greek word *kanon*, meaning "a rule" or "a fixed reference point." The phrase "the canon of Scripture" thus refers to a limited and defined group of writings, which are accepted as authoritative within the Christian church. The term "canonical" is used to refer to scriptural writings accepted to be within the canon. Thus the gospel of Luke is referred to as "canonical," whereas the gospel of Thomas is "extra-canonical" (that is, lying outside the canon of Scripture).

For the writers of the New Testament, the term "Scripture" meant primarily a writing of the Old Testament. This can be seen particularly clearly in Paul's insistence that "All Scripture is God-breathed and is useful for teaching, rebuking, correcting, and training in righteousness" (2 Timothy 3:16), which is a specific affirmation of the inspiration and authority of the writings of the Old Testament. (The phrase here translated as "all Scripture" could equally well be translated as "every Scripture" or "every writing.")

However, within a short period, early Christian writers (such as Justin Martyr) were referring to "the New Testament" (to be contrasted with the "Old Testament"), and insisting that both were to be treated with equal authority. By the time of Irenaeus, writing in the late second century, it was generally accepted that there were four canonical gospels; by the late second century, there was a widespread consensus that the four gospels, Acts, and letters had the status of inspired Scripture. Thus Clement of Alexandria recognized four gospels, Acts, fourteen letters of Paul (the letter to the Hebrews being regarded as Pauline), and Revelation. Tertullian, writing in the early second century, declared that alongside the "law and the prophets" were the "evangelical and apostolic writings (*evangelicae et apostolicae litterae*)," which were both to be regarded as authoritative within the church.

Gradually, agreement was reached on the list of books which were recognized as inspired Scripture, and the order in which they were to be arranged. This process of reception did not involve the arbitrary, authoritarian imposition of the views of influential bishops or churches. It was a gradual process of reflection and consultation, in which a consensus gradually emerged. In 367, the influential Greek Christian writer Athanasius circulated a letter which identified the twenty-seven books of the New Testament, as we now know it, as being canonical. Athanasius was not imposing his own views at this point, but reporting the views of the church as a whole – views that he clearly expected his readers to take very seriously. Christianity has always stressed the importance of the *consensus fidelium* ("the agreement of the faithful"), and the formation of the canon is an excellent example of this gradual movement towards the emergence of such a consensus.

A number of criteria were important in deciding whether a given writing was to be accepted as "canonical" or not. Three of the most important considerations in evaluating the claims to canonicity of writings were:

1   Their apostolic origins or connections. Were they to be attributed to, or based upon, the preaching and teaching of the first-generation apostles, or their immediate circle? Some were clearly works of the apostles – such as the letters of Peter and Paul. In other cases, such as the letter to the Hebrews, things were not quite so straightforward. This criterion was of major importance in the second century, when the church had to defend itself in the face of attacks from various groups, each claiming to have an "authoritative" revelation of its own.

2   To what extent had they secured general acceptance within Christian communities throughout the world? Individual churches were moving towards agreement on which texts were to be regarded as authoritative. While there were inevitably disagreements over certain texts, the process of the fixing of the canon can be seen as "crystallizing" this consensus. Eusebius of Caesarea, who wrote in the early part of the fourth century, no longer uses the criteria of apostolic authority that was so important to

writers of the second century, but rather asks whether a book was quoted by early orthodox church fathers. The debate has clearly moved on from apostolic credentials to the reception of the book within the global Christian community.

3   One of the main uses of the Bible was in Christian worship. An important criterion for canonicity was thus the extent to which a book was used liturgically – in other words, read publicly when early Christian communities gathered for worship. This practice is already referred to in the New Testament: "And when this letter has been read among you, have it read also in the church of the Laodiceans; and see that you read also the letter from Laodicea" (Colossians 4:16).

This process of determining the canonical works of the New Testament was not always an easy or straightforward process. Debate centered especially on a number of books. The western church had hesitations about including the letter to the Hebrews, in that it was not specifically attributed to an apostle; the eastern church had reservations about the book of Revelation (sometimes also referred to as "the Apocalypse"). Four of the smaller books (2 Peter, 2 and 3 John, and Jude) were often omitted from early lists of New Testament writings. Some writings now outside the canon were regarded with favor in parts of the church, although they ultimately failed to gain universal acceptance as canonical. Examples of this include the first letter of Clement (an early bishop of Rome, who wrote around 96) and the *Didache*, a short early Christian manual on morals and church practices, probably dating from the first quarter of the second century.

The arrangement of the material was also subject to considerable variation. Agreement was reached at an early stage that the gospels should have the place of honor within the canon, followed by the Acts of the Apostles. The eastern church tended to place the seven "catholic epistles" or "general letters" (that is, James, 1 and 2 Peter, 1 2 and 3 John, and Jude) before the fourteen Pauline letters (Hebrews being accepted as Pauline), whereas the western church placed Paul's letters immediately after Acts, and followed them with the catholic letters. Revelation ended the canon in both east and west, although its status was subject to debate for some time within the eastern church.

What criteria were used in drawing up the canon? The basic principle appears to have been that of the *recognition* rather than the *imposition* of authority. In other words, the works in question were recognized by Christians as already possessing authority, rather than having an arbitrary authority imposed upon them. For Irenaeus, the church does not create the canon of Scripture; it acknowledges, conserves, and receives canonical Scripture on the basis of the authority which is already inherent in it. Some early Christians appear to have regarded apostolic authorship as of decisive importance; others were prepared to accept books which did not appear to have apostolic credentials. However, although the precise details of the selection made remain unclear, it is certain that the canon was closed within the western church by the beginning of the fifth century. The issue of the canon would not be raised again until the time of the Reformation.

At the Reformation, a major debate broke out over whether some works accepted by the medieval church as canonical really deserved this status. It must be emphasized that debate centered on the Old Testament; the canon of the New Testament was never seriously questioned, despite Martin Luther's musings about the letter of James. While all the New Testament works were accepted as canonical – Luther's misgivings concerning four of them gaining little support – doubts were raised concerning the canonicity of a group of Old Testament works.

A comparison of the contents of the Old Testament in the Hebrew Bible on the one hand, and the Greek and Latin versions (such as the Vulgate) on the other, shows that the latter contain a number of works not found in the former. Following the lead of Jerome, the reformers argued that the only Old Testament writings which could be regarded as belonging to the canon of Scripture were those originally included in the Hebrew Bible.

A distinction was thus drawn between the "Old Testament" and the "Apocrypha": the former consisted of works found in the Hebrew Bible, while the latter consisted of works found in the Greek and Latin Bibles (such as the Vulgate) but *not* in the Hebrew Bible. While some reformers allowed that the apocryphal works were edifying reading, there was general agreement that these works could not be used as the basis of doctrine. Medieval theologians, however, to be followed by the Council of Trent, defined the Old Testament as "those Old Testament works contained in the Greek and Latin Bibles," thus eliminating any distinction between "Old Testament" and "Apocrypha."

A fundamental distinction thus developed between Catholic and Protestant understandings of what the term "Scripture" actually meant. This distinction persists to the present day. A comparison of Protestant versions of the Bible – the two most important being the *Revised Standard Version* (RSV) and *New International Version* (NIV) – with a Catholic Bible, such as the Jerusalem Bible, will reveal these differences. Yet the difference in question has relatively little practical importance.

One outcome of this debate was the production and circulation of authorized lists of books which were to be regarded as "scriptural." The fourth session of the Council of Trent (1546) produced a detailed list, which included the works of the Apocrypha as authentically scriptural, while Protestant congregations in Switzerland, France, and elsewhere produced lists which deliberately omitted reference to these works, or else indicated that they were of no importance in matters of doctrine. The 1559 Gallic Confession is an excellent example of this kind of work, providing a detailed list of works that are to be accepted as canonical.

The Translation of the Bible

The Bible is written in classical languages – Hebrew, Greek, and, to a very limited extent, Aramaic. So what is a modern western reader of the Bible, unable to read any of these languages, meant to do? Unlike the Muslim Qur'an, which tradition demands be read in the original classical Arabic language, many branches of Christianity have insisted that the Bible should be published and read in the language that ordinary people can understand. This "democratization" of faith reached a new level of intensity in the sixteenth century, when Protestant reformers such as Martin Luther and John Calvin asserted the right of every Christian to have access to the teaching of the Bible in their everyday language.

Although demands for the Bible to be translated into the vernacular reached fever pitch in the sixteenth century, they can be traced back much further. One of those who pressed most vigorously for an English version of the Bible in the fourteenth century was John Wycliffe (ca. 1330–1384), often seen as a forerunner of the Reformation of the sixteenth century, and widely hailed as a champion of Bible translation. Wycliffe argued that the English people had a right to read the Bible in their own language, rather than be forced to listen to what their clergy wished them to hear in Latin – the language of the church, which ordinary people did not understand. As Wycliffe pointed out, the ecclesiastical establishment had considerable vested interests in not allowing the laity access to the Bible. They might even discover that there was a massive discrepancy between the lifestyles of bishops and clergy and those commended – and practiced! – by Christ and the apostles.

Yet there was a problem: the translations that Wycliffe inspired – we are not sure how much translation work he actually did himself – were not based on the original Greek and Hebrew texts of the Bible, but on the standard medieval Latin translation, widely known as the "Vulgate." In other words, Wycliffe was translating a Latin translation into English.

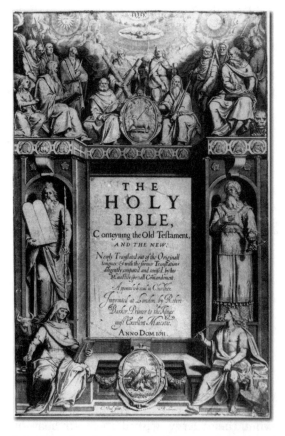

2.1 The frontispiece to the King James Bible of 1611, widely regarded as the most influential English translation of the Bible. Private collection/ www.bridgeman.co.uk.

But what if the Vulgate translation was inaccurate?

This question became of considerable importance during the sixteenth century, when the famous scholar Erasmus of Rotterdam criticized the accuracy of the Vulgate. Erasmus pointed out that the Vulgate translated the opening words of Jesus' ministry (Matthew 4:17) as "do penance, for the kingdom of heaven is at hand." This translation suggested that the coming of the kingdom of heaven had a direct connection with the sacrament of penance. Erasmus pointed out that the Greek text should be translated as "repent, for the kingdom of heaven is at hand." In other words, where the Vulgate seemed to refer to an outward practice (the sacrament of penance), Erasmus insisted that the reference was to an inward psychological attitude – that of "being repentant." These were totally different ideas!

These demands were taken up again by Luther. Luther insisted that the laity should have the right to read and interpret the Bible for themselves. Why did the Bible have to be locked away from the people, imprisoned in the fetters of a dead language which only a charmed circle could read? Why could not the educated laity be allowed to read the Bible in their own languages for themselves, and form judgments on whether what the church taught and practiced was in line with the biblical material? Giving the laity access to the Bible in their own language would let them see how they had been duped by the clergy. Having realized the need for such a translation, Luther decided the task was too important to leave to anyone else. He would do it himself, and translated the New Testament directly from the original Greek into everyday German.

The story of the translation of the Bible into English is one of the most interesting aspects of Christian history. William Tyndale, following the lead of Luther, published the first English translation of the New Testament anonymously in 1526. Although Tyndale had hopes to translate the entire Bible into English, he managed to translate only a few Old Testament books from Hebrew. In the event, the first English translation of the complete Bible to be printed – the Coverdale Bible – appeared in 1535, followed by the more accurate Matthews Bible of 1537, and the Great Bible of 1539. In 1560, a group of English émigrés based in Calvin's city of Geneva produced a particularly good translation, accompanied by illustrations and marginal notes. This rapidly became the favorite Bible of English-speaking Protestants.

However, the world's best-known English translation of the Bible dates from the early seventeenth century. In 1604, James I commissioned a new translation. More than fifty scholars were assembled for the task, working at Westminster, Oxford, and Cambridge. In 1611, the fruit of their labors was finally published. This new translation – generally known as the "Authorized Version" or the "King James Version" of the Bible – would achieve the status of a classic, and became the standard and most widely used English translation of the Bible until the end of World War I in 1918.

The King James Version of the Bible was an outstanding translation by the standards of 1611 and beyond. Yet translations eventually require revision, not necessarily because they are defective, but because the language into which they are translated itself changes over time. Translation involves aiming at a moving target, which has accelerated over the centuries. English is developing more quickly today than at any time in its previous history. Some words have ceased to be used; others have changed their meanings. Many words used by the King James translators have now changed their meaning. The English of 1611 is not the English of the twenty-first century. It can be misleading, simply because English words have changed their meaning. For example, consider the sentence:

> For this we say unto you by the word of the Lord, that we which are alive and remain unto the coming of the Lord shall not prevent them which are asleep. (1 Thessalonians 4:15)

A modern reader would find this puzzling, in that the 1611 meaning of the word "prevent" does not correspond to its modern sense. For the King James translators, "prevent" means what we now understand by "precede" or "go before" – not "hinder," which is the modern sense of "prevent." In the fact that linguistic change now means that the King James Bible has the potential to mislead and confuse, there is a clear case for revision of the translation. The extent of that revision is a matter for discussion; the need is beyond doubt. When a translation itself requires explanation, it has ceased to function as a working translation.

There is no difficulty here. Like any living language, English changes over the years. Linguistic development is simply a sign of life – it means that a language is being used and adapted to new situations. The task of translating is ongoing, not ended. Any modern translation of the Bible – whether into English, Swahili, or Mandarin – must be seen as provisional, requiring amendment as the language undergoes change and development. Translation is a never-ending task.

The Interpretation of the Bible

Every text, once translated, still needs to be interpreted. The Bible is no exception. There is a sense in which the history of Christian theology can be regarded as the history of biblical interpretation (sometimes referred to as "hermeneutics," from the Greek verb "to understand"). In what follows, we shall briefly consider some of the approaches to biblical interpretation found in the long history of the Christian engagement with the Bible.

To illustrate some of the possible approaches to biblical interpretation, we shall turn to the patristic period, widely regarded as being of formative importance to the Christian church. The *Alexandrian* school of biblical interpretation, based on the great city of Alexandria in Egypt, drew on the methods devised by the Jewish writer Philo of Alexandria (ca. 30 BC–ca. AD 45) and earlier Jewish traditions, which allowed the literal interpretation of Scripture to be supplemented by an appeal to allegory. But what is an allegory? The Greek philosopher Heracleitus had defined it as "saying one thing, and meaning something other than what is said." Philo argued that it was necessary to look beneath the surface meaning of Scripture to discern a deeper meaning which lay beneath the surface of the text. These ideas were taken up by a group of theologians based in Alexandria, of which the most important are generally agreed to be Clement, Origen, and Didymus the Blind.

The scope of the allegorical method can be seen from Origen's interpretation of key Old Testament images. Joshua's conquest of the promised land, interpreted allegorically, referred to Christ's conquest of sin upon the cross, just as the sacrificial legislation in Leviticus pointed ahead to the spiritual sacrifices of Christians. It might at first sight seem that this represents a degeneration into *eisegesis*, in which the interpreter simply reads any meaning he or she likes into the text of Scripture. However, as the writings of Didymus (which were rediscovered in an ammunition dump in Egypt during World War II) make clear, this need not be the case. It seems that a consensus developed about the images and texts of the Old Testament which were to be interpreted allegorically. For example, Jerusalem regularly came to be seen as an allegory of the church.

In contrast, the *Antiochene* school, based in the city of Antioch in modern-day Turkey, placed an emphasis upon the interpretation of Scripture in the light of its historical context. This school, especially associated with writers such as Diodore of Tarsus, John Chrysostom, and Theodore of Mopsuestia, gave an emphasis to the historical location of Old Testament prophecies, which is quite absent from the writings of Origen and other representatives of the Alexandrian tradition. Thus Theodore, in dealing with Old Testament prophecy, stresses that the prophetic message was relevant to those to whom it was directly addressed, as well as having a developed meaning for a Christian readership. Every prophetic oracle is to be interpreted as having a single consistent historical or literal meaning. In consequence, Theodore tended to interpret relatively few Old Testament passages as referring directly to Christ, whereas the Alexandrian school regarded Christ as the hidden content of many Old Testament passages, both prophetic and historical.

In the western church a slightly different approach can be seen to develop. In many of his writings, Ambrose of Milan developed a threefold understanding of the senses of Scripture: in addition to the *natural* sense, the interpreter may discern a *moral* sense and a *rational* or *theological* sense. Augustine of Hippo chose to follow this approach, although he modified it somewhat. In place of Ambrose's threefold sense of the text, Augustine instead argued for a twofold sense – a *literal-fleshly-historical* approach and an *allegorical-mystical-spiritual* sense, although he allowed that some passages could possess both senses. "The sayings of the prophets are found to have a threefold meaning, in that some have in mind the earthly Jerusalem, others the heavenly city, and others refer to both."

To understand the Old Testament at a purely historical level is unacceptable; the key to its understanding lies in its correct interpretation. Amongst the major lines of "spiritual" interpretation, the following should be noted: Adam represents Christ; Eve represents the church; Noah's ark represents the cross; the door of Noah's ark represents Christ's pierced side; the city of Jerusalem represents the heavenly Jerusalem. Augustine sets out his approach as follows:

> It is not the Old Testament that is abolished in Christ but the concealing veil, so that it may be understood through Christ. That which without Christ is obscure and hidden is, as it were, opened up . . . The secret truths are conveyed in figures that are to be brought to light by interpretation.

In this way, Augustine is able to stress the unity of the Old and New Testaments. They bear witness to the same faith, even if their modes of expression may be different (an idea developed by John Calvin). Augustine expresses this idea in a text which has become of major importance to biblical interpretation, especially as it bears on the relation between Old and New Testaments: "The New Testament is hidden in the Old; the Old is made accessible by the New."

This distinction between the *literal* or *historical* sense of Scripture on the one hand, and a deeper *spiritual* or *allegorical* meaning on the other, came to be generally accepted within the church during the early Middle Ages. The standard method of biblical interpretation used during the Middle Ages is usually known as the *Quadriga*, or the "fourfold sense of Scripture." The origins of this method lie specifically in the distinction between the literal and spiritual senses. Scripture possesses four different senses. In addition to the literal sense, three non-literal senses could be distinguished: the allegorical, defining what Christians are to believe; the tropological or moral, defining what Christians are to do; and the anagogical, defining what

Christians were to hope for. The four senses of Scripture were thus the following:

1   The *literal* sense of Scripture, in which the text could be taken at face value.
2   The *allegorical* sense, which interpreted certain passages of Scripture to produce statements of doctrine. Those passages tended either to be obscure or to have a literal meaning which was unacceptable, for theological reasons, to their readers.
3   The *tropological* or *moral* sense, which interpreted such passages to produce ethical guidance for Christian conduct.
4   The *anagogical* sense, which interpreted passages to indicate the grounds of Christian hope, pointing towards the future fulfillment of the divine promises in the New Jerusalem.

An excellent example of allegorical interpretation can be found in Bernard of Clairvaux's twelfth-century exposition of the Old Testament book of the Song of Songs. Bernard here provides an allegorical interpretation of the phrase "the beams of our houses are of cedar, and our panels are of cypress," illustrating the way in which doctrinal or spiritual meaning was "read into" otherwise unpromising passages at this time.

> By "houses" we are to understand the great mass of the Christian people, who are bound together with those who possess power and dignity, rulers of the church and the state, as "beams." These hold them together by wise and firm laws; otherwise, if each of them were to operate in any way that they pleased, the walls would bend and collapse, and the whole house would fall in ruins. By the "panels" which are firmly attached to the beams and which adorn the house in a royal manner, we are to understand the kindly and ordered lives of a properly instructed clergy, and the proper administration of the rites of the church.

A potential weakness was avoided by insisting that nothing should be believed on the basis of a non-literal sense of Scripture, unless it could first be established on the basis of the literal sense. This insistence on the priority of the literal sense of Scripture may be seen as an implied criticism of the allegorical approach adopted by Origen, which virtually allowed interpreters of Scripture to read into any passage whatever "spiritual" interpretations they liked. As Luther states this principle in 1515: "In the Scriptures no allegory, tropology, or anagogy is valid, unless that same truth is explicitly stated literally somewhere else. Otherwise, Scripture would become a laughing matter."

The *Quadriga* was a major component of academic study of the Bible within scholastic theological faculties of universities. But it was not the only option available to biblical interpreters in the first two decades of the sixteenth century. Indeed, Luther may be argued to be the only reformer to make significant use of this scholastic approach to biblical interpretation. By far the most influential approach to the subject within reforming and humanist circles in the early Reformation period was that associated with Erasmus of Rotterdam, to which we may now turn.

Erasmus' "Handbook of the Christian Soldier" (see p. 204) made much of the distinction between the "letter" and the "spirit" – that is, between the words of Scripture and their real meaning. Especially in the Old Testament, the words of the text are like a shell, containing – but not identical with – the kernel of the meaning. The surface meaning of the text often conceals a deeper hidden meaning, which it is the task of the enlightened and responsible exegete to uncover. Biblical interpretation, according to Erasmus, is concerned with establishing the underlying sense, not the letter, of Scripture. There are strong affinities here with the Alexandrian school, noted earlier.

We find similar ideas in the writings of Huldrych Zwingli, one of the leading early Swiss Protestant reformers. Zwingli's basic concern echoes that of Erasmus. The interpreter of the Bible is required to establish the "natural sense of Scripture" – which is not necessarily identical with the literal sense of Scripture. Zwingli's humanist background allows him to distinguish various figures of speech, especially alloiosis, catachresis, and synecdoche.

An example will make this difficult point clear. Take the statement of Christ at the Last Supper, in which, when breaking the bread, he spoke the words "this is my body" (Matthew 26:26). The literal sense of these words would be "this piece of bread is my body," but the natural sense is "this piece of bread signifies my body" (see p. 161).

Zwingli's search for the deeper meaning of Scripture (to be contrasted with the superficial meaning) is well illustrated by the story of Abraham and Isaac (Genesis 22). The historical details of the story are too easily assumed to be its real meaning. In fact, Zwingli argues, the real meaning of that story can only be understood when it is seen as a prophetic anticipation of the story of Christ, in which Abraham represents God and Isaac is a figure (or, more technically, a "type") of Christ.

The Devotional Reading of the Bible: Christian Spirituality

It is important to appreciate that the Bible can be read in a number of different ways. It can be read as a historical document – for example, by someone who is concerned to understand something of the history of Israel and its neighbors around the time of King Solomon. It can also be read as a sourcebook of Christian ideas – for example, by someone who wanted to find out what St. Paul thought about the nature of the church. Yet the Bible has been seen by Christians as being about far more than historical or theological information. It is both these things – and yet it is more than this. In addition to providing information, Christians have seen the Bible – when read in the appropriate manner – as a source of spiritual nourishment and refreshment. This did not mean that this way of reading the Bible was "right," where others were "wrong." Rather, Scripture was seen as a multifaceted and rich resource, which could – and should! – be read in a number of manners – some theological, some ethical, and others devotional. Our concern in this section is to note how the Bible plays a highly significant role in what is known as "spirituality." This term needs some explanation before we can proceed further.

The term "spirituality" has gained wide acceptance in the recent past as the preferred way of referring to aspects of the devotional practices of a religion, and especially the interior individual experiences of believers. It is often contrasted with a purely academic, objective, or detached approach to a religion, which is seen as merely identifying and listing the key beliefs and practices of a religion, rather than dealing with the manner in which its individual adherents experience and practice their faith.

The word "spirituality" draws on the Hebrew word ruach – a rich term usually translated as "spirit," yet which includes a range of meanings including "spirit" yet extending to "breath" and "wind." To talk about "the spirit" is to discuss what gives life and animation to someone. "Spirituality" is thus about the life of faith – what drives and motivates it, and what people find helpful in sustaining and developing it. It is about that which animates the life of believers, and urges them on to deepen and perfect what has at present only been begun.

Spirituality is the outworking in real life of a person's religious faith – what a person does

with what they believe. It is not just about ideas, although the basic ideas of the Christian faith are important to Christian spirituality. It is about the way in which the Christian life is conceived and lived out. It is about the full apprehension of the reality of God. We could summarize much of this by saying that Christian spirituality is a reflection on the whole Christian enterprise of achieving and sustaining a relationship with God, which includes both public worship and private devotion, and the results of these in actual Christian life. And for Christians, this often means reading the Bible devotionally.

Medieval conceptions

One of the most important medieval discussions of the correct way to read Scripture is provided by the Carthusian writer Guigo II (d. ca. 1188). According to Guigo, four stages were to be discerned within the process of reading the biblical text:

1   reading (lectio).
2   meditation (meditatio).
3   prayer (oratio).
4   contemplation (contemplatio).

Guigo argues that we begin by reading the text of Scripture, in full expectation that we shall encounter something of God in doing so. This leads us on to meditate on what we find – not in the sense of emptying our minds of everything, but rather allowing our minds to focus and concentrate upon the meaning and imagery of the text, with all external thoughts being excluded. This leads us to prayer as the only appropriate response to what we encounter. Finally, this leads to a quiet entrance into the presence of God in contemplation. Guigo sets out the relationship between these four activities in the following series of terse statements:

- Reading without meditation is sterile.
- Meditation without reading is prone to error.
- Prayer without meditation is lukewarm.
- Meditation without prayer is barren.
- Prayer with devotion achieves contemplation.

This general scheme was widely accepted in the Middle Ages, and offered a framework for unlocking the devotional richness of Scripture. For example, Geert Zerbolt van Zutphen (1367–1400), who is widely regarded as one of the most important early masters of the *devotio moderna*, adopted the basic themes of Guigo's approach in his major work *De spiritualibus ascensionibus* ("on spiritual ascents").

For Zerbolt, the spiritual reading of Scripture prepares the reader for meditation; meditation prepares for prayer; and prayer for contemplation. To meditate without first reading Scripture is to run the risk of being deluded or falling into error, whereas reading Scripture without turning to prayer is arid and barren. In clarifying this point, Zerbolt offers a definition of meditation which can be regarded as a synthesis of the medieval consensus on the issue:

> By meditation is meant the process in which you diligently turn over in your heart whatever you have read or heard, earnestly reflecting upon it and thus enkindling your affections in some particular manner, or enlightening your understanding.

A related approach is associated with Ignatius Loyola (ca. 1491–1556), the founder of the Society of Jesus (see pp. 225–226). Loyola developed a technique of empathetic projection or imaginative engagement, in which the reader of a biblical passage imagines herself to be projected into the biblical narrative, viewing and experiencing it from within. The idea is not original; it can be found particularly well developed in Ludwig of Saxony's *Life of Christ* (1374), in which the author sets out his intention to "recount things according to certain imaginative representations" so that his readers may "make themselves present for those things which Jesus did or said." The process involves the use of the imagination to construct a vivid and realistic mental image of the biblical scene, along with a prayerful engagement with the text in order that it might impact upon the reader in the intended manner. Loyola sets out the basic principles of his method in his "First Exercise," considering how the reader of a gospel passage relating to Jesus should approach the text.

> The first preamble is to form a visual conception of the place. It should be noted at this point that when the contemplation is on something that is visible (such as contemplating Christ our Lord during his life on earth), the image will consist of seeing with the mind's eye the physical place where the object we wish to contemplate is present. By the physical place I mean, for instance, a temple or mountain where Jesus or the Blessed Virgin is to be found, depending on the subject of the contemplation.

Protestant spirituality

The Protestant Reformation of the sixteenth century is often portrayed as a rediscovery of the Bible, and there can be no doubt that one of its leading themes was increasing the accessibility of the Bible, especially to the laity. One of the most central demands of the Reformation was that the Bible should be made available to all in a language which they could understand. The resulting translations of the Bible often had a major impact on the shaping of western European languages. For example, modern German has been recognizably shaped by the phraseology of Martin Luther's translation of the New Testament, just as modern English still contains many set phrases which derive directly from the King James Version of the Bible.

The centrality of Scripture for Reformation spirituality can be seen from the literary resources made available by the reformers. Three are of especial importance.

1   The *biblical commentary* aimed to allow its readers to peruse and understand the word of God, explaining difficult phrases, identifying points of importance, and generally allowing its readers to become familiar with the thrust and concerns of the biblical passage. Writers such as John Calvin (1509–1564), Martin Luther (1483–1546), and Huldrych Zwingli (1484–1531) produced commentaries aimed at a variety of readerships, both academic and lay.

2   The *expository sermon* aimed to fuse the horizons of the scriptural texts and its hearers, applying the principles underlying the scriptural passage to the situation of the audience. Calvin's sermons at Geneva are a model of their kind. Calvin made extensive use in his preaching of the notion of *lectio continua* – the continuous preaching through a scriptural book, rather than on passages drawn from a lectionary or chosen by the preacher. For example, during the period between March 20, 1555 and July 15, 1556, Calvin is known to have preached some two hundred sermons on a single scriptural book – Deuteronomy.

3   Works of *biblical theology*, such as Calvin's *Institutes of the Christian Religion*, aimed to allow their readers to gain an appreciation of the theological coherence of Scripture, by bringing together and synthesizing its statements on matters of theological importance. By doing this, it enabled its readers to establish a coherent and consistent worldview, which would undergird their everyday lives. For Calvin, as for the reformers in general, Scripture molded

doctrine, which in turned shaped the realities of Christian life..

An excellent illustration of the importance of the Bible for early Protestant spirituality is to be found in Martin Luther's 1535 work "A Simple Way to Pray." Luther wrote this short work for his barber, Peter Beskendorf. The treatise sets out an approach to prayer which is based on the reading of biblical passages, such as the Lord's Prayer (Matthew 6:9–13) and the Ten Commandments (Exodus 20:1–17). Luther sets out a means of praying which is based on a fourfold interaction with the biblical text. In the case of the Ten Commandments, Luther set out the method of prayer which he personally found helpful.

> I take one part after another and free myself as much as possible from distractions in order that I may pray. I then divide each commandment into four parts, so that I fashion a garland of four strands. In other words, I think of each commandment as, in the first place, instruction (which is really what it ought to be). Second, I turn it into a thanksgiving. Third, a confession. And fourth, a prayer.

Luther stresses that this framework is only an aid to prayer, and must not be allowed to obstruct the Holy Spirit. However, the framework proved popular, and was widely adopted within Lutheran circles and beyond. The four basic elements which Luther weaves together to yield his "garland of praise" can be set out as follows.

1   *Instruction.* Luther here expects the believer to be reminded of the need to trust God completely in all things, and not to depend on anything else – such as social status or wealth.

2   *Thanksgiving.* At this point, Luther turns his attention to meditation on all that God has done for him, particularly in relation to

redemption, but also recalling that God has promised to be his "comfort, guardian, guide, and strength" in times of difficulty.

3 *Confession.* Having reflected on all that God has done, Luther moves on to acknowledge and confess his own failings and weaknesses.

4 *Prayer.* In the light of the three previous items, Luther then composes a prayer, weaving together these elements, in which he asks God to renew his faith and trust, and strengthen his resolve to be obedient and faithful.

The importance of meditating on biblical passages was thus firmly established within the Protestant spiritual tradition from its earliest phases. The principle can be illustrated from virtually any period of Protestant spirituality. For our purposes, we shall note the way in which it is taken and developed in the writings of the Baptist preacher Charles Haddon Spurgeon (1834–1892), widely regarded as one of the finest preachers of the nineteenth century. For Spurgeon, the danger of an excessively technical approach to reading the Bible could be met by an emphasis upon meditation:

> The Spirit has taught us in meditation to ponder its message, to put aside, if we will, the responsibility of preparing the message we've got to give. Just trust God for that. But first, meditate on it, quietly ponder it, let it sink deep into our souls. Have you not often been surprised and overcome with delight as Holy Scripture is opened up as if the gates of the Golden City have been set back for you to enter? A few minutes' silent openness of soul before the Lord has brought us more treasure of truth than hours of learned research.

Biblical themes and imagery

To show how biblical themes and imagery are used in Christian spirituality, we may focus on one such image, and explore how it has been used over many centuries of reflection – namely, the imagery of light and darkness. In the Genesis creation account, darkness is linked with the idea of chaos and confusion (Genesis 1:1–3). When God creates light, the universe becomes a radically different place. At times, God's presence and power are described in terms of illumination – for example, the people who walked in darkness see a great light (Isaiah 9:2). Jesus is described as the "light of the world," who will overcome darkness (John 8:12).

Yet there are points where God's presence is spoken of in terms of darkness (Exodus 20:21; Deuteronomy 5:23), a reference which is probably best understood in terms of human inability to fully grasp the reality of God. Moses is spoken of as approaching God through darkness and cloud; this imagery has been widely taken to symbolize the human inability to grasp God. Similarly, Paul spoke of our present situation as being that of "seeing through a glass, darkly," even though finally we would be able to see God face to face (1 Corinthians 13:12).

The imagery of light and darkness is powerful and highly effective, and it is not surprising that many writers should have chosen to develop this biblical imagery. An emphasis on spiritual illumination can be found in the writings of the influential German spiritual theologian Meister Eckhart (ca. 1260–ca. 1328), especially in his discussion of "breaking through" the limits of human nature, in which the believer is inundated with divine goodness. This aspect of Eckhart's teaching ("der Durchbruch") is difficult to understand, and is noted here primarily to bring out the close link which Eckhart sees between the presence of God and light. One property of this "spiritual breakthrough" described by Eckhart is that it enlightens the individual:

> One property of this birth is that it comes with fresh light. It always brings a great light to the

soul, in that it is the nature of the good to diffuse itself wherever it finds itself. In this birth, God flows into the soul in such abundance of light that the nature and ground of the soul are both flooded, and it flows over and floods into the powers of the outward man.

In this section, however, we shall focus particularly on the more negative aspects of our theme, noting the way in which the idea of "darkness" is used by spiritual writers to illuminate the human situation and encourage action leading to its improvement or spiritual development. The main uses to which the image of darkness have been put include the following:

1 *Darkness as an image of doubt.* In this case, darkness is linked with the inability to see properly, and hence to gain a full understanding of what is happening. To "be in the dark" is to fail to understand what is going on. Doubt often arises from concerns about an inability to understand God's mysterious workings and presence within the world, so it is easy to see how darkness can be linked with doubt. Light is thus linked with the abolition of doubt.

2 *Darkness as a symbol of sin.* For many spiritual writers, human sin causes a barrier to be placed between God and humanity, so that God is not known or honored on account of human sinfulness. Although some writers suggest that human blindness in regard to the divine is more a consequence of being a creature than being sinful, there are others who choose to stress that spiritual blindness is linked to slavery to sin. As a result, spiritual discipline is seen as a means of obtaining spiritual illumination.

3 *Darkness as a symbol of divine unknowability.* This theme is often found within the apophatic tradition, which stresses the limits

placed upon human knowledge of God. For writers such as Gregory of Nyssa (ca. 330–ca. 395) and Gregory of Nazianzus (329–389), the human believer is plunged into a "divine night," in which God remains unknowable, even though the presence of God is beyond doubt. Precisely because of the limitations placed upon creatures, they cannot fully apprehend their creator.

This third approach can be seen particularly in the fourteenth-century writing *The Cloud of Unknowing.* The author of the work is unknown, although some have attributed it to Walter Hilton (ca. 1343–1396). Its basic theme is that there is "a sort of cloud of unknowing" which is always placed between the believer and God, with the result that God can never be seen clearly, understood by the mind, or experienced in the human affections. Although there are excellent reasons for thinking that the writer has been influenced by the apophatic theology of Dionysius the pseudo-Areopagite, it is clear that the writer develops his own distinctive approach at points of importance. Just as Moses entered into a cloud to experience God, so believers must learn to follow the dark road of unknowing and inner suffering in the present life. Despite occasional moments of rapture corresponding to a partial and temporary grasp of God, the full and permanent possession of God lies beyond the present life.

Many spiritual writers have drawn their imagery of darkness from the Old Testament writing usually referred to as the "Song of Songs," which depicts a meeting of lovers in the darkness. This is interpreted allegorically, as a reference to the encounter of the believing soul and God in the "darkness of faith." For example, John of the Cross (1542–1591) uses the image of darkness to refer to the idea of escaping at night to meet the object of the soul's desire – God. In his poem *The Dark Night*, we find him contemplating with excitement a nocturnal meeting with his beloved.

Probably the best-known exploration of the theme of darkness found in the writings of John of the Cross concerns the famous "dark night of the soul." John used the phrase "the dark night of the soul" to describe the way in which the soul is stripped of its self-assurance and self-reliance in order to open the way to a closer relationship with God. The "dark night of the soul" can be thought of in two different manners, in one of which God is active, in the other of which the believer is active. The active aspect of the "night" is voluntary discipline and self-submission on the part of the believer, in which the Christian learns to avoid sin and achieve detachment from worldly satisfaction and spiritual temptations. This is the normal way of life for most Christian believers.

Yet John also affirms that God may open up another path for those few who are thought to be ready for it. In this case, the believer is passive, and God is active. The passive aspect of the "night" involves the Christian being led or directed by God to achieve new depths of insight through contemplation. This, however, involves letting go of familiar ways of praying, and can be immensely confusing and bewildering in its early stages. In order to be led by God, it is necessary to let go of the familiar routines and insights which have sustained the spiritual life thus far.

In particular, John argues that, up to this point, the believer has relied upon the mind and imagination to depict God as a means of devotion. The passive "dark night of the soul" involves the recognition that anything concerning God that can be grasped or apprehended must be left behind. John makes extensive use of apophatic themes at this point, stressing the limitations of mediated knowledge of God. To achieve unmediated and direct knowledge of God is like being blinded by the sun, unable to see on account of its brilliance. At points, John speaks of the distress which the "dark night" causes to believers. They may feel alone, abandoned, and confused. It is thought that this aspect of John's spirituality has given him an especial appeal in more recent times, resonating with the anxiety and ambiguity of the modern world.

A further image of darkness which has proved fruitful within the Christian spiritual tradition is that of the dark wood. The theme of a great dark forest, in which individuals can become completely lost, is a major theme in many European folk tales. The Brothers Grimm, for example, collected a number of stories which center on the theme of people who find themselves lost in the great forests of Germany. In Dante's *Divine Comedy*, written in the first decades of the fourteenth century, we find this image used as a symbol of human lostness as a consequence of sin. Dante's *Divine Comedy* takes the form of an imaginary journey through hell and purgatory into paradise, set in Holy Week 1300. The drama can be read as an account of personal redemption, as well as a carefully phrased commentary on some aspects of Italian politics of the thirteenth century (especially in relation to the city of Florence). The poem opens with Dante being lost in a wood at the foot of a hill, exhausted by the journey of his life. The "dark wood" is a symbol of human lostness in a world of sin. It is from this point that his journey begins, culminating in the vision of God, "the love which moves the sun and the other stars."

Having considered some general issues concerning the Bible, we may now turn to examine its contents in more detail. We begin our exploration by turning to the Old Testament.

3
The Old Testament

The term "Old Testament" is used by Christian writers to refer to those books of the Christian Bible which were (and still are) regarded as sacred by Judaism. For Christians, the Old Testament is seen as setting the scene for the coming of Jesus, who brings its leading themes and institutions to fulfillment. Early Christians – including Jesus himself and many of the writers of the New Testament – simply used the word "Scripture" or "writing (Greek: *graphe*)" to refer to what is now known as the Old Testament. It is not clear when this specific way of referring to these books became established.

The same texts, of course, continue to be held as sacred by Jews to this day. This means that the same collection of texts is referred to in different ways by different groups. This has led to some proposals for renaming this collection of texts, none of which has gained general acceptance. Three may be noted.

1 *The Hebrew Bible.* This way of referring to the Old Testament stresses the fact that it was written in Hebrew, and is sacred to the Hebrew people. However, it fails to do justice to the way in which Christianity sees an essential continuity between the Old and New Testaments. A minor difficulty is also caused by the fact that parts of the Old Testament are written in Aramaic rather than Hebrew.

2 *The First Testament.* This way of referring to the collection of texts avoids using the word "old," which is held by some to be pejorative. "Old," it is argued, means "outdated" or "invalid." Referring to the Old Testament as the "First Testament" and the New as the "Second Testament" stresses the continuity between the two collections of texts.

3 *Tanakh* – an acronym of the Hebrew words for "law, prophets, and writings (*torah, nevi'im, ketuvim*)," which is the standard Jewish description of the works that Christians call the "Old Testament." This is perfectly acceptable for Jewish use, but does not reflect the specifically Christian understanding of continuity between Israel and the church.

There is presently no generally accepted alternative to the traditional term "Old Testament," which will therefore be used throughout this study. Nevertheless, readers should be aware of the alternatives, and the issues which led to their being proposed.

The Shape of the Old Testament

There are also significant differences between Christian groups over both the contents of the Old Testament and the order in which they should be arranged. In part, these differences arise through the influence of the Septuagint (often abbreviated as "LXX"), a Greek translation of the Old Testament which was produced in the great city of Alexandria over the period 275–100 BC. The translation was made to serve the needs of Greek-speaking Jews outside Palestine who were no longer able to read their Scriptures in the original Hebrew language.

According to tradition, the translation was carried out by a team of seventy (hence the abbreviation "LXX," which is the Roman numeric form of 70) Hellenistic Jews – that is to say, Jews who lived in a Greek-speaking culture, and had adapted to its ways of thought and life. There is textual evidence from Qumran which suggests that the Septuagint translators may have used a Hebrew original that differs from what is now regarded as the standard Hebrew text (often known as the "Masoretic text," compiled in the tenth century AD). The Septuagint version of the Old Testament was widely used by Greek-speaking Jews, and is often quoted in the New Testament. It seems that the widespread Christian use of the Septuagint led to its gradual abandonment by Jewish readers, who reverted to the original Hebrew text.

Although the historical details are not entirely clear, it seems that, at some point around the year AD 90, Jewish scholars met to determine the official canon of the Hebrew Bible. Following the Roman destruction of the Jerusalem temple in AD 70, the rabbinical school of the Pharisees in Jamnia became a center of religious thought. It was here that this process of selection was carried out. It seems that four criteria were used to determine which books should be included within the canon of Hebrew Scripture. Textually, the book had to conform to the Pentateuch. Chronologically, it could not have been written after the time of Ezra (ca. 400 BC). Linguistically, it had to have been originally written in the Hebrew language; and geographically, it had to be written in Palestine.

Some scholars suggest that this process of determining the canon was precipitated by the rise of Christianity, which used the Septuagint extensively; others suggest that the reason had more to do with internal differences within Judaism, which could be resolved by agreeing on a common understanding of which Scriptures were authoritative and which were not. The outcome of this was that Jamnia refused to accept as canonical ten books that were included in the Greek Septuagint Old Testament. The Masoretic text developed from the fifth through tenth centuries reflected the Hebrew canon of Jamnia. Jerome, in translating the Greek Septuagint into Latin in the early fifth century, noted the difference between the larger canon of the Greek Septuagint and that of Jamnia, and referred to these additional works as the "hidden or secret books," from which the word "Apocrypha" derives.

The Septuagint therefore differs from the standard Hebrew text in two important ways. As we have seen, the Septuagint included a number of texts which are not found in the Hebrew text. These Greek texts, for which there is no Hebrew original, came to be regarded as "deuterocanonical" or "apocryphal" by Christian groups. In addition, the order of books differs from the standard Hebrew arrangement. As Christianity was deeply influenced by the Septuagint, this has had important implications for Christian versions of the Bible.

To illustrate this point, we shall set out below the arrangement of the Old Testament in the Hebrew canon and Christian Bibles. To make the comparison simpler, we shall use the Protestant Old Testament canon, which excludes deuterocanonical or apocryphal works. The key point to appreciate is the different order of material, which we shall explain further presently.

Hebrew Canon: 24 Books

Torah (law)
Genesis
Exodus
Leviticus
Numbers
Deuteronomy

Nevi'im (prophets)
Joshua
Judges
Samuel
Kings
Isaiah
Jeremiah
Ezekiel
The Twelve
  Hosea
  Joel
  Amos
  Obadiah
  Jonah
  Micah
  Nahum
  Habakkuk
  Zephaniah
  Haggai
  Zechariah
  Malachi

Ketuvim (writings)
Psalms
Proverbs
Job
Song of Songs
Ruth

Christian Canon: 39 Books

Five Books of the Law
Genesis
Exodus
Leviticus
Numbers
Deuteronomy

Historical Books
Joshua
Judges
Samuel
1 Kings
2 Kings
1 Chronicles
2 Chronicles
Ezra
Nehemiah
Esther

The Writings
Job
Psalms
Proverbs
Ecclesiastes
Song of Songs

The Prophets
Isaiah
Jeremiah
Lamentations
Ezekiel
Daniel
Hosea
Joel
Amos

Lamentations
Ecclesiastes
Esther
Daniel
Ezra
Nehemiah
Chronicles

Micah
Nahum
Habakkuk
Zephaniah
Haggai
Zechariah
Malachi

The following points of comparison are of interest.

1 The Septuagint divided three large works into two. Thus in the Hebrew canon, the books of Samuel, Kings, and Chronicles are single works; in the Septuagint, they are broken down into two smaller units.

2 The Hebrew canon includes some material under the category of "prophecy" which seems actually to be *historical* rather than *prophetic*.

3 The book of Daniel is not regarded as being a prophetic work in the Hebrew canonical order, whereas the Christian canon places it firmly in this category as a "minor prophet."

4 The Hebrew canon treats the twelve minor prophets as a single book; the Christian canon separates them out, and treats each as an individual work.

5 The Christian canon places certain books alongside others where this is seen as helpful – for example, the book of Ruth (which deals with the period of the Judges) follows immediately after the historical book dealing with that era, while the book of Lamentations follows Jeremiah, on account of its historical associations.

6 While both canons agree on the identity of the first book of the Old Testament (Genesis), they end on quite different notes. The Hebrew canon ends with a historical account of the Jewish monarchy (Chronicles), where the Christian canon ends with a prophetic work (Malachi) which

foretells the coming of God to visit and redeem his people – which forms a natural link with the coming of Christ in the New Testament.

Four different configurations of what Christians refer to as the "Old Testament" can therefore be identified:

1 *Judaism*: canon and order of the Masoretic text, originally established at Jamnia.
2 *Greek Orthodoxy*: canon and order of the Septuagint.
3 *Roman Catholicism*: canon and order of the Septuagint, but with "deuterocanonical" works placed at the end.
4 *Protestantism*: canon of the Masoretic text, order of the Septuagint.

The Contents of the Old Testament

The Old Testament consists of thirty-nine canonical books, which can be broken down into four broad categories: *the five books of the law*, the *historical books*, the *prophets*, and the *"writings."* (If deuterocanonical books are included, this figure rises to forty-six). We shall consider each of these in what follows.

The five books of the law

The first five books of the Old Testament are usually referred to as "the five books of the law," or "the Pentateuch" (from the Greek words for "five scrolls"). The Pentateuch can be seen as describing the origins of the people of Israel, and especially the revelation of the God who called that people into being. It provides the foundations for a proper understanding of both the distinctive calling and identity of Israel as the people of God, and the nature and character of the "God of Israel." Above all, it sets out the specific form of law which would give and safeguard the distinctive identity and ethos of Israel as the people of God. The five books of the law were thus of considerable importance to Israel in its later period, as it sought to maintain its unique character. In many ways, the narrative which is set out in the Pentateuch sets the scene for the remainder of the Bible, which can be seen as an outworking of some of the major themes introduced in its five constituent books.

It is not clear when the Pentateuch was written. The most helpful way of understanding the distinctive nature of the work is to see it as a collection of documents, some of which are extremely old, which were brought together at a definite moment in Israel's history, possibly during the period of the exile in Babylon in the sixth century BC. This was a particularly important period in the history of the Jewish people. Cut off from their homeland, the Jewish exiles made strenuous efforts to preserve and safeguard their distinctive identity through preserving and affirming their religious roots. All the available information concerning Israel's history was gathered together and, where possible, committed to writing. The past history of the people of God was seen as a major controlling influence over its future, whenever restoration to the Jewish homeland took place. However, our understanding of the chronology of the compilation of the Pentateuch remains uncertain, and it is quite possible that we shall never know the exact circumstances of its compilation.

The Pentateuch opens with the book of *Genesis*. The book takes its name from the Greek word for "origins," reflecting the book's characteristic concern to explain the origin of the world in general, and the people of God in particular. In contrast to other accounts of creation found in the ancient near east (in which successive minor gods, goddesses, and heroes are involved in the creation of the world), Genesis

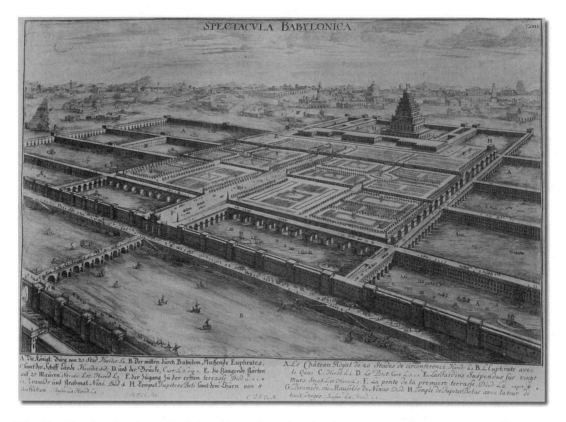

3.1 The Hanging Gardens of Babylon, after Johann Bernhard Fischer von Erlach, ca. 1700. AKG-Images.

affirms that the creation is the work of one, and only one, god. There are two accounts of the creation of the world, each told from different perspectives and with different points of focus. The first creation account in Genesis (Genesis 1:1–2:3) opens with its famous declaration that God created the heavens and the earth. Everything has its origins from God. During the six days of creation, everything that is now a familiar part of the world is surveyed, and declared to owe its existence to a sovereign act of creation on the part of God.

The account of the creation of the sun, moon, and stars is of especial interest. For many ancient peoples, these heavenly bodies represented divine or supernatural powers, and were the object of worship and supersti-

tion. Genesis puts them firmly in their place: they are parts of God's creation, and are thus subject to God's authority. They should not be worshipped, and need not be feared. God has authority and dominion over them. No part of God's creation is to be worshipped. The entire creation is the work of the creator God, who alone is to be worshipped.

The creation of humanity is of especial importance. The first creation account places the creation of humanity at the end of God's work of creation (1:26–27). This is the high point of creation, in which the only creature to bear the image of the creator God is introduced. The passage just cited is unusual, in that it opens with something like a fanfare, a declaration that something major is about to take place. It is clear that humanity is meant to be seen as the zenith of God's creative action and power. The Hebrew word often translated as "man" is here to be understood as "humanity" in general, rather than as "a male human being" in particular.

The second creation account (Genesis 2:4–25) takes a different form from the first account, yet makes many of the same points. The second account opens with the creation of humanity (2:7), affirming that humanity is the most important aspect of the creation. It is made absolutely clear that human life is totally dependent upon God. The reference to God breathing the "breath of life" into humanity (2:7) is of particular importance, in that it both emphasizes the God-given origins of life and anticipates the important life-giving role of the Holy Spirit. (The Hebrew term *ruach* can mean "spirit," "wind," or "breath," pointing to the close connections between these ideas.) It is only when God breathes upon humanity that it comes to life.

With the book of Genesis, the curtain thus lifts over the stage of world history. As the book unfolds, its readers will begin to learn about the great story of God's calling of Israel to be the people of God. Just as an operatic overture will introduce the themes of the opera to its awaiting audience, so Genesis introduces its readers to the great themes which will dominate Scripture. We learn of God's creation of the world, and of its rebellion against its creator. We learn of God's decision to restore the creation to fellowship, and the calling of a people to serve God and bring this good news to the ends of the earth. In short, Genesis sets the scene for the great drama of redemption which forms the subject of Scripture. Particular attention is focused on the person of Abraham, who is seen as the origin of a people who will inherit Canaan as their promised land, and share in the blessings promised to them by God. By the end of the book of Genesis, the people of Israel have settled in Egypt.

The narrative is then continued in the book of *Exodus*, which derives its name from the Greek term for "way out." It tells of how the people of Israel fell into slavery in Egypt, and of the way in which Moses emerged as their deliverer. A particularly important theme is that of God calling Moses, and appointing him as the deliverer of the people of God. Exodus tells of how the oppressive Egyptian monarch was forced to allow the captive people of Israel to go free, before changing his mind and pursuing them into the desert. The account of the crossing of the Red Sea is one of the high points in this dramatic narrative.

Yet Exodus tells of more than the deliverance of Israel from bondage in Egypt. It begins to narrate the way in which Israel's identity as the people of God was impressed upon her. Of central importance here is the giving of the law, or the Ten Commandments, at Mount Sinai. This code of law provided a distinctive way of living which was to be characteristic of the people of God, shaping their identity and ethos.

The book of *Leviticus* develops this aspect of the matter further. It sets out the characteristic religious and cultural practices and beliefs which marked Israel off from all other nations, and safeguarded her distinctive identity as the people of God. Leviticus gives specific guidance for the forms of worship to be adopted by Israel, and particularly the sacrifices which ensured individual and corporate purity before God. Of particular importance is the ritual associated with the Day of Atonement, which was ordained as an annual event for the removal of sin from the people of God (see p. 79).

The book of *Numbers* picks up the account of Israel's wanderings in the wilderness, as it moves from Egypt to the borders of the promised land of Canaan. Much of the book is taken up with details of the preparations being made to invade Canaan. The book ends with Israel poised on the eastern side of the River Jordan, waiting to enter the promised land.

The final book in the Pentateuch is *Deuteronomy*. This unusual word derives from the Greek words for "the second law," or perhaps "a copy of the law." This name refers to one of the distinctive features of the work, which is its repetition of the main themes of the law to Israel before she is permitted to enter Canaan. The book emphasizes the distinct identity of Israel as the people of God, and the vitally important role of the law as a means by which this unique identity and role can be safeguarded. Once Israel is established in Canaan, she is to keep the law of the Lord, not the customs of the Canaanites. Only in this way can Israel's identity and mission be preserved. As will become clear from the later historical writings, one of the most persistent features of Israel's history after the entry into the promised land is the compromise of her distinctive religious ideas and practices. Assimilation to Canaanite beliefs and rituals was a constant threat to Israel.

All this lies in the future, however. The Pentateuch ends with the death of Moses, who had led the people of Israel to the brink of Canaan, but would not himself be allowed to enter it. A new period in the history of Israel is about to dawn.

The historical books

The Old Testament places considerable emphasis on the importance of the acts of God in history. The deliverance of Israel from captivity in Egypt is often referred to by Old Testament writers as an illustration of God's power and faithfulness. The historical books serve a major purpose in relation to the Old Testament: they provide a historical narrative and theological commentary, providing its readers with an understanding of God's intentions for Israel.

Deuteronomy ended with the people of Israel waiting to cross into the promised land. The narrative of Israel is now taken up in the book of *Joshua*, named after Moses' successor as the leader of Israel. The book deals with the conquest of Canaan. One issue of particular interest concerns the dating of the conquest of Canaan. A range of dates for the conquest has been suggested, based on a variety of considerations, including archaeological evidence and the internal evidence of the biblical documents. Some factors point to an early date for the events in question, perhaps around 1400 BC; others point to a later date, perhaps in the region of 1250–1200 BC. The precise date is not, however, of vital importance to understanding the theological and cultural importance of the events.

After the crossing of the River Jordan, three major campaigns of conquest are described, focusing on the central, southern, and northern regions of Canaan. The first campaign was directed against the Gibeonites (Joshua 9:1–27), a group of peoples to the north of Jerusalem. The second campaign involved a coalition of kings from the southern regions of Canaan, including the cities of Jerusalem and Hebron (Joshua 10:1–43). Finally, Joshua dealt with a coalition of city-states in the northern region of Canaan (Joshua 11:1–23). Armies drawn from the Galilean hill country assembled at a site referred to as Merom, which is thought to be some 12 kilometers to the northwest of Lake Galilee. Joshua defeated the armies, pursuing them to the north, and eventually turning south again to take and destroy the important city of Hazor. Joshua completed his subjugation of the region by defeating the Anakites. With this, the military campaigns ended, and "the land had rest from war" (Joshua 11:23). Joshua could now divide the land amongst the tribes of Israel. This action was understood in terms of the fulfillment of the promises made to Abraham, and confirmation of God's covenant with Israel.

The history of Israel in Canaan is then taken a stage further in the book of *Judges*, which describes the consolidation of Israel's presence in the region. The book of Judges deals with the history of Israel from the death of Joshua to the rise of Samuel, before there was any permanent centralized administration (in the form of a monarchy, for example) in the land. It chronicles the decline in religious faith and obedience in the land after the death of Joshua, especially its lapse into idolatry and pagan practices. One of the most noticeable differences between the books of Joshua and Judges concerns the situations that confront Israel. In Judges, Israel has to occupy and subdue Canaan, facing threats from the various peoples already living there. Israel is portrayed as a people acting and working together against these threats from within Canaan. In Judges, however, the main threats come from outside Canaan – from peoples from the east side of the Jordan, such as the Ammonites, Midianites, and Moabites. Only on one occasion is there any reference to a threat from within Canaan itself. Israel is no longer a single centralized body of people, but a settled group of tribes who have now established themselves in various regions of Canaan. Although they share a common faith and a common story, they increasingly tend to think of their identities in terms of individual tribes and clans, rather than being members of Israel as a whole. For example, there was no national standing army; whenever a national emergency arose, volunteers had to be recruited locally to meet the challenge. The general theme of the book is the internal decline of Israel into a collection of self-serving groups, without any sense of national identity. The need for a national leader was clear.

The word "judge" needs a little explanation. During this period, a number of individuals, such as Deborah and Samuel, are referred to as "judges." In modern days, this would be understood to mean something like "an impartial arbitrator in legal debates," or "someone who passes judgment." The word is, however, used in a very different sense in this book. Its basic meaning is "a charismatic leader raised up by God to deliver Israel from danger." The emphasis is upon deliverance from danger rather than impartial legal administration. The "judges" are actually figures of salvation rather than judgment. It is against this background that the book of *Ruth* is set, documenting a love affair illustrating the issues and concerns of the period.

The book of Judges records the inner decay of Israel through a lack of national identity. It offers a graphic account of Israel's degeneration into political, religious, and moral corruption after the golden period of Joshua. So what was to happen? The closing chapters of the book of Judges frequently reiterate that "in those days Israel had no king" (Judges 17:6; 19:1; 21:25). It is clear that the establishment of the monarchy is envisaged. But how did the kingship come to be established? The two books we now know as 1 and 2 Samuel were originally one larger book, which was divided into two halves by early translators. The division is not entirely helpful, and disrupts the flow of the work. The two works together document the development of kingship in Israel, eventually leading to the recognition of Saul as the first king of Israel, and his subsequent death and replacement by David. Although David was the most significant and successful of Israel's kings, the books of Samuel offer a sympathetic yet realistic assessment of his character and achievements.

One of the developments which should be noted in this narrative is the emergence of the terms "Israel" and "Judah" to refer to the northern and southern regions of the land which was originally Canaan. The term "Israel" was originally used to refer to this land, up to and during the reign of Saul. However, after the death of Saul, open warfare broke out between the supporters of Saul in the north and the supporters of David in the south of the country. As David was himself a member of the tribe of Judah, it was probably only to be expected that the term "Judah" came to refer to both the southern tribes of Simeon and Judah (Joshua 19:1–9), who backed David against the house of Saul.

The house of Saul regarded itself as continuing the rule of Saul over all Israel, and thus retained the term "Israel" to refer to its sphere of influence, despite the fact that this now referred only to the northern region of the country. David is initially proclaimed king of Judah at the southern city of Hebron; it is only as a result of his military campaigns that he becomes king of all Israel. Up to the time of Saul's death, there had been a non-Israelite corridor separating the northern tribes from the southern tribes. This corridor included the city of Jerusalem, which was held by the Jebusites, and the city of Gezer, which was under Egyptian control. David's conquest of Jerusalem united the two halves, a process which was finally completed when Gezer was given to Solomon as a wedding present by Pharaoh (see 1 Kings 9:16–17). When the united kingdom was divided into two after the death of Solomon (930 BC), it was natural that the northern kingdom should retain the name "Israel," and the southern kingdom, centering on Jerusalem, the name "Judah."

As with 1 and 2 Samuel, the two books of *Kings* were originally one long work, which was divided into two for convenience by translators. The two books of Kings follow on directly from the two books of Samuel, with the result that the four books together provide a continuous account of the development and history of the kingdom of Israel (and subsequently of Israel and Judah) from the establishment of the monarchy until the exile in Babylon. This continuity is brought out more clearly in the title which is given to the books in the Greek translation of the Old Testament, usually referred to as the "Septuagint." In that translation, 1 and 2 Samuel are referred to as "1 and 2 Kingdoms," while 1 and 2 Kings are given the titles "3 and 4 Kingdoms."

1 Kings opens with a description of the monarchy of Israel at its high point under David, and subsequently under Solomon (970–930 BC). The description of the building of the temple is clearly seen as the climax of David and Solomon's great achievement of establishing Israel as a military, political, and religious entity. Yet Solomon's flirtations with paganism are chronicled, along with their implications for the life of the nation. Shortly after Solomon's death, the nation of Israel split apart into the northern region (still known as "Israel," but severely reduced in territory) and the southern kingdom of Judah, with Jerusalem as the capital city of the southern kingdom.

The story of decline which follows links historical narration with theological comment. The destruction of the northern kingdom by Assyria in 722 BC is clearly interpreted as a sign of God's disfavor, resulting from the paganism introduced into the region by successive kings of Israel. Among those pagan practices, Canaanite fertility cults made their reappearance. The southern kingdom survived the downfall of its northern neighbor. However, it was only a matter of time before it too collapsed. In 587 BC, Jerusalem was sacked by invading Babylonian armies, and many of the inhabitants of the city were deported to exile in Babylon.

This event marks a watershed in the Old Testament. It is widely interpreted as God's punishment of Jerusalem for her sins, and offering her a period of exile in which to repent and renew her identity as the people of God. Eventually, the community would be restored to Jerusalem, and would work to renew the faith and institutions of pre-exilic Israel. That would involve a major process of retrieval and renewal, which is described in the books of Ezra and Nehemiah.

The two books of *Chronicles* are clearly written with the needs of this restored community in mind. They are concerned to demonstrate the continuity between the past and the present, and reassure their readers of the continuing validity of God's covenant promises to the people of Jerusalem. In many ways, the books of Chronicles can be regarded as bringing together material which is spread out across the books of Samuel and Kings. However, additional material is provided in many cases, probably from archive resources. Part of the additional material relates to a much earlier period in Israel's history; its inclusion stresses the continuity of God's presence and promises throughout the history of God's people.

It is also noticeable that Chronicles tends to portray both David and Solomon in a much more favorable light than that found in the books of Samuel and Kings. The incidents which highlight David's weaker side (such as his adulterous relationship with Bathsheba) are passed over. Similarly, Solomon is portrayed in a very flattering manner. No mention is made of his foreign wives or the pagan practices or beliefs which they encouraged.

It is clear that one of the purposes of Chronicles is to stress the importance of David and Solomon, and the example and encouragement which they provide for the restored community which has now returned from exile in Babylon. They are also seen as pointing ahead to the coming of the Messiah, the ideal king of Israel, who will bring to final fulfillment all that David and Solomon tried to achieve. The work aims to encourage and inspire the nation at a time when its fortunes were often low, and reassure Israel that the God who entered into a covenant with David and Solomon remains faithful to that covenant to this very day. The temple is seen as a major focus for Israel's hope and faith, and particular attention is paid to this theme throughout the works. Thus the account of Solomon's reign is dominated by the building of the temple, which is seen as his major contribution to the wellbeing of his people.

The books of *Ezra* and *Nehemiah* document the events which resulted from the overthrow of the Babylonian empire by the Persian monarch Cyrus in 538 BC. Cyrus liberated the exiled Jewish population from Babylon, and granted them permission to return to Jerusalem and rebuild their temple. The books document various aspects of the resettlement of Jerusalem, the slow rebuilding of the temple, and the problems encountered by the returning exiles. A theme which becomes of considerable significance is the renewal of Israel's religious life, and the need for the exiles to maintain their cultural and religious identities, particularly through refusing to marry with other local peoples in the region. Finally, the book of *Esther* documents the way in which a Jewish community in the later Persian empire was spared from destruction.

The writings

One of the most important themes in the Old Testament is that of "wisdom." A number of Old Testament writings focus on this theme, noting in particular how wisdom is linked with a knowledge of God. Of the four major writings of the Old Testament, three (Job, Proverbs, and Ecclesiastes) are regarded as belonging to this specific category of "wisdom" literature. The fourth book (the Psalter) has its natural context in the worship of Israel in the temple. A fifth book is also usually included in this collection – the love poem widely known as the Song of Solomon.

The theme of "wisdom" is of considerable importance within the Old Testament. The term can refer to a form of commonsense wisdom, which notices certain patterns in human behavior. More fundamentally, however, it refers to a profound understanding of the mysteries of life, which is ultimately due to God. This can be illustrated by the history of Solomon, widely regarded as Israel's wisest king, who prays to God to give him wisdom. This request was granted on the condition that he remain faithful to God during his reign (1 Kings 3:2–15). The wisdom for which Solomon thus became famous is to be seen as a gift from God, rather than a natural endowment. That wisdom is immediately shown in action in the famous case of the two women who claimed to be the mother of the same infant (3:16–28). We later learn that, on account of his wisdom, Solomon was sought out by rulers throughout the world (4:29–34). The fundamental lesson to the reader of the Old Testament is clear: true wisdom is a gift from God, and cannot be had from any other source.

The book of *Job* is one of the most remarkable writings in the Old Testament. It focuses on a question of continuing interest and importance. Why does God allow suffering? Or, more precisely, does the fact that someone is suffering mean that he or she has fallen out of God's favor? Is suffering the direct result of sin?

The book of Job has a distinctive structure, which needs to be understood before it can be fully appreciated. The book opens by setting the scene for Job's sufferings, and allowing us to overhear Job's own understanding of his situation. We are then introduced to his three well-meaning friends, Eliphaz, Bildad, and Zophar. As the well-known phrase "Job's comforters" implies, they end up causing Job more misery and confusion than he felt in the first place. Their basic assumption is that Job's suffering results from sin – an assumption that the reader of Job knows to be incorrect, on account of the information supplied in the opening chapters of the work. The first part of the work consists of three cycles of speeches by the comforters, to which Job replies. This is then followed by some comments by Elihu, who seems to have been an onlooker who

wished to contribute to the discussion at this point. Finally God responds, clearing up the confusion which has been generated by the theological ramblings of the disputants.

The Book of *Psalms* (sometimes also known as "the Psalter") is composed of a series of collections of psalms, which was probably arranged in its final form in the third century BC. The Psalter as we now have it includes a number of smaller collections, including the "Psalms of Asaph" (Psalms 73–83), the "Psalms of the Sons of Korah" (Psalms 84–85; 87–8), and the "Psalms of David" (Psalms 138–145). The 150 psalms brought together in this collection of collections are arranged in five books, as follows:

- Book 1: Psalms 1–41.
- Book 2: Psalms 42–72.
- Book 3: Psalms 73–89.
- Book 4: Psalms 90–106.
- Book 5: Psalms 107–150.

Although the book probably took its final form in the third century BC, most of the material brought together dates from much earlier, generally in the region 1000–500 BC. The task of dating individual psalms can be difficult, although some can be assigned to dates with a reasonable degree of certainty.

Many psalms have titles attached to them. For example, Psalm 30 is entitled "A psalm. A song. For the dedication of the temple. Of David." This would naturally suggest that the psalm in question was written by David for the occasion of the dedication of the property and building materials for the temple, as recorded at 1 Chronicles 21:1–22:6. Although the reliability of the individual psalm titles has often been challenged, there are good reasons for believing that they are original and authentic. For example, psalms recorded outside the Psalter are generally given titles (such as those found at 2 Samuel 22:1, Isaiah 38:9, and

Habakkuk 3:1). Furthermore, the historical information preserved in the titles accords well with the content of the psalm in question.

The book of *Proverbs* consists mainly of a collection of short proverbial sayings, attributed to Solomon, famed for his wisdom. The Hebrew word here translated as "proverbs" has a much broader range of meaning than the corresponding English word, and can also have the sense of "parable" or "oracle" (both of which suggest God's involvement in the gathering of human wisdom). According to biblical tradition, Solomon was credited with having "spoken" some three thousand proverbs (1 Kings 4:32); the sayings collected together in the main body of the work would amount to less than one seventh of these. This suggests that the bulk of Proverbs was written in the tenth century BC, at a time of relative peace and stability suitable for the production of literary works. However, there are indications that not all the material collected in Proverbs may be due directly to Solomon. Although the work gives every indication of having been written in the tenth century BC, there are indications in the text itself that it may have received its final form at some point during the reign of Hezekiah (ca. 715–686 BC).

The book of *Ecclesiastes* is perhaps the most pessimistic in the Old Testament. Like Proverbs and Job, it belongs to the category of wisdom literature. The book takes the form of a collection of proverbs and observations, some long and some very brief. The book is best understood as a powerful and convincing commentary on the meaninglessness of life without God, and the utter despair and cynicism which will inevitably result from lacking a biblical faith. It represents a graphic portrayal of the misery and futility of human life without God, and the inability of human wisdom to discover God fully.

The author of this work introduces himself as "the teacher" (*Ekklesiastes* in the Greek translation of the Old Testament), and is traditionally identified as Solomon on account of the reference to "son of David, king of Jerusalem" (Ecclesiastes 1:1). This designation could, however, be used of any descendant of David. The book itself occasionally indicates that it was written by a subject rather than a ruler, and the style of Hebrew used suggests that the book dates from later than the time of Solomon. There is no general consensus on any particular date, and it is probable that we shall never know with certainty when the book was written.

Finally, this collection of writings ends with a brief work, sometimes referred to as the *Song of Solomon*. This is generally regarded as an outstanding love poem. The work is also known as the "Song of Songs," which literally means "the greatest of songs." The work is traditionally understood to have been written by Solomon, although there is insufficient evidence within the text of the work itself to confirm this with certainty. The book is loosely structured around five meetings between the lover and the beloved, with reflection on the periods during which they are obliged to be apart.

The prophets

The theme of prophecy is of major importance within the Old Testament (see p. 80). The prophets were understood to be individuals, inspired by God, who spoke on behalf of God to Israel. Prophecy is found in the historical books, which relate the careers and prophecies of Elijah and Elisha. However, a substantial section of the Old Testament is specifically devoted to collections of the prophecies of individual prophets. The Old Testament indicates that the prophets were often highly critical of the establishment. The themes which often recur in their writings include the need for national and individual repentance, a turning away from pagan beliefs and practices, and a rejection of dependence on military and political power. Jeremiah appears to have been particularly unpopular. Nevertheless, despite this unpopularity, the prophets were seen as maintaining a vital link between God and Israel. While the prophets were active, God continued to speak to Israel. When prophecy died out, it seemed to many that God no longer communicated with the nation.

The book of the prophet *Isaiah* is the first of the four "major prophets" (the other three books being Jeremiah, Ezekiel, and Daniel). Isaiah lived and worked in Jerusalem in the latter part of the eighth century BC. His call to prophesy came in 740 BC, the year of King Uzziah's death (6:1), and he is known to have prophesied up to at least 701 BC, when the northern kingdom of Israel fell to Assyria. At this stage, Judah and Israel were both moving out of a longer period of peace and prosperity into one of uncertainty and danger. Assyria was becoming aggressive in the region, and Israel, Judah, and Syria are uncertain as to how to react to this threat. It is against this context of political and military uncertainty that Isaiah's ministry is set. However, the prophecy is not restricted to this period in the history of Jerusalem. The later parts of the book concern prophecies of hope and restoration for the Babylonian exiles. The early parts of the prophecy cover the period between the fall of the northern kingdom of Israel in 722 and the extreme danger to Judah from Assyria in 702 BC. An important section of the work (chapters 36–39) deals with Judah's survival of this threat. A major later section (chapters 40–55) goes on to prophesy Judah's later enslavement to Babylon and its eventual deliverance from exile in that land. The final perspective of the book looks beyond events in Judah's immediate future to a glorified Jerusalem, set amidst "new heavens and a new earth."

The prophecy of *Jeremiah* is the longest book in the whole Bible. Jeremiah was called to be a prophet to Jerusalem in the year 626 BC. He would continue his ministry during the remainder of the reign of Josiah (who died in battle against the Egyptians in 609 BC), and during the reigns of Jehoahaz (609), Jehoiakim (609–598), Jehoiachin (598–597), and Zedekiah (597–586). These were turbulent years. The basic sequence of events during the period of Jeremiah's ministry can be summarized as follows. Josiah, who had instigated a series of religious reforms which led to a purification and refining of Judah's religious life, died in 609, attempting to oppose an Egyptian advance to aid the ailing Assyrian forces, who were about to fall to the sustained attacks of the Babylonians and their allies the Medes. The capital city of Assyria, Nineveh, fell to their armies in 612; it was just a matter of time before Babylon established itself as supreme in the region. The death of Josiah was something of a personal tragedy for Jeremiah, as it is clear that the king was sympathetic to both the prophet and his message from the Lord. Josiah's successors were consistently hostile towards him, and often openly contemptuous of his prophetic message. In 605, during the reign of Jehoiakim, the Babylonians laid siege to Jerusalem, and subdued it for a while. Following further unrest within the city, the Babylonians attacked it again in 598–597 BC, taking off Jehoiachin, who had succeeded the king of similar name at that time. The Babylonians attacked Jerusalem again in 588 BC, and took full possession of the city two years later. Gedaliah was appointed governor. Jeremiah found himself within the circle of the governor, which was shattered by his assassination shortly afterwards. Jeremiah sought refuge in Egypt, where he is believed to have died.

The basic themes of Jeremiah's prophecies focus on Jerusalem's need to remain faithful to God, rather than rely on military alliances with her neighbors. This theme can be found in many of the prophets of this dangerous period. A short work which is linked with the name of Jeremiah immediately follows this prophecy. The book of *Lamentations* consists of five poems or "laments" over the destruction of Jerusalem by the Babylonians in 586 BC. According to an ancient tradition, they were written by Jeremiah himself. While this cannot be proved, the book certainly seems to have been written at some point between 586 and 538 BC. The fact that the book provides such a graphic portrayal of the destruction of Jerusalem suggests that most of the material is to be dated shortly after the fall of the city in 586 BC, when the events described would still have been vivid in the memory of those who lived through them.

The book of *Ezekiel* centers on the great issues of apostasy, sin, and exile which also dominated both Isaiah and Jeremiah. Ezekiel deals with the period in the history of Judah in which the threat of exile became both real and urgent. Following the Babylonian defeat of the Egyptians at the battle of Carcemish (605 BC), the way was clear for the Babylonians to dominate the entire region which included Judah. This development is the background to some of Jeremiah's major prophecies concerning the threat of exile. That threat would be fulfilled in its totality in 586 BC, when the besieging Babylonian army would finally conquer Jerusalem and deport its population. However, an earlier deportation took place in 597 BC, when Jehoiachin and a group of about 10,000 of the population were deported. This group included Ezekiel.

Ezekiel thus prophesies about the state of affairs in Jerusalem from his exile near Babylon. There is no evidence that Ezekiel himself ever left Babylon. The exiles settled in Babylon along the "Kebar River" (Ezekiel 1:1), which was actually an irrigation canal. We learn that Ezekiel had been born into a priestly family, and would thus normally have expected to serve in the temple at Jerusalem. In 593, when he would normally have begun his priestly duties in the temple, Ezekiel was called to be a prophet to the exiles. This prophetic ministry was carried out entirely in Babylon, and covers the period 593–573 BC.

The fourth of the "major prophets" is the book of *Daniel*. This unusual work is possibly better described as an apocalyptic rather than a prophetic work, on account of the importance attached to visions of the end times. (As we saw earlier, Jewish arrangements of the books of the Old Testament treat Daniel as a "writing" rather than a "prophecy.") The book of Daniel emphasizes the importance of remaining faithful to God, even under difficult circumstances, and illustrates this from the story of Daniel and his three companions in Babylon. The later part of the book consists of visions of coming judgment and retribution, which often include symbols of peoples and nations, emphasizing God's sovereign control over history and his ultimate victory over forces which may seem to have gained the upper hand for the time being.

This is followed by the twelve minor prophets, arranged generally in terms of their dates of activity. Some of the prophets, such as Amos and Hosea, were active in the northern kingdom of Israel prior to its destruction by Assyria in 722 BC; most, including Isaiah and Micah, prophesied to the southern kingdom of Judah, and particularly its capital city, Jerusalem.

Hosea dates from the middle of the eighth century BC. It is clear that Hosea, like Amos, came from the northern kingdom of Israel, and prophesied to it during its final days before it was destroyed by the Assyrians and its peoples taken off into exile. Despite this, however, the book itself appears to have been written in the southern kingdom of Judah, suggesting that Hosea may have fled to the safety of this region after the fall of Israel. Hosea focuses on the unfaithfulness of Israel to God.

Little is known about *Joel*, apart from the name of his father. The prophecy contained in this book is difficult to date, as there are no clear references to any historical events which would allow even a provisional date to be assigned to this work. Some have suggested that the work may date from as early as the ninth century; others point to a later date, suggesting that the work may have been written after the return from exile. The central theme of the work is the coming of the "Day of the Lord." A day of darkness is at hand, in which destruction will come to Zion. Although the reference is primarily to the coming of a vast cloud of locusts, it is clear that Joel sees in this catastrophe a sign of God's judgment. This disaster is intended to move a complacent people to repentance. Joel looks forward to a coming day when the "Spirit of the Lord" will be poured out on the people of God – a prophecy which Christians regard as being fulfilled in the Day of Pentecost.

The book of *Amos* focuses on the failures of the northern kingdom of Israel. Although born in the southern kingdom of Judah, Amos appears to have ministered primarily to the northern kingdom of Israel during the reigns of Uzziah, king of Judah 792–740, and Jeroboam II, king of Israel 793–753 BC. While little is known about Amos for certain, we know that the main part of his ministry was probably carried out over a two-year period at some point during the years 767–753, centering on the shrine at Bethel. The prophecy takes the form of judgment against both the pagan nations and Israel for their sins. Israel is declared to be no better than the surrounding nations; in fact, she bears an even greater responsibility for her sins, on account of being God's chosen people. It is clear from several references in the prophecy that this was a time of national prosperity. There were few indications of the disaster that Israel would suffer at the hands of Assyria in 722–721, which would lead to the fall of the northern kingdom. The prophecy particularly complains about the lack of social justice in Israel, and her failure to remain faithful to the covenant.

The prophecy of *Obadiah* is one of the briefest works in the Old Testament, and is difficult to date. Also difficult to date is the book of *Jonah*, which describes the missionary journey of a prophet to the city of Nineveh at some point during the eighth century BC. The work is unusual in several respects, not least of which is its emphasis on the actions, rather than the words, of its central character. The book includes the famous story of "Jonah and the whale."

Micah prophesied in the southern kingdom of Judah at some point during the period 750–686 BC. The work is a powerful and spirited attack on the corruption of life in the great cities of the two kingdoms. For Micah, both Judah and Israel are guilty of a series of unacceptable offenses, including the oppression of the weak by the strong, the dispossession of people from their lands by powerful landowners, and the enslavement of helpless children. The priests and prophets, who ought to have been speaking out against these events, have totally failed to do so. Micah offers a vigorous criticism of these trends, and looks forward to the coming of a king from Bethlehem in Judaea who will put things right. Christians see this prophecy as being fulfilled in the birth of Jesus at Bethlehem.

Relatively little is known about either *Nahum* or *Habakkuk*. Both operated in the southern kingdom of Judah. *Zephaniah* prophesied during the reign of Josiah (640–609 BC), which was one of the most important periods of religious reform in Judah. The rediscovery of the "Book of the Law" led to a major religious reformation, and a corporate renewal of the covenant with the Lord which had been violated by the paganism which had flourished under earlier monarchs. It would seem that

Zephaniah's prophecies were delivered before these reforms. It is quite clear from their general tone that the religious life of Judah has reached an all-time low, and that the threat of imminent divine judgment was required to spur the king and nation into any kind of reform and renewal. The great warning of destruction in Judah (Zephaniah 1:2–13) speaks of a continuing legacy of Baal worship, worship of the stars, and devotion to the god Molech, who was chiefly noted for the cult of child sacrifice associated with his name. Zephaniah demands that these practices should end.

The prophecies of *Haggai* and *Zechariah* are both to be dated to the period when the deported population of Jerusalem was returned from exile in Babylon to rebuild their city and temple. Haggai's calling can be dated to August 520 BC; Zechariah's calling took place a few months later, in October or November of the same year. Haggai's prophecy focuses on the need to rebuild the temple as an act of honor to God. Why, he asks, are the people of Jerusalem building expensive houses for themselves, while failing to build a house for their God? Is it any wonder that Jerusalem is in such a miserable state, when they treat their God in such a way? Until the temple is rebuilt, Jerusalem will remain a wilderness. It is clear that this message has its desired effect. The rebuilding of the temple begins under Zerubbabel (Haggai 1:12). Like Haggai, Zechariah wishes to encourage the people of Jerusalem to rebuild the temple. Alongside these messages of encouragement and rebuke for inaction there are to be found a series of strongly messianic prophecies, including the famous prophecy (Zechariah 9:9–13) of the great messianic king, the descendant of David, entering into the city of Jerusalem in triumph, seated on a donkey. For Christians, this would reach its ultimate fulfillment in the triumphant entry of Jesus Christ into Jerusalem (Matthew 21:1–11).

It is generally thought that *Malachi* (whose name literally means "my messenger") was the final prophet of the Old Testament period. If this is the case, the work represents an important point of transition between the Old Testament and the New. Like Haggai and Zechariah, Malachi appears to have prophesied in the post-exilic period, at some point soon after the return of the exiles from Babylon to Jerusalem. This is suggested by a number of considerations, including the close similarity between the sins condemned in this book and those singled out for condemnation by Nehemiah. Yet a promise of forgiveness and restoration remains open. Malachi proclaims the future coming of the "Day of the Lord" (Malachi 4:1).

But when will this great day be? When will God come? Malachi declares that God will send the prophet Elijah before that day comes, to prepare the way for his coming (Malachi 4:5–6). The importance of this point in connection with the relation between the Old and New Testaments cannot be overlooked. When John the Baptist appeared by the Jordan, dressed in the kind of clothes that Elijah was known to have worn, people began to get very excited. John the Baptist declared that he had only come to prepare the way for the coming of someone greater than himself – Jesus Christ. It is clear that the New Testament can be seen as picking up where the Old Testament left off, and continuing the same story of God's involvement with Israel and the world.

Major Themes of the Old Testament

The Old Testament is a remarkably complex work, which merits much fuller study than is possible in this overview. If you have the time to take the study of the Old Testament further, you are strongly recommended to make use of one of the excellent introductions which are currently available, and which are noted in the "further reading" section at the end of the book. What follows can only serve as a very elementary introduction to some of the themes of the Old Testament, and will therefore probably tantalize and frustrate as much as inform. However, it is important to have at least some idea of some of its major themes, making the inclusion of this present section, in however brief a form, imperative.

From a Christian standpoint, the collection of writings known as "the Old Testament" refers to the history of God's actions in the world in preparation for the coming of Jesus Christ. Christians regard the New Testament as an extension of the same pattern of divine activity and presence as that declared in the Old, so that the New Testament both *continues* and *extends* the witness to the words and deeds of the God of Israel. Christians thus see the Old Testament as a preparation for the good news of Jesus Christ, in that it witnesses to the laying of the ground for the coming of Christ to fulfill the hopes and expectations of the prophets. The use made by New Testament writers of Old Testament prophecy is of particular interest in this respect. The Old Testament describes the history of the people of Israel, which is seen from a Christian perspective as an anticipation of the Christian church. We have already indicated the contents of the Old Testament, identifying some of its main books. In what follows, we shall give a very brief description of the main themes of the Old Testament, and indicate some of the ways in which they link up with the New Testament.

The creation

The Old Testament opens with an affirmation that God created the world. The fundamental theme which is affirmed in the opening chapters of the book of Genesis is that God is the originator of all that is in the world. No created thing can compare with God. This point is of particular significance, given the importance of worship of, for example, the sun or the stars among other religions of the ancient near east. For the Old Testament, God is superior to everything in creation. The height of God's creation is declared to be humanity, which alone is created in the image and likeness of God. Humanity is understood to be the steward (not the possessor!) of God's creation, and is entrusted with its care.

The account of the creation is followed by an account of the nature and origins of sin. One of the fundamental points made in Genesis 3 is that sin enters the world against God's intentions. Sin disrupts the close relationship between God and the creation, and leads to humanity rebelling against God and asserting its autonomy. This theme recurs throughout the Bible. For example, the story of the Tower of Babel (Genesis 11:1–9) is basically about human attempts at self-assertion in the face of God. God's hostility towards sin is depicted in a number of ways, including both the expulsion of Adam and Eve from the Garden of Eden and Noah's flood.

The theme of creation is the first to be encountered by readers of the Old Testament, assuming that they read the texts in their canonical order. But how important is the theme of creation to the Old Testament? In the twentieth century, the great Old Testament scholar Gerhard von Rad argued that the most characteristic insight of the Old Testament was that its God was sovereign over history, especially the history of Israel. In the Old Testament, faith in God is primarily faith in a God who acts within, and is sovereign over, cosmic human history. While von Rad is careful to stress that the faith of Israel included reference to creation, the primary emphasis lay on their God bringing Israel out of Egypt and into Canaan.

The doctrine of creation takes its place as a secondary doctrine, providing a certain context for the affirmation of the divine lordship over history. Although the Pentateuch opens with statements concerning the creative activity and authority of God, von Rad argues that the essential theological message of these historical books is summarized in a brief creed found in Deuteronomy 26:5–9:

> My father was a wandering Aramean, and he went down into Egypt with a few people and lived there and became a great nation, powerful and numerous. But the Egyptians mistreated us and made us suffer, putting us to hard labor. Then we cried out to the Lord, the God of our fathers, and the Lord heard our voice and saw our misery, toil, and oppression. So the Lord brought us out of Egypt with a mighty hand and an outstretched arm, with great terror and with miraculous signs and wonders. He brought us to this place and gave us this land, a land flowing with milk and honey.

The theme of creation is a subsidiary and secondary teaching, lending context to the more fundamental belief that God brought Israel out of Egypt.

Perhaps the Old Testament's emphasis on God's historical acts of salvation – rather than God's primordial act of creation – may be linked with polemic against Canaanite nature religion. It is clear that one of the most fundamental motivations governing the beliefs and conduct of ancient Israel around the time of the conquest was the desire to separate and distinguish itself from the religious beliefs and practices of the Canaanites. While much remains to be learned concerning Canaanite religion, it is clear that its emphasis upon *El* as the creator God, responsible for the fertility of the earth, would have caused Israel some difficulties in relation to attaching any decisive importance to the doctrine of creation. Thus when Hosea or the Deuteronomic historian engage in controversy with Canaanite religion over, for example, the fertility of the land, the debate is conducted not in terms of an appeal to the Lord as creator (and hence as the one who safeguards the fertility of the land), but through an appeal to the Lord as redeemer, who led Israel into this land – and is therefore also the one who will ensure the land's fruitfulness (Deuteronomy 8:7–9; Hosea 2:8–9). Israel's distinctiveness was better affirmed through rehearsing the acts in history by which Israel was guided and formed, rather than by appealing to concepts – such as the divine creatorship – which were shared with neighboring nations and could hence become the basis of syncretism. Just as Israel's language about her deity was designed to prevent confusion with rival claimants to this title from the nations around her, so her emphasis upon God's historical acts of redemption rather than the original act of creation was equally intended to preserve and maintain the religious distinctiveness of Israel.

Abraham: Calling and covenant

The calling of Abraham is seen as being of foundational importance to the emergence of Israel, both as a nation and as the people of God. The central theme of God's calling of Abraham (Genesis 12:1–4) is that God has chosen an individual, whose descendants will possess the land of Canaan and become a great nation. The theme of the fulfillment of this promise is of major importance throughout the Pentateuch. It is also of importance to Paul in the New Testament, who sees Abraham's willingness to trust in the promises of God as a prototype of Christian faith.

The idea of a "covenant" between God and Abraham and his descendants is introduced at this point. The ritual of circumcision is seen as the external sign of belonging to the covenant people of God. For Paul, it is of particular importance that God's promise to Abraham precedes the external sign of this covenant; this, according to Paul, implies that the promise takes precedence over the sign. As a result, Gentiles (that is, those who are not ethnic Jews) do not require to be circumcised when they convert to Christianity.

The book of Genesis traces the fortunes of Abraham and his descendants, showing the manner in which the covenant between God and Abraham is realized. The book ends with an account of the way in which Abraham's descendants settle in the land of Egypt, thus setting the scene for the next major theme of the Old Testament.

The Exodus from Egypt and the giving of the law

A major theme which now appears is that of captivity and deliverance. The story of the Exodus (a Greek word which literally means "exit" or "way out") is well known. A new ruler arises in Egypt (referred to by the term "pharaoh"), who regards the descendants of Abraham as a potential threat. The identity of this pharaoh is unknown, although there are good reasons for suggesting that it may have been Rameses II (who ruled during the period 1279–1212 BC). He subjected the Hebrews to a series of oppressive measures, designed to limit their numbers and influence. The book of Exodus describes God's call of Moses to be a liberator of Israel from its bondage in Egypt.

One of the most important Old Testament festivals is closely linked with the Exodus from Egypt. The *Passover* festival had its origins in the period before the Exodus. The origins and purpose of the festival are described at Exodus 11:1–12:30. It marks an act of divine judgment against Egypt. The regulations for the marking of the festival are laid down with some precision. Each household or group of households in Israel is to sacrifice a perfect lamb or goat, and daub its blood across the sides and tops of their doorframes. This will mark them off as God's own people, and distinguish them from their Egyptian oppressors. They are then to eat a meal, to remind them of their time in Egypt. Part of the meal consists of "bitter herbs," which symbolize the bitterness of their bondage. Another major part of the meal is unleavened bread. This "bread made without yeast" points to the haste with which the people were asked to prepare to leave Egypt. There was not even enough time for dough to rise, through the action of the yeast. The festival is named "the Lord's Passover," which refers to the fact that God will "pass over" the houses of his own people as he brings vengeance against the firstborn sons of the Egyptians. In commemoration of this act of deliverance, the Passover is to be celebrated every year as a "lasting ordinance." Further regulations concerning its celebration are mentioned later (Exodus 12:43–49).

The Passover festival thus has strong associations of divine deliverance. It is no accident that the "last supper" of Jesus was a Passover meal. In celebrating God's great act of deliverance in the past, Jesus was preparing for the great act of deliverance which would take place through his death upon the cross.

The theme of liberation comes to dominate the book of Exodus. While considerable attention is devoted to the fine details of how this liberation or redemption is accomplished (the accounts of the Ten Plagues and the crossing of the Red Sea being particularly important), the most significant point is that God acts to redeem Israel from its bondage. This theme of "God as liberator" is frequently taken up in later Old Testament writings, such as the Psalms, which recall the great act of deliverance from Egypt as an assurance of God's power and faithfulness.

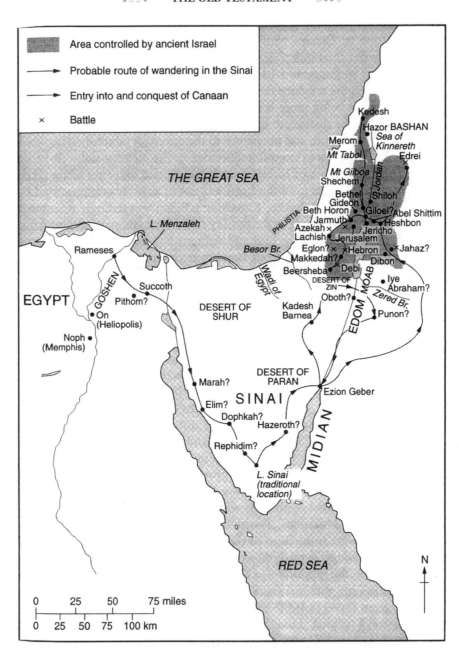

Map 3.1 The route of Israel's Exodus from Egypt and conquest of Canaan.

Earlier, we noted how circumcision was seen as a physical or external sign of the covenant between God and Israel. The theme of the covenant between God and Israel is developed significantly in the book of Exodus. Two particular points should be noted. First, a specific name is now used to refer to God. This is the term "Lord," which is the English term used to translate a cipher of four letters used to name God in this way. This group of four letters, often referred to as the "Tetragrammaton" (from the Greek words for "four" and "letters"), is sometimes represented as "Yahweh" or "Jehovah" in English versions of the Bible. Other Hebrew words could be used to refer to gods in general; this specific name "Lord" was used to refer only to the "God of Abraham, Isaac, and Jacob." It is never used to refer to any other divine or angelic being, unlike other Hebrew words for "god." These latter words act as common nouns, referring to "god" or "gods" in general, and can be used to refer to Israel's own God, or to other gods (such as the pagan gods of other nations). But the Tetragrammaton is used only to name the specific God which Israel knew and worshipped.

Second, the obligations which being the covenant people of God impose on Israel are made clear. This is the series of specific unconditional demands, which are now usually referred to as the "Ten Commandments," which Moses received at Mount Sinai. These commandments continue to be of major importance within Judaism and Christianity alike.

The entry into the promised land

One of the central themes of the book of Genesis is the promise that the descendants of Abraham will settle and dwell in the land of Canaan. The story of the wanderings of the people of Israel in the wilderness, and their final entry into the land of Canaan, takes up the remainder of the Pentateuch. Israel's period of wandering in the wilderness for a period of forty years is seen as a period of purification, in which all traces of the influence of the pagan religions of Egypt are removed. After the period of forty years, only two people

to have left Egypt in the Exodus remain alive – Moses and Joshua. Moses himself dies before the entry into the promised land of Canaan, although he is allowed to view it from a mountain peak on the far side of the Jordan.

Broadly speaking, "Canaan" refers to the territory to the west of the River Jordan, including both the Sea of Galilee to the north and the Dead Sea to the south. The occupation of Canaan is described in some detail in the book of Joshua. The initial crossing of the River Jordan into Canaan is clearly understood to parallel the earlier crossing of the Red Sea, during the Exodus from Egypt. The book of Joshua brings together accounts of three major military campaigns, undertaken by different groups of tribes, in the northern, central, and southern regions of Canaan. While it is very difficult to date the occupation of Canaan with any degree of certainty, there are strong parallels between the biblical descriptions of the events and what is known of the territory in the period 1450–1350 BC.

It is, however, the religious rather than the historical aspects of the matter which are seen as being more important. The occupation of Canaan is seen as consolidating the distinctive identity of Israel. In particular, it established the worship of the Lord, and obedience to the covenant established between the Lord and Israel, as of central importance to the identity and wellbeing of the people. The book of Joshua describes elaborate measures being taken to ensure that the worship of the Lord was not in any way compromised by indigenous Canaanite religions. Canaanite religion was strongly orientated towards fertility issues – such as the fertility of the land, animals, and humans. Its major deities – including Baal and Ashtaroth – feature regularly in the biblical accounts of the history of Israel over the next centuries. It is clear that Canaanite religion continued to exercise a fascination for Israel for some time to come.

The establishment of the monarchy

In its early period, Israel had no king. During the period following the conquest of Canaan, the region was ruled by a series of charismatic religious and political leaders, known as "judges." The book of Judges documents the serious threats to the unity of Israel at the time (partly from internal disunity, partly from external threats), and notes the role of "judges" such as Gideon, Samson, and Samuel. Under Samuel, the last of the "judges," a series of moves was made which resulted in the establishment of the monarchy. The first king was Saul, who probably reigned during the period 1020–1000 BC. Saul's reign is portrayed as divisive and tragic. One of his most significant internal opponents was David. Following Saul's death in a battle against the Philistines, David launched a military campaign which eventually led to the restoration of the unity of Israel, and the expansion of its territory. Although opposition to David continued throughout his reign, particularly from the supporters of Saul, David was able to maintain his hold on the nation until the final years of his reign.

The reign of David (ca. 1000–961 BC) saw significant developments taking place in Israel's religion. David's conquest of the city of Jerusalem led to it becoming the center of Israel's religious life, a development which would be consolidated during the reign of Solomon. The role of the king became important religiously, with the king being seen as a son of God. The theme of a future successor to David, who would rule over a renewed people of God, became a significant element of messianic hopes within Israel, and explains the importance of the "David" theme within parts of the New Testament. For New Testament writers (especially Matthew and Paul), Jesus of Nazareth is to be seen as the successor to David as king of Israel. Many Old Testament writings, particularly within the Psalter, extol the greatness of the king, the temple, and the city of Jerusalem (often referred to as "Zion"). All three are seen as tokens of God's favor towards Israel.

David was succeeded as king by Solomon, who reigned during the period 961–922 BC. During his reign, the temple was constructed as a permanent place of worship for the Lord. A strongly centralized administrative system was set in place, and extensive trading agreements negotiated with neighboring countries. Solomon's large harem caused disquiet to some, on account of the pagan religious beliefs of some of his wives. Solomon was famed for his wisdom, and some collections of proverbs in the Old Testament are attributed to him.

With the death of Solomon, the nation of Israel proved unstable. Eventually, the nation split into two sections, each with its own king. The northern kingdom, which would now be known as "Israel," would eventually cease to exist under the Assyrian invasions of the eighth century. The southern kingdom of Judah, which retained Jerusalem as its capital city, continued to exist until the Babylonian invasions of the sixth century. At this point, the monarchy ended. The Jewish hopes of restoration increasingly came to focus on the restoration of the monarchy, and the rise of a new figure like David. From a Christian perspective, these expectations could be directly related to the coming of Jesus of Nazareth.

The priesthood

The centrality of religion to the identity of Israel gave the guardians of its religious traditions a particularly important role. The emergence of the priesthood is a major theme in its own right. One of the most significant functions of the priesthood related to the cultic purity of Israel. This purity could be defiled (often referred to as "being made unclean") by various forms of pollution. The priesthood was responsible for ensuring the cleanliness of the people, which was seen as being vital for the proper worship of the Lord.

More importantly, the priesthood was responsible for the maintenance of the sacrificial system, and particularly the Day of Atonement ritual, in which sacrifices were offered for the sins of the people. A distinction is to be drawn between "uncleanliness" (which arises from natural bodily functions) and "sin" (which has strongly ethical overtones). Sin was seen as something which created a barrier between Israel and God. It is significant that most of the Old Testament images or analogies for sin take the form of images of separation. In order to safeguard the continuing relationship between the Lord and Israel, the priesthood was responsible for ensuring that the proper sacrifices were offered for sin.

One Old Testament ordinance is of particular importance, both to a full understanding of the role of the priesthood in Israel and to the meaning of the death of Jesus Christ within Christianity. This is the Day of Atonement, described in detail at Leviticus 16:1–34, which was ordained as an annual event for the removal of sin from the people of God. The full ritual is complex, involving the high priest ritually cleansing himself, and then offering a bull as a sacrifice for himself and the other priests. After this, two goats would be brought forward. One would be selected by lot as a sacrifice, while the other would become the scapegoat. The first goat would then be sacrificed as an offering for the sins of the people. Afterwards, the dead bull and goat were taken outside the camp, and burned. The high priest would then lay his hands upon the head of the second goat, and transfer all the sins of the people to the unfortunate animal. The scapegoat would then be driven out into the wilderness, carrying the guilt of the sins of Israel with it.

The Day of Atonement is of major importance as a background to understanding the death of Christ, a point brought out especially clearly in the letter to the Hebrews. Christ is seen as the perfect high priest, who makes a perfect sacrifice once and for all (instead of the annual ritual of the Day of Atonement). The sacrifice which he offers is himself; by his death, the sins of the people are transferred to him, and removed from his people. Note especially the fact that Jesus is put to death outside the walls of Jerusalem, just as the bull and goat were finally burned outside the camp of the Israelites. For the New Testament, the Levitical ritual sets the scene for the greater and perfect sacrifice which is yet to come, and which brings about what the Old Testament sacrifices could merely point to, yet not deliver.

There is ample evidence that many Jews were expecting the coming of a new priest, who would have a close personal relationship with God. An example of a text which bears witness to this hope is the *Testament of Levi*, which probably dates from about 108 BC:

> Then the Lord shall raise up a new priest, and to him all the words of the Lord shall be revealed. The heavens shall be opened, and sanctification shall come upon him from the temple of glory, with the Father's voice, as from Abraham to Isaac. And the glory of the Most High shall be spoken over him, and the spirit of understanding shall rest upon him.

The accounts of the baptism of Jesus of Nazareth (for example, see Mark 1:10–11) clearly indicate that such expectations were understood to be fulfilled in him.

A related theme is that of the temple. During the first period of its history, Israel used a moveable tent or tabernacle for its religious rites. However, when David captured the Jebusite city of Jerusalem and made it his capital, he declared his intention to build a permanent place of worship for the Lord. This was actually carried out under the direction of his successor, Solomon. The splendor of the building is a frequent theme of Old Testament writings dating from around this period. The temple was destroyed by the Babylonians in 586 BC, and rebuilt after the return from exile, half a century later. The second temple (as the building erected by the returned exiles is known) appears to have been rather less magnificent. However, with the end of the monarchy, the temple came to have increased civil significance, in that the temple authorities were responsible for both religious and civil matters.

A more splendid temple was constructed under Herod. Although work on this project appears to have begun in the decades immediately prior to the birth of Christ, the work was only completed in AD 64. It was destroyed, never to be rebuilt, during the suppression of a Jewish revolt against the Romans in the city in AD 70. The western wall of the temple largely survived; this is now widely referred to as "the wailing wall," and is an important place of prayer for Jews to this day.

Prophecy

The English word "prophet" is generally used to translate the Hebrew word *nabi*, which probably is best understood as "someone who speaks for another" or perhaps "a representative." The phenomenon of prophecy was widespread in the ancient near east, and not restricted to the "prophets of the Lord." The Old Testament refers to a number of "prophets of Baal," meaning charismatic individuals who claimed to act or speak on behalf of the Canaanite deity Baal. Early prophets of importance include Elijah and Elisha, both of whom were active during the ninth century BC. However, the most important period of prophetic activity focuses on the eighth through sixth centuries BC, and deals with the will of the Lord for Israel during a period of enormous

political turbulence, arising from the increasing power of Assyria and Babylonia. Prophets such as Jeremiah proclaimed a coming period of exile, which would be both a punishment for the past sins of the people and an opportunity for them to renew their religious practices and beliefs. After the period of exile in Babylon, post-exilic prophets such as Haggai and Malachi address some of the issues which became of importance as the returning exiles attempted to restore Jerusalem and its temple.

The prophets of Israel were seen as affirming the Lord's continued commitment to and presence within Israel. Yet with the ending of the classic period of prophecy, the Holy Spirit seemed to have ceased to operate. God became viewed in distant and remote terms. God had been active in the past, and would be active again in the future; in the present, however, there was no real sense of the presence or power of God. With the ending of the phenomenon, a period of questioning thus appears to have set in within Judaism. No longer was the "voice of God" heard within Israel. Even the most senior rabbis (or "teachers") could expect to catch nothing more than an echo of the voice of God – an idea which was expressed in the technical term *bath qol* (literally, "the daughter of the voice"). The enormous interest in both John the Baptist and Jesus of Nazareth partly reflects this concern. Might the coming of these two figures signal the renewal of prophecy and the restoration of Israel? The account of the baptism of Jesus (see Mark 1:10–11) clearly indicates that the coming of Jesus marks an inauguration of a period of renewed divine activity and presence.

The exile

One of the most important events recounted in the Old Testament is the exile of Jerusalem to Babylon in 586 BC. Jerusalem thus shared the earlier fate of its northern neighbor, Israel. The events which led to the exile of the southern kingdom of Judah are set out in 2 Kings. In 740 BC, Pekah ascended the throne of Israel. At this time, the Assyrian king Tiglath-Pilesar invaded part of the territory of the northern kingdom and deported its inhabitants to Assyria. The policy of deportation was designed to minimize the risk of rebellion on the part of conquered peoples by resettling them far from their homelands. Pekah was assassinated by Hoshea, who took the throne in his stead in the year 732. In 725 BC, Tiglath-Pilesar was succeeded by Shalmanesar, who proceeded to invade the region of Samaria in 725 BC, and laid siege to it for three years. When the fighting was over, a substantial section of the population of the region was deported to regions deep with the Assyrian empire. Israel existed no longer as a nation in its own right.

Israel, then, ceased to exist as a nation in 722 BC. But what of the southern kingdom of Judah? It is clear that a new era in Judah's history opens with the reign of Hezekiah in 729 BC. Initially reigning alongside his father Ahaz, Hezekiah took full control in 715. Hezekiah introduced a major program of religious reform. This was continued under Josiah, who began to reign in 640 BC. In the course of some work on the temple, a work referred to as the "Book of the Law" is rediscovered. It is thought that this is a reference to the book of Deuteronomy, or at least to its central chapters. On hearing it read, Josiah set in place a program of reform, including the renewal of the covenant – the declaration on the part of king and people that they will remain faithful to the law of the Lord. The Passover, which had been neglected since the days of the judges, was reinstated and celebrated at Jerusalem.

After Josiah's death in battle, he was succeeded by Jehohaz and Jehoiakim. It is during the latter's reign that the ominous events which will eventually lead to the end of Judah take place. In 605 BC, the Babylonian emperor Nebuchadnezzar defeated the massed Egyptian armies at Carcemish, establishing Babylon as the leading military and political power in the region. Along with many other territories in this region, the land of Judah became subject to Babylonian rule, possibly in 604.

Jehoiakim decided to rebel against Babylon. It is possible that he may have been encouraged in this move by a successful Egyptian counterattack against Babylon in 601, which may have seemed to suggest that Babylon's power was on the wane. It was to prove to be a terrible misjudgment. Judah was invaded by Babylonian forces, which was clearly interpreted by writers of the time as the execution of the promised judgment of the Lord against his faithless people and king. Egypt, once the hope of Judah, was also defeated, and neutralized as a military power. (These same events are also vividly described and analyzed by Jeremiah, the later chapters of whose prophecy should be read in the light of this historical narrative.)

Jehoiakim was succeeded by Jehoiachin (the close similarity of these names being a constant source of confusion to readers) towards the end of 598 BC, shortly before the Babylonians finally laid siege to the city. Early the following year, the king, the royal family, and the circle of royal advisors gave themselves up to the besieging forces. They were deported to Babylon, along with several thousand captives. The Babylonians placed Zedekiah, a relative of Jehoiachin, on the throne as their vassal, and seemed happy to leave things like that for the present. Yet Zedekiah attempted to rebel against Babylon. The Babylonian response was massive and decisive. In January 588, the Babylonians laid siege to the city; in July 586, they broke through its walls and took the city. The defending army attempted to flee, but was routed. The next month, a Babylonian official arrived in Jerusalem to supervise the destruction of the defenses of the city and its chief buildings, and the deportation of its people. The furnishings of the temple were dismantled, and taken to Babylon as booty. Any hope of a quick end to the exile soon passed. Anyone capable of leading a revolt or taking charge of a government was taken and executed. The assassination of Gedaliah, the governor appointed by the Babylonians, by Ishmael sent shock waves through the remaining inhabitants of the city. Fearing Babylonian reprisals, many fled to Egypt.

It is the interpretation of these events which is of particular interest to New Testament writers. The period of exile is interpreted as, in the first place, a judgment against Judah for its lapse into pagan religious beliefs and practices; and, in the second, as a period of national repentance and renewal, which will lead to the restoration of a resurgent people of God. It is this theme which we may consider in the final part of this section.

The restoration

The Babylonian empire finally fell. Cyrus the Great, king of Persia (559–530 BC), conquered Babylon in 539 BC. As part of his policy of religious toleration, Cyrus permitted the exiled inhabitants of Judaea to return to their homeland. The restoration of the deported inhabitants of Jerusalem to their home city after decades of exile is seen by Old Testament writers as a demonstration of the faithfulness of the Lord, and an affirmation of the repentance of the people of God.

The most important Old Testament works to deal with the restoration include the historical works of Ezra and Nehemiah, and the prophet Haggai. Although we are told little of what happened to the people of Jerusalem during their time in exile, we can nevertheless gain at least some understanding of the difficulties which they faced, and their longing to return home. The book of Ezra opens by publishing

the proclamation of Cyrus, the founder of the Persian empire who defeated the Babylonians in 539, which set the exiles free (Ezra 1:1–4). The proclamation dates from 538 BC, and shows a spirit of generosity and tolerance towards the religion of Israel which had been conspicuously absent from the Babylonians.

As a result, many of the inhabitants of Jerusalem and Judah prepared to return home, taking the captured treasures of the temple at Jerusalem with them. By September or October 537, the returning exiles had settled down in their home towns and had begun to renew their old patterns of worship. Not all the exiles returned to Jerusalem; other towns in Judah received returning exiles. The Feast of Tabernacles was celebrated with an altar built specially for that purpose, despite the risk of alienating peoples in the region around them. There was still no temple at Jerusalem; however, by building an altar dedicated to the Lord, the returning exiles could begin the process of restoring worship to what it had been before the exile.

But sooner or later, the temple would have to be rebuilt. The ruins of Solomon's temple, which had been razed to the ground by the Babylonians, would act as the foundations of the new building. Under the direction of Zerubbabel, who emerges as the natural leader in Jerusalem during this period, preparations are made to rebuild the temple in the spring of 536 BC. While many were overjoyed when the foundations were laid, older people (who could remember the great edifice built by Solomon) were distressed. It is clear that the new temple would not be on the same scale as its predecessor. On March 12, 516, the temple was finally completed and dedicated. The first major festival to be celebrated in the new building was the Passover, a festival with strong associations of deliverance from bondage and the commemoration of the faithfulness of the Lord. Although this "second temple" lacked the physical grandeur of Solomon's edifice, it nevertheless was of enormous significance. It pointed to the centrality of religious concerns to the newly restored people of God. The measures taken by Ezra to prevent foreign religious influence within Jerusalem (such as the total prohibition of intermarriage) is an indication of the seriousness of the returning exiles in this respect. The post-exilic portions of the Old Testament are notable for their emphasis on the need to maintain racial and religious purity, and the importance attached to religious festivals as national events. Jerusalem had no king; the temple and its priests gradually came to assume most of the roles of the monarchy, including responsibility for civil matters.

One point that is worth commenting on here is the use of the term "Jews" to refer to the returned exiles (see, for example, Ezra 4:23; 5:1). Up to this time, the people of God had been referred to as "Israelites" or "Judahites." The term "Jew" comes to be used in the post-exilic period to designate the people of God, and will be used regularly in later writings for this purpose.

Our attention now turns to the development of these great themes of the Old Testament in the New Testament.

4

The New Testament

The New Testament consists of twenty-seven books, which can be broken down into a number of different categories – such as the gospels and the letters. Their common theme is the identity and significance of Jesus, including the practical and ethical implications of following him. Christians were proclaiming the words and actions of Jesus almost immediately after his death. Christian churches were being established in the eastern Mediterranean within a matter of years. The earliest written documents within the New Testament take the form of letters written by prominent Christians to these churches. Yet the preaching of the words and deeds of Jesus went on in the background. It was only at a later stage, probably in the early 60s, that the words and deeds of Jesus were committed to writing, in the form that we now know as the gospels. We shall begin our study of the New Testament by examining these works.

The Gospels

The first four books of the New Testament are collectively known as "gospels." They are best to be understood as four portraits of Jesus, seen from different angles, and drawing on various sources. The first three have many features in common, and are widely regarded as drawing on common sources in circulation within early Christian circles. Each of the gospels has its own distinctive character, which needs to be appreciated. The following sections will aim to explore the distinctive features of each of the gospels. Before this, however, it is important to appreciate some features of the gospels in general.

The English word "gospel" comes from an Old English word *godspel*, meaning "good news," used to translate the Greek word *evangelion*. The word "gospel" is used in two different senses within Christianity. First, it refers to the events that center on Jesus of Nazareth, which are seen as being good news for the world. The gospel is primarily the "good news" of the coming of Jesus of Nazareth, with all that this has to offer humanity. The term is also used in a secondary and derivative sense to refer to the four books in the New Testament which focus on the life, death, and resurrection of Jesus of Nazareth. Strictly speaking, these books should be referred to as "the gospel according to Matthew," "the gospel according to Luke," and so on. This makes it clear that it is the same gospel which is being described, despite the different styles and approaches of the compilers of each of these four works.

Two related words should also be noted, deriving from the Greek word *evangelion* (which also means "good news"). The word "evangelism" refers to the bringing of the good news to people. The related word "evangelist" refers primarily to a person who brings the good news to people (such as Billy Graham). It can also, however, be used in a derivative way, to refer to the compilers of each of the four gospels. Thus commentaries on, for example, Mark's gospel may refer to Mark as an "evangelist" with this meaning in mind.

The period of oral tradition

The gospel writers were not biographers, or even historians, by our standards, nor were they interested in providing an account of absolutely everything that Jesus said and did. For example, occasionally it does not seem to have mattered to them exactly at what point in his ministry Jesus told a particular parable. The important thing was that he *did* tell it, and that it was realized to be relevant to the preaching of the early church. The gospel writers seem to have been concerned to remain as faithful as possible to the accounts of the life, death, and resurrection of Jesus which had been handed down to them.

There can be no doubt whatsoever that the gospel accounts of Jesus contain a solid base of historical information. Nevertheless, this is linked with an interpretation of this information. Biography and theology are interwoven to such an extent that they cannot be separated any more. The early Christians were convinced that Jesus was the Messiah, the Son of God, and their Savior, and naturally felt that these conclusions should be passed on to their readers, along with any biographical details which helped cast light on them. It is for this reason that fact and interpretation are so thoroughly intermingled in the gospels. The first Christians had no doubt that their theological interpretation of Jesus was right, and that it was therefore an important fact which should be included in their "biographies." To tell the story of Jesus involved explaining who he was, and why he was so important. Interpretation of the significance of Jesus is therefore found alongside the material which leads to this conclusion.

From what has just been said, it will be clear that the New Testament documents, especially the gospels, are strongly committed to their subject. They do not offer us a dispassionate account of the history of Jesus, but speak of him as Lord and Savior. For example, towards the end of John's gospel, we read the following words from the author of the gospel, as he apologizes for having had so much material concerning Jesus that he has had to omit some of it (John 20:30–31):

> Jesus did many other miraculous signs in the presence of his disciples, which are not recorded in this book. But these are written that you may believe that Jesus is the Christ, the Son of God, and that by believing you may have life in his name.

This might seem to raise a serious problem. It is pointed out, with reason, that the gospel writers were committed to Jesus. Is there not a danger that this commitment leads to them being prejudiced, and thus incapable of providing an objective picture of Jesus?

The potential bias of any historical source is of major importance, and cannot be ignored. A Christian source of the period is likely to show pro-Christian bias, just as a Jewish source might well be expected to be anti-Christian. Identification of possible bias is important in assessing potential variations in weight to be given to different sources. Yet it must be stressed that a source can be committed and correct at one and the same time. An example will make this clear. During World War II, the

German Nazi leader, Adolf Hitler, initiated an extermination program directed against Jews and others in areas of Europe occupied by the Nazis. A program of mass murder was undertaken. Gradually, news of this campaign of genocide (often referred to as "the Holocaust") filtered through to the outside world, especially the United States of America.

However, the initial reports of what was going on at the Nazi extermination camps came from Jews, who were regarded as having vested interests in the matter. Their reports were often dismissed as "biased." As a result, the recognition of the horrifying facts of the Holocaust was delayed in the United States. It was not appreciated that committed witnesses, caught up in and involved in the events in question, could nevertheless be reliable witnesses. A witness to a particularly horrifying or thrilling event is bound to be affected by what he or she has seen. Yet that does not diminish the potential reliability of his or her witness to what has happened. Precisely the same point needs to be made in relation to the New Testament writings. They are indeed written from the standpoint of faith, and with the object of bringing their readers to faith. But it does not follow that they are unreliable for that reason.

The gospels are not arranged in chronological order. As we shall see, there are reasons for thinking that Mark's gospel may have been the first to have been written, with Matthew's gospel dating from slightly later. Scholars have suggested that the reason why Matthew is placed before Mark in the canonical ordering of the New Testament has to do with the great value which the early church placed upon that gospel as a teaching resource. However, it must be appreciated that the materials which are incorporated into the gospel represent a series of recollected sayings and actions of Jesus, which were widely used for teaching purposes in the early church. These were even-

tually committed to writing in the gospels. The period of "oral tradition," during which the sayings and actions of Jesus were committed to memory by the disciples, probably dates from about 30–65.

It is thus important to appreciate that the gospels were not written by Jesus himself, nor do they date from his lifetime. It is generally thought that Jesus was crucified around the years 30–33, and that the earliest gospel (probably Mark) dates from about 65. There is probably a gap of about thirty years between the events described in the gospels taking place and subsequently being written down in the form of a gospel. By classical standards, this was an incredibly short time. The Buddha, for example, had one thing in common with Jesus: he wrote nothing down. Yet the definitive collection of his sayings (the "Tripitaka") is thought to date from around four centuries after his death, more than ten times the interval between the death of Jesus and the appearance of the first gospel.

In any case, Christians were committed to writing down their understanding of the importance of Jesus long before Mark's gospel was written. The New Testament letters (still sometimes referred to as the "epistles") date mainly from the period 49–69, and provide confirmation of the importance and interpretations of Jesus in this formative period. It is now becoming clear that Paul's letters include many references to the teaching of Jesus, providing an important link between the epistles and the gospels.

Yet despite these comments, some readers may find this gap of thirty years distressing. Why were these things not written down immediately? Might people not forget what Jesus said and did, and what happened at the crucifixion and resurrection? Yet this overlooks the fact that Christians were preaching the good news of Jesus to the world within weeks of his resurrection, making full use of this material.

There was no danger of forgetting about Jesus; his words and deeds were constantly being recalled by Christian preachers and evangelists.

This process is hinted at by Luke. After relating the early part of Jesus' life, to which his mother Mary was a central witness, Luke remarks that "his mother treasured all these things in her heart" (Luke 2:51). Is Luke hinting that Mary was his source for this part of the history of Jesus? We shall never know. But it is clear that what Jesus said and did was remembered by those around him. There are no reasons for thinking that Jesus, for example, told each parable only once. The parables were probably told numerous times, with slight variations.

It is difficult for modern readers, who are so used to information being recorded in written or other visual form, to appreciate that the classical world communicated by means of the spoken word. The great Homeric epics are good examples of the way in which stories were passed on with remarkable accuracy from one generation to another. If there is one ability which modern westerners have probably lost, it is the ability to remember a story or narrative as it is told, and then to pass it on to others afterwards.

As one study of primitive culture after another confirms, the passing down of stories from one generation to another was characteristic of the pre-modern era, including the time of the New Testament itself. Indeed, there are excellent grounds for arguing that early educational systems were based upon learning by rote. The fact that most people in the west today find it difficult to commit even a short story or narrative to memory naturally tends to prejudice them against believing that anyone else could do it; yet it is evident that it was done, and was done remarkably well. Yet this ability has not been completely lost. There is also evidence that a form of writing known as "tachygraphy" (literally, "speed writing")

was used during the first century. This way of writing, which corresponds roughly to modern shorthand, would have allowed aspects of Jesus' life or teaching to be committed to writing at an early stage. We possess, however, no evidence that this actually happened.

The period between the death of Jesus and the writing of the first gospel is usually referred to as the "period of oral tradition," meaning the period in which accounts of Jesus' birth, life, and death, as well as his teaching, were passed down with remarkable accuracy from one generation to another. In this period, it seems that certain of Jesus' sayings, and certain aspects of his life, especially his death and resurrection, were singled out as being of particular importance, and were passed down from the first Christians to those who followed them. Others were not passed down, and have been lost forever. The early Christians seem to have identified what was essential, and what was not so important, of Jesus' words, deeds, and fate, and passed down only the former to us.

An excellent example of this process of oral transmission may be found in Paul's first letter to the Christians at Corinth, almost certainly dating from the period of oral transmission:

> For I received from the Lord what I also passed on to you: The Lord Jesus, on the night he was betrayed, took bread, and when he had given thanks, he broke it and said, "This is my body, which is for you; do this in remembrance of me." In the same way, after supper he took the cup, saying, "This cup is the new covenant in my blood; do this, whenever you drink it, in remembrance of me." (1 Corinthians 11:23–25)

Paul is here passing something on to the Corinthian Christians which had been passed on to him, presumably by word of mouth. It is interesting to compare these verses with their equivalents in the synoptic gospels (Matthew 26:26–28; Mark 14:22–24; Luke 22:17–19).

The "period of oral tradition" may thus be regarded as a period of "sifting," in which the first Christians assessed what was necessary to pass down to those who followed them. Thus Jesus' sayings may have become detached from their original context, and perhaps on occasion even given a new one, simply through the use to which the first Christians put them – proclaiming the gospel to those outside the early community of faith, and deepening and informing the faith of those inside it.

Matthew

The first of the gospels is traditionally attributed to Matthew, the tax-collector who left everything to follow Jesus (Matthew 9:9–13). The same person is referred to as "Levi" in the gospels of Mark and Luke. Matthew's gospel is perhaps the most Jewish of the gospels, showing a particular interest in the relation of Jesus to the Jewish nation and its religious laws and institutions. It is of particular importance for Matthew that Jesus fulfills the great prophecies of the Old Testament. Matthew regards it as being particularly important that Jesus was a direct descendant of David, the great hero-king of Israel, and that Jesus was born in the city of David, Bethlehem. Phrases such as "this took place to fulfill what the Lord said through the prophet" can be found regularly in Matthew's presentation of the gospel, as he points out how aspects of Jesus' ministry bring to fulfillment the great expectations of the Old Testament (see the frequent use of the phrase in the first two chapters, dealing with the birth of Jesus: Matthew 1:22–23; 2:15; 2:17–18; 2:23). Similarly, Matthew brings out how Jesus does not come to abolish the Old Testament law or prophets, but to bring them to their proper fulfillment (Matthew 5:17).

Matthew emphasizes clearly the continuity between Jesus and Israel. The careful reader of the "Sermon on the Mount" (the traditional way of referring to the body of teaching presented at Matthew 5–7) will notice that Jesus seems to be being portrayed as the new Moses delivering the new law to the new Israel on a new mountain. Similarly, Matthew allows us to see a connection between the synagogue and the church, and particularly between the Twelve Tribes of Israel and the twelve disciples or apostles. The continuity between Judaism and Christianity is thus made clear.

It is not clear when Matthew was written. As noted above, the sources on which Matthew drew in compiling his gospel go back to the 30s. Matthew may have gathered his collections of material together and committed them to writing in the 70s. In part, the dating of Matthew's gospel depends on how one understands the relation of Matthew and Mark (see pp. 90–93), and it is possible that we shall never know for certain precisely when Matthew's gospel was written.

Mark

Mark is widely regarded as having been the first of the gospels to have been written down. The gospel is generally accepted to have been written by the "John Mark" who is known to have accompanied both Peter (1 Peter 1:14) and Paul (Acts 12:12, 25). The vivid details which are such a distinctive feature of this gospel (such as the specific reference to the "pillow" in the boat at 4:38), and the occasionally critical portrayal of the disciples (as at 8:14–21), are best understood if Peter was the source of the stories in question. For these and other reasons, scholars believe that Mark's gospel was the earliest of the gospels to enter general circulation within the Christian community, with Matthew and Luke expanding his accounts of the life of Jesus on the basis of additional sources available to them. Peter was executed during the Roman emperor Nero's

imago leonis

OAGI
IHA
R

US
CUS

4.1 Manuscript illumination from the Lindisfarne Gospels, ca. 698–700. AKG-Images/British Library.

Romans divided the night into four "watches": "evening" 6:00–9:00 p.m.; "midnight" 9:00–12:00 midnight; "when the cock crows" 12:00 midnight–3:00 a.m.; and "dawn" 3:00–6:00 a.m. The "cock crowing" may in fact be a reference to the trumpet blast which marked the end of the third watch of the night, rather than to the cry of a cockerel. Although some versions of the text of Mark make reference to the cock crowing twice, many early manuscripts refer to it only as crowing once.

One of the most noticeable features of this gospel is its emphasis upon the deeds of Jesus, rather than his teaching. Mark's focus on the cross, rather than the teaching, of Jesus gives his gospel a distinctive emphasis. Nevertheless, Mark passes down some major parables and sayings of Jesus. Matthew includes some important sections of teaching (such as the "Sermon on the Mount") which are not found in Mark. This is widely assumed to be due to Matthew having access to sources which Mark did not use (whether this was because he did not have access to them, or because he did not regard them as relevant to his purposes).

persecution of the Christians during the period 64–67, and it is possible that the death of Peter was the stimulus Mark needed to ensure that the gospel was committed to writing. This would suggest a date in the early 60s for the composition of the gospel.

The gospel is thought to have been written in Rome, drawing extensively on the memories of Peter (note, for example, the reference to the *praetorium* at 15:16). Mark also draws his readers' attention to the testimony of the Roman centurion, who declared that Jesus was the "Son of God" (15:39) – a vitally important testimony, coming from a Gentile. The testimony of this Roman officer would have been of especial importance to Mark's intended readership in Rome. The reference to the "cock crowing" is also important in this respect. The

Luke

Luke is the third of the synoptic gospels. Luke's gospel is actually the first part of a two-part work, the second being the Acts of the Apostles. Taken together, these two works constitute the largest piece of writing in the New Testament. Both works are dedicated to a man named Theophilus (the Greek word literally meaning "a lover of God"), who may well have been a wealthy and influential Christian sympathizer at Rome. Luke himself was probably a Gentile by birth, with an outstanding command of written Greek. He was a physician, and the traveling companion of Paul at various points during his career.

Luke's gospel has clearly been written with the interests and needs of non-Jewish readers

4.2 Gabriel's declaration to Mary that she is to bear the savior of the world, by Dante Gabriel Rossetti (1850). This incident is related early in Luke's gospel. London, Tate Gallery, AKG-Images/Erich Lessing.

in mind, apparently with a special concern to bring out the relevance of the "good news" for the poor, oppressed, and needy. He uses the word "savior" (which would already have been familiar to Greek-speaking readers) to help his readers understand the identity and significance of Jesus, and does not place as much emphasis on the messiahship of Jesus as Matthew does. His gospel includes two of the best-loved parables of Jesus: the Parable of the Good Samaritan (10:30–37) and the Parable of the Prodigal Son (Luke 15:11–32).

It is not clear when Luke's gospel was written. The abrupt ending of the account of Paul's imprisonment in the Acts of the Apostles suggests an early date for the two-part work, such as some time in the period 59–63. However, many scholars argue that Luke draws upon Mark's gospel at points, suggesting that the third gospel is to be dated later than the second, and pointing to the 70s as a possible time of writing.

John

John's gospel differs significantly in style from the first three gospels. It is sometimes referred to as "the Fourth Gospel," to bring out this difference. One of the most distinctive features of this gospel is the "I am" sayings, by which the full significance of Jesus is brought out.

Who wrote this gospel? The text of the gospel itself indicates that its author was "the disciple whom Jesus loved" (e.g., 13:23–26; 18:15–16). Tradition has identified this as the apostle John, although it should be noted that the text of the gospel itself does not make this statement explicitly. There are reasons for thinking that the gospel may have been written with the special needs of the churches in the region of Ephesus in mind. The date of writing of the gospel remains unclear. The gospel text itself suggests that both Peter and the "beloved disciple" are dead (see 21:19, 22–23), thus pointing to a date at some point after 70. This is also suggested by other factors. Most scholars suggest a date towards the end of the first century (perhaps around 85), although the possibility of an earlier date remains open.

The synoptic problem

The first three gospels include a lot of material in common. The same material is sometimes presented in one setting in Mark, another in Matthew, and perhaps even a third in Luke. The same story may be told from different

4.3   The raising of Lazarus from the dead, 1303–1305. Fresco by Giotto di Bondone. This incident is recorded in John's gospel, and linked with the sixth "I am" saying. Padua, Cappella degli Scrovegni, AKG-Images/Cameraphoto.

perspectives in different gospels. Sometimes a story is told at greater length in one gospel than in another. This is widely believed to be due to the fact that all three draw on several common sources, such as collections of the sayings of Jesus which were committed to memory at a very early stage. The opening of Luke's gospel (Luke 1:1–4) makes it clear that a number of accounts of the life and sayings of Jesus were in circulation at an early stage, also indicating that he has composed his own account of Jesus on the basis of eye-witness reports which had been made available to him. Some of this material is common to all three gospels; some is common to Matthew and Luke (which are much longer than

Mark); and some is found only in Matthew or Luke. In each case, the evangelist (as the gospel writer is known) has drawn on his own set of historical sources to allow his readers access to the details of the central figure of the Christian faith. The overlap between the first three gospels is reflected in the name that is sometimes given to them: the "synoptic gospels," from the Greek word *synopsis*, or "summary."

The academic discipline of "source criticism" attempts to clarify the sources on which the gospels are based. In general terms, it is clear that all three synoptic gospels contain common material, often reporting the same incident or teaching in exactly the same words. Much of

Mark's gospel is found in other synoptic gospels. Matthew and Luke also include some material common to each, as well as some material which is found only in one of them. Of particular importance is the observation that the material common to all three gospels follows the same order. This has led scholars to the universal conclusion that the synoptic gospels are interdependent. But how is this dependence to be explained?

The general consensus within New Testament scholarship is that four sources can be discerned for the synoptic gospels.

1   Mark's gospel itself, which seems to be used as a source by Matthew and Mark. Thus 90 percent of the contents of Mark's gospel are included in Matthew; 53 percent of Mark can be found in Luke. Mark's material is written in a style which suggests that it is older than the style found in the corresponding passages in Matthew or Luke, using many Semitic phrases. It is very difficult to explain this observation on the basis of any hypothesis other than that Matthew and Luke both based themselves on Mark, and "tidied up" his style.
2   Material common to both Matthew and Luke. This section of material, which is about two hundred verses in length, is generally referred to as "Q." There is no evidence that Q was a complete gospel in itself, or that it existed as an independent written source.
3   Material found only in Matthew (usually known as "M").
4   Material found only in Luke (usually known as "L").

What is at present the most widely accepted explanation of this event was developed in detail in its current form at the University of Oxford in the opening decade of the twentieth century. Its most celebrated statements can be found in B. H. Streeter's *Four Gospels* (1924) and W. Sanday's *Studies in the Synoptic Problem* (1911). Streeter's work represented a collection of papers reflecting the work of the Oxford gospel seminar, which met nine times a year over a period of fifteen years. Although this theory is sometimes known as "the Oxford hypothesis," it is more commonly referred to as "the two-source theory." Its basic features can be set out as follows.

Mark was the first gospel to be written down. It was available to both Matthew and Luke, who used it as a source, altering the style of the language as appropriate, but retaining Mark's ordering of the material. Matthew was written after Mark, but before Luke. Both Matthew and Luke had access to the source known as Q. In addition, Matthew had access to another source known as M; Luke had access to a different source, known as L. Although this theory acknowledges four sources (Mark, Q, M, and L), it is known as the two-source theory on account of the importance of Mark and Q in relation to its approach.

This theory is the most widely accepted in modern New Testament scholarship. Other approaches exist, but are not widely supported. For example, Augustine of Hippo argued that Matthew was written first, and that Mark abbreviated Matthew. J. J. Griesbach developed an influential hypothesis, according to which Matthew was written first, followed by Luke (who used Matthew). Finally, Mark was written, making use of both Matthew and Luke.

It must also be stressed that the "synoptic problem" concerns our understanding of the way in which the oral traditions concerning Jesus were passed down to us. It does not call their historical accuracy or theological reliability into question, but allows a deeper understanding of the formative period of the gospel traditions, in which the words and deeds of Jesus were passed down and handed over during the period ca. 30–60.

Acts

The "Acts of the Apostles," to give this work its full title, is the second installment of Luke's account of the origins of the Christian church, and follows on from the gospel which is attributed to him (see above). Taken together, Luke's gospel and history of the early church is the largest single document in the New Testament. In his gospel, Luke informed one "Theophilus" (probably a well-placed Roman official who had become interested in Christianity) of the basic details of the life, death, and resurrection of Jesus. However, by the time that Luke was writing, Christianity was well on the way to becoming a major force in the Roman empire. So how did Christianity progress from its humble origins in Palestine to the hub of the Roman empire? How did it come to wield such influence in so short a time? Luke's task was to explain this development to his (presumably Roman) reader, and particularly to show that Rome had nothing to fear from Christianity.

Luke sets out to document the rapid expansion of Christianity throughout the Roman empire. The first twelve chapters focus on Peter, and the series of events which led to the Christian gospel becoming firmly rooted in Jerusalem and the surrounding regions. Having shown how the gospel became rooted in Palestine, Luke moves on to show how it gradually became established in much of the Roman empire.

The remainder of the work focuses on Paul – a figure familiar to readers of the New Testament, who was initially a law-abiding Jew named "Saul." Luke explains Paul's background, and shows how he became first a Christian, and then the "apostle to the Gentiles." He gives a vivid account of the impact that Paul had upon the expansion of the Christian church from Palestine into the regions of modern-day Turkey and Greece. Luke gives details of the three missionary journeys Paul undertook in the eastern Mediterranean, and ends with a description of his final voyage as a prisoner to Rome itself. At several points, Luke uses the term "we" to refer to events (e.g., Acts 16:10–17; 20:5–21:18; 27:1–28:16). This clearly implies that Luke was present on these occasions, and is writing as an eye-witness.

It is not clear when the work was written. The last event to be recorded in the work dates from immediately before the outbreak of serious persecution of Christians at Rome in 64. There is no reference of any kind to the burning of Rome and the subsequent suppression of the Christian community at Rome under Nero, which began in 64, and continued on and off for several years. Nor is there any hint of the destruction of Jerusalem by Roman armies in 70. Both these events would be of relevance to Luke's narrative; the fact that neither is mentioned strongly suggests that the work predates them.

The Letters

The New Testament includes a series of letters written to individuals or churches by leading figures within the early church. These letters often clarify points of Christian doctrine and practice, and offer encouragement to Christians in the face of hostility from other religious groupings or from the secular authorities. It is clear, for example, that Christianity was subject to various forms of harassment by Jews in the first decades of its existence. It must be remembered that Christianity was very weak numerically for much of the first century, and Christians were often forced to hold their meetings in secret for fear of persecution from the local Roman authorities. In particular, the reigns of Nero and Domitian witnessed concerted efforts to eliminate the growing Christian church; some documents within the New Testament are written in the face of this kind of situation.

The letters of Paul

By far the largest collection of letters within the New Testament is due to Paul. During the course of his missionary efforts, Paul established a number of small Christian groups in Asia Minor, Macedonia, and Greece. He remained in touch with some of them subsequently by letter. Not all of these have survived; Paul himself makes reference to additional letters to the church at Corinth, and to a letter to the church at Laodicea. The use of the word "church" is potentially misleading; the early Christians did not meet in buildings designated as "churches," but gathered in secret in small groups. The word "church" is probably better translated as "congregation" or "gathering" in this context. Paul's early letters are often concerned with matters of doctrine, particularly concerning the second coming of Christ and the relation between Jews and Gentiles. The later letters reflect the growing importance of church order and structure, as Christianity increasingly becomes a permanent presence in the eastern Mediterranean region.

Paul's letters are difficult to date precisely, although it is widely believed that the earliest dates from within fifteen to twenty years of the death of Christ. In what follows, we shall consider the letters in "canonical order" – that is, in the order in which they appear in the New Testament. It must, however, be appreciated that this does not necessarily represent the order in which they were written. In general terms, the New Testament seems to arrange letters according to their length, grouping letters to the same churches or individuals together.

The first letter to be encountered is *Romans*. Paul probably wrote his letter to the Christian community at Rome in the early spring of AD 57, during his time at Corinth in the course of his third missionary journey (see p. 180). No apostle had ever visited Rome before; the letter therefore provides the church at Rome with the basic elements of Christian teaching. Most of Paul's letters were written to churches which he had personally established and taught. Romans is an exception.

The letter is of crucial importance in many ways. It sets out clearly Paul's understanding of the relation between Israel and the Christian church. In particular, it sets out Paul's doctrine of justification by faith, rather than by the works of the law. According to this teaching, both Jews and Gentiles can be justified (a word which is probably best paraphrased as "made right with God" or "put in a right relationship with God") by faith. It is not necessary to be circumcised, be a Jew, or observe the Old Testament law. What matters is faith in God. The letter is also of interest historically, in that it bears witness to the growth of the Christian church at Rome.

This is followed by the two letters to the *Corinthians*. Corinth was one of the most important cities of Greece, often being estimated as having a population of more than 500,000 people. It was a leading seaport and commercial center, and was evangelized by Paul during his third missionary journey. The letter is written from Ephesus, a leading city in Asia Minor, and probably dates from some point before the feast of Pentecost in AD 55. Paul's second letter to this church was written at some point late that same year, before winter had finally set in. The letter was written from Macedonia, the region to the north of the Roman province of Achaia (in which both Corinth and Athens were located).

The first of the two letters focuses on a number of questions. It is clear that the question of how Christians should relate to their pagan environment was of particular concern. Should Christians eat meat which had been offered to pagan idols? In addition, the church was embroiled in controversy over a number of issues relating to its worship. Were some members more important than others? What was the role of spiritual gifts? It seems that the Christians at Corinth went through something like the kind of experience now associated with the charismatic movement, and were anxious to know what to make of the phenomenon. Alongside this, we find Paul dealing with some matters of theology, including a major discussion of the nature of the resurrection.

The second letter is notable for its dark tone. Paul was obliged to cancel a planned visit to Corinth, and caused considerable resentment by doing so. The letter sets out his credentials as a minister and apostle, in the face of those who criticize him. Alongside this affirmation of his ministry, we find Paul stressing the compassion and graciousness of God.

Paul's letter to the *Galatians* is generally thought to date from around 53. Another possibility is that the letter dates from shortly after the Council of Jerusalem (Acts 15), which raised questions very similar to those which Paul addresses in this letter. This would point to an earlier date, possibly around 49. The leading theme of the letter is the freedom of Christians from the letter of the Old Testament law. Christians, according to Paul, are justified by faith, not by the works of the law. There is thus no reason for Christians to be circumcised. It seems that there were "Judaizers" (that is, people who wished to see Christians remaining faithful to the Old Testament law) within the church in Galatia.

The letter to the *Ephesians* poses some difficulties. Ephesus was the chief city of the region of Asia Minor, and the scene of some of Paul's most difficult evangelist work. This letter does not have the usual specific greetings which are customary in Paul's letters, which has led some scholars to conclude that the letter was meant to be circulated throughout the churches of the region, rather than addressed to any one specific congregation. Even the specific reference to Ephesus (Ephesians 1:1) is omitted by many manuscript versions of the text. The letter does not deal directly with any specific false teaching. This further suggests that the letter was intended to circulate throughout the churches of Asia Minor, rather than focus on the specific problems of any one congregation. It is difficult to date the letter precisely.

The letter to the *Philippians* was addressed to the Christians in the city of Philippi, an important Roman colony in Macedonia, which had been evangelized by Paul during his second missionary journey (Acts 16:11–40). It was the first European city in which Paul proclaimed the gospel. There were so few Jews in the region that there was no synagogue (Acts 16:16 refers only to a "place of prayer," not a synagogue). This may explain both why Paul does not cite the Old Testament at all during this letter, and also why the letter is virtually free of argument. Paul's letter to the church at Philippi is generally thought to have been written during a period of imprisonment, probably in Rome, around 61. The circumstances of the letter fit in well with those described in Acts 28:14–31, when Paul was under house arrest, but was still permitted to see visitors and enjoy at least some degree of freedom.

The letter to the Colossians is difficult to date, and gives some indications of being a later letter. The city of Colossae (also spelled Colosse) was located on the River Lycus in Asia Minor. Paul himself had not evangelized this city during any of his missionary journeys; however, Epaphras, one of Paul's converts during his Ephesian ministry (Acts 19:10), had traveled to the city in order to preach the gospel there.

The letter is particularly concerned to deal with a false teaching which has arisen within this young church. Although this false teaching is never specifically identified, its basic features appear to have included an emphasis upon some secret or mystical knowledge (something that would become a major theme of the movement known as Gnosticism, which became especially influential in the second century); a strict set of rules concerning what it was legitimate to eat and drink, linked with an emphasis on asceticism; and a tendency to play down the importance of Jesus Christ, and worship angels. In many ways, the ideas seem to represent a mingling of Jewish and Greek ideas. Paul counters the teaching by emphasizing that all that needs to be known about God and his purposes has been revealed supremely, uniquely, and adequately in Jesus Christ.

The two letters to the *Thessalonians* are probably the earliest of Paul's letters. As noted above, there is a possibility that Galatians may have been written as early as 49; however, the majority view among scholars remains that the Thessalonian letters are the earliest of Paul's writings. Paul's first letter to the Christians at Thessalonica was written from Corinth, probably at some point in 51, although the date cannot be fixed with certainty. Thessalonica was the largest city in Macedonia, and was evangelized by Paul during his second missionary journey (Acts 17:1–14). Paul was only able to stay there briefly, being obliged to flee from the city and seek refuge in nearby Berea, before moving on to Athens and then Corinth. While in Corinth, Paul wrote to the Christian church at Thessalonica, to offer it encouragement and guidance. The second letter to the region prob-

ably dates from about six months after the first. Both letters focus on the issue of the second coming of Christ, and the need for Christians to remain watchful. The letters indicate a concern within the very early church over the fate of Christians who have died before Christ's return.

Paul's two letters to Timothy and the letter to Titus form a special group. They are distinguished by the fact that they are written to specific individuals, rather than to churches, and also by their strongly pastoral tone. This latter is seen in their concern with issues of church government and practical Christian living. For this reason, these three letters are often referred to collectively as "the pastoral letters." The pastoral letters date from a time after the events described in Acts 28. The most obvious explanation is that Paul was released from his house arrest in Rome at some point around AD 63, and that these letters were written after this release.

The first two such letters are written to Timothy, who had played a significant role in Paul's missionary work (especially in Achaia and Macedonia: see Acts 17:14–15; 18:5), and is referred to with great affection in several of Paul's letters (Philippians 2:19–22). In addition, no fewer than six of Paul's letters name him in their opening greetings (2 Corinthians, Philippians, Colossians, 1 Thessalonians, 2 Thessalonians, and Philemon). Titus was one of Paul's many Gentile converts, and is known to have served him well and faithfully at several major stages in his ministry. Luke does not mention Titus at any point during Acts; however, there are frequent references to him elsewhere in the New Testament, indicating his importance to the early churches.

These letters differ from the earlier Pauline letters in a number of ways. They are written to individuals, rather than to churches; they focus primarily on issues of church order and ministry, rather than matters of belief and conduct; all three letters are written in a style and vocabulary which differ from those of earlier letters, such as Galatians or Romans. These observations have led some to conclude that the letters were not written by Paul; others, however, argue that Paul was simply responding to the situation which developed in the 60s.

The final letter to be grouped in this collection is the letter to *Philemon*. This short letter was written by Paul from Rome, probably during the period in which he was held under house arrest (around 60). It is a highly unusual letter, in that it deals with a purely practical matter – the fate of a runaway slave – rather than with theology.

The letters of Peter

The New Testament includes two letters attributed to *Peter*, widely regarded as preeminent of the disciples of Jesus. The first letter is addressed to Christians scattered throughout the general region of Asia Minor, who are facing the threat of persecution. Although that persecution has yet to begin, it is clearly seen as a major threat by those to whom Peter was writing. The situation which the letter presupposes could easily fit in with what we know of the difficulties faced by Christians in the reign of Nero (AD 54–68). Peter indicates that he was in "Babylon" when he wrote the letter (1 Peter 5:13). The letter aims to encourage Christians facing hardship and persecution, reminding them that Christ suffered for them. For the writer, suffering is an inevitable part of being a Christian in a hostile environment. Peter acknowledges the assistance of Silas in writing the letter (5:12). It is highly likely that Silas did more than transcribe Peter's words; secretaries were often given the task of putting a writer's thoughts into better Greek than the writer himself could manage. The letter is written in excellent Greek – much better than might be expected from a former Galilean fisherman! The second letter, in contrast, is written in much poorer Greek (there is no reference to Silas!), and seems to envisage a situation which arose at a later stage in the history of the early church.

The letters of John

The three letters of John are very similar in content and style. Their common author is the apostle John, also regarded as the author of the fourth gospel. There are very clear similarities between the style of writing and the vocabulary, particularly in the case of John's gospel and the first letter of John. It is generally thought that the letters date from the end of the first century, perhaps having been written from the city of Ephesus around 85–90. The identity of the readership of the first two letters is not clear; they are addressed to believers in general, and may have been intended as circular letters for the use of traveling evangelists. The third letter is specifically addressed to "Gaius," although his identity is not clear.

It is clear that the threat posed by some form of Gnosticism is seen as particularly important. It seems that some Gnostic ideas had found their way into the communities for which John was writing. The first letter clearly addresses at least two Gnostic teachings – that Jesus' human nature was apparent rather than real, and that a radical distinction existed between the "spiritual" and the "material." The consequence of this second idea was that sins committed in the physical nature had no negative implications for someone's spiritual nature. The first letter emphasizes the reality of Christ's human nature, and affirms that Christians should not sin.

Other letters

The letter to the *Hebrews* is one of the most fascinating letters in the New Testament, stressing how Jesus Christ represents the fulfillment of the Old Testament sacrificial system. The author of the letter is unknown. Some older translations suggest that the author is Paul. However, the text makes no such claim; in any case, the style of the writing is very different from that of Paul. The two people who are most likely to have written the work are Barnabbas and Apollos, both of whom are noted appreciatively in the Acts of the Apostles. Either would have had the deep familiarity with the Old Testament and the excellent command of the Greek language which this book demonstrates. It is not clear who the intended readers of the letter would have been. The most appropriate readers would have been Greek-speaking Jewish converts to Christianity, who wanted to know the relationship between their new faith and the old ways and ideas of Judaism. It is not clear when the letter was written, nor who its intended recipients were.

The letter of *James* is the first of a group of letters sometimes referred to as the "catholic letters" or "epistles general," in that the letters in question are not written to specific individuals, or specific churches, but seem to be intended to be read by a wide range of people. (The word "catholic" basically means "universal" or "general.") The letter of James was probably not written by James the apostle, but by James the brother of Jesus, who played an important role in the Council of Jerusalem (Acts 15:13). This council was especially concerned with clarifying whether Christian believers would be under any obligation to respect the law of Moses, especially its requirement that males should be circumcised. In the end, the council decided that this should not be a requirement (see p. 174). However, no reference is made to this controversy in the letter. The absence of any such reference to this controversy points to an early date for the letter. However, James appears to be concerned to correct a possible misunderstanding of Paul's doctrine of justification by faith, which would suggest a date at some point in the late 50s or early 60s.

The letter of *Jude* is one of the shortest books in the New Testament. The precise identity of the author of the letter remains unclear. The main concern of the letter is to counter a false teaching which appears to have become widespread. The teaching in question seems similar to that noted in 2 Peter, and seems to represent a form of Gnosticism, tinged with elements drawn from popular Jewish superstition.

The Book of Revelation

The book of *Revelation*, which brings the New Testament to its close, is traditionally regarded as having been written by John the apostle, who was also responsible for the gospel and three letters bearing his name in the New Testament. The book seems to have been written at a late date, probably during the later part of the reign of the Roman emperor Domitian (81–96), when the Roman authorities were attempting to suppress Christianity in certain regions of their empire, particularly Asia Minor.

The book is apocalyptic in its outlook, resembling the second half of the book of Daniel in the Old Testament. It takes the form largely of visions, making extensive use of symbolism and highly figurative language. In some cases, it is reasonably clear what the symbols represent; there are obvious allusions to the city of Rome, the Roman empire, and the Roman emperor at several points. In many cases, however, the interpretation of the visions is difficult and speculative. The evident purpose of the book is to encourage Christians in their present sufferings, in the knowledge that evil and oppression will finally be overcome, and that suffering and pain will be excluded from the New Jerusalem.

In the present chapter, we have considered aspects of the contents of the New Testament. One theme may be said to dominate the New Testament – Jesus Christ. Martin Luther summarized this point as follows: Jesus Christ is "the mathematical point of Holy Scripture," just as Holy Scripture "is the swaddling clothes and manger in which Christ is laid." We have already explored something of the Christian understanding of the identity and significance of Jesus. But much more needs to be said. Nor is Christian faith limited to ideas about Jesus. In the following chapters, we shall therefore move on to consider the fundamental themes of Christian belief, starting with the question of their sources and norms.

5

The Background to Christian Belief

Christians do not simply believe "in" Jesus or God; they believe certain quite definite things about them. In the first chapter of this work, we looked at some aspects of what Christians believe about Jesus. However, it is clear that a more substantial account of what Christians believe – and not simply about Jesus Christ! – is called for. This chapter will explore some of the background issues to Christian belief, before going on to a more extensive discussion of Christian beliefs in the chapter that follows.

Before we can gain a proper understanding of individual beliefs – for example, what Christians believe about God or Jesus Christ – we need to explore the background to these beliefs. What does it mean, for example, to "believe"? And where do Christian ideas come from? What are the sources and norms of Christian beliefs? What does the elusive word "theology" – often used to describe the systematic study of Christian beliefs – actually mean?

To begin this process of exploration, we shall consider what Christians mean when they talk about faith.

What is Faith?

The biblical sense of the word "faith" has a number of aspects. One biblical theme is of particular importance – the idea of trusting in God, related in the famous Old Testament account of the calling of Abraham (Genesis 15:1–6). This tells of how God promised to give Abraham countless descendants, as numerous as the stars of the night sky. Abraham believed God – that is, trusted the promise that was made to him. Similarly, the crowds around Jesus are often described as having "faith" – meaning that they believed that he had some special status, identity, or authority, and would be able to heal them from their illnesses, or deal with their concerns (e.g., Luke 5:20; 17:19). Here again the basic idea is trust, in this case mingled with discernment that there is something about Jesus which merits such an attitude of trust.

Martin Luther (1483–1546) is one of a number of writers who stressed that faith is fundamentally *trust*. Faith is about trusting a

God who makes promises, and whose promises may be relied upon. In his important 1520 essay *The Babylonian Captivity of the Church*, Luther emphasized this aspect of faith.

> Where there is the Word of the God who makes promises, there must necessarily be the faith of the person who accepts those promises. It is clear that the beginning of our salvation is a faith which clings to the Word of a promising God who, without any effort on our part, in free and unmerited mercy goes before us and offers us a word of promise.

Luther emphasizes that it is pointless to trust someone who is not worthy of trust, no matter how passionately we may try to trust them. Even a small faith in someone who is totally reliable is vastly to be preferred. Trust is not, however, an occasional attitude. For Luther, it is an undeviating trusting outlook upon life, a constant stance of conviction of the trustworthiness of the promises of God. As Karl Barth, perhaps the most significant Protestant theologian of the twentieth century, put it: "In God alone is there faithfulness, and faith is the trust that we may hold to Him, to His promise and to His guidance. To hold to God is to rely on the fact that God is there for me, and to live in this certainty."

Luther's attempts to offer a working definition of faith were developed further by John Calvin (1509–1564) in his *Institutes of the Christian Religion*, which was first published in 1536 and went through many editions until the final, definitive edition of 1559. Calvin, true to his reputation as a very precise and logical theologian, who is generally very easy to read and understand, offers us this succinct definition.

> Now we shall have a right definition of faith if we say that it is a steady and certain knowledge of the divine benevolence towards us,

5.1 Karl Barth, 1957. AKG-Images/ullstein bild.

which is founded upon the truth of the gracious promise of God in Christ, and is both revealed to our minds and sealed in our hearts by the Holy Spirit.

In the first part of this definition, Calvin states that faith is a "steady and certain knowledge of the divine benevolence towards us." Calvin here uses language that expresses confidence in God, and stresses God's reliability. While faith is defined as "knowledge," it turns out to be a certain very specific kind of knowledge. It is not just "knowledge" in general; in fact, it is not even "knowledge of God." It is specifically "knowledge of *God's benevolence towards us.*" Calvin, following Luther, argues that faith is ultimately grounded and based in God's *goodness.* It is not simply about accepting that God exists, but about encountering God's kindness to us.

For some critics of Christianity, faith is simply an evasion of critical thinking. The idea of "faith in God" is ridiculed by some rationalist writers, who argued that unless God's existence could be proved, there was no reason to pay the slightest attention to this alleged divinity. Richard Dawkins, one of the world's most prominent atheists, takes this line. Faith, Dawkins asserts, "means blind trust, in the absence of evidence, even in the teeth of evidence." This view, set out for the first time in 1976, is an expression of one of the "core beliefs" that determine Dawkins' attitude to religion. This non-negotiable core conviction surfaces again in 1992, when Dawkins delivered a lecture at the Edinburgh International Science Festival, in which he set out his views on the relation of faith and evidence. Dawkins was once more scathing over the intellectual irresponsibility of faith:

> Faith is the great cop-out, the great excuse to evade the need to think and evaluate evidence. Faith is belief in spite of, even perhaps because of, the lack of evidence . . . Faith is not allowed to justify itself by argument.

As a natural scientist, Dawkins insists on the proper place of evidence and proof in every aspect of human thought. Why, he asks, should not the same be true of faith? How can anyone take seriously a discredited and outdated notion of faith as "blind trust, in the absence of evidence, even in the teeth of evidence"?

The key point to make here is that the definition that Dawkins offers is simply not a Christian concept of faith. Dawkins offers no defense of this definition, which bears little relation to any religious (or any other) sense of the word. No evidence is offered that it is representative of religious opinion. No authority is cited in its support. I don't accept this idea of faith, and I have yet to meet a theologian who takes it seriously. It cannot be defended from any official declaration of faith from any Christian denomination.

The weakness of Dawkins' critique can be seen from the definition of faith offered by W. H. Griffith-Thomas (1861–1924), a noted Anglican theologian. The definition of faith that he offers in his *Principles of Theology* (1930) is typical of just about any Christian writer.

> [Faith] affects the whole of man's nature. It commences with the conviction of the mind based on adequate evidence; it continues in the confidence of the heart or emotions based on conviction, and it is crowned in the consent of the will, by means of which the conviction and confidence are expressed in conduct.

It's a good and reliable definition, synthesizing the core elements of the characteristic Christian understanding of faith. And this faith "commences with the conviction of the mind based on adequate evidence."

Proofs for God's Existence?

So does this mean that Christians believe that they can prove the existence of God, or any other aspect of their faith, with absolute certainty? No. The basic attitude amongst most theologians and philosophers of religion can be summarized like this. Some things can indeed be proved; but some, by their very nature, lie beyond proof. God is one of these. The basic Christian attitude to proofs for the existence of God is that it is something that reason cannot prove conclusively. Yet the fact that the existence of God lies *beyond* reason does not for one moment mean that the existence of God is *contrary* to reason. As many writers have argued, the idea of God makes a lot of sense, and also enables a lot of sense to be made of the world around us. Certain excellent reasons may be put forward for suggesting that God exists; these do not, however, count as "proofs" in the sense of "rigorous logical demonstrations" or "conclusive scientific experiments."

We can explore this by considering the writings of Thomas Aquinas (ca. 1225–1274), probably the most famous and influential theologian of the Middle Ages. Born in Italy, he achieved his fame through his teaching and writing at the University of Paris and other northern universities. His fame rests chiefly on his *Summa Theologica*, composed towards the end of his life and not totally finished at the time of his death. However, he also wrote many other significant works, particularly the *Summa contra Gentiles*, which represents a major statement of the rationality of the Christian faith, and especially the existence of God. Aquinas believed that it was entirely proper to identify pointers towards the existence of God, drawn from general human experience of the world. His "Five Ways" represent five lines of argument in support of the existence of God, each of which draws on some aspect of the world which "points" to the existence of its creator.

So what kind of pointers does Aquinas identify? The basic line of thought guiding Aquinas is that the world mirrors God, as its creator – an idea which is given more formal expression in his doctrine of the "analogy of being." Just as an artist might sign a painting to identify it as his handiwork, so God has stamped a divine "signature" upon the creation. What we observe in the world – for example, its signs of ordering – can be explained if God was its creator. If God both brought the world into existence and impressed the divine image and likeness upon it, then something of God's nature can be known from the creation.

Where might we look in creation to find evidence for the existence of God? Aquinas argues that the ordering of the world is the most convincing evidence of God's existence and wisdom. This basic assumption underlies each of the "Five Ways," although it is of particular importance in the case of the argument often referred to as the "argument from design" or the "teleological argument." We shall consider the first and last of these two "ways" to illustrate the issues.

The first way begins from the observation that things in the world are in motion or change. The world is not static, but is dynamic. Examples of this are easy to list. Rain falls from the sky. Stones roll down into valleys. The earth revolves around the sun (a fact, incidentally, unknown to Aquinas). This, the first of Aquinas' arguments, is normally referred to as the "argument from motion"; however, it is clear that the "movement" in question is actually understood in more general terms, so that the term "change" is more appropriate as a translation at points.

So how did nature come to be in motion? Why is it changing? Why isn't it static? Aquinas argues that everything which moves is moved by something else. For every motion, there is a cause. Things don't just move; they are moved by something else. Now each cause of motion must itself have a cause. And that cause must have a cause as well. And so Aquinas argues that there is a whole series of causes of motion lying behind the world as we know it. Now unless there are an infinite number of these causes, Aquinas argues, there must be a single cause right at the origin of the series. From this original cause of motion, all other motion is ultimately derived. This is the origin of the great chain of causality which we see reflected in the way the world behaves. From the fact that things are in motion, Aquinas thus argues for the existence of a single original cause of all this motion. This, Aquinas insists, is none other than God.

In more recent times, this argument has been restated in terms of God as the one who brought the universe into existence. For this reason, it is often referred to as the "cosmological" argument (from the Greek word *kosmos*, meaning "universe"). The most commonly encountered statement of the argument runs along the following lines:

1   Everything within the universe depends on something else for its existence.
2   What is true of its individual parts is also true of the universe itself.
3   The universe thus depends on something else for its existence for as long as it has existed or will exist.
4   The universe thus depends on God for its existence.

The argument basically assumes that the existence of the universe is something that requires explanation. It will be clear that this type of argument relates directly to modern cosmological research, particularly the "big bang" theory of the origins of the cosmos.

The fifth and final way is known as the teleological argument, which derives its name from the Greek word *telos*, meaning "purpose" or "goal." Aquinas notes that the world shows obvious traces of intelligent design. Natural processes and objects seem to be adapted with certain definite objectives in mind. They seem to have a purpose. They seem to have been designed. But things don't design themselves: they are caused and designed by someone or something else. Arguing from this observation, Aquinas concludes that the source of this natural ordering must be conceded to be God.

This argument was developed by William Paley (1743–1805). According to Paley, the world was like a watch. It showed evidence of intelligent design, and having been created for a purpose. If there was a watch, there must also be a watchmaker. Paley was particularly impressed by the construction of the human eye, which he argued to be so complex and highly developed that it could only be the result of intelligent design and construction.

Paley's argument was highly influential in nineteenth-century England. However, its plausibility was eroded by Charles Darwin's (1809–1882) theory of evolution, which offered an alternative explanation of how such complex structures arose. In his *Origin of Species* (1859), Darwin insisted that these could be explained on a purely natural basis, without need for an intelligent divine designer. Nevertheless, the "argument from design" remains an intriguing idea, which continues to fascinate people.

It will be obvious that Aquinas' arguments are similar in terms of their structure. Each depends on tracing a causal sequence back to its single origin, and identifying this with God. These are thus not "proofs" in the strict sense of the word, as they actually presuppose God's existence! Aquinas' approach is actually rather different. His argument is that, if we presuppose that God made the world, we end up with a way of making sense of the world that makes sense of a lot of things. In other words, Aquinas is arguing that, seen from the Christian perspective, the existence of God resonates well with what can be observed of the world. It is thus a confirmation, but not a proof, of God's existence.

But other theologians have viewed such "proofs" with skepticism. The great French mathematician and philosopher Blaise Pascal (1623–1662) had two critical concerns about the kind of approach adopted by Aquinas. First, he found it difficult to accept that the rather abstract philosophical "God" which resulted from such arguments was anything like the living God of the Old and New Testaments. In his *Pensées*, Pascal put it like this: "The metaphysical proofs for the existence of God are so remote from human reasoning, and so complex, that they have little impact."

But second, Pascal argued that these "proofs" assumed that God was known primarily through reason. For Pascal, the human heart also had its reasons for believing (or not believing!) in God. "We know the truth, not only through our reason, but also through our heart." The appeal of God to the human condition went far beyond any resonance between the world as we know it and the ideas of the Christian faith. It extends to include a deep-seated longing for God, which Pascal held to be of crucial importance in the long, unended human quest for God and final meaning.

In the end, according to Pascal, you cannot argue someone into the kingdom of God. The existence of God is not something that can be proved. Equally, it is not something that can be *disproved*. It is easy to overlook the fact that atheism is also a faith. An atheist believes that there is no God. This belief, however, is just as difficult to prove as the Christian belief that there is indeed a God.

The Sources of Christian Beliefs

Throughout its long history, Christian theology has made an appeal to three fundamental resources: the Bible, tradition, and reason. In view of their importance, we shall examine each of them in a little detail, before moving on to our first topic.

The Bible

We have already explored something of the characteristics of the Christian Bible, and noted its importance. The terms "Bible" and "Scripture," along with the derived adjectives "biblical" and "scriptural," are virtually interchangeable. Both designate a body of texts which are recognized as authoritative for Christian thinking (although the nature and

extent of that authority is a matter of continuing debate). There is widespread agreement within Christianity that the Bible has a place of especial importance in grounding and judging Christian beliefs. All the Protestant confessions of faith stress the centrality of the Bible. More recently, the Second Vatican Council (1962–1965) reaffirmed its importance for Catholic theology and preaching. The authority of the Bible is seen as linked with the idea of "inspiration" – in other words, that in some way the words of the Bible convey the words of God. This is stated clearly by most Protestant confessions of faith, such as the "Gallic Confession of Faith" (1559), which includes the following declaration:

> We believe that the Word contained in these books has proceeded from God, and receives its authority from him alone, and not from human beings.

The *Catechism of the Catholic Church* (1992) sets out a similar position, as follows:

> God is the author of Sacred Scripture. The divine revealed realities, which are contained and presented in the text of Sacred Scripture, have been written down under the inspiration of the Holy Spirit. For Holy Mother Church, relying on the faith of the apostolic age, accepts as sacred and canonical the books of the Old and the New Testaments, whole and entire, with all their parts, on the grounds that, written under the inspiration of the Holy Spirit, they have God as their author and have been handed on as such to the Church herself. God inspired the human authors of the sacred books.

As will be clear from these citations, the Bible is regarded as possessing authority for Christians in such matters as beliefs and ethics. The idea of "inspiration" is often used to explain the specific authority of the Bible for Christians.

The notion that the special status of Scripture within Christian theology rests upon its divine origins, however vaguely this may be stated, can be discerned both in the New Testament itself and in subsequent reflection on this. A classic text, often cited in this respect, is 2 Timothy 3:16–17, which speaks of Scripture as "God-breathed (*theopneustos*)." This idea was common in early Christian thought, and was not regarded as controversial. The Greek-speaking Jewish philosopher Philo of Alexandria (ca. 30 BC–ca. AD 45) regarded Scripture as fully inspired, and argued that God used the authors of scriptural books as passive instruments for communicating God's will.

The Bible is often referred to by Christians as the "word of the Lord" or the "word of God." This is especially clear in public worship, where a reading from the Bible is often accompanied by a response as follows:

Reader: This is the Word of the Lord.
Congregation: Thanks be to God!

So what is meant by this?

The first point to make is that "word" implies both action and communication. Just as a person's character and will are expressed through the words they use, so Scripture (especially the Old Testament) understands God to address people, and thus to make known God's intentions and will for them. The phrase "the word of God" thus implies action, disclosure, and communication. Traditionally, Christian theology has seen this process of disclosure as concentrated in Jesus Christ, and in the Bible. The interrelationship between Christ and Scripture is an important theme of Christian theology.

The idea of the "word of God" is complex and highly nuanced, bringing together a cluster of ideas. Three broad, and clearly related, senses of the term may be discerned both within the Christian tradition and within Scripture itself.

1   The term is used to refer to Jesus Christ as the word of God made flesh (John 1:14). This is the most highly developed use of the term in the New Testament. In speaking of Christ as the "word of God incarnate," Christian theology has attempted to express the idea that the will, purposes, and nature of God are made known in history through the person of Jesus Christ. It is the deeds, character, and theological identity of Jesus Christ, and not merely the words that he uttered, which make known the nature and purpose of God.

2   The term is also used to refer to "the gospel of Christ," or "the message or proclamation about Jesus." In this sense, the term refers to what God achieved and made known through the life, death, and resurrection of Christ.

3   The term is used in a general sense to refer to the whole Bible, which can be regarded as setting the scene for the advent of Christ, telling the story of his coming, and exploring the implications of his life, death, and resurrection for believers.

Considerations of this kind lie behind Karl Barth's use of the phrase "word of God." Barth's doctrine of "the threefold form of the word of God" distinguishes a threefold movement, from the word of God in Christ, to the witness to this word in Scripture, and finally to the proclamation of this word in the preaching of the community of faith. There is thus a direct and organic connection between the preaching of the church and the person of Jesus Christ.

Tradition

A series of controversies in the early church brought home the importance of the concept of "tradition." The word "tradition" comes from the Latin term *traditio*, which means "handing over," "handing down," or "handing on." It is a thoroughly biblical idea: St. Paul reminded his readers that he was handing on to them core teachings of the Christian faith which he had himself received from other people (1 Corinthians 15:1–4). The term can refer to both the action of passing teachings on to others – something which Paul insists must be done within the church – and to the body of teachings which are passed on in this manner. Tradition can thus be understood as a *process* as well as a *body of teaching*. The pastoral epistles (three New Testament letters that are particularly concerned with matters of church order in ensuring the continuity of Christian teaching and the preservation of orthodoxy: 1 Timothy, 2 Timothy, and Titus) in particular stress the importance of "guarding the good deposit which was entrusted to you" (2 Timothy 1:14). The New Testament also uses the notion of "tradition" in a negative sense, meaning something like "human ideas and practices which are not divinely authorized." Thus Jesus Christ was openly critical of certain human traditions within Judaism (e.g., see Matthew 15:1–6; Mark 7:13).

The importance of the idea of tradition first became obvious in a controversy which broke out during the second century. The Gnostic controversy centered on a number of questions, including how salvation was to be achieved. Christian writers found themselves having to deal with some highly unusual and creative interpretations of the Bible. How were they to deal with these? If the Bible was to be regarded as authoritative, was every interpretation of the Bible to be viewed as of equal value?

Irenaeus of Lyons, one of the church's greatest theologians, did not think so. The question of how the Bible was to be interpreted was of the greatest importance. Heretics, he argued, interpreted the Bible according to their own taste. Orthodox believers, in contrast, interpreted the Bible in ways that their apostolic authors would have approved. What had been handed down from the apostles through the church was not merely the biblical texts themselves, but a certain way of reading and understanding those texts.

> Everyone who wishes to perceive the truth should consider the apostolic tradition, which has been made known in every church in the entire world. We are able to number those who are bishops appointed by the apostles, and their successors in the churches to the present day, who taught and knew nothing of such things as these people imagine.

Irenaeus' point is that a continuous stream of Christian teaching, life, and interpretation can be traced from the time of the apostles to his own period. The church is able to point to those who have maintained the teaching of the church, and to certain public standard creeds which set out the main lines of Christian belief. Tradition is thus the guarantor of faithfulness to the original apostolic teaching, a safeguard against the innovations and misrepresentations of biblical texts on the part of the Gnostics.

This development is of major importance, as it underlies the emergence of "creeds" – public, authoritative statements of the basic points of the Christian faith, which are based upon the Bible, but which avoid maverick interpretations of biblical material. This point was further developed in the early fifth century by Vincent of Lérins, who was concerned that certain doctrinal innovations were being introduced without good reason. There was a need to have public standards by which such doctrines could be judged. So what standard was available, by which the church could be safeguarded from such errors? For Vincent, the answer was clear – tradition. For Vincent, tradition was "a rule for the interpretation of the prophets and the apostles in such a way that is directed by the rule of the universal church."

Creeds

Having noted the importance of creeds, we may explore how they came about in their present forms. Their emergence was stimulated by two factors of especial significance.

1 The need for public statements of faith which could be used in teaching, and in defense of the Christian faith against misrepresentations.
2 The need for personal "confessions of faith" at the time of baptism.

We have already touched on the first point; the second needs further exploration. It is known that the early church attached especial importance to the baptism of new members. In the third and fourth centuries, a definite pattern of instruction and baptism developed: new members of the church were instructed in the basics of the Christian faith during the period of Lent, and baptized on Easter Day. These new members of the church were asked to confirm their faith by assenting to key statements of Christian belief.

According to Hippolytus' *Apostolic Tradition*, which dates from the early years of the third century, we know that three questions were put to each baptismal candidate: "Do you believe in God, the Father Almighty? Do you believe in Jesus Christ, our Savior? Do you believe in the Holy Spirit, the holy church, and the forgiveness of sins?" As time went on, these questions were gradually changed into a statement of faith, which each candidate was asked to affirm.

The most important creed to emerge from these "baptismal creeds" is the "Apostles' Creed," which is widely used in Christian worship today. Traditionally, this creed is set out as

twelve statements, each of which is attributed to one of the twelve apostles. Although it is now widely agreed that this creed was not actually written by the apostles themselves, it is nevertheless "apostolic" in the sense that it contains the main ideas of the Christian faith that the church received from those apostles. The present form of the creed can be traced to the eighth century. In its present form, it reads as follows:

> I believe in God, the Father almighty, the creator of heaven and earth.
>
> I believe in Jesus Christ, God's only Son, our Lord, who was conceived by the Holy Spirit, born of the Virgin Mary, suffered under Pontius Pilate, was crucified, died, and was buried. He descended to the dead. On the third day he rose again; he ascended into heaven, he is seated at the right hand of the Father, and he will come again to judge the living and the dead.
>
> I believe in the Holy Spirit, the holy catholic church, the communion of saints, the forgiveness of sins, the resurrection of the body, and the life everlasting. Amen.

Note that the creed still falls into three parts, corresponding to the three questions that Hippolytus reports as being asked of baptismal candidates back in the third century. Although each of the questions has been expanded, the same basic structure can still be identified.

A longer version is usually known as the "Nicene Creed." This includes additional statements of faith concerning the identity of Jesus, in response to the fourth-century debates about his identity. The Nicene Creed makes the following statement about how Christians understand Jesus, which represents a significant expansion of the somewhat terser statement of the Apostles' Creed.

> [I believe] in one Lord Jesus Christ, the only begotten Son of God, begotten of his Father

before all worlds, God of God, Light of Light, very God of very God, begotten, not made, being of one substance with the Father; by whom all things were made; who for us and for our salvation came down from heaven, and was incarnate by the Holy Spirit of the Virgin Mary, and was made man; and was crucified also for us under Pontius Pilate; he suffered death and was buried; and the third day he rose again according to the Scriptures, and ascended into heaven, and sits on the right hand of the Father; and he shall come again, with glory, to judge both the living and the dead; whose kingdom shall have no end.

Creeds remain of great importance in contemporary Christianity. Most acts of public worship involve the reciting of a creed on a regular basis. Many parish study courses and sermon series take the form of an explanation of the creed. Christian clergy are often required to declare their assent to the creeds publicly before they are allowed to begin their ministry.

Reason

Finally, we need to note the importance of reason in Christian theology. Traditionally, Christian theology has seen reason as operating in a subservient role to revelation. Thomas Aquinas argued that supernatural truths needed to be revealed to us. Human reason, on its own, could not hope to gain access to divine mysteries. It could, however, reflect on them, once they had been revealed. This has been the position adopted by most Christian theologians. Reason allows us to reflect on revelation.

During the great "Age of Reason" in western culture – which most historians suggest is to be dated to the two hundred years between 1750 and 1950 – this judgment was challenged. Reason, it was argued, was capable of deducing anything that needed to be known about God. There was no need to propose

divine revelation. Instead, we could rely totally upon reason. This position is generally known as "rationalism," and is still encountered today in some quarters.

More recently, western culture has experienced a reaction against this emphasis on reason. The rise of postmodernism is connected with a growing awareness of the limits of the power of human reason, and the way in which an appeal to reason may be abused. Postmodern writers have emphasized that there is no single "reason" which is authoritative for all humanity.

There is, of course, continued interest today in the role of reason in theology. The most obvious sign of this is the ongoing debate over "arguments for the existence of God." Although it is open to question whether these arguments prove very much at all, let alone the existence of the Christian God, the fact that there is so much interest in them demonstrates that there is a continuing role for reason in theological debate.

We now turn to consider one of the most interesting aspects of the relation of faith and reason – the use of "helpmates" or "dialogue partners" in theology, often referred to using the term *ancilla theologiae*, a Latin phrase which literally means "a handmaid of theology."

The "Handmaid": Dialogue Between Theology and Culture

There is a long tradition within Christian theology of drawing on intellectual resources outside the Christian tradition as a means of developing a theological vision. This approach, usually referred to using the phrase *ancilla theologiae*, is grounded in the basic idea that philosophical systems can be a very helpful way of stimulating theological development, and enabling a dialogue to be opened up between Christian thinkers and their cultural environment. The two most important historical examples of this approach to theology are the dialogues with Platonism and Aristotelianism.

The dialogue with Platonism was of immense importance during the first five centuries of the Christian church, especially in the Greek-speaking world of the eastern Mediterranean. As Christianity expanded in that region, it encountered rival worldviews, of which Platonism was the most important. Such worldviews could be seen positively or negatively: they were both an opportunity for dialogue and intellectual development, and a threat to the existence of Christianity. The task faced by writers such as Justin Martyr or Clement of Alexandria was how to make use of the obvious intellectual merits of Platonism in constructing a Christian worldview, without compromising the integrity of Christianity itself. After all, despite their occasional similarities, Christianity is *not* Platonism.

A new debate opened up in the thirteenth century, during the golden age of scholastic theology. The rediscovery of Aristotle by medieval writers seemed to offer new resources to help in every aspect of intellectual life, including physics, philosophy, and ethics. It was inevitable that theologians should also want to see what use they could make of Aristotelian ideas and methods in constructing a systematic theology – such as Thomas Aquinas' massive *Summa Theologiae*, widely regarded as one of the greatest works of theology ever written.

In both these cases, using another intellectual discipline as the *ancilla theologiae* offers opportunities and risks in about equal measure. It is clearly important to appreciate what these opportunities and risks are. The two major *opportunities* offered to theology by the critical appropriation of another discipline can be summarized as follows.

1 It allows for a much more rigorous exploration of ideas than would otherwise be possible. Problems that Christian theology encounters in trying to develop its ideas often have their parallels in other disciplines. Thomas Aquinas, for example, found Aristotle's notion of an "unmoved mover" helpful in setting out some reasons for defending the existence of God.

2 It allows Christian theology to engage in a dialogue with another worldview – a major element of the church's witness to its secular context. In the second century, Justin Martyr clearly believed that many Platonists would be so impressed by the parallels between Platonism and Christianity that they might consider conversion. Similarly, in his "Areopagus address" (Acts 17:22–31), Paul draws on some themes from Stoic philosophy in attempting to communicate the Christian message to Athenian culture.

Yet alongside these positive aspects of such an engagement, an obvious risk must also be noted – that ideas which are not distinctively Christian come to play a significant (perhaps even normative) role in Christian theology. For example, Aristotelian ideas about the proper manner of logical reasoning, or Cartesian ideas about the proper starting point for any intellectual discipline, might find their way into Christian theology. On some occasions, this might turn out to be a neutral development; on others, it may eventually be recognized to have negative implications, undermining the integrity of Christian theology, and ultimately causing it to be distorted. Martin Luther, the great German reformer, argued that medieval theology had allowed a number of such distortions to arise through an excessive, and partially uncritical, use of Aristotelian ideas in the Middle Ages.

Despite these concerns, the approach continues to be widely used. Many German theologians of the nineteenth century found G. W. F. Hegel and Immanuel Kant to be helpful dialogue partners. In the twentieth century, Rudolf Bultmann and Paul Tillich both found a dialogue with existentialism to be theologically productive.

What is Theology?

Finally, we may ask what is meant by the word "theology," regularly used within Christian circles to refer to the systematic study of faith. What is it, and why do people do it? The word "theology" is easily broken down into two Greek words: *theos* (God) and *logos* (word). "Theology" is thus discourse about God, in much the same way as "biology" is discourse about life (Greek: *bios*). If there is only one God, and if that God happens to be the "God of the Christians" (to borrow a phrase from the second-century writer Tertullian), then the nature and scope of theology are relatively well defined: theology is reflection upon the God whom Christians worship and adore.

Theology was thus understood as systematic analysis of the nature, purposes, and activity of God. At its heart lay the belief that it was an attempt, however inadequate, to speak about a divine being, distinct from humans. Although "theology" was initially understood to mean "the doctrine of God," the term developed a subtly new meaning in the twelfth and thirteenth centuries, as the University of Paris began to develop. A name had to be found for the systematic study of the Christian faith at university level. Under the influence of Parisian writers such as Peter Abelard and Gilbert de la Porrée, the Latin word *theologia* came to mean "the discipline of sacred learning," em-bracing the totality of Christian doctrine, not merely the doctrine of God.

The word "theology" is not biblical, but came to be used occasionally in the early patristic period to refer to at least some aspects of Christian beliefs. Thus Clement of Alexandria, writing in the late second century, contrasted Christian *theologia* with the *mythologia* of pagan writers, clearly understanding "theology" to refer to "Christian truth claims about God," which could be compared with the spurious stories of pagan mythology. Other writers of the patristic period, such as Eusebius of Caesarea, also use the term to refer to something like "the Christian understanding of God." However, it seems that the word was not used to refer to the entire body of Christian thought, but only to those aspects relating directly to God.

Perhaps the most important moment in the history of theology as an academic discipline was the founding of universities in western Europe during the twelfth century. Medieval universities – such as Paris, Bologna, and Oxford – generally had four faculties: arts, medicine, law, and theology. The faculty of arts was seen as entry level, qualifying students to go on to more advanced studies in the three "higher faculties." This general pattern continued into the sixteenth century, as can be seen from the educational backgrounds of two leading theologians of this period. Martin Luther initially studied arts at the University of Erfurt, before going on to study within the higher faculty of theology. John Calvin began his university life by studying arts at the University of Paris, before going on to study law at the University of Orléans. The result of this development was that theology became established as a significant component of advanced study at European universities. As more and more universities were established in western Europe, so the academic study of theology became more widespread.

Initially, the study of Christianity in western Europe was focused on schools attached to cathedrals and monasteries. Theology was generally understood to be concerned with practical matters, such as issues of prayer and spirituality, rather than as a theoretical subject. However, with the founding of the universities, the academic study of the Christian faith gradually moved out of monasteries and cathedrals into the public arena. The word "theology" came to be used extensively at the University of Paris during the thirteenth century to refer to the systematic discussion of Christian beliefs in general, and not simply beliefs about God. The use of the word in this sense can be seen to a limited extent in earlier works, such as the writings of Peter Abelard. However, the work which is widely regarded as being of decisive importance in establishing the general use of the term appeared in the thirteenth century – Thomas Aquinas' *Summa Theologiae*. Increasingly, theology came to be seen as a theoretical rather than a practical subject, despite reservations about this development.

Many early thirteenth-century theologians, such as Bonaventure and Alexander of Hales, were concerned about the implications of neglecting the practical side of theology. However, Thomas Aquinas' argument that theology was a speculative and theoretical discipline gained increasing favor among theologians. This alarmed many medieval spiritual writers, such as Thomas à Kempis, who felt that this encouraged speculation about God rather than obedience to God. At the time of the Reformation, writers such as Martin Luther attempted to rediscover the practical aspects of theology. The Genevan Academy, founded by Calvin in 1559, was initially concerned with the theological education of pastors, orientated towards the practical needs of ministry in the church. This tradition of treating theology as concerned with the practical concerns of Christian ministry would continue in many Protestant seminaries and colleges. However, later Protestant writers operating in a university context generally returned to the medieval understanding of theology as a theoretical subject, even if they made it clear that it had certain definite practical implications in the areas of spirituality and ethics.

In the classic period of theology, the subject matter of theology was generally organized along lines suggested by the Apostles' Creed or Nicene Creed, beginning with the doctrine of God, and ending with eschatology. Classic models for the systematization of theology are provided by a number of writings. The first major theological textbook of western theology is Peter Lombard's *Four Books of the Sentences*, compiled at the University of Paris during the twelfth century, probably during the years 1155–1158. In essence, the work is a collection of quotations (or "sentences"), drawn from patristic writers in general, and Augustine in particular. These quotations were arranged topically. The first of the four books deals with the Trinity, the second with creation and sin, the third with incarnation and Christian life, and the fourth and final book with the sacraments and the last things. Commenting on these sentences became a standard practice for medieval theologians, such as Thomas Aquinas, Bonaventure, and Duns Scotus. Thomas Aquinas' *Summa Theologiae*, dating from a century later, surveyed the totality of Christian theology in three parts, using principles similar to those adopted by Peter Lombard, while placing greater emphasis on philosophical questions (particularly those raised by Aristotle) and the need to reconcile the different opinions of patristic writers.

Two different models were provided at the time of the Reformation. On the Lutheran side, Philip Melanchthon produced the *Loci Communes* ("Commonplaces") in 1521. This work provided a survey of the main aspects of Christian theology, arranged topically. John Calvin's *Institutes of the Christian Religion* is widely regarded as the most influential work of Protestant theology. The first edition of this work appeared in 1536, and its definitive edition in 1559. The work is arranged in four books, the first of which deals with the doctrine of God, the second with Christ as mediator between God and humanity, the third with the appropriation of redemption, and the final book with the life of the church. Other more major works of systematic theology to follow similar lines include Karl Barth's massive *Church Dogmatics*.

Having reflected on some of the questions of the sources and norms of Christian belief, we are now in a position to look at the fundamental themes of faith in the following chapter.

6

A Brief Outline of Core Christian Beliefs

It is simply impossible to study any religion, philosophy, or worldview without engaging with its ideas. Whether we are talking about Christianity or its religious or secular alternatives – ranging from Buddhism to Islam, from Marxism to Freudianism – an understanding of the movement depends on having grasped its basic principles. At one level, as we saw earlier, Christian theology can be thought of as intellectual reflection on the act, content, and implications of the Christian faith. Within the Christian tradition, this "discipleship of the mind" has long been seen as part of the process of spiritual growth. To grow in one's faith is to achieve a deeper understanding of its ideas, and to allow them to have a greater impact on one's life.

Christianity has always been resistant to the idea that spiritual growth simply takes the form of a deepened familiarity with its beliefs. This point is constantly reiterated by spiritual writers, such as Thomas à Kempis (ca. 1380–1471). In his celebrated work of spirituality *The Imitation of Christ*, Thomas sets out a strongly practical approach to the Christian faith, which focuses on the need to obey Christ rather than indulge in flights of intellectual fancy. Speculation concerning the Trinity is singled out as a case of such speculation, which he urges his readers to avoid.

What good does it do you if you dispute loftily about the Trinity, but lack humility and therefore displease the Trinity? It is not lofty words that make you righteous or holy or dear to God, but a virtuous life. I would much rather experience contrition than be able to give a definition of it. If you knew the whole of the Bible by heart, along with all the definitions of the philosophers, what good would this be without grace and love? "Vanity of vanities, and all is vanity" (Ecclesiastes 1:2) – except, that is, loving God and serving him alone.

Notice the manner in which Thomas stresses the limited value of knowledge of Christian beliefs. This kind of knowledge is not necessarily a good thing; it can be a distraction from God, and a temptation to become arrogant.

That being said, most spiritual writers argue that a deepened knowledge of the Christian faith can, and should, go hand in hand with a deepened appreciation of it, thus leading to a more profound impact at every level of life. A good example of this can be found in Thomas Merton (1915–1968), a Trappist monk who has had a critical influence on modern western spirituality. Merton affirms that there is a close link between knowing about the Christian faith (theology) and loving God (contemplation), which must be affirmed and recognized for the mutual good of each.

Contemplation, far from being opposed to theology, is in fact the normal perfection of theology. We must not separate intellectual study of divinely revealed truth and contemplative experience of that truth as if they could never have anything to do with one another. On the contrary, they are simply two aspects of the same thing . . . Unless they are united there is no fervor, no life and no spiritual value in theology; no substance, no meaning and no sure orientation in the contemplative life.

Note how Merton forges a link between the two disciplines, and indicates that their artificial separation is to their mutual impoverishment.

This chapter provides what might be thought of as a compendium of Christian belief. It is not comprehensive; rather, it tries to provide an overview of the core beliefs of the Christian faith, alongside some of the debates that are associated with them. For example, there are important divergences within Christianity over the nature of the church. For some, the church is a "mixed body," consisting of believers and unbelievers; for others, it is a "pure body," consisting only of believers. Other examples can easily be given. So where do these different approaches come from? And what are their merits? And their implications? What difference do they make to the business of Christian living?

An important aspect of studying Christian doctrine is trying to understand why the Christian churches committed themselves to ideas which, at least at first sight, seem complicated and even a little implausible. Why should Christians believe that Jesus Christ is "truly divine and truly human," when this seems much more difficult than a simpler statement such as "Jesus Christ is truly human." Or, to take another familiar example, why should anyone want to believe that God is a Trinity – "one God, three persons" – when this seems so much more complicated than simply believing in God?

There are many reasons for wanting to think about the Christian faith in more detail. Those who are not Christians will be interested in learning what Christians believe, and why. Theology offers an explanation of the Christian faith, and helps elucidate why Christians differ on certain points of importance. At least a basic understanding of Christian theology will be invaluable to anyone studying western cultural history, literature, or art.

Those who are Christians, on the other hand, might well value a brief account of the core beliefs of their faith. Reflection on those beliefs can lead to personal enrichment, and a deepened grasp of their faith. For the great Christian theologian Augustine of Hippo, there is a genuine intellectual excitement to wrestling with God. He spoke of an "eros of the mind" – a sense of longing to understand more about God's nature and ways – and the transformative impact that this could have on people's lives. Other Christian writers have stressed the practical importance of theology, noting how it is essential for the ministry of the church. Preaching, spirituality, and pastoral care, many argue, are grounded in theology. This business of "thinking about God" takes place at many levels – in church study groups, in Bible studies, through preaching, and in academic seminars.

So where shall we begin? And how shall we arrange the material that we need to cover? In what follows, we shall follow the traditional order of presentation of Christian beliefs, which is grounded in the creeds. Unsurprisingly, that means that we begin by thinking about Christian understandings of God.

God

G od lies at the heart of Christian theology. But *which* God? And what is this God like? It is clear that the little word "God" needs extensive amplification. Israel's reflections on the identity of its God – which it styled using phrases such as "the Lord God of Israel" – took place against a background of polytheism. Each nation in the region had its own god; many had highly developed pantheons, recognizing many different gods, each with its own distinctive function or sphere of influence. Simply talking about "God" was thus not particularly informative. It begged the question: which of these gods do you mean? Part of the task of Christian theology is to identify the God in which Christians believe.

This process of identification can be seen in both the Old and New Testaments. For the Old Testament prophets, Israel knew and worshipped the God who had brought her people out of Egypt, and led them into the promised land. In the New Testament, we find this idea picked up and developed further. Christians believe in the same God as Abraham; this God is, however, finally and fully disclosed in Jesus Christ. Thus Paul speaks of "the God and Father of our Lord Jesus Christ" (2 Corinthians 1:3).

The basic idea we find throughout the New Testament is that Christians worship and know the same God as Israel. Nevertheless, Christians hold that this God is revealed supremely and finally in Christ. Thus the letter to the Hebrews opens by declaring that the same God who spoke to Israel "in many times and in various ways" through the prophets has now "spoken to us through a Son," who is to be recognized as the "exact representation" of God (Hebrews 1:1–3). This point is of great importance, as it demonstrates how the Christian understanding of God is linked with the person of Christ. To know Christ is to know God. Or, as a second-century Christian writer put it, "we must learn to think of Jesus as of God" (1 Clement 1:1).

So what do Christians believe about this God? The opening words of the Apostles' Creed get us off to a good start: Christians believe in a God who is "the Father almighty, the creator of heaven and earth." We shall turn to explore the very rich and powerful theme of creation later in this chapter. To begin with, we shall look at the idea of God as "Father almighty." We can break this down into two segments, each of which really deserves a chapter to itself. However, limits on space mean that we will have to consider them both briefly, beginning with the question of what it means to speak of God as "father."

God as father

One of the most noticeable and interesting things about the biblical representation of God is that extensive use is made of *imagery*. God is depicted as a shepherd, a king, a rock – and a father. Before we begin to explore what it means to talk about God as "father," it will be helpful to look at the general question of the use of analogies in theology.

The Bible uses many analogies to speak about God. To explore some of the issues that arise from using analogies in theology, we may turn to consider one of the most familiar biblical verses, Psalm 23:1, "The Lord is my shepherd." This image of God as a shepherd is encountered frequently in the Old Testament (e.g., Psalm 80:1; Isaiah 40:11; Ezekiel 34:12), and is taken up in the New Testament to refer to Jesus, who is the "good shepherd" (John 10:11).

To speak of "God as a shepherd" is to affirm that "God is *like* a shepherd." In other words, the image of a shepherd helps us think about the nature of God, and allows us to gain insights into his nature. It does not mean that God is *identical* to a human shepherd. Rather, it means that some aspects of a human shepherd help us think about God more effectively.

But is *every* aspect of the human analogy to be carried over to God? Every analogy breaks down at some point. How far can we press this analogy before it ceases to be reliable? To explore this issue, we could draw up a brief list of things that are true about shepherds.

1 Shepherds look after sheep.
2 Shepherds protect their sheep against danger.
3 Shepherds lead their sheep to food and water.
4 Shepherds are human beings.

It is immediately clear that the first three aspects of the analogy can be carried over to our thinking about God. God cares, protects, and leads. In all these respects, the analogy of the shepherd works well, and illuminates the character of God.

Yet shepherds are ultimately human beings. Is *this* aspect of the analogy to be carried over? It is quite clear we are not meant to think of God as a human being. While God is *not* a human being, it is still true that the behavior of one particular group of human beings is seen as helping us to get a better understanding of the nature of God. So it would seem that this is one aspect of the analogy which we are not meant to press too far.

Having explored the use of analogies in theology in general, we may now turn to the specific analogy that we encounter in the creed – the analogy of God as a *father*. What does it mean to speak of God in this way? The image of God as father is deeply embedded within the Christian faith, not least because of the prayer that Christ taught his disciples, now known as the "Lord's Prayer." Its opening words will be familiar to every reader: "Our Father . . . " If Jesus Christ referred to God in this way, it is clearly of major importance to Christian faith. But how are we to interpret this image?

Once more, we are dealing with an analogy. So what sort of ideas does the analogy convey? The following ideas might come to mind, and we shall explore each of them briefly.

1 Fathers are human beings.
2 Fathers bring their children into existence.
3 Fathers care for their children.
4 Fathers are male..

The first of these characteristics is clearly not meant to be transferred to our thinking about God. As we saw in the case of the shepherd analogy, this is the inevitable consequence of using language drawn from the created order to refer to the creator.

The second is clearly important. God is our originator. Without God, we would not be here. Both the Old and New Testaments stress our complete dependence upon God from beginning to end. There is also no doubt that the analogy of God as father conveys the idea of care. The Old Testament in particular often compares God's relation with his people to a father's relationship with his young son. When the son is very young, he is totally dependent upon his father for everything, and their relationship is very close. But as the son grows older, he gradually comes to exercise his independence and break away from his father, so that the relationship becomes more distant. The prophet Hosea uses this illustration to bring out how Israel has become a virtual stranger to the God who called her into existence:

> When Israel was a child, I loved him, and out of Egypt I called my son. But the more I called Israel, the further they went away from me. They sacrificed to the Baals, and they burned incense to images. It was I who taught Ephraim to walk, taking them by the arms, but they did not realize it was I who healed them. I led them with the cords of human kindness, with ties of love. (Hosea 11:1–4)

As Jesus Christ pointed out in the Sermon on the Mount (Matthew 7:9–11), even human fathers want to give their children good things. So how much more will God, as our heavenly father, want to give good things to those who ask for them in prayer.

It is the fourth aspect of this analogy which has generated most debate, and which needs further discussion. Both Old and New Testaments use male language about God. The Greek word for "god" (*theos*) is unquestionably masculine, and most of the analogies used for God throughout Scripture – such as father, king, and shepherd – are male. Does this mean that God *is* male?

It is important to note that the Bible also uses female imagery to refer to the love of God for humanity. Just as a mother can never forget or turn against her child, so God will not forget or turn against his people (Isaiah 49:15). There is a natural bond of affection and sympathy between God and his children, simply because he has brought them into being. Thus God loved us long before we loved God (1 John 4:10, 19). Psalm 51:1 refers to God's "great compassion." It is interesting to note that the Hebrew word for "compassion" (*rachmin*) is derived from the word for "womb" (*rechmen*). God's compassion towards his people is that of a mother towards her child (cf. Isaiah 66:12–13). Compassion stems from the womb.

So is God male? Does speaking of God as "father" mean that Christianity believes in a male deity? Earlier, we noted the analogical nature of theological language. Individual persons or social roles, largely drawn from the rural world of the ancient near east, are identified as models for the divine activity or personality. One such analogy is that of a shepherd; another is that of a father.

Yet the statement that "a father in ancient Israelite society is a suitable analogy for God" is not equivalent to saying that "God is male." To speak of God as father is to say that the role of the father in ancient Israel allows us insights into the nature of God. It is not to say that God *is* a male human being. Yet the Old Testament

is clear that mothers were also analogies for aspects of God's love for Israel. Although there are many more references to paternal role models than to maternal, there is no doubt that both fathers and mothers function as analogies for God in the Bible.

The important point to appreciate here is that *neither* male *nor* female sexuality is to be attributed to God. For sexuality is an attribute of the created order, which cannot be assumed to correspond directly to any such polarity within the creator God. Indeed, the Old Testament completely avoids attributing sexual functions to God, on account of the strongly pagan overtones of such associations. The Canaanite fertility cults emphasized the sexual functions of both gods and goddesses; the Old Testament refuses to endorse the idea that the gender or the sexuality of God is a significant matter.

Talking about God as "shepherd" or "father" leads us on to another important theme of Christian thinking about God – namely, the concept of a *personal* God, to which we now turn.

A personal God

Down the ages, theologians and ordinary Christian believers alike have had no hesitation in speaking about God in personal terms. For example, Christianity has ascribed to God a whole series of attributes such as love, trustworthiness, and purpose which seemed to have strongly personal associations. Many writers have pointed out that the Christian practice of prayer seems to be modeled on the relationship between a child and a parent. Prayer expresses a gracious relationship which "is simply trust in a person whose whole dealing with us proves him worthy of trust" (John Oman). Similarly, one of Paul's leading images for the change that Christ effects in humanity – reconciliation – is clearly modeled on human personal relationships. It implies that the transformation through faith of the relationship between God and sinful human beings is like the reconciliation of two persons, such as an alienated husband and wife.

For early Christian writers, the word "person" is an expression of the individuality of a human being, as seen in his or her words and actions. Above all, there is an emphasis upon the idea of social relationships. A person is someone who plays a role in a social drama, who relates to others. A person has a part to play within a network of social relationships. "Individuality" does not imply social relationships, whereas "personality" relates to the part played by an individual in a web of relationships, by which that person is perceived to be distinctive by others. The basic idea expressed by the idea of "a personal God" is thus a God with whom we can exist in a relationship which is analogous to that which we could have with another human person.

It is helpful to consider what overtones the phrase "an impersonal God" would convey. The phrase suggests a God who is distant or aloof, who deals with humanity (if God deals with us at all) in general terms which take no account of human individuality. The idea of a personal relationship, such as love, suggests a reciprocal character to God's dealings with us. This idea is incorporated into the notion of a personal God, but not into impersonal conceptions of the nature of God. There are strongly negative overtones to the idea of "impersonal," which have passed into Christian thinking about the nature of God.

It is also important to appreciate that personal relationships establish the framework within which such key biblical themes as "love," "trust," and "faithfulness" have their meaning. Both the Old and New Testaments are full of statements concerning the "love of God," the "trustworthiness of God," and the "faithfulness of God." "Love" is a word which

is used primarily of personal relationships. Furthermore, the great biblical theme of promise and fulfillment is ultimately based upon a personal relationship, in that God promises certain quite definite things (such as eternal life and forgiveness) to certain individuals. One of the great themes which dominates the Old Testament in particular is that of the covenant between God and people, by which they mutually bind themselves to each other. "I will be their God, and they will be my people" (Jeremiah 31:33). The basic idea underlying this is that of personal commitment of God to God's people, and of God's people to their God.

A twentieth-century philosophical analysis of what it means to speak of a "person" is also helpful in clarifying what it means to speak of a personal God. In his major work *I and Thou* (1927), the Jewish writer Martin Buber (1878–1965) drew a fundamental distinction between two categories of relations: *I–Thou* relations, which are "personal," and *I–It* relations, which are impersonal. We shall explore these basic distinctions briefly, before considering their theological importance.

- *I–It relations.* Buber uses this category to refer to the relation between subjects and objects, for example between a human being and a pencil. The human being is active, whereas the pencil is passive. This distinction is often referred to in more philosophical language as a *subject–object relation*, in which an active subject (in this case, the human being) relates to an inactive object (in this case, the pencil). According to Buber, the subject acts as an *I*, and the object as an *It*. The relation between the human being and pencil could thus be described as an *I–It* relation.
- *I–Thou relations.* At this point, we come to the core of Buber's philosophy. An *I–Thou* relation exists between two active subjects – between two *persons*. It is something

which is *mutual* and *reciprocal* that links two persons. This idea lies at the heart of Buber's concept of an *I–Thou* relation.

So how does Buber's philosophy help us to understand and explore the idea of God as a person? A number of key ideas emerge, all of which have important and helpful theological applications. Furthermore, Buber anticipated some of these himself. In the final sections of *I and Thou*, he explores the implications of his approach to thinking and speaking about God – or, to use his preferred term, "the Absolute Thou."

First, Buber's approach affirms that God cannot be reduced to a concept, or to some neat conceptual formulation. According to Buber, only an "It" can be treated in this way. For Buber, God is the "Thou who can, by its nature, never become an It. That is, God is a being who escapes all attempts at objectification and transcends all description." Theology must learn to acknowledge and wrestle with the presence of God, realizing that this presence cannot be reduced to a neat package of contents.

Second, the approach allows valuable insights into the idea of revelation. For Christian theology, God's revelation is not simply a making known of facts about God, but a self-revelation of God. Revelation of ideas about God is to be supplemented by revelation of God as a person, a presence as much as a content. We could make sense of this by saying that revelation includes knowledge of God as an "It" and as a "Thou." We come to know things about God; yet we also come to know God. Similarly, "knowledge of God" includes knowledge of God as both "It" and "Thou." "Knowing God" is not simply a collection of data about God, but a personal relationship.

In the third place, Buber's "dialogical personalism" also avoids the idea of God as an object, perhaps the weakest and most heavily criticized aspect of some nineteenth-century

liberal Protestant theology. The characteristic non-inclusive nineteenth-century phrase "man's quest for God" summed up the basic premise of this approach: God is an "It," a passive object, waiting to be discovered by (male) theologians, who are viewed as active subjects. Writers within the dialectical school, especially Emil Brunner in his *Truth as Encounter*, argued that God had to be viewed as a Thou, an active subject. As such, God could take the initiative away from humans, through self-revelation and a willingness to be known in a historical and personal form, namely, Jesus Christ. Theology would thus become the human response to God's self-disclosure, rather than the human quest for God.

God as almighty

The Apostles' Creed goes on to speak of God as "almighty." What do we mean when we say that God is "almighty" in this way? At first sight, this might seem to be rather pointless. The meaning of the word "almighty" is perfectly obvious in everyday language. It means "capable of doing anything." And as we believe that God is indeed almighty, we are simply saying that God can do anything. This would appear to bring discussion of the matter to an end. What more is there to say?

Yet one of the tasks of theology is to encourage us to use language critically – to make us think about what we really mean when we talk about God. Is it really quite as simple as this? Might not the word "almighty" have a subtle difference when applied to God than when applied to a human? To explore this, let's consider a simple statement, as follows:

"To say that God is almighty means that God can do anything."

At first, this definition seems fairly straightforward. Yet it runs into some difficulties at an early stage. Consider the following question: "Can God draw a triangle with four sides?" It does not take much thought to see that this question has to be answered in the negative. Triangles have three sides; to draw something with four sides is to draw a quadrilateral, not a triangle.

However, on further reflection, it is not clear that this question causes problems for the Christian understanding of God. Four-sided triangles do not and cannot exist. The fact that God cannot make such a triangle is not a serious issue. It just forces us to restate our simple statement in a more complicated way. "To say that God is almighty means that God can do anything that does not involve logical contradiction." Or we can follow Thomas Aquinas, who remarked that it was not that God could not do such things, it was simply that such things cannot be done.

Yet theology is about rather more than such logical riddles. The real issue concerns the divine nature itself. We can begin to engage with this important matter by considering a question that intrigued medieval philosophers, such as William of Ockham:

"Can God make someone who loves him hate him?"

At first sight, this question seems a little strange. Why should God want to turn someone's love for him into a hatred? The question appears unreal and pointless. On closer examination, however, the question begins to make sense. At one level, there is no problem. "To say that God is almighty means that God can do anything that does not involve logical contradiction." There is clearly no such contradiction here. God must have the ability to turn someone's love into hatred. Yet there is obviously a deeper issue, concerning the *character* of God. Can we ever imagine God *wanting* to do this?

To make this important point clearer, let us ask another question. "Can God break promises?" There is no logical contradiction involved in breaking promises. It happens all the time. It may be regrettable, but there is no intellectual difficulty about it. If God can do anything that does not involve a logical contradiction, God can certainly break a promise.

Yet for Christians, this suggestion is outrageous. The God whom we know and love is one who remains faithful to what has been promised. If we cannot trust God, whom can we trust? The suggestion that God might break a promise contradicts a vital aspect of God's character – namely, God's faithfulness and truthfulness. One of the great themes of both Old and New Testaments is the total trustworthiness and reliability of God. Humans may fail; God remains faithful. Consider these biblical verses.

> Know therefore that the Lord your God is God. He is the faithful God, keeping his covenant of love to a thousand generations. (Deuteronomy 7:9)
> The Lord is faithful to all his promises. (Psalm 145:13)

The point here is that there is a tension between power and trust. An all-powerful cheater can make promises which cannot be relied upon. Yet one of the greatest insights of the Christian faith is that we know a God who *could* do anything – but who *chose* to redeem us. God did not need to enter into a covenant with Israel – but God chose to do so, and having done so, remains faithful to this promise. We see here the important idea of divine self-limitation – the notion that God freely chooses to behave in certain ways, and in doing so, places limits on divine action. God cannot be accused of acting arbitrarily or whimsically; rather, God acts reliably and faithfully.

So we come back to the question with which we began. Can God do *anything*? The commonsense answer would be simple and straightforward. If God is almighty, God must be capable of doing anything. Yet Christian theology insists that God's omnipotence is to be set within the context of God's nature – that of a righteous and faithful God, whose promises are to be trusted.

The doctrine of the Trinity

For many, the doctrine of the Trinity is one of the most baffling areas of Christian theology. How can God be thought of as "three persons"? There are many who suspect that this is simply an attempt by theologians to make their subject inaccessible to outsiders. Thomas Jefferson, third President of the United States of America, was severely critical of what he termed the "incomprehensible jargon of the Trinitarian arithmetic." Why on earth do we need to speak of God in this convoluted and puzzling way?

The best way of understanding the doctrine is to suggest that it is the inevitable and legitimate way of thinking about God which emerges from a sustained engagement with the biblical witness to the words and works of God. The doctrine of the Trinity can be regarded as the outcome of a process of prolonged and critical reflection on the pattern of divine activity revealed in Scripture, and continued in Christian experience. This is not to say that Scripture contains a doctrine of the Trinity; rather, Scripture bears witness to a God who demands to be understood in a Trinitarian manner.

At first sight, there are only two biblical verses which are open to a Trinitarian interpretation: Matthew 28:19 and 2 Corinthians 13:14. The first commands the disciples to baptize people "in the name of the Father, Son, and Holy Spirit"; the second speaks of the Father, Son, and Spirit in the familiar words of "the grace." Both these verses have become deeply rooted in the Christian consciousness, the former on account of its baptismal associations, and the latter through the common use of the formula in Christian prayer and devotion. Yet these two verses, taken together or in isolation, can hardly be thought of as constituting a doctrine of the Trinity.

The ultimate grounds of the doctrine of the Trinity are not to be sought exclusively in these two verses. Rather, the foundations of the doctrine are to be identified in the pattern of divine activity to which the New Testament bears witness. The Father is revealed in Christ through the Spirit. There is the closest of connections between the Father, Son, and Spirit in the New Testament writings. Time after time, New Testament passages link together these three elements as part of a greater whole. The totality of God's saving presence and power can only, it would seem, be expressed by involving all three elements (for example, see 1 Corinthians 12:4–6; 2 Corinthians 1:21–22; Galatians 4:6; Ephesians 2:20–22; 2 Thessalonians 2:13–14; Titus 3:4–6; 1 Peter 1:2).

The development of the doctrine of the Trinity is best seen as being directly related to the evolution of Christology. The more emphatic the church became that Christ was God, the more it came under pressure to clarify how Christ related to God. The development of the doctrine of the Trinity took place in three stages, and was essentially complete by the end of the fourth century.

- Stage 1: the recognition of the full divinity of Jesus Christ.
- Stage 2: the recognition of the full divinity of the Spirit.
- Stage 3: the definitive formulation of the doctrine of the Trinity, embedding and clarifying these central insights, and determining their mutual relationship.

This sequential development of the doctrine of the Trinity is acknowledged by Gregory of

6.1 One of the most famous attempts to represent the Trinity – Andrei Rubljov's icon of 1411, depicting the three angels with Abraham, widely interpreted as an analogue of the Trinity. Moscow, Tretjakov Gallery, AKG-Images.

Nazianzus, who pointed to a gradual progress in clarification and understanding of the mystery of God's revelation in the course of time.

The starting point for Christian reflections on the Trinity is the New Testament witness to the presence and activity of God in Christ and through the Spirit. For Irenaeus of Lyons, writing in the second century, the whole process of salvation, from its beginning to its end, bore witness to the action of Father, Son, and Holy Spirit. Irenaeus made use of a term which would feature prominently in future discussions of the Trinity: "the economy of salvation." The use of the term "economy" here needs a little explanation. The Greek word *oikonomia* basically means "the way in which

one's affairs are ordered" (the relation to the modern sense of the word will thus be clear). For Irenaeus, the "economy of salvation" meant "the way in which God has ordered the salvation of humanity in history."

At the time, Irenaeus was under considerable pressure from Gnostic critics, who argued that the creator God was quite distinct from (and inferior to) the redeemer God. Marcion argued that the Old Testament God was merely a creator God, and totally different from the redeemer God of the New Testament. As a result, the Old Testament should be shunned by Christians, who should concentrate their attention upon the New Testament. Irenaeus vigorously rejected this idea. He insisted that the entire process of salvation, from the first moment of creation to the last moment of history, was the work of one and the same God. There was a single economy of salvation, in which the one God – who was both creator and redeemer – was at work to redeem the creation.

In his *Demonstration of the Apostolic Preaching*, Irenaeus insisted upon the distinct yet related roles of Father, Son, and Spirit within the economy of salvation. He affirmed his faith in:

God the Father uncreated, who is uncontained, invisible, one God, creator of the universe; this is the first article of our faith . . . And the *Word of God*, the Son of God, our Lord Jesus Christ, . . . who, in the fullness of time, in order to gather all things to himself, became a human being amongst human beings, capable of being seen and touched, to destroy death, bring life, and restore fellowship between God and humanity. And the *Holy Spirit* . . . who, in the fullness of time, was poured out in a new way on our human nature in order to renew humanity throughout the entire world in the sight of God.

This passage brings out clearly the idea of the Godhead in which each person is responsible for an aspect of the economy of salvation. Far from being a rather pointless piece of theological speculation, the doctrine of the Trinity is grounded directly in the complex human experience of redemption in Christ, and is concerned with the explanation of this experience.

The real difficulty for most people lies in the *visualization* of the Trinity. How can we make sense of such a complex and abstract idea? St. Patrick, the patron saint of Ireland, is rumored to have used the leaf of a shamrock to illustrate how a single leaf could have three different elements. Gregory of Nyssa uses a series of analogies in his letters to help his readers grasp the reality of the Trinity, including:

1   The analogy of a spring, fount, and stream of water. The one flows from the other and they share the same substance – water. Although different aspects of the stream of water may be *distinguished*, they cannot be *separated*.
2   The analogy of a chain. There are many links in a chain; yet to be connected to one is to be connected to all of them. In the same way, Gregory argues, someone who encounters the Holy Spirit also encounters the Father and the Son.
3   The analogy of a rainbow. Drawing on the Nicene statement that Christ is "light from light," Gregory argues that the rainbow allows us to distinguish and appreciate the different colors of a sunbeam. There is only one beam of light, yet the colors blend seamlessly into one another.

More recently, the contemporary American theologian Robert Jenson has argued that the Trinitarian formula can be thought of as a *proper name* – a shorthand way of identifying exactly what God we are talking about. The doctrine of the Trinity is a summary of the story of God's dealings with Israel and the church. It narrates the story of how God created and redeemed humanity, affirming that it is the story of one and the same God throughout. Jenson develops this approach in a fresh and helpful direction, offering a creative restatement of the traditional doctrine of the Trinity. He argues that "Father, Son, and Holy Spirit" is the proper name for the God whom Christians know in and through Jesus Christ. It is imperative, he argues, that God should have a proper name – a name that we can use when speaking to him in prayer, or appealing to him in worship. "Father, Son, and Holy Spirit" is a *proper name*, which we are asked to use in naming and addressing God. "Linguistic means of identification – proper names, identifying descriptions, or both – are a necessity of religion. Prayers, like other requests and praises, must be addressed."

Jenson also points out that ancient Israel was set in a polytheistic context, in which the term "god" conveyed relatively little information. It was necessary to *name* the god in question. A similar situation was confronted by the writers of the New Testament, who were obliged to identify the God at the heart of their faith, and distinguish this God from the many other gods worshipped and acknowledged in the region, especially in Asia Minor.

The doctrine of the Trinity thus *identifies* and *names* the Christian God – but identifies and names this God in a manner consistent with the biblical witness. It is not a name which we have chosen; it is a name which has been chosen for us, and which we are authorized to use. The Trinity is thus an instrument of theological precision, which forces us to be explicit about the God under discussion. Christians do not believe in a generic god, but in a very specific God who is known in and through a series of actions in history.

The doctrine of the Trinity plays a major role in contemporary Christian worship, spirituality,

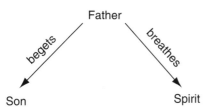

Figure 6.1 The eastern approach to the Trinity.

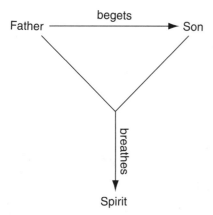

Figure 6.2 The western approach to the Trinity.

and theology. It explains the trajectory of revelation and salvation: God is revealed through Jesus Christ, and that revelation is interpreted by the Holy Spirit. God redeems humanity through Jesus Christ, and that salvation is applied to humanity through the agency of the Holy Spirit. It is an explanation of the pathway to knowledge of God, and fellowship with God. Christians believe in a saving encounter with God through Christ in the power of the Holy Spirit.

At one level, the doctrine emphasizes the sheer immensity of God. There is no way that a fallen and finite human mind is going to be able to comprehend the fullness of God. At another, it provides a framework both for making sense of, and deepening the quality of, Christian worship. Christians pray *to* the

Father *through* the Son *in* the Spirit. Once more, we find a trajectory identified: the goal of Christian prayer and worship is God; the medium or means through which this is channeled is the risen Christ; and the power which inspires and elicits these actions is the Holy Spirit.

In the past, Christian theologians were primarily concerned with rebutting rationalist criticisms of the doctrine of the Trinity, which held it to be incomprehensible nonsense. Yet the influence of rationalism is on the wane, and the twentieth century saw a massive recovery of confidence in the doctrine, largely through the pioneering theological work of Karl Barth and Karl Rahner. Yet the fading of rationalism must be set against the increasing importance of a new critic of Christian theology, especially at this point. In recent years, increasing attention has been paid to Islamic criticism of the doctrine of the Trinity. The three great monotheistic faiths of the world – Christianity, Judaism, and Islam – share a belief that there is only one supreme being, the Lord and creator of the universe. "Hear, O Israel, the Lord your God is one Lord" (Deuteronomy 6:4). Islamic critics of Christianity regularly criticize Christians, however, for deviating from this emphasis upon the unity of God (often referred to by the Arabic word *tawhid*) through the doctrine of the Trinity. Muslim writers argue that this doctrine is a late invention which distorts the idea of the unity of God, and ends up teaching that there are three gods.

The teaching of the Qur'an on what Christians believe is not quite as clear as might be hoped for, and has led some Christian interpreters of Islam to suggest that it believes that Christians worship a trinity consisting of God, Jesus, and Mary (Qur'an, 5:116). Although there are reasons for suspecting that Mohammed may have encountered heterodox forms of Christian belief in Arabia, including unorthodox statements of the Trinity, it seems more likely that the doctrine has simply been misunderstood as implying that Christians either worship three gods, or worship a single God with three component parts. Christian responses to this Islamic criticism of the doctrine of the Trinity argue that it fails to appreciate the Christian emphasis upon the unity of God, or the Christian experience of the complexity of God's engagement with the world, which leads Christians to formulate the doctrine of God in this particular way.

Finally, we need to note an important debate over the Trinity, often referred to as the *"filioque"* controversy. The name of this debate needs explanation. We have already explained how eastern and western approaches to the Trinity have different understandings of the relationship of the Father and Spirit (see figures 6.1 and 6.2 above). The Nicene Creed referred to the Holy Spirit "proceeding from the Father," which reflects the eastern approach. The western church, however, preferred Augustine's approach, which tended to present the Spirit as proceeding from both the Father and the Son.

By the ninth century, however, the western church routinely altered this phrase, speaking of the Holy Spirit "proceeding from the Father and the Son." The Latin term *filioque*, which literally means "and from the Son," has since come to refer to this addition, now normative within the western church, and the theology which it expresses. This idea of a "double procession" of the Holy Spirit was a source of intense irritation to Greek writers: not only did it raise serious theological difficulties for them, it also involved tampering with the supposedly inviolable text of the creeds. Many scholars see this bad feeling as contributing to the growing tensions between the eastern and western churches, which eventually led to a split around the year 1054. It remains a topic of debate between theologians to this day.

Creation

All the Christian creeds emphasize that God is the creator of the world. For example, the Apostles' Creed opens by affirming belief in a God who is "creator of heaven and earth." This theme is found throughout the Christian Bible. In fact, it is the first theme that the reader of the Bible encounters when approaching that work in its canonical order – in other words, when beginning with the book of Genesis (a Greek word, which literally means "beginning" or "origin"). However, it must be appreciated that the theme is deeply

6.2 William Blake's watercolor *The Ancient of Days* (ca. 1821), depicting God in the act of creating the world. Fitzwilliam Museum, University of Cambridge, UK/www.bridgeman.co.uk.

embedded in the wisdom and prophetic literature of the Old Testament. For example, Job 38:1–42:6 sets out what is unquestionably the most comprehensive understanding of God as creator to be found in the Old Testament, stressing the role of God as creator and sustainer of the world.

Models of creation

It is possible to discern two distinct, though related, contexts in which the notion of "God as creator" is encountered: first, in contexts which reflect the praise of God within Israel's worship, both individual and corporate; and secondly, in contexts which stress that the God who created the world is also the God who liberated Israel from bondage, and continues to sustain her in the present.

Of particular interest for our purposes is the Old Testament theme of "creation as ordering," and the manner in which the critically important theme of "order" is established on and justified with reference to cosmological foundations. It has often been pointed out how the Old Testament portrays creation in terms of an engagement with and victory over forces of chaos. This "establishment of order" is generally represented in two different ways:

1 Creation is an imposition of order on a formless chaos. This model is especially associated with the image of a potter working clay into a recognizably ordered structure (e.g., Genesis 2:7; Isaiah 29:16; 44:8; Jeremiah 18:1–6).
2 Creation concerns conflict with a series of chaotic forces, often depicted as a dragon or another monster (variously named "Behemoth," "Leviathan," "Nahar," "Rahab," "Tannim," or "Yam") which must be subdued (Job 3:8; 7:12; 9:13; 40:15–32; Psalm 74:13–15; 139:10–11; Isaiah 27:1; 41: 9–10; Zechariah 10:11).

It is clear that there are parallels between the Old Testament account of God engaging with the forces of chaos and similar accounts found in other religious texts of the ancient near east – for example, Ugaritic and Canaanite mythology. Nevertheless, there are significant differences at points of importance, not least in the Old Testament's insistence that the forces of chaos are not to be seen as divine. Creation is not to be understood simply as the forming of the universe, but in terms of God's mastery of chaos and ordering of the world.

Perhaps one of the most significant affirmations which the Old Testament makes is that *nature is not divine.* The Genesis creation account stresses that God created the moon, sun, and stars. The significance of this point is too easily overlooked. Each of these celestial entities was worshipped as divine in the ancient world. By asserting that they were created by God, the Old Testament is insisting that they are subordinate to God, and have no intrinsic divine nature.

One of the most important developments of the doctrine of creation arose in response to the Gnostic controversy of the second century. For Gnosticism, in most of its significant forms, a sharp distinction was to be drawn between the God who redeemed humanity from the world, and a somewhat inferior deity (often termed "the demiurge") who created that world in the first place. The Old Testament was regarded by the Gnostics as dealing with this lesser deity, whereas the New Testament was concerned with the redeemer God. As such, belief in God as creator and in the authority of the Old Testament came to be interlinked at an early stage. Of the early writers to deal with this theme, Irenaeus of Lyons is of particular importance.

A distinct debate centered on the question of creation *ex nihilo* ("out of nothing"). It must be remembered that Christianity initially took root and then expanded in the eastern

Mediterranean world of the first and second centuries, which was dominated by various Greek philosophies. The general Greek understanding of the origins of the world could be summarized as follows. God is not to be thought of as having *created* the world. Rather, God is to be thought of as an architect, who ordered preexistent matter. Matter was already present within the universe, and did not require to be created; it needed to be given a definite shape and structure. God was therefore thought of as the one who fashioned the world from this already existing matter. Thus in one of his dialogues (*Timaeus*), Plato developed the idea that the world was made out of preexistent matter, which was fashioned into the present form of the world.

This idea was taken up by most Gnostic writers, who were here followed by individual Christian theologians such as Theophilus of Antioch and Justin Martyr. They professed a belief in preexistent matter, which was shaped into the world in the act of creation. In other words, creation was not *ex nihilo*; rather, it was to be seen as an act of construction, on the basis of material which was already to hand, as one might construct an igloo out of snow, or a house from stone. The existence of evil in the world was thus to be explained on the basis of the intractability of this preexistent matter. God's options in creating the world were limited by the poor quality of the material available. The presence of evil or defects within the world are thus not to be ascribed to God, but to deficiencies in the material from which the world was constructed.

However, the conflict with Gnosticism forced reconsideration of this issue. In part, the idea of creation from preexistent matter was discredited by its Gnostic associations; in part, it was called into question by an increasingly sophisticated reading of the Old Testament creation narratives. Reacting against this Platonist worldview, several major Chris-tian writers of the second and third centuries argued that *everything* had to be created by God. There was no preexistent matter; everything required to be created out of nothing. Irenaeus argued that the Christian doctrine of creation affirmed the inherent goodness of creation, which contrasted sharply with the Gnostic idea that the material world was evil.

Tertullian emphasized the divine decision to create the world. The existence of the world is itself due to God's freedom and goodness, not to any inherent necessity arising from the nature of matter. The world depends on God for its existence. This contrasted sharply with the Aristotelian view that the world depended on nothing for its existence, and that the particular structure of the world was intrinsically necessary. Yet not all Christian theologians adopted this position at this early stage in the emergence of the Christian tradition. Origen, perhaps one of the most Platonist of early Christian writers, clearly regarded the doctrine of creation from preexistent matter to have some merit.

The central issue relating to the doctrine of creation which had to be debated in the first period of Christian theology was thus that of *dualism*. The classic example of this is found in some of the forms of Gnosticism, so forcefully opposed by Irenaeus, which argued for the existence of two gods – a supreme god, who was the source of the invisible spiritual world, and a lesser deity who created the world of material things. This approach is strongly dualist, in that it sets up a fundamental tension between the spiritual realm (which is seen as being good) and the material realm (which is seen as being evil). The doctrine of creation affirmed that the material world was created good by God, despite its subsequent contamination by sin. A similar outlook is associated with Manicheism, a Gnostic worldview which Augustine found attractive as a young man.

By the end of the fourth century, most Christian theologians had rejected the Platonist approach, even in the form associated with Origen, and argued for God being the creator of both the spiritual and material worlds. The Nicene Creed opens with a declaration of faith in God as "maker of heaven and earth," thus affirming the divine creation of both the spiritual and material realms. During the Middle Ages, forms of dualism once more made their appearance, particularly in the views of the Cathari and Albigenses, who taught that matter is evil, and was created *ex nihilo* by the devil. Against such views, the Fourth Lateran Council (1215) and the Council of Florence (1442) taught explicitly that God created a good creation out of nothing.

Implications of the doctrine of creation

To believe in God as our creator affects the way we live in the world. It is not simply a notional adjustment to the way we view things, which makes little difference to everyday life. Rather, it gives us a "big picture" of our place in this world, and above all in relation to God. Martin Luther (1483–1546) knew of the importance of the practical application of Christian beliefs, and developed the "Catechism" as a means of educating ordinary people about the implications of their belief. In his *Lesser Catechism* (1529), Luther explains in simple terms what it means to believe in God as creator:

> I believe that God created me, along with all creatures. He gave me my body and soul, eyes, ears and all the other parts of my body, my mind and all my senses, and preserves them as well. He gives me clothing and shoes, food and drink, house and land, spouse and children, fields, animals and all I own. Every day He abundantly provides everything I need to nourish this body and life. He protects me against all danger, shields and defends me from all evil. He does all this because

of His pure, fatherly and divine goodness and His mercy, not because I have earned it or deserved it.

The doctrine of God as creator has several additional major implications, of which four may be noted here.

First, a distinction must be drawn between God and the creation. A major theme of Christian theology from the earliest of times has been to resist the temptation to merge the creator and the creation. The theme is clearly stated in Paul's letter to the Romans, the opening chapter of which criticizes the tendency to reduce God to the level of the world. According to Paul, there is a natural human tendency, as a result of sin, to serve "created things rather than the creator" (Romans 1:25). A central task of a Christian theology of creation is to distinguish God from the creation, while at the same time to affirm that it is *God's* creation.

This process may be seen at work in the writings of Augustine; it is of considerable importance in the writings of reformers such as Calvin, who were concerned to forge a world-affirming spirituality in response to the general monastic tendency to renounce the world, evident in writings such as Thomas à Kempis' *Imitation of Christ*, with its characteristic emphasis upon the "contempt of the world." There is a dialectic in Calvin's thought between the world as the creation of God himself, and the world as the fallen creation. In that it is God's creation, it is to be honored, respected, and affirmed; in that it is a fallen creation, it is to be criticized with the object of redeeming it. These two insights could be described as the twin foci of the ellipse of Calvin's world-affirming spirituality. A similar pattern can be discerned in Calvin's doctrine of human nature, where – despite his stress upon the sinful nature of fallen humanity – he never loses sight of the fact that it remains God's creation. Though stained by sin, it remains the creation and possession of God, and is to be valued for that reason. The doctrine of creation thus leads to a critical world-affirming spirituality, in which the world is affirmed, without falling into the snare of treating it as if it were God.

In the second place, creation implies God's authority over the world. A characteristic biblical emphasis is that the creator has authority over the creation. Humans are thus regarded as part of that creation, with special functions within it. The doctrine of creation leads to the idea of *human stewardship of the creation*, which is to be contrasted with a secular notion of *human ownership of the world*. The creation is not ours; we hold it in trust for God. We are meant to be the stewards of God's creation, and are responsible for the manner in which we exercise that stewardship. This insight is of major importance in relation to ecological and environmental concerns, in that it provides a theoretical foundation for the exercise of human responsibility towards the planet.

In the third place, the doctrine of God as creator implies the goodness of creation. Throughout the first biblical account of creation, we encounter the affirmation: "And God saw that it was good" (Genesis 1:10, 18, 21, 25, 31). (The only thing, incidentally, that is "not good" is that Adam is alone. Humanity is created as a social being, and is meant to exist in relation with others.) There is no place in Christian theology for the Gnostic or dualist idea of the world as an inherently evil place. As we shall explore elsewhere, even though the world is fallen through sin, it remains God's good creation, and capable of being redeemed.

This is not to say that the creation is presently perfect. An essential component of the Christian doctrine of sin is the recognition that the world has departed from the trajectory upon which God placed it in the work of creation. It has become deflected from its intended course. It has fallen from the glory in which it was created. The world as we see it is not the world as it was intended to be. The existence of human sin, evil, and death is itself a token of the extent of the departure of the created order from its intended pattern. For this reason, most Christian reflections on redemption include the idea of some kind of restoration of creation to its original integrity, in order that God's intentions for his creation might find fulfillment. Affirming the goodness of creation also avoids the suggestion, unacceptable to most theologians, that God is responsible for evil. The constant biblical emphasis upon the goodness of creation is a reminder that the destructive force of sin is not present in the world by God's design or permission.

In the fourth place, the doctrine of creation affirms that human beings are created in the image of God (Genesis 1:26–27). This insight, central to any Christian doctrine of human nature, is of major importance as an aspect of the doctrine of creation itself. "You made us for yourself, and our hearts are restless until they find their rest in you" (Augustine of Hippo). With these words, the significance of the doctrine of creation for a proper understanding of human experience, nature, and destiny is established.

Models of God as creator

The manner in which God acts as creator has been the subject of intense discussion within the Christian tradition. A number of models of, or ways of picturing, the manner in which God is to be thought of as creating the world have been developed, each of which casts some light on the complex and rich Christian understanding of the notion of "creation."

(1) *Emanation*. This term was widely used by early Christian writers to clarify the relation between God and the world. Although the term is not used by either Plato or Plotinus, many patristic writers sympathetic to the various forms of Platonism saw it as a convenient

and appropriate way of articulating Platonic insights. The image that dominates this approach is that of light or heat radiating from the sun, or from a human source such as a fire. This image of creation (hinted at in the Nicene Creed's phrase "light from light") suggests that the creation of the world can be regarded as an overflowing of the creative energy of God. Just as light derives from the sun and reflects its nature, so the created order derives from God, and expresses the divine nature. There is, on the basis of this model, a *natural* or *organic* connection between God and the creation.

However, the model has weaknesses, of which two may be noted. First, the image of a sun radiating light, or a fire radiating heat, implies an involuntary emanation, rather than a conscious decision to create. The Christian tradition has consistently emphasized that the act of creation rests upon a prior decision on the part of God to create, which this model cannot adequately express.

This naturally leads on to the second weakness, which relates to the impersonal nature of the model in question. The idea of a personal God, expressing a personality both in the very act of creation and in the subsequent creation itself, is difficult to convey by this image. Nevertheless, the model clearly articulates a close connection between creator and creation, leading us to expect that something of the identity and nature of the creator is to be found in the creation. Thus the beauty of God – a theme which was of particular importance in early medieval theology, and has emerged as significant again in the later writings of the Swiss theologian Hans Urs von Balthasar – would be expected to be reflected in the nature of the creation.

(2) *Construction.* Many biblical passages portray God as a master builder, deliberately constructing the world (for example, Psalm 127:1). The imagery is powerful, conveying the ideas of purpose, planning, and a deliberate intention to create. The image is important, in that it draws attention to both the creator and the creation. In addition to bringing out the skill of the creator, it also allows the beauty and ordering of the resulting creation to be appreciated, both for what it is in itself, and for its testimony to the creativity and care of its creator.

However, the image has a deficiency, which relates to a point we noted in connection with Plato's dialogue *Timaeus.* It portrays creation as involving preexistent matter. Here, creation is understood as giving shape and form to something which is already there – an idea which, we have seen, causes at least a degree of tension with the doctrine of creation *ex nihilo.* The image of God as a builder would seem to imply the assembly of the world from material that is already to hand, which is clearly deficient.

Nevertheless, despite this difficulty, it can be seen that the model expresses the insight that the character of the creator is, in some manner, expressed in the natural world, just as that of an artist is communicated or embodied in her work. In particular, the notion of "ordering" – that is, the imparting or imposing of a coherence or structure to the material in question – is clearly affirmed by this model. Whatever else the complex notion of "creation" may mean within a Christian context, it certainly includes the fundamental theme of ordering – a notion which is especially significant in the creation narratives of the Old Testament.

(3) *Artistic expression.* Many Christian writers, from various periods in the history of the church, speak of creation as the "handiwork of God," comparing it to a work of art which is both beautiful in itself and expresses the personality of its creator. This model of creation as the "artistic expression" of God as creator is particularly well articulated in the writings of the eighteenth-century North

American theologian Jonathan Edwards, as we shall see presently.

The image is profoundly helpful, in that it supplements a deficiency of both of the models noted above – namely, their impersonal character. The image of God as artist conveys the idea of personal expression in the creation of something beautiful. Once more, the potential weaknesses need to be noted: for example, the model could easily lead to the idea of creation from preexistent matter, as in the case of a sculptor with a statue carved from an already existing block of stone. However, the model offers us at least the possibility of thinking about creation from nothing, as with the author who writes a novel, or the composer who creates a melody and harmony. It also encourages us to seek for the self-expression of God in the creation, and gives added theological credibility to a natural theology. There is also a natural link between the concept of creation as "artistic expression" and the highly significant concept of "beauty."

Creation and natural theology

So if God created the world, what may be known of God from the world? What can be known of the creator from the creation? This question has been debated within Christian theology for centuries. "The heavens declare the glory of God; the heavens proclaim the work of God's hands" (Psalm 19:1). This well-known text can be seen as representing a general theme within the Christian Bible – that something of the wisdom of the God who made the world can be known through the world that was created. The exploration of this theme has proved to be one of the most fruitful areas of theology.

A number of major Christian theologians have developed natural theologies based on the sense of beauty which arises from contemplating the world. Hans Urs von Balthasar and Jonathan Edwards offered such an approach in the twentieth and eighteenth centuries respectively, the former from a Roman Catholic and the latter from a Reformed perspective. The seventeenth-century physicist and chemist Robert Boyle developed the image of nature as a temple and the natural scientist as a priest, thus drawing attention to the sense of wonder evoked by the study of nature in all its beauty.

Augustine of Hippo argued that there was a natural progression from an admiration of the beautiful things of the world to the worship of the one who had created these things, and whose beauty was reflected in them. The great medieval theologian Thomas Aquinas set out "Five Ways" of inferring from the orderliness of the world to the reality of God; the fourth of those ways is based upon the observation of the existence of perfection in the world. Although Aquinas does not specifically identify "beauty" as one of these perfections at this point, it is clear that this identification can be made without difficulty, and is made elsewhere in Aquinas' work. This general line of argument was developed in the early twentieth century by the noted philosophical theologian F. R. Tennant, who argued that part of the cumulative case for the existence of God was the observation of beauty within the world.

Within the Reformed tradition, a recognition of the importance of "beauty" as a theological theme can be discerned in the writings of Calvin. However, its most powerful exposition within this tradition is generally agreed to be found in the writings of the leading eighteenth-century American theologian Jonathan Edwards. Edwards argues that the beauty of God is to be expected – and duly found – in the derived beauty of the created order.

It is very fit and becoming of God who is infinitely wise, so to order things that there should be a voice of His in His works, instructing those that behold him and painting forth and shewing divine mysteries and things more immediately appertaining to Himself and His spiritual kingdom. The works of God are but a kind of voice or language of God to instruct intelligent beings in things pertaining to Himself.

The most theologically sustained and sophisticated exploration of the significance of "beauty" of the present century can be found in the writings of the Swiss Roman Catholic theologian Hans Urs von Balthasar (1905–1988). "The fundamental principle of a theological aesthetics . . . is the fact that, just as this Christian revelation is absolute truth and goodness, so also it is absolute beauty." Von Balthasar thus describes his own work as "an

attempt to develop a Christian theology in the light of the third transcendental, that is to say: to complement the vision of the true and the good with that of the beautiful."

Humanity

"What are human beings, that you are mindful of them?" (Psalm 8:4). From the beginning of history, people have wondered about their place in the greater scheme of things. Why are we here? What is our destiny? What is the meaning of human existence? The doctrine of creation offers the

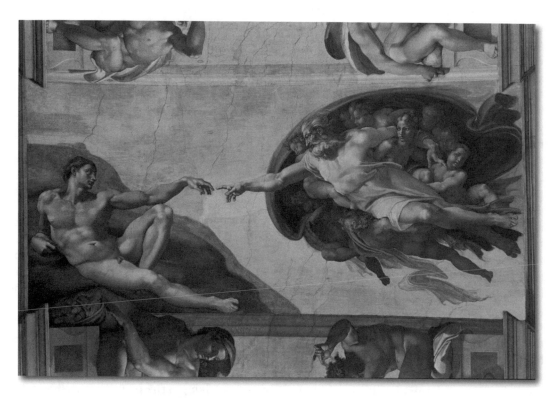

6.3 Michelangelo's fresco *The Creation of Adam* (1511–1512), from the Sistine Chapel. Rome, Vatican, Capella Sistina, AKG-Images/Erich Lessing.

beginnings of an answer. It helps us to deepen our understanding and appreciation of the world in which we find ourselves placed.

The Christian understanding of creation is that humanity is part of God's creation, and must learn and accept its place within that created order. Yet although Christians believe that humanity is part of the created order, this does not mean that we are *indistinguishable* from the remainder of creation. We have been set a little lower than the angels, and been "crowned with glory and honor" (Psalm 8:5). Men and women are created "in the image of God" (Genesis 1:27). In what follows, we shall explore this idea further.

Humanity and the "image of God"

This brief yet deeply significant phrase opens the way to a right understanding of human nature, and our overall place within the created order. Although humanity is not divine, it possesses a relationship with God which is different from that of other creatures. *Humanity bears the image of God.* For some, this is a statement of the privileged position of humanity within creation. Yet for most Christian theologians, it is above all an affirmation of *responsibility* and *accountability* towards the world in which we live.

So how are we to understand this relationship to God? How can we visualize it? What does it mean to speak of "being made in the image of God"? A number of models have been developed within Christian theology, of which we may note three.

First, the "image of God" can be seen as a reminder of the authority of God over humanity. In the ancient near east, monarchs would often display images of themselves as an assertion of their power in a region (see, for example, the golden statue of Nebuchadnezzar, described in Daniel 3:1–7). To be created in the "image of God" could there be understood as being owned by God, or, to put this another way, to be *accountable to God*.

This important point underlies an incident in the ministry of Jesus Christ (Luke 20:22–25). Challenged as to whether it was right for Jews to pay taxes to the Roman authorities, Jesus requested that a coin be brought to him. He asked, "Whose image and title does it bear?" Those standing around replied that it was Caesar's. Christ then tells the crowd to give to Caesar what is Caesar's, and to God what is God's. While some might take this to be an evasion of the question, it is nothing of the sort. It is a reminder that those who bear God's image – that is, humanity – must dedicate themselves to him.

Second, the idea of the "image of God" can be taken to refer to some kind of correspondence between human reason and the rationality of God as creator. On this understanding of things, there is an intrinsic resonance between the structures of the world and human reasoning. This approach is set out with particular clarity in Augustine's major theological writing *On the Trinity*:

> The image of the creator is to be found in the rational or intellectual soul of humanity…[The human soul] has been created according to the image of God in order that it may use reason and intellect in order to apprehend and behold God.

For Augustine, we have been created with the intellectual resources which can set us on the way to finding God by reflecting on the creation.

In more recent years, the importance of this point has been explored by the physicist turned theologian John Polkinghorne, formerly professor of theoretical physics at Cambridge University. Polkinghorne points out that some of the most beautiful patterns thought up by the mathematicians are found actually to occur in the structure of the physical world around us. There seems to be some deep-seated relationship between the reason within (the rationality of our minds – in this case mathematics) and the reason without (the rational order and structure of the physical world around us).

Polkinghorne argues that there seems to be some kind of "resonance" or "harmonization" between the ordering of the world and the capacity of the human mind to discern and represent it. "If the deep-seated congruence of the rationality present in our minds with the rationality present in the world is to find a true explanation, it must surely lie in some more profound reason which is the ground of both. Such a reason would be provided by the Rationality of the Creator." The "image of God" is thus an affirmation that humanity and the cosmos were shaped by the same divine rationality – and that, since humanity shares this rationality, it is able to make sense of the created order.

A third approach suggests that the "image of God" is about the capacity to relate to God. To be created in the "image of God" is to possess the potential to enter into a relationship with God. The term "image" here expresses the idea that God has created humanity with a specific goal – namely, to relate to God. We are thus meant to exist in a relationship with our creator and redeemer. As the Oxford literary critic and writer C. S. Lewis argued, if we do not do this, there is an absence where there ought to be a presence. Following Blaise Pascal, he suggests that there is a God-shaped gap within us, which only God can fill. And in the absence of God, we experience a deep sense of longing – a longing which is really for God, but which fallen and sinful humanity misreads, accidentally or deliberately, as a longing for things within the world. And these things never satisfy. If we are made for God, and God alone, then there is nothing else

that will satisfy. As Lewis constantly pointed out, this God-given sense of longing proves a key to answering the great questions of life with which humanity has wrestled.

Yet the Christian understanding of human nature is not totally determined by the idea of being made in the image of God. Important though this idea may be, it needs to be supplemented with the idea of the fall, and especially that of sin.

Humanity, the fall, and sin

For Christianity, humanity is sinful – that is to say, alienated from God, and as a result of this fundamental disruption of our identity, alienated from society, from other humans, and from our environment. For many theologians, the essence of the human predicament is our deep-seated longing to be with God. Humanity was present in creation as a creature, not as its Lord. Unwilling to accept the limitations placed upon them by virtue of being human, they chose to rebel against their position within the order of things. Latent within human nature is an unwillingness to accept this order, and our place within it. Humanity is an eternal rebel, wanting more and constantly challenging boundaries. Some would argue that this restlessness and desire to overcome any limitations is part of being human.

Two incidents from the book of Genesis are widely seen as offering a superb commentary on the profound contradictions within human nature – eating the fruit of the "tree of the knowledge of good and evil," and the construction of the Tower of Babel. Genesis tells how Adam and Eve were placed within their paradise, and given complete freedom to eat of all its trees – except one (Genesis 2:15–17). This limitation on their freedom proves too much for them. If they were to eat the fruit of the "tree of the knowledge of good and evil," they would become like God himself, determining what is good and what is evil (Genesis 3:1–5). We long for autonomy; we do not want to be accountable to *anyone*. As the great Russian novelist Fyodor Dostoyevsky pointed out in his novel *The Devils* (1871–1872), if there is no God, we are able to do as we please. This was one of the great themes of the "golden age of atheism," which began with the French Revolution in 1789, and ended with the fall of the Berlin Wall in 1989, with its great revolt against God.

Much the same theme is found in the account of the Tower of Babel (Genesis 11:1–9). This is memorably depicted in the great painting of Pieter Breughel the Elder (1563), which represents the tower as a giant construction reaching up into the heavens. Karl Barth, one of the twentieth century's greatest theologians, saw in this construction another aspect of sinful human nature – the desire to assert human authority and power in the face of God. Barth suggested that the Tower of Babel could be interpreted as a symbol of the human longing to be able to have knowledge of God on our own terms. Instead of waiting for God to reveal himself on terms of his own choosing, humanity believed it could take charge of things, and peep into heaven as it pleased. Yet this desire for human control contained within itself the seeds of its own negation. When we take charge, we seem to mess things up.

Over the years, Christian theologians have developed two fundamental images to help make sense of this puzzling human predicament: *deflection* and *defection*. For the second-century writer Irenaeus of Lyons, humanity has been deflected from its true path by sin. We have lost our way, and need to be helped back onto the right road. Irenaeus tends to see humanity as weak and easily misled. We were created as infants, not as mature human beings, and must learn and grow. Asked why God did not create humanity already endowed with perfection, Irenaeus replied that they

were simply not ready to cope with it. "A mother is able to offer food to an infant, but the infant is not yet able to receive food unsuited to its age."

For Augustine, humanity has defected from its true calling. Instead of using our God-given freedom to love God, we used it to advance our own agendas. We are now caught in a trap of our own making: Augustine argues that we are unable to break free from our entanglement with sin. As Paul points out, we are captivated by indwelling sin, unable to do the good that we would like to do, and instead doing the bad things we do not want to do (Romans 7:17–25). Our only hope lies in being set free by God himself. The freedom to love that ought to have led to fellowship with God – as Adam and Eve walked with God in the garden of Eden – led instead to self-love, and a desertion of God for the lesser good.

Augustine uses a series of images to illuminate how we have become trapped by sin in this way. It is like an illness which we have contracted, and are unable to cure. It is like having fallen into a deep pit, and being unable to get out. The essential point he wants to make is that once sin – which he conceives as an active force in our lives – has taken hold of us, we are unable to break free from its grasp. To use a modern analogy, it is like being addicted to heroin, and unable to break the habit.

On the Christian understanding of things, human nature, intended to be the height of God's creation, lies in ruins. It is in need of radical remodeling and internal renewal. Like a once great palace fit for a king, it has fallen into disrepair and decay. Yet the situation can be redeemed. God's presence itself within human nature would bring about the renewal, restoration, and repristination of what was now languishing in sin and death. If God were to enter into the human situation, it could be transformed from within. We can see here the outlines of a doctrine of the incarnation – the idea that God entered into our world and our history as one of us, in order to bring us to heaven.

And this brings us to the central theme of Christian belief – the identity and significance of Jesus Christ, as savior and redeemer of fallen humanity.

Jesus

I n chapter 1, we explored some aspects of the biblical understanding of the identity and significance of Jesus. Christian doctrine can be seen as the outcome of an extended and ongoing process of reflection on these biblical ideas, which weaves them together into a coherent whole. Part of the task of Christian theology is to weave together the various elements of the biblical witness to the identity and significance of Jesus. The various biblical motifs that need to be integrated in this way include:

1　The terms that the New Testament uses to refer to Jesus.
2　What Jesus is understood to have achieved, which is understood to be directly related to his identity. There is a close link between the Christian understanding of the *person* of Christ and the *work* of Christ. In other words, discussion of the *identity* of Christ is interlocked with discussion of the *achievement* of Christ. We shall explore this issue further when reflecting on salvation later in this chapter.
3　The impact that Jesus made upon people during his ministry – for example, through his healing.
4　The resurrection, which New Testament writers interpret as an endorsement and validation of Jesus' exalted status in regard to God. Thus for Paul, the resurrection

demonstrates that Jesus is the Son of God (Romans 1:3–4).

In this section, we shall consider how Christian theology wove these various insights into a coherent understanding of the person of Christ.

Before exploring this, however, we may note an especially significant response to Jesus, which has a particularly important place in today's world – that of Islam.

Islamic approaches to the identity of Jesus

The growing global importance of Islam makes the question of how Muslims view Jesus of increasing significance to Christianity. Islam acknowledges that Jesus was a prophet, and a messenger of God. The name "Jesus" (Arabic *isa*) is used twenty-five times in the Qur'an. In most cases, his name is linked with the title "Son of Mary" (*ibn Mariam*), although it is less frequently linked with that of Moses. Although the New Testament makes it clear that the name "Jesus" means "God saves" (Matthew 1:21), the Qur'an offers no explanation of the name *isa*. The related term "Messiah" (*al masih*) is also used in the Qur'an. Again, the rich Old Testament associations of this term as "God's anointed" are not noted or understood. It is not clear why the Qur'an should refer to Jesus as the "son of Mary." This title is used very rarely in the New Testament (Mark 6:3). It is also unusual (but not unknown) in the Semitic world for any major figure to be named after his mother, rather than father. The Qur'an also refers to Jesus using quite elevated language. Thus Jesus is referred to as the "word of God" and "spirit of God," giving him a place of honor within the Islamic understanding of the progression of revelation, which is held to reach its definitive climax in the revelation to Mohammed, committed to writing in the Qur'an.

The Islamic view of the significance of the death and resurrection of Jesus is somewhat complex. Although there are points where the Qur'an refers to the death of Christ, indicating that this was in accord with the will of God, the precise manner and significance of his death remain unclear. One passage seems to teach that Jesus was neither killed by the Jews nor crucified by his enemies, "although it seemed so to them" (*shubbiha la-hum*). Rather, Jesus was translated to heaven, with some other unnamed person taking his place on the cross. The phrase "it seemed so to them" would thus bear the sense of either "the Jews thought that Jesus died on the cross" or "the Jews thought that the person on the cross was Jesus." The mainstream Sunni position thus allows for some form of divine exaltation of Jesus, either as resurrection or ascension. Although the Qur'an itself does not mention any hope of Jesus' return to earth before the final judgment at the end of history, such ideas are found in at least some popular Islamic writings. There are reasons for supposing that this idea may have developed in the post-Qur'anic era, possibly as a result of growing familiarity with Christian views of the end of time.

Perhaps most significantly, the idea of the incarnation is completely unacceptable to Islam. The Christian belief that Christ is the Son of God is interpreted by many Islamic writers as meaning that God has physical children. Islam regards this as an unacceptable pagan idea. There is a misunderstanding here. The traditional Christian doctrine of Jesus as the "Son of God" has never been understood to mean that God physically fathered Jesus. The point being made by this title for Jesus is fundamentally relational, not physical. The doctrine of the incarnation affirms the unique status of Jesus in relation to God, and hence the unique role of Jesus within the Christian tradition as a bearer of divine revelation and the agent of divine salvation.

We shall explore more of the Christian understanding of the concept of incarnation presently. As background to the definitive statement of this idea at the Council of Chalcedon (451), we shall explore some aspects of the process of reflection on the New Testament within the earlier Christian tradition.

Early Christian approaches to Christology

As we have seen from our analysis of the view of Jesus found in the New Testament, the first Christians were confronted with something so exciting and novel in the life, death, and resurrection of Jesus that they were obliged to employ a whole range of images, terms, and ideas to describe it. There was simply no single phrase available which could capture the richness and profundity of their impressions and experience of Jesus. They were forced to use a whole variety of expressions to illuminate the different aspects of their understanding of him. Taken together, these combine to build up an overall picture of Christ.

At times they may even have drawn upon ideas or concepts ultimately deriving from paganism to try to build up this picture. For example, it is often thought that the opening section of John's gospel (John 1:1–18), with its distinctive emphasis on the "Word" (Greek: *Logos*), is trying to show that Jesus occupies the same place in the Christian understanding of the world as the idea of the *Logos* occupies in secular Greek philosophy. But this does not mean that Christians invented their understanding of Jesus' significance because they happened to read a few textbooks of Stoic philosophy. Rather, they noticed an analogy or parallel, and saw the obvious advantages to be gained by exploiting it to express something which they already knew about. It also went some way to make Christianity more understandable to an educated Greek audience. Even at this early stage in the Christian tradition, we can see a principled determination to make the gospel both intelligible and accessible to those outside the church. The gospel was thus expressed using ideas and concepts which helped to bring out its central themes, and make them understandable to non-believers.

An excellent example of this process within the New Testament is provided by Paul's "Areopagus Sermon" (Acts 17:16–34). This sermon, preached to philosophers at the Areopagus (or "Mars Hill") in Athens, seems to have aimed to gain a hearing for the gospel by engaging with ideas and terms which were already familiar to Paul's audience. Luke's gospel is another case in point. Luke is clearly writing for an audience which includes non-Jews (usually referred to as "Gentiles"). The word "Messiah" would have meant little to such a readership, who would not have been fully aware of its implications and nuances. However, many of the Greek religions were already used to terms such as "Savior" or "Redeemer." By using such terms, and always interpreting them in a rigorously Christian manner, Luke could express the significance of Jesus Christ in terms which would have made sense to his readers.

The first period of the development of Christology centered on the question of the divinity of Jesus. That Jesus was human appeared to be something of a truism to most early patristic writers. What required explanation about Jesus concerned the manner in which he differed from, rather than the ways in which he was similar to, other human beings.

Two early viewpoints were quickly rejected as heretical. *Ebionitism*, a primarily Jewish sect which flourished in the early first centuries of the Christian era, regarded Jesus as an ordinary human being, the human son of Mary and Joseph. This reduced Christology was regarded as totally inadequate by its opponents, and soon passed into oblivion. More significant was the diametrically opposed view, which

came to be known as *Docetism*, from the Greek verb "*dokein*" (to seem or appear). This approach – which is probably best regarded as a tendency within theology rather than a definite theological position – argued that Christ was totally divine, and that his humanity was merely an appearance. The sufferings of Christ are thus treated as apparent rather than real. Docetism held a particular attraction for the Gnostic writers of the second century, during which period it reached its zenith. By this time, however, other viewpoints were in the process of emerging, which would eventually eclipse this tendency. These culminated in the Chalcedonian doctrine of the incarnation – so called because it received definitive formulation at the Council of Chalcedon – to which we now turn.

The concept of the incarnation

The Christian doctrine of the person of Jesus Christ is often discussed in terms of "incarnation." "Incarnation" is a difficult yet important word, deriving from the Latin term for "flesh," summarizing and affirming the basic Christian belief that Jesus Christ is both divine and human. The idea of the incarnation is the climax of Christian reflection upon the mystery of Christ – the recognition that Jesus Christ reveals God; that he represents God; that he speaks as God and for God; that he acts as God and for God; that he is God. In short, we must, in the words of a first-century writer, learn to "think about Jesus as we do about God" (2 Clement 1:1–2). We are thus in a position to take the crucial step which underlies all Christian thinking on the incarnation – to say that, as Jesus Christ acts as God and for God in every context of importance, we should conclude that, for all intents and purposes, he is God.

The classic Christian position is therefore summarized in the "doctrine of the two

6.4   Mosaic depicting Jesus Christ in the Byzantine church of Hagia Sophia, Istanbul, ca. 1260. AKG-Images/Erich Lessing.

natures'' – that is to say, that Jesus is perfectly divine and perfectly human. This view was definitively stated by the Council of Chalcedon (451). This laid down a controlling principle for classical Christology, which has been accepted as definitive within orthodox Christian theology ever since. The principle in question could be summarized as follows: provided that it is recognized that Jesus Christ is both truly divine and truly human, the precise manner in which this is articulated or explored is not of fundamental importance.

Chalcedon simply stated definitively what the first five centuries of Christian reflection on the New Testament had already established. It defines the point from which we start – the recognition that, in the face of Christ, we see none other than God himself. That is a starting point, not an end. But we must be sure of our starting point, the place at which we begin, if the result is to be reliable. Chalcedon claims to have established that starting point, and whatever difficulties we may find with its turgid language and outdated expressions, the basic ideas which it lays down are clear and crucial, and are obviously a legitimate interpretation of the New Testament witness to Jesus Christ.

Chalcedon did not commit itself to any one philosophical system or outlook in setting out the identity of Jesus. Any such attempt would probably have been abandoned as outdated within centuries, and been an embarrassment to the church ever afterwards. Rather, it attempted to safeguard an essential fact, which could be interpreted in terms of philosophical ideas or concepts which might make sense at any particular point in history, provided these explanations do not deny or explain away any part of the fact. As a result, Christian theologians and apologists have enjoyed a considerable degree of liberty in defending and explaining this central Christian doctrine to different audiences throughout Christian history.

Every explanation of the person and work of Jesus Christ must, in the final analysis, be recognized to be inadequate, and Chalcedon merely stated with great clarity what the essential fact was which required explanation and interpretation: Jesus really is both God and a human being. To make this point absolutely clear, the Council used a technical term, already well established by this time. This is the Greek term *homoousios*, which is usually translated into English as "of one substance," or "of one being." Jesus is "of one substance" with God, just as he is "of one substance" with us. In other words, Jesus is the *same* as God; it really is God himself whom we encounter in Jesus, and not some messenger sent from God. Although this term was not itself biblical, it was widely regarded as expressing a thoroughly biblical insight.

An important minority viewpoint must, however, be noted. The Council of Chalcedon did not succeed in establishing a consensus throughout the entire Christian world. A minority viewpoint became established during the sixth century, and is now generally known as *Monophysitism* – literally, the view that there is "only one nature" (Greek: *monos*, "only one," and *physis*, "nature") in Christ. The nature in question is understood to be divine, rather than human. The intricacies of this viewpoint lie beyond the scope of this volume; the reader should note that it remains normative within most Christian churches of the eastern Mediterranean world, including the Coptic, Armenian, Syrian, and Abyssinian churches.

Jesus as mediator

The doctrine of the incarnation established that Jesus Christ was to be thought of as per-

fectly human, and perfectly divine. Important though this idea may be, it is not easy to visualize. So what models or analogies may be helpful as we try to visualize the place of Jesus Christ on the map of divine and human possibilities? In this section, we shall explore one New Testament title for Christ which has been explored in some detail by Christian theologians – namely, the idea that Jesus Christ is a *mediator* between God and humanity at several points (Hebrews 9:15; 1 Timothy 2:5). Christ is here understood to mediate between a transcendent God and fallen humanity.

So what is mediated? Two basic complementary answers are given within the New Testament, and the long tradition of Christian theological engagement with Scripture: *revelation* and *salvation*. Christ mediates both *knowledge of God* and *fellowship with God*.

The so-called *"Logos-*Christology" of Justin Martyr and other early patristic writers is an excellent instance of the notion of the mediation of knowledge of God through Christ. The *Logos* is understood to be a mediating principle which bridges the gap between a transcendent God and God's creation. Although present in a transient manner in the Old Testament prophets, the *Logos* becomes incarnate in Christ, and thus provides a point of mediation between God and humanity. A related approach is found in Emil Brunner's *The Mediator* (1927), and in a more developed form in *Truth as Encounter* (1938). In the latter, Brunner argued that faith was primarily an encounter with the God who meets us personally in Jesus Christ.

The idea of mediation is also developed in the theological writings of Dorothy L. Sayers, who is perhaps best known for her crime novels, which introduced Lord Peter Wimsey as an amateur aristocratic sleuth. However, she also developed a considerable interest in Christian theology, evident in works such as *The Mind of the Maker* and *Creed or Chaos?* In this second work, Sayers argues that it is not good enough to agree that Jesus was a good teacher with some useful ideas, unless we have good reasons for asserting that there is something distinctive about Jesus which requires us to take those ideas with compelling seriousness. Hence, Sayers argues, the great questions of Christology are inevitable, and must be addressed. This book was published during World War II (1939–1945), and Sayers uses a comparison with Adolf Hitler to make her point here.

> It is quite useless to say that it doesn't matter particularly who or what Christ was or by what authority He did those things, and that even if He was only a man, He was a very nice man and we ought to live by His principles: for that is merely Humanism, and if the "average man" in Germany chooses to think that Hitler is a nicer sort of man with still more attractive principles, the Christian Humanist has no answer to make.

Having made this point, she then turns to consider the issue of mediation. Under what conditions is mediation between God and humanity possible? And in what way is Jesus capable of acting in this capacity? Her answer is that the "two natures" – in other words, the doctrine that Jesus is both truly human and truly divine – safeguards this idea.

> The central dogma of the Incarnation is that by which relevance stands or falls. If Christ was only man, then He is entirely irrelevant to any thought about God; if He is only God, then He is entirely irrelevant to any experience of human life.

Other writers have stressed the importance of Christ as the one who mediates salvation. This approach can be seen in John Calvin's *Institutes* (1559). Christ is here seen as a unique channel or focus, through which God's redeeming work is directed towards and made available to humanity. Humanity, as originally created by God, was good in every respect. On account of the fall, natural human gifts and faculties have been radically impaired. As a consequence, both the human reason and human will are contaminated by sin. Unbelief is thus seen as an act of will as much as of reason; it is not simply a failure to discern the hand of God within the created order, but a deliberate decision *not* to discern it and *not* to obey God.

Calvin develops the consequences of this at two distinct, although clearly related, levels. At the revelational level, humans lack the necessary rational and volitional resources to discern God fully within the created order. There are obvious parallels here with the *Logos*-Christology of Justin Martyr. At the soteriological level, humans lack what is required in order to be saved; they do not *want* to be saved (on account of the debilitation of the mind and will through sin), and they are *incapable* of saving themselves (in that salvation presupposes obedience to God, now impossible on account of sin). True knowledge of God and salvation must both therefore come from outside the human situation. In such a manner, Calvin lays the foundations for his doctrine of the mediatorship of Jesus Christ.

Calvin's analysis of the knowledge of God and of human sin lays the foundation for his Christology. Jesus Christ is the mediator between God and humanity. In order to act as such a mediator, Jesus Christ must be both divine and human. In that it was impossible for us to ascend to God, on account of our sin, God chose to descend to us instead. Unless Jesus Christ was himself a human being, other human beings could not benefit from his presence or activity. "The Son of God became the Son of Man, and received what is ours in such a way that he transferred to us what is his, making that which is his by nature to become ours through grace."

Calvin's stress upon the mediatorial presence of God in Christ leads him to insist upon a close connection between the person and the work of Christ. Drawing on a tradition going back to Eusebius of Caesarea (ca. 260–ca. 340), Calvin argues that Christ's work may be summarized under three offices or ministries (the *munus triplex Christi*) – prophet, priest, and king. The basic argument is that Jesus Christ brings together in his person the three great mediatorial offices of the Old Testament. In his *prophetic* office, Christ is the herald and witness of God's grace. He is a teacher endowed with divine wisdom and authority. Through his *priestly* office, Christ is able to reinstate us within the divine favor, through offering his death as a satisfaction for our sin. Finally, in his *kingly* office, Christ has inaugurated a kingship which is heavenly, not earthly; spiritual, not physical. This kingship is exercised over believers through the action of the Holy Spirit. In all these respects, Christ brings to fulfillment the mediatorial ministries of the Old Covenant, allowing them to be seen in a new and clearer light as they find their fulfillment in his mediatorship.

Salvation

The Apostles' Creed is emphatic that Jesus was a real historical person, who lived and died. Jesus was a first-century Jew, who lived in Palestine in the reign of Tiberius Caesar, and who was executed by crucifixion under Pontius Pilate. The Roman historian Tacitus refers to Christians deriving their name from "Christ, who was executed at the hands of the procurator Pontius Pilate in the reign of Tiberius." The Christian faith certainly holds that Jesus existed as a real historical figure, and that he was crucified. Christianity is, however, most emphatically not about the mere facts that Jesus existed and was crucified.

As we have seen, the *interpretation* of his life and death is of critical importance. In what follows, we shall look at some of the interpretations of the death of Christ which are sometimes referred to as "theories of the atonement." Each of these has had widespread influence within Christianity, impacting significantly upon its worship.

Christ the victor: The defeat of death and sin

"Thanks be to God, who gives us the victory through our Lord Jesus Christ" (1 Corinthians 15:57). The early church gloried in the triumph of Christ upon the cross, and the victory which he won over sin, death, and Satan. The gates of heaven had been thrown wide open through the conquest of Calvary. The powerful imagery of the triumphant Christ rising from the dead and being installed as "ruler of all" (*pantokrator*) seized the imagination of the Christian east. The cross was seen as the site of a famous battle, comparable to the great Homeric epics, in which the forces of good and evil engaged, with the good emerging victorious.

The early church was more concerned to affirm Christ's victory over the enemies of humanity than to speculate over precisely how it came about. Christ's resurrection and his triumphant opening of the gates of heaven to believers were something to be proclaimed and celebrated, rather than subjected to the desiccations of theological analysis.

The Roman cultural context led to the theme of the victory of Christ being depicted as a triumphant procession, comparable to those of ancient Rome. In its classical form, the triumphal parade proceeded the *triumphator* from the Campus Martius through the streets of Rome, finally ending up at the temple of Jupiter on the Capitoline Hill. The parade was led by the general's soldiers, often carrying placards with slogans describing the general and his achievements (e.g. Julius Caesar's troops carried placards which bore the words: *Veni, Vidi, Vici* ["I came, I saw, I conquered"]) or showing maps of the territories he conquered. Other soldiers led carts containing booty that would be turned over to Rome's treasury. A section of the parade included prisoners, often the leaders of the defeated cities or countries, bound in chains.

It was a small step for Christian writers to transform this imagery into the liturgical proclamation of *Christus Triumphator*. This powerful symbolism was firmly grounded in the New Testament, which spoke of the victorious Christ as "making captivity a captive" (Ephesians 4:8). While this theme can be seen in some Christian art of this early period, its most dramatic impact was upon the hymnody of the time. One of the greatest hymns of the Christian church, dating from this period, portrays Christ's triumphant procession and celebrates his defeat of his foes.

Venantius Honorius Clementianus Fortunatus (ca. 530–ca. 610) was born in Ceneda, near Treviso, in northern Italy. He became a Christian at an early age, and went on to study at Ravenna and Milan. He gained a reputation for excellence in poetry and rhetoric, and went on to become elected bishop of Poitiers around 599. He is chiefly remembered for his poem, *Vexilla regis prodeunt* – "the banners of the king go forth." According to a well-established tradition, in the year 569, St. Radegunde presented

6.5   A triumphal procession in Rome celebrating Titus' victory over the Jews in AD 70, carved on the Arch of Titus, erected in AD 81. The idea of *Christus Triumphator* was developed using this model. AKG-Images/Erich Lessing.

a large fragment of what was believed to be the true Cross to the town of Poitiers, in southern Gaul. Radegunde had obtained this fragment from the emperor Justin II. Fortunatus was the one chosen to receive the relic on its arrival at Poitiers. When the bearers of the holy fragment were some 2 miles distant from the town, Fortunatus, with a great gathering of believers and enthusiasts – some of whom were carrying banners, crosses, and other sacred emblems – went forth to meet them. As they marched, they sang this hymn, which Fortunatus had composed for the occasion. This was soon incorporated within the Passiontide office of the western church, and is still widely used today in marking Holy Week within western Christianity. The English translation is taken from the Mediaeval Hymns and Sequences (1851) of the great Victorian hymnologist and medievalist John Mason Neale (1818–1866).

> The royal banners forward go,
> The cross shines forth in mystic glow;
> Where he in flesh, our flesh Who made,
> Our sentence bore, our ransom paid.
>
> There whilst He hung, His sacred side
> By soldier's spear was opened wide,
> To cleanse us in the precious flood
> Of water mingled with His blood.
>
> Fulfilled is now what David told
> In true prophetic song of old,
> How God the heathen's King should be;
> For God is reigning from the tree.
>
> O tree of glory, tree most fair,
> Ordained those holy limbs to bear,
> How bright in purple robe it stood,
> The purple of a Savior's blood!
>
> Upon its arms, like balance true,
> He weighed the price for sinners due,
> The price which none but He could pay,
> And spoiled the spoiler of his prey.

> To Thee, eternal Three in One,
> Let homage meet by all be done:
> As by the cross Thou dost restore,
> So rule and guide us evermore.

Christ the harrower of hell: Atonement as restoration

A further development of the theme of "Christ the victor" depicts Christ as extending the triumph of the cross and resurrection to the netherworld. The medieval idea of "the harrowing of hell" holds that, after dying upon the cross, Christ descended to hell, and broke down its gates in order that the imprisoned souls might go free. The idea rests (rather tenuously, it has to be said) upon 1 Peter 3:18–22, which makes reference to Christ "preaching to the spirits in prison." However, the text which proved the most significant stimulus to the development of this idea was the apocryphal gospel of Nicodemus. While the final version of this work is generally thought to date from the fifth century, the specific section dealing with the "harrowing of hell" may date from as early as the second century.

The hymn "You Choirs of New Jerusalem," written by Fulbert of Chartres (ca. 970–1028), expresses this idea in two of its verses, picking up the theme of Christ as the "lion of Judah" (Revelation 5:5) defeating Satan the serpent (Genesis 3:15):

> For Judah's lion bursts his chains
> Crushing the serpent's head;
> And cries aloud through death's domain
> To wake the imprisoned dead.
>
> Devouring depths of hell their prey
> At his command restore;
> His ransomed hosts pursue their way
> Where Jesus goes before.

The idea rapidly became established in popular English literature of the Middle Ages. One of the most important pieces of Christian literature of this period is *Piers Plowman*, traditionally attributed to William Langland. In this poem, the narrator tells of how he falls asleep, and dreams of Christ throwing open the gates of hell, and speaking the following words to Satan:

> Here is my soul as a ransom for all these sinful souls, to redeem those that are worthy. They are mine; they came from me, and therefore I have the better claim on them... You, by falsehood and crime and against all justice, took away what was mine, in my own domain; I, in fairness, recover them by paying the ransom, and by no other means. What you got by guile is won back by grace... And as a tree caused Adam and all mankind to die, so my gallows-tree shall bring them back to life.

It is clear that this highly dramatic understanding of the way in which Christ threw open the gates of death and hell, allowing their imprisoned masses to escape and enter into the joys of heaven, made a potent appeal to the imagination of the readers of *Piers Plowman*.

Such is the power of the image that it lingers, often unrecognized, in later writings. A particularly powerful example of this can be found in C. S. Lewis' children's tale *The Lion, the Witch and the Wardrobe*. The book tells the story of Narnia, a land which is discovered by accident by four children rummaging around in an old wardrobe. In this work, we encounter the White Witch, who keeps the land of Narnia covered in a perpetual wintry snow. As we read on, we realize that she rules Narnia not as a matter of right, but by stealth. The true ruler of the land is absent; in his absence, the witch subjects the land to oppression. In the midst of this land of winter stands the witch's castle, within which many of the inhabitants of Narnia have been imprisoned as stone statues.

6.6   The harrowing of hell, as depicted in Jean de Berry's *Petites Heures* (fourteenth century). Bibliothèque Nationale de France, Paris.

As the narrative moves on, we discover that the rightful ruler of the land is Aslan, a lion. As Aslan advances into Narnia, winter gives way to spring, and the snow begins to melt. The witch realizes that her power is beginning to fade, and moves to eliminate the threat posed to her by Aslan. Aslan surrenders himself to the forces of evil, and allows them to do their worst with him – yet by so doing, disarms them. Lewis' description of the resurrection of Aslan is one of his more tender moments, evoking the deep sense of sorrow so evident in the New Testament accounts of the burial of Christ, and the joy of recognition of the reality of the resurrection. Lewis then describes how Aslan – the lion of Judah, who has burst his chains – breaks into the castle, breathes upon the statues, and restores them to life, before leading the liberated army through the shattered gates of the once-great fortress to freedom. Hell has been harrowed, and its inhabitants liberated from its dreary shades.

Christ the redeemer: Atonement as satisfaction

An interpretation of the cross which gained considerable influence at the time of the Renaissance may be traced back to the eleventh century. Anselm of Canterbury, seeking to offer a logically and morally persuasive construal of the crucifixion and resurrection, appealed to the legal conventions of his day. Anselm argued that the purpose of the incarnation was that God, through Christ, might be able to offer forgiveness, while at the same time satisfying and not offending against his own strict justice. For Anselm, sin is an offense against God, and therefore requires some kind of payment in return (he may have got this idea from the feudal requirements of guilty peasants to their lords in medieval society, or simply from the penitential practice of the church at the time). Humanity cannot pay this debt, as the price demanded is the forfeit of life itself ("the wages of sin is death" – Romans 6:23). So Christ as the divine human both has the divine ability and the human obligation to pay the debt and enable satisfaction to be made.

For Anselm, Christ's death on the cross could therefore be interpreted as a *satisfaction* offered to God for human sin. The value of the satisfaction thus offered had to be equivalent to the weight of human sin. Anselm argued that the Son of God became incarnate in order that, as the God-man, Christ would possess both the human *obligation* to pay the satisfaction and the divine *ability* to pay a satisfaction of the magnitude necessary for redemption. This idea is faithfully reproduced by Mrs. Cecil F. Alexander in her famous nineteenth-century hymn "There is a Green Hill Far Away":

There was no other good enough
To pay the price of sin;
He only could unlock the gate,
Of heaven, and let us in.

Much the same theme was developed centuries earlier by the devotional poet George Herbert (1593–1633). Herbert spent the final part of his life as rector of the parish of Fugglestone with Bemerton near Salisbury. At Bemerton, George Herbert conducted what is widely regarded as an exemplary parish ministry. He rebuilt the parish church at his own expense; he visited the poor, consoled the sick, and sat by the bed of the dying. "Holy Mr. Herbert" became the talk of the countryside in the three short years before he died of consumption on March 1, 1633.

While on his deathbed, Herbert sent the manuscript of a collection of poems to his friend Nicholas Ferrar, and requested him to arrange for their publication. The resulting volume of poems, entitled *The Temple: Sacred Poems and Personal Ejaculations*, was published later in the year of Herbert's death. It met with popular acclaim, and had run to seven editions by 1640. The poem known as "Redemption" is a particularly important exploration of the associations of the Old Testament notion of "redeeming land." Herbert here develops the idea of the death of Christ as the price by which God takes legitimate possession of a precious piece of land. While also exploring the idea of the shame and humility of the cross, Herbert is able to bring out the legal and financial dimensions of redemption.

Having been tenant long to a rich Lord,
   Not thriving, I resolved to be bold,
   And make a suit unto Him, to afford
A new small-rented lease, and cancell th' old.
In heaven at His manour I Him sought:
   They told me there, that He was lately gone
   About some land, which he had dearly bought

Long since on Earth, to take possession.
I straight return'd, and knowing His great birth,
   Sought Him accordingly in great resorts –
   In cities, theatres, gardens, parks, and courts:
At length I heard a ragged noise and mirth
   Of theeves and murderers; there I Him espied,
   Who straight, "Your suit is granted," said, and
                        died.

The central image here is the "lease" – that is to say, the right to inhabit a certain place. Herbert wants to "afford" – for he cannot at present hope to pay the high cost of – a lease on a new property, and cancel his old. The transition implied is theological as much as physical; Herbert wants to dwell in heaven, not remain on earth. Yet the cost of this transition is immense. The basic theme enunciated by Herbert in this poem is that of the costliness of redemption; that is to say, that the admission price of the believer to heaven is the death of the Son of God.

Christ the lover: Atonement as the enkindling of love

A leading theme of the New Testament understanding of the death of Christ is that it demonstrates the love of God for humanity, and elicits a matching love in response. This theme is developed within Christian theology in terms of God stooping down to enter the created world, becoming incarnate in Christ. The love of God for wounded humanity is thus focused on the act of divine humility in leaving the glory of heaven to enter the poverty and suffering of the created order, and finally to suffer death upon the cross.

Such thoughts have proved a powerful stimulus to the Christian imagination. The English poet John Donne (1571–1631) offers what is widely regarded as one of the most significant poetic reflections on the love of God in Holy Sonnet XV:

Wilt thou love God, as he thee? then digest
My soul, this wholesome meditation,
How God the Spirit, by angels waited on
In heaven, doth make his temple in thy breast.
The Father having begot a Son most blessed,
And still begetting (for he ne'er begun)
Hath deigned to choose thee by adoption,
Coheir to his glory, and Sabbath's endless rest;
And as a robbed man, which by search doth find
His stol'n stuff sold, must lose or buy it again:
The Son of glory came down, and was slain,
Us whom he had made, and Satan stol'n, to unbind.
T'was much, that man was made like God before,
But, that God should be made like man, much more.

The poem engages with the entire process of incarnation and atonement, focusing on the divine determination to redeem humanity, whatever the cost might be. The poem develops the idea that humanity has unjustly come under the power and authority of Satan, obliging God to act justly in order to deliver us from this Satanic thrall. Not only did the "Son of Glory" come down from heaven, entering into this world of sin and death; he "was slain" on our behalf, in order to secure our freedom.

One of the most celebrated literary explorations of the love of God is the third poem to bear the title "Love" in George Herbert's collection *The Temple*, which we considered earlier. The closing poem of this remarkable collection can be seen as an extended musing on how it can be that Christ can possibly love sinners, and welcome them to the heavenly banquet.

Love bade me welcome, yet my soul drew back,
   Guilty of dust and sin.
But quick-ey'd Love, observing me grow slack
   From my first entrance in,
Drew nearer to me, sweetly questioning
   If I lack'd anything.

"A guest," I answer'd, "worthy to be here";
   Love said, "You shall be he."

"I, the unkind, the ungrateful? ah my dear,
    I cannot look on thee."
Love took my hand and smiling did reply,
    "Who made the eyes but I?"

"Truth, Lord, but I have marr'd them; let my shame
    Go where it doth deserve."
"And know you not," says Love, "who bore the
                                            blame?"
    "My dear, then I will serve."
"You must sit down," says Love, "and taste my
                                            meat."
    So I did sit and eat.

Throughout the poem, Christ himself is personified as "Love." The first verse of the poem invites its readers to imagine themselves approaching Christ, at once attracted to him yet at the same time aware of their weakness and failings. Why should such a Christ want to receive, still less welcome, anyone who was "guilty of dust and sin"? Why should the creator stoop down to greet the creature, or the savior to embrace the sinner? Yet Herbert asks us to imagine Christ noticing our hesitation, and moving swiftly to greet and reassure us.

Is there anything that you would like? Herbert's answer to Love's question was simple yet profound: he wanted to be worthy to be Love's guest at the heavenly banquet, the marriage supper of the Lamb. Yet the request seemed utterly beyond his reach. How could someone so insignificant and guilty ever be welcomed into the presence of the glorious Son of God? Herbert believes himself to be so unworthy that he should not even be allowed to gaze upon Christ from a distance, let alone be welcomed into his presence. Yet Love reassures him once more – this time, through *taking him by the hand*. The words instantly evoke a series of gospel images – as in the healing of a blind man or the raising of a dead young girl – in the language of the King James Bible that Herbert knew so well. "And *he* *took the blind man by the hand*, and led him out of the town; and when he had spit on his eyes, and put his hands upon him, he asked him if he saw ought" (Mark 8:23). "And *he took the damsel by the hand*, and said unto her, Talitha cumi; which is, being interpreted, Damsel, I say unto thee, arise" (Mark 5:41). Just Christ was willing to touch and hold these unfortunates, so he takes hold of Herbert. Christ "bore the blame" for his sin, so that it need no longer be a barrier between sinner and savior. And having taking him by the hand, Christ leads him to sit down at table with him – as a guest.

In the third verse of the poem, we find a deeply moving reflection on the sense of unworthiness felt by Herbert. Even though he knows that Christ loves him, and has willingly borne his guilt, he believes that he has been welcomed into Christ's presence as a *servant* – as one who is to *wait upon* Christ. The poem ends with an exquisite portrayal of Herbert, the hesitant believer, being welcomed as an honored guest, not as an attendant servant, in the portals of the New Jerusalem.

A final issue which must be addressed at this early stage concerns the chronology of salvation. Is salvation to be understood as something which has happened to the believer? Or is it something currently happening? Or is there an eschatological dimension to it – in other words, is there something which has yet to happen? The only answer to such questions which can be given on the basis of the New Testament is that salvation includes past, present, and future reference. Salvation is an exceptionally complex idea, embracing not simply a future event, but something which has happened in the past (Romans 8:24; 1 Corinthians 15:2), or which is taking place now (1 Corinthians 1:18). The Christian understanding of salvation thus presupposes that something *has* happened, that something *is now happening*, and that something further *will still happen* to believers. We shall return to this point when we consider the teachings of the Christian creeds about eternal life and the hope of heaven.

Grace

A central theme in the Bible is that God's choice of peoples or individuals is not determined by their merits, but by God's love and through God's will. This can be seen particularly in God's decision to choose Israel as his people. The Old Testament regularly affirms that Israel was chosen, not because of anything it had to offer, but solely because of the grace of God and by his sovereign choice (Deuteronomy 7:7; Isaiah 41:8–9; Ezekiel 20:5). This, of course, does not abrogate Israel's responsibility to live up to her duties as God's people. Many of the Old Testament prophets stressed the *conditionality* of Israel's election. Unless Israel behaved in ways appropriate to her identity and calling as God's chosen people, that status would be revoked.

Our attention in this section focuses on this idea of God's choice not being determined by merit or achievement – an idea that is often expressed using the idea of "grace." This term is used frequently in the New Testament. For Paul, Christians are saved by grace, not by works (Ephesians 2:1–10) – in other words, their salvation does not depend upon their achievements, but upon the generosity and graciousness of God. Grace affirms the sheer generosity and goodness of God, in that salvation is made possible and available to those who have neither the merit nor the intrinsic capacity to secure it for themselves.

These ideas were developed and clarified in the long process of wrestling with the Bible within the Christian church. This process of reflection initially focused on the person of Christ and the doctrine of the Trinity. The

question of what it means to speak of a "gracious God" did not received detailed attention until the late third and early fourth centuries. One especially important debate helped crystallize Christian perceptions about how best to systematize the New Testament's teaching on grace – the Pelagian controversy of the early fifth century.

The central figure in the controversy was Augustine of Hippo. Augustine had been converted to Christianity after a long struggle with a series of questions concerning the meaning of life – such as the origin of evil, and how the good life may be lived out in practice. One of Augustine's favorite biblical texts is John 15:5, in which Christ declares that "apart from me you can do nothing." In Augustine's view, we are totally dependent upon God for our salvation, from the beginning to the end of our lives. Augustine draws a careful distinction between the natural human faculties – given to humanity as its natural endowment – and additional and special gifts of grace. God does not leave us where we are naturally, incapacitated by sin and unable to redeem ourselves, but gives us grace in order that we may be healed, forgiven, and restored.

Augustine's view of human nature is that it is frail, weak, and lost, and needs divine assistance and care if it is to be restored and renewed. Grace, according to Augustine, is God's generous and quite unmerited attention to humanity, by which this process of healing may begin. Human nature requires transformation through the grace of God, so generously given. An integral aspect of his thinking at this point is the idea of "original sin" – that is, the idea that we are contaminated by sin from the moment of our entry into the world.

For Augustine, humanity is universally affected by sin as a consequence of the fall. The human mind has become darkened and weakened by sin. Sin makes it impossible for the sinner to think clearly, and especially to understand higher spiritual truths and ideas. Similarly, as we have seen, the human will has been weakened (but not eliminated) by sin. For Augustine, the simple fact that we are sinners means that we are in the position of being seriously ill, and unable to diagnose our own illness. Using the gospel analogy of Christ as the physician, Augustine argues that Christ both diagnoses our situation (sin), and offers us a cure that we cannot secure for ourselves (grace). It is through the grace of God alone that our illness is recognized for what it is, and a cure is made available.

So what are the implications of this for our understanding of human nature? For Augustine, humanity is now imperfect: it is wounded, and has been robbed of grace. God may have made humanity perfect; as a consequence of sin, humanity is now sinful, and needs to be healed. One of the symptoms of sin which Augustine discusses in detail is the captivity of the human free will. For Augustine, our freedom is compromised by sin. Our desires and longings, which should have been directed towards God, are misdirected towards things of the world. "We look for happiness not in you," Augustine wrote in a prayer, "but in what you have created." The human free will has thus been weakened and incapacitated – but not eliminated or destroyed – through sin. In order for that free will to be restored and healed, it requires the operation of divine grace. Free will really does exist; it is, however, distorted by sin.

In order to explain this point, Augustine uses an everyday analogy. Consider a pair of scales, with two balance pans. One balance pan represents good, and the other evil. If the pans were properly balanced, the arguments in favor of doing good or doing evil could be weighed, and a proper conclusion drawn. The parallel with the human free will is obvious: we weigh up the arguments in favor of doing good and evil, and act accordingly. But what, asks Augustine, if the balance pans are loaded?

What happens if someone puts several heavy weights in the balance pan on the side of evil? The scales will still work, but they are seriously biased towards making an evil decision. Augustine argues that this is exactly what has happened to humanity through sin. The human free will is biased towards evil. It really exists, and really can make decisions – just as the loaded scales still work. But instead of giving a balanced judgment, a serious bias exists towards evil. Using this and related analogies Augustine argues that the human free will really exists in sinners, but that it is compromised by sin.

The essential point which Augustine makes is that we have no control over our sinfulness. It is something which contaminates our lives from birth, and dominates our lives thereafter. It is a state over which we have no decisive control. We could say that Augustine understands humanity to be born with a sinful disposition as part of human nature, with an inherent bias towards acts of sinning. In other words, sin causes sins: the state of sinfulness causes individual acts of sin. Augustine develops this point with reference to three important analogies: original sin as a "disease," as a "power," and as "guilt."

The first analogy treats sin as a hereditary disease, which is passed down from one generation to another. As we saw above, this disease weakens humanity, and cannot be cured by human agency. Christ is thus the divine physician, by whose "wounds we are healed" (Isaiah 53:5), and salvation is understood in essentially sanative or medical terms. We are healed by the grace of God, so that our minds may recognize God and our wills may respond to the divine offer of grace.

The second analogy treats sin as a power which holds us captive, and from whose grip we are unable to break free by ourselves. The human free will is captivated by the power of sin, and may only be liberated by grace. Christ is thus seen as the liberator, the source of the grace which breaks the power of sin.

The third analogy treats sin as an essentially judicial or forensic concept – guilt – which is passed down from one generation to another. In a society which placed a high value on law, such as the later Roman empire, in which Augustine lived and worked, this was regarded as a particularly helpful way of understanding sin. Christ thus comes to bring forgiveness and pardon.

Augustine's opponent in this debate was Pelagius, a British Christian who had settled in Rome in the late fourth century. Pelagius was disturbed by the moral laxity of Roman Christians, and argued vociferously against Augustine's doctrine of grace. It encouraged moral laxity, he insisted, and failed to emphasize the need for Christians to actively seek perfection. For Pelagius, there was nothing wrong with human nature. If God told people to be perfect, they were capable of being perfect. Where Augustine argued that sinfulness frustrated the human desire to be and do good, Pelagius argued that the real problem was simply laziness.

In 413, Pelagius wrote a lengthy letter to a Roman woman of high birth, named Demetrias, who had recently decided to turn her back on wealth in order to become a nun. In this letter, Pelagius made clear the consequences of his views on human nature and free will. God has made humanity, and knows precisely what it is capable of doing. Hence all the commands given to us can be obeyed, and are meant to be obeyed. It is no excuse to argue that human frailty prevents these commands from being fulfilled. God has made human nature, and only asks of it what it can manage.

[Instead of regarding God's commands as a privilege] . . . we cry out at God and say, "This is too hard! This is too difficult! We cannot do it! We are only human, and hindered by the weakness of the flesh!" What blind madness!

What blatant presumption! By doing this, we accuse the God of knowledge of a twofold ignorance – ignorance of God's own creation and of God's own commands. It would be as if, forgetting the weakness of humanity – which, after all, is God's own creation! – God had laid upon us commands which we were unable to bear.

Pelagius makes the uncompromising assertion that "since perfection is possible for humanity, it is obligatory." As things turned out, the moral rigor of this position, and its unrealistic view of human nature, served only to strengthen Augustine's hand as he developed the rival understanding of a tender and kindly God attempting to heal and restore wounded human nature.

Perhaps the sharpest contrast between Augustine and Pelagius concerns the basis of salvation. What do we need to do to be saved? The two writers offer very different answers. To summarize them briefly: Augustine emphasizes trusting God's promises, and receiving what they promise; Pelagius emphasizes living a good life, and securing salvation by moral integrity and good works. As this debate is so important, we shall consider it in more detail.

For Augustine, humanity is justified as an act of grace: even human good works are the result of God working within fallen human nature. Everything leading up to salvation is the free and unmerited gift of God, given out of love for sinners. Through the death and resurrection of Jesus Christ, God is enabled to deal with fallen humanity in this remarkable and generous manner, giving us that which we do not deserve (salvation), and withholding from us that which we do deserve (condemnation).

Augustine's exposition of the parable of the laborers in the vineyard (Matthew 20:1–10) is of considerable importance in this respect. As we shall see, Pelagius argued that God rewarded each individual strictly on the basis of merit. Augustine, however, pointed out that this parable indicates that the basis of the reward given to the individual is the promise made to that individual. Augustine emphasized that the laborers did not work for equal periods in the vineyard, yet the same wage (a denarius) was given to each. The owner of the vineyard had promised to pay each individual a denarius, providing he worked from the time when he was employed to sundown – even though this meant that some worked all day, and others only for an hour.

Augustine thus drew the important conclusion that the basis of our justification is the divine promise of grace made to us. God is faithful to that promise, and thus justifies sinners. Just as the laborers who began work in the vineyard so late in the day had no claim to a full day's wages, except through the generous promise of the owner, so sinners have no claim to justification and eternal life, except through the gracious promises of God, received through faith.

For Pelagius, however, humanity is justified on the basis of its merits: human good works are the result of the exercise of the totally autonomous human free will, in fulfillment of an obligation laid down by God. A failure to meet this obligation opens the individual to the threat of eternal punishment. Jesus Christ is involved in salvation only to the extent that he reveals, by his actions and teaching, exactly what God requires of the individual. If Pelagius can speak of "salvation in Christ," it is only in the sense of "salvation through imitating the example of Christ."

In the end, the western church opted for Augustine's approach, while not following it through to some of the conclusions that his more enthusiastic supporters advocated – especially in relation to the idea of predestination. Many historians suggest that the basic issues of the Pelagian controversy are regularly replayed throughout the history of the church. The Reformation of the sixteenth century is widely regarded as taking up the fundamental ideas of the Pelagian debate, but this time using the language of "justification by faith" rather than "salvation by grace." Earlier Christian theologians – such as Augustine – had given priority to those New Testament texts which used the language of "salvation by grace" (e.g., Ephesians 2:5). However, Martin Luther's wrestling with the issue of how God was able to accept sinners led him to focus on those passages in which Paul spoke primarily of "justification by faith" (e.g., Romans 5:1–2). Although it can be argued that the same fundamental point is being made in both contexts, the *language* used to express that point is different. One of the most important influences of the Reformation was the displacement of the language of "salvation by grace" by that of "justification by faith."

The doctrine of justification came to be seen as dealing with the question of what an individual had to do in order to be saved. As contemporary sources indicate, this question came to be asked with increasing frequency as the sixteenth century dawned. The rise of humanism brought with it a new emphasis upon individual consciousness, and a new awareness of human individuality. In the wake of this dawn of the individual consciousness came a new interest in the doctrine of justification – the question of how human beings, *as individuals*, could enter into a relationship with God. How could a sinner hope to do this?

This question lay at the heart of the theological concerns of Martin Luther, and came to dominate the early phase of the Reformation. For Luther, God graciously accepted sinners, and bestowed upon them the gift of righteousness which allowed them to stand in God's presence. Although believers remain sinners, they are clothed with the righteousness of Christ, which is freely given to them by grace. Luther develops a number of concepts to clarify this important idea, including his famous slogan *simul iustus et peccator* ("at one and the same time a righteous person and a sinner"). This expresses the critically important idea that God can accept a sinner without the need for prior moral transformation. For Luther, we do not need to be good in order to be accepted by God; rather, it is by being accepted by God that we can become good.

The Church

The Apostles' Creed includes a clause which declares that Christians believe in the church. So what is meant by this? How is the church to be defined, and what is its purpose? This area of theology is traditionally designated "ecclesiology" (from the Greek word for "church," *ekklesia*). The New Testament actually uses the word "church" in two somewhat different manners. At many points, the term "church" is used to designate individual Christian congregations – local visible gatherings of believers. For example, Paul wrote letters to churches in the cities of Corinth and Philippi. The book of Revelation makes reference to the "seven churches of Asia," probably meaning seven local Christian communities in the region of Asia Minor (modern-day Turkey). Yet at other points, we find the term being used in a wider, more general sense, meaning something like "the total body of Christian believers." The tension between the local and universal senses of the word "church" is of considerable importance, and needs careful examination. How could both aspects be maintained?

The unity of the church

Traditionally, this tension is resolved through arguing that there is one universal church which exists in local communities. On the basis of this approach, there is one universal church, consisting of all Christian believers, which takes the form of individual local churches in a given region. One influential way of conceiving this idea is due to John Calvin, who drew an important distinction between the *visible* and the *invisible* church. At one level, the church is the community of Christian believers, a visible group. It is also, however, the fellowship of saints and the company of the elect – an *invisible* entity. In its invisible aspect, the church is the invisible assembly of the elect, known only to God; in its visible aspect, it is the community of believers on earth. The former consists only of the elect; the latter includes both good and evil, elect and reprobate. The former is an object of faith and hope, the latter of present experience. The distinction between them is eschatological (that is, to do with the end times): the invisible church is the church which will come into being at the end of time, as God ushers in the final judgment of humanity.

The importance of this way of thinking, and others like it, is best appreciated by considering the following question. How can we talk about "one" Christian church, when there are so many different Christian denominations? Faced with an apparent tension between a theoretical belief in "one church" and the observable reality of a plurality of churches, Christian writers developed a number of approaches to allow the later observation to be incorporated within the framework of the former.

Some have adopted a basically *Platonic* approach, which draws a fundamental distinction between the empirical church (that is, the church as a visible historical reality) and the ideal church. Others have favored an *eschatological* approach. On this understanding, the present disunity of the church will be abolished on the last day. The present situation is temporary, and will be resolved on the day of judgment. This viewpoint lies behind Calvin's distinction between the "visible" and "invisible" churches, which we considered above.

Some have found a *biological* approach helpful, comparing the historical evolution of the church to the development of the branches of a tree. This image, developed by the eighteenth-century German Pietist writer Nicolas von Zinzendorf, and taken up with enthusiasm by Anglican writers of the following century, allows the different empirical churches – e.g., the Roman Catholic, Orthodox, and Anglican churches – to be seen as possessing an organic unity, despite their institutional differences. The various churches are thus seen as branches on the same root, possessing a fundamental unity, despite their diversity.

The universality of the church

The Christian creeds refer to the church as "universal" or "catholic." This term "derives from the Greek phrase *kath' holou* ("referring to the whole"). The Greek words subsequently found their way into the Latin word *catholicus*, which came to have the meaning "universal or general." This sense of the word is retained in the English phrase "catholic taste," meaning a "wide-ranging taste" rather than a "taste for things that are Roman Catholic." Older versions of the English Bible often refer to some of the New Testament letters (such as those of James and John) as "catholic epistles," meaning that they are directed to all Christians (rather than those of Paul, which are directed to the needs and situations of individual identified churches, such as those at Rome or Corinth). The word "universal" is now widely used as an alternative to "catholic."

The developed sense of the word is perhaps best seen in the fourth-century catechetical writings of Cyril of Jerusalem. In his eighteenth catechetical lecture, Cyril teases out a number of senses of the word "catholic":

The church is thus called "catholic" because it is spread throughout the entire inhabited world, from one end to the other, and because it teaches in its totality (*katholikos*) and without leaving anything out every doctrine which people need to know relating to things visible and invisible, whether in heaven or earth. It is also called "catholic" because it brings to obedience every sort of person – whether rulers or their subjects, the educated and the unlearned. It also makes available a universal (*katholikos*) remedy and cure to every kind of sin.

It will be clear that Cyril is using the term "catholic" in four ways, each of which deserves a little further comment.

1   Catholic is to be understood as "spread throughout the entire inhabited world." Here, Cyril notes the geographical sense of the word. The notion of "wholeness" or "universality" is thus understood to mandate the church to spread into every region of the world.

2   Catholic means "without leaving anything out." With this phrase, Cyril stresses that the "catholicity" of the church involves the complete proclamation and explanation of the Christian faith. It is an invitation to ensure that the totality of the gospel is preached and taught.

3   Catholic means that the church extends its mission and ministry to "every sort of person." Cyril here makes an essentially sociological point. The gospel and the church are for all kinds of human beings, irrespective of their race, gender, or social status. We can see here a clear echo of St. Paul's famous declaration that "there is neither Jew nor Greek, there is neither slave nor free, there is neither male nor female; for you are all one in Christ Jesus" (Galatians 3:28).

4   Catholic means that the church offers and proclaims "a universal remedy and cure to

every kind of sin." Here, Cyril makes a soteriological statement: the gospel, and the church which proclaims that gospel, can meet every human need and distress. Whatever sins there may be, the church is able to offer an antidote.

The various senses of the term "catholic" are also brought out clearly by Thomas Aquinas, in his discussion of the section of the Apostles' Creed dealing with the doctrine of the church. In this analysis, Aquinas singles out three essential aspects of the idea of "catholicity."

> The church is catholic, i.e. universal, first with respect to place, because it is throughout the entire world (*per totum mundum*), against the Donatists. See Romans 1:8: "Your faith is proclaimed in all the world"; Mark 16:15: "Go into all the world and preach the gospel to the whole creation." ... Secondly, the Church is universal with respect to the condition of people, because no one is rejected, whether master or slave, male or female. See Galatians 3:28: "There is neither male nor female." Thirdly, it is universal with respect to time. For some have said that the church should last until a certain time, but this is false, because this church began from the time of Abel and will last to the end of the world. See Matthew 28:20: "And I am with you always, to the close of the age." And after the close of the age it will remain in heaven.

Note how catholicity is here understood in terms of geographical, cultural, and chronological universality.

The holiness of the church

One of the most interesting debates concerning the doctrine of the church relates to whether its members are required to be holy. The debate is seen at its most intense during the Donatist controversy of the fourth century, which fo-

cused on the question of whether church leaders were required to be morally pure. Under the Roman emperor Diocletian (284–313), the Christian church was subject to various degrees of persecution. The origins of the persecution date from 303; it finally ended with the conversion of Constantine, and the issuing of the Edict of Milan in 313. Under an edict of February 303, Christian books were ordered to be burned and churches demolished. Those Christian leaders who handed over their books to be burned came to be known as *traditores* – "those who handed over [their books]." The modern word "traitor" derives from the same root. One such *traditor* was Felix of Aptunga, who later consecrated Caecilian as bishop of the great North African city of Carthage in 311.

Many local Christians were outraged that such a person should have been allowed to be involved in this consecration, and declared that they could not accept the authority of Caecilian as a result. The new bishop's authority was compromised, it was argued, on account of the fact that the bishop who had consecrated him had lapsed under the pressure of persecution. The hierarchy of the Catholic church was thus tainted as a result of this development. The church ought to be pure, and should not be permitted to include such people.

The Donatists believed that the entire sacramental system of the Catholic church had become corrupted on account of the lapse of its leaders. How could the sacraments be validly administered by people who were tainted in this way? It was therefore necessary to replace these people with more acceptable leaders, who had remained firm in their faith under persecution. It was also necessary to rebaptize and reordain all those who had been baptized and ordained by those who had lapsed. Inevitably, this resulted in the formation of a break-away faction. By the time Augustine – destined to be a central figure in the controversy – returned to North Africa from Rome in 388, this breakaway faction had established itself as the leading Christian body in the region, with especially strong support from the local African population.

Augustine responded by putting forward a theory of the church which he believed was more firmly grounded in the New Testament than the Donatist teaching. In particular, Augustine emphasized the *sinfulness of Christians*. The church is not meant to be a "pure body," a society of saints, but a "mixed body" (*corpus permixtum*) of saints and sinners. Augustine finds this image in two biblical parables: the parable of the net which catches many fishes, and the parable of the wheat and the weeds (or "tares," to use an older word familiar to readers of the King James Bible). It is this latter parable (Matthew 13:24–31) which is of especial importance, and requires further discussion.

The parable tells of a farmer who sowed seed, and discovered that the resulting crop included both wheat and weeds. What could be done about it? To attempt to separate the wheat and the weeds while both were still growing would be to court disaster, probably involving damaging the wheat while trying to get rid of the weeds. But at the harvest, all the plants – whether wheat or weeds – are cut down and sorted out, thus avoiding damaging the wheat. The separation of the good and the evil thus takes place at the end of time, not in history.

For Augustine, this parable refers to the church in the world. It must expect to find itself including both saints and sinners. To attempt a separation in this world is premature and improper. That separation will take place in God's own time, at the end of history. No human can make that judgment or separation in God's place.

So in what sense is the church holy? For Augustine, the holiness in question is not that of its members, but of Christ. The church cannot be a congregation of saints in this world, in that its members are contaminated with original sin. However, the church is sanctified and made holy by Christ – a holiness which will be perfected and finally realized at the last judgment. In addition to this theological analysis, Augustine makes the practical observation that the Donatists failed to live up to their own high standards of morality. The Donatists, Augustine suggests, were just as capable as Catholics of getting drunk or beating people up.

Yet the Donatist vision of a "pure body" remains attractive to many. As is so often the case with theological debates, the evidence is never entirely on one side of the argument. A strong case continues to be made for the idea of the church as a "pure body," especially in denominations which trace their identity back to the more radical wing of the Protestant Reformation, often known as "Anabaptism." The radical Reformation conceived of the church as an "alternative society" within the mainstream of sixteenth-century European culture. For Menno Simmons, the church was "an assembly of the righteous," at odds with the world, and not a "mixed body," as Augustine argued:

> In truth, those who merely boast of his name are not the true congregation of Christ. The true congregation of Christ is those who are truly converted, who are born from above of God, who are of a regenerate mind by the operation of the Holy Spirit through the hearing of the Word of God, and have become the children of God.

It will be clear that there are strong parallels with the Donatist view of the church as a holy and pure body, isolated from the corrupting influences of the world, and prepared to maintain its purity and distinctiveness by whatever disciplinary means proved necessary.

Other writers have pointed out how the term "holy" is often equated with "morality," "sanctity," or "purity," which often seem to bear little relation to the behavior of fallen human beings. Yet the Hebrew term *kadad*, which underlies the New Testament concept of "holiness," has a rather different meaning, bearing the sense of "being cut off," or "being separated." There are strong overtones of *dedication*: to be "holy" is to be set apart for and dedicated to the service of God.

A fundamental element – indeed, perhaps *the* fundamental element – of the Old Testament idea of holiness is that of "something or someone whom God has set apart." The New Testament restricts the idea almost entirely to personal holiness. It refers the idea to individuals, declining to pick up the idea of "holy places" or "holy things." People are "holy" in that they are dedicated to God, and distinguished from the world on account of their calling by God. A number of theologians have suggested a correlation between the idea of "the church" (the Greek word for which can bear the meaning of "those who are called out") and "holy" (that is, those who have been separated from the world, on account of their having been called by God).

To speak of the "holiness of the church" is thus primarily to speak of the holiness of the one who called that church and its members. The church has been separated from the world, in order to bear witness to the grace and salvation of God. The term "holy," in this sense, therefore affirms both the calling of the church and its members and the hope that the church will one day share in the life and glory of God.

The apostolicity of the church

Fourthly and finally, the church is declared to be "apostolic." What does this mean? The primary sense of the term is "originating with the Apostles" or "having a direct link with the Apostles." It is a reminder that the church is founded on the apostolic witness and testimony. In the New Testament, the word "apostle" has two related meanings:

1 Someone who has been commissioned by Christ, and charged with the task of preaching the good news of the kingdom.
2 Someone who was a witness to the risen Christ, or to whom Christ revealed himself as risen.

In declaring the church to be "apostolic," the creeds emphasize the historical roots of the gospel, the continuity between the church and Christ through the Apostles whom he appointed, and the continuing evangelistic and missionary tasks of the church.

The church can therefore be thought of as being "apostolic" in three ways, each laying emphasis on a different aspect of the church's history, calling, and function.

(1) Historically, the origins of the church are to be traced back to the apostles. The New Testament tells something of this historical development, especially in the Acts of the Apostles, and brings out the critical role played by the apostles, as Christ's appointed representatives, in the expansion of the church.

(2) Theologically, the church is "apostolic" in that it maintains and transmits the teaching of the apostles. Earlier, we noted how the first Christians, when agreeing on the contents of the New Testament, regarded apostolic authorship as of major importance. The New Testament can be thought of as a repository of apostolic teaching. In declaring that the church is "apostolic," the creeds are insisting that an integral part of the church's task, and an essential precondition for its right to call itself "Christian," is faithfulness to the apostolic tradition. This theme can be seen in some of the later writings of the New Testament, which are

especially concerned with maintaining Christian faithfulness in the post-apostolic period. Thus Paul asks his successor Timothy to remain faithful to what he has been taught, and pass this down to those who will succeed him:

> Hold to the standard of sound teaching that you have heard from me, in the faith and love that are in Christ Jesus. Guard the good treasure entrusted to you, with the help of the Holy Spirit living in us. (2 Timothy 1:13–14)

(3) The church is apostolic, in that it is charged with the responsibility of carrying on the succession of apostolic ministry. The patterns of ministry found in the New Testament, although in an emerging form – for example, deacons, presbyters or "elders," and bishops – are to remain normative for Christianity. More importantly, the tasks entrusted by Christ to the apostles – such as the pastoral care of the poor and needy, teaching, and the preaching of the gospel to the world – are passed on down within the church to their successors.

Among the tasks passed on to the church in this way is Christ's command to do certain specific things, both as a reminder of his life, death, and resurrection and as a celebration and proclamation of his ongoing presence within the church. In view of the importance of these "sacraments" to the life of the church, we may consider them in a little detail.

The Sacraments

The word "sacrament" is widely used to refer to certain acts of worship which are understood to possess special importance in maintaining and developing the Christian life. The term derives from the Latin word *sacramentum*, which originally meant "a military oath." The third-century theologian Tertullian used this parallel as a means of bringing out the importance of sacraments in relation to Christian commitment and loyalty within the church. Baptism, for example, is a sign of allegiance to Christ, and of commitment to the Christian community.

There has been considerable debate within the Christian community over both the identity and function of sacraments, and what to call them. The fundamental Christian practice of using bread and wine to recall the last supper is referred to in different ways by different Christian groups. The most commonly encountered ways of referring to this are: the mass, the eucharist, the Lord's Supper, and the holy communion. In general terms, Protestantism tends to accept only two sacraments – baptism and the eucharist – where Roman Catholicism and Greek Orthodoxy recognize seven. The seven sacraments of the Roman Catholic church are generally grouped together in three categories: the sacraments of initiation (baptism, confirmation, and the eucharist), the sacraments of healing (reconciliation or penance, and the anointing or "unction" of the sick), and sacraments of vocation (marriage and ordination). The Greek Orthodox church also recognizes these seven sacraments, while using the term "chrismation" in place of confirmation.

What is a sacrament?

Although earlier Christian writers often refer to the sacraments, we find relatively little reflection on what determines whether something is a sacrament or not. The word was used somewhat uncritically, without any attempt to achieve any theological precision on what the term entailed. Augustine of Hippo is generally regarded as having laid down the general principles relating to the definition of sacraments. The principles he adopted can be set out as follows:

In the first place, sacrament is fundamentally a *sign*. "Signs, when applied to divine things, are called sacraments." In the second, this sign must bear some relation to the thing which is signified. "If sacraments did not bear some resemblance to the things of which they are the sacraments, they would not be sacraments at all."

These definitions, though useful, are still imprecise and inadequate. For example, does it follow that every "sign of a sacred thing" is to be regarded as a sacrament? In practice, Augustine understood by "sacraments" a number of things that are no longer regarded as sacramental in character – for example, the creed and the Lord's Prayer. As time passed, it became increasingly clear that the definition of a sacrament simply as "a sign of a sacred thing" was insufficient. It was during the earlier Middle Ages that further clarification took place.

In the late twelfth century, Peter Lombard developed Augustine's definition, giving it a new clarity and precision. Peter's definition takes the following form:

> A sacrament bears a likeness to the thing of which it is a sign. "For if sacraments did not have a likeness of the things whose sacraments they are, they would not properly be called sacraments" (Augustine)... Something can properly be called a sacrament if it is a sign of the grace of God and a form of invisible grace, so that it bears its image and exists as its cause. Sacraments were therefore instituted for the sake of sanctifying, as well as of signifying... Those things which were instituted for the purpose of signifying alone are nothing more than signs, and are not sacraments, as in the case of the physical sacrifices and ceremonial observances of the Old Law, which were never able to make those who offered them righteous.

This definition embraces each of the seven traditional sacraments noted above, and excludes such things as the creed and the incarnation. As the definition was included in Peter's widely used and authoritative theological textbook *The Four Books of the Sentences*, it passed into general use in later medieval theology, and remained virtually unchallenged until the time of the Reformation.

Martin Luther challenged this way of thinking about the sacraments, insisting that there were three basic elements which were essential to the definition of a sacrament: a physical sign; a promise; and an explicit command from Christ that this physical sign should be used in this way. Luther's more radical definition limited the list of sacraments to baptism and the eucharist.

In what follows, we shall explore some questions linked with each of these sacraments, which continue to be debated and discussed within Christian circles.

Baptism

Should children be baptized? Matthew's gospel records Jesus Christ as commanding his disciples to go and make disciples, and baptize them (Matthew 28:17–20). But what about children? Does this command extend only to adults, or does it include infants? The New Testament includes no specific references to the baptism of infants. However, neither does it explicitly forbid the practice, and there are also a number of passages which could be interpreted as condoning it – for example, references to the baptizing of entire households, which would probably have included infants (Acts 16:15, 33; 1 Corinthians 1:16). Paul treats baptism as a spiritual counterpart to circumcision (Colossians 2:11–12), suggesting that the parallel may extend to its application to infants.

Most mainline Christian churches accept that the baptism of infants is a valid practice, with its roots in the apostolic period. Martin

Luther and John Calvin, though severely critical of the Catholic church over many points of doctrine and practice, held that infant baptism was an authentic biblical practice. The reasons given for infant baptism vary. Augustine of Hippo argued that, since Christ is the savior of all people, all people require salvation. As baptism is a recognition both of the need for human salvation and of God's gracious willingness to provide it, all should be baptized. After all, he argued, little children were as much in need of salvation as adults.

Another line of defense of the baptism of infants lies in the Old Testament, which stipulated that male infants born within the bounds of Israel should have an outward sign of their membership of the people of God. The outward sign in question was circumcision – that is, the removal of the foreskin. Infant baptism was thus to be seen as analogous to circumcision – a sign of belonging to a covenant community. Writers such as Huldrych Zwingli argued that the more inclusive and gentle character of Christianity was publicly affirmed by infant baptism. The more *inclusive* character of Christianity was affirmed by the baptism of both male and female infants; Judaism, in contrast recognized only the marking of male infants. The more *gentle* character of the gospel was publicly demonstrated by the absence of pain or the shedding of blood in the sacrament. Christ suffered – in being circumcised himself in addition to his death on the cross – in order that his people need not suffer in this manner.

But not all are persuaded of the case for infant baptism. Many Baptist writers reject the traditional practice of baptizing infants. Baptism was to be administered only when an individual showed signs of grace, repentance, or faith. The practice of baptizing infants is held to be without biblical foundation. It may have become the norm in the post-apostolic period, but not in the period of the New Testament itself. It is also argued that the practice of infant baptism leads to the potentially confusing idea that individuals are Christians as a result of their baptism, thus weakening the link between baptism and Christian discipleship.

The eucharist

At the last supper, Jesus commanded his disciples to remember him through the bread and wine. It is clear that this was done from the earliest of times. The New Testament itself makes reference to the first Christians obeying Jesus Christ's command to remember him in this way (1 Corinthians 11:20–27). This act of celebration and remembrance is referred to in different ways by Christian churches, including the mass, the holy communion, the Lord's Supper, and the eucharist (this last term deriving from the Greek word for "thanksgiving").

An important debate within Christianity concerns whether, and in what manner, Christ may be said to be present at the Lord's Supper. This is often linked with the words spoken by Christ at the last supper. Taking the bread, he told his disciples: "this is my body" (Matthew 26:26). What does this mean? The majority opinion within global Christianity is that Christ's words can only mean that, in some sense, Christ's body is present in the bread of the Lord's Supper. The doctrine of "transubstantiation," which was formalized in 1215, holds that the outward appearance of the bread remains unchanged, whereas its inward identity is transformed. In other words, the bread continues to look, taste, smell, and feel as if it were bread; at its most fundamental level, however, it has been changed. By a similar argument, the wine is held to have become the blood of Christ. This position is often stated using the Aristotelian ideas of "substance" (that which gives something its inward identity) and "accidents" (mere external appearances). On this view, the substance of the bread and wine is changed, but their accidents remain unaltered.

Although this position is especially associated with the Roman Catholic church, related viewpoints can be found in eastern Orthodoxy. Martin Luther developed a slightly different idea, often known as "consubstantiation," which holds that the bread remains bread, but is *additionally* the body of Christ. Luther illustrated this idea by pointing to how a piece of iron, when placed in a hot fire, becomes red hot. Although remaining iron, it has heat added to it. In the same way, the bread of the Lord's Supper remains bread, but additionally contains or conveys the body of Christ.

Not all Christians take this position. Some, following John Calvin, argue that the bread is an "efficacious sign." In other words, although the bread is not the body of Christ, it represents this in such a way that what is signified is effectively conveyed. Others follow the Swiss reformer Huldrych Zwingli, who argued that the bread symbolized Christ's body. The bread and the wine of the Lord's Supper are there to help believers recall the events of Calvary, and to encourage them to recommit themselves to the church, to God, and to each other. Zwingli's approach is sometimes known as "memorialism." It holds that there is no objective change in either the bread or the wine. Any change that takes place is subjective, taking place in the mind of the beholder, who now "sees" the bread as a sign of Christ's body, and a reminder of his sacrifice upon the cross.

These, of course, represent only a few positions that Christians have defended. Nevertheless, they illustrate the ongoing debates within Christianity over how best to interpret both the biblical witness to the last supper and the long Christian history of repeating the actions Christ commanded, as a "reminder (Greek: *anamnesis*)" of him.

Christianity and Other Faiths

How does Christianity understand itself to relate to other religious traditions? What do Christians believe about the place of other faiths? The question is not in the least modern; it has been asked throughout Christian history. Initially the question focused on Christianity's relationship with Judaism, from whose matrix it emerged in the period AD 30–60 (see pp. 172–175). And as Christianity expanded, it encountered other religious beliefs and practices, such as classical paganism. The Acts of the Apostles often relates incidents illustrating the tensions between Christianity and classic pagan culture. As it became established in India in the fifth century, it encountered the diverse native Indian cultural movements which western scholars of religion have misleadingly grouped together, and termed "Hinduism." Arab Christianity has long learned to coexist with Islam in the eastern Mediterranean.

In recent years, this question has become particularly important in the western church, on account of the presence of other faiths in hitherto Christian nations as a result of immigration from predominantly Islamic, Hindu, or Buddhist regions. However, the question has been debated throughout the long period of Christian reflection, and has long been important to Christians outside the west, who live in situations in which they are a minority faith in the midst of other, often more aggressive, religious traditions.

The "commonsense" approach to other religions

A naive, commonsense, view of religion might be that it is an outlook on life which believes in, or worships, a Supreme Being. This outlook, characteristic of Deism and Enlightenment rationalism, is easily shown to be inadequate. Buddhism is classified as a religion by most people; yet here a belief in some supreme being is conspicuously absent. The same problem persists no matter what definition of "religion" is offered. No unambiguously common features can be identified among the religions, in matters of faith or practice. Thus Edward Conze, the great scholar of Buddhism, recalled that he "once read through a collection of the lives of Roman Catholic saints, and there was not one of whom a Buddhist could fully approve...They were bad Buddhists though good Christians."

For the last two decades, there has been a growing consensus that it is seriously misleading to regard the various religious traditions of the world as variations on a single theme. "There is no single essence, no one content of enlightenment or revelation, no one way of emancipation or liberation, to be found in all that plurality" (David Tracy). John B. Cobb, Jr. also notes the enormous difficulties confronting anyone wishing to argue that there is an "essence of religion": "Arguments about what religion truly is are pointless. There is no such thing as religion. There are only traditions, movements, communities, peoples, beliefs, and practices that have features that are associated by many people with what they mean by religion."

Cobb also stresses that the assumption that religion has an essence has bedeviled and seriously misled recent discussion of the relation of the religious traditions of the world. For example, he points out that both Buddhism and Confucianism have "religious" elements – but that does not necessarily mean that they can be categorized as "religions." Many "religions" are, he argues, better understood as cultural movements with religious components.

The idea of some universal notion of religion, of which individual religions are subsets,

appears to have emerged at the time of the Enlightenment. To use a biological analogy, the assumption that there is a genus of religion, of which individual religions are species, is a very western idea, without any real parallel outside western culture – except on the part of those who have been educated in the west, and uncritically absorbed its presuppositions.

What, then, of Christian approaches to understanding the relation between Christianity and other religious traditions? In what way can such traditions be understood, within the context of the Christian belief in the universal saving will of God, made known through Jesus Christ? It must be stressed that Christian theology is concerned with evaluating other religious traditions from the perspective of Christianity itself. Such reflection is not addressed to, or intended to gain approval from, members of other religious traditions, or their secular observers.

Two main approaches can be identified: *particularism*, which holds that only those who hear and respond to the Christian gospel may be saved; and *inclusivism*, which argues that, although Christianity represents the normative revelation of God, salvation is nonetheless possible for those who belong to other religious traditions. A third approach, usually referred to as "pluralism," holds that all the religious traditions of humanity are equally valid paths to the same core of religious reality. This position is not typical of historical Christianity, and is often regarded as a culturally accommodated response to western pluralist culture, adopting the "commonsense" model of religion now recognized to be seriously flawed. We shall explore it briefly in what follows.

The pluralist approach

The most significant exponent of a pluralist approach to religious traditions is John Hick (b. 1922). In his *God and the Universe of Faiths*

(1973), Hick argued for a need to move away from a Christ-centered to a God-centered approach. Describing this change as a "Copernican Revolution," Hick declared that it was necessary to move away from "the dogma that Christianity is at the centre to the realization that it is *God* who is at the centre, and that all religions . . . including our own, serve and revolve around him." Developing this approach, Hick suggests that the aspect of God's nature of central importance to the question of other faiths was his universal saving will. If God wishes everyone to be saved, it is inconceivable that God should be revealed in such a way that only a small portion of humanity could be saved. In fact, as we shall see, this is not a necessary feature of either particularist or inclusivist approaches. However, Hick draws the conclusion that it is necessary to recognize that all religions lead to the same God. Christians have no special access to God, who is universally available through all religious traditions.

This suggestion is not without its problems. For example, it is fairly clear that the religious traditions of the world are radically different in their beliefs and practices. Hick deals with this point by suggesting that such differences must be interpreted in terms of a "both–and" rather than an "either–or." They should be understood as complementary, rather than contradictory, insights into the one divine reality. This reality lies at the heart of all the religions; yet "their differing experiences of that reality, interacting over the centuries with the different thought-forms of different cultures, have led to increasing differentiation and contrasting elaboration." (This idea is very similar to the "universal rational religion of nature," propounded by Deist writers, which became corrupted through time.) Equally, Hick has difficulties with those non-theistic religious traditions, such as Advaitin Hinduism or Theravada Buddhism, which have no place for a god.

These difficulties relate to observed features of religious traditions. In other words, the beliefs of non-Christian religions make it difficult to accept that they are all speaking of the same God. But a more fundamental theological worry remains: is Hick actually talking about the Christian God at all? A central Christian conviction – that God is revealed definitively in Jesus Christ – has to be set to one side to allow Hick to proceed. Hick argues that he is merely adopting a theocentric, rather than a Christocentric, approach. Yet the Christian insistence that God is known normatively through Christ implies that authentically Christian knowledge of God is derived through Christ. For a number of critics, Hick's desertion of Christ as a reference-point means abandoning any claim to speak from a Christian perspective.

Traditional Christianity is strongly resistant to the homogenizing agenda of religious pluralists, not least on account of its high Christology. The suggestion that all religions are more or less talking about vaguely the same "God" finds itself in difficulty in relation to certain essentially Christian ideas – most notably, the doctrines of the incarnation and the Trinity (see above). For example, if God is Christ-like, as the doctrine of the divinity of Christ affirms in uncompromising terms, then the historical figure of Jesus, along with the witness to him in Scripture, becomes of foundational importance to Christianity. Many pluralists thus find themselves rejecting a series of central Christian teachings – such as that of the divinity and the resurrection of Jesus, and the doctrine of the Trinity. This strongly reductionist approach to Christianity is regarded with distaste by many Christians, who feel that serious liberties are being taken with their faith to serve the notion that all religions are saying the same thing.

In what follows, then, we shall explore the two main lines of approach found within the Christian tradition in relation to other religions.

The particularist approach

Perhaps the most influential statement of this position may be found in the writings of Hendrik Kraemer (1888–1965), especially his *Christian Message in a Non-Christian World* (1938). Kraemer emphasized that "God has revealed *the* Way and *the* Truth and *the* Life in Jesus Christ, and wills this to be known throughout the world." This revelation is absolutely distinctive; it exists in a category of its own, and cannot be set alongside the ideas of revelation found in other religious traditions.

At this point, a certain breadth of opinion can be discerned within this approach. Kraemer himself seems to suggest that there is real knowledge of God outside Christ when he speaks of God shining through "in a broken, troubled way, in reason, in nature and in history." The question is whether such knowledge is only available through Christ, or whether Christ provides the only framework by which such knowledge may be discerned and interpreted elsewhere.

Some particularists (such as Karl Barth) adopt the position that there is no knowledge of God to be had apart from Christ; others (such as Kraemer) allow that God reveals himself in many ways and places – but insist that this revelation can only be interpreted correctly, and known for what it really is, in the light of the definitive revelation of God in Christ.

What, then, of those who have not heard the gospel of Christ? What happens to them? Are not particularists denying salvation to those who have not heard of Christ – or who, having heard of him, choose to reject him? This criticism is frequently leveled against particularism by its critics, especially from a pluralist perspective. Thus John Hick suggests that the doctrine that salvation is only possible through Christ is inconsistent with belief in the universal saving will of God. That this is not, in fact,

the case is easily demonstrated by considering the view of Karl Barth, easily the most sophisticated of twentieth-century defenders of this position.

Barth declares that salvation is only possible through Christ. He nevertheless insists on the ultimate eschatological victory of grace over unbelief – that is, at the end of history. Eventually, God's grace will triumph completely, and all will come to faith in Christ. This is the only way to salvation – but it is a way that, through the grace of God, is effective for all. For Barth, the particularity of God's revelation through Christ is not contradicted by the universality of salvation.

In closing this brief discussion of particularism, it should be noted that a number of works published in the 1980s termed this type of approach as "exclusivism." This term has now been generally abandoned, mainly because it is considered to be polemical. The approach is now generally described as "particularism," on account of its affirmation of the particular and distinctive features of the Christian faith.

The inclusivist approach

The most significant advocate of this model is the leading Jesuit writer Karl Rahner (1904–1984). In the fifth volume of his *Theological Investigations*, Rahner develops four theses, setting out the view not merely that individual non-Christians may be saved, but that the non-Christian religious traditions in general may have access to the saving grace of God in Christ.

1   Christianity is the absolute religion, founded on the unique event of the self-revelation of God in Christ. But this revelation took place at a specific point in history. Those who lived before this point, or who have yet to hear about this event, would thus seem to be excluded from

salvation – which is contrary to the saving will of God.

2 For this reason, despite their errors and shortcomings, non-Christian religious traditions are valid and capable of mediating the saving grace of God, until the gospel is made known to their members. After the gospel has been proclaimed to the adherents of such non-Christian religious traditions, they are no longer legitimate, from the standpoint of Christian theology.

3 The faithful adherent of a non-Christian religious tradition is thus to be regarded as an "anonymous Christian."

4 Other religious traditions will not be displaced by Christianity. Religious pluralism will continue to be a feature of human existence.

We may explore the first of these theses in more detail. It will be clear that Rahner strongly affirms the principle that salvation may only be had through Jesus, as he is interpreted by the Christian tradition. "Christianity understands itself as the absolute religion, intended for all people, which cannot recognize any other religion beside itself as of equal right." Yet Rahner supplements this with an emphasis upon the universal saving will of God: God wishes that all shall be saved, even though not all know Christ. "Somehow all people must be able to be members of the church." For this reason, Rahner argues that saving grace must be available outside the bounds of the church – and hence in other religious traditions. He vigorously opposes those who adopt too-neat solutions, insisting either that a religious tradition comes from God or that it is an inauthentic and purely human invention. Where Kraemer argues that non-Christian religious traditions were little more than self-justifying human constructions, Rahner argues that such traditions may well include elements of truth.

Rahner justifies this suggestion by considering the relation between the Old and New Testaments. Although the Old Testament, strictly speaking, represents the outlook of a non-Christian religion (Judaism), Christians are able to read it and discern within it elements which continue to be valid. The Old Testament is evaluated in the light of the New, and as a result, certain practices (such as food laws) are discarded as unacceptable, while others are retained (such as the moral law). The same approach can and should, Rahner argues, be adopted in the case of other religions.

The saving grace of God is thus available through non-Christian religious traditions, despite their shortcomings. Many of their adherents, Rahner argues, have thus accepted that grace, without being fully aware of what it is. It is for this reason that Rahner introduces the term "anonymous Christians" to refer to those who have experienced divine grace without necessarily knowing it. This term has been heavily criticized. For example, John Hick has suggested that it is paternalist, offering "honorary status granted unilaterally to people who have not expressed any desire for it." Nevertheless, Rahner's intention is to allow for the real effects of divine grace in the lives of those who belong to non-Christian traditions. Full access to truth about God (as it is understood within the Christian tradition) is not a necessary precondition for access to the saving grace of God.

Rahner does not allow that Christianity and other religious traditions may be treated as equal, or that they are particular instances of a common encounter with God. For Rahner, Christianity and Christ have an exclusive status, denied to other religious traditions. The question is: can other religious traditions give access to the same saving grace as that offered by Christianity? Rahner's approach allows him to suggest that the beliefs of non-Christian religious traditions are not necessarily true, while allowing that they may, nevertheless, mediate the grace of God by the lifestyles which they evoke – such as a selfless love of one's neighbor.

A somewhat different approach is associated with the Second Vatican Council (Vatican II). In its decree on other faiths (*Nostra Aetate*, October 28, 1965), the Council followed Rahner in affirming that rays of divine truth were indeed to be found in other religions. However, where Rahner allowed other faiths to have soteriological potential, the Council maintained the distinctiveness of the Christian faith at this point.

> The Catholic Church rejects nothing of what is true and holy in these religions. She has a high regard for the manner of life and conduct, the precepts and doctrines which, although differing in many ways from her own teaching, nevertheless often reflect a ray of that truth which enlightens all men. Yet she proclaims and is in duty bound to proclaim without fail, Christ who is the way, the truth and the life (John 14:6). In him, in whom God reconciled all things to himself (2 Corinthians 5:18–19), men find the fullness of their religious life.

The distinction between Rahner and Vatican II can be summarized as follows, using some theological jargon. Rahner is both revelationally and soteriologically inclusive; Vatican II tends to be revelationally inclusive, yet soteriologically particularist. To put this in plain English: Rahner holds that, before the advent of Christianity, any religion can give knowledge of God and bestow salvation. Vatican II, on the other hand, holds that while other religions may bring some knowledge of God, salvation is only possible through the church.

Once more, this debate continues. It can only become more important. As Christianity expands in parts of the world once dominated by other faiths, and as other faiths become part of western society through immigration, the question continues to be forced on Christians: how are these other faiths to be understood? This brief summary of the debate has outlined the main approaches currently adopted, which are likely to remain significant for some considerable time.

The Last Things: Heaven

Finally, we come to the theme of the Christian hope – an idea often expressed in terms of the phrase "the last things" (Greek: *ta eschata*, from which the word "eschatology" is derived). In this closing section of this chapter, we shall focus on Christian beliefs concerning heaven, the most important of these "last things."

The word "heaven" is traditionally used to refer to the hope of dwelling in the presence of God for ever. The term is not understood geographically or spatially, as if it referred to a country or a region of the world. The dominant sense of the word is relational – that is, it is used to designate the state of dwelling with God, without attaching this to any particular understanding of precisely where this dwelling is located. As we shall see in what follows, the Christian vision of heaven is shaped by two controlling images or themes – the New Jerusalem, and the restoration of creation. A radical transformation of all things will bring about a new order of things, reversing the devastating effects of sin upon humanity and the world. The image of resurrection conveys the ideas of both radical change and continuity – that is to say, that the new order of things, though utterly different from what we currently know and experience, nevertheless demonstrates continuity with the present order. The present age will be *transformed* and *renewed*, just as a seed is transformed utterly in becoming a living plant.

But how are we to understand this hope of our future resurrection? What will be the relationship of our earthly bodies to our heavenly bodies? The New Testament is very restrained at this point. The image of a seed, used by Paul in 1 Corinthians 15, was taken by many writers to mean that there was some organic connection between the earthly and heavenly body. Gregory of Nyssa is a good example of a writer who reasons like this:

> The resurrection is nothing other than the reconstitution of our nature to its pristine state. For we read in Scripture that, in the first act of creation, the earth initially brought forth the green plant; then seed was produced from this plant; and from this seed, when it had been scattered on the earth, the same form of the original growth sprang up. Now the inspired Apostle says that this is precisely what also happens at the resurrection. Thus we learn from him not only that human nature is changed into a far nobler state, but also that we are to hope for the return of human nature to its primal condition.

Some early Christian writers thought that it was best to imagine the streets of the New Jerusalem as inhabited by disembodied souls. On this model, the human being consists of two entities – a physical body and a spiritual soul. Death leads to the liberation of the soul from its material body. This view was commonplace within the Hellenistic culture of the New Testament period. However, this idea was vigorously opposed by most early Christian theologians. The most significant minority voice in this matter belonged to Origen, a highly creative theologian with a strongly Platonist bent, who held that the resurrection body was purely spiritual. This view was contested by most Christian writers, who insisted that the phrase "the resurrection of the body" was to be understood as the permanent resurrection of both the body and the soul of the believer.

But what would these resurrected individuals look like? Many early Christian writers argued that the "citizens of heaven" would be naked, recreating the situation in paradise. This time, however, nakedness would give rise neither to shame nor to sexual lust, but would simply be accepted as the natural and innocent state of humanity. Others, however, argued that the inhabitants of the New Jerusalem would be clothed in finery, reflecting their status as citizens of God's chosen city.

So how did this process of transformation take place? What is the connection between the present human state of humility and mortality, and the future state of glory and immortality? What sort of reconstitution of human nature took place at the resurrection? Methodius of Olympus offered an analogy for this process of reconstitution which would prove highly influential in discussing this question. The resurrection could, he argued, be thought of as a kind of "rearrangement" of the constituent elements of humanity. It is like a statue which is melted down, and reforged from the same material – yet in such a manner that any defects or damage are eliminated.

> It is as if some skilled artificer had made a noble image, cast in gold or other material, which was beautifully proportioned in all its features. Then the artificer suddenly notices that the image had been defaced by some envious person, who could not endure its beauty, and so decided to ruin it for the sake of the pointless pleasure of satisfying his jealousy. So the craftsman decides to recast this noble image . . . Now the melting down of a statue corresponds to the death and dissolution of the human body, and the remolding of the material to the resurrection after death.

A similar argument is found in the *Four Books of the Sentences*, the masterpiece of the great twelfth-century theologian Peter Lombard. This book, which served as the core textbook for just about every medieval theologian, took the view that the resurrected body was basically a reconstituted humanity, from which all defects had been purged:

> Nothing of the substance of the flesh from which humanity is created will be lost; rather, the natural substance of the body will be reintegrated by the collection of all the particles that were previously dispersed. The bodies of the saints will thus rise without any defect, shining like the sun, all their deformities having being removed.

A final question that has caused considerable debate among Christian theologians concerns the *age* of those who are resurrected. If someone dies at the age of 60, will they appear in the streets of the New Jerusalem as an old person? And if someone dies at the age of 10, will they appear as a child? This issue engendered much debate, especially during the Middle Ages. By the end of the thirteenth century, an emerging consensus can be discerned. As each person reaches their peak of perfection around the age of 30, they will be resurrected as they would have appeared at that time – even if they never lived to reach that age. Peter Lombard's discussion of the matter is typical of his age: "A boy who dies immediately after being born will be resurrected in that form which he would have had if he had lived to the age of thirty." The New Jerusalem will thus be populated by men and women as they would appear at the age of 30 (the age, of course, at which Christ was crucified) – but with every blemish removed.

A further issue concerning the form of the resurrection body became especially important during the twentieth century, when the practice of cremation became increasingly common in Christian nations, partly on account of the ever more prohibitive cost of burial. Was cremation inconsistent with belief in the resurrection? Was our resurrection to eternal life dependent on being buried intact? The question had been debated in earlier periods. For example, during a second-century persecution of Christians in southern France, pagan oppressors burned the bodies of the Christians they had just martyred, and threw their ashes in the River Rhône. This, they believed, would prevent the resurrection of these martyrs, in that there was now no body to be raised. Christian theologians responded by arguing that God was able to restore all that the body had lost through this process of destruction. God would still be able to raise the bodies of those who had been mutilated in this way.

For centuries cremation was expressly forbidden in the Roman Catholic church. Two reasons were often given for this. In the first place, cremation was seen as a pagan practice that denied the doctrine of the resurrection. Secondly, there was the belief that the body is the temple of the Holy Spirit. However, some significant changes in Roman Catholic practice took place in the twentieth century. In 1963, the Vatican lifted the ban on cremation for Catholics. However, no allowance was made for any prayer or rituals to be used with the cremated remains. This meant that all funeral services were to occur in the presence of the body, with cremation taking place afterwards. In 1997, the Vatican granted permission for the cremated remains of a body to be brought into church for the liturgical rites of burial. It is still, however, the official church's preference to have the full complement of funeral rites take place with the body present, and for cremation to follow afterwards.

In Protestant circles, perhaps the most influential answer to this question was offered by the famous American evangelist Billy Graham, who wrote thus in a nationally syndicated newspaper column:

In Corinthians 5, Paul makes the contrast between living in a tent, a temporary home that can be pulled down and put away, and living in a permanent home that will last forever. Our bodies are our temporary tents. Our resurrected bodies will be our permanent homes. They are similar in appearance but different in substance. Cremation is therefore no hindrance to the resurrection.

Graham's point was clear: the Christian hope of resurrection is grounded in the trustworthi-ness of the divine promises, not the precise circumstances of a person's funeral arrangements.

These ideas are important in a number of respects, not least in relation to Christian funeral services. We shall consider these in a later chapter. Our attention now turns to the broad sweep of Christian history, as we survey some of the landmarks in the development of the Christian presence in the world.

7

A Brief History of Christianity

History, in the view of many, is rather dull and uninteresting. At best, it is the prelude to the study of more interesting matters – such as what is happening in the present. Yet very often we simply cannot understand what is taking place right now without a knowledge of the background to the present. It is impossible to understand the rise of Adolf Hitler without a knowledge of the Weimar Republic, and the tensions arising from the Treaty of Versailles. To make sense of the "troubles" in Northern Ireland requires some basic knowledge of the history of Ireland, and especially the Protestant "Plantations" established in the late sixteenth century. The present political tensions in the Middle East, Iraq, or many parts of sub-Saharan Africa cannot be understood in isolation from the history of western involvement in those regions. And, in precisely the same way, the present situation within Christianity globally cannot be understood without a working knowledge of its history and development.

The present chapter offers a brief overview of the history of Christianity. During the course of this analysis, we shall examine some of the landmarks of the history of Christianity – the conversion of the Roman emperor Constantine, the rise of scholasticism, the dawn of the Reformation, the American and French Revolutions of the eighteenth century, and the

Russian and Chinese Revolutions of the twentieth. We shall explore the way in which a religion which came to birth in Palestine gradually established a presence in Europe, and thence in the Americas, sub-Saharan Africa, and parts of Asia.

The overview to be offered is woefully inadequate for those wishing to gain a detailed understanding of the emergence and development of the world's largest faith. Virtually every paragraph in this chapter demands a book-length treatment, and raises difficult and often controversial questions that cannot be properly discussed in the limited space available. Yet it is ideal for the purposes of the present book, which has a more restricted and modest goal – to enable its readers to understand Christianity as it is presently experienced in the world. This is the subject of the next chapter, to which this chapter is an extensive prologue.

It is hoped, however, that the present survey will also be of use and interest to those wishing to study church history in greater detail. Years of teaching have taught me that the best way to approach a vast and complex subject is often to give a broad survey – rather like drawing a basic map of a region. This allows people to fill in the fine detail later, to the extent that is appropriate for their own purposes.

This survey chapter is broken down into four major sections, following a fairly conventional approach to church history. We begin by considering the patristic period, during which Christianity emerged as a new religious movement in the Mediterranean world, and began to consolidate both its ideas and its physical presence in the region. This period is often thought of as closing politically with the fall of the Roman empire, and theologically with the Council of Chalcedon (451). But such markers are ultimately arbitrary, even though they are useful as landmarks.

The second major phase embraces what some historians used to call the "Dark Ages," leading in to the great revival of western culture in the Middle Ages. During this period, Christianity became one of the most important (in the view of many scholars, *the* most important) forces of cohesion and continuity in western Europe, with a growing impact in eastern Europe and a continuing presence in the great Byzantine empire in southeastern Europe. Once more, any landmarks used to designate the end of this period are ultimately arbitrary. However, the fall of Constantinople to Islamic armies in 1453 is unquestionably of decisive importance.

The third major phase is marked by the flowering of the Renaissance and the onset of the Reformation in western Europe. These two sixteenth-century developments can be said to have shaped the contours of global Christianity, by creating the divisions within western Christianity which were then exported to much of the rest of the world through immigration to the Americas, and the work of missionary societies in the eighteenth, nineteenth, and twentieth centuries. Although this is a relatively short period, it is of such importance to an understanding of modern Christianity that it demands to be considered in some detail.

Finally, we consider the modern period, which is usually held to begin in the eighteenth century, and was of such importance in shaping Christianity. This period is marked by significant reversals of fortunes for Christianity in many parts of the west, coupled with expansion and consolidation in many other parts of the world, above all Africa and Asia. It is a complex and fascinating story, which helps us understand the multifaceted composition, character, and fortunes of Christianity at the beginning of the twenty-first century.

We begin by considering the early history of Christianity in the patristic period.

The Early Church

The first two major periods of Christian history are usually understood to be the period of the New Testament itself (often referred to as "the apostolic era"), and the period between the closing of the New Testament (ca. 100) and the Council of Chalcedon in 451. During this period, the distinctive shape of the Christian faith emerged. In the present section, we shall explore some of the events and issues which emerged as significant during this first phase in the global expansion of Christianity. We begin by exploring an issue which is of major importance within the New Testament, and continues to be important today – the relation between Christianity and Judaism.

Christianity and Judaism

In one sense, Christianity can be said to begin with the coming of Jesus Christ. Yet Christians themselves have always been clear that Christianity is continuous with Judaism. The "God of Abraham, Isaac, and Jacob" is the same as the "God of Jesus Christ." Early Christianity emerged within Judaism, and most of the first converts to the movement were Jews. The New

Testament frequently mentions Christians preaching in local synagogues. So similar were the two movements that outside observers, such as the Roman authorities, tended to treat Christianity as a sect within Judaism, rather than as a new movement with a distinct identity.

This relationship was usually expressed in terms of two "covenants." This terminology is used in the New Testament, especially the letter to the Hebrews, and became normative within Christian thought over the following centuries. The "Old Covenant" refers to God's dealings with Israel, expressed in Judaism; the "New Covenant" refers to God's dealings with humanity as a whole, revealed in Jesus Christ. The Christian belief that the coming of Christ inaugurates something *new* expresses itself in a distinctive attitude towards the Old Testament, which could basically be summarized thus: *religious principles and ideas* (such as the notion of a sovereign God who is active in human history) are appropriated; religious *practices* (such as dietary laws and sacrificial routines) are not.

One option which has generally been rejected completely is to treat the Old Testament as the writings of a religion which had nothing to do with Christianity. This approach is especially associated with the second-century writer Marcion, who was excommunicated in the year 144. According to Marcion, Christianity was a religion of love, which had no place whatsoever for law. The Old Testament relates to a different God than the New; the Old Testament God, who merely created

7.1 The destruction of the Jewish temple in Jerusalem by the Romans under Titus, August 30, AD 70. AKG-Images/Peter Connolly.

the world, was obsessed with the idea of law. The New Testament God, however, redeemed the world, and was concerned with love. According to Marcion, the purpose of Christ was to depose the Old Testament God (who bears a considerable resemblance to the Gnostic "demiurge," a semi-divine figure responsible for fashioning the world), and usher in the worship of the true God of grace.

The emphasis on the continuity between Christianity and Judaism raised a number of serious difficulties for the early Christians. First, there was the question of the role of the Jewish law in the Christian life. Did the traditional rites and customs of Judaism have any continuing place in the Christian church? There is evidence that this issue was of particular importance during the 40s and 50s, when non-Jewish converts to Christianity came under pressure from Jewish Christians to maintain such rites and customs. The issue of circumcision was particularly sensitive, with Gentile converts to Christianity often being pressed to become circumcised, in accord with the law. This controversy is recorded in the Acts of the Apostles, which notes how, in the late 40s, a section of the church argued that it was essential that male Christians should be circumcised. In effect, they seemed to regard Christianity as an affirmation of every aspect of contemporary Judaism, with the addition of one extra belief – that Jesus was the Messiah. Unless males were circumcised, they could not be saved (Acts 15:1).

In order to resolve this issue, Paul and Barnabas set out to Jerusalem from Antioch. Luke provides us with an account of the first General Council of the Christian church – the Council of Jerusalem in 49 (Acts 15:2–29). The debate is initially dominated by converted Pharisees, who insist upon the need to uphold the law of Moses, including the circumcision requirements. Yet Paul's account of the growing impact of the Christian gospel among the Gentiles causes the wisdom of this approach to be questioned. If so many Gentiles are becoming Christians, why should anything unnecessary be put in their way? Paul conceded the need to avoid food which had been sacrificed to idols – an issue which features elsewhere in his letters (1 Corinthians 8:7–13). But there is no need for circumcision. This position won widespread support, and was summarized in a letter which was circulated at Antioch (Acts 15:30–35).

Yet although the issue was resolved at the theoretical level, it would remain a live concern for many churches in the future. Having sorted out this issue in Palestine, Paul determined to return to the region of Galatia (in the center of modern-day Turkey) to make sure that the churches which he had planted would know of this decision. Paul's letter to the Galatians, probably written around 53, deals explicitly with this question, which had clearly become a contentious topic in the region. Paul notes the emergence of a Judaizing party in the region – that is, a group within the church which insisted that Gentile believers should obey every aspect of the law of Moses, including the need to be circumcised. According to Paul, the leading force behind this party was James – not the apostle James, who died in AD 44, but the brother of Jesus Christ who was influential in calling the Council of Jerusalem, and who wrote the New Testament letter known by his name.

For Paul, this trend was highly dangerous. If Christians could only gain salvation by the rigorous observance of the law, what purpose did the death of Christ serve? It is faith in Christ, not the scrupulous and religious keeping of the law of Moses, which is the basis of salvation. Nobody can be justified (that is, put in a right relationship with God) through keeping the law. The righteousness on which our salvation depends is not available through the law, but only through faith in Christ. Aware of the importance and sensitivity of this issue, Paul then explores this question in some detail (see Galatians 3:1–23). The Galatians have fallen into the trap of believing that salvation came by doing works of the law, or by human achievement. So what has happened to faith? Did the gift of the Holy Spirit ever come through keeping the law? Paul then makes an appeal to the example of Abraham to make his point. Paul argues that Abraham was "justified" (that is, put in a right relationship with God) through his faith (Galatians 3:6–18). The great patriarch was not put in a right relationship with God through circumcision; that came later. That relationship with God was established through Abraham's faith in God's promise to him (Genesis 15:6). Circumcision was simply the external sign of that faith. It did not establish that faith, but confirmed something that was already there. Nor does the law, or any aspect of it, abolish the promises which God had already made. The promise to Abraham and his descendants – which includes Christians as well as Jews – remains valid, even after the introduction of the law.

So the basic point is that the promise of God to Abraham was made before either circumcision or the law of Moses was delivered. Thus all who share in the faith of Abraham are the children of Abraham. It is possible for the Gentiles to share Abraham's faith in the promises of God – and all the benefits that result from this faith – without the need to be circumcised, or be bound to the fine details of the law of Moses. It is Christ's death and resurrection, not external observance of the law, which constitute the ultimate grounds of our relationship with God.

This controversy is important for several reasons. It casts light on tensions within the early church; it also raises the question of whether Jewish Christians enjoyed special privileges or status in relation to Gentile Christians. The final outcome of the debate was that Jews and Gentiles were to be given equal status and acceptance within the church. The chronological priority of Israel over the church did not entail the privileging of Jews over Gentiles within the Christian community. While the theological and ethical teaching of the Old Testament was to be honored and accepted by Christians, they were under no obligation to obey the ceremonial or cultic aspects of the law, including circumcision or sacrifice. Those were both fulfilled and superseded by the coming of Jesus Christ. For many early Christians, the fact that Jesus was circumcised removed any need for them to undergo the same painful process.

Yet the relationship of Jew and Gentile within the church was not the only subject of discussion. What about the relationship between men and women?

Christianity and women

Our most important source for the history of early Christianity is the Acts of the Apostles, written by the same Luke who compiled the third of the four gospels. Acts emphasizes the vitally important role of women in providing hospitality for missionaries, which was of major importance in establishing the church in Europe, with women converts such as Lydia making their homes available as house churches and staging-posts for missionaries. Luke appears to be concerned to bring out clearly the important historical point that the early church attracted significant numbers of prominent women in cultures which gave them a much greater social role than in Judaism, and offered them considerable responsibility in the overall evangelistic and pastoral ministry of the early church.

In particular, Luke singles out Priscilla and Aquila as a husband-and-wife team who were engaged in an evangelistic and teaching ministry (Acts 18:1–3, 24–26), not least in relation to Apollos. Interestingly, the name of the woman precedes that of her husband. As many scholars of antiquity point out, it is unusual for a woman's name to precede that of her husband. Perhaps Priscilla had a higher social rank than her husband, or was more significant in Christian circles. The priority given to Priscilla clearly suggests that Luke regards her as taking precedence over Aquila in terms of the teaching ministry exercised by the couple. Many other examples could be given. Paul commends to the Roman church "our sister Phoebe, a servant of the church at Cenchrea" (Romans 16:1), commenting on how helpful she had been to him. 1 Timothy 3:11 and 5:9–10 also clearly point to women having a ministerial role, exercising a recognized and authorized ministry of some form within the church.

"There is neither Jew nor Greek, slave nor free, male nor female, for you are all one in Christ Jesus" (Galatians 3:28). This verse stands as the foundation of Paul's approach to differences of gender, class, or race. Paul affirms that being "in Christ" transcends all social, ethnic, and sexual barriers. Perhaps this vigorous and unambiguous statement was provoked by the local situation in Galatia, in which Judaizers (that is to say, people who wished Christians to retain the traditions of Judaism) were attempting to retain customs or beliefs which encouraged or justified such distinctions. Paul does not mean that people stop being Jews or Greeks, or male and female, as a result of their conversions. It does mean that these distinctions, while remaining, cease to have any saving significance. They may have importance in the eyes of the world; yet in the sight of God, and within the Christian community, they are transcended by the union between Christ and the believer. Paul's affirmation has two major consequences. First, it declares that there are no barriers of gender, race, or social status to the gospel. The gospel is universal in its scope. Secondly, it clearly implies that, while Christian faith does not abolish the particularities of one's existence, they are to be used to glorify God in whatever situation we find ourselves.

Christianity thus laid the foundations for the radical undermining of traditional attitudes towards both women and slaves at two levels:

1   It asserted that all were one in Christ – whether Jew or Gentile, whether male or female, whether master or slave. Differences of race, gender, or social position were declared to place no obstacles between all believers sharing the same common relationship with the risen Christ.
2   It insisted that all – whether Jew or Gentile, whether male or female, whether master or slave – share in the same Christian fellowship, and worship together. Society might force each of these groups to behave in different manners; but within the Christian community, all were to be regarded as brothers and sisters in Christ.

These developments did not lead to an immediate alteration in existing attitudes towards either women or slaves. Theory always appears to have preceded practice, with the practice being affected by a variety of factors, including the cultural acceptability of the development in question. Nevertheless, it was equivalent to placing a theoretical time bomb under them. It was only a matter of time before the foundations of these traditional distinctions would be eroded to the point at which they could no longer be maintained. As the Roman historian Harold Mattingley once pointed out, "Christianity made no attempt to abolish slavery at one blow, but it undermined its basis by admitting slaves into the same religious fellowship as their masters."

The general principle which thus emerges can be stated as follows. The New Testament makes it clear that there is a theoretical equality amongst Christians. Differences of racial origin, gender, or class are relativized and abolished by the new relationship with the risen Christ which arises through faith in him. Yet the practical outworking of these developments is seen as a long-term issue. Cultural attitudes modify these radical theoretical beliefs. The theoretical equality of all believers may not be culturally acceptable in certain contexts. As a result, theory may not be able to pass into practice in one cultural context, while it may in another.

It is clear that Paul's approach is profoundly liberating, implying new freedoms for women. Spiritual gifts, Paul insists, are not bestowed on the basis of gender, race, or class. Whatever gifts God has bestowed must be recognized and put to use. But Paul is clearly aware that this universalization will raise problems in terms of its practical application in matters of church life and within Christian families. His letters therefore include discussion of a number of sensitive areas, which I propose to deal with. Both the passages in question are drawn from Paul's letters to Corinth.

It must be stressed that the Corinthian situation appears to have been especially difficult, with the issue of personal freedom emerging as being of major importance. Paul is obliged to lay down limits to Christian freedom, particularly in relation to spiritual gifts, in order to prevent the church from degenerating into chaos, or hindering the spread of the gospel by scandalizing people for cultural, not theological, reasons.

A passage which is often singled out for discussion in relation to this question is 1 Corinthians 11:2–16, which raises the issue of whether women should cover their heads in public worship. The passage in question is notoriously difficult to interpret, largely because we do not know enough about the Corinthian church, or local Corinthian culture, to be sure that we have understood Paul's point. There seems to be no explanation forthcoming from modern scholars as to why Paul regards it as obvious that men should have their heads uncovered, and women their heads covered, at worship. One suggestion has been that a woman with an uncovered head might have been mistaken for a prostitute. In that Corinth was noted as a center of prostitution, partly on account of the fact that it was a port, it is possible that this explanation would make sense of Paul's recommendation. However, there is not enough evidence to support this contention. Nor is it clear quite why he regards it as obvious that men should cut their hair shorter than women.

The issue of length of hair is generally thought to relate to pagan religious beliefs and practices, which Paul would have wished to forbid in his congregation. For example, a number of scholars have pointed out that, within contemporary Corinthian culture, hair style or length was a sign of sexual or religious practices. Long hair for a man could indicate homosexuality, as could short hair on a women. Equally, disheveled hair on the part of a woman was often linked with the ecstatic mystery cults, such as the frenzied rituals associated with the Isis cult. If this is the case, we are dealing with recommendations from Paul which are grounded in the particularities of the Corinthian situation of the time, and which need not be regarded as binding upon Christians for all time. Paul's recommendations would seem to relate to local Corinthian circumstances, which no longer apply.

On the basis of what has been said, it is clear that the Christian gospel gave a new status to women, as it did to others (such as Gentiles and slaves) who had hitherto been regarded as marginalized within Judaism. However, there was, as we have seen, a genuine tension between these new attitudes and values and the generally patriarchal structure of family and society in the first century. The New Testament is not revolutionary, in the sense that it does not make demands for a radical and violent overthrow of the existing order of things. Rather, it lays the foundations for a new set of attitudes which, if generally accepted, would have transformed society.

But how could the church get those values accepted in a society which was clearly not ready to receive them? To get society to accept Christian values and attitudes, society had first to be made Christian. This meant that evangelism was seen as a priority. Yet evangelism, then as now, had to proceed by ensuring that people outside the church were not unnecessarily scandalized. The acceptance of the gospel itself was prior to the acceptance of the new values which it embodied. As a result, there is a tension between the theological affirmation of the equality of all, and the apologetic recognition of divergence and diversity.

Many scholars have noted how Christianity was treated with contempt by educated Romans and Greeks in its first two centuries. In order to gain any kind of hearing for the good news of the gospel, at least some degree of cultural accommodation was necessary. The early Christians chose not to dilute the gospel message, but attempted to demonstrate the social acceptability of Christianity. Inevitably, this meant bringing Christian attitudes towards women more into line with those which prevailed in the wider community. By the end of the fourth century, such social pressures seem to have led to the neglect, or perhaps even suppression, of the ministerial roles of women within the church. But this is to be regarded as a response to a set of specific historical circumstances encountered during this early period in the development of the church, rather than something which is permanently binding on all Christians.

The expansion of the gospel: Paul

The gospel had its origins in Palestine – a backwater of the vast Roman empire. However, despite these somewhat unpromising credentials, it spread rapidly throughout the Roman empire. One of the most important agents of this development was the Jewish leader once known as "Saul of Tarsus," now known as "Paul." We possess two significant sources for Paul's life: the letters written by Paul himself, and the Acts of the Apostles, compiled by Luke. These two sources are notably different. Paul's primary concern in his letters is to establish his credentials as an apostle. In affirming that God has called both Jews and Gentiles to be equal partners in the Christian faith, Paul often finds it appropriate to emphasize his Jewish pedigree and in particular his high standing within Judaism as a Pharisee. For example, in defending the view that Christians are under no obligation to be circumcised, Paul appeals to his earlier period as a zealous defender of Jewish traditions. He knew their value and importance; he was now, however, convinced that they had been superseded by the new revelation through Christ.

Paul particularly draws attention to the radical changes in values and outlook which he experienced as a result of his conversion, but gives little historical detail concerning the manner in which this conversion took place. Luke's account, however, is told from the standpoint of the overall development of Christianity in the first two or three decades after the crucifixion and resurrection of Jesus of Nazareth. Luke brings out the way in which there is a close connection between the conversion or calling of Paul and the origins of the mission to the Gentiles, while providing historical details concerning the conversion itself.

There are five explicit references to this "conversion" or "calling" of Paul in the New Testament (Acts 9:1–19; 22:1–21; 26:2–23;

Galatians 1:11–17; Philippians 3:3–17). Of the three accounts in Acts, two take the form of statements by Paul in defense of his activities, in which he relates his personal narrative to his critics (in one case, a Jewish audience; in the other, King Agrippa). Both statements highlight Paul's Jewish background, and show a clear concern to address Jewish sensitivities. The first account takes the form of a historical narrative, relating the events which took place on the road to Damascus. It is this account (Acts 9:1–19) which has had the greatest impact on Christian thinking.

This narrative tells of how Paul originally bore the name of "Saul." He had established a reputation as a zealous persecutor of the church in Palestine during its initial period of growth. (Paul elsewhere mentions that he was a Pharisee, an established teacher of the Jewish law.) As he travels to the city of Damascus, in order to extend his persecutions of Christians in the region, he experiences a vision of Jesus of Nazareth. This is then interpreted by Ananias, a Christian at Damascus, in terms of a divine commissioning to be an apostle to the Gentiles. It must be noted that this account places its emphasis more on the theme of "calling" than of "conversion." The impact of the experience relates to its significance for Paul's mission rather than to his personal experience, although a link between the two is clearly assumed.

The narrative now shifts to the realization of this calling to be an apostle to the Gentiles. Acts subsequently records three major missionary journeys undertaken by Paul, and hints at a fourth. Paul's first missionary journey (described in Acts 13:4–15:35) would probably have taken place at some time around AD 46–48. At this stage, Paul would probably have been around 44 years old. Some fourteen years had passed since his conversion, during which time he had been occupied primarily with missionary work in the region

of Syria. Paul and Barnabas are joined by John Mark, more usually known as Mark, and generally thought to have been the author of the gospel now known by his name. In 46 these three companions set out on their way to the south coast of Asia Minor, a region of the northeastern Mediterranean coast which constitutes modern-day Turkey. Their journey initially takes them to the island of Cyprus, and subsequently to Iconium, Lystra, and Derbe in the region of Galatia. Paul established small Christian communities in the area, before revisiting those he had already planted as he traced his steps back to Antioch.

Paul's second missionary journey (described in Acts 15:36–18:22) was undertaken in the aftermath of the Council of Jerusalem, which had given equal status to Jews and Gentiles within the church. The first stage of the journey took them overland once more to Galatia, where they are joined by Timothy, who will become one of Paul's most trusted colleagues. They then proceeded to Troas, at the northwestern tip of Asia Minor, close to the site of the ancient city of Troy. There they are joined by Luke himself, who is generally regarded as a primary source for many of the accounts relating to this part of the journey (notice the use of "we" in many of the reports from this section). Crossing the Aegean Sea, they landed in the area of Macedonia, where they spent some time in the city of Philippi, a major Roman colony.

The visit to Philippi was of especial importance on account of its symbolic role. For the first time, the Christian gospel was preached on the continent of Europe. After establishing a church in the city, to which he would later write, Paul and his companions moved on to the region of Thessalonica, further south. Here, Paul may have taken temporary employment as a tentmaker to support himself while undertaking missionary work in the region.

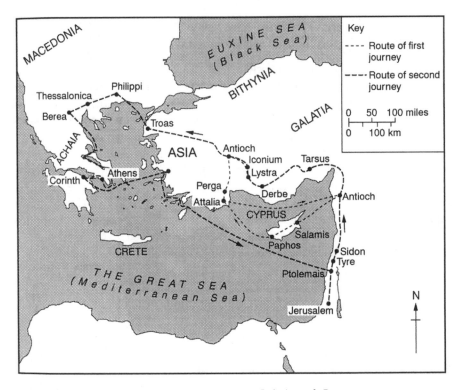

Map 7.1 Paul's first and second missionary journeys to Galatia and Greece.

As a result of his preaching in the local synagogue (17:1–9), a church was established (to which he would later write his two earliest letters, 1 Thessalonians and 2 Thessalonians).

From there, they moved on to Athens, still widely regarded as the intellectual center of the ancient world (Acts 17:15–34). The city had a reputation for its short-lived interest in the latest ideas and intellectual fashion, and appears to have seen in Paul the course of some exciting new ideas. It was here that Paul delivered his famous address on the Areopagus, or "Mars Hill," in which he argued that Christianity put a name to the god whose existence ancient philosophy had recognized. There is no letter from Paul to the Athenians; it seems that no church was founded in this city. But in the port city of Corinth, further south, Paul gained a much more sympathetic

hearing (Acts 18:1–28). Corinth was a huge seaport, with many openings for evangelism within the local Jewish community, as well as within the vastly larger Gentile population. Paul stayed there for eighteen months. It was clearly an important time in his ministry. Encouraged by the reports of church growth in the region of Macedonia, Paul wrote both his letters to the Thessalonian Christians.

At some point in AD 53, Paul set off from Corinth on his third missionary journey, described in Acts 18:23–21:17. His visit to the city of Ephesus was of particular importance. At the time of his visit, the city was a stronghold of pagan superstition, centering on the goddess Diana. As a result of Paul's visit to the city, a church was established, which seems to have acted as a crucial resource for the evangelization of the region in later years.

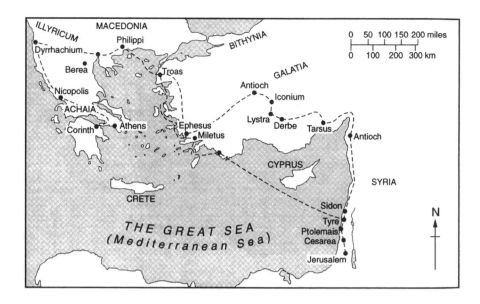

Map 7.2 Paul's third missionary journey in the Aegean Sea.

Paul's letters are fascinating for many reasons. Not only do they provide us with an understanding of the fundamental ideas of early Christianity, and their importance to the Christian communities, but also his personal comments and casual greetings to those he knows offer important insights into how the gospel was developing and spreading. Paul's references to women are of especial interest. For example, he greets Prisca, Junia, Julia, and the sister of Nereus, who worked and traveled as missionaries in pairs, either with their husbands or with their brothers (Romans 16:3, 7, 15). He praises Junia as a prominent apostle, who had been imprisoned for her activities. Mary and Persis are commended for their hard work (Romans 16:6, 12), and Euodia and Syntyche are called his fellow-workers in the gospel (Philippians 4:2–3).

We can also gain some insight into how the early Christian communities worshipped, and how they were organized. One of the most intriguing aspects of Paul's letters is the refer-

ence he makes to women in leadership roles within the house churches that were then springing up. This pattern is already evident in some of the historical material found elsewhere in the New Testament – such as Lydia of Thyatira (Acts 16:15). In Paul's letters, we read of others in such positions of leadership, such as Apphia (Philemon 2), Prisca (1 Corinthians 16:19), and Nympha of Laodicea (Colossians 4:15).

The expansion of the gospel: Rome

Rome was the administrative center of the empire which embraced the whole Mediterranean region. Indeed, the Romans tended to refer to the Mediterranean as "Mare Nostrum" – "our sea." Judaea was part of this vast empire – and a rather insignificant part at that. Although the languages spoken in this region of the empire were Aramaic (a language closely related to Hebrew) and Greek, Latin was used for administrative purposes. John's gospel makes reference to the charge against Jesus, to the effect that he claimed to be "king of the Jews," being written in all three languages (John 19:19–20). In many paintings and representations of the crucifixion, this inscription is shown by four letters: INRI – the initial letters of the Latin phrase *Iesus Nazarenus Rex Iudaeorum*, meaning "Jesus of Nazareth, King of the Jews."

It is clear that Greek was the first language of the early Christians. It is no accident that the entire New Testament was written in an everyday form of Greek (usually referred to as *koine*). Yet Christianity is soon a presence at Rome. There is evidence that Mark's gospel may have been written in Rome at some point around 64, on the eve of Nero's persecution of Christians in the city. (Mark 12:42 notes that two copper coins make one *quadrans*, a coin not in circulation in the eastern part of the empire. Similarly, Mark 15:16 explains that a Greek word corresponds to the Latin *praetorium*.) Paul's letter to the Romans, dating from around 57, refers to a number of individuals with Latin names, such as Urbanus, Aquila, Rufus, and Julia. Yet the letter is written in Greek! So how could a Greek-speaking movement gain such acceptance in a Latin-speaking city?

The answer is quite simple. Many Romans knew Greek. Huge numbers of Greek-speaking immigrants from the eastern regions of the empire had made their home in Rome, to the irritation of many indigenous Romans. Seneca is one of many Roman writers to complain about the vast numbers of immigrants in his city, and the cultural disruption which they caused. To speak Greek was, in the eyes of many Romans, a sign of being an immigrant, and hence of lower social status.

However, the situation was more complex than this. Many educated Romans cultivated the study of Greek as a result of their interest in Greek philosophy and poetry. To be able to speak the refined Greek of the philosophers and poets (as opposed to the common Greek of the masses) was a sign of cultural accomplishment. Claudius, the emperor who was responsible for the expulsion of large numbers of Jews (along with some Jewish Christians) from Rome in 49, spoke both Latin and Greek; indeed, he even attempted to modify the Latin alphabet, adding three new letters based on Greek originals.

It was therefore relatively easy for Greek-speaking Christians to gain a hearing at Rome. The evidence indicates that the movement had acquired a considerable following by the end of the century, although a significant Christian literature in Latin only begins to emerge in the following century.

The consolidation of Christianity

As we have seen, Christianity had its origins in Palestine – more specifically, the region of Judaea, especially the city of Jerusalem. Christianity regarded itself as a continuation and development of Judaism, and initially flourished in regions with which Judaism was traditionally associated, supremely Palestine. However, it rapidly spread to neighboring regions, partially through the efforts of early Christian evangelists such as Paul of Tarsus. By the end of the first century, Christianity appears to have become established throughout the eastern Mediterranean world, and even to have gained a significant presence in the city of Rome, the capital of the Roman empire. As the church at Rome became increasingly powerful, tensions began to develop between the Christian leadership at Rome and at Constantinople, foreshadowing the later schism between the western and eastern churches concentrated in these respective centers of power.

In the course of this expansion, a number of regions emerged as significant centers of

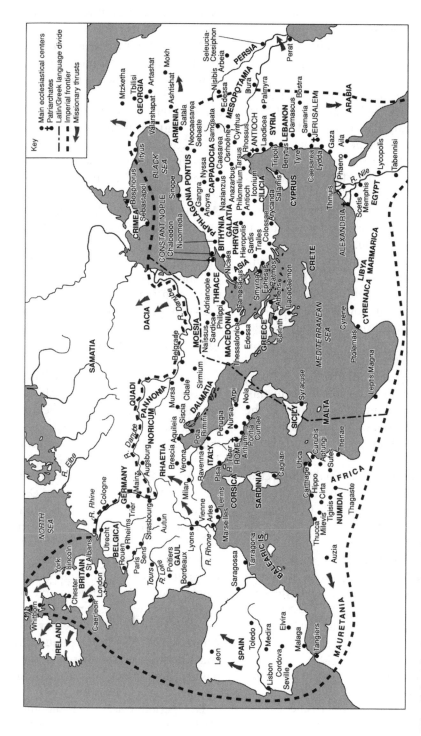

Map 7.3 The Roman empire and the church in the fourth century.

Key
- Main ecclesiastical centers
- † Patriarchates
- Latin/Greek language divide
- Imperial frontier
- Missionary thrusts

IRELAND

BRITAIN
Whithorn
York
Lincoln
Chester
Caerleon
St Albans
London

NORTH SEA

R. Elbe

SAMATIA

GERMANY
Cologne
Rheims
Trier
Mainz
Strasbourg
Augsburg
R. Rhine
R. Danube

BELGICA
Utrecht
Rouen
Paris
Sens

GAUL
Tours
Poitiers
Bordeaux
Autun
Vienne
Lyons
Arles
Marseilles
Lerins

R. Loire
R. Rhone

SPAIN
Leon
Toledo
Medira
Cordova
Seville
Malaga
Elvira
Saragossa
Tarragona
Lisbon

BALEARIC IS.

MAURETANIA
Tangiers
Auzia

QUADI

PANNONIA
NORICUM
RHAETIA
Brescia
Aquileia
Mursa
Siscia
Cibale
Sirmium
Belgrade

DACIA

R. Danube

MOESIA
Naissus
Sardica
Adrianople
Philippi

DALMATIA
Pola
Ravenna
Rimini

ITALY
ROME
Milan
Verona
Pisa
Perugia
Nursia
Arpi
Nola
Antium
Pontia
Cumae
R. Tiber

CORSICA

SARDINIA
Cagliari

SICILY
Syracuse

MALTA

AFRICA
Utica
Carthage
Hippo
Cirta
Curubis
Sufes
Thenae

NUMIDIA
Thucca
Milevis
Tigisis
Thagaste

Lepcis Magna

MEDITERRANEAN SEA

MACEDONIA
Thessalonica
Edessa

GREECE
Corinth
Athens
Lacedaemon

CRETE

CYRENAICA
Cyrene
Ptolemais

LIBYA

MARMARICA

THRACE

BLACK SEA

CONSTANTINOPLE
Chalcedon
Nicomedia
Nicaea

CRIMEA
Bosphorus
Sébastopol
Tityus
Sinope

PAPHLAGONIA
PONTUS
Gangra
Neocaesarea
Sebaste
Satala

BITHYNIA

PHRYGIA
Hieropolis
Sardis
Tralles
Colossae
Philomelium

GALATIA
Ancyra
Nyssa
Nazianzus

CAPPADOCIA
Caesarea
Anazarbus
Samosata
Osrhoëne

ASIA
Smyrna
Ephesus
Patmos
Stampsacus

CILICIA
Iconium
Anatarbus
Tarsus
Antioch

GEORGIA
Mtzketha
Tbilisi
Artashat

ARMENIA
Valarshapat
Ashtishat
Mokh

PERSIA
Perat
Arbeia
Seleucia-Ctesiphon

MESOPOTAMIA
Edessa
Nisibis
Dura
Palmyra

SYRIA
† ANTIOCH
Rhossus
Cyrrhus
Laodicea
Tripoli
Berytus
Tyre

LEBANON
Damascus
Samaria
Bostra

† JERUSALEM
Caesarea
Salamis
Lydda
Gaza
Aila

ARABIA

CYPRUS

EGYPT
† ALEXANDRIA
Memphis
Scetis
Phaeno
Thmuis
Lycopolis
Tabennisi
R. Nile

theological debate. Three may be singled out as having especial importance, the first two of which were Greek-speaking, and the third Latin-speaking.

1 The city of Alexandria, in modern-day Egypt, which emerged as a center of Christian theological education. A distinctive style of theology came to be associated with this city, reflecting its long-standing association with the Platonic tradition. The political importance of this great cosmopolitan city was such that it was of major significance as a center for Christian mission and education.

2 The city of Antioch and the surrounding region of Cappadocia, in modern-day Turkey. A strong Christian presence came to be established in this northern region of the eastern Mediterranean at an early stage. As we have already seen, Paul's missionary journeys often involved church planting in this region, and Antioch features significantly at several points in the history of the very early church, as recorded in the Acts of the Apostles. Antioch itself soon became a leading center of Christian thought.

3 Western north Africa, especially the area of modern-day Algeria. In the late classical period, this was the site of Carthage, a major Mediterranean city and at one time a political rival to Rome for dominance in the region. During the period when Christianity expanded in this area, it was a Roman colony. Major Christian writers active in this region include Tertullian, Cyprian of Carthage, and Augustine of Hippo.

This is not to say that other cities in the Mediterranean were devoid of significance. Rome, Constantinople, Milan, and Jerusalem were also centers of Christian theological reflection, even if none was destined to achieve quite the importance of its rivals.

The period during which Christianity established itself as a dominant religious force in the Mediterranean region is usually referred to as "the patristic period." The term "patristic" comes from the Latin word *pater*, "father," and designates both the period of the church fathers and the distinctive ideas which came to develop within this period. The term "patristic period" is rather vaguely defined, but is usually often taken to refer to the period from the closing of the New Testament writings (ca. 100) to the definitive Council of Chalcedon (451). However, many scholars argue that the term ought to be used in a broader sense, and include developments up to about 750. A third term which is often encountered in the literature is "patristics," which is usually understood to mean the branch of theological study which deals with the study of "the fathers."

The patristic period is one of the most exciting and creative periods in the history of Christian life and thought. This feature alone is enough to ensure that it will continue to be the subject of study for many years to come. The period is also of importance for theological reasons. Every mainstream Christian body – including the Anglican, eastern Orthodox, Lutheran, Reformed, and Roman Catholic churches – regards the patristic period as a definitive landmark in the development of Christian doctrine. Each of these churches regards itself as continuing, extending, and, where necessary, criticizing the views of the early church writers. For example, the leading seventeenth-century Anglican writer Lancelot Andrewes (1555–1626) declared that orthodox Christianity was based upon two testaments, three creeds, four gospels, and the first five centuries of Christian history.

The period was of crucial importance in clarifying a number of issues. A task of initial significance was sorting out the relationship between Christianity and Judaism. The letters of Paul in the New Testament bear witness to the importance of this issue in the first century of Christian history, as a series of doctrinal and practical questions came to the fore. Should Gentile (that is, non-Jewish) Christians be obliged to be circumcised? How was the Old Testament to be correctly interpreted?

However, other issues soon emerged. One which was of especial importance in the second century is that of *apologetics* – the reasoned defense and justification of the Christian faith against its critics. During the first period of Christian history, the church was often persecuted by the state. Its agenda was that of survival; there was limited place for theological disputes when the very existence of the Christian church could not be taken for granted. This observation helps us understand why apologetics came to be of such importance to the early church, through writers such as Justin Martyr (ca. 100–ca. 165), concerned to explain and defend the beliefs and practices of Christianity to a hostile pagan public. Although this early period produced some outstanding theologians – such as Irenaeus of Lyons (ca. 130–ca. 200) in the west, and Origen (ca. 185–ca. 254) in the east – theological debate could only begin in earnest once the church had ceased to be persecuted.

Those persecutions were often extremely violent. In August 177, many Christians were martyred by pagans in the city of Lyons, in southern Gaul. Their bodies were burned and thrown into the River Rhône, in the belief that this would prevent them from being raised from the dead. Among them was Blandina, a slave girl. In March 202, two women were martyred at Carthage. Perpetua and Felicitas – the former with a newly born son, and the latter being pregnant – were martyred for refusing to offer sacrifices to the emperor.

One of the most serious of these persecutions was undertaken in North Africa by the emperor Decius. The Decian persecution ended in June 251, when Decius was killed on a military expedition. The persecution led to many Christians lapsing or abandoning their faith. Division arose immediately within the church over how these individuals should be treated: did such a lapse mark the end of their faith, or could they be reconciled to the church by penance? Opinions differed sharply, and serious disagreement and tension resulted. Very different views were promoted by Cyprian of Carthage and Novatian. Both of these writers were martyred during the persecution instigated by the emperor Valerian in 257–258.

One of the most severe outbursts of persecution came about in February 303, under the emperor Diocletian. An edict was issued ordering the destruction of all Christian places of worship, the surrender and destruction of all their books, and the cessation of all acts of Christian worship. Christian civil servants were to lose all privileges of rank or status and reduced to the status of slaves. Prominent Christians were forced to offer sacrifice according to traditional Roman practices. It is an indication of how influential Christianity had become that Diocletian forced both his wife and daughter, who were known to be Christians, to comply with this order. The persecution continued under successive emperors, including Galerius, who ruled the eastern region of the empire.

In 311, Galerius ordered the cessation of the persecution. It had been a failure, and had merely hardened Christians in their resolve to resist the reimposition of classical Roman pagan religion. Galerius issued an edict which permitted Christians to live normally again and "hold their religious assemblies, provided that they do nothing which would disturb public order." The edict explicitly identified

Christianity as a religion, and offered it the full protection of the law. The legal status of Christianity, which had been ambiguous up to this point, was now resolved. The church no longer existed under a siege mentality.

Christianity was now a legal religion; it was, however, merely one among many such religions. The conversion of the emperor Constantine changed this irreversibly, and brought about a complete transformation in the situation of Christianity throughout the Roman empire. Constantine was born to pagan parents in 285. (His mother would eventually become a Christian, apparently through her son's influence.) Although he showed no particular attraction to Christianity in his early period, Constantine certainly seems to have regarded toleration as an essential virtue. Following Maxentius' seizure of power in Italy and North Africa, Constantine led a body of troops from western Europe in an attempt to gain authority in the region. The decisive battle took place on October 28, 312 at the Milvian Bridge, to the north of Rome. Constantine defeated Maxentius, and was proclaimed emperor. At some point shortly afterwards, he declared himself to be a Christian.

This point is affirmed by both Christian and pagan writers. What is not clear is precisely why or when this conversion took place. Some Christian writers (such as Lactantius and Eusebius) suggest that the conversion may have occurred before the decisive battle, with Constantine seeing a heavenly vision ordering him to place the sign of the cross on his soldier's shields. Whatever the reasons for the conversion, and whether it dates from before or after the battle of Milvian Bridge, the reality and consequences of this conversion are not in doubt. Gradually, Rome became Christianized. On his own instructions, the statue of the emperor erected in the Forum depicts Constantine bearing a cross – "the sign of suffering that brought salvation," according to the inscrip-

7.2 Constantine, the first Christian Roman emperor. AKG-Images/Nimatallah.

tion provided by Constantine. In 321, Constantine decreed that Sundays should become public holidays. Christian symbols began to appear on Roman coins. Christianity was now more than just legitimate; it was on its way to becoming the established religion of the empire.

As a result, constructive theological debate became a public affair. Apart from a brief period of uncertainty during the reign of Julian the Apostate (361–363), the church could now count upon the support of the state. Theology thus emerged from the hidden world of secret church meetings to become a topic of public interest and concern throughout the

Roman empire. Increasingly, doctrinal debates became a matter of both political and theological importance. Constantine wished to have a united church throughout his empire, and was thus concerned that doctrinal differences should be debated and settled as a matter of priority.

The later patristic period (from about 310 to 451) can therefore rightly be regarded as a high water mark in the history of Christian theology. Theologians now enjoyed the freedom to work without the threat of persecution, and were able to address a series of issues of major importance to the consolidation of the emerging theological consensus within the churches. That consensus involved extensive debate, and a painful learning process in which the church discovered that it had to come to terms with disagreements and continuing tensions. Nonetheless, a significant degree of consensus, eventually to be enshrined in the ecumenical creeds, can be discerned as emerging within this formative period.

Theological debates of the early Christian period

The patristic period saw a number of major disputes developing within the church. Three can be singled out as being of particular importance to the development of Christian theology. The three debates were:

1   *The Donatist controversy.* This debate centered on Roman North Africa, particularly the region around Carthage. Christians in this region suffered particularly during the Diocletian persecution. Such was the ferocity of the persecution that many Christians, including some senior church figures, collaborated with the Roman authorities, in the hope that the storm would pass and they could get back to a normal way of life. Others fiercely resisted the persecution. As a result, controversy developed within the church over the treatment of those who had compromised their principles during the persecution. One group, which centered on the figure of Donatus, took a hard line. No compromise could be permitted. Clergy who had collaborated in any way during the persecution could not be readmitted within the church. This controversy, which became particularly important during the fourth century, forced the western church to give careful thought to two areas of Christian doctrine – the doctrine of the church and the doctrine of the sacraments (see pp. 154–162).

2   *The Arian controversy.* This controversy broke out in the eastern section of the church during the fourth century. It focused on Arius, based in the Egyptian city of Alexandria. Arius argued that Jesus Christ could not be described as being fully divine. Rather, Jesus was to be thought of as supreme among God's creatures. Arius met stiff resistance from various opponents, especially Athanasius. The resulting dispute became so serious that the unity of the Roman empire was threatened. As a result, the emperor Constantine convened a council of 220 bishops at the city of Nicaea in Asia Minor. He demanded that they settle the issue. The Council of Nicaea decided against Arius, and affirmed that Jesus Christ was "of one substance" with God – in other words, that Jesus was both human and divine. This doctrine, which is generally referred to as "the doctrine of the two natures" (see pp. 139–143), is of particular importance to Christian thought.

3   *The Pelagian controversy.* This debate broke out in the final years of the fourth century, and continued into the first two decades of the fifth century. The basic question under

debate was the respective roles played by God and humanity in salvation. Does God have the upper hand? Or do we? Is salvation something which is given to us by God? Or is it something which we earn or merit by our good works? Such questions caused significant divisions within the church at the time, and would become controversial once more during the sixteenth century (see pp. 150–154).

The origins of monasticism

One of the most important developments to take place during the patristic period was the development of monasticism. The origins of the movement are generally thought to lie in remote hilly areas of Egypt and parts of eastern Syria. Significant numbers of Christians began to make their homes in these regions, in order to get away from the population centers, with all the distractions that these offered. One such person was Anthony of Egypt, who left his parents' home in 273 to seek out a life of discipline and solitude in the desert.

The theme of withdrawal from a sinful and distracting world became of central importance to these communities. While some lone figures insisted on the need for individual isolation, the concept of a communal life in isolation from the world gained the ascendancy. One important early monastery was founded by Pachomius during the years 320–325. This monastery developed an ethos which would become normative in later monasticism. Members of the community agreed to submit themselves to a common life which was regulated by a rule, under the direction of a superior. The physical structure of the monastery was significant: the complex was surrounded by a wall, highlighting the idea of separation and withdrawal from the world. The Greek word

koin_ōnia (often translated as "fellowship"), frequently used in the New Testament, now came to refer to the idea of a common corporate life, characterized by common clothing, meals, furnishing of cells (as the monks' rooms were known), and manual labor for the good of the community.

The monastic ideal proved to have a deep attraction for many. By the fourth century, monasteries had been established in many locations in the Christian east, especially in the

7.3 Saint Augustine of Hippo in a monastic cell, as depicted by Sandro Botticelli, ca. 1495. AKG-Images/Rabatti-Domingie.

regions of Syria and Asia Minor. It was not long before the movement was taken up in the western church. By the fifth century, monastic communities had come into existence in Italy (especially along the western coastline), Spain, and Gaul. Augustine of Hippo, one of the leading figures of the western church at this time, established two monasteries in North Africa at some point during the period 400–425. For Augustine, the common life (now designated by the Latin phrase *vita communis*) was essential to the realization of the Christian ideal of love. He supplemented this emphasis on community life with an appreciation of the importance of intellectual activity and spiritual study.

During the sixth century, the number of monasteries in the region grew considerably. It was during this period that one of the most comprehensive monastic "rules" – the "Rule of Benedict" – made its appearance. Benedict of Nursia (ca. 480–ca. 550) established his monastery at Monte Cassino at some point around 525. The Benedictine community followed a rule which was dominated by the notion of the unconditional following of Christ, sustained by regular corporate and private prayer, and the reading of Scripture. Benedict's sister, Scholastica, was also active in the monastic movement.

The rise of Celtic Christianity

The rise of Christianity in the Celtic regions of Europe – more specifically, Ireland, Scotland, Cornwall, Brittany, and Wales – is of considerable interest, not least in that this form of Christianity found itself in opposition to the more Romanized forms which rapidly gained the ascendancy in England. Although the origins of Celtic Christianity seem to lie in Wales, it is Ireland which established itself as a missionary

7.4   The abbey of Monte Cassino. AKG-Images/Pirozzi.

center of distinction in the fifth and sixth centuries. Other centers of missionary activity in the Celtic sphere of influence are known from this period, most notably Candida Casa (modern-day Whithorn, in the Galloway region of Scotland), which was established by Bishop Ninian in the fifth century. The significance of this missionary station was that it lay outside the borders of Roman Britain, and was thus able to operate without the restrictions then associated with Roman forms of Christianity.

The person who is traditionally held to be responsible for the evangelization of Ireland was a Romanized Briton by the name of Magonus Sucatus Patricius, more usually known by his Celtic name "Patrick" (ca. 390–ca. 460). Born into a wealthy family, Patrick was taken captive by a raiding party at the age of 16, and sold into slavery in Ireland, probably in the region of Connaught. Here, he appears to have discovered the basics of the Christian faith, before escaping and making his way back to his family. He had been in captivity for six years. It is not clear precisely what happened between Patrick's escape from captivity and his subsequent return to Ireland as a missionary. A tradition, dating back to the seventh or eighth century, refers to Patrick spending time in Gaul before his return to Ireland. It is possible that some of Patrick's views on church organization and structures may reflect first-hand acquaintance with the monasticism of certain regions of southern France. There is excellent historical evidence for trading links between Ireland and the Loire Valley around this time.

At any rate, Patrick returned to Ireland, and established Christianity in the region. It is clear that some form of Christianity already existed. Not only does Patrick's conversion account presuppose that others in the region knew about the gospel; contemporary records dating from as early as 429 also speak of one Palladius as the bishop of Ireland, indicating that at least some form of rudimentary ecclesiastical structures existed in the region. Irish representatives are also known to have been present at the Synod of Arles (314). Patrick's achievement is perhaps best understood in terms of the consolidation and advancement of Christianity, rather than its establishment in the first place.

The monastic idea took hold very quickly in Ireland. Historical sources indicate that Ireland was largely a nomadic and tribal society at this time, without any permanent settlements of any importance. The monastic quest for solitude and isolation was ideally suited to the Irish way of life. Whereas in western Europe as a whole monasticism was marginalized within the life of the church, in Ireland it rapidly became its dominant form. It is no exaggeration to say that the Irish church was monastic, with the abbot rather than the bishop being seen as preeminent.

The authority structures which emerged within Celtic Christianity were thus rather different to those which came to dominate the Roman British church at this time. The Irish monastic model came to be seen as a threat to the Roman model of the episcopate, in which the government of the church resided firmly in the hands of the bishops. None of the abbots of Iona ever allowed bishops to formally ordain them, rejecting the need for any such "official" recognition. In Ireland, some of the older bishoprics (including Ramah) were reorganized on a monastic basis, with others being absorbed by monasteries. Abbeys were responsible for the pastoral care of the churches which grew up in their vicinity. The Roman episcopal system was thus marginalized. The Celtic church leaders were openly critical of worldly wealth and status, including the use of horses as a mode of transport, and any form of luxury. Theologically, Celtic Christianity also stressed the importance of the world of nature as a means of knowing God. This is especially clear from the ancient Irish hymn traditionally ascribed to Patrick, and known as "St. Patrick's Breastplate." The theme of a "breastplate" was common in Celtic Christian spirituality. It is based upon Paul's references to the "armor of God" (Ephesians 6:10–18), and develops the theme of the believer being protected by the presence of God and a whole range of associated powers. Although strongly Trinitarian in its structure, it shows a fascination with the natural world as a means of knowing God. The God who made the world is the same God who will protect Christians from all dangers.

The Irish monasteries acted as centers for missionary activity, often using sea lanes as channels for the transmission of Christianity. Brendan (d. ca. 580) and Columba (d. ca. 597) are excellent examples of this type of missionary. In a poem entitled "The Navigation of St. Brendan" (ca. 1050), Brendan is praised for his journeys to the "northern and western isles" (usually assumed to be the Orkneys and Hebrides, off the coast of Scotland). Columba brought Christianity from the north of Ireland to the western isles of Scotland, and established the abbey of Iona as a missionary outpost. From there, Christianity spread southwards and eastwards. Aidan (d. 651) is an outstanding example of a monk from Iona who acted as a missionary in this way. At the invitation of the king of the region of Northumbria, he established a missionary monastery on the island of Lindisfarne, off the east coast of northern England. Celtic Christianity began to penetrate into France, and become increasingly influential in the region.

The tensions between Celtic Christianity and its Roman rivals could not be ignored. Celtic Christianity threatened to undermine the episcopate, reduce the power of Rome, make it more difficult for Christianity to become culturally acceptable, and make monasticism the norm for Christian living. By 597, the ascend-

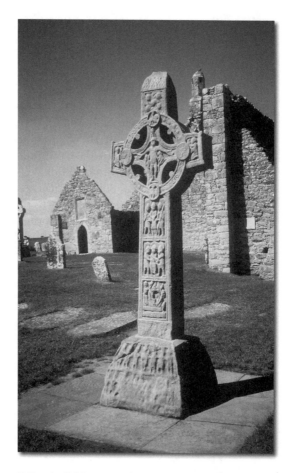

7.5 A Celtic cross from Ireland. AKG-Images/ Juergen Sorges.

ancy of the Celtic vision seemed inevitable. However, the following century saw a series of developments which led to its gradual eclipse outside its heartlands of Ireland. By a coincidence of history, the event which led to its eclipse took place in the very year of Columba's death. In 597, Augustine was sent to England by Pope Gregory to evangelize the English. As Roman forms of Christianity became established in England, tensions arose between northern and southern English Christians, the former remaining faithful to Celtic traditions, and the latter to Roman.

The northeastern English town of Streanae-shalch – later renamed "Whitby" – had risen to fame on account of the work of the Anglo-Saxon noblewoman Hild (614–680), who established an abbey and convent there in 657. The Synod of Whitby (664) is widely seen as establishing the dominance of Roman Christianity in England. Although the Synod focused on the question of when Easter should be celebrated (Celtic and Roman traditions differing on the issue), the real debate concerned the growing influence of the see of Canterbury. The Saxon invasions of England in the previous century had resulted in major cultural changes in the region, making inevitable the gradual erosion of Celtic culture, including its distinctive approach to Christianity.

The year 700 may be seen as marking the end of the growth of Celtic Christianity, and also a convenient point at which to pause this narrative briefly. A period of cultural and intellectual consolidation lay ahead, as what is now known as "the Middle Ages" began to dawn. We shall resume our account of the growth of Christianity by exploring this development.

The Middle Ages

By the fifth century, Christianity had begun to establish itself securely in the Mediterranean region. Five major centers emerged within the region, each of which served as the nucleus of groups of churches: Alexandria, Antioch, Constantinople, Jerusalem, and Rome. These five centers, generally referred to as "patriarchates," were intended to be seen as equal partners within the church as a whole. In fact, however, there was a considerable degree of rivalry between them, with frequent jostling for position as the preeminent center of the Christian faith. The growing power of the Roman church was a cause of particular concern to the four eastern patriarchates.

Instability: The church in a period of uncertainty

An event of fundamental importance to the history of the church took place during this period. For a variety of reasons, relations between the eastern church, based at Constantinople, and the western, based at Rome, became increasingly strained during the ninth and tenth centuries. Growing disagreement over the wording of the Nicene Creed was of no small importance to this increasingly sour atmosphere. However, other factors contributed, including the political rivalry between Latin-speaking Rome and Greek-speaking Constantinople, and the increasing claims to authority of the Roman pope. The final break between the Catholic west and Orthodox east is usually dated to 1054; however, this date is slightly arbitrary.

The patristic period focused on the Mediterranean world, and centers of power such as Rome and Constantinople. Instability was widespread throughout the region during this period. The following developments were of particular importance in relation to this unstable situation.

1   *The fall of Rome.* The northern frontier of the Roman empire was more or less defined by the River Rhine. In 404, this frontier collapsed in the face of assault by "barbarians." Huge areas of the Roman empire were now under the control of the Franks, Goths, and Vandals. Rome itself was sacked twice, most notably by the forces of Alaric the Goth in 410. By 476, the western regions of the Roman empire were in ruins. The political stability of the region was eroded, with the result that

Christianity found itself facing a period of considerable uncertainty.

2 *The Arab invasions.* Islam became a significant religious movement amongst the Arab people in the seventh century. A program of conquest was initiated, which eventually led to Arab forces taking control of the entire coastal region of north Africa by about 750. Islamic forces also moved north, posing a serious threat to Constantinople itself. Arab forces laid siege to the city during the period 711–778, eventually being forced to withdraw. The enforcement of Islam in the conquered regions of the Holy Land led to intense concern in the western church, and was one of the factors which led to the crusades during the period 1095–1204.

By the eleventh century, a degree of stability had settled upon the region, with three major power groupings having emerged to take the place of the former Roman empire.

1 *Byzantium,* centered on the city of Constantinople (now Istanbul, in modern-day Turkey). The form of Christianity which predominated in this region was based on the Greek language, and was deeply rooted in the writings of patristic writers of the eastern Mediterranean region, such as Athanasius, the Cappadocians, and John of Damascus.

2 *Western Europe,* centered on regions such as France, Germany, the Lowlands, and northern Italy. The form of Christianity which came to dominate this region was centered on the city of Rome and its bishop, known as "the pope." (However, for the period known as the "Great Schism," some confusion developed: there were two rival claimants for the papacy, one based at Rome, the other at the southern French city of Avignon.) Here, theology came to focus on the great cathedral and university schools of Paris and elsewhere, based largely on the Latin writings of Augustine, Ambrose, and Hilary of Poitiers.

3 *The Caliphate,* an Islamic region embracing much of the extreme eastern and southern parts of the Mediterranean. The expansion of Islam continued, with the fall of Constantinople (1453) sending shock waves throughout much of Europe. By the end of the fifteenth century, Islam had established a significant presence in several regions of the continent of Europe, including Spain, parts of southern Italy, and the Balkans. This advance was eventually halted by the defeat of the Moors in Spain in the final decade of the fifteenth century, and the defeat of Islamic armies outside Vienna in 1523.

Nevertheless, the Islamic advance in Europe was consolidated through the Ottoman empire, which created pockets of Islamic populations in parts of southeastern Europe such as the Balkans. The history of Europe in the twentieth century showed the continuing influence of this important historical development.

Christianity in the east to the fall of Constantinople

The particular style of Christianity which flourished in the eastern region of the Roman empire is generally referred to as "Byzantine," taking its name from the Greek city of Byzantium, which Constantine chose as the site of his new capital city in 330. At this point, it was renamed "Constantinople" ("city of Constantine"). However, the name of the older town remained, lending itself to the distinctive type of Christianity which flourished in this region until the fall of Constantinople to invading Islamic armies in 1453. Constantinople was not the only center of Christian thought in the eastern Mediterranean. Egypt and Syria had been centers of theological reflection for some time. However, as political power increasingly came to be concentrated on the imperial city, so its status as a theological center advanced correspondingly.

Constantinople soon became a hub of missionary activity. At some point around the year 860, the Moravian ruler Rastislav asked the Byzantine emperor to send missionaries to his people in central Europe. Two Greek brothers, Cyril and Methodius, were sent in response to this request. This development was of particular importance to the formation of eastern European culture. Not only did it eventually lead to the dominance of Orthodoxy in the region of eastern Europe; it also had a major impact on the alphabets used in the region. Cyril devised an alphabet suitable for writing down the Slavic languages. This became the basis for the modern Cyrillic alphabet, named after the younger of the two "apostles of the Slavs." The conversion of Moravia was followed by that of Bulgaria and Serbia later that century. This was followed by the conversion of the Russians, at some point around the year 988, partly through the influence of Olga of Kiev (d. 969), widow of the great Ukrainian king Vladimir.

As the eastern and western churches became increasingly alienated from each other (a process which had begun long before the final schism of 1054), so Byzantine thinkers often emphasized their divergence from western theology (for example, in relation to the *filioque* clause: see p. 126), thus reinforcing the distinctiveness of their approach through polemical writings. For example, Byzantine writers tended to understand salvation in terms of *deification* rather than western legal or relational categories. Any attempt to achieve a degree of reunion between east and west during the Middle Ages was thus complicated by a complex network of political, historical, and theological factors. By the time of the fall of Constantinople, the differences between east and west remained as wide as ever. With the fall of Byzantium, intellectual and political leadership within Orthodoxy tended to pass to Russia. The Russians, who had been converted through Byzantine missions in the tenth century, took the side of the Greeks in the schism of 1054. By the end of the fifteenth century, Moscow and Kiev were firmly established as patriarchates, each with its own distinctive style of Orthodox Christianity, which remains of major significance today. Other regions which converted to Orthodoxy during this period include Serbia and Bulgaria.

It is clear that the flourishing of the eastern Orthodox church in Russia during the Middle Ages was of considerable importance to the shaping of Muscovite Russia. It is estimated that during the fourteenth, fifteenth, and sixteenth centuries, more than 250 monasteries and convents were established in the region. The monastic revival, under the guidance of leaders such as St. Sergius of Radonezh (d. 1392), gave further impetus to the missionary efforts of the Russian church. During the thirteenth century, for example, the Finnish-speaking peoples of the Karelia region were converted to Orthodoxy.

The fall of Constantinople in 1453 caused a major development within Russian Orthodoxy. Traditionally, each new metropolitan of the Russian church was installed by the patriarch of Constantinople, and looked to the Byzantine emperor (based in Constantinople) for its political leadership. The Russian church was very much a daughter of the Byzantine church. But with the fall of Constantinople, this traditional approach became a thing of the past. What could replace it? In the event, the eastern Orthodox church in Moscow became autocephalous — that is, self-governing. As a result, the political and cultural links between the Russian church and state became deeper. By 1523, the relation between church and state was so close that some writers began to refer to Moscow as the "Third Rome," to be treated with respect equal to Rome and Constantinople. Philotheus of Pskov proclaimed that, now that Rome and Byzantium had become corrupt, the leadership of the Christian world had passed to Moscow: "Two Romes have fallen; the third stands; there will be no fourth."

Two controversies are of particular importance within eastern Christianity during this period. The first of these, which broke out during the period 725–842, is usually referred to as the iconoclastic ("breaking of images") controversy. It erupted over the decision of emperor Leo III (717–742) to destroy icons, on the grounds that they were barriers to the conversion of Jews and Muslims. The controversy was mainly political, although there were some serious theological issues at stake, most notably the extent to which the doctrine of the incarnation justified the depiction of God in the form of images (see pp. 322–323). The second, which broke out in the fourteenth century, focused on the issue of hesychasm (Greek: *hesychia* = silence), a style of meditation through physical exercises which enabled believers to see the "divine light" with their own eyes. Hesychasm placed considerable emphasis upon the idea of "inner quietness" as a means of achieving a direct inner vision of God. It was particularly associated with writers such as Simeon the New Theologian and Gregory Palamas (ca. 1296–1359), who was elected as archbishop of Thessalonica in 1347. Its opponents argued that its methods tended to minimize the difference between God and creatures, and were particularly alarmed by the suggestion that God could be "seen."

The renewal of western Christianity

After the collapse of the western section of the Roman empire in the later fifth century, Christianity was forced to go through a period of reconstruction. Since the conversion of Constantine, the church could more or less rely on the support of the emperor. With the destruction of the western Roman empire, the church was suddenly exposed to uncertainty and instability. Christianity had become quite Roman in its culture and outlook; it now found itself having to adapt to a new environment in which Roman ideas and values carried little weight. Furthermore, Christianity had never really taken hold in the extreme regions of the empire. Its future in the regions seemed highly uncertain.

However, a program of consolidation and expansion began to get under way. Pope Gregory the Great encouraged missionary work in the outlying regions of the empire. As we noted above, Ireland had been converted to Christianity in the fifth century by Patrick and Palladius; it soon became a center for missionary activity in Wales and England. This was supplemented by missionary work undertaken by Augustine, with the support of the pope. As a result, two rather different styles of Christianity were established in England by the seventh century, one Celtic, the other Roman. This led to tensions – for example, over the date of Easter. These were largely resolved by the Synod of Whitby (664), which settled this particular debate.

With the conversion of England, a base was established for the evangelization of other northern European nations. Missionaries from England became active in Germany. Under the rule of Charlemagne (ca. 742–814), Christianity was given new institutional and social stability. The importance of Charlemagne in the consolidation of Christianity in western Europe was given formal recognition by the pope, who crowned him as the first "Holy Roman Emperor" on Christmas Day, 800. Although this coronation further strained relations between the eastern and western churches, it nevertheless gave Christianity a new authority in the western regions of Europe. Missionaries such as Boniface and Walburga, abbess of the monastery at Heidenheim, carried out significant missionary work in Germany. By the end of the first millennium, Christianity was more or less established as the dominant religion of much of the region. The scene was set for further consolidation and renewal.

The rise of scholasticism

An important aspect of the Christian renaissance of the period was a new flowering of interest in Christian theology. The period 1050–1350 saw a remarkable consolidation of Christian thought at the intellectual level. When the Dark Ages finally lifted from over western Europe, giving birth to the Middle Ages, the scene was set for revival in every field of academic work. The restoration of some degree of political stability in France in the late eleventh century encouraged the re-emergence of the University of Paris, which rapidly became recognized as the intellectual center of Europe. A number of theological "schools" were established on the Left Bank of the Seine, and on the Île de la Cité, in the

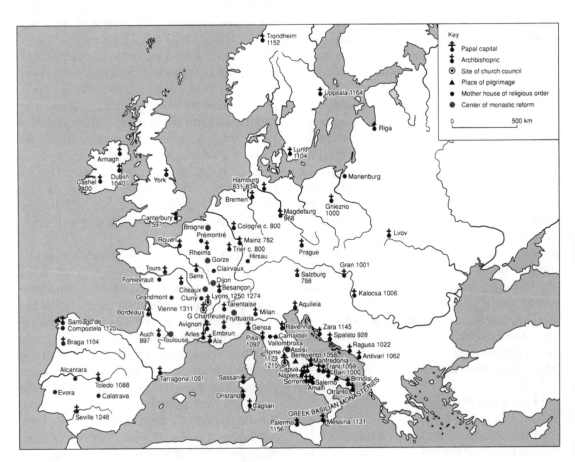

Map 7.4 Main ecclesiastical centers in western Europe during the Middle Ages.

shadow of the newly built cathedral of Notre Dame de Paris.

One such school was the Collège de la Sorbonne, which eventually achieved such fame that "the Sorbonne" came to be a shorthand way of referring to the University of Paris. Even in the sixteenth century, Paris was widely recognized as a leading center for theological and philosophical study, including among its students such names as Erasmus of Rotterdam and John Calvin. Other such centers of study were soon established elsewhere in Europe. A new program of theological development began, concerned with consolidating the intellectual, legal, and spiritual aspects of the life of the Christian church.

The early part of the medieval period is dominated by developments in France. Several monasteries produced outstanding Christian writers and thinkers. For example, the monastery at Bec, in Normandy, gave rise to such writers as Lanfranc (ca. 1010–1089) and Anselm (ca. 1033–1109). One of the most renowned figures of this period was the German nun and abbess Hildegard of Bingen (1098–1179), who wrote about music, art, medicine, natural history, spirituality, and theology. Her musical compositions are stilled played today.

The University of Paris soon established itself as a remarkable center of theological speculation, producing such leading writers as Peter Abelard (1079–1142), Albert the Great (ca. 1200–1280), Thomas Aquinas (ca. 1225–1274), and Bonaventure (ca. 1217–1274). The fourteenth and fifteenth centuries witnessed an expansion of the university sector in western Europe, with major new universities being founded in Germany and elsewhere.

A central resource for the new medieval interest in theology is also linked with Paris. At some point shortly before 1140, Peter Lombard arrived at the university to teach. One of his central concerns was to get his students to wrestle with the thorny issues of theology. His

7.6 Thomas Aquinas, from the series of portraits of famous men in the Palazzo Ducale in Urbino, ca. 1476, by Justus van Gent (active between 1460 and 1480). Paris, Musée du Louvre, AKG-Images/Erich Lessing.

contribution was a textbook – perhaps one of the most boring books that has ever been written. The *Four Books of the Sentences* brings together quotations from Scripture and the patristic writers, arranged topically. The task Peter set his students was simple: make sense of the quotes. The book proved to be of major importance in developing the Augustinian heritage, in that students were obliged to wrestle with the ideas of Augustine and reconcile apparently contradictory texts by devising suitable theological explanations of the inconsistencies. By 1215 the work was firmly established as the most important textbook of the age. It became obligatory for theologians to comment on the work. The resulting works, known as *Commentaries on the Sentences*, became one of the most familiar theological genres of the Middle Ages. Outstanding examples include those of Thomas Aquinas, Bonaventure, and Duns Scotus.

Perhaps the most critical intellectual development associated with this period was the rise of scholasticism. Scholasticism is best regarded as the medieval movement, flourishing in the period 1200–1500, which placed emphasis upon the rational justification of religious belief, and the systematic presentation of those beliefs. "Scholasticism" thus refers not to a *specific system of beliefs* but to a *particular way of organizing theology* – a highly developed method of presenting material, making fine distinctions and attempting to achieve a comprehensive view of theology. It is perhaps understandable why, to its humanist critics, scholasticism seemed to degenerate into little more than logical nit-picking. However, scholasticism may be argued to have made vitally important contributions to a number of key areas of Christian theology, especially in relation to the role of reason and logic in theology. The writings of Thomas Aquinas, Duns Scotus, and William of Ockham – often singled out as the three most influential of all scholastic writers – make massive contributions to this area of theology, and have served as landmarks ever since.

The rise of the religious orders

Yet it was not only the life of the mind which underwent renewal during this period. The western church was subjected to a sustained program of reform under Gregory VII (ca. 1021–1095), who was elected pope in 1073. Although the "Gregorian Reform" was intensely controversial at the time, modern scholars are generally agreed that it led to the renewal of the church at this critical period in its history. In particular, Gregory managed to achieve an inversion of the existing understanding of the relation of church and state. Whereas it had been assumed that the church was subservient to the state, Gregory managed to establish the principle that, at least in some areas, the church has authority over the state.

The scene was set for further consolidation of papal authority during the later Middle Ages. One crucial development was the weakness of the empire following the death of emperor Henry IV in 1197. Henry's predecessor as emperor, Frederick I (also known as "Barbarossa"), ruled during the period 1152–1190. He established his authority over much of northern Italy. Henry consolidated these gains. Yet in 1197, Henry died, leaving his empire to his 3-year-old son. Chaos resulted, leaving the empire weak and divided. As it happened, a strong pope was elected the following year, who seized the opportunity to reestablish the authority of the papacy. Under Innocent III (pope from 1198 through 1216), the medieval papacy reached an unprecedented level of power throughout western Europe. Innocent adopted the title of "Vicar of Christ" (the term "vicar" here means "representative" or "substitute"). For Innocent, "no king can reign correctly unless he serves the Vicar of Christ."

Nevertheless, other developments undermined this process of consolidation. Of particular importance was the emergence of the Avignon papacy during the period 1378–1417. This development resulted from the temporary withdrawal of the papacy from Rome to Avignon for political reasons during the period 1309–1377. On the return of the papacy to Rome in 1378, two pro-French antipopes ruled in Avignon. The resulting schism was finally settled through the Council of Pisa (1409) and the Council of Constance (1417).

The period was of enormous importance in other respects. Several major new religious orders were founded in the region. In 1097, the Cistercian order was founded at Cîteaux, in the middle of the wild countryside around the River Saône. This order placed an emphasis on the importance of manual labor rather than of scholarship, and on private rather than corporate prayer. The Cistercian order was noted for its severe rule, which denied virtually all of the comforts of life. For example, fires were permitted only once a year, on Christmas Day. One of the most noted Cistercian leaders was the great spiritual writer and preacher Bernard of Clairvaux (1090–1153). By the dawn of the fourteenth century, it is estimated that some 600 Cistercian monasteries or convents had come into being.

Two other major orders were founded more than a century later – the Franciscans and Dominicans. The Franciscans were founded by Francis of Assisi (ca. 1181–1226), who renounced a life of wealth to live a life of prayer and poverty. He was joined by Clare of Assisi, formerly a noblewoman, who founded the order of "Poor Clares." The Franciscans were often referred to as "the Gray Friars," on account of the dark gray habits they wore. The order was distinguished by its emphasis on individual and corporate poverty. It was often viewed as anti-intellectual; nevertheless, some of the greatest theologians of the period, such as Bonaventure, were members of the order.

The Dominicans (sometimes referred to as "Black Friars" on account of their black mantle worn over a white habit) were founded by the Spanish priest Dominic de Guzman (1170–1221), with a particular emphasis on education. By the end of the Middle Ages, the Dominicans had established houses in most major European cities, and made a significant contribution to the intellectual life of the church. Perhaps the greatest medieval theologian, Thomas Aquinas, was a member of this order.

The rebirth of western culture: The Renaissance

The French term "Renaissance" is now universally used to designate the literary and artistic revival in fourteenth- and fifteenth-century Italy. In 1546 Paolo Giovio referred to the fourteenth century as "that happy century in which Latin letters are conceived to have been reborn," anticipating this development. Certain historians, most notably Jacob Burckhardt, argued that the Renaissance gave birth to the modern era. It was in this era, Burckhardt argued, that human beings first began to think of themselves as *individuals*. In many ways, Burckhardt's definition of the Renaissance in purely individualist terms is highly questionable. But in one sense, Burckhardt is undoubtedly correct: *something* novel and exciting developed in Renaissance Italy, which proved capable of exercising a fascination over generations of thinkers.

It is not entirely clear why Italy became the cradle of this brilliant new movement in the history of ideas. A number of factors have been identified as having some bearing on the question.

1 Scholastic theology – the major intellectual force of the medieval period – was never particularly influential in Italy. Although many Italians achieved fame as theologians (such as Thomas Aquinas and Gregory of Rimini), they generally operated in northern Europe. There was thus an intellectual vacuum in Italy during the fourteenth century. Vacuums tend to be filled – and Renaissance humanism filled this particular gap.

2 Italy was saturated with visible and tangible reminders of the greatness of antiquity. The ruins of ancient Roman buildings and monuments were scattered throughout the land, and appear to have

aroused interest in the civilization of ancient Rome at the time of the Renaissance, acting as a stimulus to its thinkers to recover the vitality of classical Roman culture at a time that was culturally arid and barren.

3 As Byzantium began to crumble – Constantinople finally fell to Islamic invaders in 1454 – there was an exodus of Greek-speaking intellectuals westward. Italy happened to be conveniently close to Constantinople, with the result that many such émigrés settled in her cities. A revival of the Greek language was thus inevitable, and with it a revival of interest in the Greek classics.

It will be clear that a central component of the worldview of the Italian Renaissance is a return to the cultural glories of antiquity, and a marginalization of the intellectual achievements of the Middle Ages. Renaissance writers had scant regard for the latter, regarding them as outweighed by the greater achievements of antiquity. What was true of culture in general was also true of theology: Renaissance thinkers regarded the late classical period as totally overshadowing the theological writings of the Middle Ages, both in substance and in style. Indeed, the Renaissance may partly be regarded as a reaction against the type of approach increasingly associated with the faculties of arts and theology of northern European universities. Irritated with the technical nature of the language and discussions of the scholastics, the writers of the Renaissance bypassed them altogether. In the case of Christian theology, the key to the future lay in a direct engagement with the text of Scripture and the writings of the patristic period.

The intellectual force within the Renaissance is generally referred to as "humanism." Humanism as a cultural and educational movement is primarily concerned with the promotion of eloquence in its various forms. Its interest in morals, philosophy, and politics is of secondary importance. To be a humanist is to be concerned with eloquence first and foremost, and with other matters incidentally. Humanism was essentially a cultural program which appealed to classical antiquity as a model of eloquence. In art and architecture, as in the written and spoken word, antiquity was seen as a cultural resource, which could be appropriated by the Renaissance. Humanism was thus concerned with *how ideas were obtained and expressed* rather than with *the actual substance of those ideas*. A humanist might be a Platonist or an Aristotelian – but in both cases the ideas involved derived from antiquity. A humanist might be a skeptic or a believer – but both attitudes could be defended from antiquity.

The form of "humanism" which proved to be of especial importance to Christianity is primarily northern European humanism. We must therefore consider what form this northern European movement took. It is becoming increasingly clear that northern European humanism was decisively influenced by Italian humanism at every stage of its development. Three main channels for the diffusion of the methods and ideals of the Italian Renaissance into northern Europe have been identified.

1 Through northern European scholars moving south to Italy, perhaps to study at an Italian university or as part of a diplomatic mission. On returning to their homeland, they brought the spirit of the Renaissance back with them.

2 Through the foreign correspondence of the Italian humanists. Humanism was concerned with the promotion of written eloquence, and the writing of letters was seen as a means of embodying and spreading the ideals of the Renaissance. The foreign correspondence of Italian humanists was

considerable, extending to most parts of northern Europe.

3 Through printed books, originating from sources such as the Aldine Press in Venice. These works were often reprinted by northern European presses, particularly those at Basle in Switzerland. Italian humanists often dedicated their works to northern European patrons, thus ensuring that they were taken notice of in potentially influential quarters.

Although there are major variations within northern European humanism, two ideals seem to have achieved widespread acceptance throughout the movement. First, we find the same concern for written and spoken eloquence, after the fashion of the classical period, as in the Italian Reformation. Second, we find a religious program directed towards the corporate revival of the Christian church. The Latin slogan *Christianismus renascens*, "Christianity being born again," summarizes the aims of this program, and indicates its relation to the "rebirth" of letters associated with the Renaissance.

A central element of the humanist agenda was the return to the original sources of western European culture in classical Rome and Athens. The theological counterpart to this agenda was the direct return to the foundational resources of Christian theology, supremely in the New Testament. This agenda proved to be of major significance, as will be seen below. One of its most important consequences was a new appreciation of the foundational importance of Scripture as a theological resource. As interest in Scripture developed, it became increasingly clear that existing Latin translations of this source were inadequate. Supreme among these was the "Vulgate," a Latin translation of the Bible which achieved widespread influence during the Middle Ages. The Old Testament was written in Hebrew (although small sections are written in Aramaic); the New Testament was written in Greek. The Vulgate provided a Latin translation of these texts for the benefit of writers who knew Latin, but no Hebrew or Greek. Yet the reliability of this translation was soon called into question.

The rise of humanist scholarship would expose the distressing discrepancies between the Vulgate and the texts it purported to translate – and thus open the way to doctrinal reformation as a consequence. It is for this reason that humanism is of decisive importance to the development of medieval theology: it demonstrated the unreliability of this translation of the Bible – and hence, it seemed, of theologies based upon it. The biblical basis of scholasticism seemed to collapse, as humanism uncovered error after error in its translation. We shall explore this point further in what follows.

The literary and cultural program of humanism can be summarized in the slogan *ad fontes* – "back to the original sources." The "filter" of medieval commentaries – whether on legal texts or on the Bible – is abandoned, in order to engage directly with the original texts. Applied to the Christian church, the slogan *ad fontes* meant a direct return to the title-deeds of Christianity – to the patristic writers, and supremely to the Bible, studied in their original languages. This necessitated direct access to the Greek text of the New Testament.

The first printed Greek New Testament was produced by Erasmus of Rotterdam in 1516. Erasmus' text was not as reliable as it ought to have been: Erasmus had access to a mere four manuscripts for most of the New Testament, and only one for its final part, the book of Revelation. As it happened, that manuscript left out five verses, which Erasmus himself had to translate into Greek from the Latin of the Vulgate. Nevertheless, it proved to be a literary milestone. For the first time, theologians had the opportunity of comparing the original Greek text of the New Testament with the later Vulgate translation into Latin.

Drawing on work carried out earlier by the Italian humanist Lorenzo Valla, Erasmus showed that the Vulgate translation of a number of major New Testament texts could not be justified. As a number of medieval church practices and beliefs were based upon these texts, Erasmus' allegations were viewed with consternation by many conservative Catholics (who wanted to retain these practices and beliefs) and with equally great delight by the reformers (who wanted to eliminate them). For example, the Vulgate translated the opening words of Jesus' ministry (Matthew 4:17) as "do penance, for the kingdom of heaven is at hand." This translation suggested that the coming of the

7.7 Erasmus of Rotterdam, ca. 1525/1530, after the painting, 1517, by Quentin Massys (1465/1466–1530). Rome, Galleria Nazionale, Palazzo Barberini, AKG-Images/Pirozzi.

kingdom of heaven had a direct connection with the sacrament of penance. Erasmus, again following Valla, pointed out that the Greek should be translated as "repent, for the kingdom of heaven is at hand." In other words, where the Vulgate seemed to refer to an outward practice (the sacrament of penance), Erasmus insisted that the reference was to an inward psychological attitude – that of "being repentant."

Such developments undermined the credibility of the Vulgate translation, and opened the way to theological revision on the basis of a better understanding of the biblical text. It also demonstrated the importance of biblical scholarship in relation to theology. Theology could not be permitted to base itself upon translation mistakes! The recognition of the vitally important role of biblical scholarship to Christian theology thus dates from the second decade of the sixteenth century. It also led to the theological concerns of the Reformation, which we shall consider later in this chapter.

Western Christianity in the late Middle Ages

The Christianity which flourished in western Europe in the period 1350–1500 is widely regarded as having great strengths and equally great weaknesses. Historians have tended to concentrate on the weaknesses, partly to understand the developments of the sixteenth century, in which the Reformation got under way. While it is important to understand the nature of these weaknesses, it must be understood that there were considerable strengths.

It is clear that the fifteenth century witnessed a remarkable growth in popular versions of Christianity. It is true that this "popular Christianity" often bore little relation to the official teachings of the church. For example, the gospel was often linked to a series of popular concerns about illness, crop failures, personal romance, and individual prosperity. Many were attracted to the cult of relics – that is, objects or personal possessions associated with the great men and women of faith, or perhaps even with Jesus himself. Thus merchants were known to carry "splinters of the cross" as they made potentially dangerous trading journeys, in much the same way as soldiers wore relics of the saints to protect them from their enemies. In countless such ways, Christianity had become deeply rooted in the popular consciousness by the end of the Middle Ages.

One particularly striking example of this is to be found in the practice of making pilgrimages. In England, a tradition developed of making a pilgrimage to the cathedral city of Canterbury, celebrated in Geoffrey Chaucer's famous work the *Canterbury Tales*. Other sites of major importance included the city of Rome, venerated as the burial place of both the apostles Peter and Paul, and the northwestern Spanish shrine of Santiago de Compostela.

The growing literature of the late fifteenth and early sixteenth centuries listing complaints about the church – once thought by some scholars to point to a decline in the influence of religion in the period – is now thought to point to a growing ability and willingness on the part of the laity to criticize the church, with a view to reforming it. For example, the period 1450–1520 saw a considerable increase in popular religion in Germany. Just about every conceivable objective criterion – the number of masses endowed, the fashion for forming religious brotherhoods, the donations to religious charities, the building of new churches, the number of pilgrimages made, and the growth in popular religious literature – points to a remarkable growth in popular interest in religion. This was often linked with a very deep devotion to the Virgin Mary. A major cult came to center on Mary, often linked with the recitation of the rosary – a series of fifteen prayers, counted off using a string of beads as a memory aid.

A renewed interest in the Christian faith on the part of more academic individuals, linked with a perception of the need to refashion and renew it if it was to regain its vitality, is also evident from the final decade of the fifteenth century onwards. The dynamism unleashed by the remarkably sudden (and still largely unexplained) development of Spanish mysticism in the 1490s was harnessed through the Cisnerian reforms, leading to a new concern for religious education and a revival of religious vocations in Spain. The University of Alcalà and the Complutensian Polyglot (a multilingual version of the Bible) were perhaps the most tangible results of these reforms.

The church was probably the most important sponsor of the arts during this period, commissioning a series of major works – such as Michelangelo's Sistine Chapel roof – which continue to be regarded as cultural high points. Important advances were also made in the area of spirituality. Works such as Thomas à Kempis' *Imitation of Christ* came to be regarded as a classic. Many other works of similar importance appeared, demonstrating the commitment of the church of this period to the pastoral and spiritual care of its members.

The rise of humanism led to a new concern to relate the Christian faith to the personal experience of individuals. One of the most subtle and significant developments in the self-understanding of Christianity began to take place, as a religion which had grown used to expressing and defining itself in external forms began to rediscover its appeal to the inward consciousness. The Christian writers of the Renaissance recognized the need to implant the gospel firmly in the experiential world of the individual, as something which could and should be personally and inwardly appropriated. The age-old appeal of both Paul and Augustine to the introspective conscience of the individual led to these writers being reappropriated with fresh interest, whether in the sonnets of Petrarch or the new religious writings of Renaissance theologians, preachers, and biblical commentators.

A generation of thinkers subsequently rose to the challenge on the eve of the Reformation. In Paris, Lefèvre d'Etaples explored the relevance of Paul's understanding of faith for the individual. At Oxford, John Colet stressed the importance of a personal encounter with the risen Christ in the Christian life. In Italy, the movement often known as "Catholic evangelicalism" or "evangelism," with its stress on the question of personal salvation, became firmly established within the church, even penetrating deeply within its hierarchy, without being regarded as in any way heretical.

In the Low Countries, Erasmus won the hearts and minds of the educated elite of Europe with the reforming program outlined in the *Enchiridion* or "Handbook of the Christian Soldier," which appeared in 1503. This book was notable for its stress on a personally assimilated and inward faith, which Erasmus contrasted unfavorably with the concern for external matters characteristic of the institutional church. The work was reprinted in 1509, and entered its third edition in 1515. From that moment onwards it became a cult work, apparently going through twenty-three editions in the next six years. It was devoured by educated laity throughout western Europe. The work developed the radical and – to lay minds – attractive idea that the church could be reformed and renewed by its laity. The clergy may assist the laity in their understanding of their faith, but do not have any superior status. Religion is an inner spiritual affair, in which the individual believer seeks to deepen his or her knowledge of God by the reading of Scripture. Significantly, the *Enchiridion* plays down the role of the institutional church in order to emphasize the importance of the individual believer.

Despite these obvious strengths, some serious challenges to the established forms of Christianity in western Europe can be identified, which are of relevance to the increasing demands for reform within the late medieval church at the time. In what follows, we shall explore three of these, each of which significantly affected the development of western Christianity.

The growth in adult literacy

By the dawn of the sixteenth century adult literacy was increasingly common, made possible by the development of printing, the growth of the paper industry, and the growing appeal of the humanist movement. In the early Middle Ages, literacy was restricted to the clergy. Written material took the form of manuscripts which had to be painstakingly copied out by hand, and were generally confined to the libraries of monasteries on account of their scarcity. In order to save precious parchment, words were abbreviated, making manuscripts difficult to decipher. Humanism, however, made adult literacy a social achievement, a skill which opened the way to social refinement and advancement. As the newly emerging professional classes began to gain power in the cities, gradually wresting control from the old patrician families, they brought to their practice and interpretation of the Christian faith much the same critical acumen and professionalism they employed in their secular careers. The clerical monopoly on literacy was thus decisively broken. This development opened the way for an increasingly critical lay assessment of the abilities of the clergy, and growing lay confidence in religious matters.

A surge in anti-clericalism

Among the more significant elements in our understanding of the background to the Reformation is the new contempt with which clergy were viewed by an increasingly literate and articulate laity. The phenomenon of anti-clericalism was widespread, and not specifically linked to any area of Europe. In part, the phenomenon reflects the low quality of the rank and file clergy. In Renaissance Italy, it was common for parish priests to have had virtually no training; what little they knew, they gleaned from watching, helping, and imitating. Diocesan visitations regularly revealed priests who were illiterate, or had apparently permanently mislaid their breviaries. The poor quality of the parish clergy reflected their low social status: in early sixteenth-century Milan, chaplains had incomes lower than those of unskilled laborers. Many resorted to horse and cattle trading to make ends meet. In rural France during the same period, the clergy enjoyed roughly the same social status as vagabonds: their exemption from taxation, prosecution in civil courts, and compulsory military service apart, they were virtually indistinguishable from other itinerant beggars of the period.

The tax privileges enjoyed by clergy were the source of particular irritation, especially in times of economic difficulty. In the French diocese of Meaux, which would become a center for reforming activists in the period 1521–1546, the clergy were exempted from all forms of taxation, including charges relating to the provisioning and garrisoning of troops – which provoked considerable local resentment. In the diocese of Rouen, there was a popular outcry over the windfall profits made by the church by selling grain at a period of severe shortage. Clerical immunity from prosecution in civil courts further isolated the clergy from the people.

In France, the subsistence crises of the 1520s played a major role in the consolidation of anti-clerical attitudes. In his celebrated study of Languedoc, Le Roy Ladurie pointed out that the 1520s witnessed a reversal of the process

of expansion and recovery which had been characteristic of the two generations since the ending of the Hundred Years' War. From that point onwards, a crisis began to develop, taking the form of plague, famine, and migration of the rural poor to the cities in search of food and employment. A similar pattern has now been identified for the period in most of France north of the Loire. This subsistence crisis focused popular attention on the gross disparity between the fate of the lower classes and the nobles and ecclesiastical establishment.

By the end of the Middle Ages, there was significant local hostility to the clergy in many regions of Europe. The pattern is not uniform, and varies considerably from region to region. It seems that this hostility was greatest in the cities, and least in the countryside. It is widely agreed that anti-clericalism was a significant contributing factor to the growing clamor for the reformation of the church, which became increasingly strident in the late fifteenth century.

The rise of doctrinal pluralism

It is widely agreed that the confusion that began to emerge within the church over matters of doctrine during the fourteenth and fifteenth centuries caused difficulties for the enforcement of religious orthodoxy. Indeed, it can be further argued that doctrinal unclarity was of major importance in relation to the origins of the Reformation in the following century. It became increasingly unclear who had authority to speak on behalf of the church. If a novel theological opinion developed, who was to determine whether it was consistent with the teachings of the church? And there was no shortage of new opinions in the late medieval church. The reasons for this are not difficult to understand.

The rapid expansion of the university sector throughout western Europe in the late fourteenth and fifteenth centuries led to an increased number of theology faculties, with a corresponding increase in the number of theological treatises produced as a result. Then, as now, theologians had to do something to justify their existence. These works frequently explored new ideas. But what was the status of these ideas? The general failure to draw a clear distinction between theological opinions and church teaching, between private opinion and communal doctrine, caused considerable confusion. Who was to distinguish between opinion and doctrine? The pope? An ecumenical council? A professor of theology? Failure to clarify such crucial questions contributed in no small manner to the crisis of authority in the late medieval church. In many centers in western Europe, a "long period of magnificent religious anarchy" (to use a phrase from the historian Lucien Febvre) set in.

Confusion over the official teaching of the church contributed in no small manner to the origins of Luther's program of reform in Germany. Of central importance to Luther was the doctrine of justification – the question of how an individual enters into a relationship with God. The most recent known authoritative pronouncement on the part of a recognized ecclesiastical body relating to this doctrine dated from 418, more than a millennium before the Reformation – and its confused and outdated statements did little to clarify the position of the church on the matter in 1518, eleven hundred years later. It seemed to Luther that the church of his day had lapsed into Pelagianism, an unacceptable understanding of how an individual entered into fellowship with God. The church, he believed, taught that individuals could gain favor and acceptance in the sight of God on account of their personal achievements and status, thus negating the whole idea of grace. Luther may well have been mistaken in this apprehension – but

there was such confusion within the church of his day that none was able to enlighten him on the authoritative position of the church on the matter.

We therefore turn to consider the turmoil of the sixteenth century, which saw major divisions arise within the western church that remain of crucial importance to the present day.

The Reformation

The sixteenth century proved to be a period of remarkable importance, setting the scene for the development of many of the features now associated with western Christianity. One particularly critical feature which can be traced back to this period and its aftermath is the rise of "denominations" – that is, distinctive types of Christians, such as Anglicans, Baptists, Lutherans, and Methodists. The period proved to be remarkably creative. Not only did the period give rise to what is loosely called "Protestantism"; it also gave birth to a theologically and spiritually renewed Catholicism. Such is the importance of this period to the emergence of modern Christianity in the west that it demands careful attention. While the terms used to refer to periods of Christian history can be misleading or controversial, there is a widespread tendency to refer to the events of this period collectively as "the Reformation."

The term "Reformation" is used by historians and theologians to refer primarily to the western European movement, centering upon individuals such as Martin Luther, Huldrych Zwingli, and John Calvin, concerned with the moral, theological, and institutional reform of the Christian church in that region. Initially, up to about 1525, the Reformation may be regarded as centering upon Martin Luther and the University of Wittenberg, in

7.8 Portrait of Martin Luther, 1528, from the studio of Lucas Cranach the Elder (1472–1553). Wittenberg, Lutherhalle, AKG-Images.

modern-day northeastern Germany. However, the movement also gained strength, initially independently, in the Swiss city of Zurich in the early 1520s. Through a complex series of developments, the Zurich Reformation gradually underwent a succession of political and theological changes, eventually coming to be associated primarily with the city of Geneva (now part of modern-day Switzerland, although then an independent city-state) and John Calvin. Although initially focusing on regions such as Germany and Switzerland, the Reformation had a considerable impact on most of western Europe during the sixteenth century, provoking either a positive response to at least one aspect of the movement (as, for example, in England, Holland, and Scandinavia) or a reaction against the movement resulting in a consolidation of Catholicism (as, for example, in Spain and France).

The Reformation movement was complex and heterogeneous, and concerned an agenda far broader than the reform of the doctrine of the church. It addressed fundamental social, political, and economic issues, too complex to be discussed in any detail in this volume. The growing power of nationalism was unquestionably important in some regions of Europe, including England and Germany. The agenda of the Reformation varied from one country to another, with the theological issues which played major roles in one country (for example, Germany) often having relatively little impact elsewhere (for example, in England). In response to the Reformation, the Catholic church moved to put its own house in order. Prevented from calling a council at an early date owing to political instability in Europe resulting from tensions between France and Germany, the pope of the day was eventually able to convene the Council of Trent in 1545. This set itself the task of clarifying and defending Catholic thought and practice against its evangelical opponents.

The term "Reformation" is used in a number of senses, and it is helpful to distinguish them. Each represents a perfectly valid use of the term. In what follows, we shall explore the main facets of this complex movement, before examining aspects of the growing alienation of Catholic and Protestant during this turbulent period.

The Lutheran Reformation

The Lutheran Reformation is particularly associated with the German territories and the pervasive personal influence of one charismatic individual – Martin Luther. Luther was particularly concerned with the doctrine of justification, which formed the central point of his religious thought. The Lutheran Reformation was initially an academic movement, concerned primarily with reforming the teaching of theology at the University of Wittenberg. Wittenberg was an unimportant university, and the reforms introduced by Luther and his colleagues within the theology faculty attracted little attention. It was Luther's personal activities – such as his posting of the famous Ninety-Five Theses (October 31, 1517) – which attracted considerable interest, and brought the ideas in circulation at Wittenberg to the attention of a wider audience.

Strictly speaking, the Lutheran Reformation only began in 1522, when Luther returned to Wittenberg from his enforced isolation in the Wartburg. Luther was condemned by the Diet of Worms in 1521. Fearing for Luther's life, certain well-placed supporters removed him in secrecy to the castle known as the "Wartburg," until the threat to his safety ceased. In his absence, Andreas Bodenstein von Karlstadt, one of Luther's academic colleagues at Wittenberg, began a program of reform at Wittenberg which seemed to degenerate into chaos. Convinced that he was needed if the Reformation was to survive Karlstadt's neptitude, Luther emerged from his place of safety and returned to Wittenberg.

From this point onwards, Luther's program of academic reform changed into one of reform of church and society. No longer was Luther's forum of activity the university world of ideas; he now found himself regarded as the leader of a religious, social, and political reforming movement which seemed to some contemporary observers to open the way to a new social and religious order in Europe. In fact, Luther's program of reform was much more conservative than that associated with his Reformed colleagues, such as Huldrych Zwingli. Furthermore, it met with considerably less success

than some anticipated. The movement remained obstinately tied to the German territories, and – Scandinavia apart – never gained the foreign power bases which seemed to be like so many ripe apples, ready to fall into its lap. Luther's understanding of the role of the "godly prince" (which effectively ensured that the monarch had control of the church) does not seem to have had the attraction which might have been expected, particularly in the light of the generally republican sentiments of Reformed thinkers such as Calvin.

An integral part of Luther's reforming program was to give a new role to the laity, including women. Luther's doctrine of the "priesthood of all believers" laid down that every Christian – irrespective of gender or social status – was a priest in God's sight. Luther reacted against the isolation of Christians from the world, arguing that monasteries and convents prevented them from living out their calling in their world. One of Luther's most interesting exploits took place in 1523, when he arranged for the liberation of a dozen nuns from the cloister of Marienthron. They were smuggled out in herring barrels, provided by a merchant friend. Luther married one of them, Katia von Bora, in 1525. Up to this point, women tended to exercise religious leadership only in monastic contexts, on account of the segregation of the genders. Katia's role as mistress of the family household set the pattern for Lutheran women for many years, and offered a significant social role for women outside the confines of monastic life.

The Calvinist Reformation

The origins of the Calvinist Reformation, which brought the Reformed churches (such as the Presbyterians) into being, lie with developments within the Swiss Confederation. Whereas the Lutheran Reformation had its origins in an academic context, the Reformed church owed its origins to a series of attempts to reform the morals and worship of the church (but not necessarily its doctrine) according to a more biblical pattern. It must be emphasized that although Calvin gave this style of Reformation its definitive form, its origins are to be traced back to earlier reformers, such as Huldrych Zwingli and Heinrich Bullinger, based at the leading Swiss city of Zurich.

Although most of the early Reformed theologians – such as Zwingli – had an academic background, their reforming programs were not academic in nature. They were directed towards the church as they found it in the Swiss cities, such as Zurich, Berne, and Basle. Whereas Luther was convinced that the doctrine of justification was of central significance to his program of social and religious reform, the early Reformed thinkers had relatively little interest in doctrine, let alone one specific doctrine. Their reforming program was institutional, social, and ethical, in many ways similar to the demands for reform emanating from the humanist movement.

The consolidation of the Reformed church is generally thought to begin with the stabilization of the Zurich Reformation after Zwingli's death in battle (1531) under his successor, Heinrich Bullinger, and to end with the emergence of Geneva as its power base, and John Calvin as its leading spokesman, in the 1550s. The gradual shift in power within the Reformed church (initially from Zurich to Berne, and subsequently from Berne to Geneva) took place over the period 1520–1560, eventually establishing the city of Geneva, its political system (republicanism), and its religious thinkers (initially Calvin, and after his death Theodore Beza) as predominant within the Reformed church. This development was consolidated through the establishment of the Genevan Academy (founded in 1559), at which Reformed pastors were trained.

7.9 Portrait of John Calvin. Rotterdam, Museum Boymans-van Beuningen, AKG-Images.

The term "Calvinism" is often used to refer to the religious ideas of the Reformed church. Although still widespread in the literature relating to the Reformation, this practice is now generally discouraged. It is becoming increasingly clear that later sixteenth-century Reformed theology draws on sources other than the ideas of Calvin himself. To refer to later sixteenth- and seventeenth-century Reformed thought as "Calvinist" implies that it is essentially the thought of Calvin – and it is now generally agreed that Calvin's ideas were modified subtly by his successors. The term "Reformed" is now preferred, whether to refer to those churches (mainly in Switzerland, the Lowlands, and Germany), religious thinkers (such as Theodore Beza, William Perkins, or John Owen) who based themselves upon Calvin's celebrated religious textbook, *Institutes of the Christian Religion*, or church documents (such as the famous Heidelberg Catechism) based upon it.

Of the three constituents of the Protestant Reformation – Lutheran, Reformed or Calvinist, and Anabaptist – it is the Reformed wing which is of particular importance to the English-speaking world. Puritanism, which figures so prominently in seventeenth-century English history and is of such fundamental importance to the religious and political views of New England in the seventeenth century and beyond, is a specific form of Reformed Christianity. To understand the religious and political history of New England or the ideas of writers such as Jonathan Edwards, for example, it is necessary to come to grips with at least some of the theological insights and part of the religious outlook of Puritanism which underlie their social and political attitudes.

The Radical Reformation (Anabaptism)

The term "Anabaptist" owes its origins to Zwingli (the word literally means "rebaptizers," and refers to what was perhaps the most distinctive aspect of Anabaptist practice – the insistence that only those who had made a personal public profession of faith should be baptized). Anabaptism seems to have first arisen around Zurich, in the aftermath of Zwingli's reforms within the city in the early 1520s. It centered on a group of individuals (among whom we may note Conrad Grebel) who argued that Zwingli was not being faithful to his own reforming principles. He preached one thing, and practiced another. Although Zwingli professed faithfulness to the *sola scriptura*, "by Scripture alone," principle, Grebel argued that he retained a number of practices – including infant baptism, the close link between church and magistracy, and the participation of Christians in warfare – which were

not sanctioned or ordained by Scripture. In the hands of such radical thinkers, the *sola scriptura* principle would be radicalized; reformed Christians would only believe and practice those things explicitly taught in Scripture. Zwingli was alarmed by this, seeing it as a destabilizing development which threatened to cut the Reformed church at Zurich off from its historical roots and its continuity with the Christian tradition of the past.

A number of common elements can be discerned within the various strands of the movement: a general distrust of external authority, the rejection of infant baptism in favor of the baptism of adult believers, the common ownership of property, and an emphasis upon pacifism and non-resistance. To take up one of these points: in 1527, the governments of Zurich, Berne, and St. Gallen accused the Anabaptists of believing "that no true Christian can either give or receive interest or income on a sum of capital; that all temporal goods are free and common, and that all can have full property rights to them." It is for this reason that "Anabaptism" is often referred to as the "left wing of the Reformation" (Roland H. Bainton) or the "radical Reformation" (George Hunston Williams). For Williams, the "radical Reformation" was to be contrasted with the "magisterial Reformation," which he broadly identified with the Lutheran and Reformed movements. These terms are increasingly being accepted within Reformation scholarship, and you are likely to encounter them in your reading of more recent studies of the movement.

The Catholic Reformation

This term is often used to refer to the revival within Roman Catholicism in the period following the opening of the Council of Trent (1545). In older scholarly works, the movement is often designated the "Counter-Reformation":

as the term suggests, the Roman Catholic church developed means of combating the Protestant Reformation in order to limit its influence. It is, however, becoming increasingly clear that the Roman Catholic church countered the Reformation partly by reforming itself from within, in order to remove the grounds of Protestant criticism. In this sense, the movement was a reformation of the Roman Catholic church, as much as it was a reaction against the Protestant Reformation.

The same concerns underlying the Protestant Reformation in northern Europe were channeled into the renewal of the Catholic church, particularly in Spain and Italy. The Council of Trent, the foremost component of the Catholic Reformation, clarified Catholic teaching on a number of confusing matters, and introduced much needed reforms in relation to the conduct of the clergy, ecclesiastical discipline, religious education, and missionary activity. The movement for reform within the church was greatly stimulated by the reformation of many of the older religious orders, and the establishment of new orders (such as the Jesuits). The more specifically theological aspects of the Catholic Reformation will be considered in relation to its teachings on Scripture and tradition, justification by faith, and the sacraments. As a result of the Catholic Reformation, many of the abuses which originally lay behind the demands for reform – whether these came from humanists or Protestants – were removed.

In its broadest sense, the term "Reformation" is used to refer to all four of the movements described above. The term is also used in a somewhat more restricted sense, meaning "the Protestant Reformation," excluding the Catholic Reformation. In this sense, it refers to the three Protestant movements noted above. In many scholarly works, however, the term "Reformation" is used to refer to what is sometimes known as the "magisterial

Reformation," or the "mainstream Reformation" – in other words, that linked with the Lutheran and Reformed churches (including Anglicanism), and excluding the Anabaptists.

The rise of Protestantism

The term "Protestant" is widely used to refer to the forms of Christianity which emerged in western Europe during the sixteenth century in response to medieval Christianity. The term requires some comment, in that it is not particularly helpful. It derives from the aftermath of the Diet of Speyer (February 1529), which voted to end the toleration of Lutheranism in Germany. In April of the same year, six German princes and fourteen cities protested against this oppressive measure, defending freedom of conscience and the rights of religious minorities. The term "Protestant" derives from this protest. It is therefore not strictly correct to apply the term "Protestant" to individuals prior to April 1529, or to speak of events prior to that date as constituting "the Protestant Reformation." The term "evangelical" is often used in the literature to refer to the reforming factions at Wittenberg and elsewhere (e.g., in France and Switzerland) prior to this date. Although the word "Protestant" is often used to refer to this earlier period, this use is, strictly speaking, an anachronism. The term "evangelical" is generally more accurate and helpful.

The origins of Protestantism are enormously complex, involving social, political, economic, and theological matters. It has, for example, often been noted that Protestantism had an especial appeal to the rising middle classes of the sixteenth century, offering opportunities and status denied to them in more traditional societies, in which the aristocracy held power. Equally, the adoption of one form of Protestantism by England's Henry VIII is partly due to Henry's desire to establish a national English church, free of interference from Rome. While it is thus not true to say that the origins of Protestantism are purely religious in nature, it is nevertheless important to appreciate that religious matters were of major importance to its emergence.

To explore the origins of Protestantism, it is probably most helpful to look at three of its leading representatives: Martin Luther (1483–1546), Huldrych Zwingli (1484–1531), and John Calvin (1509–1564). Each can be seen as in some way contributing to the emergence of the movement.

Martin Luther began his career with the intention of studying law. He initially studied at the University of Erfurt, a noted stronghold of scholasticism. Following what seems to have been a traumatic experience during a violent thunderstorm, Luther decided to enter the Augustinian monastery in Erfurt and train for the priesthood. After a period spent studying theology and serving his religious order in several capacities, Luther took up a teaching position at the recently founded University of Wittenberg in 1511. As a professor of biblical studies, he gave courses of lectures on a number of biblical works, including the Psalter, Romans, Galatians, and Hebrews. During the course of these lectures, he appears to have gone through some kind of theological conversion.

The nature of this conversion is quite complex; however, it is generally agreed to focus on the doctrine of justification – the question of how human beings enter into a right relationship with God. Luther's initial position seems to have been that this right relationship can be brought into being through human achievement. In other words, people can do certain quite definite things, through their own efforts. As a result, they are put in a right relationship with God. However, Luther came to regard this understanding as seriously deficient. At some point around the year 1515 (although the precise date is disputed), Luther seems to have decided that this relationship could only be established from God's side. It is to be understood as a divine gift, rather than a human achievement. On the basis of this changed understanding of how human beings are put in a correct relationship with God (pp. 150–154), Luther embarked on a program of reform within the church.

Perhaps the most famous aspect of that program was the posting of the Ninety-Five Theses on October 31, 1517. This collection of ninety-five points relating to the practice of selling indulgences caused considerable controversy, and resulted in Luther's name becoming widely known. This was followed up in 1519 by the Leipzig Disputation, in which Luther and Johann Eck entered into public debate over a number of important issues, including that of the authority of the pope. The following year saw the publication of three major reforming works, which set an agenda for the reformation and renewal of the church and its theology: *The Appeal to the German Nobility*, *The Babylonian Captivity of the Church*, and *The Freedom of a Christian*. These increased considerably the pressure on the church authorities, particularly in Germany, for a reform of some of the current practices and beliefs of the church.

It was not long before Luther's ideas were being widely discussed and debated within western Europe. A group met regularly in the English university town of Cambridge to discuss Luther's writings. Known as "the White Horse" group after the tavern in which they were prone to gather, the group included several figures who would have a crucial impact on the development of the Reformation in England during the 1530s.

Yet reforming movements were springing up elsewhere in Europe, including in Switzerland. The Swiss reformer Huldrych Zwingli was educated at the universities of Vienna

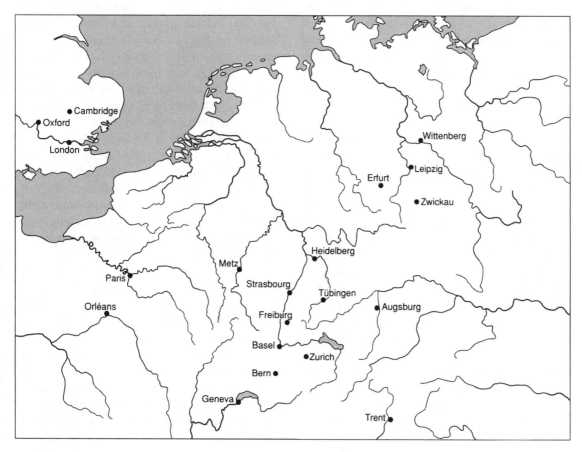

Map 7.5 Major centers of Protestant theological and ecclesiastical activity at the time of the Reformation.

and Basle, before taking up parish duties in eastern Switzerland. It is clear that he took a keen interest in the agenda of Christian humanism, especially the writings of Erasmus, and became committed to belief in the need to reform the church of his day. In 1519, he took up a pastoral position in the city of Zurich. Zwingli used the pulpit of the Great Minster, the chief church within the city, to propagate a program of reform. Initially, this program was primarily concerned with the reformation of the morals of the church. However, it soon extended to include criticism of the existing theology of the church, especially in relation to sacramental theology. The term "Zwinglian" is used especially to refer to the belief, associated with Zwingli, that Christ is not present at the eucharist, which is best seen as a memorial of Christ's death.

After the first wave of the Reformation had passed, a new agenda emerged. John Calvin belongs to the second generation of reformers, who were more concerned with the consolidation of the ideas and practices of the Reformation. Calvin was born in Noyon, northeast of Paris, in 1509. Educated at the scholasticism-dominated University of Paris, he subsequently moved to the more humanist University of

Orléans, at which he studied civil law. Although initially inclined to a career of scholarship, he underwent a conversion experience in his mid-twenties, which led to his becoming increasingly associated with reforming movements in Paris, and eventually being forced into exile in Basle.

The second generation of reformers were far more aware of the need for works of systematic theology than the first. Calvin, the major figure of the second period of the Reformation, saw the need for a work which would set out clearly the basic ideas of evangelical theology, justifying them on the basis of Scripture and defending them in the face of Catholic criticism. In 1536, he published a small work entitled *Institutes of the Christian Religion*, a mere six chapters in length. For the next quarter of a century Calvin worked away at this material, adding extra chapters and rearranging the content. By the time of its final edition (1559), the work had eighty chapters and was divided into four books. The first book deals with God the creator, and his sovereignty over that creation. The second book concerns the human need for redemption, and the manner in which this redemption is achieved by Christ the mediator. The third book deals with the manner in which this redemption is appropriated by human beings, while the final book deals with the church and its relation to society. Although it is often suggested that predestination stands at the center of Calvin's system, this is not the case; the only principle which seems to govern Calvin's organization of his theological system is a concern to be faithful to Scripture on the one hand, and to achieve maximum clarity of presentation on the other.

After winding up his affairs in Noyon early in 1536, Calvin decided to settle down to a life of private study in the great city of Strasbourg. Unfortunately, the direct route from Noyon to Strasbourg was impassable, due to the outbreak of war between Francis I of France and the emperor Charles V. Calvin had to make an extended detour, passing through the city of Geneva which had recently gained its independence from the neighboring territory of Savoy. Geneva was then in a state of confusion, having just evicted its local bishop and begun a controversial program of reform under the Frenchmen Guillaume Farel and Pierre Viret. On hearing that Calvin was in the city, they demanded that he stay and help the cause of the Reformation. They needed a good teacher. Calvin reluctantly agreed.

His attempts to provide the Genevan church with a solid basis of doctrine and discipline met intense resistance. After a series of quarrels, matters reached a head on Easter Day 1538: Calvin was expelled from the city, and sought refuge in Strasbourg. Having arrived in Strasbourg two years later than he had anticipated, Calvin began to make up for lost time. In quick succession he produced a series of major theological works. As pastor to the French-speaking congregation in the city, Calvin was able to gain experience of the practical problems facing Reformed pastors. Through his friendship with Martin Bucer, the Strasbourg reformer, Calvin was able to develop his thinking on the relation between the city and church.

In September 1541, Calvin was asked to return to Geneva. In his absence, the religious and political situation had deteriorated. The city appealed to him to return and restore order and confidence there. The Calvin who returned to Geneva was a wiser and more experienced young man, far better equipped for the tasks awaiting him than he had been three years earlier. His experience at Strasbourg lent new realism to his theorizing about the nature of the church, which is reflected in his subsequent writings in the field. By the time of his death in 1564, Calvin had made Geneva the center of an international movement, which came to bear his name. Calvinism is still one of the most potent and significant intellectual movements in human history.

The Reformation in England

The English Reformation took a somewhat different direction than its continental counterpart. Although there was at least some degree of popular pressure for a reform within the church, the leading force for reform was Henry VIII, who ascended the throne in 1509. In 1527, Henry took the first steps to dissolve his marriage to Catherine of Aragon. This decision resulted from Henry's desire to ensure the succession to the English throne. The only child of this marriage, Mary Tudor, was female; Henry wanted a male heir. The pope refused to dissolve or annul the marriage.

It is quite improper to suggest that the English Reformation resulted from the pope's refusal to grant Henry his divorce. Nevertheless, it was a factor. Henry gradually appears to have shifted towards a policy which involved the replacement of papal authority in England with his own authority. The creation of an English national church was part of this vision. Henry seems not to have been particularly interested in matters of doctrine or theology, preferring to concentrate upon the practicalities of religious and political power. His decision to appoint Thomas Cranmer (1489–1556) as archbishop of Canterbury led to at least some Protestant influences being brought to bear on the English church.

When Henry died in 1547, he was succeeded by his son, Edward VI. Edward was a minor on his accession; as a result, real power was exercised by his advisors, who were generally of a strongly Protestant persuasion. Cranmer, who remained in office as archbishop during Edward's reign, was able to bring in noticeably Protestant forms of public worship, and encouraged leading Protestant

7.10 Henry VIII, 1540, by Hans Holbein the Younger (1497–1543). Rome, Galleria Nazionale, Palazzo Barberini, AKG-Images/Nimatallah.

thinkers (such as Martin Bucer and Peter Martyr Vermigli) to settle in England and give theological direction to the Reformation. However, Edward died in 1553, leaving the nation in a state of religious flux.

Edward was succeeded by Mary Tudor, who was strongly Catholic in sympathy. She set in motion a series of measures which suppressed Protestantism and restored Catholicism. Some of the measures were deeply unpopular, most notably the public burning of Thomas Cranmer at Oxford in 1556. Cranmer was replaced as archbishop of Canterbury by Reginald Pole, a moderate Catholic. At the time of Mary's death in 1558, Catholicism had not yet been totally reestablished. When Elizabeth I succeeded to the throne, it was not entirely clear what direction her religious policies might take. In the event, Elizabeth pursued a complex policy, which seems to have been aimed at appeasing both Protestants and Catholics, while allowing the queen to have supreme authority in matters of religion. What is usually referred to as "the Elizabethan Settlement" (1558–1559) established the national English church as a reformed episcopal church, having broadly Protestant articles of faith with a more Catholic liturgy. Nobody was really entirely happy with the outcome, which was widely seen as a compromise; however, it enabled England to emerge from a period of religious tension and avoid the serious religious conflicts that were raging elsewhere in Europe at the time.

The leading features of Protestantism

Protestantism was, as we have noted, a remarkably diverse movement. However, examination of Protestant church practice and key documents – such as the Augsburg Confession (Lutheran, 1530); the Heidelberg Catechism (Reformed, 1562); the Thirty-Nine Articles (Anglican, 1563) – shows that a number of central themes can be seen as typical of the movement. These include the following.

1   A rejection of papal authority. Protestants regarded the authority of the pope as resting on a series of unjustifiable developments, and wished to return to simpler models of church leadership, such as those found in the New Testament. As a result, some Protestant churches retained an episcopal system of church government, regarding this as a legitimate and biblical means of maintaining faith and order within the churches.

2   Particular emphasis was placed on the priority of the Bible. The Reformation introduced what is generally known as the "Scripture principle" – that is, the insistence that the ultimate foundation and criterion of Christian thinking is the Bible.

This does not mean that Protestant writers rejected reason or tradition in their thinking; it simply means that they regarded these as playing a subordinate role to the Bible. The English writer William Chillingworth (1602–1644) gave a particularly distinctive statement of this belief in his famous declaration that "the Bible only is the religion of Protestants.".

3   Protestant churches rejected the medieval sacramental system, which recognized seven sacraments. Instead, they affirmed that there were only two "sacraments of the gospel" – baptism and what was variously referred to as the Holy Communion, Lord's Supper, mass, or commemoration.

4   One of the most visible distinctions between Catholics and Protestants centered on the second sacrament referred to above. Catholic churches practiced "communion in one kind" – that is, they allowed the laity to receive only bread at the communion. (Priests were allowed to receive both bread and wine.) While the origins of this practice are not clear, it became widespread within medieval western Christianity. In contrast, Protestant churches practiced "communion in both kinds" – that is, the laity were allowed to receive the bread and the wine.

5   In the medieval Catholic church, a strong distinction was maintained between priests and laity. The sacrament of ordination was understood to confer some distinct and indelible character upon ministers, which marked them off from the laity. The distinction between clergy and laity was generally maintained within Protestantism, but understood in a rather different way. The doctrine of the "priesthood of all believers," which was widely accepted among leading Protestant thinkers, affirmed that all believers were to be regarded as priests, at least in some sense. As a result, professional

ministers differed from the laity only in that they exercised specific functions within the church.

6 Protestants rejected a series of Catholic beliefs concerning purgatory, arguing that they were without biblical foundation. The related practice of praying for the dead was also abandoned.

7 Protestants generally adopted a suspicious attitude towards Mary, seeing in her as much a potential source of idolatry as an example of Christian obedience. The practice of Marian veneration was generally rejected within Protestantism, along with a series of beliefs concerning the ability of the saints to intercede for either the living or the dead.

Many other examples of differences between Catholics and Protestants could be given; interested readers are referred to the analysis on pp. 261–274 for further discussion of differences between contemporary forms of Christianity. However, it is important to appreciate that there are considerable areas of agreement between Catholics and Protestants, which can easily be overlooked in the face of their obvious differences.

The confessionalization of faith: Protestant orthodoxy

As we have seen, the initial period in the life of Protestantism was enormously dynamic. From about 1520 to 1560, the movement was concerned to conquer new territories and make new advances. Yet a change of outlook appears to have settled in at some point in the 1560s, perhaps around the time of the death of Calvin in 1564. The movement was now concerned to defend itself. Something along the lines of a siege mentality seems to have evolved. Two general themes appear to have contributed to this change of outlook.

First, following the Council of Trent, Catholicism underwent a dramatic renewal of confidence. Protestants were forced to realize that the vision of nation after nation accepting the agenda of the Reformation was unrealistic. Catholicism began to regain territories which had once been sympathetic to the Reformation, and consolidated its hold on others which had remained loyal. The task now facing Protestantism was that of maintaining its present position. Part of that defensive strategy was the formulation of rigorous theological criteria of identity, so that Protestants could distinguish themselves from Catholics. The issue of doctrinal purity or "theological correctness" became crucial. Increasingly, Protestant theologians came to concentrate their attention on the formulation and defense of theological orthodoxy.

Second, increasing tensions developed between the two main types of Protestantism in mainland Europe – Lutheran and Reformed (or Calvinist). It had been generally assumed that those parts of Germany which were Protestant would be Lutheran. However, in the 1560s, Calvinism began to make significant inroads in Germany, increasing the tension between the Lutheran and Reformed churches in this region. Lutheran theologians now found themselves fighting on two fronts – against Catholics on the one hand, and Calvinists on the other. As a result, it became increasingly important to distinguish these two types of Protestantism. This led to a deliberate attempt to draw rigorous theological or doctrinal distinctions between them. As a result, a concern for "right doctrine" became of decisive importance. It is for this reason that the term "Protestant orthodoxy" is used to refer to Protestantism during this period.

The term "confessionalism" or "Second Reformation" is used to refer to the process of emphasizing doctrinal correctness, which is so typical of this period in the history of the

Protestant churches. The growing religious and political tensions within Germany in the 1560s and beyond caused an increasingly sharp distinction to be drawn between "Lutheran" and "Reformed" as epithets applied to the two main confessions that developed within the Reformation. In the early period of the Reformation, the reformers regarded themselves as evangelicals committed to a common program of theological education and reform. By the second half of the century, however, it was evident that a major bifurcation had occurred within the movement (if, indeed, it had not always been there from the beginning). The political roots of this fissure may be traced back to the abortive Colloquy of Marburg (1529), although its intellectual roots must be traced back further.

By the 1550s, this political bifurcation was more or less complete. One section of the movement, broadly corresponding to the German territories, regarded Luther, his catechisms, and the Augsburg Confession as theological authorities, whereas the cities of the Rhineland and Switzerland recognized the rival authority of Calvin and his *Institutes*, and the Heidelberg Catechism. Although it is evident that the two movements still regarded themselves as heirs to a common tradition, political and ecclesiological developments, particularly the rise of confessionalism, led to an emphasis upon their divergence, rather than upon their convergence upon matters once held to be fundamental to the Reformation. Disputes between various Protestant schools became of almost as great importance as disputes with Roman Catholicism.

This critical transition is associated with the rise of "Protestant scholasticism," similar in many ways to the forms of scholasticism which developed within the medieval church several centuries earlier. An emphasis came to be placed on the rational justification and defense of key doctrines, which were in turn used to justify and defend the integrity of the particular type of Protestantism in question, over and against other types of Protestantism on the one hand, and Catholicism on the other. To many observers, it seemed that this type of Christianity placed too much weight on matters of the head, and not enough on matters of the heart. It is this belief which underlies the rise of Pietism, to which we shall turn presently. First, we consider the specifically English version of Protestant orthodoxy usually known as "Puritanism," which had considerable cultural and political influence in the seventeenth century.

English-language Protestantism: Puritanism

The term "Puritan" was originally intended to be abusive. It was used to stigmatize those members of the Church of England during the reign of Elizabeth I who wanted to adopt more Reformed beliefs and practices (such as the abolition of bishops). The University of Cambridge was a vital center for Puritan activity, with Emmanuel College establishing itself as a significant seedbed of Puritan theological and pastoral thinking. Official hostility towards these trends led to the formation of small separatist congregations, which "withdrew" from the national church as a protest against its failure to reform itself completely. The most important of these separatist groups was the "Brownists," named after Robert Browne (ca. 1550–1633).

Following official harassment, the separatists initially found refuge in the Netherlands; some, however, were able to return to England later and establish congregations there. These groups, which may be regarded as forerunners of modern Baptists, flourished particularly during the period of the Puritan commonwealth, when it is estimated that there were 300 such congregations in England. Following the restoration of Charles II, the Baptists found themselves facing official hostility once more; it was not until the late eighteenth century that they would achieve a significant degree of acceptance and stability.

One group of particular interest should be noted. A separatist congregation was established at Scrooby, Nottinghamshire, in 1606, with John Robinson (ca. 1575–1625) as its pastor. Growing official hostility forced the congregation to move to Leiden in the Netherlands in 1609. However, the Dutch situation was still not ideal. The congregation set its sights on America, which was then being opened up to European settlers. On September 6, 1620, 102 members of the congregation set sail for America in the *Mayflower*. The resulting colony established in Massachusetts would be seen as a model by many Europeans, dissatisfied with the restrictions of religious life in the region.

Despite its growing influence within the national English church, Puritanism continued to encounter strong hostility from both church and state in the early seventeenth century. However, growing popular discontent with the monarchy at the time led to Puritanism becoming identified with the forces of democracy. As the tension between king and parliament grew, Puritanism was seen as a vigorous supporter of parliamentary authority. The resulting Civil War led to the execution of Charles I and the establishment of a Puritan commonwealth under Oliver Cromwell during the 1650s. However, the restoration of Charles II led to the withering of Puritanism as a significant political and social force in England.

Yet Puritanism was set to exercise a crucial influence elsewhere. Dissatisfaction with the religious situation in England led many English Puritans to emigrate to America, taking their faith with them. Massachusetts Bay became a center of Puritanism. The impact of this development on American history was decisive, in the opinion of many scholars, and

laid the foundations for the emergence of the United States of America as a nation with a strong sense of a distinctively religious identity.

One figure worth noting here is the Puritan poet Anne Bradstreet (1612–1672), who sailed to New England on the *Arbella*, exchanging a life of relative comfort and culture for the comparative wilderness of Massachusetts. Her poetry, which is still read today, reflects her attempts to relate faith and life, especially in the midst of the challenges and dangers of her new environment. One of her more poignant poems was written in July 1666, when her house was destroyed by fire. In the poem, she contrasts the frailty and transience of her earthly home with her hope of an indestructible home in heaven:

> Thou hast an house on high erect
> Fram'd by that mighty Architect,
> With glory richly furnished,
> Stands permanent tho' this bee fled.
> It's purchased, and paid for too
> By him who hath enough to doe.

A Protestant religion of the heart: Pietism

As orthodoxy became increasingly influential within mainstream Protestantism, so its defects became clear. At its best, orthodoxy was concerned with the rational defense of Christian truth-claims and a concern for doctrinal correctness. Yet too often this came across as an academic preoccupation with logical niceties, rather than a concern for relating theology to the issues of daily life. The term "Pietism" derives from the Latin word *pietas* (best translated as "piety" or "godliness"), and was initially a derogatory term used by the movement's opponents to describe its emphasis upon the importance of Christian doctrine for the everyday Christian life.

The movement is usually regarded as having been inaugurated with the publication of Philip Jakob Spener's *Pia Desideria* ("Pious Wishes," 1675). In this work, Spener lamented the state of the German Lutheran church in the aftermath of the Thirty Years' War (1616–1648), and set out proposals for the revitalization of the church of his day. Chief among these proposals was a new emphasis upon personal Bible study. These proposals were treated with derision by academic theologians; nevertheless, they were to prove influential in German church circles, reflecting a growing disillusionment and impatience with the sterility of orthodoxy in the face of the shocking social conditions endured during the war. For Pietism, a reformation of doctrine must always be accompanied by a reformation of life.

Pietism developed in a number of different directions, especially in England and Germany. In Germany, the movement became influential in the first half of the eighteenth century. Nikolaus Ludwig Graf von Zinzendorf (1700–1760) founded the Pietist community generally known as the "Herrnhuter," named after the village of Herrnhut. Alienated from what he regarded as the arid rationalism and barren orthodoxy of his time, Zinzendorf stressed the importance of a "religion of the heart," based on an intimate and personal relationship between Christ and the believer. A new emphasis was placed upon the role of "feeling" (as opposed to reason or doctrinal orthodoxy) within the Christian life, which may be regarded as laying the foundations of Romanticism in later German religious thought. Zinzendorf's emphasis upon a personally appropriated faith finds expression in the slogan "a living faith," which he opposed to the prevailing nominalism of Protestant orthodoxy.

Many of these ideas took root in England through the influence of John Wesley (1703–1791), a founder and early leader of the Methodist movement within the Church of England,

which subsequently gave birth to Methodism as a denomination in its own right. Convinced that he "lacked the faith whereby alone we are saved," Wesley paid a visit to Herrnhut in 1738 and was deeply impressed by what he found. The Pietist emphasis upon the need for a "living faith" and the role of experience in the Christian life led to Wesley's conversion experience at a meeting in Aldersgate Street in May 1738, in which he felt his heart to be "strangely warmed." Wesley's emphasis upon the experiential side of Christian faith, which contrasted sharply with the dullness of contemporary English Deism, led to a minor religious revival in England. Selina, Countess of Huntingdon (1707–1791), played a particularly significant role in this revival

7.11 John Wesley, from a nineteenth-century engraving. Private collection/www.bridgeman.co.uk.

by establishing pulpits throughout England served by leading revivalist preachers in rotation.

Tensions emerged within English Pietism, particularly in relation to the doctrine of grace: both Wesleys, John and his brother Charles, were Arminians, while their colleague George Whitfield was Calvinist. Yet despite their differences, the various branches of Pietism succeeded in making Christian faith relevant to the experiential world of ordinary believers. It is of some importance to note that the strongly anti-religious tone of the French Revolution during the eighteenth century is partly due to the absence of any real equivalent of Pietism in the region. The movement may be regarded as a reaction against a one-sided emphasis upon doctrinal orthodoxy, in favor of a faith which relates to the deepest aspects of human nature.

The Great Awakening: American Protestantism

Christianity was brought to North America largely by refugees seeking to escape from religious persecution then endemic in Europe. As a result, the first settlers in North America were generally deeply committed to their Christian beliefs. Most early settlers were English-speaking Protestants, fleeing from persecution in England, especially during the reigns of James I and Charles I.

The earliest New England settlements were in the Massachusetts Bay area. However, the Tidewater district of Virginia was also of importance. Jamestown was founded in 1607, and the colony attracted many refugees from England, especially under the reign of Charles I. Relationships with local Native American tribes were a matter of particular concern. John Eliot, who arrived in Massachusetts in 1631, was interested in the culture and language of the Native Americans who lived in the Boston area, and made a point of studying and learning Natic (as this regional variant of Algonquian is known). He began to preach in this language, and was able to attract support for his missionary work in the region, eventually managing to gain parliamentary approval in 1649 for the establishment of the Society for the Propagation of the Gospel in New England.

Perhaps the most celebrated encounter between Christianity and Native American culture is associated with Pocahontas (1595–1617), an Indian princess, who was the daughter of Powhatan, the powerful chief of the Algonquian Indians in the Tidewater region of Virginia. Although much legend has become attached to her conversion to Christianity and her relationship with Captain John Smith, there is no doubt that these are based on a solid historical core. Her marriage to John Rolfe in 1614 brought about a significant period of peace between the settlers and the Native Americans. Pocahontas was baptized and christened Rebecca. She died after a voyage to England to promote the work of the Virginia Company.

Although some of those settling in this region at this time were Anglicans, the evidence suggests that many were Puritans, fleeing what they regarded as an oppressive England to find religious toleration in the New World. America was to be their promised land, the Atlantic Ocean the Red Sea, and England under Charles I and Archbishop William Laud was the new Egypt. The resonances with the great biblical account of the Exodus of the people of God from Egypt and the settlement in a new land, prepared for them by God, were too obvious to miss.

In 1620 the Pilgrim Fathers made their landmark voyage from Plymouth. Between 1627 and 1640 some 4,000 individuals made the hazardous crossing of the Atlantic Ocean, and settled on the coastline of Massachusetts Bay. For them, America was the promised land, and they were the chosen people. Expelled from their Egypt by a cruel Pharaoh, they had settled in a land flowing with milk and honey. They would build a new Jerusalem, a city upon a hill, in this strange land. They might be far from the country of their birth, but they were close to God. Puritan communities emerged as strongly cohesive social and political bodies, with a firm sense of calling by God.

By the end of the first quarter of the eighteenth century, however, it seemed to many that Christianity had lost its way in the New World. In the early seventeenth century, New England churches would only admit to full membership individuals who could testify to a personal experience of conversion. As the century progressed, fewer and fewer individuals could testify to such an experience. Yet most individuals wanted some kind of connection with the church – for example, to have their children baptized, or to have a Christian burial service. From about 1660 onwards, a "halfway" membership was recognized: anyone who was prepared to accept the truth of Christianity and the moral discipline of the church could have his or her children baptized.

The result of this was inevitable: by the beginning of the eighteenth century a large proportion of church members were "nominal" or "half-way." They might attend church, and learn from the preaching of the word of God; they might have their children baptized; they might recognize Christianity as true and morally helpful – but they were, in the final resort, unconverted. Christianity and church membership were viewed as just another part of American society. Being baptized and attending church were two aspects of being a good citizen.

Growing material prosperity brought with it an indifference to faith, which soon became reduced to morality. The future of Christianity in the New World seemed to be in doubt. A sense of listlessness, of despondency, appears in many Christian writings of the period. The sense of purpose which pervaded the lives and writings of earlier generations of Christians in North America began to fade away. Older Christians began to become intensely nostalgic, longing for the old days of their youth.

In 1734, the religious landscape of the American colonies changed radically. The "Great Awakening" erupted, especially at Northampton, Massachusetts, in response to the preaching of Jonathan Edwards. Edwards published accounts of the events at Northampton in the form of a book, *A Faithful Narrative of the Surprising Work of God*, which drew international attention to the awakening. As the revival continued in New England, it was given a new sense of direction by George Whitefield (1714–1770), recently arrived from England.

The revival had a lasting impact on American Christianity. It established the role of wandering preachers, unattached to any particular church. It undermined the authority of the clergy of established churches, who felt their positions to be deeply threatened by the upsurge in popular religious interest. The foundations of a mass popular culture were laid, in which Christianity was not the preserve of a clerical elite committed to the preservation of the existing social order, but a popular movement with a direct appeal to the masses. The established clergy refused to allow Whitefield to preach in their churches; he responded by preaching in the fields around towns, and attracting vast audiences which could never have been contained within the churches from which he was barred. Perhaps the group to be most deeply threatened by this development was the colonial clergy of the Church of England – the guardians of the existing social order. It is no exaggeration to say that the roots of the American Revolution lay in the growing religious alienation between the new popular

American religion and the established religion of England. Within a generation of the Great Awakening, the colonies were in revolt against the colonial power.

The resurgence of Roman Catholicism

The evidence suggests that the Catholic church was poorly prepared to meet the challenges thrown at it by the Reformation. As a result, the new ideas of the Reformation were able to gain a considerable advantage over their Catholic rivals. For example, relatively few Catholic theologians were able or willing to write in the everyday languages of Europe, such as French or German. Luther and Calvin, by addressing audiences directly in their own languages (rather than the Latin favored by scholars), were able to outmaneuver their opponents.

A particularly important example of an evangelical work to appear in a major European language is provided by the anonymous *The Benefits of Christ*, which was published in Italian in 1543. Although its author remains uncertain, its impact was dramatic. According to one contemporary source, the second edition of the work, published at Venice, sold 40,000 copies over a period of six years. Perhaps most important of all, the Bible was translated into the everyday languages of Europe, making its ideas widely available to ordinary people. One of the most influential translations was Martin Luther's *German Bible*, which had a massive influence on the shaping of the German language. William Tyndale (ca. 1494–1536) produced an English translation of the New Testament in 1526, which had a similar impact on the English language. Catholics, meanwhile, had to continue relying on the Latin translation of the Vulgate – a translation which was increasingly regarded as inaccurate and unreliable at critical points.

A second point concerns Catholic knowledge of the thought of the early church. Early evangelical writers, such as Philip Melanchthon, were able to argue that the Reformation represented a return to the ideas and practices of the early church. Their Catholic opponents simply did not have enough knowledge of the writings of the period to contest this position. An excellent illustration of this point is provided by the Lausanne Disputation of October 1536, in which John Calvin responded to the suggestion that evangelicals despised the fathers (that is, the Christian writers of the first five centuries), regarding them as possessing no authority in matters of doctrine. Calvin declared that this was simply not true: not merely did the evangelicals respect the fathers more than their Catholic opponents; they also knew them better. Reeling off a remarkable chain of references to their writings, including their location – apparently totally from memory – Calvin virtually destroyed the credibility of his opponent. Cyprian is quoted to the letter ("in the second book of his letters, the third letter"), Chrysostom even more precisely ("the twenty-first homily, about half-way through"). The dramatic effect of this intervention was considerable. Yet looking into Calvin's quotations more closely, it is clear that the fathers are generally quoted out of context, often omitting material which points to a different interpretation than that which Calvin suggested. Nevertheless, his Catholic opponents at Lausanne (and, indeed, as time would prove, elsewhere) lacked the ability to refute him.

A third difficulty was that the Catholic church found itself outpaced by the pedagogy of the Reformation. The first phase of the Reformation recognized the importance of catechetical material – that is to say, material designed to make the ideas of the Reformation as accessible and intelligible as possible. A classic example of this is provided by Luther's *Short*

Catechism (1527), which set out his ideas in a clear and simple format. It proved to be a long time before a Catholic equivalent was forthcoming.

To add still further to Catholic difficulties in combating the rise of Protestantism, the Habsburg–Valois conflict, which rumbled on during the critical period of the 1530s until 1544, meant that two major Catholic power blocks were engaged in fighting each other. This provided a window of opportunity for the various forms of Protestantism to expand and consolidate their influence in Germany and elsewhere. The formation of the "Schmalkaldic League" (February 1531) united Lutheran and Reformed forces in the face of a military threat from emperor Charles V, and ensured the safety of Protestantism in the meantime.

Yet in the end, all of these proved to be nothing more than temporary difficulties. It was not long before Catholic writers were producing high-quality literature in the everyday languages of Europe. As Catholics devoted more time to studying the patristic period, they became increasingly confident concerning the continuity between the early church and their own period. Catholic catechisms began to appear. And the resolution of the Habsburg–Valois conflict in 1544 allowed the armies of Charles V to turn their attention to the military defeat of Lutheranism. By the end of 1544, the Schmalkaldic League had been routed. The Religious Peace of Augsburg (1555) eventually established the principle widely known as *"cuius regio, eius religio"* (which can be roughly translated as "the region determines the religion"). This more or less fixed the boundaries of Lutheranism, the Reformed churches, and Catholicism in central Europe.

The most important achievement of the Catholic church during this period, however, is widely regarded as being the Council of Trent's magisterial response to the Reformation, which placed the church in a much stronger position to consolidate itself. In view of the importance of this development, we may consider it in more detail.

The Council of Trent

Scholars agree that the convening of the Council of Trent was a decisive landmark in sixteenth-century religious history. This Council, which began its discussions in December 1545, was suspended at various points. In 1547, the outbreak of an epidemic at Trent forced its relocation to Bologna, followed by its suspension until 1551. A further suspension resulted in 1552, as a result of the revolt of the German princes against the authority of the emperor (which was eventually settled by the Religious Peace of Augsburg, noted above). It was not until 1562 that the Council could meet again; it concluded its work the following year.

Why did the Council of Trent not meet earlier? The most important reason relates to a war which was raging in Europe at the time, as noted above. The emperor Charles V was engaged in battle with the king of France. While this war was taking place, it would have been impossible for French and German bishops to sit down at the same conference table. An attempt was made to convene a reforming council at Mantua in 1537; it had to be aborted, due to the war. Another attempt was made in 1542; once more, it failed. However, in September 1544 the Peace of Crépy brought hostilities between the French and Germans to an end. Two months later Pope Paul III issued a document convening the Council of Trent with the objectives of settling theological disputes, reforming the church, and liberating Christians from Turkish invaders. The Council was scheduled to begin in March 1545, although delays crept in for a number of reasons.

The impact of the Council on the development of Catholicism during the remainder of the sixteenth century and beyond was considerable. It is widely regarded as the most important church council between the Council of Nicaea (325) and the Second Vatican Council (1962–1965). Its main achievements can be summarized as follows.

1   *The clarification of Catholic teaching.* As noted earlier, there was considerable confusion within Catholicism over what counted as the "official teaching of the church," and what was to be regarded simply as the "private opinions of individuals." This was particularly important in relation to the doctrine of justification (see pp. 153–154), which lay at the heart of Martin Luther's campaign for reform back in the late 1510s. Many traditional Catholic doctrines and practices were affirmed, including the practice of communion in one kind, the authority of the Vulgate translation of the Bible (although a revision of the translation was ordered in 1546, and completed in 1592), and the necessity of seven sacraments.

2   *The elimination of abuses within the church.* The late medieval church was plagued by a series of abuses, which did little to enhance its popular reputation. Clergy and bishops were known to be permanently absent from their parishes or dioceses, entrusting their care to minor officials while they pursued their careers elsewhere. Occasionally, clergy would hold several parishes in plurality, receiving a larger income without providing the necessary pastoral care in return. Trent moved to eliminate such abuses, by laying down strict guidelines for bishops and clergy.

An important development which took place around this period was the development of the "Society of Jesus," more generally known as "the Jesuits," to which we now turn.

The Society of Jesus

The Jesuits were founded by Ignatius Loyola (ca. 1491–1556). Loyola was a professional soldier invalided out of service in 1521 on account of a leg wound. While convalescing, he read biographies of the saints and became convinced of the need for a tightly disciplined life of faith, modeled on military lines. The importance of discipline can be seen clearly in Loyola's most significant contribution to the field of Christian spirituality – the *Spiritual Exercises*, which he drew up during the period 1522–1523 (see below). These set out a four-week program of prayer, meditation, and reflection, aimed at deepening the commitment

7.12   Ignatius Loyola, founder of the Society of Jesus, 1556, by Jacopino del Conte (1510–1598). Rome, Curia Generalizia of the Society of Jesus, General's study, AKG-Images.

of the reader to Christ. The work can be seen as a training manual for future combatants in a spiritual war.

Loyola and six colleagues constituted the original nucleus of the Society of Jesus, which was formally founded in Paris in 1534, and given papal approval by Paul III in 1540. From that point onwards, it expanded rapidly. The constitution of the order was unusual, in that it added a fourth vow to the traditional list of three vows associated with religious orders. In addition to vows of poverty, chastity, and obedience, Jesuits were required to give an oath of absolute obedience to the pope. In effect, the Jesuits became a spiritual elite, personally and directly responsible to the pope, who was free to use them in whatever way he thought best for the defense of the Christian faith and the Christian church. Although the Jesuits were not founded with the religious controversies of the Reformation period in mind, it is clear that combating Protestantism soon became one of the central goals pursued by the Jesuits, especially after the final session of the Council of Trent.

By 1556, the year of Loyola's death, there were more than a thousand members of the order, which became a significant presence in Italy, Spain, and Portugal. Their influence was felt especially in the fields of missionary work and education. Jesuit missions were established during the sixteenth century in areas as diverse as Brazil, China, India, Japan, and Malaya. In the field of education, the Jesuits established a rigorous program of studies, designed to ensure the intellectual excellence of the order. The "Ratio Studiorum" ("Method of Studies") issued in 1599 focused on literature, philosophy, and theology, and went some considerable way towards establishing the preeminence of Jesuits in the theological and cultural debates of the time. The legacy of this educational development can still be seen, particularly in the United States.

The renewal of Catholic spirituality

It is widely accepted that one of the more significant developments within the sixteenth-century Catholic church relates to the renewal of spirituality, especially in Spain. One of the best-known figures from this period is John of the Cross (1542–1591), a Carmelite who had a link with the town of Avila, where he served during the period 1572–1577. In a series of writings, such as *The Dark Night of the Soul* and *The Ascent of Mount Carmel*, John stressed the need for believers to achieve a mystical union with God. The idea of the "dark night of the soul" proved immensely helpful to those undergoing spiritual trials, and is widely regarded as his most significant and enduring contribution to spirituality.

Accounts of this fascinating period in the revival of spirituality often focus on Teresa of Avila (1515–1582), who developed an interest in spirituality while still a relatively young girl. At an early stage, she decided to enter an order of Carmelite nuns at Avila in 1535. At this stage, the convent in question did not make particularly severe demands of its members. Teresa found the life of prayer dry, difficult, and unrewarding, and came close to abandoning it altogether. However in 1554 she had a powerful religious conversion experience, which led her to the conclusion that she had, up to this point, been trusting in her own efforts, rather than allowing God to refresh and renew her in "sweetness and glory." Her enthusiasm over her new experience of God received something of a setback when the spiritual directors she initially consulted informed her that they were probably satanic. However, Diego de Cetina suggested that her experiences were valid, and recommended that she focus her thoughts on the passion of Christ.

For Teresa, spiritual and institutional renewal were closely linked. She began a program of reform within the Carmelite order in 1562, founding the first "discalced" (that is, shoeless) Carmelite convent with a considerably stricter rule than that found elsewhere. The reform gained momentum, and was extended to male Carmelites in 1568. One of the first male discalced Carmelites was John of the Cross (born Juan de Yepes). Throughout her later career, she encountered serious (and occasionally violent) opposition from the "calced" Carmelites, who took exception to her more rigorous understanding of the religious life. Although her writings were initially placed on the Index of banned books, it was only a matter of time before their spiritual and literary merit were appreciated. She was canonized in 1622. On July 18, 1970, Pope Paul VI named Teresa of Avila the first ever woman doctor of the church.

The three most important of Teresa's writings are her *Life*, *The Way of Perfection*, and *The Interior Castle of the Soul*. Her *Life* was written to serve two purposes: to provide an account of her spiritual development on the one hand, and on the other to describe her spiritual experiences and methods of prayer, which were regarded as controversial. (Her later work, *The Way of Perfection*, focused on these experiences and methods, and aimed to make them more widely known.) The first draft of the *Life* was completed by June 1562; the work was revised over the period 1563–1565 in response to the comments of her advisors. A particularly important addition is the section now contained as chapters 11–22, in which Teresa, at the insistence of García de Toledo, set out a systematic account of her understanding of prayer. Initially, reaction was generally favorable; however, Teresa had made enemies, and the manuscript was confiscated by the Inquisition in 1574. It was only after her death that the work was recovered, and began to be read more widely.

However, many consider Ignatius Loyola – the founder of the Society of Jesus – to be the greatest figure in the Spanish spiritual renaissance of the sixteenth century. Initially, Loyola's career was fairly typical of his age. After a period of service in the household of the Royal Treasurer of Castille, he joined the army of the Duke of Nájera. Any hopes he may have held for future advancement were called into question when he was wounded during the siege of Pamplona (May 1521). The leg wound which he received required a prolonged period of convalescence at the family home, the castle of Loyola. He had hoped to alleviate the boredom of this period of enforced rest by reading some novels; the family library, however, was not particularly well stocked. In the end, Loyola found himself reading Ludwig of Saxony's *Life of Christ* (1374), a work that develops the idea of an imaginative projection of the reader into the biblical narrative.

The result of Loyola's immersion in this work was a decision to reform his life by selling his possessions and making a pilgrimage to Jerusalem. The latter task proved abortive. He was obliged to spend a period of ten months (March 1522–February 1523) at the town of Manressa waiting to be allowed to travel to Rome, prior to a further journey onward to Jerusalem. During that period, he developed the general approach to spirituality which is now embodied in the *Spiritual Exercises*. This book is primarily intended for those who conduct retreats, and is not really intended to be read by others. However, it has found a wide readership beyond its anticipated audience.

The most characteristic features of the *Spiritual Exercises* can be summarized as follows:

1 An imaginative approach to the reading of Scripture and prayer, in which those undertaking the exercises (often referred to as "exercitants") form mental images as aids to prayer and contemplation.

2 A structured and progressive program of reflection and meditation, which proceeds sequentially through the major themes of

the Christian life. The four weeks specified for the *Exercises* focus on sin and its consequences; the life of Christ; the death of Christ; and the resurrection.

3 The use of a retreat director, who guides the exercitant through the exercises, allowing reflection on both God and self, leading to the taking of decisions for personal reform and renewal.

The "Ignatian retreat" soon became a well-established feature of Christian life. Though their origins lie in the sixteenth century, Ignatian approaches to prayer have been welcomed by many in the twenty-first century who have found more cognitive or intellectual approaches to be spiritually dry and unhelpful.

The Wars of Religion

The rise of Protestantism and the renewal of Catholicism inevitably caused political and social tensions to rise throughout Europe. The emperor Charles V had felt the force of these tensions, and was eventually obliged to establish an uneasy truce through the 1555 Religious Peace of Augsburg, which put an end to the long-standing conflicts between the Lutheran princes and the Catholic emperor. Yet it was not long before conflict broke out elsewhere.

The first major European war which can be shown to be directly due to religious issues broke out in France. The specific tension in this case was between Catholics and Calvinists (the term "Huguenots" was used locally to refer to the latter). Earlier, we noted that Calvin was French. Calvin appears to have seen part of his mission in life as being to convert his native country to the Reformed faith, using Geneva as a base. In April 1555, Genevan records document several agents sent out from Geneva to evangelize parts of France likely to be fertile ground for Calvinism. Others followed rapidly, in response to requests for help from French Calvinist congregations.

The whole affair was cloak-and-dagger. Secrecy was essential to the entire operation, at both the Genevan and French ends of the operation. Safe houses, complete with hiding places, were established, a day's journey apart. An underground network, similar to that employed by the French Resistance during World War II, allowed men from Geneva to slip undetected into France. By 1560, Calvinism was firmly established in many leading French cities, and gaining influential converts. There had been an explosion in the growth of Calvinist congregations and influence; the complete reformation of France seemed a real possibility. Perhaps one third of the nobility had signaled its acceptance of his religious ideas.

According to a list prepared for Admiral de Coligny in March 1562, there were 2,150 Huguenot churches in France at that point. It is difficult to verify these figures; it would, however, seem reasonable to suggest that there were at least 1,250 such churches, with a total membership in excess of 2,000,000 out of a national population of 20,000,000. Tensions rose. In 1562, war broke out. The issue was only settled through the Edict of Nantes (1598), which guaranteed the rights of French Protestants. However, it was widely ignored by subsequent French monarchs, and was finally revoked by Louis XIV in 1685, resulting in a substantial exodus of Protestants from the country.

Other religious conflicts erupted in the region. The Dutch War of Independence (1560–1618) had strongly religious dimensions. An increasingly Calvinist Dutch population wished to rid themselves of a Catholic Spanish colonial power. In England, the Civil War (1642–1649) clearly had religious aspects, reflecting deep-seated disagreements between Royalists and Puritans over the manner of government and the doctrines of the national Church of England.

By far the most important religious conflict, however, was the Thirty Years' War, which rumbled on from 1618 through 1648. The context within which this war emerged was the tension after the Peace of Augsburg in 1555. The Peace did not take account of Calvinism, which became a major presence in the region from 1560. As a result, Calvinism was given no official protection, in contrast to both Lutheranism and Catholicism. As Calvinism continued to expand, tensions increased. The trigger for the conflict was the outbreak of anti-Protestant riots in Bohemia, partly reflecting the vigorous Catholicism of Ferdinand II. The Bohemian nobles protested to the emperor over these developments. On failing to receive any satisfactory assurances for their safety, they revolted, and demanded to be ruled by a local Calvinist prince instead.

The revolt sparked a wider conflict, drawing in surrounding states and principalities. Its impact on the German economy was disastrous. When the war was finally resolved through the Peace of Westphalia (1648), any remaining enthusiasm for religious warfare had evaporated. People had had enough. A yearning for peace led to a new emphasis on toleration, and growing impatience with religious disputes. The scene was set for the Enlightenment insistence that religion was to be a matter of private belief rather than state policy. Our attention now turns to the curious cultural climate which amalgamated rationalism, revival, and revolution which gained the ascendancy in the eighteenth century.

The Modern Period

During the second half of the fifteenth century, Christianity became increasingly a European religion. Islam had launched a *jihad* ("holy war") against Christianity several centuries earlier. By about 1450, as a direct result of its military conquests, Islam was firmly established in the southwestern and southeastern parts of Europe. Although Christian communities continued to exist outside Europe (most notably in Egypt, Ethiopia, India, and Syria), Christianity was becoming geographically restricted. Its future seemed insecure.

One of the most dramatic developments to take place during the last few centuries has been the recovery of Christianity from this crisis. By the twentieth century, Christianity was firmly established as the dominant religion in the Americas, Australasia, southern Africa, and throughout many of the island nations of the South Pacific. Despite this dramatic expansion outside Europe, however, Christianity suffered a series of internal setbacks within Europe. In this section, we shall explore something of this complex story of advances and retreats, consolidations and weakening. We begin by noting one of the most significant reactions against wars of religion in Europe – the rise of indifference to religion.

The rise of indifference to religion in Europe

With the ending of the European Wars of Religion, a degree of stability settled upon the continent. Although religious controversy continued intermittently, it became generally accepted that certains parts of Europe were Lutheran, Catholic, Orthodox, or Reformed. The sense of weariness which had been created by the Wars of Religion led to a new interest in religious toleration. The classic argument for toleration of diversity in matters of religion may be found in John Locke's *Letter Concerning Toleration*.

Locke argued for religious toleration on the basis of three general considerations, as follows. First, it is impossible for the state to adjudicate between competing religious truth-claims. Locke points out that no earthly judge can be brought forward to settle the matter. For this reason, religious diversity is to be tolerated. Second, Locke suggests that, even if it could be established that one religion was superior to all others, the legal enforcement of this religion would not lead to the desired objective of that religion. Third, Locke argues, on pragmatic grounds, that the results of trying to impose religious uniformity are far worse than those which result from the continuing existence of diversity. Religious coercion leads to internal discord, or even civil war. Toleration is the only way of coping with the religious diversity of early modern Europe.

Locke's analysis can be seen as leading to the view that religion is a private matter of public indifference. What individuals believe should be regarded as private, with no relevance to the public field. This approach at one and the same time upheld religious toleration, while indicating that religion was a purely private matter. This perception was strengthened by the rise of the Enlightenment, which regarded the religions as different expressions of the same ultimate reality, which could be known through reason.

Locke's views on toleration were one response to the growing hostility towards those who took their religion too seriously, threatening the peace and prosperity of Europe. Another was the rise of rationalism. If religion was such a source of rage, abuse, and intolerance, why not undermine it completely? The Enlightenment saw reason, rather than God, as the source and arbiter of all good and true beliefs – as we shall see in what follows.

The Enlightenment: The rise of rationalism

The movement which is now generally known as "the Enlightenment" ushered in a period of considerable uncertainty for Christianity in western Europe and North America. The trauma of the Reformation and the resulting Wars of Religion had barely subsided on the continent of Europe before a new and more radical challenge to Christianity arose. If the sixteenth-century Reformation challenged the church to rethink its external forms and the manner in which it expressed its beliefs, the Enlightenment saw the intellectual credentials of Christianity itself (rather than any one of its specific forms) facing a major threat on a number of fronts. The growing emphasis upon the need to uncover the rational roots of religion had considerable negative implications for Christianity, as subsequent events were to prove.

The Enlightenment criticism of traditional Christianity was based upon the principle of the omnicompetence of human reason. A number of stages in the development of this belief may be discerned. First, it was argued that the beliefs of Christianity were rational, and thus capable of standing up to critical examination. This type of approach may be found in John Locke's *Reasonableness of Christianity* (1695), and within the early Wolffian school in Germany. Christianity was a reasonable supplement to natural religion. The notion of divine revelation was thus maintained.

Second, it was argued that the basic ideas of Christianity, being rational, could be derived from reason itself. There was no need to invoke the idea of divine revelation. As this idea was developed by John Toland in his *Christianity not Mysterious* (1696) and Matthew Tindal's *Christianity as Old as Creation* (1730), Christianity was essentially the republication of the religion of nature. It did not transcend natural religion, but was merely an example of it. All so-called "revealed religion" is actually nothing other than the reconfirmation of what can be known through rational reflection on nature. "Revelation" was simply a rational reaffirmation of moral truths already available to enlightened reason.

Third, the ability of reason to judge revelation was affirmed. As critical reason was omnicompetent, it was argued that it was supremely qualified to judge Christian beliefs and practices, with a view to eliminating any irrational or superstitious elements. This view placed reason firmly above revelation, and may be seen as symbolized in the enthronement of the Goddess of Reason in Notre Dame de Paris in 1793, in the aftermath of the French Revolution.

The Enlightenment was primarily a European and American phenomenon, and thus took place in cultures in which the most numerically significant form of religion was Christianity. This historical observation is of importance: the Enlightenment critique of religion in general was often particularized as a criticism of Christianity in general. It was Christian doctrines that were subjected to a critical assessment of a vigor without any precedent. It was Christian sacred writings – rather than those of Islam or Hinduism – that were subjected to an unprecedented critical scrutiny, both literary and historical, with the Bible being treated "as if it were any other book" (Benjamin Jowett). It was the life of Jesus of Nazareth that was subjected to critical reconstruction, rather than that of Mohammed or Buddha.

The Enlightenment attitude to religion was subject to a considerable degree of regional variation, reflecting a number of local factors peculiar to different situations. One of the most important such factors is Pietism, perhaps best known in its English and American form of Methodism. As noted earlier, this movement placed considerable emphasis upon the experiential aspects of religion (for example, see John Wesley's notion of "experimental religion"). This concern for religious experience served to make Christianity relevant and accessible to the experiential situation of the masses,

contrasting sharply with the intellectualism of, for example, Lutheran orthodoxy, which was perceived to be an irrelevance. Pietism forged a strong link between Christian faith and experience, thus making Christianity a matter of the heart as well as of the mind.

As noted earlier, Pietism was well established in Germany by the end of the seventeenth century, whereas the movement only developed in England during the eighteenth century, and in France not at all. The Enlightenment thus preceded the rise of Pietism in England, with the result that the great evangelical revivals of the eighteenth century significantly blunted the influence of rationalism upon religion. In Germany, however, the Enlightenment followed after the rise of Pietism, and thus developed in a situation which had been significantly shaped by religious faith, even if it would pose a serious challenge to its received forms and ideas. (Interestingly, English Deism began to become influential in Germany at roughly the same time as German Pietism began to exert an influence in England.) The most significant intellectual forces in the German Enlightenment were thus directed towards the reshaping (rather than the rejection or demolition) of the Christian faith.

In France, however, Christianity was widely perceived as both oppressive and irrelevant, with the result that the writers of the French Enlightenment were able to advocate the total rejection of Christianity as an archaic and discredited belief system. In his *Treaty on Tolerance*, Denis Diderot argued that English Deism had compromised itself, permitting religion to survive where it ought to have been eradicated totally. As it happened, something very like this nearly occurred during the French Revolution of 1789. But what of the earlier American Revolution of 1776, which served as a model for many French revolutionaries?

Christianity in the American Revolution

The causes of the American Revolution are complex, involving a number of interrelated issues. Perhaps the dominant theme is that of a desire to break free from the influence of England, which was increasingly seen as paternalist, oppressive, and exploitative. This desire for freedom expressed itself in the political, economic, and religious arenas. The Church of England was increasingly viewed as the religious dimension of British colonialism.

During the 1760s, vigorous efforts were made by American Protestants to resist the expansion of the Church of England's authority in the region. The Church of England was established by law in all the southern colonies, and its influence seemed destined to increase still further. The Quebec Act of 1774, which established Catholicism in French-speaking regions of Canada, was seen as particularly provocative. If Britain could decide what was the established religion in Canada, what would it do in America? Suspicion and hostility grew unchecked.

The imposition of the Stamp Tax (1764) brought cries of "no taxation without representation." The 1773 decision of the British parliament to give the East India Company exclusive rights to sell tea in North America led to the "Boston Tea Party," and widespread unrest in Massachusetts. British troops were sent to restore order; this action was interpreted as an act of war by the colonists. A series of battles was fought in 1775, leading to the Declaration of Independence on July 4, 1776. A full-scale war of independence ensued, in which church pulpits often served as rallying points for revolutionary activity. In effect, the revolution united Christian groups of more or less all persuasions in the service of a greater goal.

The American revolutionaries saw themselves as called to break the spiritual and temporal power of the Church of England in America. Like their forebears at the time of the English Civil War, they saw the conflict as a moment of purification, a time in which the true identity of a nation would be shaped. The battle was not between Christianity and atheism, but between a compromised state church and a pure gospel church. It would be a battle for the soul of America. While some revolutionaries had economic and political goals, others had religious objectives – objectives that demanded the *purification* of religion, not its *elimination*. Political republicanism was not seen as entailing atheism. Was not Calvin's Geneva, that city of God set upon a hill for all to see and imitate, itself a republic? And might not republicanism and the cause of true religion thus be united, where in England they were seen as opposing?

The constitutional separation of church and state can be argued to rest upon a fundamental desire to avoid any specific form of Christianity defining the establishment, after the manner of the Church of England, which was widely regarded as corrupt and degenerate in American republican circles. The First Amendment to the Constitution declared that "Congress shall make no law respecting an establishment of religion or restricting the free exercise thereof." The Constitution thus prevented any formal establishment of religion, meaning that no Christian church (such as the Church of England) was to be given a favored legal status by the state. Although some modern constitutional theorists argue that this was intended to remove religion from American public life, or that it justifies this practice today, it is clear that the intention of the Constitution was simply to avoid giving legal or social precedence to any specific Christian grouping.

The American Revolution thus led to the consolidation of Christianity in the United States. However, on the continent of Europe, another revolution was about to break out. In this case, the consequences were more far reaching and negative.

The great revolt against God: The origins of western atheism

If any event signals the dawn of the golden age of atheism in the west, it is the French Revolution of 1789. Generations of accumulated popular resentment and intellectual hostility against king and church could finally be contained no longer. The storming of the Bastille on July 14 of that year was widely seized upon as an icon of liberation, symbolizing the sweeping aside of an old order, based on superstition and oppression. A brave new world lay ahead, firmly grounded in nature and reason, and equally firmly committed to the liberation of humanity from "tyranny" and "superstition." The wisdom of the day was as simple as it was powerful: eliminate God, and a new future would dawn. It was a vision which thrilled many across Europe, drawing aside a curtain on a once forbidden world, which now seemed about to become reality.

It was clear that both the pillars of traditional French society – the monarchy and the church – needed reform. Even late in the summer of the momentous year 1789, the general feeling was that the French monarch had allowed a series of measures which would abolish feudalism and remove some of the grievances felt by ordinary people against the power and privileges of the church. On November 2, it was agreed that all church lands should be nationalized, with a basic minimum wage for priests being set in place, guaranteed by the state. The Civil Constitution of the Clergy (July 1790) rejected the authority of the pope, and reorganized and slimmed down the dioceses and the cathedral clergy. Although radical, the measures were not anti-Christian. The clergy split into a group which wished to remain loyal to Rome, and another wishing to comply with the new civil authority.

All changed soon afterwards. A more radical revolutionary faction, headed by Robespierre, gained power and launched its celebrated "Reign of Terror." Louis XVI was publicly guillotined on January 21, 1793. A program of dechristianization was put in place during the period 1793–1794. The cult of the Goddess Reason was given official sanction. The old calendar was replaced by a republican calendar which eliminated Sundays and Christian festivals, replacing them with secular alternatives. Priests were placed under pressure to renounce their faith. A program of church closure was initiated. Although the impact of these measures seems to have been felt mostly in urban areas, they caused considerable disruption and hardship to the church throughout France.

The religious policies of the French Revolution were soon extended to neighboring areas. In November 1792, French revolutionary armies embarked on a campaign of conquest in the region. By 1799, six satellite republics had been established, embracing areas such as the Netherlands, Switzerland, parts of northern Italy, and areas of the Rhineland. In February 1798, the papal states were occupied, and the pope was deported to France, where he died six months later. The French Revolution, it seemed to many, had destroyed not only the French church but also the papacy.

On the eve of the nineteenth century, the future of Christianity in Europe thus seemed remarkably fragile. Many saw it as linked with the politics of a bygone era, an obstacle to progress and liberty. Its faith and its institutions seemed to be in irreversible decline. In fact, this would prove to be a false perception. The revolutionary experimentation with a secular state eventually fizzled out. Under Napoleon, relations with the pope were reestablished, although on very different terms to those in operation before the revolution. The Bourbon monarchy was restored. In 1814, Louis XVIII returned to claim the throne of France, and reestablished Catholicism. The situation was never easy, and real tensions between church and state continued unabated throughout most of the nineteenth century. Nevertheless, the church was able to regain at least some of its lost influence, prestige, and clergy. The period 1815–1848 witnessed a series of popular revivals (usually referred to as "le Réveil") in French-speaking Europe.

Yet the atheist experiment, however short-lived, had created immense interest throughout Europe, and galvanized both religious and political radicals. Atheism began to seem an immensely attractive option, particularly in Germany. In view of the importance of atheism to the fortunes of Christianity in western Europe in the nineteenth and twentieth centuries, we shall consider this development in more detail.

Karl Marx and the consolidation of atheism

Marxism, probably one of the most significant worldviews to emerge during the modern period, has had a major impact upon Christianity during the twentieth century. "Marxism" is usually understood to refer to the ideas associated with the German writer Karl Marx (1818–1883). Until about 1989, the term also referred to a state ideology, characteristic of a number of states in eastern Europe and elsewhere, which regarded Christianity and other religions as reactionary, and adopted repressive measures to eliminate them.

The notion of materialism is fundamental to Marxism. This is not some metaphysical or philosophical doctrine which affirms that the world consists only of matter. Rather, it is an assertion that a correct understanding of human beings must begin with material production. The way in which human beings respond to their material needs determines everything else. Ideas, including religious ideas, are responses to material reality. They are the superstructure which is erected upon a socioeconomic substructure. In other words, ideas and belief-systems are a response to a quite definite set of social and economic conditions. If these are radically altered (for example, by a revolution), the belief-systems which they generated and sustained will pass away with them.

This first idea flows naturally into the second – alienation of humanity. A number of factors bring about alienation within the material process, of which the two most significant are the division of labor and the existence of private property. The former causes the alienation of the worker from his product, whereas the second brings about a situation in which the interests of the individual no longer coincide with those of society as a whole. As productive forces are owned by a small minority of the population, it follows that societies are divided along class lines, with political and economic power being concentrated in the hands of the ruling class.

If this analysis is correct, Marx believed that the third conclusion naturally followed. Capitalism – the economic order just described – was inherently unstable, due to the tensions arising from productive forces. As a result of these internal contradictions, it will break down. Some versions of Marxism present this breakdown as happening without any need for assistance. Others present it as the result of a social revolution, led by the working class. The closing words of the *Communist Manifesto* (1848) seem to suggest this latter: "Workers have nothing to lose but their chains. They have a world to gain. Workers of the world, unite!"

So how do these ideas relate to Christian theology? In his 1844 political and economic manuscripts, Marx develops the idea that religion in general (he does not distinguish the individual religions) is a direct response to social and economic conditions. Religion has no real independent existence. It is a reflection of the material world, a spiritual superstructure built upon an economic and social substructure. "The religious world is but the reflex of the real world." Thus Marx argues that "religion is just the imaginary sun which seems to man to revolve around him, until he realizes that he himself is the center of his own revolution." In other words, God is simply a projection of human concerns. Human beings "look for a superhuman being in the fantasy reality of heaven, and find nothing there but their own reflection."

But why should religion exist at all? If Marx is right, why should people continue to believe in such a crude illusion? Marx's answer centers on the notion of alienation. "Humans make religion; religion does not make humans. Religion is the self-consciousness and self-esteem of people who either have not found themselves or who have already lost themselves again." Religion is the product of social and economic alienation. It arises from that alienation, and at the same time encourages that alienation by a form of spiritual intoxication which renders the masses incapable of recognizing their situation and doing something about it. Religion is a comfort, which enables people to tolerate their economic alienation. If there were no such alienation, there would be no need for religion. The division of labor and the existence of private property introduce alienation and estrangement into the economic and social orders.

Materialism affirms that events in the material world bring about corresponding changes in the intellectual world. Religion is thus the result of a certain set of social and economic conditions. Change those conditions, so that economic alienation is eliminated, and religion will cease to exist. It will no longer serve any useful function. Unjust social

conditions produce religion, and are in turn supported by religion. "The struggle against religion is therefore indirectly a struggle against *the world* of which religion is the spiritual fragrance."

Marx thus argues that religion will continue to exist, as long as it meets a need in the life of alienated people. "The religious reflex of the real world can . . . only then vanish when the practical relations of everyday life offer to man none but perfectly intelligible and reasonable relations with regard to his fellow men and to nature." In other words, a shake-up in the real world is needed to get rid of religion. Marx thus argues that when a non-alienating economic and social environment is brought about through communism, the needs which gave rise to religion will vanish. And with the elimination of those material needs, spiritual hunger will also vanish.

In practice, Marxism had virtually no influence until the period of World War I (1914–1918). This can be put down partly to some internal problems, and partly to the lack of any real opportunities for political expansion. The internal problems are especially interesting. The suggestion that the working class could liberate itself from its oppression, and bring about a political revolution, soon proved to be illusory. It rapidly became clear that Marxists, far from being drawn from the ranks of the politically conscious working class, were actually depressingly middle class (like Marx himself). Aware of this problem, Vladimir Ilyich Lenin developed the idea of a "vanguard party." The workers were so politically naive that they needed to be led by professional revolutionaries, who alone could provide the overall vision and practical guidance that would be needed in bringing about and sustaining a world revolution.

The Russian Revolution gave Marxism the break it needed. However, although Marxism established itself in a modified form

(Marxism-Leninism) within the Soviet Union, it proved unsuccessful elsewhere. Its successes in eastern Europe after World War II (1939–1945) can be put down mainly to military strength and political destabilization. Its successes in Africa were largely due to the seductive appeal of Lenin's carefully devised concept of "imperialism," which allowed alienated elements in certain African and Asian countries to put their backwardness down to their ruthless and systematic exploitation by the external agency of western capitalism rather than to any inherent deficiencies.

The economic failure and political stagnation which resulted when such countries experimented with Marxism in the 1970s and 1980s soon led to disillusionment with this new philosophy. In Europe, Marxism found itself locked into a spiral of decline. Its chief advocates increasingly became abstract theoreticians, detached from working-class roots, with virtually no political experience. The idea of a socialist revolution gradually lost its appeal and its credibility. In the United States and Canada, Marxism had little, if any, social appeal in the first place, although its influence upon the academic world was more noticeable. The Soviet invasion of Czechoslovakia in 1968 resulted in a perceptible cooling of enthusiasm for Marxism within western intellectual circles. However, Marx's ideas found their way, suitably modified, into modern Christian theology. Latin American liberation theology (see pp. 258–260) can be shown to have drawn appreciatively on Marxist insights, even if the movement cannot really be described as "Marxist" as a result.

The globalization of Christianity: The age of mission

Although missionary work had always been undertaken by the church, it is widely agreed that a new age of evangelism began in the eighteenth century, with England playing a particularly significant role in the spreading of Christianity. The twentieth century, for some nineteenth-century pundits, was to be the Christian century. A series of triumphalistic congresses and writings in the late nineteenth century had confidently proclaimed the inevitability of the conversion of the world within the next generation. The First International Convention of the Student Volunteer Movement met in Cleveland in 1891, and adopted as its motto the slogan "the evangelization of the world in this generation." It was the largest student conference assembled in its time, and was carried along by an ebullient confidence typical of its age. In what follows, we shall offer an overview of the "great age of mission," which came to an end with the outbreak of World War I in 1914.

A major cultural concern may be noted from the outset. The interplay of British economic agendas and imperial ambitions with religious issues has always been conceded to be complex. There is no doubt that many missionaries – and by no means all English – saw the adoption of western culture as going hand in hand with the spread of the Christian faith. Inevitably, this led to the growing perception that Christianity was essentially a western religion.

This was a particularly sensitive matter in parts of Asia, such as India and China. The first major Protestant mission to India was based at Tranquebar on the Coromandel Coast, about 200 kilometers south of Madras. Among the German Lutheran missionaries of note were Bartholomäus Ziegenbalg (who directed the mission from its founding in 1706 to 1719) and Christian Frederick Schwartz (director from 1750 to 1787). However, the growing political power of Britain in the region inevitably favored the activities of British missionaries, the first of which (the Baptist William Carey) began work in Bengal in 1793. This work was assisted in no small measure by the decision of Clement XIV to suppress the Society of Jesus. The bull *Dominus ac Redemptor* (July 21, 1773) formally terminated "all and every one of its functions and ministries." The missionary activity of the Jesuits in India and elsewhere was thus brought to an end. Nevertheless, at least fifty Jesuits are known to have continued missionary work in India after the suppression of their order, despite the efforts of the Portuguese to repatriate them.

British missionary societies and individuals were thus able to operate in India without any major opposition from other European agencies. Nevertheless, they received no support from the British authorities; the East India Company, for example, was opposed to their activities, on the grounds that they might create ill-will amongst native Indians and thus threaten the trade upon which it depended. However, the Charter Act (passed by the British parliament on July 13, 1813) revised the conditions under which the Company was permitted to operate: the new charter gave British missionaries protected status, and a limited degree of freedom to carry out evangelistic work on the Indian subcontinent. The result was inevitable: "since 1813, Christian missions have never been wholly free from the stigma of undue dependence on government" (Stephen Charles Neill). The new Charter also made provision for the establishment of an Anglican bishopric at Calcutta. Under Reginald Heber (1783–1826; bishop of Calcutta 1823–1826), missionary work was expanded considerably, and restricted to Anglicans (Lutheran missionaries were obliged to be reordained to allow them to continue operating in the region). Further revisions to the East India Company's charter in 1833 removed some of the restrictions imposed earlier upon missionary work.

It was inevitable that religious tensions would develop. In 1830, the Dharma Sabha was formed, apparently as a reaction against intrusive forms of westernization in Bengal. The uprising of 1857 (generally referred to as "the Indian Mutiny" by contemporary English writers) is often regarded as the outcome of this growing resentment at westernization.

Western missionary efforts in China also met with limited results. One of the many effects of the Opium War of the 1840s was to open the "Middle Kingdom" up to at least some western attitudes. China chose to remain isolated from the west until the nineteenth century, when growing interest in commerce opened up the region to western missionaries. However, Christianity continued to be seen as something western, and hence in conflict with traditional Chinese values. As Chinese nationalism became an increasingly important political force, hostility deepened towards the west. Christianity was widely regarded as a western influence, which needed to be eliminated from China. The I Ho Ch'uan crusade of 1899–1900, with its fanatical opposition to foreign investment and religious activity, was particularly difficult for the Christian churches in China. Further opposition to Christianity developed for ideological reasons under Mao Zedong, especially during the years of the "cultural revolution" (1966–1976), which aimed to eliminate religion. In recent years, however, there has been growing unofficial acceptance of Christianity within China.

If missionary work in Asia met with limited success, this was compensated for by successes elsewhere, especially in Africa and Australasia. Growing missionary interest in Africa developed during the late eighteenth century, especially in reaction to the brutality of the slave trade. Major British missionary societies which were active in Africa during the late eighteenth or early nineteenth centuries include the Baptist Missionary Society (BMS, founded 1792, and initally known as "The Particular Baptist Society for the Propagation of the Gospel''); the London Missionary Society (LMS, founded 1795, and initially known as ''The Missionary Society''); and the Church Missionary Society (CMS, founded 1799, and originally known as ''The Church Missionary Society for Africa and the East''). Each of these societies developed a particular focus on specific regions: the BMS focused on the Congo basin, the LMS on southern Africa (including Madagascar), and the CMS on West and East Africa. All of these societies were Protestant, and generally strongly evangelical in their outlook. It was not until the middle of the nineteenth century that Catholic mission groups began to become seriously involved in the region. The trauma of the French Revolution (1789) and its aftermath had severely shaken the Catholic church. Only after the Congress of Vienna (1815) had settled the future shape of Europe could the church turn its attention to evangelism.

The dominant feature of sub-Saharan Africa in the nineteenth century is the growing importance of colonialism. Belgium, Britain, France, and Germany had all established colonies in this region during the period. The forms of Christianity dominant in these European nations varied considerably, with the result that a considerable diversity of churches became established in Africa. Anglicanism, Catholicism, and Lutheranism were all well established by the end of the century; in South Africa, the Dutch Reformed church had a particularly strong influence among European settlers. It must, however, be stressed that other missionaries from radically different backgrounds were also active in the region. For example, at least 115 black American missionaries are known to have been present and active in Africa during the period 1875–1899.

Reports of the voyages of Captain Cook during the eighteenth century, including the discovery of Australia, led to a renewed interest in evangelizing this hitherto unknown region. In 1795, the London Missionary Society was founded with the primary objective of sending missionaries to ''the islands of the South Sea.'' The first major missionary expedition to the region set off in August 1796, when thirty missionaries set sail for Tahiti. Although this mission faced considerable difficulties – not least of which related to the very different sexual mores of England and Tahiti – it can be seen as marking the beginning of a sustained effort to establish Christianity in the area.

The geographical nature of the region made one of the most reliable means of evangelization – the establishment of mission stations – impossible. The populations of the islands were generally too small to justify the building and maintenance of such settlements. The most successful strategy to be adopted was the use of missionary vessels, which allowed European missionaries to direct and oversee the operations of native evangelists, pastors, and teachers.

The most significant Christian missions in the region were located in Australia and New Zealand, which eventually came to serve as the base for most missionary work in the area. Christianity came to Australia in 1788. The circumstances of its arrival were not entirely happy. The fleet which arrived in New South Wales was transporting convicts to the penal settlements which were being established there. At the last moment, William Wilberforce persuaded the British naval authorities to allow a chaplain to sail with the fleet. With the dramatic increase in immigration to the region from Britain in the following century, the various forms of British Christianity became established. The formation of the ''Bush Brotherhoods'' in 1897 laid the basis for the evangelization of the interior of the continent.

The first missionaries arrived in New Zealand in 1814. The consolidation of Christianity in the region was largely due to Bishop George

Selwyn (1809–1878), who was appointed missionary bishop of New Zealand in 1841. During his time there, he had a marked impact on the development of Christianity, particularly in relation to education. He returned to England in 1867.

This brief overview of the "great age of mission" helps explain how Christianity broke free from its European context to become a global religion. Although apparently landlocked in Europe as a result of Islamic expansion in the sixteenth century, the growing maritime ambitions of western European nations led to Christianity being diffused throughout the world – yet often in a decidedly westernized form. This legacy of western influence, as events demonstrated, was often a mixed blessing. One of the most remarkable developments of late twentieth- and early twenty-first-century Christianity has been the process of "indigenization," in which Christianity in many parts of Latin America, Asia, and Africa broke free from its western origins and evolved in forms much more adapted to those areas' distinct cultural heritages.

The shifting fortunes of Roman Catholicism

After the trauma of the French Revolution, Catholicism began to regain something of the confidence it had known in earlier periods. The rise of Romanticism had a powerful effect on the reawakening of interest in Catholicism, particularly in Germany and France. Chateaubriand's *Génie du Christianisme* ("Genius of Christianity"), which appeared in 1802, did much to develop this new interest in the Christian faith, which can be seen reflected in many aspects of nineteenth-century culture. Other writers who drew on Romanticism in their defense of Catholicism included Allessandro Manzoni (1785–1873) in Italy and Friedrich von Stolberg (1750–1819) in Germany. Rationalism

was widely regarded as having led to the catastrophes of the past; there was a new sympathy for the view that Christianity was a major source of artistic inspiration and cultural excellence.

There can be no doubt that Catholicism needed to renew itself after the devastation of the French Revolution and its aftermath. It is helpful to reflect on the extent of Catholicism after the end of the Napoleonic era in 1814. Although Catholic missions had led to the establishment of Catholic communities in regions such as South America, Japan, and India, Catholicism was largely a European religion at this stage, bounded by the new nation of Belgium in the northwest, Spain in the southwest, Austria in the northeast, and Italy in the southeast. Most of the 100 million European Catholics were to be found in the Habsburg empire, Italy, and France. It fell to Pius VII to renew his church after his return to Rome in May 1814. The undertaking seemed enormous; nevertheless, he proved equal to the task. The groundwork for this endeavor was laid by the papal Secretary of State, Consalvi, who negotiated concordats with a series of states during the Congress of Vienna (1815). The Congregation for Extraordinary Ecclesiastical Affairs was established in 1814, with the objective of rebuilding Catholicism throughout Europe. The success of these measures can be seen in a traditionally strongly Protestant nation such as England, in which the Catholic hierarchy was reestablished in 1850.

Catholicism became a major influence in the United States during this period. Although revolutionary America was dominated by Protestantism, waves of immigrants from Ireland and Italy began to alter the religious balance of power decisively as the nineteenth century progressed. Archbishop John Carroll (1735–1815) did much to encourage the social acceptance of Catholicism at a time during which its numbers were rapidly increasing. During the 1840s, it is estimated that 2.5 million Irish Catholics emigrated to the east coast of the United States, with dramatic demographic consequences for eastern cities such as Boston and New York. The emergence of American Catholicism as a major force in the life of the nation was partly due to the ethnic loyalty of its adherents, who saw Catholicism as an integral aspect of their identity. Their European origins thus served to mold the religious views of American immigrants at this critical period in the history of the nation. The founding of major Catholic educational institutions, such as the University of Notre Dame in 1842, created the basis for the emergence of Catholicism as a significant intellectual force in the life of the nation.

The reemergence of the pope as a major figure within Catholicism during the nineteenth century can be attributed, at least in part, to the aftermath of the Napoleonic wars. In the decades prior to the French Revolution, the pope seems to have been largely ignored by the Catholic faithful, who regarded him as isolated and distant. However, Napoleon's fairly vicious treatment of the pope caused him to regain his prestige in the eyes of both the faithful and European governments. Even in France, the heartland of movements which advocated nationally governed churches, there was a new respect for the pope. The scene was set for the return of the papacy as a leading institution within Catholicism and beyond. The movement which advocated increased papal authority was known as "ultramontanism," and merits further attention in its own right, not least because of its importance in connection with the First Vatican Council – to which we now turn.

The First Vatican Council

The term "ultramontanism" derives from two Latin words bearing the sense of "beyond the mountains." The mountains in question are the Alps, and the issue at stake is the extent to which the pope had authority "beyond the Alps" – that is to say, beyond Italy into Europe itself. There was considerable sympathy for this view in the 1820s, partly due to the influence of Joseph de Maistre (1754–1821), whose *Du pape* ("On the Pope") appeared in 1819. The rise of revolutionary movements in France, Italy, and Germany during the late 1840s led to increased concern over the political stability of Catholic countries, and particularly the position of the pope himself. Faced with the prospect of steadily decreasing political power, culminating in his unhappy eviction from many of his former possessions in 1870, Pius IX (pope from 1846 to 1878) concentrated on establishing his spiritual authority within the church.

7.13 The Vatican. AKG-Images/Joseph Martin.

The most significant aspect of this program is widely agreed to be the opening of the First Vatican Council in 1869. This Council can be seen as marking a decisive confrontation between liberal Catholics on the one hand, and ultramontanists on the other. The issue which brought this controversy to sharp focus was the location of supreme authority within the church. Was supreme authority invested in the great Councils of the church, or in the papacy itself? In the end, the outcome was a decisive victory for the ultramontanists. This was given formal expression in the famous dogma of papal infallibility, promulgated on July 13, 1870. This affirmed that the pope, when speaking *ex cathedra* (that is, in his formal capacity as teacher and defender of the faith), is infallible.

This dogma caused some concern, particularly in Germany. Otto von Bismarck (1815–1898) was appointed chancellor of Prussia in 1864. He embarked on a policy of German unification, which was pursued with increasing vigor after the end of the Franco-Prussian War in 1871. Bismarck regarded the dogma as an insult to German Protestants, and a potential threat to the emerging authority of the German state. As a result, Bismarck embarked on a policy of discrimination against German Catholics during the 1870s. This *Kulturkampf* ("Culture-War") eventually fizzled out in 1886. Yet anti-religious feeling was growing elsewhere in Europe, most notably in France, where the 1901 Association Law and the 1905 Separation Law virtually eliminated religion from public life, including education.

In Italy, the position of the pope became difficult following the rise to power of Victor Emmanuel (1820–1878), who in effect stripped the pope of all his territories except for the Vatican, the Lateran, and Castel Gandolfo. While the Law of Papal Guarantees ensured his independence and safety, it nevertheless placed restrictions on his rights. This was eventually replaced by the Lateran Treaty of 1929, which was more favorable to the pope.

The Victorian crisis of faith

In his important book *God's Funeral*, A. N. Wilson documents and analyzes the rise of atheism in Victorian Britain. One of the most interesting things about the book is his careful documentation of the ambivalence felt within late nineteenth-century England over its loss of faith. The secular enterprise, begun with great enthusiasm, had achieved substantial successes by the end of the century. Politically and socially, Christianity remained highly significant in national life, and would remain so until after World War I. Yet its ideas were increasingly seen as discredited, unattractive, and outdated by its novelists, poets, and artists. Christianity had been tried and tested at the imaginative and rational levels, and found wanting on both counts. Although it might be thought that this grand retreat from faith would have been greeted with delight and celebration, Wilson brings out the deep sense of emotional loss and confusion which the inexorable elimination of God brought in its wake.

It is difficult to seize on a single figure as illustrating or causing this crisis of faith. However, the poet Algernon Swinburne is of importance. For Swinburne, Christianity had dulled the west's imagination, and was now suffering extinction because of its inability to capture the imagination of its culture. The key to Swinburne's importance lies in a line from what is widely regarded as one of his greatest poems, the "Hymn to Proserpine":

Thou has conquered, O pale Galilean; the world has grown grey from thy breath.

These words point to Swinburne's fundamental conviction of the *imaginative deficit* of the Christianity he knew and so thoroughly detested. Religion takes away a sun, and offers a mere star in its place. God was the great oppressor of the human soul. What was there in the pallid Christ of popular devotion that could enrich the imagination of his day? The Victorian Christ might make the world meek and mild; he would never capture its allegiance through an appeal to beauty or joy. Christianity triumphed by impoverishing culture and diminishing humanity's delight in itself. Yet, perhaps most significantly of all, there was no link between Christ and the transcendent – no reason to suppose that, in encountering and wrestling with the person of Jesus Christ, one was stepping over the threshold of a mystery and passing into the presence of something (or someone) of compelling beauty or delight.

The novelist George Eliot is also regularly seen as a major figure in this emerging climate of suspicion and hostility towards religious faith. Many of Eliot's misgivings about Christianity concerned its apparent lack of concern for issues of morality in its own doctrine. Why, Eliot asked, did it devalue human love, except when directed towards the praise of God? We can see here a leading theme of the Victorian crisis of faith – a growing moral revolt against Christianity on account of its leading ideas. Writers such as J. A. Froude, Matthew Arnold, and F. W. Newman abandoned their faith on account of a growing sense of the immorality of such doctrines as original sin, predestination, and substitutionary atonement. Theological terms and slogans which had been the proud watchwords of an earlier generation of Protestant writers now became embarrassments which could no longer be tolerated. Where Puritans had exulted in the thought of a sovereign God who could deal unaccountably with his creatures in any way he liked, many Victorians found this deeply disturbing, and in open conflict with their increasingly developed sense of morality and justice.

Eliot, like many others, therefore turned to a "religion of human sympathy" in place of this rather dark and dismal conception of God. Similar patterns of alienation from conventional religion are found thoughout her novels, from *Adam Bede* through to *Middlemarch*. The moral aspects of faith can, she believed, be maintained without the metaphysical basics of Christianity. We can be good without God. Indeed, belief in the Christian God can be a significant obstacle to the achievement of "individual and social happiness." These views became the received wisdom of the age, defining the emerging late Victorian consensus on the ability of humanity to shape its own destiny. While some – Thomas Hardy comes to mind – were more pessimistic about humanity's ability to construct morality without God than Eliot, they were a distinguished minority in this discussion.

The Victorian era is widely regarded as undergoing major changes from about 1870 to 1900, which can be seen as ultimately subverting the values and beliefs of its earlier phases. Many writers of the period were conscious of standing at the threshold of a new age, uncertain of what it might bring, yet suspecting that the old ways of thinking were on their way out. In his *Stanzas from the Grand Chartreuse*, written around this time, Matthew Arnold (1822–1888) spoke of being caught

> Between two worlds, one dead,
> The other powerless to be born,
> With nowhere to lay my head.

Arnold's journey through the Alps is the backdrop against which he explores his sense of displacement, focusing especially on the erosion of faith in his culture – and perhaps even in himself. His once robust faith, he comments, more than a little wistfully, now seems "but a dead time's exploded dream." Arnold expresses a sense of melancholy and sadness over his nation's loss of faith, which he saw pathetically mirrored in the ebbing of the tide on Dover beach:

> The Sea of Faith
> Was once, too, at the full, and round earth's shore
> Lay like the folds of a bright girdle furl'd.
> But now I only hear
> Its melancholy, long, withdrawing roar,
> Retreating, to the breath
> Of the night-wind, down the vast edges drear
> And naked shingles of the world.

That tide was now ebbing, and Arnold never expected to see it return. It is impossible to read his poem "Dover Beach" without glimpsing something of his pain and bewilderment over his nation's willing loss of its religious soul.

Yet Arnold's sadness was shared by others, who might have been expected to be rather more positive about the nation's loss of faith. There is something almost tender in Thomas Hardy's marking the end of the era of faith, as he envisages God's funeral procession:

> I did not forget
> That what was mourned for, I, too, long had prized.

The more radical elements of the French Revolution believed, with a passion and depth that seem slightly misplaced today, that the elimination of God would lead to public rejoicing and the end of craven submission to the crass ideologies of the past. In the event, the fading of God, like a slow but inevitable sunset, was marked by a sense of loss, of bereavement, which earlier generations would have found difficult to comprehend. Suddenly, it became meaningful to speak of the "death of God" in western culture – a theme which became increasingly important in the aftermath of the Russian Revolution of 1917.

The Armenian genocide of 1915

The history of Christianity in the twentieth century opened with a catastrophe which traumatized Christians in the eastern Mediterranean region, and which was an ominous portent of things to come later that century. Turkey was a predominantly Islamic country which found itself caught up in World War I. The region was home to a significant number of non-Islamic peoples, including Armenian Christians. The Armenian people had adopted the Christian faith in 301, and were proud of the fact that they were the oldest Christian nation in the region. The events of 1915 did not come entirely as a bolt from the blue. There had been a series of massacres of Armenian Christians at twenty-four major centers during October 1895. These are now generally seen as a small-scale rehearsal for the much more extensive and systematic killings of 1915. These massacres were not, it seems, specifically directed against Christians but against non-Islamic religious minorities in general.

The events of 1895 paled into insignificance in the light of the massive assaults of twenty years later, specifically directed against Armenian Christians by the Young Turks. It is thought that one and a half million Armenian Christians were slaughtered during the genocide of April 1915. These events took place deep within the Ottoman empire, under wartime conditions which made communication and intervention virtually impossible. Nevertheless, what had happened could not be concealed. A month later, the governments of France, Great Britain, and Russia issued a declaration denouncing the massacres as "crimes against humanity and civilization," for which the entire Turkish government would be held responsible. The early use of the phrase "crimes against humanity" is of no small importance, as this prefigures the modern concern to prevent such criminal events ever happening again.

The draft peace treaty with Turkey known as the "Treaty of Sèvres" (August 10, 1920) contained a specific provision by which the Turkish government undertook to hand over to the Allied Powers the persons responsible for the massacres committed during the war on Turkish territory. However, the Treaty of Sèvres was not formally ratified and never came into force. It was replaced by the Treaty of Lausanne (July 24, 1923), which did not contain any provisions respecting the punishment of war crimes. Instead, it set out a "Declaration of Amnesty" for all offenses committed by Turkish agents between August 1, 1914 and November 20, 1922 – including the Armenian genocide. No action was taken against Turkey, leading many to conclude that the international community was prepared to tolerate such acts of genocide. Moral outrage might be expressed; no decisive action would be taken. Such, at any rate, was the conclusion of Adolf Hitler, as he gave thought to his own plans for genocide, which would also take place under wartime conditions. In fact, there are uncomfortable historical parallels between the Ottoman attitude towards their substantial Christian minority and the Nazi treatment of Jews throughout the Third Reich which have not been given the attention they merit.

The impact of this genocide upon world Christianity has been mixed. Regionally, it was seen as a catastrophe. Christians in the Middle East were stunned and numbed by the events. Many of them lived as religious minorities under Islamic rule. Might not these shocking events presage a more general repression of Christians by other Islamic powers in the region? In the event, these fears proved unfounded. The Turkish massacres seemed to reflect the political situation within the country at the time, which encouraged xenophobia. Unaware of this, the survivors of the massacres

believed they had no place in post-war Turkey, even with a secularist constitution which denied Islam the power it had enjoyed under the Ottomans. Dispersion seemed the only viable solution. Today, the largest Armenian Christian community is found in the United States.

The genocide raised dark and difficult questions within the worldwide Christian community. Would the twentieth century mark the beginning of a more sustained attack on Christianity by its rivals? The nineteenth century had witnessed an intellectual attack of unprecedented ferocity upon the ideas of Christianity, especially in Victorian England. Might the twentieth century see a new type of attack, in which the target was the lives, not just the ideas, of Christians?

In the event, things moved more quickly and drastically than anyone could have expected. In the dark days of 1915, some Armenians had looked to Russia for help. Was not this great nation a bastion of Orthodox Christianity? Might not its great resources be brought to bear on their desperate situation? In the event, no help was forthcoming. But in 1917, events took a turn which few could have predicted. The Russian Revolution overthrew the tsarist state and ushered in an altogether new state ideology. No longer was Russia an Orthodox nation. If anything, she would be a nation committed to the elimination of religion from her territory – and, if possible, far beyond.

The Russian Revolution and the state enforcement of atheism

As we noted earlier, the radical political ideas of Karl Marx never really seemed to catch on in nineteenth-century Europe. They attracted attention from a few academics and social critics; yet they failed to gain acceptance from those who really mattered – those who actually had power. The Russian Revolution of 1917 changed the situation radically and irreversibly. Suddenly, Marx's ideas were being taken seriously and put into practice by a state. For Vladimir Ilyich Lenin, religion was a tool of oppression, cynically used against the peasants by the Russian ruling classes. The Soviet Union now became the first state to have as its ideological objective the total elimination of religion.

Yet a problem was immediately apparent. Marx's theories predicted that religion would vanish with the revolution, in that its causes would be eliminated. With the revolutionary abolition of socioeconomic alienation, there was no need for any spiritual narcotic to dull the pain of life. There should be no reason for religious belief to continue to exist. Yet it soon became clear that religion was obstinately persisting. The outcome of this observation was inevitable: it would be necessary to enforce what the theory predicted would happen spontaneously. A barrage of repressive measures, from banners to bullets, from pamphlets to prison camps, was unleashed against the religionists of the Soviet Union.

Initially, attention was directed towards the religious group that was dominant in Russia itself – Orthodoxy. On January 23, 1918, Lenin issued a decree depriving the church of any right to own property or to teach religion in private or state schools or to any group of minors. In a Soviet variant of Henry VIII's suppression of the English monasteries, Lenin proposed the confiscation of the wealth of churches and monasteries, and the execution of any who opposed it. Lenin ordered his lieutenants to "put down all resistance with such brutality that they will not forget it for several decades."

The persecution continued under Joseph Stalin, but became much more serious. Under the ruthless Stalinist repressions of the 1930s, virtually all of the Orthodox clergy were shot or deported to labor camps. A separate campaign was waged against the Roman

7.14   V. I. Lenin. AKG-Images.

Catholic church in the Ukraine. Here, other factors lent this suppression a peculiar urgency – a desire to suppress the national identity of the region and to eliminate forms of Christianity which recognized the authority of religious figures outside the Soviet Union – such as the pope. By 1939, 99 percent of Russia's churches had been closed.

Stalin's suppression of religion, however, extended to other faiths, in line with his general ideological commitment to the forcible elimination of religion. Attacks on Jews were endemic throughout the period of the Soviet Union. Stalin was especially fearful of a secessionist Islamic movement gaining momentum in the southeastern republics of the Soviet Union, and forcibly suppressed Islam throughout the region.

Things changed briefly in 1941, following Hitler's attack on the Soviet Union, which for a time seemed as if it might lead to the defeat of Stalin and the overthrow of Marxism-Leninism. Realizing that he needed to secure broad popular support for a costly and destructive war, Stalin loosened his iron grip on the religious life of the country. Church bells rang again in Moscow, and a limited amount of freedom was granted to the Orthodox church. Yet these proved to be temporary measures. With Stalin's successful installation of puppet regimes throughout eastern Europe and the victory of Mao Zedong's Red Army in China in the late 1940s, it seemed that the future of religion in a substantial portion of the world was genuinely in doubt. What hope was there for Christianity in a world from which religion was being eliminated as a deliberate matter of policy? The future seemed bleak.

The general mood of despondency around this time was heightened by a growing awareness of the failure of the German churches to prevent Hitler's war plans, and the genocidal agenda which developed during its course. As we shall see, some began to wonder whether Christianity had what was needed to resist tyranny.

The Nazi crisis: The failure of "Culture Protestantism"

After a period of sustained economic failure and political crisis, Adolf Hitler was installed as the German chancellor in 1933. Under Hitler, the German churches would be tested as never before. National Socialism was not in any sense a Christian philosophy, being based instead on long-standing beliefs concerning Germanic culture, especially the role of a pan-Germanic alliance in dominating central Europe. These were often tinged with pagan ideas, derived from the great pre-Christian Norse mythologies. Hitler's program demanded control over most aspects of German life, including the German churches. Unlike Stalin, however, Hitler believed that it might be possible to secure the compliance of the churches through cajoling, flattery, and deceit.

Hitler's program of Nazification was relatively easily presented in terms of the renewal of German culture. This had particular resonance with the movement within German Christianity often referred to as "Culture Protestantism," which proposed a close link between religion and culture. Nazi rule was at first welcomed by many German churchmen, partly because it offered a bulwark against the ominous state atheism sponsored within the Soviet Union, and partly because it seemed to offer a new cultural role for religion. Yet division arose from September 1933, partly over the Aryan clause that demanded that no Jew should hold office in the church. A furious debate broke out between the "Confessing Church," led by figures such as Martin Niemöller, who were not willing to cooperate with Hitler in church matters, and the "German Christians," who saw Hitler as the savior of the German nation and church. There were unquestionably many Christians who took a courageous stance against the Nazi regime, including Dietrich Bonhoeffer, executed in the final phase of World War II. Yet the German churches as institutions failed to provide a credible and cogent alternative to the rise of Nazism.

This failure of the German churches to make a significant impact on Hitler's rise to power, and his gradual move towards reaffirmation of German imperial claims, raised serious questions concerning the moral credentials of Christianity, which continue to trouble thoughtful Christians. One of Nazism's more reflective critics was Dietrich von Hildebrand, who argued that the Nazis gained credibility through the relativism of the German culture of the period; the best critique of the movement would be a vigorous reassertion of objective moral values, such as those of Christianity. A form of Christianity which failed to resist cultural trends, or which lent them active support, would thus be powerless to resist Nazism – or similar movements in the future.

One issue of major continuing concern is the way in which mainline churches and their theologians showed an uncomfortable tendency to go with the flow – to accept, endorse, and incorporate the latest cultural trends without subjecting them to penetrating examination. It was as if their critical faculties had been suspended in a frenzy of excitement over the "renewal of German culture." The church, they insisted, had to become up to date and align itself with modern thought forms. And was not Nazi ideology the authentic voice of the German people, which the churches should heed? Was not God speaking a new word to the German people, which should lead to a reform of Christian life and thought? Had not the philosopher Martin Heidegger enthusiastically embraced this worldview in his 1933 rectoral address at Heidelberg in May 1933, declaring it to be the way of the future?

The history of the German churches during the Third Reich exposed the fatal vulnerability of any form of Christianity which took its lead from cultural norms or the "modern world." Writers such as Karl Barth and Dietrich Bonhoeffer vigorously opposed this trend, arguing that Christianity and the churches should seek their norms and legitimation in Jesus Christ and the Bible, not in cultural norms. But they were a decided minority.

What Bonhoeffer and Barth offered the German churches was an understanding of the basis of Christian life and thought which was not dependent on accepting contemporary cultural norms. Both these writers stressed

7.15 Dietrich Bonhoeffer in the garden of a hotel in London shortly before the outbreak of World War II. AKG-Images.

that, since "Culture Protestantism" mirrored the norms of contemporary culture, it had no adequate basis for critiquing that culture. The situation was especially serious in the case of state or other established churches, which were under particular pressure to provide religious endorsement for cultural and political programs.

It is therefore not surprising that many Christian thinkers found both Bonhoeffer and Barth immensely congenial resources as they struggled with similar issues. For example, John de Gruchy pointed out the importance of Bonhoeffer for Christians in South Africa at the time of apartheid. Bonhoeffer, it was argued, provided a model for challenging prevailing cultural norms and taking a stand against a state which enjoyed a substantial degree of support from the established church of the region.

Barth and Bonhoeffer vigorously contested any Faustian pact between faith and politics. Although both writers had pronounced political commitments, they regarded these as subservient to the overriding task of remaining faithful to Jesus Christ. A church which scents the powerful fragrance of power and influence shows a worrying ability to become accommodating and flexible on matters which some might regard as non-negotiable.

The widespread failure of the German churches to identify the threat posed by Nazism, let alone to confront it, has left many Christians despondent and anxious. Might the historical European link between church and state culture inevitably lead to Christianity being caught up in similar fiascos in the future? Was the traditional European model of the religious denomination as state church now shown to be fatally flawed? And if so, what might be the implications for those Protestant denominations in North America and Australasia, whose origins were to be traced back to their European forebears?

The Second Vatican Council

The 1960s are now widely regarded as marking the high water mark of a period of secular optimism in western culture. The question of the relevance of Christianity within such a context became of crucial importance. Sensitive to a whole range of issues, John XXIII (pope from 1958 to 1963) summoned the Second Vatican Council (Vatican II) to deal with the issue of "updating" the agenda of the church. The Council began its meetings in October 1962. In four sessions, spread over the fall of each year during the period 1962–1965, more than

7.16 Pope John XXIII, previously Angelo Guiseppe Roncalli, pictured in 1962. AKG-Images/ Erich Lessing.

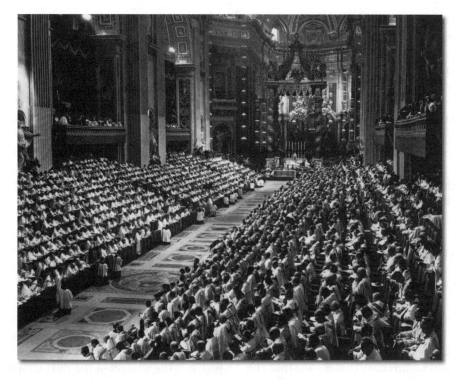

7.17   The opening of the second session of the Second Vatican Council, September 29, 1963, with Pope Paul VI (formerly Giovanni Battista Montini). Hulton/Getty Images.

2,450 bishops from all over the world met at Rome to discuss the future direction of the Catholic church. The death of John XXIII on June 3, 1963 did not interrupt the work of the Council, which was continued by his successor, Paul VI (pope from 1963 to 1978).

The agenda set before the Council was enormous. In general terms, the Council considered the place of the Christian faith in the modern world, particularly the relation between Christians and non-Christians, and between Catholics and other Christians. The importance of evangelism was affirmed, within a context of respecting the identities and integrities of non-Christians. Particular attention was paid to the nature of the church itself, and the relation of the bishops and pope.

After Vatican II, the Catholic church increasingly came to see itself more as a community of believers than as a divinely ordained and hierarchically ordered society. The laity were given an increasingly important place in the life of the church. The importance of ecumenism – that is, the program of relating to and increasing understanding between different styles of Christianity – was recognized. The Council also followed the example of Leo XIII in stressing the social aspects of the Christian faith, including its implications for human rights, race relations, and social justice. Within the church, the idea of "collegiality" became of increasing importance. This expresses the notion that the church is itself a community of member churches, with authority dispersed to some extent among its bishops rather than concentrated in the pope.

Vatican II is a landmark in the history of Catholicism. It remains to be seen how it will influence the development of Christianity in the new millennium. While many Catholics welcomed the new atmosphere which it introduced, others felt that it had betrayed many central concerns of traditional Catholic teaching and practice. Traces of this tension remain in the modern Catholic church. It is, however, a creative tension, and can be expected to lead to a healthy process of self-examination in the future.

Other tensions have emerged as significant within post-Vatican II Catholicism. Increasingly, Christianity is becoming a religion of the developing world, with its numerical center of gravity moving away from the western world towards the emerging nations of Africa and Asia. Much the same pattern is reflected in other Christian churches. This means that the agenda of the developing world is increasingly coming to dominate Catholicism, as the traditional concerns of the west become of lesser importance. For many observers, the ultimate confirmation of this trend would be the election of a non-western Catholic as pope. During the papal election of April 2005, a number of Latin American and African candidates were being seriously discussed as potential popes. In the end, the German Cardinal Joseph Ratzinger was elected, choosing to be known as Pope Benedict XVI. The future election of a non-western pope is now widely seen as inevitable, and would mark the final stage in the rebirth of Catholicism since the disaster of the 1790s. It would have moved decisively from being a western European to a global faith.

This very brief sketch of the development of Christianity has laid the background for the present state of Christianity in the world, which is the subject of the next chapter.

8

Christianity: A Global View

By the opening years of the twenty-first century, Christianity has become a global religion. Christianity has never really been a western religion. Its origins lie in Palestine, and its future lies predominantly in South America, Asia, and Africa. Christianity reached a position of considerable influence in western Europe in the Middle Ages and early modern period, and continues to be of immense significance in the shaping of western culture. Yet this is now being seen as an extended yet temporary phase in its complex development. Its historical roots and its future flowering lie elsewhere. One of the most dramatic developments of the final decade of the twentieth century has been the growing realization within the established churches of the west – who traditionally regarded themselves as the epicenters of faith – that the numerical center of gravity of Christianity now lies in the developing world.

One outcome of this massive expansion and variegation will be obvious. Never has the movement been so numerous; never has it been so diverse; and never has it been so difficult to understand. Contemporary Christianity is shaped by complex cultural factors, the lingering shadows of historical events and figures, significant divergences over issues of theology, and local concerns. This chapter provides a comprehensive overview of this complex movement, broken down according to regions of the world and denominations, designed to allow readers to gain something of an understanding of the contemporary shape of the movement.

A Regional Survey of Christianity

Traditionally, global surveys of Christianity have begun by considering western Europe and North America, on the basis of the assumption – which probably came easily to European and American authors – that these were the most significant regions of the Christian world. Yet the center of gravity of Christianity has shifted decisively elsewhere – to the developing world, especially Africa and Asia. The arrangement of material in this section reflects this development.

Africa

As the nineteenth century came to an end, Christianity represented a tiny minority faith in Africa. It was widely seen as a colonial religion, imposed by the European powers in their quest for influence in the region, and had very slight influence outside European circles.

The Christian leaders of the region were imported from Europe – as in the case, for example, of the colonial bishops of the Church of England. By the end of the twentieth century, sub-Saharan Africa was a predominantly Christian region, with Europeans marginalized in an increasingly indigenized Christian community.

Christianity became established in North Africa during the first centuries of the Christian era. Churches were established along much of the North African coast, in the areas now known as Algeria, Tunisia, and Libya. A particularly strong Christian presence developed in Egypt, with the city of Alexandria emerging as a leading center of Christian thought and life. Much of this Christian presence was swept away through the Arab invasions of the seventh century. Christianity survived in Egypt, although as a minority faith. Only the small kingdom of Ethiopia (which designates a territory much smaller than the modern nation of the same name) can be said to have remained a Christian nation. At the opening of the sixteenth century, Africa was dominated by Islam in its north, and by native forms of religion in the south. Apart from the isolated case of Ethiopia, there was no significant Christian presence whatsoever.

The situation began to change gradually during the later sixteenth century. Portuguese settlers occupied previously uninhabited islands off the West African coast, such as the Cape Verde Islands. However, such settlements had little impact on the mainland of Africa. The coming of Christianity to southern Africa is to be dated from the eighteenth century, and is closely linked with the great evangelical awakening in England at this time. Major British missionary societies began to become active in Africa during the late eighteenth or early nineteenth centuries. Yet the Christian missionaries were far from optimistic concerning their prospects. Islam was deeply embedded in many parts of Africa, and seemed far more attuned to the African soul. How could Christianity possibly take root in this region? As late as 1897, senior figures of the British religious establishment believed that Christianity had quite simply failed to establish a lasting presence in Africa. The twentieth century would see the erosion or elimination of what little Christian presence had been established in that region.

African Christians of the late nineteenth century can be broadly divided into two categories: expatriate Europeans and indigenous Africans. The former tended to maintain as much of the Christian life of their homeland as possible, often for sentimental or cultural reasons. Thus the external trappings of the Church of England found themselves replicated to various extents in the many British colonies to spring up in southern Africa during this period.

More significant, however, was the gradual adoption of Christianity by native African people. The early converts to Christianity were often those who were on the margins of traditional African societies – such as slaves, women, and the poor. The dramatic growth in African Christianity is now thought to be mainly the result of the establishment of indigenous African Christian communities, which provided catechists and pastors to the growing number of converts that they attracted, rather than to the activities of European missionaries.

Christianity caused tensions to arise within traditional African societies. Western Christianity was strongly monogamist; African culture had long recognized the merits of polygamy. Increasingly, the European Christian insistence upon a man having only one wife was seen as a western import, having no place in traditional African society. The United African Methodist church, an indigenous African church which recognized polygamy, traces its origins back to a meeting of the

Methodist church in Lagos, Nigeria, in 1917, when a large group of leading lay people were debarred from the church on account of their polygamous beliefs. They responded by forming their own Methodist church, which adopted native African values frowned on by the European missionaries.

In the period following World War I (1914–1918), Christianity underwent significant transformation and development in this region, becoming the majority religion in most parts of sub-Saharan Africa by the end of the twentieth century. Statistics are notoriously difficult to garner, not least because many of the churches in the region have no interest in compiling membership data for the benefit of scholars. However, a widely cited statistic has it that there were roughly 10 million African Christians in 1900, 145 million in 1970, and 400 million in 2000. Christianity has clearly established a permanent indigenous presence in the region.

The growing numerical strength of Christianity in Africa is having major effects on the politics of the region. Of particular importance is the Islam–Christianity interface, which is potentially the cause of considerable regional conflict. For example, the southern part of Nigeria is predominantly Christian, and the north predominantly Muslim. This raises the question of whether Nigeria can survive as a single nation, or whether some form of partition – such

8.1 Pope John Paul II ordains priests in the West African state of Nigeria. © Vittoriano Rastelli/ CORBIS.

as that introduced between predominantly Muslim Pakistan and predominantly Hindu India in 1947 – will be necessary in future.

One of the most significant developments of the twentieth century was the rise of African independent churches, a term that refers to a very broad range of Christian churches which place an emphasis on retaining a traditional African heritage within the context of their Christian faith. These churches are often strongly charismatic, stressing the importance of spiritual healing, exorcism, the interpretation of dreams, and prophetic guidance. A good example is provided by the Eternal Sacred Order of Cherubim and Seraphim, which is based in Nigeria. Reacting against the word-based culture of the nineteenth-century west, these churches emphasize experience and symbolism. A further factor of importance here is the racism of some white churches, particularly in South Africa under the apartheid regime. The Zionist churches of this region can be seen as a celebration and affirmation of black African identity in the face of such official hostility. In the last few decades, these churches have often been influenced by the charismatic movement, which has proved to be an important catalyst for further growth in the region. It is thought that these churches have something like 50 million adherents throughout Africa.

So what does the African situation tell us about the future of Christianity? Gone is the stereotype of western-led churches following western-style worship, as if Christianity was just some aspect of European colonialism. African Christianity is led by Africans, preached by Africans, and shows little interest in mimicking western ways of thinking. If anything, African Christian leaders seem to be of the view that western Europe needs to be reconverted to Christianity, and have offered to undertake this rather awesome task if the churches in the west are not up to it. In the eighteenth century,

Europeans brought Christianity to Africa. Today, the situation has been inverted.

Southeast Asia

In 1521, the great Spanish explorer Ferdinand Magellan discovered a group of some 3,141 islands. The islands, now known as "the Philippines," became a Spanish colony. Under Spanish rule, a program of evangelization was undertaken by various religious orders, especially the Franciscans and Dominicans. The islands came under American rule in 1898. The Philippines are unusual in that they constitute the only predominantly Christian country in Southeast Asia. Although Catholicism is currently the dominant form of Christianity in the region, many Protestant missionary societies established a presence following the end of Spanish rule. While various forms of Protestantism are now firmly rooted in the region, they constitute a minority.

Elsewhere in Southeast Asia, Christianity is best described as a growing minority presence. In Japan, Christianity first gained a foothold in 1549, when the Jesuit missionary Francis Xavier landed at Kagoshima. The small church in the country experienced a long period of isolation from the west during the Tokugawa shogunate. It was only in 1865 that Japan opened its doors to the west, revealing the continuing presence of about 60,000 Christian believers in the country. During the Meiji period (1868–1912), Christianity gained a growing following in the country. However, it has never achieved the substantial levels of growth seen in China or Korea in recent years. For many Japanese, Christianity, like butter, is seen as a western import. This is evident from the colloquial Japanese term for Christianity, which can be translated as "it tastes of butter."

Perhaps the most interesting developments in Southeast Asia are to be found in China and

Korea. It is known that Christianity established a presence in China in 1294, when Franciscan missionaries reached the country. There is, however, evidence that Christianity reached China much earlier. The Sigan-Fu Tablet, generally thought to date from 781, refers to a Nestorian missionary who had arrived in the region 146 years earlier, pointing to the strongly missionary activity of this eastern form of Christianity around this time. However, the church never achieved any great success in conversions. One of the many effects of the Opium War of the 1840s was to open the "Middle Kingdom" up to at least some western attitudes. China chose to remain isolated from the west until the nineteenth century, when growing interest in commerce opened up the region to western missionaries. Of these, James Hudson Taylor (1832–1905) may be singled out for special comment.

Hudson Taylor was initially a missionary with the Chinese Evangelization Society. Dissatisfaction with this organization led him to found the China Inland Mission in 1865. This Mission was unusual in several aspects, not least its willingness to accept single women as missionaries and its interdenominational character. Hudson Taylor showed an awareness of the cultural barriers facing Christian missionaries in China, and did what he could to remove them – for example, he required his missionaries to wear Chinese, rather than western, dress.

Nevertheless, western attempts to evangelize Christianity were of very limited value. Christianity was seen as something western, and hence un-Chinese. The defeat of China by Japan in an ill-fated war during the years 1894–1895 was widely regarded as a direct result of the presence of foreigners in the country. This led to the I Ho Ch'uan crusade of 1899–1900, with its fanatical opposition to foreign investment and religious activity. With the establishment of the Republic of

China in 1911, Christianity received a degree of official toleration. This ended abruptly in 1949, with the communist victory which led to the foundation of the People's Republic of China, and the ejection of all western missionaries from the country. The "cultural revolution" of the 1960s involved the forcible suppression of Christianity. It was far from clear what was happening to Christians; many came to the conclusion that it had been eradicated.

In 1979, the horrors of the cultural revolution came to an end. It became clear that Christianity had survived the revolution. In broad terms, three main strands can be discerned within modern Chinese Christianity.

1   The Three Self Patriotic Movement, founded in 1951, is the "official" church. The phrase "Three Self" refers to the three principles of self-supporting, self-administering, and self-propagating. The general idea was to ensure that the church was totally independent of any foreign influence. However, it is also clear that the state exercises considerable control over this church.

2   The Catholic church remains important within China. The government insistence that churches shall not be dependent on or obedient to foreign agencies clearly causes some difficulties for Catholics, on account of their loyalty to the pope. In general terms, there seem to be two groups within modern Chinese Catholicism, one of which is independent of the Vatican (the "Catholic Patriotic Association"), the other of which is not. The former group seems to be in the ascendancy.

3   The house church movement is now the most important Christian movement within China. Strongly charismatic in orientation, the movement has witnessed spectacular numerical gains, particularly

in the rural areas of China. While it is impossible to obtain reliable figures, there are indications that possibly as many as 50 million Chinese belong to such churches.

The situation in Korea is of importance to the future of Christianity in the region. The origins of Christianity in Korea go back to the late eighteenth century, when a small Catholic community was established following initiatives from Beijing, China. The small Christian community was vigorously persecuted during the nineteenth century. Of the total Christian population of about 18,000, it is thought that 8,000 were massacred. However, a degree of stability resulted when a friendship treaty was signed with the United States in 1882. Shortly afterwards, American Protestant missionaries arrived in Korea and began to establish major medical and educational missions in the country. Nevertheless, at the dawn of the twentieth century only a tiny proportion of the country was Christian – perhaps 1 percent. The latest survey of the religious commitments of the Korean publication published by the Central Intelligence Agency determines the population of South Korea in 2000 to be just under 50 million, of which 49 percent are Christian and 47 percent Buddhist. So how and why did this massive change come about? How did a country with virtually no Christian presence come to be, in effect, a Christian nation?

As might be expected, the situation is complex. However, it is clear that Christianity was perceived as an ally, rather than an enemy, by Koreans in the twentieth century. Korea was annexed by Japan in 1910, and remained under Japanese rule until the end of World War II. Unusually, Christianity was seen as allied with Korean nationalism, especially in the face of Japanese oppression. Elsewhere in Asia, Christianity was easily depicted by its critics as the lackey of western imperialism. In Korea, however, the enemy was not the

west but Japan. Throughout this time, Christians played an active role in the Korean independence movement out of all proportion to their numbers. Of the 123 people tried for insurgence by the Japanese in the 1911 popular revolt against Japanese rule, 98 were Christians. At this time, Christians made up just over 1 percent of the Korean population. The significance of this point could hardly be overlooked.

After World War II, Korea underwent partition into a communist north and democratic south following the Korean War, which broke out on June 25, 1950. The heavy involvement of Christian missionary agencies in the relief programs which followed the ending of the war created a powerful stimulus to the development of Christianity, which was catalyzed still further by the Korean churches' programs of social action during the 1960s. Growth continued unabated, especially within Korean Protestantism. In 1957, there were about 800,000 Protestants in Korea. This figure had more than doubled by 1968 (1,873,000), and had soared further by 1978 (5,294,000). The Catholic church also enjoyed a surge in its growth, rising from 285,000 (1957) to 751,000 (1968), then to 1,144,000 (1986).

Today, Korea sends out Christian missionaries to nations throughout Asia. The large Korean diasporas in major western cities, from Sydney to Los Angeles, from Melbourne to New York, are closely linked with a network of churches, which increasingly serve as a focal point for community action, mutual support, and spiritual nourishment. And as North Korea shows every sign of being about to collapse, economically and politically, the question of the future religious development of this hardline communist state remains completely open. The anecdotal evidence suggests that Christianity has already made deep inroads within the population, and is expected to grow further in the next decade.

Christianity is in decline in the west. Yet the Korean situation reminds us that the global story is far from simple, and forces us to ask which of its present scenarios will determine Christianity's future. For example, the available evidence strongly suggests a major growth in Christianity within China, despite continuing official hostility towards its presence, particularly during the period of the "cultural revolution." Outside mainland China, Christianity has made considerable inroads into Chinese expatriate communities in Singapore, Indonesia, and Malaysia. A similar picture emerges in Chinese communities in large western cities, such as Los Angeles, Vancouver, Toronto, and Sydney.

North America

The United States of America is widely seen as the powerhouse of modern Christianity. Unlike the French Revolution of 1789, which led to a revolt against both the ideas and institutions of Christianity, the American Revolution of 1776 led to Christianity playing an increasingly significant role in American life and culture. The constitutional separation of church and state isolated Christianity from any position of privilege, thus reducing any possibility that it might be compromised by social status or power.

Although the forms of Christianity which predominated in the early colonial period were essentially Protestant, immigration from Italy and Ireland in the nineteenth century led to a significant increase in the Roman Catholic population of the United States. Nevertheless, at the time of writing, Protestantism remains the most numerous form of Christianity in the United States.

Since the United States is widely regarded as playing such a significant role in global Christianity, it is both interesting and important to explore its contemporary shape. Many polls have surveyed the religious affiliations of Americans, and provided a breakdown along denominational lines. The results of these polls are open to debate, chiefly due to difficulties with the reliability of sampling techniques. The most reliable sampling method is generally held to be "self-identification" – that is, allowing individuals to state their own religious commitment. A 2002 survey by the Pew Forum on Religion and Public Life came up with the following statistics.

Religious affiliation	%
Christianity	76.5
Judaism	1.3
Islam	0.5
Buddhism	0.5
Hinduism	0.4
Unitarian Universalist	0.3
Wiccan/Pagan/Druid	0.1

First, in terms of the overall shape of American religious life, Christianity is by far the most numerous religion. Patterns of churchgoing – as many as 40 percent of Americans attend church regularly – are far greater than most other nations with a Christian cultural tradition, especially western Europe. The Pew survey reveals the growing importance of non-Christian religions, including Islam and Hinduism, but notes that both continue to represent very small segments in American public life.

The survey also allowed Christianity to be broken down denominationally, making it possible for the respective strengths of various styles of Christianity to be identified. Although Protestantism continues to be the most numerous form of Christianity in the United States, it is distributed over a wide range of denominations. Roman Catholicism remains the largest single religious group.

Denomination	%
Roman Catholic	24.5
Baptist	16.3
Methodist/Wesleyan	6.8
Lutheran	4.6
Presbyterian	2.7
Pentecostal/Charismatic	2.1
Episcopalian/Anglican	1.7
Latter-Day Saints/Mormon	1.3
Churches of Christ	1.2
Congregational/United Church of Christ	0.7
Assemblies of God	0.5

Yet the traditional pattern of analyzing American Christianity along purely denominational lines cannot do justice to its complexity. John C. Green, a political scientist who heads up the Bliss Institute at the University of Akron, conducted a National Survey of Religion and Politics in the spring of 2004 for the Pew Forum on Religion and Public Life. This careful study attempted to explore transdenominational trends by identifying tendencies within religious groups. The three most important such groups are identified as evangelical Protestants (the conservative, mainline, and liberal wings of fundamentalist, other evangelical, Pentecostal, and charismatic denominations), mainline Protestants (the left, center, and liberal wings of the Episcopal Church, the Evangelical Lutheran Church in America, the Presbyterian Church (USA), the Reformed Church in America, the United Church of Christ, the United Methodist Church, and smaller denominations with similar beliefs), and Roman Catholics. Each can be subdivided into three distinct factions: traditionalists, modernists, and centrists.

"Traditionalists" are here defined as individual conservative believers with levels of orthodox belief in God, heavy religious involvement (as judged by attendance, financial support, prayer, Scripture reading, small group participation), and a desire to hold fast to their beliefs and practices and resist pressures for change coming from society as a whole. "Modernists" are here defined as believers with liberal tendencies, such as a high level of heterodox belief, relatively low level of religious involvement, and a desire to accommodate change. "Centrists" are just defined as those in between traditionalists and modernists!

The survey noted a number of important trends since 1992, particularly a growth in conservative attitudes within evangelical Protestantism and a clear consensus that Americans regard it as important for their President to have strong religious beliefs. It was also noted that mainline Protestantism, once thought to be aligned with Republicans, has increasingly sided with the Democrats in the last two decades.

The survey is especially helpful in illuminating the "culture wars" within American society, especially on issues such as gay marriage, abortion, and stem cell research. In general terms, the greatest hostility to such trends in American society has come from within evangelical Protestantism, whereas mainline Protestantism has tended to be supportive of them.

In a later section of this chapter, we shall explore some of the developments within American Protestantism during the twentieth century which have had a major impact elsewhere.

South America

In the sixteenth century, western Europe was thrown into confusion by the massive religious and social upheaval generally known as "the Reformation." The birth of Protestantism led to major changes in patterns of religious life throughout the region, and arguably to more resilient and dynamic forms of Christianity. The Catholic church, initially caught off guard by the rapid changes triggered by the religious protests and programs of Martin Luther and others, finally got its act together and launched its own program of renewal and reform, usually referred to as the "Catholic Reformation." By the end of the sixteenth century, the Catholic church was in far better shape than at its beginning, despite the traumatic events which had shaken it in the critical period 1517–1545.

Is something similar now happening in Latin America? The question was first raised seriously in 1990, when David Stoll published a work provocatively entitled *Is Latin America Turning Protestant?* The work fell like a bombshell into the North American religious studies community. It had long got used to the idea that Latin America was a bastion of Roman Catholicism, which had recently undergone major renewal through the movement known as "liberation theology." The academics loved liberation theology, which resonated with some of the core values of academic culture, and tended to treat it in a distressingly naive and uncritical manner. It proved fatally easy for North American scholars, observing the situation from afar, to allow their perceptions of this complex situation to be shaped to an unwise extent by the writings of liberation theologians and political activists. As a result they failed to listen to what the ordinary people were saying about their situation, and what they longed for.

The simple fact of the matter is that liberation theology was essentially an academic movement, whose concerns resonated with those of the poor of the region but were stated in terms which they couldn't understand. It proposed reform programs which seemed to just about everyone to be totally unrealistic, given the history and social realities of the region.

Stoll's book provided hard figures which pointed to the inexorable long-term growth of certain types of Protestantism in this hitherto strongly Catholic region of the world. The rapid spread of Pentecostalism in the region had transformed the situation. Evangelical communities had sprung up, apparently from nowhere, and were drastically changing the religious landscape of the region. It is now estimated that at least 50 million of the 450 million population of South and Central America are Protestants. And the trend is growing. Interestingly, the styles of Protestantism that were expanding seemed to be the newly emerging revivalist forms known as "Pentecostalism" and "evangelicalism," not the traditional Protestant denominations of the region.

How is this change to be explained? And what are its implications? Some hinted darkly that it was all due to the work of the Central Intelligence Agency (CIA) during the Reagan era. The statistics do not support this view, even after the most generous massaging; the trend goes back further than that, and continues today. A more plausible explanation is that Catholicism is seen as a colonial religion, planted by the *Conquistadores* in the sixteenth-century Spanish and Portuguese expansions in the territory. The forms of evangelicalism and Pentecostalism which have developed in Latin America are much more attuned to local realities, and are seen by some as being more acceptable for that region.

The most likely explanation of the developments of recent years has to do with the ideas and worship styles of the forms of evangelicalism which are sweeping through the region. They were popular, accessible, and made their appeal to the world of personal religious experience. Liberation theology appeared well intentioned towards popular Latin American culture, but was perceived to be bookish, intellectualist, and out of touch with the ordinary people. You'd need a degree of some kind to understand, for example, what Leonardo Boff was saying. The evangelical pastors operate at grassroots level and are deeply attuned to the concerns of their people. People wanted to take control of their lives, and saw evangelical or Pentecostal religion as a means of achieving this goal. Rather than transform society – which they saw as a laudable, but decidedly long-term, goal – they would change themselves, their families, and their communities.

The experiential religion of Pentecostalism (pp. 266–268) resonated especially well with these concerns, and also allowed important bridges to be built with significant elements of popular Latin American culture – such as a pervasive belief in spirits. The Pentecostal worldview includes elements such as the exorcism of demons (which tends to make western academic theologians cringe with embarrassment) that related easily and naturally to the folk religion of the region. It transferred itself effortlessly to Latin American soil, and seems set for further growth. The most telling indicator of future trends is that the movement is being spread from Latino to Latino, not from evangelical missionaries from outside the region. The movement may well owe its origins to North Americans; it is now firmly in the hands of the locals.

We see here a pattern which has already been observed in the case of Korea and sub-Saharan Africa. Forms of Christianity originally planted in the region by Europeans or North Americans were taken over by an indigenous leadership, and went on to flourish in their new forms. The initial stages of growth may well have been encouraged and sustained by Europeans or North Americans. Yet that was then. What we have now are indigenized forms of Christianity in these regions, with a native leadership and locally thought-through understandings of the gospel. The decentralization of Christianity is well under way.

Finally, it must be pointed out that the Roman Catholic church in Latin America has hardly overlooked these developments, and has moved to counter them. The answer, it is clear, does not lie with the rather cerebral approach of liberation theology, which is increasingly being seen as having little relevance to the new situation. It may be of importance to the social policies of the churches; it does not relate well to ordinary people. One answer has been to develop contemporary worship styles which mimic the informality of evangelicalism and Pentecostalism, while retaining the basic structure and content of Catholic worship.

The situation is still in flux, and the outcome impossible to predict. Yet, like the Reformation of the sixteenth century, it is likely that this will lead to renewed and more resilient forms of both Protestantism and Catholicism emerging from this process – perhaps both now concerned to export their dynamic new ideas back to their original European contexts?

Europe

The twentieth century witnessed a considerable decline in attendance at church in western Europe, once seen as the heartland of the Christian faith. Whether this perception was accurate is, of course, very much open to debate. Nevertheless, it is evident that attendance at church – perhaps the most obvious indicator of popular support for Christianity – was eroded in this region during the twentieth century. The influence of Christianity upon popular culture, academic debate, and governmental policy-making diminished throughout the period. World War I is often seen as marking a turning point, catalyzing the process of decline which continues unabated to this day. However, many point out that the trends which emerged at this point had their origins deep in the Victorian period. It was only a matter of time before Europe transferred the secularization of its intellectuals to popular culture as a whole.

In that many sociologists of religion and other futurologists live and work in western Europe, it is entirely understandable that the western European paradigm should be treated as global in its significance and validity. Eurocentrism has always been an immensely attractive philosophy to Europeans, from Erasmus of Rotterdam onwards. Just as medieval thinkers believed that the entire solar system orbited the earth, so many European academics seem to believe that what happens in Europe prefigures what will happen everywhere else. Where Europe leads, others must follow.

This perspective is not shared outside western Europe. The fate of Christianity in western Europe is one paradigm among many for the future of Christianity, and it is essential to appreciate that it is by no means the self-evidently universal paradigm that some might suggest. Europe, for example, was the conspicuous exception to one of the most remarkable phenomena of the 1990s – the surge in interest in spirituality which led many sociologists to speak of the "desecularization" of the world. The western European context thus cannot be taken as typical of the global religious situation. To take the present western European situation as a paradigm for the future global situation makes little sense.

The contrast with eastern Europe is especially significant in this respect. For much of the period 1950–1989, Christianity found itself severely repressed by Marxist regimes in eastern Europe. The rapid increase of Soviet political and military influence in the region after World War II led to the installation of regimes with strongly anti-religious agendas. Whereas western Europeans, with the example of the French Revolution in mind, had tended to think of atheism as a liberator and the church as an oppressor, eastern Europeans thought in precisely inverted terms. The church was the people's support in the face of atheistic state oppression.

If any one event crystallized this perception, it was the election of a Polish cardinal as the successor to the short-lived Pope John Paul. Taking the title John Paul II, he rapidly established the Catholic church's credentials as a force opposed to Marxist repression, especially in his native Poland. The collapse of Marxism as a state ideology in this region throughout the 1980s is widely credited to his influence. While the church in eastern Europe faces many challenges in the twenty-first century, its role as the defender of human rights against Marxism has done much to ensure it enjoys popular goodwill as it faces them.

Christianity: A Survey of its Contemporary Forms

In the previous section, we explored the shape of Christianity in some important regions of the world. Yet contemporary Christianity is variegated, characterized by quite different understandings of church government, styles of worship, and cultural roots. In the section that follows, we shall examine some of the major forms of Christianity in today's world, beginning with the most important, numerically speaking – Roman Catholicism.

Roman Catholicism

Roman Catholicism is by far the world's largest Christian grouping, and is universally expected to be the most successful such grouping in the next century. It represents the largest religious group in the United States, with four times the membership of its nearest rival, the Southern Baptists. Recent statistics suggest a modest growth in its membership in the United States over the last few years. It is by far the most widely distributed Christian group in the world, and continues to expand. It can expect to face problems everywhere;

nevertheless, its past history suggests that it will be able to face these, and make the necessary adjustments.

Yet the future of Roman Catholicism was once seen to be in doubt. To appreciate this point, we need to go back two centuries and consider the situation of the Catholic church in western Europe following the French Revolution of 1789. As the nineteenth century cautiously opened, there was a general feeling that the future of Roman Catholicism was very much in doubt. The French Revolution had virtually wiped out the influence and presence of the church in France. Revolution was to be exported, both through the spread of its leading ideas and through the activities of French revolutionary troops, who invaded parts of hitherto Catholic Europe. Things looked grim. The Napoleonic era was widely seen as presaging the end of any role for Catholicism in Europe. Yet with the defeat of Napoleon and the reshaping of Europe at the Congress of Vienna (1815), the situation began to stabilize.

It is important to appreciate that, although at this time Catholicism was a growing presence in regions such as South America, Japan, and India, it was still primarily a European religion. One of the most significant developments in Catholicism during the nineteenth and early twentieth centuries was its rapid expansion outside Europe. Catholicism became a major influence in the United States around this time, largely through immigration from Ireland and Italy. Archbishop John Carroll (1735–1815) did much to encourage the social acceptance of Catholicism at a time during which its numbers were rapidly increasing. Carroll became the first Catholic bishop of Baltimore in 1789, and went on to become the nation's first Catholic archbishop in 1810. The founding of major Catholic educational institutions – such as the University of Notre Dame in 1842 – laid the foundations for the emergence of Catholicism as one of the most significant intellectual forces in American cultural life.

Yet our attention in this section focuses on a question which is of central importance to the theme of this chapter. What part will Catholicism play in the future of Christianity? If this question had been asked in 1800, it is highly doubtful that any informed observer, basing herself on the western European situation, would see a significant future for Catholicism in particular, or Christianity in general. To ask the question in 2006 is to invite a rather different response. Most observers are convinced that Catholicism will remain the dominant and most successful form of Christianity in the next century. One of the reasons for this is the achievement of the Second Vatican Council (1962–1965), especially the reforming and renewing agenda which it imposed upon a hesitant church (see pp. 248–250).

However, tensions have since emerged as significant within Catholicism, including a startling decline in the number of men offering themselves for the priesthood. This is especially evident in the Irish Republic, traditionally a Roman Catholic bastion in western Europe. Allegations of child abuse have seriously eroded the status of the priesthood. In 1979, there were just under 8,000 priests in Ireland, of whom fewer than 400 were under the age of 29. More than 6,000 are over the age of 40. A serious shortage of priests confronts the Irish church, and it is difficult to see what can be done about it. Similar patterns can be discerned throughout the western world. In the developing world, however, things are much more encouraging.

Since the Second Vatican Council, Catholicism has continued to grow in the non-western world. This means that the agenda of the developing world is increasingly coming to dominate Catholicism, as the traditional agenda of the west becomes of lesser importance. For many observers, the ultimate confirmation of this trend would be the election of a non-western Catholic as pope – a possibility that was being seriously considered during the papal elections of April 2005. This development, which is now widely seen as inevitable, would demonstrate that Catholicism has moved decisively from being a western European to a global faith in the last two centuries. There are no compelling reasons to assume anything other than that the Catholic church will continue to be the major player in global Christianity in the next century.

The distinctive ethos of Catholicism is difficult to summarize, on account of the complexity of the movement. However, the following points are important.

1   The Catholic church has traditionally had a strongly hierarchical understanding of

8.2 Pope Benedict XVI, formerly Cardinal Joseph Ratzinger, enthroned in April 2005. Domenico Stinellis/AP/EMPICS.

church government, focusing on the pope, cardinals, and bishops. The pope has considerable influence over the appointment of bishops throughout the Catholic world. The College of Cardinals meets in secret sessions following the death of a pope, in order to elect his successor. A cardinal is a priest or bishop, nominated by the pope, who is entrusted with special administrative responsibilities.

2   Partly on account of the importance of the pope, the city of Rome has a particularly significant place within the Catholic ethos. The term "Roman Catholic," often used by Protestants to refer to this church, reflects the importance of Rome as a center for the movement. The Vatican City is widely regarded as the spiritual epicenter of Catholicism, and served as the venue for the two most recent councils: Vatican I (1869–1870) and Vatican II (1962–1965). Many Catholics will make a pilgrimage to Rome, on account of its strong historical associations with early Christianity (the apostles Paul and Peter being widely believed to have been martyred and buried in the city).

3   The church is generally seen as a visible divine institution, whose structures are grounded in divine reality. Although this view of the church was modified slightly by Vatican II, it remains of importance for modern Catholicism. Particular significance is attached to the role of the teaching office of the church (usually referred to as the *magisterium*). The Council of Trent affirmed that no one was free to interpret Scripture "contrary to the sense in which Holy Mother Church, who is to judge the true sense and interpretation of the Holy Scriptures, has held and does hold." Lying behind this is a strongly corporate

conception of the Christian life and of authority within the church, contrasting sharply with the individualism which has become characteristic of modern western culture during the twentieth and early twenty-first centuries.

4 The Catholic clergy are of crucial local importance in everyday Catholic life. Catholic clergy are not permitted to marry. This is one of the most noticeable practical differences between Catholicism and other forms of Christianity. Orthodoxy and Protestantism permit their priests (or ministers) to marry. Catholic priests are exclusively male. Although women are permitted to undertake some pastoral and liturgical responsibilities (the precise details of which vary from place to place), the Catholic church currently remains committed to an exclusively male priesthood.

5 Catholicism is strongly liturgical. In other words, the forms of worship used by the church are fixed and laid down centrally, reflecting the conviction that the way in which the church prays and worships is inextricably linked to what the church believes (a point sometimes made using the Latin slogan *lex orandi, lex credendi*). The liturgy is seen as a public statement of the beliefs and values of the church, and a means by which continuity with the apostolic tradition is maintained. Until the Second Vatican Council, the language of the liturgy was Latin; the use of native languages is now permitted, although considerable care is taken to ensure that vernacular translations accurately reflect the sense of the original Latin versions of the liturgy.

6 Catholicism is strongly sacramental, placing considerable emphasis on the "sacramental economy" (that is, the view that the benefits of Christ, which result from his death and resurrection, are communicated to the church through the sacraments). The Catholic church recognizes seven sacraments (whereas Protestants recognize only two). In terms of the regular liturgical life of the church, the most important such sacrament is the mass, which is understood to make present the body and blood of Christ.

7 The monastic life continues to be of importance to shaping and articulating the Catholic ethos. Although there has been a decline in the traditional religious orders, they nevertheless continue to play a vital role, such as acting as retreat centers for laity. Growing popular interest in Ignatian spirituality is of particular interest in this respect. The role of the religious orders in establishing and maintaining educational centers at every level should also be noted.

8 Catholicism places an emphasis on the role of the saints in general, and the Virgin Mary in particular. The saints and Mary are understood to act as intercessors for both the living and the dead. The doctrine of the immaculate conception of Mary states that Mary was conceived without her sharing in the common human condition of original sin, thus providing a theological formalization for the high place of Mary in Catholic life and devotion. Nevertheless, Catholic writers are careful to draw attention to the distinction between the *veneration* due to Mary (which is honorific) and the *worship* which is due to God and to Jesus Christ as the Son of God.

Eastern Orthodoxy

Eastern Orthodoxy – often referred to simply as "Orthodoxy" – whether in its Greek or Russian forms, represents a form of Christianity which retains a strong degree of continuity with the early Greek church, and traces its liturgy and doctrines directly back to the early church.

Orthodoxy is numerically strongest in eastern Europe, particularly in Russia and Greece, where it has had a critical influence in shaping a sense of national identity. However, it has also established a major presence in North America and Australia through emigration. The Australian city of Melbourne, for example, is home to one of the largest Greek Orthodox communities in the world.

Any attempt to describe the distinctive ethos of Orthodoxy would include the following elements.

1   A very strong sense of historical continuity with the early church. Orthodoxy is thus strongly orientated towards the idea of

8.3   Greek Orthodox priests outside the Church of the Holy Sepulchre in Jerusalem in 1895 (photograph Carl Raad). AKG-Images.

paradosis ("tradition"), particularly the writings of the Greek fathers. Writers such as Gregory of Nyssa, Maximus the Confessor, and the writer who adopted the pseudonym "Dionysius the Areopagite" are of particular importance in this respect. Tradition is seen as a living entity, which remains essentially unchanged while being capable of meeting the new challenges of each succeeding age. This is reflected in the fixed liturgical forms used within Orthodoxy. Russian Orthodoxy places importance on the use of Old Slavonic in the liturgy, stressing both the theological and linguistic continuity with previous generations.

2   Orthodoxy recognizes only seven Ecumenical Councils, and does not accept any council after the Second Council of Nicaea (787) as having binding authority. Although local councils met to deal with various matters, these are not understood to have the same authority as these earlier councils.

3   Orthodoxy has been very resistant to the ideas of authority which emerged within western Catholicism. In the twentieth century, increasing attention was also paid by western theologians to the notions of "catholicity" which were dominant in the Orthodox churches. This is often expressed using the Russian word *Sobornost*, which has no exact equivalent in other languages. While the term denotes the general idea of "universality," it also expresses the unity of believers within the fellowship of the church. The idea, which is developed most fully in the writings of Sergei Bulgakov and A. S. Khomiakoff, attempts to do justice to both the distinctiveness of the individual members of the church and the overall harmony of its corporate life. This is linked with the notion of "conciliarity" (the Russian word

sobor means "a council" or "an assembly"), by which the life of the church is governed in such a way that authority is dispersed among all the faithful, rather than centralized and concentrated in any single quasi-papal figure.

4 Theologically distinctive ideas include an insistence that the Holy Spirit proceeds from the Father alone (rather than, as in western churches, from the Father and the Son: see pp. 122–123), and the understanding of salvation as "deification." "God became human, in order that humans might become God." This theological refrain may be discerned as underlying much of the soteriological reflections of the eastern Christian tradition, both during the patristic period and in the modern Greek and Russian Orthodox theological traditions. As the citation suggests, there is an especially strong link between the doctrine of the incarnation and this understanding of salvation. For Athanasius, salvation consists in the human participation in the being of God. The divine Logos is imparted to humanity through the incarnation. On the basis of the assumption of a universal human nature, Athanasius concluded that the Logos assumed not merely the specific human existence of Jesus Christ, but human nature in general. As a consequence, all human beings are able to share in the deification which results from the incarnation. Human nature was created with the object of sharing in the being of God; through the descent of the Logos, this capacity is finally realized.

5 The Orthodox use of icons – that is, pictures of Jesus Christ, Mary, or some other religious figure – is of particular importance. The strong emphasis on the incarnation of the Son of God is understood to have consequences for prayer and spirituality. Icons are "windows of perception," through which the believer may catch a glimpse of the divine reality.

6 Monasteries continue to play a critically important role in the articulation and defense of the Orthodox ethos. Perhaps the most important monastic center remains Mount Athos, a peninsula stretching into the Aegean Sea. Most bishops are drawn from monasteries.

7 Orthodox clergy are permitted to marry (providing they do so before ordination), unlike their Catholic counterparts. Bishops, however, are generally unmarried, on account of their predominantly monastic backgrounds. Orthodoxy insists that only males can be ordained, and rejects the possibility of female priests, largely on the basis of continuity with tradition on this matter.

Pentecostalism

The origins of Pentecostalism are complex, but are usually traced back to the first day of the twentieth century – January 1, 1901. Charles Parham (1873–1929) had launched the Bethel Bible College in Topeka, Kansas, a few months earlier. One of his particular interests was the phenomenon of "speaking in tongues," which is described in Acts 2:1–4. Most Christians had taken this to be something that happened in the early church but was no longer part of the Christian experience. On New Year's Day, 1901, one of Parham's students experienced this phenomenon. A few days later, Parham experienced it for himself.

Parham began to teach about this apparent recovery of the "gift of tongues." One of those who heard him speak was the African American preacher William J. Seymour (1870–1922), who opened the "Apostolic Faith Mission" at 312 Azusa Street, Los Angeles, in April 1906. Over the next two years, a major revival broke out, characterized by the phenomenon of "speaking in tongues." The term "Pentecostalism" began to be applied to the movement, taking its name from the "Day of Pentecost" – the occasion, according to the New Testament, when the phenomenon was first experienced by the early Christian disciples (Acts 2:1–4).

The movement spread rapidly in America, appealing especially to the marginalized. Unusually, it seemed to appeal to and be embraced by both white and African American Christian groupings. Although Pentecostalism can be thought of as traditionalist in its Christian theology, it differs radically from other Christian groupings in the emphasis which it placed on speaking in tongues, and its forms of worship. These are strongly experiential, and involve prophesying, healings, and exorcisms. The worship style and lack of intellectual sophistication of the movement led to its being ignored by mainline denominations and the academy. Yet after World War II, a new phase of its expansion began, which paved the way for its massive growth in the second half of the twentieth century.

The incident which brought Pentecostalism to wider public attention took place in Van Nuys, California, in 1960. The rector of the local Episcopalian church, Dennis Bennett, told his astonished congregation that he had been filled with the Holy Spirit and had spoken in tongues. Reaction varied from bewilderment to outrage; the local Episcopalian bishop promptly banned speaking in tongues from his churches. However, it soon became clear that others in the mainline denominations had shared Bennett's experience. They came out of their closet and made it clear that they believed that they had experienced an authentic New Testament phenomenon, which would lead to the renewal of the churches.

By the late 1960s, it was evident that some form of renewal based on charismatic gifts (such as "speaking in tongues") was gaining

a hold within Anglican, Lutheran, Methodist, and Presbyterian circles. Perhaps most importantly of all, a growing charismatic movement began to develop within the Roman Catholic church. Using the term "Pentecostal" to describe this now became problematic, as this term was used to refer to a family of churches – such as the Assemblies of God – which placed particular emphasis on "speaking in tongues." Accordingly, the term "charismatic" was used to refer to movements within the mainline churches based upon the ideas and experiences of the Pentecostalist movement. Charismatic renewal within the mainline churches has led to new and informal worship styles, an explosion in "worship songs," a new concern for the dynamics of worship, and an increasing dislike of the traditionalism of formal liturgical worship, especially when this involves the cumbersome use of hymn books or service books.

The Pentecostalist movement – which we shall here take to include charismatic groups within mainline churches – has changed considerably since World War II. The most obvious change is the massive surge in growth. It is now estimated that there are 500 million Pentecostalists in the world, with a very wide geographical distribution. Although the movement may be argued to have its origins primarily within African American culture, it has taken root in South America, Asia, Africa, and Europe.

Why has this form of Christianity become so popular? Two factors are generally recognized as playing a significant role in the growing global appeal of Pentecostalism. First, Pentecostalism stresses a direct, immediate experience of God, and avoids the rather dry and cerebral forms of Christianity which many find unattractive and unintelligible. It is thus significant that Pentecostalism has made huge inroads in working-class areas of Latin America, in that it is able to communicate the divine without the need for the alienating impedimenta of a

8.4   A Pentecostal worship service. © David Gallant/CORBIS.

bookish culture. Second, the movement uses a language and form of communication which enable it to bridge cultural gaps highly effectively. Pentecostalism is best seen as an oral religion, which communicates its vision of life in stories, testimonies, and songs.

Protestantism

The term "Protestantism" is widely used to refer to those churches which trace their historical origins back to the European Reformation of the sixteenth century. The term is potentially misleading, in that most Protestant churches stress their historical and theological continuity with the early church. It must be stressed that the term "Protestant" is not in tension with the idea of being "catholic." The orthographical distinc-

tion between "catholic" and "Catholic" is of critical importance! To be "Catholic" is to be "catholic" *in a particular way*, which Protestants reject. Anglican and Lutheran writers, for example, place particular stress on their continuity with the life and thought of the early church, and affirm their "catholic" credentials. Similarly, in 1536 John Calvin, the reformer of the city of Geneva, vigorously defended the Reformation against the charge that it had no place for the patristic heritage. In what follows, we shall follow the general convention of using the term "Protestant" to refer to those churches whose historical origins are to be traced back to the divisions which opened up in the sixteenth century.

Protestant churches have had particularly close links with the state in a number of areas of Europe. Lutheranism, for example, has had close links with the state in Scandinavia, just as various forms of Presbyterianism have been influential in Scotland and the Netherlands, and Anglicanism in England. Partly on account of those links, and more generally through their continuity with the mainline Reformation, these churches offer baptism to infants who are too young to confess the Christian faith. This serves to distinguish the Baptists, who insist that baptism should be administered only to those who are believing Christians (see p. 161).

The term "denomination" is often used to refer to specific Protestant churches, such as Lutheranism or Methodism. A number of trends have developed within Protestant denominations in recent times, of which two are of particular importance. Evangelicalism (see pp. 273–275) is now a major influence within most mainline Protestant denominations in the English-speaking west, although its influence has been, until relatively recently, significantly lesser in continental Europe. A number of independent churches have now sprung up with a distinctively evangelical ethos, especially in South America and southern Africa. The charismatic movement has been of significance in the life of many mainline Protestant churches, and its influence has also been felt within Catholicism. A number of specifically charismatic denominations (such as the Assemblies of God) are now of growing importance in global Protestantism. In what follows, we shall focus on five major Protestant denominations; it must be appreciated that the rapid growth of evangelicalism and the charismatic movement means that numerical growth within Protestantism is now increasingly likely to happen outside the mainline denominations.

All Protestant denominations permit their ministers to marry. In recent years, most – but not, it must be stressed, all – Protestant denominations have permitted women to be ordained to full-time ministry within the church. Other means by which Protestants can be distinguished from Catholics include the following:

1 The authority of the pope is rejected. While some Protestants treat the pope with respect, he is not regarded as carrying any moral or doctrinal weight for Protestants.
2 Protestantism recognizes only two sacraments (see p. 159), and administers communion in both kinds (see p. 304). In other words, the laity are permitted to receive both bread and wine at communion. However, it should be noted that Methodism has traditionally insisted that unfermented grape juice, rather than wine, should be used at communion.
3 A cluster of characteristic Catholic beliefs are rejected, or treated as strictly optional private beliefs for individuals rather than the official teaching of the denomination. These include: purgatory, the intercession of the saints, and any form of devotion to the Virgin Mary.
4 Until the Second Vatican Council, the liturgy of the Catholic church was required to be read in Latin. This contrasted with the views of the reformers, who argued that all forms of public worship had to be in a language which the common people could understand.

Readers interested in following up on some of these historical and theological points are recommended to read works which deal with the history and theology of the Reformation, which will provide considerably more detailed explanations of these points, as well as expanding on them.

Anglicans

"Anglicanism" is the term usually employed to denote the distinctive features of the *ecclesia*

Anglicana – the national church of England, as it emerged from the sixteenth-century Reformation. The worldwide expansion of English influence, initially through the annexation of Ireland and Scotland, and subsequently through the colonization of North America in the seventeenth century, the Indian subcontinent in the late eighteenth century, and sub-Saharan Africa in the nineteenth, brought with it a significant enlargement of the sphere of influence of Anglicanism. The parody of Anglicanism as "the British empire at prayer" contains at least an element of truth; Anglicanism has exercised relatively little influence outside those realms once subject to British presence or rule.

The main features of Anglicanism are the following.

1   Anglicanism is an episcopal church, which sees the episcopacy as a means of demonstrating historical continuity with the early church. This is of particular importance to the more catholic sections of the Anglican church.
2   Particular importance is attached to the English city of Canterbury. The archbishop of Canterbury is seen as the spiritual head of Anglicanism, although he lacks the powers invested in a pope. All the bishops of the Anglican churches are invited to Canterbury every ten years for the Lambeth Conference, which aims to review the directions taken by Anglicanism in the last decade, and plan for the future.
3   Anglicanism is defined and distinguished theologically by the Thirty-Nine Articles, dating from the reign of Elizabeth I.
4   Anglicanism is a strongly liturgical church, which originally found one of its central foci in the Book of Common Prayer (1662), which embodied the "spirit of Anglicanism" in a fixed liturgical form. Anglican churches throughout the world had this in common,

along with a common ecclesiastical structure. Yet the process of liturgical revision, which became of major importance in the 1970s, resulted in the Anglican churches in England, Canada, the United States, and Australia adopting different liturgical forms, thus severely weakening the theological convergence of the movement.
5   The growing trend towards decentralization, linked with an increasing concern on the part of nations such as Australia and Canada to shake off their "colonial" image, has led to a new concern to develop distinctively national or ethnic approaches to Anglican identity. In its traditional forms, Anglicanism has been perceived as too "English" or "colonial" to maintain its credibility in the post-colonial era. As a result, Anglicanism has become increasingly diverse, reflecting its local concerns and resources. This trend gives every indication of continuing in the years ahead.
6   Anglicanism is predominantly an English-language church, although there are small Anglican presences outside Anglophone contexts (such as Francophone Africa).

Baptists

The origins of the Baptist churches are to be found in the seventeenth century. The more radical sections of the Reformation had always insisted that the church was to be a pure society of believers, rather than a mixed body. During the seventeenth century, particularly in England, there was growing support not only for the idea that congregations should consist only of those who explicitly and publicly affirmed their faith, but also for the related idea that baptism should be reserved only for those who affirmed their faith in this way. This contrasted with the Church of England, which permitted infants to be baptized.

The movement gained momentum in England during the nineteenth century, with great preachers such as C. H. Spurgeon drawing huge audiences for their sermons. The foundation of the Baptist Missionary Society by William Carey in 1792 led to considerable effort being invested in mission. Baptist congregations were established in North America, where the movement has grown to have considerable influence in public life in the United States. The Southern Baptist Convention is one of the most important forces in modern American Christianity; its six seminaries have been of major importance in shaping the distinctive ethos of the denomination. Perhaps the best-known Protestant Christian of the twentieth century – Billy Graham – is a Baptist.

The Baptist ethos is difficult to summarize, on account of the diversity within the denomination worldwide. However, the following will be helpful in gaining something of an understanding of the movement.

1 Baptists insist that baptism should be reserved for believers. Infant baptism is regarded as unjustified. This is probably one of the most distinctive aspects of the Baptist ethos. Some Baptist churches maintain an open policy towards baptism, accepting both adult and infant baptism; nevertheless, the emphasis upon adult baptism remains distinctive.

2 Baptists tend to be theologically conservative, placing a high value on the role of the Bible. The use of the term "the Bible Belt" to refer to the southern states of the United States reflects the importance of the Bible in Baptist church life, especially in preaching. Although the term "evangelicalism" is sometimes regarded with suspicion (it is seen as a "Yankee" – i.e., northern – word), it is clear that the Southern Baptists are increasingly becoming evangelical in orientation.

3 Baptist churches deliberately avoid the traditional form of church architecture, by which the altar is central and the pulpit to one side. This is seen as having the effect of focusing the attention of the congregation on the sacrament of the eucharist. Instead, Baptist church designs tend to place the pulpit at the center of things, to stress that the public reading of the Bible and the subsequent sermon preached on the biblical text are of central importance.

4 Baptists have tended to be critical of fixed liturgies, seeing in them an unhealthy tendency towards a purely formal expression of faith, and a suppression of extempore prayer on the part of both minister and congregation.

5 Baptist clergy are referred to as "ministers" (from the Latin word for "servant") or "pastors" (from the Latin word for "shepherd"). The term "priest" is completely avoided. The episcopal system of church government is rejected.

Lutherans

Lutheranism is the form of Protestantism which derives directly from Luther's reformation of the German church in the 1520s. Lutheranism was initially restricted to parts of northeastern Germany; however, by a gradual process of expansion, the movement established itself in Scandinavia and the Baltic states. Although there were early indications that Lutheranism might establish itself as the dominant form of Christianity in England during the late 1530s, it never gained the influence which some expected it to. The movement was active in missionary work, especially in India. However, its greatest expansion came about through the emigration of Lutheran communities from Scandinavia and Germany to North America. The settlement of Swedish communities in Minnesota is a particularly good example of this phenomenon. Lutheran communities also settled in Australia through a similar process. As a result, Lutheranism today is to be found chiefly in Germany, Scandinavia, the Baltic states, and especially the northern states of the USA. North American and European Lutheranism have tended to pursue somewhat different agendas during the past century, reflecting their different contexts. However, the formation of the Lutheran World Federation has gone some considerable way towards giving Lutherans a common sense of identity and purpose.

The Lutheran ethos reflects, to some degree, the central themes of Luther's personal program of reformation, which stressed continuity with the medieval church while at the same time introducing doctrinal and other changes where these were regarded as necessary.

1   Lutheranism is a strongly liturgical church, seeing the liturgy as a means of ensuring historical continuity with the past, and of maintaining doctrinal orthodoxy.
2   Lutheranism is defined theologically by both the Augsburg Confession (1530) and the Formula of Concord (1577). As a result, the words "Augsburg" and "Concord" are frequently incorporated into the titles of Lutheran seminaries and publishing houses.
3   Lutheranism retains a sacramental emphasis, going back to Luther, which is absent from many other Protestant denominations. It adopts a causative approach to baptism, arguing that baptism is "necessary and effectual to salvation." This contrasts with the view of other Protestant denominations (particularly the Baptists), who tend to regard baptism as a sign of grace rather than as something which is necessary before that grace can be given.

Methodists

Methodism was a movement within the Church of England, which subsequently gave birth to Methodism as a denomination in its own right. Its origins are especially associated with John Wesley (1703–1791), a founder and early leader of the Methodist movement. Contrary to the intentions of Wesley, Methodism broke away from the Church of England and became a distinct denomination. The distinctive emphasis of the early Methodists was the need for personal holiness. The term "Methodist" was originally a nickname, based on the methodical nature of the devotions and disciplines of the Wesleys and their circle. In general terms, Methodism has tended to be found primarily in English-speaking regions of the world, showing a parallelism with Anglicanism in this respect. As a result of various union schemes, Methodism has ceased to exist as a distinct denomination in various parts of the world, including Canada and Australia. The formation of the World Methodist Council has gone some way towards maintaining Methodism as a distinct entity within global Christianity.

1   Since its inception, Methodism has placed particular emphasis on the role of the laity. The office of the "lay preacher" illustrates this emphasis, which can also be exemplified in aspects of Methodist church government.
2   Methodism has taken considerable trouble to attempt to integrate personal faith and social action, seeing the gospel as involving both personal and social transformation.
3   Since the time of the Wesleys, Methodism has been characterized by a theological stance best described as "an optimism of grace." This contrasts with the more

Calvinist approach to this issue adopted by Reformed churches.

Presbyterians and other Reformed Christians

If the Lutheran churches owed their historical origins to Luther, the Reformed churches owed theirs to Calvin. Reformed versions of Christianity were soon established in western Europe, from where they spread to North America. In Europe, Scotland and the Netherlands were soon established as particularly important centers of Reformed thought. In England, the two major Reformed traditions have been referred to conventionally as "Presbyterianism" and "Congregationalism," reflecting two different systems of church government. As a result of Dutch colonial policy during the nineteenth century, forms of Reformed Christianity were established in South Africa, the northeastern parts of South America, and parts of Southeast Asia. In the United States, Princeton Theological Seminary was established as a leading center of Presbyterian thought and practice. In recent years, South Korea has become a leading center of Reformed church life, as a result of the very rapid growth of Christianity in that region (see above). The World Alliance of Reformed Churches, constituted in its present form in 1970 (although tracing its origins back to 1875), provides a means of allowing the various Reformed churches to maintain their common identity.

The diversity within Reformed churches is such that it is difficult to generalize concerning them. However, the following aspects of the Reformed ethos are of importance.

1   Reformed churches are generally governed by "presbyters" or "elders" (the word "Presbyterianism" derives from this practice). Some Reformed churches regard the elders as ministers in their own right, with pastoral or teaching responsibilities; others see them as assistants, with specific responsibilities in relation to the administration and government of the church. The term "minister" is used.

2   Reformed worship traditionally places considerable emphasis upon the reading and preaching of the Word of God. Holy Communion is celebrated regularly but infrequently. This emphasis upon preaching, rather than the sacraments, is especially evident from the regular Sunday worship of the Reformed churches.

3   In the English-speaking west, and regions influenced by it, the Reformed faith is defined theologically by the Westminster Confession (1647). As a result, the word "Westminster" is frequently incorporated into the titles of Reformed seminaries and publishing houses.

4   Most Reformed churches place an emphasis upon the sovereignty of God in predestination, which contrasts with the more "optimistic" view associated with Wesleyan Methodism.

Evangelicalism

Evangelicalism has become of major importance in the mainline Protestant churches since 1945. Although some new Protestant denominations have been formed which are explicitly evangelical in orientation, the general pattern which has emerged is that evangelicalism is a movement within the mainline denominations. Hence evangelicals within the Reformed churches retain much of the ethos of those churches (including its church structures), while supplementing these with at least some of the characteristics of evangelicalism, noted below. Similarly, evangelicals within Anglicanism adopt many

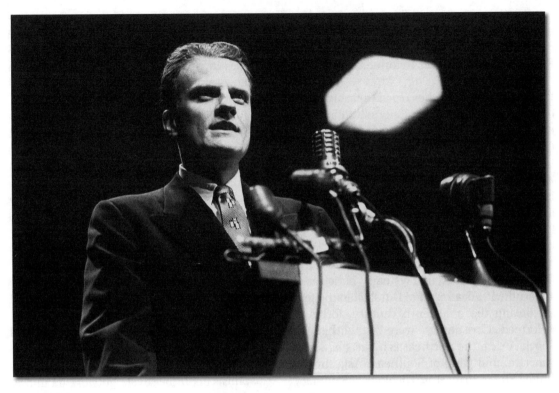

8.5 Billy Graham, pictured in 1954. © POPPERFOTO/Alamy.

of the characteristics of the latter (such as the episcopal system of church government and the use of a fixed liturgy), while retaining an evangelical ethos within this church.

The four main distinctive features of the evangelical ethos are the following.

1   Evangelicalism is strongly biblical in its emphasis. This is especially evident in the styles of preaching found within the movement. This emphasis is carried over into other aspects of evangelical life, including the importance attached to small Bible study groups within the life of the church, and to the regular reading of the Bible in personal devotion.

2   Evangelicalism places a particular emphasis on the cross of Jesus. Although Jesus is of central importance to evangelicalism, its emphasis has tended to fall upon the saving death of Jesus on the cross. This is especially reflected in evangelical hymns and songs.

3   Evangelicalism stresses the need for personal conversion. Considerable emphasis is placed on the dangers of "nominalism," meaning by this "a purely formal or external acceptance of Christian teachings, without any personal transformation in consequence." Evangelical preaching often stresses the need for Christians to be "born again" (see John 3:1–16).

4   Evangelical churches and individual evangelicals have a deep commitment to evangelism – that is, to converting others to the Christian faith. Billy Graham is a good example of a twentieth-century evangelical

who has become well known on account of this emphasis. It should be noted that the words "evangelicalism" and "evangelism" are often confused, on account of their similar spelling. The former refers to a movement, the latter to an activity – but an activity which is especially associated with this specific movement.

Christianity: A Survey of its Global Concerns

Thus far, we have explored some of the regional developments and denominational groupings that shape Christianity today. But what of the issues that concern Christianity? What are its internal debates? What are the points of conflict within the movement? And what are the potential or actual tensions between Christianity and its broader cultural context? In what follows, we shall explore some of these concerns, and comment on their significance for the present shape and future development of the Christian faith. We begin by considering some of the issues that have arisen as a result of Christianity's global presence.

The globalization of Christianity

Globalization is generally held to represent the emergence of an increasingly global culture, which displaces local cultures. So how does this process impact on Christianity? The world has been undergoing a massive change through technological innovation and global restructuring. Many social theorists argue that the world is now structured by global forces, which reinforce the dominance of a worldwide capitalist economic system. This leads to the erosion of the primacy of the "nation-state" through multinational and transnational cor-

porations, and the degrading of local cultures and traditions through the emergence of a global culture.

One possibility is that globalization necessarily leads to secularization. On this view, the modernization process implicit in globalization inevitably entails ideological progress, leading to the erosion of religion. This approach does not sit easily with the events of recent years, such as the Islamic revolution in Iran, and the resurgence of religion as a marker of national identity in the former territories of the Soviet Union. Additional hypotheses thus have to be introduced to accommodate the theory to the happenings of the real world. Here, religious revival is seen as an attempt to resist the advance of globalization. The Islamic revolution in Iran and the rise of the Hindu National Party in India can both be seen as irrational reactions against the imposition of a global culture upon these regions. However, these reverses are to be seen as transient. In the course of time, modernization must prevail.

The difficulty with this view is that it clearly rests on some of the core assumptions of the Enlightenment – a movement which arose within western culture, affirming the autonomy of reason and logic and which reacted against religion as an improper persistence of irrational ideas. The Enlightenment was not a global phenomenon, and its ideas cannot be regarded as possessing universal validity or as commanding global support. In effect, this approach to religion only works if globalization is explicitly understood as *westernization*, and if the ethos of the west is defined in terms of the secularism which was typical of the immediate post-war period, especially in western Europe. In the twenty-first century, however, many would regard such an analysis of western culture as seriously skewed. A new interest in spirituality is likely to lead to increasing respect, for example, for the religions of Asia in the west, rather than any kind of pressure for them to conform to the rather dry and sterile secular creed of the now-defunct Enlightenment – a creed which is irreducibly ethnocentric rather than universal.

A second approach argues that religion will continue to be part of a global culture. In contrast to the previous view, which envisaged the secularist agenda of the west being imposed upon – or accepted by – global culture, this viewpoint sees the emergence of a global religion which is basically a fusion of the religious traditions of the world. The rise of consumerism points to the desire of many to construct their own worldviews, rather than accept prepackaged non-negotiable ideologies. This can only lead to the idea that the global religion of the future will not be any one of the present-day contenders but an amalgam, constructed according to taste.

Yet perhaps the most reliable prediction is the simplest: that today's religions will continue to be of significance in the twenty-first century. A process of adaptation and development will unquestionably take place, especially within Christianity. Some theorists suggest that Christianity might respond to continuing pressure from other religions and anti-religious forces through a process of convergence between its leading elements – Roman Catholicism, Eastern Orthodoxy, and revivalist or conservative forms of Protestantism.

One thing, however, is clear. English is rapidly becoming the preferred language of the global Christian community. Partly on account of the massive historical impact of the United Kingdom in relation to the propagation of Christianity, and the continuing importance of American Christian television and radio shows, religious publications, and major conference speakers, English is well on its way to becoming the dominant language of the international Christian community. What Latin was once to the Catholic church, English is becoming for the church at large. The growing size and cultural importance of Chinese Christianity must be noted here; the predominance of English as the language of faith may be a temporary development.

The challenge of fundamentalism

The word "fundamentalism" is generally taken to mean something like "a revivalist conservative religious orthodoxy," and designates a phenomenon which can be discerned within Christianity, Islam, Judaism, and Hinduism. The term is used particularly to refer to styles of religious belief and behavior which are opposed to change, and seek to restore an ideal past. Often, that past is viewed in hopelessly unrealistic terms, partly as a means of stressing the contrast between the past glories and present failures of a religious movement. A 1969 study by Anthony F. C. Wallace on cultural revival within the Iroquois peoples in the eighteenth century, focusing on the figure of "Handsome Lake," offers important insights into the origins and development of religious fundamentalism, which merit close attention by all concerned with this phenomenon. To paraphrase Wallace's analysis, three general stages can be seen in the process of cultural or religious revitalization:

1　Social change takes place within a people or social grouping, which results in cultural tension.
2　Initially, this tension leads to an attempt to accommodate the changes. This inevitably leads to a change or perceived degeneration in social patterns, which in turn leads to social disruption.
3　In reaction to this, a reaffirmation of traditional cultural patterns takes place, usually through the emergence of charismatic figures who champion this return to such patterns.

Although the development of fundamentalism is generally discussed with reference to Christianity, it is particularly helpful to note an Islamic case study in exploring the factors involved.

The origins of the modern Islamic movement can be traced back to about 1875, when Jamal al-Din al-Afghani urged Muslims to resist the growing western influence in the Middle East by a reaffirmation of their Muslim heritage. He encouraged Muslims to believe that, prior to the arrival of the westerners, a golden age of wise Islamic rule held sway. This situation could be retrieved by a return to personal religious piety, a reform and renewal of Islamic *sharia* law, and violent resistance to western presence and influence in the region. Since then the establishment of the State of Israel has contributed powerfully to the resurgence of Islamic fundamentalism. The Iranian revolution of 1978–1979 may be seen as evidence of the importance of this vision. Every time the United States intervenes in the politics of the Middle East (and especially when it supports Israel), it stimulates the growth and sustains the passion of Islamic fundamentalism.

The paradox of fundamentalism is that it depends upon secularism for its credibility. What drives fundamentalism is the perception that the modern world is out to eliminate religion. Fundamentalism and western secular materialism thus exist in a paradoxically symbiotic relationship. Dislike of religious fundamentalism motivates the growth of secularism, which in turn generates a reaction, leading to the swelling of the ranks of the fundamentalists. Are we locked into a vicious cycle of co-dependency? And is the west actually unintentionally feeding the growth of religious fundamentalism, at home and abroad, through a failure to appreciate the genesis of this movement? There are some hard questions that need to be asked.

From what has been said, it will be clear that fundamentalism is essentially a *reactive* movement, which emerges in response to the perception of a threat to the core values of a people or group. That threat may be external (as with western influence in the Middle East) or internal (as with the modernization process, which can be argued to erode traditional beliefs). The Pharisees of biblical times can easily be categorized as "fundamentalists," in that they sought to recapture and reassert traditional Jewish beliefs and practices that they believed to have been threatened by Hellenism. The word may indeed be a recent coinage; the phenomenon which it designates has been with us for at least two thousand years.

Our concern is primarily with the events of the twentieth century, and their longer-term implications for the twenty-first century. Fundamentalism arose as a religious reaction within American conservative Protestantism especially during the period 1920–1940 to the threat which it discerned in the rise of a secular culture. It is not correct to regard the movement simply as a return to or reaffirmation of older positions, although aspects of fundamentalist teachings may indeed be discerned in the writings of classic Reformed orthodoxy, or in those of the Old Princeton School, such as those of Benjamin B. Warfield and Charles Hodge. Fundamentalism cannot be equated with "a basic unaltered orthodoxy," as this fails to take into account the reactive nature of the movement. Fundamentalism is a deliberate and considered reaction to developments in the twentieth and early twenty-first centuries. It was from its outset, and has remained, a counter-cultural movement, using central doctrinal affirmations as a means of defining cultural boundaries.

It did not take long for fundamentalist Protestants to appreciate that they were locked into a spiral of decline, and were incapable of challenging or changing the cultural trends which they so abhorred. Fundamentalism signally failed to turn back the rising tide of liberalism; it failed to achieve any significant impact upon the thought world of its day, and it simply turned its back on the social problems of its time, vilifying them without engaging with the issues constructively. A protest movement arose within American fundamentalism demanding a new strategy. While honoring the objectives of their elders, the younger generation could see that their tactics were fatally flawed.

The emergence of evangelicalism (or, as it was then known, "neo-evangelicalism") as a distinctive option, avoiding the fatal weaknesses of fundamentalism, dates from the period immediately following World War II. Carl F. H. Henry argued that fundamentalists did not present Christianity as a worldview, with a distinctive social vision, but chose to concentrate on only one aspect of the Christian proclamation. As a result, an impoverished and reduced gospel was presented to the world, radically defective in its social vision. Fundamentalism was too other-worldly and anti-intellectual to gain a hearing amongst the educated public, and unwilling to concern itself with exploring how Christianity related to culture and social life in general. Henry argued for the need for sustained cultural engagement on the part of evangelicals.

Initially, the term "new evangelicalism" was used to refer to this third force in North American Protestantism; gradually, this was displaced by the simpler and more economical term "evangelicalism," distinguished by its stalwart defense of orthodox Christian faith, backed up by solid theological scholarship and its commitment to the social application of the gospel message. Evangelicalism, then, may be thought of as a revivalist conservative Christian movement which eschews the social isolationism of its fundamentalist counterpart.

Fundamentalism, however, is also likely to have a continuing appeal in the modern world.

Where traditional religious beliefs, practices, or freedoms are perceived to be jeopardized, fundamentalism is a likely response. The history of Christianity does not suggest that this will take the form of a violent reaction. Unlike Islamic fundamentalism, which appears to regard acts of violence against its opponents as sanctioned by the greater good of restoring allegedly "pure" Islamic beliefs, Christian fundamentalists have generally (but not without exception) remained within the law. So what could trigger off violence? Perhaps the most obvious would be the legal enforcement of de-Christianization – the process of removing a country's Christian past from its present.

While there are social theorists who argue that the world will become an increasingly homogeneous place in the twenty-first century, there is an alternative vision, which cannot be dismissed or ignored. According to this alternative vision, the world will become increasingly like the Lebanon or the Balkans, with its territories divided along tribal lines rather than taking the form of organized nation-states. Whether western politicians like it or not, religious issues matter to these communities. Indeed, it could be argued that a failure to appreciate the importance of religious issues has befuddled the foreign policies of both the United States and the European Union in the last decade. We may develop this point by considering how conflict might flare up between Christian and Muslim communities in the twenty-first century.

Tensions between Christianity and Islam

The two global religions which are most passionately committed to expansion are Christianity and Islam, both of which made considerable advances in the twentieth century. The last five hundred years have seen something of an inversion of their relationship. Up to about 1520, Islam was the dominant global religion, having made substantial territorial inroads into Europe. However, the expansion of Christianity in North and South America, Africa, Asia, and Australasia has led to the relation being changed. Today, Christianity is by far the largest faith grouping in the world.

It is important to appreciate that Christianity is a growing presence in traditionally Islamic regions of the world – such as Malaysia and Indonesia – while Islam has gained a presence in the west, largely through patterns of economic migration. Large Islamic communities have developed in Britain, for example. However, these tend to conceive their identities in terms of the ethnic origins of their communities, and have made relatively little impact on traditional British society.

Islamic and Christian expansion into geographical areas in which neither traditionally had a significant presence, and the establishment of presences in regions historically dominated by each other, clearly raises some difficult questions. One possible outcome of this situation is peaceful coexistence and the growth of mutual understanding. Another is social unrest, possibly leading to civil war – or partition. Large nations with significant religious communities may find that the Indian situation of 1947 repeats itself, with the only viable solution being to allow regions with distinctive religious identities to form their own states.

So what does the future hold here? In many ways, the issue will be determined by the styles of Islam in the ascendancy in the regions of potential conflict. Traditional Islamic nations treated Christian minorities well and were content to allow them to dwell in peace, providing they did not try to convert their Muslim neighbors or resist conversion to Islam, did not build places of worship, and paid an appropriate poll tax (*jizya*) to the state for offering them its protection. This continues to be the case in Egypt, where a significant number of impoverished Coptic Christians convert to Islam each year because they cannot afford to pay the poll tax.

However, there are more aggressive forms of Islamic fundamentalism which are supportive of a more militant attitude towards Christianity. The potential danger of the situation can be see from events in the populous and potentially wealthy West African state of Nigeria, which has long been troubled by political corruption and economic instability. Muslims and Christians each make up about 45 percent of Nigeria's 110 million people. The northern region of the country is predominantly Muslim, the southern Christian. Over the period 1999–2000, some of the northern states introduced *sharia* law – traditional Islamic law – in an attempt to cut down on lawlessness. However, the measure caused rioting in these states, as Christians took to the streets to protest at what they regarded as victimization. For example, *sharia* law prescribes the death sentence for "blasphemy," which is generally taken to mean criticism of the prophet Mohammed. In Pakistan, accusations of blasphemy have been leveled against Christians, sometimes as young as 13.

Critics of this law argue that it inevitably discriminates against religious minorities, not least because *sharia* regards non-Islamic witnesses as possessing a lesser status in the eyes of the law. *Sharia* law is intended to be applied only to a Muslim community, and cannot be enforced on religious minorities. However, religious minorities often complain that they suffer discrimination in various ways. The situation is particularly tense in hardline Islamic nations, such as Afghanistan, Sudan, and Saudi Arabia. It is clear that the twenty-first century may witness growing tension and unrest at the interfaces of these two expansionist world religions.

One of the most trenchant criticisms directed against western Christians by their colleagues in Asia and Africa is that they seem to have no idea of the significance of this point. This, for example, became clear at the Lambeth Conference of 1998, which brought together Anglican bishops from throughout the world. Traditionally, this conference has been dominated by the agendas and concerns of western Anglicans, especially in North America. This time round, the developing world made its mark on proceedings. Resolution 61 of the conference expressed "concern that the emergence of Islamic religious fundamentalism" has resulted in serious violation of some basic human rights, including "the right of religious belief, practice, and propagation, as well as destruction of property of Christian churches in such places as Northern Nigeria and the Sudan."

The uncertain future of the Protestant denomination

In recent years there has been increasing interest in whether traditional Protestant denominations can survive in the twenty-first century. The discussion has tended to focus on the American experience, which is often seen as setting the trend for the remainder of the Christian world. In what follows, we shall consider the debate, and its potential implications.

In 1929, H. Richard Niebuhr published a book entitled *The Social Sources of Denominationalism*. This study of the origin of the modern American religious denominations argued that they represented the distinguishing mark of American religious life, and they were here to stay. They were rooted in historical differences of social class, wealth, national origin, and race, which remained normative in American culture.

The next decades seemed to confirm everything Niebuhr argued. Throughout the 1950s, the growth of the traditional Protestant denomination surged in the United States.

Congregationalists, Episcopalians, Methodists, and Presbyterians reported net annual membership gains. Their membership reflected precisely the issues Niebuhr had noted. When Methodists got rich, they became Episcopalians. Each denomination vigorously defended its sovereignty and vested interests. In 1956, a survey showed that 80 percent of Episcopalians believed that it was wrong to hold worship service with other Christian groups. A year earlier, a Gallup poll showed that 96 percent of the adult population of the United States belonged to the same denomination as their parents. Their churchgoing habits had not changed over a generation.

Yet by 1990, something had gone wrong for many of these denominations. It was not simply that their growth had stalled. They were in decline. By 1990, the denominations just mentioned had lost between one fifth and one third of their 1965 memberships, at a time when the population growth of the United States had surged. A real numerical decline thus converted into a massive slump in the proportion of America's population choosing to associate with these denominations. Anglicanism, Methodism, and Presbyterianism are among those which are particularly vulnerable to these major demographic shifts.

Alongside the numerical decline of the traditional American denomination, another trend can be observed, calling into question whether the "denomination" has any real future. The denomination is increasingly being seen as a historical anomaly which the future does not seem to want. Christian denominations in America are one of the very few institutional expressions of European culture still in existence. But why, many Americans began to wonder, should modern America's religious life be made dependent upon a European model – especially when that model was now seen as having failed back in its homelands?

Both individual churches and Christians in America are showing an increasing reluctance to define themselves denominationally. I have attended churches in California which have described themselves as "in the Presbyterian tradition" – meaning that they do things like the Presbyterians used to, but do not care to be associated with the institutional politics and policies of this mainline denomination. Is this because it has become slightly outdated to do so? Or because it is seen as associating with an outmoded establishment? Many churches have named themselves after their localities, skillfully dropping any reference to their denomination. The inclusion of denominational identities is no longer viewed as a positive in marketing terms.

A quite different scenario may develop in South America, Asia, and Africa, in which more dynamic and adapted forms of these mainline faiths have developed. However, there is little indication that the western denominations are likely to benefit from these trends. At present, the only sections of western mainline denominations which are showing any signs of life or growth are those affected by evangelical or charismatic renewal.

The commodification of Christianity in the west

In 1993, sociologist George Ritzer coined the term "McDonaldization" to designate a trend he believed was characteristic of modern American culture – "the process by which the principles of the fast-food restaurant are coming to dominate more and more sectors of American society." Why should Ritzer have fixed on a hamburger chain as a paradigm for social change in the west, especially America? Because he saw in McDonald's a way of creating and marketing a product which seemed to have become a way of life for many.

An excellent example is provided by the service industries which have sprung up in response to the migration of industrialization to the developing world (where labor costs are lower), and growing affluence in the west. Recreation – the idea of taking time out to relax – has become a product. And once a product has been identified, Ritzer argues, the quest begins to be able to create, deliver, and market that product as effectively and efficiently as possible. A human quest thus becomes a bureaucratic matter, as a series of rules, regulations, and procedures is developed to ensure that the resulting product is delivered to its intended market with the minimum difficulty.

Ritzer identifies four defining characteristics of the McDonaldization process: efficiency, calculability, predictability, and control. These are the moral values of the production line, not of living human beings – and they have, he argues, come to shape western society as a whole, with disturbing results. Instead of expressing their basic human skills and talents, people are forced through the labor market to perform a number of highly simplified tasks on a regular and tedious basis.

While Ritzer made no attempt to apply his ideas to the life of the churches, there is no doubt that these trends can be seen at work in modern western Christianity, especially within the burgeoning evangelical movement. They sit ill at ease, however, with some core traditional Christian ideas and values. In his excellent study *The McDonaldization of the Church*, leading Scottish religious analyst John Drane has explored how the four key features of this process can be seen at work within highly successful churches – yet, paradoxically, threaten to undermine the very faith on which these churches seek to build.

- *Efficiency.* Drane notes how Christian bookstores display and sell countless books offering quick and efficient fixes to spiritual difficulties. Issues of discipleship which, in previous generations, would have been seen as requiring dedication, prayer, and commitment, perhaps extended over many years, can be sorted out in a few moments. "Christian maturity" used to be seen as something that arose over decades, as Christians read their Bibles, listened to sermons, prayed about the future directions of their lives, took care of the sick and elderly, and generally came to internally assimilate the ideas and values of Christianity through living it out over many years.

- *Calculability.* During the 1970s and 1980s, the "Church Growth Movement" set out a series of strategies (all of which, it argued, could be found in the New Testament) for increased church membership. Spirituality became a matter of numbers, with bigger numbers meaning better spirituality.
- *Predictability.* Drane regards this as the "McDonaldization" characteristic that is easiest to discern within the church. Worship patterns can be totally predictable, generating a comfortable and familiar environment for worship, yet running the risk of failing to challenge and excite. The political and social makeup of congregations leads to a certain predictability about moral values and choices. The theme of predictability inevitably leads to the desire to *control* what happens – which leads us to the next category that Drane discusses in illustrating the McDonaldization of the church.
- *Control.* An efficient production and marketing system requires a high degree of control. In the case of McDonald's, this is not really a problem. The quality of the product is assured; it remains to make sure that it is properly cooked, packaged, and delivered.

Western Christianity shows similar traits. There is a set pattern to how you get to see things. Many people encounter Christianity for the first time through the Alpha Course, or through some major evangelistic rally, such as those once led by Billy Graham. These tend to offer introductions to the Christian faith which are highly structured and preprogrammed, with one step leading on to the next. It works – and many find this immensely helpful. When there is so much to discover, it helps to have someone manage the process of familiarization for you.

The Alpha Course is an excellent example of an efficient, predictable, and controlled presentation of the Christian faith, which has been widely adopted by churches throughout the world precisely on account of its proven track record. Like McDonald's, the concept travels well. The basic idea is that of a ten-week program which introduces some of the fundamentals of the Christian faith in a generally relaxed environment, in which inquirers are invited to ask any questions they may have. The group of people who assemble for the course rapidly become a community, sharing in the experience of encountering Christianity and each other at the same time. The sharing of meals is an important element in this community-building dimension to the program, which brings together the dual themes of "believing" and "belonging." The style matters as much as the content. Precisely because so much careful thought has been given to its format, the Alpha Course has succeeded where others have stalled.

There has, of course, been much resistance to this commodification of Christianity. It is argued that it distorts the Christian gospel. Evangelism now becomes a matter of developing a slick sales technique, and discipleship a matter of efficient processing of individuals through church programs. Nevertheless, it seems to be working – at least, in terms of the number of people that are impacted by this marketing approach. It remains to be seen what this will mean for the future of Christianity as a whole.

The demands for de-westernization of Christianity

Old habits of thinking die hard. One of the working assumptions underlying most discussions of the future of Christianity in the twentieth century was that it represented a western faith, and that its future was predicated upon trends in western society. By 1990, it was perfectly obvious that this was no longer true. Over the century, the center of gravity of Christianity had moved south, and now lies in the developing world. To its critics in the third world, western Christianity continues to behave as if the entire Christian world is simply a clone of western Christianity. The reality, however, is rather different.

Albert Vun, the rector of St. Patrick's Anglican Church, in Sabah, Malaysia, tells a story to illustrate this point. The church of St. Michael's, in the neighboring region of Sandakan, was built according to a European model, with a high sloping roof. Vun told his congregation about the shape of the roof, and asked his audience to imagine why it was built like this. The answer, of course, was simple: to allow the snow to slide off easily. Now there has never been any snow in tropical Sandakan. The church was simply constructed according to a European design, adapted to the heavy snowfalls of northern European winters.

In much the same way, Vun argues, Europeans developed understandings of what it meant to be a church which reflected their own situation. These ideas did not relate well to Malaysia or Singapore, and should not be used in that context. Local understandings of church identity and function would be needed, sensitive to both the limitations and possibilities of the context. Western understandings of what it meant to be "church" were so culturally conditioned by western society and values that they were a liability rather than an asset in a non-western context.

But there are deeper issues than this. We shall consider one – the growing critique of western systematic theology within African and Asian Christianity. The massive shift of the Christian epicenter from the western world to the developing worlds of Africa and Asia is laden with implications for the future of academic theology. The discipline of systematic theology has generally been developed in a western context and is, at least to some extent, shaped by the audiences which it addresses and the issues which are debated within that culture. The noted German Protestant theologian Wolfhart Pannenberg has argued that western theology has been shaped by its engagement with the rise of the natural sciences and the secular critique of authority. Yet precisely because these critiques are especially associated with the western world, might not very different styles of systematic theology arise when the engagement in question is not western but reflects issues in the emerging world – such as an encounter with Hinduism rather than secularism?

This predominantly western orientation of systematic theology thus raises some important questions. Why, for example, should an Asian feel in the slightest degree obligated to continue such a tradition? Is not the correct and obvious way ahead in the twenty-first century to develop theologies which arise out of a local engagement with the realities of the gospel, rather than accept what someone else – generally from a western context – has bequeathed?

For example, let us consider the case of John Calvin (1509–1564), a noted western theologian who continues to be an important resource for Reformed theology today. For Calvin, the task of theology was to relate Scripture to sixteenth-century Geneva; for others, it will be to relate that same Scripture to the Hong Kong of the twenty-first century. Calvin's approach and the results which it yields may be helpful to Christians in Hong Kong as they seek to undertake this task. Yet his answers cannot be identical to theirs. For instance, it is well known that Calvin was interested in – and, to some extent, influenced by – the language and concepts of the classical Roman philosophical and rhetorical tradition. China has an older philosophical and rhetorical tradition. Why should Chinese theologians feel under the slightest obligation to make use of the same ideas that Calvin borrowed, when they have a distinguished heritage of their own to draw upon?

Much western theology of the modern period was based upon the flawed assumption of the universality of the modes of western thought and discourse. There existed certain universally valid ways of thinking, which western philosophy and theology had uncovered. The styles of theology which had gained the ascendancy in the west were thus valid for all people. It was simply a matter of exporting these theological methods to the rest of the world, colonizing the unsophisticated areas of the world in order that they might benefit from these insights. These modern theologians, of course, did not think of themselves as colonists; this distasteful image would suggest that they were implanting an essentially alien way of thinking into a native culture. Yet that is precisely what it was. And there were lots of problems associated with the approach.

First of all, what the Enlightenment thought was universal turned out to be ethnocentric. For example, the philosophies of Immanuel Kant and G. W. F. Hegel can be argued to embody the core values of western culture at the time. Kant is the philosopher of the classical Newtonian worldview, and Hegel the philosopher of German culture. They are both locked into a specific cultural context, and their ideas, far from being universally valid, are determined by their social contexts. As many western theologians happened to share the same, or similar, contexts, they found the use of these systems generally unproblematic. But what conceivable justification could be offered for imposing such Eurocentric philosophies upon China, India, or Japan, with significantly different intellectual histories and inherited modes of thought?

Second, the dominance of western theology in global Christianity was defended (by westerners) on the basis of the general cultural influence of the west. Non-western theologians, however, argue that western Christianity exploited the military and economic strengths of the west as a means of smuggling in its approach to theology, suppressing and dismissing local approaches which might well have something important to say. With the advent of postmodernity, a welcome sense of openness has developed in the west towards non-western modes of thought. Postmodernity's critics suggest that this has not yet really progressed beyond lip service. However, it is a step in the right direction.

The most important development, however, has been the general trend within many sections of the developing church to ignore the history and agendas of western systematic theology altogether, and simply to see theology as a direct engagement with the text of the Bible. A growing number of Christian thinkers argue that theology is fundamentally nothing more and nothing less than attentiveness to Scripture, and a desire to express and communicate what is to be found there to the church and the world. Christian theology is under an obligation to pay respectful and obedient attention to the biblical testimony, and allow itself to be shaped and reshaped by what it finds expressed here.

This means that the Bible is interpreted against the backdrop of the culture within which the interpretative process takes place. A Hong Kong Christian will need to ask how what she reads in Scripture illuminates and informs her situation, and will feel no pressing need to involve western academics as intermediaries in this process of reflection. To use an economic analogy, the new theological trends involve the elimination of the middleman. The issue is that of Christian thinkers applying Scripture to their own contexts, rather than slavishly repeating interpretations of Scripture originally developed with a very different cultural context in mind.

The emergence of new ways of "being church"

Christianity is like a plant: it grows and develops. In many of his parables, Jesus Christ compared the kingdom of God to a seed, which undergoes growth. Growth and development are sure signs of life; an absence of change tends to point to an organization being moribund. A living faith grows, like a plant – yet by growing, undergoes change. As the great English Victorian writer John Henry Newman once pointed out, if the church is to remain the same, it must change. To stay still, we must move.

The paradox captured by Newman lies at the heart of many of the impassioned debates and anxieties within Christian churches and communities over the future direction of Christianity. Many of those debates center on how congregations should respond to the changing situations and needs of their members, and those whom they hope to reach in the wider culture. The debate is about new ways of "being church," to use the jargon that has developed in recent years. In what follows, we shall consider three such new ways of "being church": the community church, the cell church, and the "seeker-sensitive" church.

The *community church* has emerged in recent years, especially in the United States, as a powerful vehicle of social renewal and Christian fellowship. Such churches see themselves as "islands in the stream." They are like the monasteries of the Middle Ages, offering safety and community to travelers. Where the rationality of European churches often seemed to rest on Descartes' celebrated (if enigmatic) axiom, "I think, therefore I am," such churches rest their appeal on a totally different axiom – "I belong, and therefore I am." Identity is about belonging somewhere – and these churches see themselves as providing a community for their members. Saddleback Church, in Lake Forest, California, models the way ahead for many, stressing the importance of being affirmed by God and loved by the Christian community.

A community church is like small-town America of bygone days, with a population numbered in the low thousands. There is a sense of belonging to a common group, of shared common values, and of knowing one another. People don't just go to community churches; they see themselves as belonging there. At a time when American society appears to be fragmenting, the community churches offer cohesion.

Community churches offer their members a whole range of social activities, all designed to meet needs, offer services, and forge community. A typical community church – such as Mariners Church, in Irvine, California – might offer seminars on such pressing matters as single parenting, recovery from alcohol and drugs abuse, and divorce dynamics. As a result, these congregations foster a deep sense of personal renewal and human interconnectedness.

Once, community was defined by where you lived. It was part of the inherited order of things, something that you were born into. Now, it has to be *created* – and the agency that creates this community is increasingly the voluntary organization. Unsurprisingly, Christian churches are strategically placed to create community, where social forces are destroying it in American society as a whole. The community churches have proved especially effective in this role.

So what is the significance of these new churches, which are often recent creations, with large congregations? Most community churches are non-denominational, and have no interest in ecclesiastical politics. They see themselves as being there primarily for their members, and they have no interest in supporting or sustaining the unwieldy and increasingly self-serving denominational hierarchies. Their growth is likely to catalyze further the decline of the Protestant denomination in the west – something touched on earlier in the present section.

The *cell church* movement offers a quite different approach. Since World War II, many churches have experimented with "small groups." In addition to meeting regularly in the main church building for worship on Sundays, many congregation members would also meet in smaller groups during the week for the purpose of Bible study and prayer. Many churches found that these small groups became the basis of numerical growth. To put the situation in a nutshell, the groups grew because they attracted additional members; once they reached a certain critical size, the group was no longer "small," and – like an amoeba – it split into two. Many mainline churches reported that small groups seemed to be the engines of church growth.

A careful study of church attendance in England during the 1990s revealed the fact that larger churches found it difficult to sustain growth. It seemed that, having reached a critical mass, larger churches began to lose the sense of "belonging" that is such an important theme in postmodern culture. Growth seems to take place in smaller churches, possibly because of the greater intimacy and sense of belonging that this engenders. No one pastor seems able to cope with more than about 150 people, if they are to be cared for properly. Clearly, a large church with active small groups might be in a position to benefit from the economies of scale and resources possible with a larger church, while at the same time using its small groups as a means of nourishing and sustaining the fellowship, personal intimacy, and sharing which many find such an important aspect of being church. It is this basic idea which underlies the "cell church" movement.

This new approach to "being church" is now widespread, especially in the Far East, and is seen as offering a radical new understanding of the role of small groups within the life of the church. Faith Community Baptist Church in Singapore has experienced remarkable growth, and has attracted attention throughout the Pacific Rim. One of the largest Anglican cell churches in the world is located in Tawau, Sabah, in East Malaysia (formerly known as British North Borneo). St. Patrick's Church has grown from around 700 to 3,000 since it decided to make the transition to being a "cell church" in 1992. Although the "cell church" approach makes use of the small group, it does so in a quite different manner. Most significantly of all, it abandons traditional European assumptions about what churches are, and how they ought to be run.

It is estimated that as many as 75 million people are now members of cell churches. The basic idea behind the movement can be found in the patterns of church life which are related in the New Testament, especially the Acts of the Apostles (e.g., Acts 2:42–46). Like the early church, the movement forms small cells, sometimes called "Basic Christian Communities," which are typically based in members' houses. The life of the church lies in the cells, which are seen as primary; the gathered congregation on Sundays is secondary.

The cells generally start off with anything between six to eight people, growing over a period of months to fifteen. At this point each cell splits into two smaller groups and grows again, before dividing once more. New members are drawn into the group through personal witness or evangelism, and are cared for within the group. The primary purpose of the cell is often described as being for edification and multiplication – that is, to build up believers, and to enable them to reach out into their communities and bring new converts within the church. The cells will gather together for corporate worship on Sundays – but the real pastoral work and outreach take place within the cells themselves.

Seeker-sensitive churches aim to remove the ecclesiastical trappings that often seem to place a barrier between the unchurched and the Christian faith. Willow Creek Community Church is the archetypal example of such a way of "being church." Anything that might alienate the unchurched is removed. Bill Hybels and other leaders of Willow Creek noted that many Americans were unchurched, and hence had no experience of clerical robes, hard pews, collection plates, and old-fashioned hymns. They did not know the language of the Christian tradition, and the Bible was a closed book to them. Why, its leaders wondered, did newcomers to the faith have to fight their way through a jungle of obsolete Christian cultural trappings to find out about Jesus? For an unchurched person, the first experience of a traditional church worship service was likely to be the last. Old-fashioned music, dusty old hymnals, uncomfortable pews, and a pompous liturgy were in stark contrast to the everyday life experienced by modern Americans. Why place such barriers in the way of people? They are not essential to the Christian faith. Why should people

be put off Christianity by the habits of a church culture of a bygone era, when there were so many ways of reaching out to them?

So the decision was taken: the Sunday services at Willow Creek would be "seeker-sensitive." They would take into account the alienating impact of traditional church architecture and practice. Where secular buildings – such as banks and colleges – once modeled themselves on Gothic churches, many churches are now modeling themselves on secular gathering places, with huge auditoriums and atriums. The Sunday services at Willow Creek avoid hymn books, prayer books, kneelers, clerical robes – in fact, just about anything that a seeker might find alienating. Just where, Willow Creek asked, does it say that you have to wear sixteenth-century clerical dress, sing only eighteenth-century hymns, and use nineteenth-century church architecture in order to be authentically Christian? Digital projectors provide everything that is needed, and the music is modeled on the best the secular market can offer. It's not *traditional western* Christianity – but it is certainly Christianity. And more and more churches are following this lead.

In this section, we have considered three trends that may well change the shape of global Christianity in the present century. Others could easily be added. The essential point to appreciate is that Christianity is not "frozen" in a permanent institutional form but is undergoing growth, adaptation, and development as it moves into new contexts and acclimatizes to the challenges of familiar – yet changing – situations.

So what, then, is the future of Christianity? There is little doubt as to where that future lies – in the developing world. The Christianity of 2050 is likely to be predominantly the faith of poor non-whites living south of Europe and the United States of America. It can be predicted to show substantial interest in reviving Christianity's root emphases on healing and prophecy, not least because its adherents will identify themselves with the poor and oppressed who first embraced the redemption, healing, and blessing that Jesus promised.

It remains to be seen how the western church will cope with this shift, and what it can learn from it. The forms of Christian lifestyle, worship, and theology favored by believers in the west seem to have diminishing attraction to Christians in the developing world. Christianity unquestionably has a future, and a bright one at that – but not in the regions and in the forms that those in the west have come to accept as normative.

9

The Life of Faith: Encountering Christianity as a Lived Reality

In earlier parts of this work, we explored Christianity from several aspects, focusing particularly on its teachings and history. Although this is valuable in helping students to gain a sense of what Christianity is all about, the approach to date has one major disadvantage. It may create the unhelpful and deeply misleading impression that Christianity is simply a set of ideas. While it is certainly true that Christianity is based on a set of core beliefs, it is essential to appreciate that these beliefs have a significant effect on the personal lives and values of individual Christians, on the way in which Christian communities behave and worship, and the cultures in which Christianity has secured a presence.

The final chapter of this book aims to explore Christian life in the modern world. It is intended particularly for those who, though not Christians, need at least a basic understanding of Christianity as a major force in modern global culture. Many people experience Christianity as a living presence in the world rather than as a set of ideas. This part of the work examines the nature of that presence, wherever possible explaining the beliefs underlying Christian customs, values, and activity in the modern world.

We shall consider the structure of the Christian year, focusing both on the religious significance of major Christian festivals and on the customs which have come to be attached to them. Anyone wishing to understand Christianity needs to know that, for Christians, Christmas is most emphatically not just about giving people presents, nor is Easter just about giving people eggs. Considerable care is taken to ensure that the Christian understanding of the significance of all major festivals is accurately described. We then move on to consider the way in which Christianity has impacted – and continues to impact – on culture, including its significance for music, art, and poetry. We begin, however, by considering the life of the church – the institution to which Christians belong. Although there are considerable differences between individual Christian denominations, most of the material which follows is applicable to all.

The Life of the Church

At the heart of the Christian life is a worshipping community. Those who are encountering Christianity from the outside are most likely to experience it through various forms of worship. That worship takes an incredible variety of styles – from the sumptuous, ornate, and elaborate worship of Russian Orthodoxy within a gilded cathedral to the informal, laid-back, and guitar-led worship of Latin American Pentecostalism, packed inside a makeshift church. It is therefore appropriate to engage with at least some aspects of Christian worship as it is encountered today.

The Christian services that are most likely to be experienced by those who are not themselves Christians are weddings, funerals, and the great Christmas "Service of Nine Lessons and Carols." For this reason, we shall begin with these, and offer a greater degree of explanation and comment than normal to allow these services to act as "gateways" to Christianity.

Christian weddings

The basic structure of a Christian wedding is very simple. It consists of the bride and groom consenting to marriage in the sight of human witnesses and of God, asking for God's blessing on their union. The basic structure of the service is shaped partly by theological considerations shared by all Christians, and partly by legal and cultural factors which are specific to a given locality. Christianity has long been adept at intermingling its own distinctive ideas with cultural norms. Alongside specifically Christian ideas, you will therefore find customs which originate from elsewhere – such as the placing of a ring (or rings) on the fourth

9.1 A Russian Orthodox wedding at the Church of the Transfiguration, St. Petersburg. © Robert Harding Picture Library Ltd./Alamy.

fingers, which has no specifically Christian significance and is widely held to represent an older tradition taken over by Christianity.

The Christian marriage service emphasizes that marriage is a voluntary commitment of two individuals, and that this is part of the creation ordinance of God. Often, a passage from the book of Genesis is read to make this point: "And the Lord God said, 'It is not good for the man to be alone' " (Genesis 2:18). Humanity was created for fellowship with other people, and also with God. Many Christian marriage liturgies make reference to Jesus Christ attending the wedding at Cana in Galilee, where he performed the miracle of turning water into wine (John 2). For an example of such a liturgy, we may turn to the Episcopal Church of Scotland's marriage service of 2002, which interweaves these ideas into the ceremony:

> We have come together in the presence of God, to witness the marriage of N. and N., to ask his blessing on them, and to share their joy. Our Lord Jesus Christ was himself a guest at a wedding in Cana of Galilee, and through his Spirit he is with us now.
> The Scriptures teach us that marriage is a gift of God in Creation and a means of his grace, a holy mystery in which man and woman become one flesh. It is God's purpose that, as husband and wife give themselves to each other in love throughout their lives, they shall be united in that love as Christ is united with his Church.

This brief excerpt from the marriage service makes reference to a deeper, spiritual significance of marriage. For Christians, the union of a man and woman in marriage symbolizes the spiritual union between a believer and Jesus Christ. Christian spiritual writers often speak of the "spiritual marriage" between Christ and the believer. Martin Luther, for example, speaks of faith as the "wedding ring" that unites Christ and the believer, pointing to both the personal relationship that exists between the two parties and their mutual exchange of goods. For Luther, Christ receives the sin and guilt of the believer, and gives the believer his righteousness and the gift of eternal life.

Christian funerals

The central theme of a Christian funeral service is the proclamation of the hope of resurrection, the celebration of the life of the deceased, and the entrustment of the person who has died to God's tender care. "Christians celebrate the funeral rites to offer worship, praise, and thanksgiving to God for the gift of life which has been returned to God, the author of life and the hope of the just" (Roman Catholic *Order of Christian Funerals*).

In the traditional English funeral service set out in the Book of Common Prayer (1662), the theme of resurrection is sustained throughout. The service opens with the priest meeting the funeral party at the churchyard gate, and speaking some words from John's gospel (John 15:25–26), in which the theme of the Christian hope is clearly set out:

> I am the resurrection and the life, saith the Lord: he that believeth in me, though he were dead, yet shall he live; and whosoever liveth and believeth in me shall never die.

The service then proceeds with the reading of 1 Corinthians 15, a chapter in which Paul stresses the importance of the resurrection, and the difference it makes to Christians. This reading includes the following words:

> Death is swallowed up in victory. O death, where is thy sting? O grave, where is thy victory? The sting of death is sin, and the strength of sin is the law. But thanks be to

God, which giveth us the victory through our Lord Jesus Christ. Therefore, my beloved brethren, be ye stedfast, unmoveable, always abounding in the work of the Lord, forasmuch as ye know that your labor is not in vain in the Lord.

Finally, as the corpse is lowered into the grave, the priest speaks these words. Again, note the theme of hope.

Forasmuch as it has pleased Almighty God of his great mercy to take unto himself the soul of our dear *brother* here departed, we therefore commit *his* body to the ground; earth to earth, ashes to ashes, dust to dust; in sure and certain hope of the resurrection to eternal life, through our Lord Jesus Christ.

The theme of the resurrection hope is often emphasized using appropriate symbols. For example, in the Roman Catholic rite, the coffin or casket is met at the entrance to the church and sprinkled with holy water as a reminder of the believer's baptism, which is seen as affirming that the believer has passed from death to life (Romans 6:1–4). Family members then place a pall over the casket, and may place Christian symbols – such as a cross or Bible – upon it as a sign of the Christian hope of resurrection.

Alongside these fundamental themes, a number of ancillary themes are often developed. For example, consider the following directions (or "liturgical norms"), laid down by the Roman Catholic archdiocese of Vancouver. Note the emphasis on the equality of believers, in death and in life.

The casket remains closed during the funeral rite and should be covered with a pall in remembrance of the baptismal garment – a sign of the Christian dignity of the person entering in Christ a new life beyond this life. The pall may be ornamented with Christian symbols. In addition to its liturgical significance, the pall serves very practical purposes: it avoids ostentation, prevents embarrassment of the poor, and emphasizes the Christian's equality before God.

The "pall" is a simple cloth that covers the coffin or casket. Here, it is interpreted as a reminder of baptism. The same custom is used outside the Catholic tradition. For example, the First United Methodist Church in Austin, Texas, offers a bereaved family the use of a pall at its funeral services, for the following reason:

First Church has a white funeral pall with a gold antique satin cross covering the full length and width, symbolic of God's power to cover sin with forgiveness, fear with hope, and death with life. This pall is available to you and is appropriate in place of casket flowers.

The Service of Nine Lessons and Carols

The Victorian period witnessed the institutionalization of Christmas as a national religious festival in England. The practice of having Christmas trees was introduced by Queen Victoria's consort, Albert, from his native Germany. Christmas cards were circulated using the newly established national postal service, making extensive use of a device invented by the novelist Anthony Trollope – the post box. The Victorian period witnessed an explosion in the writing of Christmas carols; some of the best-known carols date from this hugely influential and formative period in English history, including "In the Bleak Midwinter" and "Once in Royal David's City."

As Christmas became an increasingly important festival in the later nineteenth century, it became painfully clear that no adequate provision had been made by the English church for celebrating it publicly in church. The 1662 Book of Common Prayer offered no special arrangements for the Christmas season, other than specifying certain appropriate collects and readings. As the celebration of Christmas became more and more prominent in the national consciousness, the demand grew for a special church service for this time of year, incorporating both carols and biblical readings. One such service was devised for late on Christmas Eve, 1880, by Edward White Benson (1829–1896), then bishop of the diocese of Truro in southwestern England. The format was both simple and elegant. The service consisted of nine carols and nine lessons, to be read by various officials of the church in ascending order, beginning with a chorister and ending with the bishop himself. Benson went on to become archbishop of Canterbury; the service went on to be adopted, in a new format, by King's College, Cambridge.

The origins of the distinctive Cambridge format are to be traced to Christmas Eve 1918, the first Christmas celebration after the trauma and devastation of the Great War. (At this stage, there was no hint that another massive conflict lay only twenty years ahead; the term "World War I" was introduced later.) Eric Milner-White had just been appointed chaplain and dean of King's College, Cambridge, having served as an army chaplain during the war. He was acutely aware of the need to make worship more relevant and attractive to a hardened and skeptical post-war generation, and realized that the Christmas story could be used as a showcase for Christian worship. Exploiting the long-established choral tradition of King's College, Milner-White developed the format of the "Nine Lessons and Carols" which has become so influential and well known. Some modifications were introduced in December 1919; the format has remained more or less the same ever since.

The backbone of the service consists of nine Christmas carols, sung by the entire congregation, and nine biblical readings, taken from the King James Version. These are interspersed with choral items, reflecting the Christmas themes. While the service includes some prayers – such as the Collect for Christmas Eve – taken from the 1662 Book of Common Prayer, the Bidding Prayer is original and specific to this service. Yet even though the prayer dates from the early twentieth century, its language and imagery reflect those of the seventeenth, especially the King James Version itself.

In terms of the prayers and readings, the structure of the service is as follows:

The Bidding Prayer, read by the Dean
Lesson 1: Genesis 3:8–15; 17–19, read by a chorister
Lesson 2: Genesis 22:15–18, read by a choral scholar
Lesson 3: Isaiah 9:2, 6–7, read by a member of the college staff
Lesson 4: Isaiah 11:1–3a; 4a; 6–9, read by a representative of the City of Cambridge
Lesson 5: Luke 1:26–35; 38, read by the Director of Music
Lesson 6: Luke 2:1, 3–7, read by a representative of the Cambridge churches
Lesson 7: Luke 2:8–16, read by a fellow of the college
Lesson 8: Matthew 2:1–12, read by the Vice-Provost
Lesson 9: John 1:1–14, read by the Provost
The Collect for Christmas Eve
The Blessing

The lessons follow the same principle established by Benson some forty years earlier, in which the most junior representative of the institution reads the first lesson, and the most senior gives the final reading. (The "Provost" is the head of house of King's College; other Oxford and Cambridge colleges use terms such as "President," "Master," "Warden," or "Principal" to refer to their heads.)

The opening Bidding Prayer sets the scene for the public reading of the Christmas tale; the closing Collect summarizes the significance of the great themes which have been reaffirmed in reading and praise throughout the service. The opening prayer makes clear what Christmas is all about, from a Christian perspective.

> Beloved in Christ, be it this Christmas Eve our care and delight to prepare ourselves to hear again the message of the angels: in heart and mind to go even unto Bethlehem and see this thing which is come to pass, and with the shepherds and the wise men adore the Child lying in his Mother's arms. Let us read and mark in Holy Scripture the tale of the loving purposes of God from the first days of our disobedience unto the glorious Redemption brought us by this Holy Child; and in company with the whole Church let us make this chapel, dedicated to his pure and lowly Mother, glad with our carols of praise.

The fundamental theme of the service is simple: Christ is the long-promised savior of the world, God incarnate, who has entered into our world as one of us in order to redeem it.

Christian worship

There are clear indications of an emerging style of worship within the New Testament. The Acts of the Apostles records that the first Christians met regularly, and "devoted themselves to the apostles' teaching and to the fellowship, to the breaking of bread and to prayer" (Acts 2:42). In addition to the "breaking of bread," the New Testament also highlights the significance of baptism as a sign of personal commitment to Jesus Christ, and of entrance into the Christian community. The importance of singing and thanksgiving can be seen from a number of passages: "Speak to one another with psalms, hymns, and spiritual songs. Sing and make music in your heart to the Lord, always giving thanks to God the Father for everything, in the name of our Lord Jesus Christ" (Ephesians 5:19–20). The styles of Christian worship

which are encountered in Christian churches today can all be traced back, in different ways, to the New Testament.

The New Testament tends to use the word "church (Greek: *ekklesia*)" to refer to a gathering of people rather than a building. Indeed, the threat of persecution was such that the early church tended to meet in secret, "borrowing" buildings which were normally used for other purposes in order to avoid drawing attention to its activities. The strong element of secrecy associated with early Christian worship led to all kinds of rumors concerning what Christians did during their worship. The accusation of cannibalism, widespread in the late first century, appears to reflect a misunderstanding of the idea of eating the body and drinking the blood of Jesus Christ; that of orgies seems to rest on the early Christian love-feast, or *agape*, which was fundamentally a celebration of the love of Jesus Christ for his people, and the mutual love of Christians.

Christian worship is particularly associated with one day of the week – Sunday. It is clear that Christians regarded the first day of the week as being of especial importance, as it was the day on which Jesus rose again from the dead. Whereas Jewish worship was particularly associated with the seventh day of the week (the Sabbath, or Saturday), the first Christians did not retain this traditional Jewish custom. Sunday was seen as the first day of God's new creation, and therefore was the day appropriate for all major public Christian worship. Justin Martyr, writing ca. 165, is an important witness to this tradition:

> On the day which is called Sunday, all who live in the cities or in the countryside gather together in one place. And the memoirs of the apostles or the writings of the prophets are read, so long as there is time. Then, when the reader has finished, the president delivers a discourse in which he invites the people to

follow the examples of virtue which these provide. Then we all stand up together and offer some prayers. And when we have finished these prayers, bread and wine mixed with water are presented. The president then offers prayers and a thanksgiving, according to his ability, and the people indicate their assent by saying "Amen." The elements for which thanks have been given are then distributed and received by all present, and are taken to those who are not present by the deacons.

It is impossible to understate the place of worship in sustaining the Christian life. Especially within the Greek Orthodox tradition, the public worship of the church represents a drawing close to the threshold of heaven itself, and peering through its portals to catch a glimpse of the worship of heavenly places. The Orthodox liturgy celebrates the notion of being caught up in the worship of heaven, and the awesome sense of mystery that is evoked by the sense of peering beyond the bounds of human vision.

A biblical text which has played no small part in shaping this immense respect for mystery in worship may be noted here. The sixth chapter of the prophecy of Isaiah relates the call of the prophet, portraying him as undergoing a liminal experience as he enters the "holy of holies":

In the year that King Uzziah died, I saw the Lord sitting on a throne, high and lofty; and the hem of his robe filled the temple. Seraphs were in attendance above him; each had six wings: with two they covered their faces, and with two they covered their feet, and with two they flew. And one called to another and said: "Holy, holy, holy is the Lord of hosts; the whole earth is full of his glory." The pivots on the thresholds shook at the voices of those who called, and the house filled with smoke. And I said: "Woe is me! I am lost, for I am a man of unclean lips, and I live among a people of unclean lips; yet my eyes have seen the King, the Lord of hosts!" (Isaiah 6:1–5)

The central insight which many theologians gleaned from this passage is that human beings are simply not capable of beholding the worship of heaven itself; it must be accommodated to their capacity through being reflected through created things – such as the created order, the sacramental bread and wine, or the liturgy itself.

To share in worship is thus to stand in a holy place (Exodus 3:5) – a place in which humanity, strictly speaking, has no right to be. Whenever the divine liturgy is celebrated on earth, the boundaries between heaven and earth are removed, and earthly worshippers join in the eternal heavenly liturgy chanted by the angels. During these moments of earthly adoration, worshippers have the opportunity of being mystically transported to the threshold of heaven. Being in a holy place and about to participate in holy things, they on the one hand become aware of their finitude and sinfulness, and on the other gain a refreshing glimpse of the glory of God – precisely the pattern of reflection set out in Isaiah's vision.

The association between worship and heaven is often enhanced musically. Just as Gothic churches embodied a sense of the spaciousness of heaven, allowing and encouraging worshippers to visualize the worship of heaven, so the judicious use of music has widely been held to bring about a corresponding effect. It is difficult to make this point purely verbally, without listening to the music itself. However, to listen to the *Vespers* (1915) of Sergei Rachmaninoff (1873–1943), or the motets "Assumpta est Maria" and "Missa Assumpta est Maria" of Giovanni Pierluigi da Palestrina (ca. 1525–1594), is to gain something of an appreciation of how the vision of heaven can be mediated musically in worship.

The idea of liminality – that is, being on the threshold of the sacred, peering into the forbidden heavenly realms – is represented visually in the structure of Orthodox churches, especially the way in which the sanctuary and the altar are set apart from the people on account of a deep sense of the awesomeness of the mystery of God. In their treatises on worship, Chrysostom and other Greek patristic writers repeatedly draw attention to the liturgical importance of this sense of the sacred. The altar is the "terrifying table"; the bread and the wine are "the terrifying sacrifice of the body and blood of Christ which worshippers must approach with fear and trembling." For the Orthodox, there is an especially close link between the eucharist – the sacrament celebrated with and through bread and wine – and the experience of the worship of heaven.

All generalizations are dangerous, and must be treated with a degree of caution. However, they are also useful to those who are trying to gain an understanding of an exceptionally complicated matter. What follows is a listing of the various elements which will be encountered in Christian worship. The types of Christian worship vary considerably, and not all of the elements to be discussed below will be found in all types of worship. However, they are useful as a starting point for exploring modern worship. The reader who is approaching Christianity from outside must be warned that it is of very limited value to simply read about Christian worship; worship is something which demands to be experienced. You are strongly recommended to supplement your reading with involvement in the worshipping life of a local Christian church, in order to gain an appreciation of its structures, rhythms, and appeal.

Prayer

Prayer is an integral element of all forms of Christian worship. It could be defined as "a covenant relationship between God and humanity in Christ...In the New Covenant, prayer is the living relationship of the children of God with their Father who is good beyond measure, with his Son, Jesus Christ, and with the Holy Spirit" (*Catechism of the Catholic Church*). Prayer takes a variety of forms. A distinction is made between the *private* prayers of individuals and the *public* prayer of the church. Prayer can also take the form of *thanksgiving*, in which thanks are offered to God for blessings which have been received, whether by individuals or by the church as a whole. Perhaps the most important is *petitionary* prayer, in which the congregation, or individuals within that congregation, make specific requests of God. This type of prayer can be illustrated from the teaching of Jesus, who compared this type of prayer to human requests.

Praise

The Christian Bible regularly exhorts believers to praise God. This has become incorporated into Christian worship from the earliest of times. In contemporary Christianity, it is especially associated with hymns and worship songs. These are set to various forms of music, often with the cultural preferences of congregations in mind.

Many classic hymns date from the eighteenth century, from writers such as Isaac Watts ("When I survey the wondrous cross") and John and Charles Wesley. Given the importance of hymns to Christian life and thought, we shall consider one hymn writer in detail – John Newton (1725–1807), author of one of the church's most famous hymns, "Amazing Grace."

John Newton was the main author of the *Olney Hymns*, a remarkable collection of songs of praise, many of which are still widely used today. He was converted after spending some time in the slave trade. Although there is ample evidence that Newton disliked the slave trade, and had considerable sympathy for those whom he transported to the Americas, he still went on to become the captain of his own slave ship. In 1748, at the age of 23, he underwent a religious conversion, which led him to fully realize the inhumanity of his actions. He left his life as a slave ship captain and settled down as a "surveyor of tides" at the port of Liverpool. He was ordained as a priest for the Church of England in 1764, and served in the village of Olney. That same year he published his "Authentic Narrative," which detailed his exploits commanding a slave vessel.

In 1779, he published the collection of hymns for which he is best known. In his preface to this work, Newton explained his objectives in writing these hymns – to "promote the faith and comfort of sincere Christians." The most famous of these hymns celebrates the theme of amazing grace.

Amazing grace! How sweet the sound
That saved a wretch like me!
I once was lost, but now am found;
Was blind, but now I see.

'Twas grace that taught my heart to fear,
And grace my fears relieved;
How precious did that grace appear
The hour I first believed.

Through many dangers, toils, and snares,
I have already come;
'Tis grace hath brought me safe thus far,
And grace will lead me home.

The Lord has promised good to me,
His Word my hope secures;
He will my Shield and Portion be,
As long as life endures.

When we've been there ten thousand years,
Bright shining as the sun,
We've no less days to sing God's praise
Than when we'd first begun.

It is impossible to read this hymn without connecting it with Newton's own life-experience.

There is no doubt that he hated both the slave trade and those who promoted it – including himself. How could God love such a degraded and vile person? Why would God want anything to do with him? In the hymn, Newton tries to express the great paradox of grace – that God loves sinners, even before they have repented of their sins. The hymn reflects Newton's own amazement that he could know and serve God, and write songs of praise dedicated to him.

A similar theme is explored in his hymn "Praise for the Fountain Opened," based on Zechariah 13:1. In this hymn, Newton again explores the way in which the death of Christ is sufficient to pardon, purge, and purify even a sinner such as himself.

There is a fountain filled with blood
Drawn from Emmanuel's veins;
And sinners, plunged beneath that flood,
Lose all their guilty stains.

The dying thief rejoiced to see
That fountain in his day;
And there have I, as vile as he,
Washed all my sins away.

Hymns are thus primarily acts of praise – declaring God's goodness, faithfulness, and love, or extolling his glory. Yet, as will be clear from the theologically rich imagery of Newton's hymns, they have a secondary role – educating people in the basics of Christian belief.

Reading Scripture

The public reading of the Bible is an integral element of Christian worship. Many churches use a structured program of Bible readings (often referred to as a "lectionary"), which aims to ensure that the Bible is read in its totality throughout the course of the regular worship of the church. Others allow individual ministers to determine what biblical passages shall be read at any given time. The principle, however, remains the same. Part of Christian worship is the hearing and responding to the word of God. Sometimes that response may take the form of believing certain doctrines; at others, it may involve the recognition of the need to behave in certain ways, to do certain things.

In the early church, priority was given to the reading of a passage from the gospels. This was seen as a public declaration of the words and deeds of Jesus Christ. Many churches adopted the practice of standing in order to hear the gospel reading, as a way of demonstrating that the good news of Jesus Christ was central to the life and worship of the church and its individual members. This practice gradually developed into that of having two or three readings, typically arranged sequentially as a reading from the Old Testament; a reading from one of the New Testament letters; a reading from one of the gospels. In many churches, the public reading of Scripture is followed by the explanation or application of the passage of Scripture through a sermon. We shall explore this in what follows.

Preaching

Many Christian services include a sermon. The word "sermon" derives from the Latin term *sermo*, literally meaning "a word." A sermon is fundamentally a statement or application of the Christian faith, and often takes the form of the exegesis (literally, "the drawing out") of a biblical passage (for example, the passage chosen or set for the day), a biblical theme, or an article of the creed. Collections of excellent or reliable sermons were in circulation within Christianity by an early stage. The Latin term *homilarium* is used to refer to books of sermons, such as those assembled by Paul the Deacon (ca. 790) or Alan of Farfa (d. 770). Styles of sermon vary considerably, with some preachers seeing the sermon as primarily catechetical (that is, aimed at

teaching the congregation more about their faith), and others as exhortatory (that is, aimed at encouraging their audience to lead better lives as Christians, or to take to heart some basic Christian teaching or principle).

Although preaching is a regular part of the worship of many Christian traditions, it was given an especially vital role at the time of the Reformation. The new emphasis on the importance of the Bible, and particularly the Reformation emphasis on the "priesthood of all believers," made the creation of a biblically literate laity of considerable significance. The especial emphasis placed by writers such as John Calvin on the crucial nature of Bible-based preaching reflects these concerns.

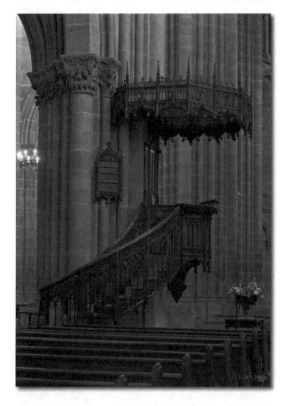

9.2 The pulpit in St. Peter's Cathedral, Geneva. J.-P. Scherrer/Geneva 2005.

The reciting of the creeds

Many more formal Christian services of worship involve reciting one of the creeds – usually the Apostles' Creed or the Nicene Creed. These creeds are intended to remind believers of the basic themes of their faith, and enable them to avoid false teachings as a result. The recitation of the creeds also establishes a strong sense of "belonging," in that it affirms the basic continuity between the Christian communities of today and those of the classic period.

The creeds are statements of faith which are common to all Christians, whether Protestant, Orthodox, or Catholic. They are regarded as possessing a universal significance for all Christians, which transcends the particular importance of individual statements of faith of certain historic churches. Thus, for example, Anglicans might regard the Thirty-Nine Articles as having considerable importance in defining their specifically Anglican beliefs, just as Presbyterians might feel similarly about the Westminster Confession. But these two documents would never be incorporated into the public worship of these churches, in that they are seen to lack the *universal* authority of the creeds.

The sacraments

In general terms, a sacrament may be thought of as an external rite or sign, which in some way conveys or represents the grace of God to believers. A minimalist definition of a sacrament might take the form of "an external physical sign of an interior spiritual grace." The New Testament does not actually make use of the specific term "sacrament." Instead, we find the Greek word *mysterion* (which is probably best translated as "mystery") used to refer to the saving work of God in general. This Greek word is never used to refer to what would now be regarded as a sacrament (for

example, baptism). However, it is clear from what we know of the history of the early church that a connection was made at an early stage between the "mystery" of God's saving work in Christ and the "sacraments" of baptism and the eucharist. We shall explore each presently.

As we saw earlier, most Christians, irrespective of their backgrounds, regard the sacraments as important signs of God's grace and presence. For Luther, sacraments were like promises with signs attached, intended to reassure us of the reality and trustworthiness of those promises. The bread and wine of the eucharist, and the water of baptism, are visible and tangible signs of the spiritual reality which lies behind them. The bread and wine point to the richness of life which the gospel offers, and the water to the cleansing which it brings.

This aspect of the role of sacraments in spirituality is brought out clearly in the famous hymn "Adoro te devote," traditionally ascribed to Thomas Aquinas (ca. 1225–1274). We shall cite three verses from this work, and note the general line of its argument.

Godhead here in hiding, whom I do adore
Masked by these bare shadows, shape
      and nothing more;
See, Lord, at thy service low lies here a heart
Lost, all lost in wonder at the God thou art.

O thou our reminder of Christ crucified.
Living bread the life of us for whom he died,
Lend this life to me then: feed and feast my mind,
There be thou the sweetness man was
      meant to find.

Jesus whom I look at shrouded here below,
I beseech thee send me, what I thirst for so;
Some day to gaze on thee, face to face in light
And be blessed forever, with thy glory's sight.

The initial idea is that the sacrament offers a means of discerning the presence of God, even though that presence takes the form of "bare shadows" rather than reality. Yet even though the sacrament is only a sign of the greater reality to which it points, it nevertheless possesses the ability to focus the worshipper's thoughts on God. More specifically, the sacrament reminds us of the saving death of Christ, and the benefits which this brings to humanity. It also serves to uplift the mind to think of its future contemplation of the face of God in heaven. The sacrament thus serves as an important *visible and tangible* reminder of the Christian hope, as well as a reminder of the pain and suffering of the cross.

Baptism

The word "baptism" comes from the Greek word *baptizein*, meaning "to wash" or "to cleanse." In the New Testament, the term refers initially to the baptism offered by John the Baptist in the River Jordan as a sign of repentance. Jesus himself was baptized by John. For Christians, the necessity of baptism is partly grounded in the command of the risen Christ to the disciples to baptize people everywhere in the name of the Father, Son, and Holy Spirit (Matthew 28:17–20). In the New Testament, baptism is clearly understood as both a

9.3 Christian baptism by total immersion in the Indian Ocean off the island of Zanzibar. © World Religions Photo Library/Alamy.

condition for and a sign of membership of the Christian community.

The Acts of the Apostles records Peter ending an early sermon with the following words, addressed to those who wanted to know what to do if they were to be saved: "Repent and be baptized, every one of you, in the name of Jesus Christ for the forgiveness of your sins. And you will receive the gift of the Holy Spirit" (Acts 2:38). In the writings of Paul, baptism is affirmed as a practice, and interpreted theologically, both in terms of dying and rising with Christ (Romans 6:1–4) and in terms of "being clothed with Christ." "You are all sons of God through faith in Christ Jesus, for all of you who were baptized into Christ have clothed yourselves with Christ" (Galatians 3:26–27).

Although the New Testament seems to indicate that baptism was administered to adults, it was not long before young children were being baptized as well. The origins of this practice are not clear. The New Testament refers to both individuals and entire households being baptized; it is possible that the baptism of households extended to include infants (Acts 16:15, 33; 1 Corinthians 1:16). Paul treats baptism as a spiritual counterpart to circumcision (Colossians 2:11–12), suggesting that the parallel may extend to its application to infants. The early church saw a clear link between baptism under the New Covenant and circumcision under the Old Covenant. There are hints of this idea in the New Testament itself. The early church argued that, just as circumcision was a covenantal sign, demonstrating that someone belonged to the people of Israel, so baptism was a sign of belonging to the covenant community of the church. Since Israel circumcised infant boys, why should not the church baptize infants? More generally, there seems to have been a pastoral need for Christian parents to celebrate the birth of a child within a believing household. Infant baptism may well have had its origins partly in response to this concern. However, it must be stressed that there is genuine uncertainty concerning both the historical origins and the social or theological causes of the practice.

It is clear, however, that the practice of infant baptism was widespread by the end of the second century. In the second century, Origen treats infant baptism as a universal practice, which he justifies on the basis of a universal human need for the grace of Christ. A similar argument would later be deployed by Augustine: in that Christ is the savior of all, it follows that all – including infants – require redemption which baptism confers, at least in part. Opposition to the practice can be seen in the writings of Tertullian, who argued that the baptism of children should be deferred until such time as they "know Christ."

The practice of infant baptism – in, for example, the Catholic church – leads to the process of Christian initiation having at least two phases. First, the person is baptized as an infant. The infant has no faith, but relies upon the faith of the church and the commitment of the parents to bring him or her up within a Christian environment, and teach and embody the Christian faith in the home. The second phase is confirmation, when the child is able to affirm the Christian faith in his or her own right. Within the Catholic tradition, baptism is carried out by a local priest, whereas confirmation is carried out by the bishop, as a representative of the whole church. However, the Orthodox church has always insisted on the continuity between baptism and confirmation (known as "chrismation," on account of the use of oil to anoint the person being confirmed in this way), and thus aims to allow the same priest to baptize and confirm a given person.

The eucharist

The origins of the Christian practice of using bread and wine in public worship go directly back to Jesus. It is clear from the New Testament witness that Jesus expected his church to continue to use bread and wine in remembrance of him. There are strong associations with the Jewish Passover meal, not least its commemoration of an act of divine deliverance. According to John's gospel, John the Baptist declared that Jesus Christ is "the lamb of God, who takes away the sin of the world" (John 1:29). The image of the "Lamb of God" immediately calls to mind the great Passover celebrations of Israel, which recalled God's faithfulness in delivering his people from captivity in Egypt (Exodus 12). A Passover lamb would be slain, as a reminder of God's continuing care for his people and commitment to them in conditions of adversity and suffering. To think of Jesus as this lamb of God is to see him as linked with God's great actions of deliverance, including the liberation of his people from their bondage to sin and the fear of death.

It is clear that Christians obeyed this explicit command of Jesus from the earliest of times. The Acts of the Apostles reports that the disciples were "breaking bread" within weeks of the death and resurrection of Jesus. Paul's first letter to the Corinthians plainly refers to the practice in the most solemn of terms, making it clear that Paul is passing on something of the utmost importance to his readers. Justin Martyr, writing about 165, indicates that the normal practice had been established as reading and expounding the Bible, followed by giving thanks and distributing the bread and the wine (see above, p. 161). Note that the wine in question was always mixed with water. The

9.4   The Last Supper, according to Jacopo da Ponte Bassano (ca. 1510–1592), celebrated and commemorated in the eucharist. Rome, Galleria Borghese, AKG-Images/Cameraphoto.

reason for this practice is unclear; it may have been a practical measure designed to avoid dehydration on the part of those receiving the wine. Theological explanations of the practice soon developed, including the idea that the mingling of the wine and water symbolized the mingling of Jesus Christ and his people.

This fundamental pattern, in a wide variety of forms, has passed into modern Christian practice. One major difference between Christians should, however, be noted at this point.

Eucharist, Mass, or Supper: What's in a Name?

Christians have proved unable to agree on the best way to refer to the sacrament which focuses on the bread and wine. The main terms used to refer to it are the following. Note the specific associations of each word with particular Christian traditions.

EUCHARIST

This term derives from the Greek verb *eucharistein*, and means "a thanksgiving." The theme of thanksgiving is an important element of the breaking of the bread, making this an entirely appropriate term for the service in question. The term "eucharist" is particularly associated with the Greek Orthodox tradition, but has found acceptance beyond this.

THE MASS

This term derives from the Latin word *missa*, which really just means "a service of some sort." As the main service of the western church in the classic period was the breaking of the bread, the term came to refer to this one service in particular. The term "mass" is now especially associated with the Catholic tradition.

HOLY COMMUNION

The phrase "holy communion" points to the idea of "fellowship" or "sharing." It highlights the bond of fellowship both between Jesus and the church, and between individual Christians. The term is used in more Protestant circles, particularly in churches tracing their origins back to the English Reformation.

LORD'S SUPPER

This phrase picks up the theme of the breaking of the bread as a memorial of the last supper. To share in the "Lord's Supper" is to recall with thanks all that Jesus achieved for believers through his death on the cross. The term is used in more Protestant circles, particularly in churches tracing their origins back to the English Reformation. This is sometimes abbreviated to the simple term "supper."

As a general rule, Catholics have taught that only priests are permitted to receive *both* the bread and the wine at communion; Protestant churches permit both priests and laity to receive both bread and wine. The origins of the Catholic practice of denying the wine to the laity remain uncertain; it may represent the outcome of a practical desire to avoid spillage. Although the Second Vatican Council clearly wished to encourage the laity to receive the wine as well as the bread, this remains the exception rather than the rule. In the Orthdox church, both priests and laity are permitted to receive both bread and wine, although the general practice is for the communion to be received from a spoon, which contains the bread to which a few drops of wine have been added. The more general western custom is the direct handing of the bread to the communicant.

The Rhythms and Seasons of the Christian Life

From the earliest of times, Christians developed ways of structuring time which reflected fundamental Christian beliefs and the historical events on which they were grounded. This structuring of time appears to have arisen for a number of reasons. The fact that Christianity was grounded on historical events immediately established the basics of a structuring of the year. Good Friday and Easter Day, for example, were located at quite specific positions in the annual calendar. Pentecost and Ascension were easily added to this annual structure. The structure of the Christian year thus reflected some landmark events, of fundamental importance to Christianity.

The structuring of the year also had an important educational role. It allowed the church to focus its attention on certain themes at certain times of the year. Although the great themes of the Christian faith were taught and preached at all times, the structure of the Christian year allowed certain ideas or themes to be emphasized at appropriate points. Thus Pentecost marked an obvious time to celebrate the person and work of the Holy Spirit. Good Friday was a particularly appropriate time to reflect on the meaning of Christ's death. Easter Day allowed the theme of the resurrection to be developed and applied to Christian living.

Yet a third reason must also be noted. The New Testament speaks about "redeeming the time" (Ephesians 5:16). Time does not simply mark the location of Christian existence; it offers Christians an arena within which they may grow and develop. To structure time is thus seen as a means of encouraging spiritual growth, allowing the passing of time to reinforce some basic Christian ideas and deepen their impact on the Christian mind, imagination, and heart. The structuring of the Christian day, week, or year is thus a means of enhancing its potential to remind, recall, and represent some fundamental themes of faith.

One of the most obvious developments in the Christian structuring of time was the setting aside of Sunday – the first day of the week – as the day on which the resurrection of Christ would be celebrated. The letters of Paul clearly presuppose that Christians were meeting for worship on Sunday, breaking with the Jewish tradition of observing the sabbath (Saturday) as a day of rest. In 321, following his conversion to Christianity, the Roman emperor Constantine formally declared that Sunday would be the official imperial day of rest.

Sunday was thus seen by Christian writers as a "space" which was set aside, in God's goodness, to allow for physical rest and spiritual refreshment. One of the writers who stresses this point is Susanna Wesley (1669–1742), the mother of John and Charles Wesley, who was persuaded of the importance of creating space for God in the midst of a busy life. For Susanna, Sunday was a space which had been created by God for exactly this purpose, and was meant to be used joyfully and profitably.

It is also known that early Christian communities set aside Wednesdays and Fridays as fast-days. The reason for the selection of these particular days is not clear; a later explanation suggested that Wednesday was thus observed because it was the day on which Christ was betrayed, and Friday the day on which he was crucified. The practice of eating fish (rather than meat) on Friday, still widely encountered in Catholic circles, reflects this early development.

Perhaps the most important manner of structuring time concerns the Christian year, to which we now turn.

The Christian year

As we have emphasized, Christianity is not just a set of ideas; it is a way of life. Part of that life is a richly structured yearly pattern of living, in which various aspects of the Christian faith are singled out for particular attention during the course of a year. The two such festivals which are most familiar outside Christian circles are Christmas and Easter, celebrating the birth and resurrection of Jesus respectively. This section will focus on the major festivals of the Christian year, explaining their religious basis and noting some of the customs which have come to be attached to them in parts of the Christian world.

It should be noted that there are major variations within the Christian world over the festivals of the Christian faith. In general terms, evangelical and charismatic Christians tend to place a relatively low value on such festivals, whereas Catholic and Orthodox Christians tend to place a considerably greater emphasis upon them. Indeed, the importance attached by Christians to festivals such as Advent and Lent is generally a useful indication of the type of Christianity which they have adopted.

Festivals tend to fall into a number of different categories. A major distinction is drawn between *fixed* and *movable* feasts. A "fixed feast" refers to a festival which takes place on the same date each year. Thus in the western church, Christmas Day is invariably celebrated on December 25. Other feasts are determined with reference to events whose dates vary from year to year. For example, the date of Easter is determined in relation to the full moon, and could fall at any point between March 21 and April 25. A series of other festivals is dependent on the date of Easter, as follows:

- Ash Wednesday, which falls forty weekdays before Easter Day.
- Maundy Thursday, which is the Thursday before Easter Day.
- Good Friday, which is the Friday before Easter Day.
- Ascension Day, which is the fortieth day after Easter Day (and thus always falls on a Thursday).
- Pentecost, which is the fiftieth day after Easter Day (and thus always falls on a Sunday).
- Trinity Sunday, which is the Sunday following Pentecost.

Other festivals focus on individual saints, some of which have particular regional or professional associations. Examples of these associations include:

- St. David, patron saint of Wales, whose feast is observed on March 1.
- St. Patrick, patron saint of Ireland, whose feast is observed on March 17.
- St. Cecilia, patron saint of church music, whose feast is observed on November 22.

St. Christopher, patron saint of travelers, whose feast is celebrated in some parts of the church on July 25.

In each case, the association of saints with a particular profession is usually linked with events in their lives. Other saints have developed associations that have no apparent connection with their original figure. For example, St. Valentine is thought to have been a Roman Christian who was martyred at Rome in the third century. His feast day, which is celebrated on February 14, now has strong associations with personal romance in some western societies.

In addition to festivals, two periods are often observed as times of fasting or penitence – Advent and Lent. While many Christians no longer observe the tradition of fasting once associated with these periods, particularly during the Middle Ages, some continue to regard these as being of importance as times of personal reflection or penitence.

It should be noted here that the Orthodox church follows a liturgical year which is broadly divided into three parts, focusing on Easter. These three parts are the *triodion*, the *pentecostarion*, and the *octoechos*. We shall explore each of these briefly. The "triodion" refers to the ten weeks prior to Easter, which can be seen as a preparation for this great festival. The "pentecostarion" refers to the entire Easter period, which is understood to embrace the period between Easter and the Sunday after Pentecost (in the western church, this final date is often celebrated as "Trinity Sunday"). The "octoechos" refers to the remainder of the year.

In what follows, we shall explore the highlights of the western Christian year, which have a major impact on the way in which many Christian churches worship and pray, and which often percolate into society as a whole. In each case, the foundation of the festival or season will be noted, and some of the customs which have come to be associated with it will be outlined. The order in which the festivals will be discussed is chronological rather than alphabetical. The western Christian year opens with the time of advent, to which we now turn.

Advent

The term "Advent" derives from the Latin word *adventus*, meaning "coming" or "arrival." It refers to the period immediately before Christmas, during which Christians recall the background to the coming of Jesus. Traditionally, four Sundays are set apart in order to prepare for the full appreciation of Christmas, of which the first is referred to as "Advent Sunday," and the final as the "Fourth Sunday in Advent." This period of four Sundays is often observed by the making of "advent crowns," consisting of four candles in a wooden or metal frame. A candle is then lit for each of the four Sundays in Advent. Some churches use purple clerical clothing at this time as a symbol of the need for penitence (a custom which also applies to Lent, which also has a penitential character).

Strictly speaking, Advent is intended to focus on the relationship of two "advents" or "comings" of Jesus: his first coming in humility, during his time on earth (which is especially associated with Christmas); and his second coming in glory as judge, which will take place at the end of time.

Christmas

Christmas is a fixed or immovable feast, and is always celebrated on December 25. It must be stressed that this has never been understood to mean that Christians believe that Jesus was born on this date; rather, this date was chosen for the celebration of the birth of Jesus, irrespective of the precise date of that birth. It is likely that the date was chosen at Rome during the fourth century to provide a Christian alternative to a local pagan festival. The date of the festival is actually something of an irrelevance, despite the association with the imagery of winter and snow found in many Christian writings originating in the northern hemisphere.

The central theme of Christmas is the birth of Jesus, which is often commemorated in special carol services. Of these, the most famous is widely regarded as the "Service of Nine Lessons and Carols" associated with King's College, Cambridge. The nine lessons (that is, readings from the Bible) are designed to trace the steady progress of God's work of redemption in the world, beginning with the call of Israel, and culminating in the coming of Jesus Christ. This pattern of service is now used throughout the Christian world, and is familiar to many non-Christians. We considered it in some detail earlier in this chapter.

Many customs have come to be associated with Christmas, the more famous of which have their origins in the nineteenth century. "Santa Claus" is an American corruption of the Dutch form of "Saint Nicolas," the patron saint of children. This saint was celebrated on December 6 by the giving of gifts to children. Dutch settlers in New Amsterdam (later renamed "New York") brought this custom to the New World, where it became firmly established, and was merged into the festival of Christmas itself. The practice of bringing a Christmas tree into houses and decorating it had its origins in Germany, and was brought to England in the 1840s by Queen Victoria's husband, Prince Albert. The origins of this custom in Germany go back to the dawn of its Christian history, when missionaries were confronted with pagan beliefs concerning tree-gods.

Epiphany

The unusual name of this festival derives from the Greek word *epiphaneia*, which literally means "manifestation" or "making known." The festival takes place on January 6. In the eastern church, the festival is specifically linked to the baptism of Jesus. In the western church, however, it is linked with the visit of the "wise men" or "Magi" to the infant Jesus. The festival is understood to mark the beginning of the long process by which the identity and significance of Jesus was "made known" to the world. The visit of the Magi (described in Matthew 2:1–11) is here seen as an anticipation of the recognition and worship which would subsequently be associated with the ministry of Jesus in Galilee and Judaea, which culminated in the resurrection.

Lent

The period of Lent begins with Ash Wednesday, which falls in the seventh week before Easter. The term "Ash Wednesday" needs explanation. The Old Testament occasionally refers to putting ashes on one's face or clothing as a symbol of repentance or remorse (e.g., Esther 4:1; Jeremiah 6:26). Lent is seen as a period of repentance; the wearing of ashes was therefore seen as a proper external sign of an inward attitude of remorse or repentance. In earlier periods in the history of the church, particularly during the Middle Ages, the first day of Lent was therefore marked by imposing ashes on the heads of the clergy and people. In more recent years, the ashes in question are made by burning the palm crosses handed out on Palm Sunday during the previous Lent. The theme of repentance is also symbolized in some churches by the wearing of purple clerical dress during this season.

Lent is widely regarded as a time of preparation for Easter, and in the past was commonly associated with a period of fasting. Lent is based on the period of forty days spent by Jesus in the wilderness before the beginning of his public ministry in Galilee (see p. 16). Just as Jesus fasted for forty days, so his followers were encouraged to do the same thing. A period of forty days of fasting before Easter was thus encouraged. The origins of this seem to go back to the fourth century. In earlier times, a shorter period of fasting was recommended (two or three days). The precise nature of the "fasting" varied from one location and period to another. In general terms, the western church has understood "fasting" primarily in terms of a reduced intake of food, and eating fish rather than meat. The emphasis has generally been placed on devotional reading or attendance at church rather than fasting.

An issue which needs to be noted at this point concerns the length of Lent. The period intervening between Ash Wednesday and Easter Day is actually forty-six days. So how does this relate to the forty days of fasting? The answer lies in the tradition, established at a very early stage in the development of Christianity, that every Sunday was to be regarded as a celebration of the resurrection of Christ. For this reason, fasting was forbidden on Sundays. The period of forty-six days thus consists of forty days of fasting, plus the six Sundays which fall between Ash Wednesday and Easter Day.

One of the most interesting customs linked with Lent concerns the day before Lent begins. As noted above, Lent begins on a Wednesday. The day before this therefore signified the last day before this official period of fasting began. In England, this day was called "Shrove Tuesday," although it is more widely known as "Pancake Day." The origins of this name lie in the practice of clearing out larders immediately before Lent. The simplest way of using up the accumulation of eggs, flour, milk, and other ingredients was to make pancakes. The same day is referred to as "Mardi Gras" in some European countries and their former colonies, and is marked by major carnivals, such as that now associated with Rio de Janeiro in Brazil.

The final week of Lent, leading up to Easter Day itself, should be singled out for special mention. This period, which is generally known as "Holy Week," begins with Palm Sunday (the Sunday before Easter) and ends on the day before Easter Day. It is a time often set aside for reflection on the suffering and death of Christ – a period sometimes referred to as "Passiontide." One of the devotional aids that has become of considerable importance in Roman Catholicism is the "Stations of the Cross." This involves fourteen representations of different aspects of Christ's last day on earth – Good Friday, which we shall consider in a moment. The fourteen "stations" are as follows:

1 Christ's condemnation by Pontius Pilate.
2 Christ receives the cross.
3 Christ's first fall under the weight of the cross.
4 Christ's meeting with his mother, Mary.
5 The carrying of the cross by a passerby, Simon of Cyrene.
6 The wiping of Christ's face by Veronica. The name "Veronica" is not told in the gospels, but it is found in early apocryphal writings, such as The Acts of Pilate. This relates that Veronica was the woman Jesus cured of a blood ailment (Matthew 9:20–22), and that she came to his trial before Pilate to claim his innocence.
7 Christ's second fall under the weight of the cross.
8 Christ's exhortation to the women of Jerusalem.
9 Christ's third fall under the weight of the cross.
10 The stripping of Christ's garments.

11 The crucifixion of Christ.
12 The death of Christ.
13 The presentation of Christ's body to Mary.
14 The burial of Christ.

Many churches have fourteen panels illustrating each of these stations built into their walls. Others use removable panels, which are displayed at this time of the year. Worshippers are encouraged to walk round the church, pausing at each station for contemplation, reflection, and prayer.

"Holy Week" includes four days which are worth special mention. These are:

- Palm Sunday.
- Maundy Thursday.
- Good Friday.
- Holy Saturday.

Note that Easter Day – which is always a Sunday – follows immediately after Holy Saturday. However, Easter Day is seen as lying outside the season of Lent, and marks the end of the period of fasting. We shall consider each of these four days within Holy Week separately.

Palm Sunday is the Sunday immediately before Easter. On this day, the church commemorates the triumphal entry of Jesus into Jerusalem, during which the crowds threw palm fronds into his path (see Matthew 21:1–11). This day, which marks the beginning of Holy Week, is now widely marked by the distribution of crosses made from palm fronds to congregations.

Maundy Thursday focuses on one of the final acts concerning Jesus to be related in John's gospel – the washing of the disciples' feet by Jesus (John 13:1–15). The ceremony of the "washing of the feet" of members of the congregation came to be an important part of the liturgy of the medieval church, symbolizing the humility of the clergy, in obedience to the example of Christ. The unusual term

"Maundy" is related to this medieval practice. In the Middle Ages, church services were held in Latin. The opening words of a typical service on this day are based on the words of Jesus recorded in John 13:34: "A new command I give you: Love one another. As I have loved you, so you must love one another." In Latin, the opening phrase of this sentence is "mandatum novum do vobis." The word "Maundy" is a corruption of the Latin word "mandatum" ("command").

In England, a particularly interesting ceremony has come to be associated with this day. As an affirmation of humility, the monarch would wash the feet of a small number of his or her subjects. This has now been replaced by the ceremony of the "Maundy Money," in which the monarch distributes specially minted coins to the elderly at cathedrals throughout England.

Good Friday is observed as the day on which Jesus died on the cross. It is the most solemn day in the Christian year, and is widely commemorated by the removing of all decorations from churches. In Lutheran churches, the day was marked by the reading of the passion narrative in a gospel, a practice which lies behind the "passions" composed by Johann Sebastian Bach (1685–1750). Both the Matthew Passion and the John Passion have their origins in this observance of Good Friday. The practice of observing a period of three hours' devotion from 12:00 a.m. to 3:00 p.m. on Good Friday has its origins in the eighteenth century. The "Three Hours of the Cross" often take the form of an extended meditation on the "Seven Last Words from the Cross," with periods of silence, prayer, or hymn-singing.

The events of Good Friday are also marked dramatically in various ways throughout the world. Perhaps the best known of these is the enactment of the passion and death of Christ which takes place every ten years in the little Upper Bavarian village of Oberammergau.

9.5 Queen Elizabeth II hands out Maundy Money during the Royal Maundy Service held at Liverpool's Anglican Cathedral in 2004. The purses containing the coins were given to 78 men and 78 women, the number selected to mark the queen's 78th year. PA/EMPICS.

As a way of expressing their gratitude to God for delivering them from the plague in 1633, the villagers undertook to act out the passion and death of Christ every decade. The event, which lasts six hours and involves about 700 people, is now a major tourist attraction. In the Philippines, the only Asian nation in which Christianity is the dominant religion, Good Friday is observed with particular fervor. In villages and towns throughout the nation, the crucifixion of Christ is reenacted by young men who are willing to be nailed to crosses briefly as a sign of their commitment to the Christian faith.

Holy Saturday is the final day of Lent, immediately before Easter Day. Especially in the eastern Orthodox churches, the day is marked by the "Paschal Vigil" – a late evening service which leads directly into the following Easter Day and makes extensive use of the imagery of light and darkness.

Easter

Easter Day marks the resurrection of Jesus and is widely regarded as the most significant festival of the Christian year. The religious importance of the festival is fundamental. In the first place, it affirms the identity of Jesus as the risen Savior and Lord. In the Orthodox tradition, this point is often made through icons or pictures in churches, which show a triumphant and risen Christ (often referred to as *Christos pantocrator*, "Christ the all-powerful") as ruler over the universe as a result of his being raised from the dead. In the second place, it affirms the Christian hope – that is, the fundamental belief that Christians will be raised from the dead, and hence need fear death no more. Both these themes dominate Easter hymns and liturgies. A good example is provided by an early eighteenth-century collection of hymns known as the *Lyra Davidica*.

Similar themes are found in the poems of the Christian tradition. The words of the English poet George Herbert (1593–1633) illustrate this point well. For Herbert, Easter is about the believer's hope of rising with Christ:

Rise, heart, thy Lord is risen. Sing his praise
Without delays,
Who takes thee by the hand, that thou likewise
With him mayst rise.

In the Greek Orthodox church, the following traditional Easter greeting is widely used, and has become familiar within other Christian traditions during the present century:

Christos anestos ("Christ is risen").
Alethos anestos ("He is risen indeed").

Easter is marked in a wide variety of ways throughout the Christian world. In Catholic and Orthodox churches, particular emphasis

Dates of Easter Sunday, 1995–2020

Year	Date	Year	Date
1995	April 16	2008	March 23
1996	April 7	2009	April 12
1997	March 30	2010	April 4
1998	April 12	2011	April 24
1999	April 4	2012	April 8
2000	April 23	2013	March 31
2001	April 15	2014	April 20
2002	March 31	2015	April 5
2003	April 20	2016	March 27
2004	April 11	2017	April 16
2005	March 27	2018	April 1
2006	April 16	2019	April 21
2007	April 8	2020	April 12

Once the date of Easter Day is established, the dates of all other related festivals can be determined. Palm Sunday occurs one week earlier than Easter Day. Pentecost occurs seven weeks after Easter Day, and Trinity Sunday eight weeks later. Thus in the year 2000, the dates of these four festivals were as follows:

Palm Sunday	April 16
Easter Day	April 23
Pentecost	June 11
Trinity Sunday	June 18

is often placed on the importance of the symbolism of light and darkness. In the ancient church, baptisms took place on Easter Day, as a way of showing that the believers had passed from darkness to light, from death to life. The custom of giving Easter eggs, widespread in western culture, seems to go back to the idea of an egg as a symbol of new life, pointing to the new life brought by the Christian gospel.

The liturgy and hymns of the Christian church are a particularly powerful witness to the importance of the message of the resurrection of Jesus Christ from the dead. The "Troparion of Easter" within the Byzantine liturgy sets out clearly the significance of the Easter event for the world:

> Christ is risen from the dead!
> Dying, he conquered death!
> To the dead, he has given life!

Ascension

Ascension Day, which always falls on a Thursday, can be seen as completing the sequence of events celebrated at Easter. The feast recalls the final ascension of Christ after he had been raised from the dead and recommissioned the disciples. Theologically, ascension marks the end of the period of appearances of the risen Christ to his disciples. These appearances, which are recorded in some detail in the gospels and hinted at in the letters of the New Testament, began immediately after the resurrection. The theme of "exaltation" is important at this point, in that Jesus is understood to have been exalted (raised) to the right hand of God.

Pentecost

Pentecost is the feast on which the church celebrates the gift of the Holy Spirit to the apostles, leading to the dramatic expansion of the church in its formative period. The Holy Spirit is of major importance to Christian thought and life. In recent times, the rise of the charismatic movement within the worldwide church has led to an increased awareness of the particular role of the Spirit. Pentecost falls on the fiftieth day after Easter. In the account of the death and resurrection of Jesus set out by Luke in his gospel and the Acts of the Apostles, there is a continuous sequence of events leading from the resurrection to the giving of the Spirit. After the resurrection, Jesus appears to his disciples on a number of occasions, to promise them the gift of the Holy Spirit. This is described as "the gift the Father promised," and is clearly linked with the theme of empowerment for evangelism and mission.

John's gospel refers to Jesus promising the gift of the Spirit after he had been taken from his disciples. The basic theme is that the Spirit is given to the disciples after Jesus is no longer present with them physically, in order to remind them of his words and works. Note that the Spirit is referred to in John's gospel as the "Counselor." The Greek word *parakletos* could also be translated as "Comforter" or "Advocate."

The specific event which is commemorated at Pentecost is the coming of the Holy Spirit, which is described in the Acts of the Apostles. Luke relates how the disciples had gathered together, when they were filled with the Holy Spirit. Luke's description of the event focuses on the impact of the event: the disciples were empowered to preach the gospel, and to break down the barriers of language separating them and their audiences. Theologically, the coming of the Spirit thus occupies a significant role in the scheme of salvation, in that it can be seen as a reversal of the "tower of Babel" (Genesis 11:1–32).

Pentecost is a major feast in the Christian year. In many Christian traditions, it is seen as second in importance only to Easter itself.

Pentecost is sometimes referred to in older English writings as "Whitsun" (literally, "white Sunday"), on account of the tradition of the clergy wearing white robes on this occasion.

Trinity

The final important feast of the Christian year is Trinity Sunday, which follows immediately after Pentecost. This festival completes the Easter sequence of events by celebrating the distinctively Christian doctrine of the Trinity, in which God is understood to be revealed as Father, Son, and Holy Spirit. It is placed immediately after Pentecost, which celebrates the gift of the Holy Spirit. The early church did not regard the doctrine of the Trinity as marking the occasion of a church festival. The Orthodox Christian year, for example, does not include any direct equivalent of this festival. The feast first became of crucial importance in the Middle Ages, and was eventually given official sanction by John XXII in 1334. Trinity Sunday is the last major festival in the Christian year. The remainder of the year is reckoned in terms of "Sundays after Trinity," until the cycle resumes again on Advent Sunday.

The monastic day

While there is no doubt that the Christian year represents one of the most important ways of structuring time, another should also be noted. One of the most significant ways of structuring time developed within the monasteries. Monasticism can be seen, in part, as a reaction against the secularization of the church as a result of the conversion of Constantine. Monasteries were established in part to allow for constant prayer, which was seen as increasingly problematical for Christians who chose to remain active in the world. Increasingly, monasticism came to be seen as an ideal, in which the goal of continuous prayer was pursued with a dedication which was impossible outside a monastic context.

This emphasis upon constant prayer led to the restructuring of the day. The pattern which gradually emerged was that of seven times of prayer during the day, and one during the night. These times of prayer were given the name "offices," from the Latin term *officium*, meaning "an obligation." The biblical basis for this pattern was found in the Psalter. For example, Psalm 119:64 commends prayer at seven points during the day, and many of the psalms refer to prayer during the night. The evolution of the monastic day can be seen as the gradual institutionalization of this pattern of seven daytime offices and one at night.

The precise evolution of this pattern is not completely understood. The following factors seem to have been involved.

1   There was already a widespread trend within ordinary church life to pray corporately in the early morning and evening. These offices came to be referred to as "Matins" and "Vespers" (from the Latin terms for "morning" and "evening"). The monasteries appear to have incorporated this regular pattern of prayer into their own more rigorous structures. These two times of prayer were often referred to as "the principal offices.".

2   A second major factor was the structure of the classical Roman working day. This led to prayer being specified for the third, sixth, and ninth hours (that is, 9:00 a.m., noon, and 3:00 p.m.). These were designated as "terce," "sext," and "none" respectively (from the Latin words for "third," "sixth," and "ninth").

3   Two additional offices were specified. *Compline* was, in effect, the final time of prayer before retiring to bed. *Prime* was an early morning form of prayer, apparently introduced by Cassian, who was concerned that

monks might go back to bed after the night office and sleep until 9:00 a.m.

4   There appears to have been considerable variation as to the time of the night office, reflecting local patterns of worship and understandings of personal discipline. If the day is divided into eight periods of three hours, it might be expected that the night office would be set for 3:00 a.m.; however, there appears to have been some variation on this matter.

The basic point to be made here is that the monastic day was systematically structured into segments, which included prayer and the reading of Scripture, especially the Psalms. Psalms 148, 149, and 150 were used with particular frequency. The pattern of daily offices was seen as an important framework for the development of personal and corporate spirituality, offering monks the opportunity to achieve the ideal of continual prayer, and at the same time saturate them with biblical passages. The internalization of Scripture, so important an aspect of monastic spirituality, is partly grounded in the rich use of the Bible in the monastic offices, as well as the emphasis within some monastic traditions on personal devotion on the part of individual monks in their cells.

It should be noted that some aspects of this structuring of the day remain important outside the monastic tradition. An excellent example is provided by the tradition of evangelical "Quiet Time," a daily period set aside for private reading of the Bible, meditation, and prayer. For many evangelicals, the early morning provides an ideal opportunity to begin the day with the reading of Scripture. Although the pressures of modern life have undermined this practice somewhat, the basic principle remains unaltered. Many study aids have emerged to encourage and assist the practice of the "Quiet Time," typically through assigning a passage to each day and offering brief devotional comments and reflections on the passage as an aid to prayer. Similarly, Dietrich Bonhoeffer (1906–1945) stressed the positive value of setting aside a daily period for personal Bible study and meditation. In his *Life Together* (1938), Bonhoeffer set out the importance of "being alone with the Word," allowing it to challenge and inspire its readers.

Christian Attitudes to Culture: Some General Considerations

Christianity is both a private and a public faith. It affects the way that individuals think and behave; it also impacts on society as a whole. Yet while some Christian writers advocate withdrawal or disengagement from society, others support full engagement with culture as a whole. Some Christians hold that it is not proper to attend any form of public entertainment – such as the cinema – where others believe that it is important to engage fully and appreciatively with culture at large.

The history of the interaction between Christianity and culture is very complex. Some Christian groups have deliberately defined themselves as countercultural, and hence worn clothes and adopted practices which mark them off from those around them. The Mennonite and Amish communities in modern America are a particularly good example of this trend. Holding that their faith demands that they separate from mainstream culture, and clearly distinguish themselves by physical and visible means, the Amish adopt clothing styles that encourage humility and separation from the world. The Amish dress in a very simple style, avoiding all but the most basic ornamentation. Clothing is made at home of plain fabrics and is primarily dark in color. This, however, is a minority perspective. Most Christians see no need to distinguish themselves from the world.

To understand the complexities of the interrelationship of Christianity and culture, we need to consider the first phase of Christian history. Since it first established a significant presence at Rome in the 40s, Christianity had had a decidedly ambiguous legal status. On the one hand, it was not legally recognized, and so did not enjoy any special rights; on the other, it was not forbidden. However, its growing numerical strength led to periodic attempts to suppress it by force. Sometimes these persecutions were local, restricted to regions such as North Africa; sometimes they were sanctioned throughout the Roman empire as a whole.

So how should Christians respond to this situation? Prior to the conversion of Constantine, many Christians were content to maintain a low profile, keeping their religious views to themselves. Many – including Tertullian – took the view that Christianity must preserve its distinctive identity by avoiding such secular influences. "What," he famously asked, "has Athens to do with Jerusalem?" But with the conversion of Constantine, new possibilities emerged.

Augustine of Hippo is widely, and rightly, seen as mapping out the mainstream Christian response to the relation of faith and culture. Augustine's approach is probably best described as the "critical appropriation of classical culture." For Augustine, the situation is comparable to Israel fleeing from captivity in Egypt at the time of the Exodus. Although they left the idols of Egypt behind, they carried the gold and silver of Egypt with them, in order to make better and proper use of such riches, which were thus liberated in order to serve a higher purpose than before. In much the same way, the philosophy and culture of the ancient world could be appropriated by Christians, where this seemed right, and thus allowed to serve the cause of the Christian faith.

Augustine's fundamental idea is to make use of a way of thinking – or writing, or speaking – which had hitherto been imprisoned within a purely pagan use, and liberate it from this captivity so that it might be put to the service of the gospel. Augustine argues that what are essential neutral yet valuable ways of thinking or self-expression have been quarried in "the mines of the providence of God"; the difficulty is the use to which they were put within pagan culture, in that they had been "improperly and unlawfully prostituted to the worship of demons."

Augustine's approach thus laid the foundation for the assertion that whatever was good, true, or beautiful could be used in the service of the gospel. It was this approach which would prove dominant in the western church, providing a theological foundation for the critical appropriation by Christian writers of literary genres whose origins lay outside the church. In addition to literary forms already known within the church and widely recognized as entirely appropriate in Christian usage – such as the sermon and the biblical commentary – might be added others, whose cultural pedigree was thoroughly secular. Examples would include drama and – to anticipate a later development – the novel.

Yet Augustine's view never secured total acceptance. The study of Christian history reveals a complex pattern of interactions with culture, some inspired by Augustine, others by more countercultural ways of thinking. For some Christians, the world is to be seen as a hostile environment for Christian belief and practice. The values of the kingdom of God stand in contrast to those of the world. This type of spirituality was of considerable importance in the first few centuries of Christian history, when Christianity was viewed with intense distrust and suspicion by the secular authorities, and on occasion actively perse-cuted. Once the Roman emperor Constantine was converted to Christianity, however, a very different situation resulted. Christianity rap-idly became the official religion of the Roman empire. In the eyes of many, this resulted in a compromise with secular values. Bishops began to imitate the dress and customs of secu-lar rulers – for example, by wearing purple robes (a symbol of wealth and power).

This led to many Christians believing that some authentically Christian ideals were being jeopardized. The rise of the monastic move-ment is widely seen as a revolt against the easy accommodation which began to emerge between church and state, with the result that it began to become difficult to tell them apart. The monasteries saw themselves as centers of authentic Christianity, insulated from the temptations of power and wealth, in which the true Christian vision could be pursued. Many works of monastic spirituality spoke of the cultivation of "contempt for the world," meaning a studied rejection of the temptations offered by the world, which were seen as an obstacle to salvation and personal spiritual growth. Withdrawal from the world was the only guaranteed means of ensuring one's sal-vation.

Although the Protestant Reformation rejected the monastic ideal, the dual themes of the renunciation of the world and the hos-tility of the world for authentic Christianity were taken up and developed by the more radical wing of the movement. Anabaptist writers stressed the need to form alternative Christian communities, often in rural areas. Anabaptist writers refused to have anything to do with secular power or authority, reject-ing the use of force. A tension can be discerned at this point between radical writers and the mainline reformers (such as Luther and Cal-vin), who encouraged a more positive and interactive approach to society and culture.

Similar attitudes can be found within North American fundamentalist circles today.

The relationship between Christianity and culture is thus complex. Some Christians see no difficulty in interacting positively and fully with the local culture; others fear that any such engagement will lead to the erosion of Christian distinctiveness.

The Impact of Christianity on Culture

C hristianity possesses the potential to change culture. This can be seen in both the ancient and the modern world. In the late third century, many Romans were convinced that the diminishing prosperity and influence of Rome were directly due to the rise of Chris-tianity. The old religious cults were being abandoned in favor of Christianity. There is no doubt that one of the most significant con-tributing causes to the slow and inexorable death of classical pagan culture was the rise of Christianity. A similar pattern can be seen in modern Chinese culture, where there is a wide-spread interest in Christianity amongst the younger generation. Traditional Chinese cus-toms, such as "grave-sweeping" (in which children are regarded as being under an obli-gation to honor their ancestors by tidying their graves), are regarded with suspicion by younger Chinese Christians, who feel that the practice is linked with a set of beliefs which are not Christian. This traditional Chinese custom is being eroded, owing to the growth of Chris-tianity. Countless other examples could be given of cultural changes resulting from the growth of Christianity, including the decline of traditional religious beliefs and their associated practices in Africa and Southeast Asia.

One of the most marked differences between Christianity and the two other great monothe-istic religions – Judaism and Islam – is that

Christianity makes no religious requirements of its followers concerning food or clothing. Judaism and Islam both regard certain foods – such as pork – as being "unclean," and forbid their followers to eat them. Jesus of Nazareth declared all foods to be clean, insisting that moral and religious purity depended on what lay within a person's heart, rather than what entered their bodies through their mouths (Mark 7:18–19). In a similar way, Judaism and Islam require animals to be slaughtered in a particular fashion to meet strict religious laws (*kosher* and *halal*, respectively). Christianity has never made any such demands of its followers, despite pressure from Judaizing factions within the early church to adopt such requirements.

It must, however, also be appreciated that Christianity exists in a mutual relationship with culture. Christianity had an impact on its surrounding culture; that culture also molded Christianity. This process was entirely natural: in that Christianity did not lay down precise rules concerning food, dress, or lifestyle, Christians regarded themselves as able to incorporate aspects of their culture according to their beliefs. As the history of Christian expansion makes clear, Christians did not impose a uniform culture on peoples who had chosen to accept the Christian faith. It is quite evident that Christianity fostered an attitude of tolerance towards traditional cultural beliefs and norms, where these were not seen as having a direct relevance to the Christian faith. The wide range of cultural diversity within Christianity is perhaps one of the most striking differences between Christianity and Islam.

A broad assortment of traditional cultural customs and practices thus find their way into Christianity. Some have achieved almost universal acceptance. Two examples will illustrate this. The traditional color associated with Christian bishops is purple. This was a sign of social status in the classical world, and was adopted by Christians as a means of designating the importance of bishops within the Christian community and beyond. Had Christianity had its origins in China, it is entirely possible that bishops would have worn yellow (the traditional Chinese color associated with royalty). This aspect of classical culture was regarded as acceptable by Christians, and thus eventually found its way into the church. A second example is the Christian practice (now widespread within western culture) of placing a wedding ring on the fourth finger of the bride's left hand. This reflects a traditional Roman custom, which Christians found perfectly acceptable – and thus incorporated into their marriage customs.

A further area of interest concerns the need for a supply of wine in order to comply with the explicit commandment of Jesus that his followers should use bread and wine to remember him. The great medieval monasteries in Spain, France, and Italy soon fell into the habit of establishing vineyards, in order to ensure a regular supply of communion wine. It was a monk – one Dom Perignon – who discovered how wine could be preserved by the use of the bark of the Portuguese cork oak.

In what follows, we shall explore some of the ways in which Christianity has influenced – and continues to influence – culture. It must be made clear that the restriction of the subject in this way is entirely due to lack of space. What follows must be regarded as illustrative of the way in which Christianity interacted with culture; in no way can this brief analysis be considered to be definitive!

Christianity and the development of the natural sciences

The emergence of the natural sciences is one of the most distinctive features of modern culture. It is therefore of importance to explore the impact of Christianity on this development.

As might be expected, this turns out to be rather complex. Although there is a popular perception that science and Christianity are in permanent conflict, this does not really fit the facts. The most reliable accounts of the relationship of Christianity and the natural sciences note that it is complex.

The insight that God created the world is widely agreed to offer a fundamental motivation for scientific research. To explore this point, let us consider three broad positions on the question of the status of nature:

1   The natural world is divine.
2   The natural world is created, and bears some resemblance to its creator – this is the Christian view, as we noted earlier.
3   The natural world has no relation to God.

Clearly, a degree of simplification has been introduced here. However, it allows us to make a point of fundamental importance about the relation of Christianity and science. Suppose that someone is strongly religious. If the natural world has no relation to God, there will be no motivation to study it. On the other hand, if the natural world does bear some relation to God, there will clearly be a very good reason for studying it, in that it offers to allow deeper insights into the nature of the God who created it. It is clearly therefore of considerable interest to explore the way in which a doctrine of creation – such as that associated with Judaism or Christianity – establishes a connection between God and the natural order.

A point which is stressed by many religious writers of the sixteenth and seventeenth centuries is that the invisible God can be studied through the visible creation. This idea (which is sometimes expressed in terms of the "two books" of Scripture and Nature) gave additional impetus to the study of nature. If God could not be seen, yet had somehow imprinted his nature on the creation, it would be possible to gain an enhanced appreciation of the nature and purpose of God by studying the natural order.

A second related issue concerns the order of nature. One of the fundamental themes of a doctrine of creation (such as that associated with Christianity and Judaism) is that in creation God imposes order, rationality, and beauty upon nature. The doctrine of creation leads directly to the notion that the universe is possessed of a regularity which is capable of being uncovered by humanity. This theme, which is expressed in terms of "the laws of nature," is of fundamental significance. This religious undergirding of the notion of the regularity of nature is known to have been of crucial historical importance to the emergence and development of the natural sciences.

Yet the picture is far more complex than this. Alongside these positive interactions of Christianity and the natural sciences, we should note some points at which there is clearly conflict, or at least the potential for conflict.

Our first point concerns the generally conservative character of much traditional religion. Christian churches have often tended to think of themselves as guardians of tradition, and thus as opposed to radical new ideas. This is not necessarily a result of Christian theology but reflects the social role which the churches played over a long period in western European history. On the other hand, the natural sciences were often seen as radical, calling into question received wisdom.

As Freeman Dyson points out in an essay entitled "The Scientist as Rebel," a common element of most visions of science is that of "rebellion against the restrictions imposed by the local prevailing culture." Science is thus a subversive activity, almost by definition – a point famously stated in a lecture delivered to the "Society of Heretics" at Cambridge by the biologist J. B. S. Haldane in February 1923. For the Arab mathematician and astronomer Omar Khayyam, science was a rebellion against the intellectual constraints of Islam; for nineteenth-century Japanese scientists, science was a rebellion against the lingering feudalism of their culture; for the great Indian physicists of the twentieth century, their discipline was a powerful intellectual force directed against the fatalistic ethic of Hinduism (not to mention British imperialism, which was then dominant in the region). And in western Europe, scientific advance inevitably involved confrontation with the culture of the day – including its political, social, and religious elements. In that the west has been dominated by Christianity, it is thus unsurprising that the tension between science and western culture has often been viewed as a confrontation between science and Christianity.

It is also important to note that the rise of the scientific worldview called into question many traditional religious views. For example, the rise and gradual acceptance of the Copernican model of the solar system posed a serious challenge to an earth-centered view of the universe, which had become implicit in much traditional religious thinking. It is, however, arguable whether such geocentric approaches should have become so deeply embedded in traditional religious thinking. As a matter of fact, the older view that the Bible supports such a geocentrism rests largely on the implicit assumption that, as the earth is at the center of everything, the Bible must say the same thing. Techniques of biblical interpretation which allowed for the "stripping out" of culturally conditioned elements in the Bible or on the part of the biblical interpreter proved able to deal with this difficulty.

It is the Darwinian controversy, however, which presented the most radical threat to traditional religious beliefs, in that it posed a direct challenge to the belief that God created each species directly (the idea of "special creation"), and particularly the idea that humanity was the apex of God's creation, created in such a manner that it was set apart from the rest of the animal kingdom. Darwin's ideas (which, aware of their sensitivity, he tended to state rather cautiously) clearly implied that human beings were rather less special than they might like to think.

Where Copernicanism called into challenge one aspect of the traditional interpretation of the Genesis creation narrative, Darwinism called another into question. Although there were many who believed that it was perfectly possible to reconcile the Bible, Copernicus, and Darwin (and the idea of "theistic evolution" needs to be noted here), the general perception arose that there was a fundamental, perhaps even fatal, contradiction between the two disciplines of science and religion. Although this was polarized by social and political factors typical of western Europe (and especially England) in the later nineteenth century, the fact remains that some such tension exists – and thus potentially makes religion hostile to scientific advance.

It will therefore be clear that any analysis of the historical interaction of science and religion which portrays the matter in purely negative or purely positive terms is being unacceptably selective in its approach. The simple fact is that the historical interaction has been ambivalent. Religious belief has both encouraged and discouraged the emergence of the natural sciences. The simplistic view that faith and science are locked in mortal combat is nonsense. But there can be no denying that it is a very ambivalent relationship. Perhaps it should not surprise anyone that surveys regularly demonstrate that natural scientists are pretty evenly split on whether God exists.

Our attention now turns away from one specific component of modern culture – the natural sciences – to the world of art, music, and literature. In what way has Christianity shaped the way we represent and reflect the world? We may begin by considering how Christian symbols have developed.

Christian symbolism: The cross

We have already seen how the figure of Jesus Christ dominates the Christian faith. In particular, we noted how the death of Jesus on the cross is understood by Christians to be the foundation of the salvation of humanity. The cross is thus a symbol of salvation. It is also a symbol of the Christian hope, in that it affirms that death has been defeated through the resurrection of Jesus. The cross – an instrument of execution – thus became a sign of the hope and transformation which are fundamental to Christianity.

The cross has been the universally acknowledged symbol of the Christian faith from a very early period, probably as early as the late second century. Indeed, it is fair to suggest that there is no symbol other than the cross which carries such weight, authority, or recognition within the Chrisian faith. Christians are baptized with the sign of the cross. Churches and other Christian places of meeting do not merely include a cross; they are often built in the shape of a cross. The Christian emphasis on the cross has had considerable implications for the design of churches. Indeed, it is probably at this point that Christian theology has had its most profound impact on western culture. To walk around a great medieval cathedral or church is to view theology embodied in stone.

Many Christians find it helpful to make the sign of the cross in times of danger or anxiety. The graves of Christians – whether Catholic, Orthodox, or Protestant – are marked with crosses. Careful studies of the origins and development of Christian symbolism have made it clear that the cross was seen as the symbol of the Christian gospel from the earliest of times. Even in the earliest writings of the New Testa-ment, the phrase "the message of the cross" is used as a shorthand summary of the Christian gospel (see 1 Corinthians 1:18–25). Two second-century writers bring out the importance of the cross with particular clarity: for Tertullian, Christians are "those who believe in the cross"; for Clement of Alexandria, the cross is "the supreme sign of the Lord." There is an anti-Christian graffito which has been preserved from ancient Rome, which depicts a man adoring a crucified man with the head of an ass. The inscription reads: "Alexander worships his god."

The final stage in the global acceptance of the cross as the supreme symbol of the Christian faith is generally regarded as having been the conversion of the future Roman emperor Constantine. At some point shortly before or after the decisive battle of the Milvian Bridge (312), Constantine saw a vision of a cross, which ordered him to place the sign on his soldiers' shields. During the reign of Constantine, crosses of various types were erected in Rome, and began to appear on Roman coinage. Crucifixion had continued as a means of execution under previous Roman emperors. Constantine outlawed the practice, and directed that the scaffolds used for execution would no longer be referred to as "crosses (*cruces*)" but as "patibula."

Early Christian writers regarded the cross as a teaching aid for the great themes of the Christian faith. Not only did it affirm the reality of salvation and hope in a world of death; it also affirmed the full humanity of Jesus. Early Christian writers were also prepared to read more ambitious ideas into the cross. As Justin Martyr argued, was there not a direct parallel between the Christian cross and the Platonic cosmic symbol of the Greek letter *chi* (which is cross-shaped: "X")?

There is evidence that Christians in the first century were reluctant to portray the crucifixion of Jesus. It was one thing to make the sign of the cross; it was quite another to depict Jesus on the cross of Calvary, especially on account of the issues of taste and decency involved in portraying Jesus naked. However, these inhibitions were gradually overcome. Christian art, in both the east and west, began to focus on the crucifixion for devotional purposes. In response to the view that Jesus was purely divine, lacking any real human nature, Christian leaders encouraged artists to produce depictions of the crucifixion of Jesus as a way of emphasizing his full humanity. What better way of stressing the suffering and death of Jesus than to portray him on the cross? The implications of these considerations are momentous, and help understand the importance attached by many Christian writers to the devotional depiction of the crucifixion.

Although depictions of the resurrection were of considerable importance in Christian art at this time, the cross remained of fundamental importance to Christian thought and devotion. This focus on the cross found its expression at many levels of culture, including the design of churches. Many churches are built in the shape of crosses, and display crosses prominently within them. Of particular significance to many Christians is the *crucifix* – that is, a wooden carving of Jesus stretched out on the cross, with the inscription "INRI" above his head (these letters spell out the Latin words *Iesus Nazarenus Rex Iudaeorum*, which are to be translated as "Jesus of Nazareth, King of the Jews"; see John 19:1–16 for the background). The crucifix is intended to remind Christians of the sufferings of Jesus, and thus emphasizes the costliness and reality of the salvation which resulted from his death on the cross.

The cross has found its way into the symbolism of nations whose history has been steeped in the Christian faith. For example, the "Union Flag" of the United Kingdom consists of three different crosses – the crosses of St. George (England), St. Patrick (Ireland), and St. Andrew (Scotland) – combined into a single design. Celtic crosses – that is, crosses with a circle embracing their four arms – are a particular feature of the Irish landscape. Other forms of the cross with specific national or regional associations include the "Cross of Lorraine" and the "Maltese Cross." The background to this incorporation of this Christian symbol into national flags can probably be traced back to the second century. Justin Martyr and others then drew a parallel between the way in which conquering Roman armies marched behind their "banners and trophies (*vexilla et tropaia*)." In the same way, such writers argued, Christians marched behind the banner of the cross, which bore the trophy of a defeated death. This theme is brought out particularly clearly in the great processional hymn of Bishop Venantius Fortunatus (ca. 530–ca. 610), entitled *Vexilla regis prodeunt* ("The banners of the king go forth") (see pp. 144–145). In this processional hymn, Venantius Fortunatus compares the cross to a banner in a great triumphant procession. The cross symbolizes the reality of the victory gained by the death of Jesus on the cross.

Although the cross is the most familiar and widely encountered of Christian symbols, it is important to note that other symbols were significant in early Christianity. One of these may be noted. A fish was used as a symbol of Christian identity, on account of its potential as a teaching aid. The Greek term for fish is *ichthus*. The five letters of the Greek word for fish are ΙΧΘΥΣ ("I-CH-TH-U-S"); these letters act as an acronym, spelling out the central Christian beliefs concerning the identity and significance of Jesus.

Greek letter	Greek word	English translation
Ι (iota)	Iesous	Jesus
Χ (chi)	Christos	Christ
Θ (theta)	Theou	of God
Υ (upsilon)	Huios	Son
Σ (sigma)	Soter	Savior

The word *ichthus* thus spells out the Christological affirmation: "Jesus Christ, Son of God, Savior." References to "the fish" can be found in a number of early Christian writings, particularly on tombs. The Greek word *ichthus* and the symbol of a fish are both still widely used by Christians. If the automobile in front of you has a symbol of a fish on its bumper, it is probably owned by a Christian. If an organization or an Internet address has the word "ichthus" in it, you can be fairly certain it has something to do with Christianity.

Christian art

God is invisible, and cannot be seen by mortal human beings. This insight is fundamental to most religions with a strongly transcendent understanding of God. Yet throughout the history of Christian thought, human beings have shown a marked longing to be able to depict God in some manner. If God cannot be visualized, the idea of God becomes potentially abstract and impersonal, remote from the world of human experience. One of the most significant themes in Christian spirituality is that of *visualization* – the development of ways in which the divine may be represented visually, as something to be contemplated, without compromising the transcendence of God. Can the face of God be seen?

We begin our discussion of this question by considering an issue which inevitably emerges in this matter – the problem of idolatry. To create an image of God runs the risk of constructing something which we ourselves have generated. In other words, every image of God which we generate could become an idol. Presumably for this reason, the Old Testament absolutely prohibited the production of any images of God. The Second Commandment – regarded as binding by all Christians – is quite explicit on this point (Exodus 20:4–5):

You shall not make yourself an idol in the form of anything in heaven above or on the earth beneath or in the waters below. You shall not bow down to them or worship them.

This concern has been of major importance within the Reformed tradition within Christianity. This tradition, which is grounded in the works of the Protestant reformer John Calvin (1509–1564), holds that there is at least a theoretical risk of worshipping something of our own construction associated with the production of any form of religious imagery. The Reformed tradition therefore discourages any form of religious art, including the depiction of God or Jesus Christ.

Below, we note the importance of icons within the Orthodox tradition. It is important to note that the Orthodox use of icons has not met with universal approval. The iconoclastic controversy within the Byzantine world (715–843) raised the question of whether icons were, in fact, idols. Leading defenders of icons (including John of Damascus and Theodore of Studios) insisted that it was perfectly legitimate to represent the humanity of Christ in icons. Through faith, it was possible to pass through the humanity of Christ and discern his divinity.

It will also be clear from what has just been said that the Reformed tradition within western theology generally holds that the use of icons is potentially idolatrous, in that it encourages the worship of images which have been constructed by human hands. The Orthodox response to such criticisms is that it is not the image, but the reality which it attempts to depict, that is the object of worship. For Orthodoxy, an icon is a method of prayer, and as such it is a window into heaven, not simply a piece of art to be gazed upon for aesthetic pleasure. In the Byzantine tradition, the theology of icons has normally been applied to two-dimensional painted icons and mosaics alone rather than statues.

The Heidelberg Catechism sets out the general lines of the Reformed objection to the use of icons. It also indicates why religious art never developed within the Reformed churches to anything like the same extent as within Catholicism or Orthodoxy. This Catechism, written in German in 1563, develops the idea that images of God are neither necessary nor helpful for Christian believers. There is an interesting parallel with Islam here, in that both Islam and Reformed theology are concerned to avoid images of God becoming objects of worship in themselves, instead of being aids to the worship of God.

Question 96. What does God require in the next commandment?
Answer: That we should not portray God in any way, nor worship him in any other manner than he has commanded in his Word.

Question 97. So should we not make any use of images?
Answer: God cannot and should not be depicted in any way. As for creatures, although they may indeed be depicted, God forbids making use of or having any likeness of them, in order to worship them or to use them to serve him.

Question 98. But should we allow pictures instead of books in churches, for the benefit of the unlearned?
Answer: No. For we should not presume to be wiser than God, who does not want Christendom to be taught by means of dumb idols, but through the living preaching of his Word.

Note how the Heidelberg Catechism indicates that biblical preaching should take the place of religious art as a means of instruction and devotion. This concern serves to distinguish the Reformed tradition from other Reformation churches (including Lutheranism and Anglicanism), as well as from Catholicism and Orthodoxy. Most other Christian traditions regard religious art as a helpful aid to devotion, and encourage the display of appropriate works of religious art in places of worship. It may also be noted that several recent theologians within the Reformed tradition have used works of religious art as a means of encouraging theological reflection and personal devotion. Thus Karl Barth (1886–1968) had a copy of Matthias Grünewald's Isenheim altarpiece, depicting the crucifixion, on his desk. Jürgen Moltmann (b. 1926) had a copy of Marc Chagall's *Crucifixion in Yellow* in front of him as he wrote *The Crucified God*, widely regarded as one of the theological masterpieces of the twentieth century.

So how can the charge of idolatry be avoided, if religious imagery is to be used to depict the divine? The simplest answer is perhaps the most persuasive: *because we are meant to*. The New Testament affirms that Jesus is the "image of the invisible God" (Colossians 1:15) and the "exact representation" of God (Hebrews 1:4). St. John's gospel includes a number of important sayings of Jesus which indicate that to have seen him is to have seen God (see, for example, John 14:6). The basic theme that emerges from such texts is that Jesus is the authorized visual image for God. In other words, Jesus makes God known in a visible and tangible manner.

This insight has enormous implications for Christian spirituality, some of which we have already explored (pp. 139–141). God is like Jesus. To focus our thoughts upon Jesus is to pass through a window into the living God. The love of Jesus for the outcast, poor, and helpless mirrors the love of God for these people. The importance of this insight for Christian spirituality is immense. It allows us to visualize God in a manner of which God approves. It is not as if we have decided to treat Jesus as if he were an image of the invisible God. It is that we have been told that Jesus is indeed an image of that God, and we are meant to act upon that knowledge. The noted Scottish theologian Hugh Ross Mackintosh (1870–1936) expressed this insight as follows: "When I look into the face of Jesus, and see there the very face of God, I know that I have not seen that face elsewhere and cannot see that face elsehow."

The relevance of this point for spirituality can be demonstrated from a number of sources. We shall examine a particularly well-known case. On May 8, 1373, the English religious writer Julian of Norwich experienced a series of visions concerning the love of God. These were triggered off by a very specific stimulus. Julian had become ill, and those around her were convinced that she was about to die. The local parish priest was sent for. He held before her a crucifix (that is, a carving of Christ upon the cross), and spoke these words to her: "I have brought you the image of your Creator and Savior. Look at it, and be strengthened." The image of Christ upon the cross proved to be a gateway to a series of extended meditations on the goodness of God, and God's overwhelming generosity and courtesy to sinners.

A development of this point can be seen in religious art. If contemplation of the life and person of Jesus led people to a deeper knowledge of God, it seemed to many that vivid depictions of incidents in the life of Christ could assist that process still further. The Middle Ages and Renaissance witnessed a dramatic increase in the use of religious art for both public and private devotion. Panel painting was widely used to depict narratives concerning Jesus, or static portraits of Jesus and his mother. In the early Middle Ages, the two dominant religious images were the madonna and child, and the crucifixion. By the later Renaissance, the same attention once paid to the crucifixion was being devoted to other religious subjects. Renaissance artists regarded many incidents in the life of Jesus as of poten-

tial importance. Particular attention was paid to the Annunciation (that is, to the scene in Luke's gospel in which Gabriel informs Mary that she is to bear a son), the baptism of Jesus, and the resurrection. The appearance of the risen Jesus to Mary Magdalene (John 20:17) was also the subject of many classic works, including Fra Angelico's fresco *Noli me tangere* ("Do not touch me"), painted over the period 1440–1441 in the convent of San Marco in Florence. In addition, emotions – especially pain and sadness – came to be conveyed through the expressions on the faces of those being depicted. Painted panels could be displayed singly in churches, but were often combined in the form of diptychs, triptychs, or even polyptychs, as in the Ghent altarpiece by Hubert and Jan van Eyck or the Isenheim altarpiece by Matthias Grünewald.

Two scenes in the life of Christ may be singled out for special comment: his birth (often referred to as "the nativity") and his death on the cross (the crucifixion). We shall explore these in more detail, to illustrate the way in which Christian themes and values found their artistic expression.

The "nativity" – that is, the birth – of Christ has long played a central role in Christian iconography. Christians have always appreciated the theological and spiritual importance of the birth of the savior, and have found picturing this event to be helpful to personal and corporate devotion. The incarnation is about God's descent into this world of sin, so that he might raise us up to the heavenly places. The more we are reassured that God really did enter into our history as one of us, the more we can be reassured that we shall be raised up into those heavenly places in which the Christ-child now reigns in glory.

In the west, the dominant approach to depicting the nativity is to set Mary and her child at the center of the picture. An excellent example of this approach can be found in *The*

Mystic Nativity by Sandro Botticelli (1447–1515). In this work, executed around the year 1500, Mary is depicted in terms appropriate to the era of the painter rather than to the New Testament. Botticelli here follows other Renaissance painters of the fourteenth and fifteenth centuries, who portrayed Mary dressed as a noblewoman of their time. The point being made is that Christ's entry into history is of importance to all ages, not simply the Palestine of the first century. Representing Mary as a lady of the Renaissance was a means of emphasizing the transformative potential of the Christ-child for the Renaissance, as well as for all ages.

Botticelli follows a long-standing tradition in including an ox and ass in the nativity scene. Yet a quick reading of the gospel nativity accounts soon discloses that no mention is made of oxen or asses. So why are these traditionally included in the scene? From the second century onwards, commentators on the birth of Christ linked the scene with Isaiah 1:3, which speaks of the ox and the ass knowing their true master and his crib. It seems that this prophetic passage was then linked with the birth of Christ, thus reminding us that the whole of the created order is involved in the birth of Christ and the new creation which will result from his incarnation, death, and resurrection. Botticelli follows this tradition, and portrays the angels in heaven as rejoicing over the transformation of the created order that will take place through Christ. Indeed, in the lower section of the painting, angels are even depicted as dancing with humans, as they celebrate the possibility of a new heaven and a new earth.

In some cases, the themes of Christmas and Epiphany are merged. For example, in Rembrandt's *Shepherds worshipping the Child*, we see the first visitors to the newborn king – the shepherds from the fields around Bethlehem, along with some of their sheep. These are sometimes joined by the three "wise men" or kings from the east, who brought the newborn child the exotic and costly gifts of gold, frankincense, and myrrh. Traditionally, it is assumed that each "wise man" brought one of the three gifts (the gospels do not tell us how many "wise men" actually came).

Churches, private chapels, and houses were often decorated with depictions of the crucifixion as a means of encouraging personal devotion. Christian writers and artists have always been aware of the need to reflect on this pivotal event, and its life-changing implications. Unlike the Docetic heresy (which held that Jesus merely had the "appearance" of humanity, and did not really suffer), Christian orthodoxy stressed both the reality of Christ's agony on the cross and the salvation which it achieved. Visual representations of Christ's suffering on the cross thus served to stress the costliness of our redemption, and to deepen our appreciation of what he achieved for us. The more we appreciate the pain he suffered, the more we shall adore him for what he did for us.

Depictions of the passion of Christ often reveal significantly different interests and emphases. Some depict Christ as raised up on this cross, high above the crowds around him. This is meant to focus our attention on the way in which Christ was "raised up" on the cross, so that we might in turn be "raised up" to heaven by his cross and resurrection. Others focus on the crowds around him, sometimes depicting the rage and fury on the faces of those who mocked him. The point being made here is that those who crucified Christ were actually quite ordinary people, just like us. So deep-rooted is sin in human nature that our natural instinct is not to adore Christ, but to crucify him. It is a telling reminder of the power of sin to distort and destroy, and an equally powerful reminder of our need for redemption – the redemption, of course, that Christ died on the cross in order to bring to us.

Others focus on those who are standing around the cross. An excellent example of this is provided by Matthias Grünewald's famous altarpiece at Isenheim, painted during the years 1513–1515. On the left of the cross, three people mourn the dead Christ: Mary, the mother of Jesus; John, the beloved disciple; and Mary Magdalene. This is intended to help us appreciate the appalling impact that Christ's death had on his disciples. In the case of Mary, we are invited to imagine how she must have felt when her son – the one whom she held in her arms as an infant – was taken away from her and spread out on the arms of the cross.

On the right of the cross, we see John the Baptist. Grünewald wants to remind us of the words of John on seeing Jesus: "Behold the lamb of God, who takes away the sin of the world." The death of Christ is the means by which the sin of the world was removed. By pointing to the crucified Christ, John proclaims that this Christ is the lamb of God, whose death purges us of our sins. In case we miss this allusion, Grünewald includes a lamb in the lower part of the picture, along with a cross and chalice to point to the importance of its saving death. John the Baptist also symbolizes the continuity between the Old and New Testaments. Jesus is the fulfillment of the great Old Testament prophecies of redemption. He is indeed the one by whose stripes we are healed, and whose wounds bring us salvation (Isaiah 53).

9.6 The crucifixion, as depicted by Matthias Grünewald in the Isenheim altarpiece, executed ca. 1513–1515. Colmar, Unterlinden Museum, AKG-Images/Erich Lessing.

Church architecture

Initially, Christians had to borrow buildings in which they could worship. Until Christianity was a recognized religion within the Roman empire, it was not free to build its own distinctive structures. Christians met in private homes, or borrowed pagan temples as places of worship. However, from the fourth century onwards, Christians were free to construct places of meeting and worship which reflected their own distinct ideas and beliefs. This led to the development of several distinctive styles of church architecture, each of which is grounded in a set of beliefs about the nature of God, the place of the institution of the church in God's plan of salvation, and the ultimate destiny of human nature.

To appreciate the importance of church architecture throughout the Middle Ages – the golden age of church architecture – it is essential to understand the exceptionally high value attached to the institution of the church at this time. In the third century of the Christian era, Cyprian of Carthage penned a slogan which would have a decisive impact on Christian understandings of the role of the church as the mediator and guarantor of redemption. "Outside the church, there is no salvation." This pithy maxim was open to a number of interpretations. That which predominated throughout the Middle Ages can be argued to result directly from the growth in institutional authority of the church after the collapse of the Roman empire. Salvation was only to be had through membership of the church. Christ may have made the hope of salvation possible; only the church could make it available. There was an ecclesiastical monopoly on the dispensation of redemption.

This theological position was undergirded by new approaches to biblical interpretation which gained ground after the fall of Rome. Increasingly, western theologians argued that the Bible had four "senses" or meanings. In addition to the *literal* sense of a passage, three deeper *spiritual* meanings could be discerned: the allegorical sense of the passage, referring to a matter of doctrine; the tropological sense, concerning matters of ethics; and the anagogical sense, which pointed to the Christian hope. For Bede, the great early historian of English Christianity, this approach to the interpretation of biblical passages was pregnant with meaning when applied to passages dealing with the Old Testament temple.

> The temple of the Lord in the literal sense is the house which Solomon built; allegorically, it is the Lord's body or his church ... tropologically, it is each of the faithful ... anagogically, it is the joys of the heavenly mansion.

Each of these senses was reflected in medieval reflections on the nature and significance of the church, particularly in developing the connection between the physical structure of a church building and the theological truths which that institution sought to proclaim.

The insight that the institution of the church was the guarantor of the hope of human salvation was rapidly assimilated into church architecture. The great portals of Romanesque churches were often adorned with elaborate sculptures depicting the glory of heaven as a tactile affirmation that it was only by entering the church that this hope could be achieved. Inscriptions were often placed over the great west door of churches, declaring that it was only through entering the church that heaven could be attained. The doorframe was allowed to be identified with Christ for this purpose, speaking words directed to those passing by, or pausing to admire its magnificent ornamentation.

An excellent example is provided by the Benedictine priory church of St.-Marcel-lès-Sauze, which was founded in 985 and extensively developed during the twelfth century. The portal to the church depicts Christ as addressing these words to all who draw near:

> You who are passing through,
> you who are coming to weep for your sins,
> pass through me,
> since I am the gate of life.

Although the words are clearly to be attributed to Christ (picking up on the image of Christ as the "gate of the sheepfold" from John 10), a tactile link has been forged with the building of the church itself. This is often reinforced visually through the physical location of the baptismal font close to the door of the church, thereby affirming that entrance to heaven is linked with the sacrament of baptism.

A similar theme is found in the inscription placed over the portal of the Benedictine church of Santa Cruz de la Serós, located close to the main pilgrimage route from Jaca to Puente la Reina in Spain.

> I am the eternal door; pass through me, faithful ones.
> I am the fountain of life; thirst for me more than for wine.

The door of the church of San Juan de la Peña, possibly dating from the twelfth century, bears the following message:

> Through this gate, the heavens are opened to every believer.

Perhaps the most famous literary variant on this theme actually constitutes an ironic inversion of its contents. The third canto of Dante's *Inferno* – the first of the three books of his *Divine Comedy* – includes a famous description of the portal of hell, on which are inscribed the words *Lasciate ogni speranza voi ch'entrate* ("Abandon hope, all you who enter here"). Dante's description clearly assumes familiarity with the conventions of ecclesiastical architecture of the period, and playfully parodies its leading theme.

One particularly important function of church architecture is to stress the transcendence of God. The great soaring arches and spires of medieval cathedrals were intended to emphasize the greatness of God, and raise the thoughts of worshippers heavenwards. The symbolism is that of the eternal impinging upon the temporal, with the church building symbolizing the mediation between heaven and earth offered through the gospel. This emphasis on representing the transcendent here on earth is especially associated with the Gothic style of church architecture, which merits further discussion.

The term "Gothic" was coined in the sixteenth century by Giorgio Vasari to denote the style between Romanesque and Renaissance, characterized by pointed arches, extended door and window space, structural complexity, immense size, and (especially in northern Europe) large stained glass windows and sculptured doorways. (It is worth noting that Vasari intended the term to be pejorative, emphasizing associations with the barbarism of the Gothic tribes who destroyed Roman civilization.) The rise of Gothic architecture is usually traced back to the twelfth century, a period of relative political stability in western Europe which encouraged the rebirth of art and architecture. Within a period of a century (1130–1230) some twenty-five Gothic cathedrals were built in France. One of the most distinctive features of this architectural style is its deliberate and programmatic use of height and light to generate and sustain a sense of the presence of God and heaven on earth. The extensive use of buttresses allowed the weight of the building to be borne by outside supports, thus allowing the external walls to have large glass windows, which ensured that the building was saturated with the radiance of the sun. The use of stained glass helped generate an other-worldly brilliance within the cathedral, while simultaneously allowing gospel scenes to be depicted to worshippers. The use of tall, thin internal columns created an immense sense of spaciousness, again intended to evoke the hope of heaven. The cathedral thus became a sacred space, bringing the vast expansiveness and brilliance of heaven within the reach of believers. Worship there was seen as an anticipation of the life of heaven, allowing the worshipper to step into another world, to savor its delights, before returning to the dull routines of everyday life.

While it might be a little ambitious to speak of a coherent "theology of the Gothic cathedral," there can be no doubt of the spiritual aspirations of its designers and the importance of its sacred spaces in anticipating its heavenly counterparts. The theological significance of these tactile values is perhaps best explored by considering the ideas of Abbot Suger (1080–1151), who devoted much of his later life to the restoration of the abbey church of Saint-Denis, near Paris. This early example of the classic Gothic style embodies many of its characteristic emphases. Yet perhaps most importantly, Suger's three books of commentary on the renovation process allow us insights into both the physical process of construction and the spiritual and aesthetic principles which governed his design. The inscription he placed above the great bronze doors of the church point to his theological interpretation of the sense of radiance and spaciousness he had created within the building:

The work shines nobly,
but the work which shines nobly should clear minds,
so that they may travel through the true lights to the true light,
where Christ is the true door.

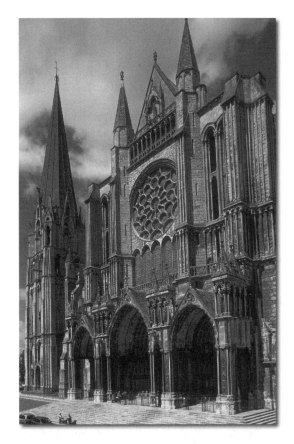

9.7 The south transept of the cathedral of Notre Dame de Chartres, one of the best examples of Gothic church architecture. The façade was completed in the mid-thirteenth century. AKG-Images/Archives CDA/St.-Genes.

The point being made is clear: Suger wants the human mind to be drawn upwards through the light of the building to the true light, who is the enthroned Christ in heaven.

While not all were persuaded by this theology of the church, which placed such emphasis upon the role of the church – considered both as institution and as physical structure – as guarantor and visualization of the hope of heaven, there is no doubting its massive impact upon the culture of the Middle Ages and beyond.

In addition to this emphasis on the transcendence of God, architecture reflects a concern to focus on what is deemed to be important by specific Christian groupings. Three such foci can be singled out.

1   Especially within Catholicism, the altar was selected for special attention, reflecting an emphasis upon the importance of the mass. Gregory the Great chose to erect an altar over the tomb of St. Peter, thus combining a focus on the "sacrament of the altar" with a veneration of the relics of saints.
2   Within the eastern Orthodox tradition, particular emphasis came to be placed on the iconostasis – that is, the stand on which icons were placed. In later Orthodox churches, the iconostasis became such a prominent feature that it in effect cut off the entire altar area from the sight of the laity. The icon placed upon the iconostasis thus assumed a much higher profile than the altar.
3   Within the Protestant tradition, the emphasis upon preaching led to the pulpit being elevated above the altar, both physically and in terms of the emphasis placed upon it. The distinguished Swiss reformed theologian Karl Barth notes how Reformed churches stress God's "otherness" through the design of churches and other liturgical means:.

> Preaching takes place from the pulpit (a place which by its awesome but obviously intended height differs from a podium), and on the pulpit, as a warning to those who ascend it, there is a big Bible. Preachers also wear a robe – I am not embarrassed to say this – and they should do so, for it is a salutary reminder that from those who wear this special garment, people expect a special word.

More recently, church architecture has come to be influenced by other factors. For example,

North American revivalism of the late nineteenth century saw worship partly in terms of entertainment, and thus designed church buildings with stages suitable for the performance of music and worship. The rise of "base ecclesial communities" or "house churches" has led to a new informality of worship, often within private homes or borrowed premises, in which the emphasis has been placed on fellowship, prayer, and worship, with architectural considerations being of minimal importance. For some, this can be regarded as a return to the earliest Christian practice, and is thus more authentic than later developments.

Stained glass

There are many points at which the Christian interest in church architecture and art forms converges – for example, the use of altarpieces to remind congregations of the reality of the sufferings of Jesus Christ on the cross as an aid to devotion. Yet it is widely agreed that the most distinctively Christian art form to be linked with the design of church buildings is the use of stained glass. Why did this take place? And what was its significance?

Early Christian buildings did not use stained glass. Windows were widely used, but were seen primarily as functional. They were necessary to allow light into the building. Wall paintings were commonly used to represent incidents in the life of Christ or the saints. They were intended to inspire devotion on the part of congregations. And if they were to do this, they needed to be seen. Windows allowed sunlight into the church building, so that these devotional aids could be properly viewed and appreciated. These windows were often quite narrow, and did not need to be filled with glass.

The origin of the stained glass window is lost in history. We know that it was in production, but on a very small scale, in the seventh century. St. Paul's church in Jarrow – the home of Bede, the great historian of English Christianity – still contains a very small round stained glass window, dating from the Anglo-Saxon period. To view this small window helps appreciate how the art form was developed on a much grander scale in later centuries.

The flourishing of the Gothic architectural style propelled stained glass design and technology into the forefront. Churches became taller and lighter, walls became thinner, and windows larger. They needed to be filled with glass. So why not use glass to create devotional images? Instead of seeing a window as a means of illuminating wall paintings, why not allow the window itself to represent biblical images?

The technology of creating stained glass windows was well established by the year 1100. Glass was colored during its manufacture, by adding metallic salts or oxides. The addition of gold produced a cranberry color, silver produced yellows and golds, while cobalt produced a deep blue, ideal for representing the heavens. Most of what is known about medieval stained-glass making comes from the book *On Diverse Arts* by a twelfth-century German monk known as Theophilus. An artist and metalworker himself, Theophilus described how he carefully studied glaziers and glass painters at work in order to provide detailed directions for creating windows of "inestimable beauty." He then provided precise instructions for the production of a stained glass window, which were followed meticulously throughout the Middle Ages.

If you want to assemble simple windows, first mark out the dimensions of their length and breadth on a wooden board, then draw scroll work or anything else that pleases you, and select colors that are to be inserted. Cut the glass, and fit the pieces together with the grouting iron. Enclose them with lead and solder on both sides. Surround it with a wooden frame strengthened with nails, and set it up in the place where you wish.

As windows became larger, more elaborate means of supporting windows were developed, making use of saddle bars.

In France, the best early exemplars of Gothic stained glass are to be found in the north of France in the church of Saint Denis (founded 1144), and the cathedrals of Chartres (1150), Laôn (1160), Notre Dame de Paris, (1163), Reims (1211), and Amiens (1220). All are graced by spectacular stained glass windows. Several of these are circular, and are known as "rose windows." Of these, the best is probably the great cathedral of Chartres, which has 152 of its original windows still intact, including the three great rose windows, which date from around 1200. Other important examples include the cathedral of Évora in Portugal (founded 1186), Canterbury cathedral, and York Minster (the largest Gothic cathedral in northern Europe).

From 1550 to 1850, stained glass came to be seen as unsophisticated by many artists. New technology allowed glass to be painted, opening up new possibilities. Instead of assembling tiny fragments of stained glass to produce a picture, it was possible to paint directly onto glass. Many medieval stained glass windows were removed from churches and replaced with the new painted forms. The revival of stained glass as an ecclesiastical art form dates from the second half of the nineteenth century, and is especially associated with the pre-Raphaelite movement. Perhaps the best example is found in the three windows by Sir Edward Burne-Jones, "Hope, Charity, and Faith," designed for St. Martin's Church in Brampton, Cumbria, and manufactured by William Morris' workshop. This unique pre-Raphaelite church was built in 1889 according to a design by the architect Philip Webb.

9.8   The great rose window above the main portal of the cathedral of Notre Dame, Strasbourg, France, one of the finest examples of stained glass in Europe. AKG-Images/Hedda Eid.

9.9   A panel from one of the stained glass windows in the Sainte-Chapelle, Paris, built 1243–1248 by Pierre de Montreuil. The thirteenth-century windows, which illustrate scenes from the Old and New Testaments, are remarkable for the vitality of the characters they depict. AKG-Images/Joseph Martin.

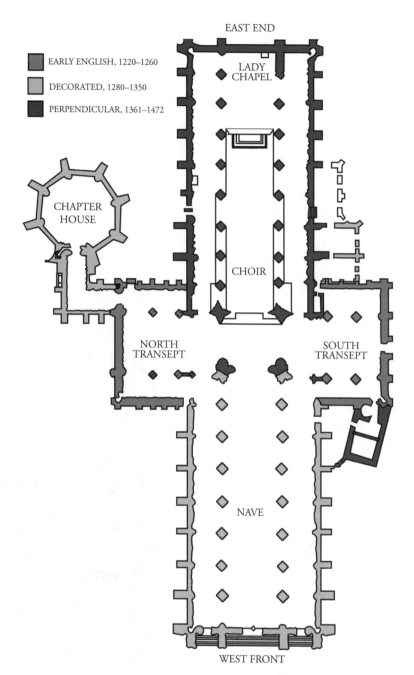

9.10 Ground plan of York Minster, one of the greatest Gothic cathedrals of Europe. Note especially its cruciform structure. © The Dean and Chapter of York.

Icons

The use of icons in public worship and private devotion, though especially associated with eastern Orthodoxy, is now widespread within Christianity. An "icon" (derived from the Greek word *eikon*, "image") has come to mean a portable, sacred image, typically painted on a wooden base, following the traditions and conventions of Byzantine art.

The history of the use of icons is somewhat unclear. However, there is substantial evidence to indicate that the use of such sacred images originated in the region of Palestine and Syria. It seems that the first icons were pictures of martyrs, often illustrating aspects of their histories. The homilies of eastern Christian writers of the fourth century – such as Basil the Great and Gregory of Nyssa – are an important witness to this practice. However, from the fifth century onwards, it became increasingly common for icons to depict Jesus Christ and Mary.

The iconoclast controversy led to a hiatus in the production of icons, and the destruction of many older icons. While Orthodox writers conceded that the Old Testament prohibited the production and use of religious images, they argued that this was an essentially temporary provision, reflecting the widespread use of idols in Canaanite culture. With the defeat of Roman paganism through the conversion of Constantine, Orthodox theologians argued that this was no longer a significant issue. Furthermore, they pointed out that the incarnation of the Son of God further undermined this Old Testament prohibition: was not Jesus the image of God, displayed to humanity? The resolution of this question in favor of the "iconophiles" led to a golden age of iconography, based at Constantinople from about 850 to 1200. During this time, a special style of icon-painting developed, and became characteristic of Byzantine art.

So what are icons understood to achieve? What is their purpose? Orthodox Christian writers emphatically reject what they regard as two serious misunderstandings: that icons are themselves objects of worship, and that they are merely a form of religious art whose significance lies in beautifying religious sites. (Frescoes in the Roman catacombs, dating from the second and third centuries, seem to have been executed with this objective in mind.)

To turn to the first misunderstanding. For Orthodoxy, icons are not the object of adoration or worship, which is proper alone to Christ or God; they are the object of veneration.

9.11 Byzantine icon of the late thirteenth or early fourteenth century, showing Mary with the infant Jesus. Venice, Galleria dell' Accademia, AKG-Images/Cameraphoto.

Furthermore, this veneration is derivative rather than direct. In other words, the respect shown to an icon is – as Basil the Great put it – "passed on to the one who is represented by it."

In the case of the second misunderstanding, Orthodoxy holds that icons are windows to the transcendent. They can be thought of as a "visible gospel," proclaiming the same truths as Scripture, yet in a pictorial rather than verbal form. Thus Nicephorus, patriarch of Constantinople (806–815), considered that icons are especially significant for those who lack the conceptual skills to understand Scripture. Indeed, very often what eludes people when reading or hearing words is captured when viewing icons.

Image and word are thus not seen to be in conflict but offer the possibility of mutual reinforcement. Orthodox writers tend to speak about the "scriptural vision" and the "pictorial formation" as the two symbolic ways through which humanity gains access to transcendent realities. Where the iconoclasts argued that the "uninstructed and illiterate" would be unable to distinguish the image and the divine reality it depicted (hence lapsing into idolatry), the iconophiles held that these same people could use icons as "Scripture in color" to lead them to the divine reality – if they were properly instructed in how to use them.

Christian music

The richness of Christian worship inevitably led to the adoption of all kinds of musical styles in the life of the Christian church. Although early Christian writers were hesitant over the use of music in worship, fearing that it would paganize what was a thoroughly Christian occasion, the value of music as an aid to Christian devotion was soon realized.

The most important early use of music can be traced back to the use of certain set forms of words, usually derived from the Bible, for monastic services (often known as "offices") – for example, the *Magnificat* ("My soul magnifies the Lord") at the early evening office of Vespers, and the *Nunc Dimittis* ("Lord, now allow your servant to depart in peace"), set for the late evening office of Compline. Each of these set pieces is known by its opening words in Latin. It was not long before plainsong was introduced as a means of permitting these central texts to be sung, rather than just recited. The form of chanting which is probably best known in the modern world is "Gregorian chant," which is readily available in high-quality modern recordings, often made in monastic settings.

Gradually, the patterns became more complex and ornate, with increasingly complicated musical forms being used to express the various emotions associated with the biblical passages being sung. Among the most important hymns set to music in this way, the following should be noted:

- *Te lucis ante terminum* ("To you before the ending of the day"), a hymn sung at Compline, in which believers commit themselves to the care of God during the hours of darkness.
- *Pange lingua gloriosa* ("Now, my tongue, the glorious mystery proclaiming"), a medieval hymn, often ascribed to Thomas Aquinas, which explains the meaning of the communion service. It was often used on Maundy Thursday (see p. 309).
- *Puer natus* ("A boy is born"), a short hymn sung at the entry of the choir, celebrating the birth of Jesus.

With the Reformation, controversy developed over the role of music. Zwingli and Calvin did not regard music as having a proper place in Christian worship. In other Protestant traditions, however, music continued to play an important role. Martin Luther composed settings for a number of traditional hymns, as well as writing hymns of his own. The most famous of these is *Ein feste Burg ist unsere Gott* ("A safe stronghold is our God"), which remains widely used in modern Protestant church life, particlarly in Lutheranism. The Church of England encouraged the setting of the Psalms and other canticles as chants.

The most dynamic form of musical development within Protestantism was due to the rise of Methodism, with John and Charles Wesley both recognizing the enormous potential of hymns to convey Christian teachings. Charles Wesley pioneered the use of "borrowing" secular tunes for Christian purposes. For example, the English composer Henry Purcell had written a superb tune to accompany John Dryden's text praising England, entitled "Fairest isle, all isles excelling." Wesley altered the words to reflect Christian interests, but retained Purcell's operatic tune, resulting in the well-known hymn "Love divine, all loves excelling." Perhaps the most well known of all Protestant musical pieces is Handel's *Messiah*, which sets to music a series of biblical texts focusing on the coming of Jesus and his subsequent glorification.

The most important musical developments within western Christianity, however, are linked with Catholicism. The great cathedrals of Europe demanded increasingly sophisticated and prestigious musical settings of standard Catholic liturgical texts. Of these, the most important were the texts of the mass and the requiem. Virtually every major European composer contributed to the development of church music. Monteverdi, Haydn, Mozart, Beethoven, Rossini, and Verdi are all examples of composers to have made significant contributions in this sphere. The Catholic church was without question one of the most important patrons of musical developments, and a crucial stimulus to the development of the western musical tradition.

Music continues to be an integral part of modern Christian life. The classics of the past continue to find service in modern Christian worship. However, it is clear that more popular styles of music are having an increasing influence on Christian worship, especially in evangelical and charismatic congregations.

Christianity and literature

"The church, as a body, has never made up her mind about the Arts." Thus wrote Dorothy L. Sayers, herself an important contributor to the shaping of Christian literature in the twentieth century. There can be no doubt that she is correct in her judgment. Some Christian writers have adopted strongly positive attitudes to literature, seeing it as a powerful ally

9.12 J. S. Bach, 1746, by Elias Gottlob Haussmann. AKG-Images/Erich Lessing.

in the quest to foster the Christian vision and interact with the world. Others have regarded literature as alien to the Christian faith, with a potential to mislead.

One of the most important debates in the early church concerned the extent to which Christians could appropriate the immense cultural legacy of the classical world – poetry, philosophy, and literature. In what way can the *ars poetica* be adopted by Christian writers, anxious to use such classical modes of writing to expound and communicate their faith? Or was the very use of such a literary medium tantamount to compromising the essentials of the Christian faith? It was a debate of immense significance, as it raised the question of whether Christianity would turn its back on the classical heritage or appropriate it, even if in a modified form.

In the early period of the Christian church, a critical and hostile attitude towards contemporary pagan culture – including its literature – tended to prevail. This attitude can be argued to be rooted in Paul's insistence that Christians should avoid compromising their faith through inappropriate adoption of worldly attitudes and viewpoints. "What do righteousness and wickedness have in common? Or what fellowship can light have with darkness? What harmony is there between Christ and Belial? What does a believer have in common with an unbeliever?" (2 Corinthians 6:14–15). Yet Paul himself shows a clear familiarity with classic literature and poetry. He appeals to the authority of Cleanthes, Aratus, and Epimenides in a speech delivered at the Areopagus in Athens (Acts 17:28). He cites from the native Cretan poet Epimenides when commenting on the moral state of the inhabitants of Crete (Titus 1:12–13). Allusions to Homer, Plato, and Menander can be found elsewhere in his writings.

Yet the classical culture which helped shape early Christian attitudes to literature was itself uncertain as to literature's precise role. Plato deliberately excluded poets from his ideal republic, an attitude warmly commended by Augustine. For Augustine, the poets "composed fictions with no regard to the truth or set the worst possible examples before wretched people under the pretense that they were divine actions." Yet the rhetorical skills developed by Aristotle and others were recognized as important means of enhancing the effectiveness of communication. There are many points in Paul's speeches, as recorded in the Acts of the Apostles, where a positive influence of Hellenistic rhetoric has been observed. It is therefore no cause for surprise that early Christian attitudes to literature are complex, nuanced, and difficult to characterize. Writers such as Tertullian and Chrysostom were intensely suspicious of Greek and Latin literature, and sought to minimize its importance and influence within the church; Jerome and Augustine were considerably more positive, even though they shared some of the anxieties voiced elsewhere.

At many points, literature was seen by Christian apologists as a means of further enhancing the appeal of their faith to the wider world. Might not the obvious attractions of the gospel be augmented if it were to be presented in words of beauty and power, in which theological precision was supplemented by the lyricism of poetry and the rhetoric of prose? Gravity of form and sublimity of expression in an argument could assist in both the communication and commendation of its substance. The anonymous *Cursor Mundi*, written about 1300, argues along such lines when it suggests that, since people enjoy reading secular literature so much, it makes sense to present religious truth in literary forms. In this way, a work of religious literature will result which will both be a delight to read and nourish the human soul. Yet the tension which this approach generated can be seen from other works of this period. For example, Geoffrey Chaucer concludes his *Canterbury Tales* with a "retraction," in which he asks his readers to forgive him for his "translations and compositions of worldly vanity."

The implication is clear; works of literature are potentially vain, whereas purely religious works, written for the purpose of doctrinal and ethical instruction, are acceptable. Chaucer's obvious concern at this point raises the question of whether the notion of "Christian literature" is inherently indefensible, in that the desire to please and amuse is potentially in tension with the seriousness of Christian doctrine and ethics. This is certainly the view that we find in the noted Puritan writer Richard Baxter, who argued that literature encouraged its readers to waste their time in recreation when they could be doing something more productive, and that it possessed a disquieting potential to be morally corrupting. Baxter's most severe criticism was directed against works of fiction, which he held to actively promote a culture of falsehood which "dangerously bewitcheth and corrupteth the minds of young and empty people."

One manner of reconciling this tension was known throughout Christian history, and became of especial importance during the Romantic period. The language of literature, it was argued, served to elevate its readers, and inspire them to devotion and passion. Was not this sufficient justification for a religious literature? In his *Preface* to the *Lyrical Ballads*, William Wordsworth complained of the "frantic novels, sickly and stupid German Tragedies, and deluges of idle and extravagant stories in verse" by which his age had been seduced, and urged a recovery of the language and concerns of writers such as Shakespeare and Milton. For Wordsworth himself, there was an obvious affinity between religion and poetry; indeed, Wordsworth's literature increasingly adopted the characteristics of religion. This develop-

ment is of particular importance to the development of seeing the Bible as literature. For Percy Bysshe Shelley, the Bible is revered on account of its literary character, rather than the religious views which it propounded.

Yet it must not be assumed that a Christian interest in literature was a purely pragmatic consequence of a desire for church growth and a consolidation of religious faith. From the outset, Christian writers have found the notion of "God as author" as offering a substantial theological foundation and encouragement for the writing of literature. In the beginning, God created through God's word, spoken over the face of chaos. Did this not point to the critical role of words in the Christian understanding of the world? And was there not the most natural of connections between the verbal origins of the world and a concern with words, revelation, texts, literature, and reading and writing? The production of Christian literature was thus seen by some as resting upon rigorous theological foundations, rather than being opportunistic.

But this raises the difficult question of precisely what is to be understood by "Christian literature." Although this continues to be debated, there is at least some agreement on the categories of writing that deserve to be included. These writings fall into three broad types:

1 Works of literature which are specifically written to serve the needs of Christians or the church as an institution – such as prayers, devotional works, and sermons. The Christian faith has given rise to certain specific forms of writing, which Christians have sought to develop to the highest standards of cultural excellence. These works are a response to the nature of the Christian faith, and can be seen as both responding to the needs of that faith and expressing its nature.

2 Works of literature in general – such as stories and poems – which are not specific to the Christian faith, but which have been shaped or influenced by Christian ideas, values, images, and narratives. Christian poetry, in particular, reflects a quite distinct set of ideas and images, and it is important to appreciate the way in which these are reflected or assimilated in such writings. Although most Christian literature is written by Christians, it is important to note that there are many examples of writings which have unquestionably been shaped by Christian influences, even though their writers would not regard themselves as Christians. The lyrical ballads of both William Wordsworth and Samuel Taylor Coleridge might be included within this category.

3 Works of literature which involve interaction with Christian ideas, individuals, schools of thought, or institutions, often written by those who would regard themselves as observers or critics of Christianity. George Eliot or Thomas Hardy fall within this category. Here, the influence of Christianity is evident, at least through the subject matter of the writing itself. Yet even the mode of criticism itself often reflects a subtle appropriation, development, or modification of Christian assumptions – such as an assumption concerning what Christianity *ought* to be, which is then contrasted with what is observed through experience.

It lies beyond the scope of this brief discussion to offer a detailed analysis of the nature and development of Christian literature. However, something of its scope can be appreciated by considering some representative examples of the field – such as Dante's *Divine Comedy*, the devotional religious poems of George Herbert, the more metaphysical religious poems of T. S. Eliot, and the works of the twentieth-century literary critic and novelist C. S. Lewis.

Dante Alighieri (1265–1321) was born into a well-established family in the city of Florence, and became embroiled in the complex world of Florentine politics. Florence had been severely disrupted by a political crisis in 1293, which had seen the traditional power of the established families shaken by a rising mercantile class. Alongside this tension between established families and the rising middle classes there remained serious tensions between two such families – the Guelfs and Ghibellines – compounded by divisions within the Guelfs, which led to acrimonious infighting between sections of that family. In such a convoluted and politically unstable situation, it was easy to take a wrong step. Dante was unwise enough to ally himself with the wrong faction within the Guelf family. Realizing that his situation was untenable, he fled the city in October 1301. He was initially exiled and then condemned to death in his absence by the Florentine courts.

Exile was an established way of life in the world of the Italian city-states, and Dante would hardly have been alone in his situation. Although it is virtually impossible to be sure what happened to Dante after his departure from Florence in 1301, it is entirely possible that he was able to secure some kind of patronage from the Ghibelline family in another part of Italy, away from his native Tuscany. What we do know is that his exile from Tuscany was of momentous importance to his understanding of his own destiny, and that he regarded it as a turning point in his life. It was at this stage that he conceived and began to write the major work which we now know as the *Divine Comedy*.

The *Divine Comedy*, a vernacular poem in 100 cantos (more than 14,000 lines), was composed during this period of exile. It is the tale of the poet's journey through Hell and

Purgatory and hence to Paradise. Written in a complex pentameter form known as "terza rima," it is a magnificent synthesis of the medieval theological outlook, depicting a changeless universe ordered by God. The title is perhaps misleading to modern readers, in that the term "comedy" implies something amusing or funny. The Italian term *commedia* is better translated as "drama." The term "divine" appears to have been added by a Venetian publisher at a later stage.

The *Divine Comedy* takes the form of three major interconnected poems, respectively entitled *Inferno* ("Hell"), *Purgatorio* ("Purgatory"), and *Paradiso* ("Paradise"). The work makes substantial use of the leading themes of Christian theology and spirituality, while at the same time including comment on contemporary political and social events. The poem describes a journey which takes place in Holy Week 1300 – before Dante's exile from Florence. From the substantial number of clues in the text, it can be worked out that the journey begins at nightfall on Good Friday. After entering Hell, Dante journeys downwards for an entire day, before beginning his ascent towards Purgatory. After climbing Mount Purgatory, Dante rises further until he eventually enters into the presence of God.

Throughout the journey, Dante is accompanied by guides. The first guide is Virgil, the great Roman poet who wrote the *Aeneid*. It is widely thought that Dante uses Virgil as a symbol of classic learning and human reason. As they draw close to the peak of Mount Purgatory, Virgil falls behind, and Dante finds himself in the company of Beatrice, who leads him through the outer circles of Heaven. Finally, he is joined by Bernard of Clairvaux, who leads Dante into the presence of God – the "love which moves the sun and the other stars."

The structure of the poem is immensely intricate, and it can be read at a number of levels. It can, for example, be read as a commentary on medieval Italian politics, particularly the intricacies of Florentine politics over the period 1300–1304; or it can be seen as a poetic guide to Christian beliefs concerning the afterlife. More fundamentally, it can be read as a journey of self-discovery and spiritual enlightenment, in which the poet finally discovers and encounters his heart's desire.

The devotional poet George Herbert (1593–1633) was elected as a fellow of Trinity College in 1614, and was appointed Public Orator at Cambridge University six years later. This position required him to make public speeches on major university occasions, using the rather florid academic Latin of the period. While there is little doubt that Herbert could have used this prestigious position as a stepping-stone to high political office, he chose not to do so. It is possible that the death of James I in 1625 may have caused him to reconsider his future ambitions; it is also highly likely that the personal influence of Nicholas Ferrar led him to study divinity. He thus gave up his secular ambitions, took holy orders in the Church of England in 1630, and spent the rest of his life as rector of the parish of Fugglestone with Bemerton near Salisbury.

Herbert's poems are characterized by a precision of language, a metrical versatility, and an ingenious use of imagery or "conceits" that was favored by the metaphysical school of poets. They include almost every known form of song and poem, but they also reflect Herbert's concern with speech – conversational, persuasive, proverbial. Carefully arranged in related sequences, the poems explore and celebrate the ways of God's love as Herbert discovered them within the fluctuations of his own personal experience.

Yet Herbert must be seen as an "ecclesiastical" rather than just a "religious" poet. His writings concern the rhythms of the church year as much as his personal religious experiences. Although Herbert was strongly Anglican in his outlook, his religious poetry won admirers across the entire religious spectrum. For example, it was read and admired by Charles I before his execution, as it was by Oliver Cromwell's personal chaplain. John Donne may be the greatest of the metaphysical poets; Herbert, however, is widely regarded as supreme among the English devotional poets.

Although Herbert is remembered primarily as a poet, his literary activities were by no means restricted to this genre. One of his most famous works of prose is *A Priest to the Temple; or the Country Parson* (1652). This is probably best seen as a Baconian manual of practical advice to country parsons, which bears witness to both the intelligence and devotion which he brought to his responsibilities as the rector of Fugglestone with Bemerton. Its elegance of style has been much admired, making its inclusion in this collection essential.

Thomas Stearns Eliot (1888–1965) rose to fame primarily on account of his poem *The Waste Land* (1922). Although Eliot would later establish a reputation as a literary critic as much as a poet, this early work was widely seen as a manifesto of "modernism" in English literature, making a deliberate and conscious break with the past. That Eliot had developed a religious agenda became clear when he was baptized into the Church of England on June 29, 1927. In the early years of his first marriage, Eliot would visit churches to admire their beauty; in later years, he visited them for the sake of peace, contemplation, and spiritual refreshment. In 1926, while visiting Rome with his brother and sister-in-law, Eliot caused considerable surprise by kneeling before Michelango's *Pietà*. His biographers have suggested that Eliot had a sense of tradition and an instinct for order within himself and found the church and faith gave him this security within a life of frustrations and struggles. Perhaps Eliot's awareness of what he came to term "the void" in all human affairs led him to look for a framework of meaning which allowed him both to understand and to endure the disorder, meaninglessness, and futility which he found in his own experience.

His poems now began to include explicitly religious themes, even in their titles – such as "Ash-Wednesday" (1930), "A Song for Simeon" (1928), and "The Visit of the Magi" (1927). Eliot's Christian concerns are perhaps best seen in *The Four Quartets* (1943), which are regularly cited in sermons and works of popular Christian theology and spirituality. Eliot was awarded the Nobel Prize for Literature in 1948, and died in London in 1965.

C. S. Lewis (1898–1963) is widely agreed to be one of the most engaging and accessible Christian writers of the twentieth century. Originally an atheist, Lewis found his attitude to Christianity undergoing a dramatic change in the 1920s. The story of his return to the faith he abandoned as a boy is described in great detail in his autobiography, *Surprised by Joy*. After wrestling with the clues concerning God he found in human reason and experience, he eventually decided that intellectual honesty compelled him to believe and trust in God.

After his conversion, Lewis began to establish his reputation as a leading authority on medieval and Renaissance English literature. *The Allegory of Love*, published in 1936, is still regarded as a masterpiece, as is his *Preface to Paradise Lost*. Alongside his scholarly writings, however, Lewis wrote books of a very different nature. Aiming at clarity and conviction, Lewis produced a series of works aimed at communicating the reasonableness of Christianity to his own generation. The works brought him popular acclaim, but seemed to some to destroy his scholarly reputation. This was especially the case with *The Screwtape*

Letters, which alienated many of his academic colleagues on account of their "populist" or "vulgar" tone. In 1946, he was passed over for the Merton professorship of English Literature at Oxford.

Lewis' first popular book was *The Pilgrim's Regress*, based loosely on John Bunyan's *Pilgrim's Progress*. It was not a great publishing success. Nevertheless, Lewis continued writing at this popular level. *The Problem of Pain*, which appeared in 1940, was well received, and on the basis of its clarity and intelligence of argument, Lewis was invited to give a series of radio talks by the British Broadcasting Corporation. In 1942, these talks were published as *The Case for Christianity*. Such was their success that Lewis combined them with two other short works – *Christian Behaviour* (1943) and *Beyond Personality* (1944) – to yield the composite work *Mere Christianity*. The year 1942 also saw the publication of *The Screwtape Letters*, whose wit and insight firmly established Lewis' reputation as a leading defender of the Christian faith, at the cost of estranging many of his academic colleagues.

A significant part of his reputation as a Christian writer rests on his Narnia chronicles. The first novel in the series was published in 1950. *The Lion, the Witch and the Wardrobe* introduces its readers to the land of Narnia, which is discovered by four English children (Peter, Susan, Edmund, and Lucy) at the back of a seemingly ordinary wardrobe. The series ended in 1956, with the publication of *The Last Battle*. The series can be seen as standing in the "fairy-tale" tradition established by George MacDonald in the nineteenth century. Its success did much to publicize Lewis' notion of "the baptized imagination," which emphasized the importance of the human imagination in grasping and appreciating the essence of the Christian faith. As Lewis once pointed out, "while reason is the natural organ of truth, imagination is the organ of meaning."

Pilgrimage and the Christian life

Many Christian traditions ascribe particular spiritual importance to certain places, or the process of traveling to these. Once more, it is necessary to note that this is not a uniform tendency within Christianity. While immediately conceding the dangers of generalization, it seems that Protestantism has usually been more critical than affirmative of the notion of a "holy place." In the present section, we shall explore some aspects of this notion of "holy places," and their significance for spirituality.

The Old Testament clearly regarded the city of Jerusalem as a holy place. Jerusalem and its temple were seen as the central focus of the religion of Israel. God had chosen Jerusalem as a dwelling-place, and the city and its temple were thus set apart as possessing a religious significance denied to other locations in Israel. Earlier in Israel's history, sites such as Shiloh and Mizpah were seen as being of especial religious importance. It was at these sites that shrines were established during the period of the conquest of Canaan. Nevertheless, the temple erected at Jerusalem came to be seen as possessing supreme significance. Some Old Testament passages spoke of Jerusalem or its temple as the "dwelling place" of God. As a result, Jerusalem came to play a special role in Israel's hopes for the future. It was from Jerusalem that the knowledge of God was to spread to all nations (Isaiah 2:2–4; Micah 4:1–3). It was by worshipping God in Jerusalem that the nations of the world would find their true unity (Isaiah 19:23; Zechariah 8:3). The modern Jewish Passover ends with the expression of the hope that, next year, the Passover will be celebrated in Jerusalem.

It is therefore clear that Jerusalem came to play a special role in Judaism. In that the central events upon which the Christian faith is founded – supremely, the death and resurrection of Jesus – took place in Jerusalem, it might therefore be expected that the New Testament should take over this Old Testament understanding of the special place of the city. This, however, proves not to be the case. The special sacred status of Jerusalem within the Old Testament is not endorsed by the New Testament, which affirms the historical *but not the theological* importance of Jerusalem. The theme of the "new Jerusalem" is certainly found, as a statement of the Christian hope (see Hebrews 12:22; Revelation 21:2). Yet this is not seen as legitimizing any present spiritual significance for the city of Jerusalem.

The significance of Jerusalem is not discussed in any detail by Christian writers of the first three centuries, in itself an indication that this was not seen as being of crucial importance. Two very different views emerge in the fourth century. Eusebius of Caesarea (ca. 260–339) argued that the spirtuality of the New Testament was concerned not with physical entities (such as the "land of Israel" or the "city of Jerusalem") but with spiritual matters, of which these physical entities were at best convenient physical symbols. Cyril of Jerusalem (ca. 320–386), in contrast, was quite clear that Jerusalem remained a "holy city." It is, of course, entirely possible that ecclesiastical politics may have entered into this debate. Cyril was anxious to maintain the prestige of his own city; Eusebius was interested in promoting the claims of Rome as the new city to be granted special divine favor.

An important document dating from this period, which illustrates the spiritual importance of pilgrimage, is known as the "Peregrinatio" or "Pilgrimage of Egeria." This document, discovered in 1884 and probably dating from 381–384, is in effect the personal journal of a woman visiting the Holy Land and recording all that she observes. Although the text is often read for its important first-hand testimony concerning liturgical practices in

the Holy Land at this time, it is also a vital witness to the benefits that such pilgrimages were understood to bring.

In the course of Christian history, a number of sites have emerged as having potential spiritual importance. These include (but are by no means limited to) the following.

- Jerusalem, the scene of the last supper, betrayal, crucifixion, and resurrection of Jesus.
- Rome, widely believed to be the site of the martyrdom and burial of both St. Peter and St. Paul.
- Canterbury, the site of the martyrdom of Thomas à Becket in 1170. The bawdy escapades accompanying pilgrimages to Canterbury were set out by Geoffrey Chaucer in his *Canterbury Tales*.
- Santiago de Compostela, in northwestern Spain, the traditional burial place of St. James the Apostle.
- Lourdes, in southern France, the site of a vision of the Virgin Mary in 1858, which has become associated with reports of healings.

What role do pilgrimages to such sites play in Christian spirituality? Clearly, the answer to such questions will be complex and nuanced, given the considerable variation within Christianity concerning issues of theology. For example, Protestants generally do not accept any kind of "theology of sacred places," and would not give any particular place of honor to Mary. Pilgrimages to Lourdes, therefore, do not feature prominently in Protestant spirituality. In general, it is thought that the following factors are of crucial importance in relation to a spirituality of pilgrimage.

1 The act of making a pilgrimage involves at least a degree of commitment and hardship. This makes a pilgrimage an act of

THE LIFE OF FAITH

9.13 Santiago de Compostela. AKG-Images/ Andrea Jemolo.

self-denial or personal discipline, the virtues of which would be widely accepted. The degree of hardship can be enhanced in various ways: for example, medieval penitents were in the habit of placing small stones inside their shoes to make the journey more painful.

2 The pilgrimage offers an opportunity to reflect on the life and teaching of the person who is associated with the pilgrimage site. For example, a pilgrimage to Santiago de Compostela offers an opportunity to read about St. James, just as a pilgrimage to Rome can be the focus for reflection on the life and teaching of both St. Peter and St. Paul.

3 The notion of "pilgrimage" helps reinforce the Christian idea that believers are "strangers and pilgrims on earth"

(Hebrews 11:13), whose true home is a city in heaven (Philippians 3:20). The idea of passing through life en route to the heavenly city, rather than making oneself at home in the world, is clearly embodied in the act of pilgrimage.

4 For some, the sites of pilgrimage are themselves endued with some spiritual quality, which can be experienced by those who travel there..

As was noted above, Protestants generally regard the notion of "pilgrimage" with suspicion. However, it is important to appreciate that the idea is present, although in a slightly redirected manner, within many Protestant spiritualities. Many Protestants find it helpful to make journeys to the Holy Land or sites of relevance to the New Testament – for example, the seven churches of Asia (mentioned in the book of Revelation) or the churches established by or written to by St. Paul. These journeys are seen, however, primarily as bringing a new depth to Bible study, in that biblical passages take on a new personal significance through a visit to the site in question. Visiting religious sites is thus seen as an aid to more effective Bible study.

The image of "pilgrimage" gained new importance through the Second Vatican Council's use of the idea as a model of the church. The *Dogmatic Constitution of the Church* comments as follows on the place of the church in the world:

Already the final age of the world is with us (cf. 1 Corinthians 10:11) and the renewal of the world is irrevocably under way – it is even now anticipated in a certain real way, for the Church on earth is endowed already with a sanctity that is real though imperfect. However, until there be realized new heavens and a new earth in which justice dwells (cf. 2 Peter 3:13) the pilgrim Church, in its sacraments and institutions, which belong to this present age, carries the mark of this world which will pass, and she herself takes her place among the creatures which groan and travail yet and await the revelation of the sons of God (cf. Romans 8:19–22).

This brief survey of the complex and rich shape of Christian life in today's world brings to an end this introduction to Christianity. Restric-tions on space have severely limited the amount of material which has been presented. However, it is hoped that what has been in-cluded will enable you to gain a deeper under-standing and appreciation of the most influential religious movement in today's world. If this introduction has left you feeling that you would like to know more, it will have served its purpose.

A Glossary of Christian Terms

W hat follows is a brief discussion of a series of techical terms relating to Christianity that the reader is likely to encounter in the course of reading. The following work is particularly recommended to those wishing to gain more detailed understanding of Christian terms:

Livingstone, Elizabeth A., and F. L. Cross, *The Oxford Dictionary of the Christian Church*, 3rd edn (Oxford: Oxford University Press, 1997).

Adoptionism The heretical view that Jesus was "adopted" as the Son of God at some point during his ministry (usually his baptism), as opposed to the orthodox teaching that Jesus was Son of God by nature from the moment of his conception.

Alexandrian School A patristic school of thought, especially associated with the city of Alexandria in Egypt, noted for its Christology (which placed emphasis upon the divinity of Christ) and its method of biblical interpretation (which employed allegorical methods of exegesis). A rival approach in both areas was associated with Antioch.

Anabaptism A term derived from the Greek word for "rebaptizer" and used to refer to the radical wing of the sixteenth-century Reformation, based on thinkers such as Menno Simons or Balthasar Hubmaier.

Analogy of being (*analogia entis*) The theory, especially associated with Thomas Aquinas, that there exists a correspondence or analogy between the created order and God, as a result of the divine creatorship. The idea gives theoretical justification to the practice of drawing conclusions from the known objects and relationships of the natural order concerning God.

Analogy of faith (*analogia fidei*) The theory, especially associated with Karl Barth, which holds that any correspondence between the created order and God is only established on the basis of the self-revelation of God.

Anthropomorphism The tendency to ascribe human features (such as hands or arms) or other human characteristics to God.

Antiochene School A patristic school of thought, especially associated with the city of Antioch in modern-day Turkey, noted for its Christology (which placed emphasis upon the humanity of Christ) and its method of biblical interpretation (which employed literal methods of exegesis). A rival approach in both areas was associated with Alexandria.

Anti-Pelagian writings The writings of Augustine relating to the Pelagian controversy, in which he defended his views on grace and justification. See **Pelagianism**.

Apocalyptic A type of writing or religious outlook in general which focuses on the last things and the end of the world, often taking the form of visions with complex symbolism. The book of Daniel (Old Testament) and Revelation (New Testament) are examples of this type of writing.

Apologetics The area of Christian theology which focuses on the defense of the Christian faith, particularly through the rational justification of Christian belief and doctrines.

Apophatic A term used to refer to a particular style of theology, which stressed that God cannot be known in terms of human categories. "Apophatic" (which derives from the Greek *apophasis*, "negation" or "denial") approaches to theology are especially associated with the monastic tradition of the eastern Orthodox church.

Apostolic era The period of the Christian church, regarded as definitive by many, bounded by the resurrection of Jesus Christ (ca. AD 35) and the death of the last apostle (ca. AD 90?). The ideas and practices of this period were widely regarded as normative, at least in some sense or to some degree, in many church circles.

Appropriation A term relating to the doctrine of the Trinity, which affirms that while all three persons of the Trinity are active in all the outward actions of the Trinity, it is appropriate to think of those actions as being the particular work of one of the persons. Thus it is appropriate to think of creation as the work of the Father, or redemption as the work of the Son, despite the fact that all three persons are present and active in both these works.

Arianism A major early Christological heresy, which treated Jesus Christ as the supreme of God's creatures, and denied his divine status. The Arian controversy was of crucial importance in the development of Christology during the fourth century.

Atonement An English term originally coined by William Tyndale to translate the Latin term *reconciliatio*, which has since come to have the developed meaning of "the work of Christ" or "the benefits of Christ gained for believers by his death and resurrection."

Barthian An adjective used to describe the theological outlook of the Swiss theologian Karl Barth (1886–1968), and noted chiefly for its emphasis upon the priority of revelation and its focus upon Jesus Christ. The terms "neo-orthodoxy" and "dialectical theology" are also used in this connection.

Beatific vision A term used, especially in Roman Catholic theology, to refer to the full vision of God, which is allowed only to the elect after death. However, some writers, including Thomas Aquinas, taught that certain favored individuals – such as Moses and Paul – were allowed this vision in the present life.

Calvinism An ambiguous term, used with two quite distinct meanings. First, it refers to the religious ideas of religious bodies (such as the Reformed church) and individuals (such as Theodore Beza) who were profoundly influenced by John Calvin (1510–1564), or by documents written by him. Second, it refers to the religious ideas of John Calvin himself. Although the first sense is by far the more common, there is a growing recognition that the term is misleading.

Cappadocian fathers A term used to refer collectively to three major Greek-speaking writers of the patristic period: Basil of Caesarea, Gregory of Nazianzen, and Gregory of Nyssa, all of whom date from the late fourth century. "Cappadocia" designates an area in Asia Minor (modern-day Turkey), in which these writers were based.

Cartesianism The philosophical outlook especially associated with René Descartes (1596–1650), particularly in relation to its emphasis on the separation of the knower from the known, and its insistence that the existence of the individual thinking self is the proper starting point for philosophical reflection.

Catechism A popular manual of Christian doctrine, usually in the form of question and answer, intended for religious instruction.

Catholic An adjective which is used to refer both to the universality of the church in space and time, and to a particular church body (sometimes also known as the Roman Catholic church) which lays emphasis upon this point.

Chalcedonian definition The formal declaration at the Council of Chalcedon that Jesus Christ was to be regarded as having two natures, one human and one divine.

Charisma, charismatic A set of terms especially associated with the gifts of the Holy Spirit. In medieval theology, the term "charisma" is used to designate a spiritual gift, conferred upon individuals by the grace of God. Since the early twentieth century, the term "charismatic" has come to refer to styles of theology and worship which place particular emphasis upon the immediate presence and experience of the Holy Spirit.

Christology The section of Christian theology dealing with the identity of Jesus Christ, particularly the question of the relation of his human and divine natures.

Circumincession See *Perichoresis*.

Conciliarism An understanding of ecclesiastical or theological authority which places an emphasis on the role of ecumenical councils.

Confession Although the term refers primarily to the admission to sin, it acquired a rather different technical sense in the sixteenth century – that of a document which embodies the principles of faith of a Protestant church, such as the Lutheran Augsburg Confession (1530), which embodies the ideas of early Lutheranism, and the Reformed First Helvetic Confession (1536).

Consubstantial A Latin term, deriving from the Greek *homoousios*, literally meaning "of the same substance." The term is used to affirm the full divinity of Jesus Christ, particularly in opposition to Arianism.

Consubstantiation A term used to refer to the theory of the real presence, especially associated with Martin Luther, which holds that the substance of the eucharistic bread and wine are given together with the substance of the body and blood of Christ.

Creed A formal definition or summary of the Christian faith, held in common by all Christians. The most important are those generally known as the "Apostles' Creed" and the "Nicene Creed."

Deism A term used to refer to the views of a group of English writers, especially during the seventeenth century, the rationalism of which anticipated many of the ideas of the Enlightenment. The term is often used to refer to a view of God which recognizes the divine creatorship, yet which rejects the notion of a continuing divine involvement with the world.

Dialectical theology A term used to refer to the early views of the Swiss theologian Karl Barth, which emphasized the "dialectic" between God and humanity.

Docetism An early Christological heresy, which treated Jesus Christ as a purely divine being who only had the "appearance" of being human.

Donatism A movement, centering upon Roman North Africa in the fourth century, which developed a rigorist view of the church and sacraments.

Doxology A form of praise, usually especially associated with formal Christian worship. A "doxological" approach to theology stresses the importance of praise and worship in theological reflection.

Ebionitism An early Christological heresy, which treated Jesus Christ as a purely human figure, although recognizing that he was endowed with particular charismatic gifts which distinguished him from other humans.

Ecclesiology The section of Christian theology dealing with the theory of the church.

Enlightenment, the A term used since the nineteenth century to refer to the emphasis upon human reason and autonomy, characteristic of much of western European and North American thought during the eighteenth century.

Eschatology The section of Christian theology dealing with the "end things," especially the ideas of resurrection, hell, and eternal life.

Eucharist The term used in the present volume to refer to the sacrament variously known as "the mass," "the Lord's Supper," and "holy communion."

Evangelical A term initially used to refer to reforming movements, especially in Germany and Switzerland, in the 1510s and 1520s, but now used of the movement, especially in English-language theology, which places especial emphasis upon the supreme authority of Scripture and the atoning death of Christ.

Exegesis The science of textual interpretation, usually referring specifically to the Bible. The term "biblical exegesis" basically means "the process of interpreting the Bible." The specific techniques employed in the exegesis of Scripture are usually referred to as "hermeneutics."

Exemplarism A particular approach to the atonement, which stresses the moral or religious example set to believers by Jesus Christ.

Fathers An alternative term for "patristic writers."

Feminism A movement in western theology since the 1960s, which lays particular emphasis upon the importance of "women's experience" and has directed criticism against the patriarchalism of Christianity.

Fideism An understanding of Christian theology which refuses to accept the need for (or sometimes the possibility of) criticism or evaluation from sources outside the Christian faith itself.

Five Ways, the A standard term for the five "arguments for the existence of God" associated with Thomas Aquinas.

Fourth gospel A term used to refer to the gospel according to John. The term highlights the distinctive literary and theological character of this gospel, which sets it apart from the common structures of the first three gospels, usually known as the "synoptic gospels."

Fundamentalism A form of American Protestant Christianity, which lays especial emphasis upon the authority of an inerrant Bible.

Hermeneutics The principles underlying the interpretation, or exegesis, of a text, particularly of Scripture, especially in relation to its present-day application.

Hesychasm A tradition, especially associated with the eastern church, which places considerable emphasis upon the idea of "inner quietness" (Greek: *hesychia*) as a means of achieving a vision of God. It is particularly associated with writers such as Simeon the New Theologian and Gregory Palamas.

Historical Jesus A term used, especially during the nineteenth century, to refer to the historical person of Jesus of Nazareth, as opposed to the Christian interpretation of that person, especially as presented in the New Testament and the creeds.

Historico-critical method An approach to historical texts, including the Bible, which argues that proper meaning must be determined only on the basis of the specific historical conditions under which it was written.

History of Religions School The approach to religious history, and Christian origins in particular, which treats Old and New Testament developments as responses to encounters with other religions, such as Gnosticism.

Homoousion A Greek term, literally meaning "of the same substance," which came to be used extensively during the fourth century to designate the mainline Christological belief that Jesus Christ was "of the same substance as God." The term was polemical, being directed against the Arian view that Christ was "of similar substance (*homoiousios*)" to God. See also **Consubstantial**.

Humanism In the strict sense of the word, an intellectual movement linked with the European Renaissance. At the heart of the movement lay, not (as the modern sense of the word might suggest) a set of secular or secularizing ideas, but a new interest in the cultural achievements of antiquity. These were seen as a major resource for the renewal of European culture and Christianity during the period of the Renaissance.

Hypostatic union The doctrine of the union of divine and human natures in Jesus Christ, without confusion of their respective substances.

Ideology A group of beliefs and values, usually secular, which govern the actions and outlooks of a society or group of people.

Incarnation A term used to refer to the assumption of human nature by God, in the person of Jesus Christ. The term "incarnationalism" is often used to refer to theological approaches which lay especial emphasis upon God's becoming human.

Justification by faith, doctrine of The section of Christian theology dealing with how the individual sinner is able to enter into fellowship with God. The doctrine was to prove to be of major significance at the time of the Reformation.

Kenoticism A form of Christology which lays emphasis upon Christ's "laying aside" of certain divine attributes in the incarnation, or his "emptying himself" of at least some divine attributes, especially omniscience or omnipotence.

Kerygma A term used, especially by Rudolf Bultmann (1884–1976) and his followers, to refer to the essential message or proclamation of the New Testament concerning the significance of Jesus Christ.

Liberal Protestantism A movement, especially associated with nineteenth-century Germany, which stressed the continuity between religion and culture, flourishing between the time of F. D. E. Schleiermacher and Paul Tillich.

Liberation theology Although this term designates any theological movement laying emphasis upon the liberating impact of the gospel, the term has come to refer to a movement which developed in Latin America in the late 1960s, which stressed the role of political action and orientated itself towards the goal of political liberation from poverty and oppression.

Liturgy The written text of public services, especially of the eucharist.

Logos A Greek term meaning "word," which played a crucial role in the development of patristic Christology. Jesus Christ was recognized as the "word of God"; the question concerned the implications of this recognition, and especially the way in which the divine "logos" in Jesus Christ related to his human nature.

Lutheranism The religious ideas associated with Martin Luther, particularly as expressed in the Lesser Catechism (1529) and the Augsburg Confession (1530).

Manicheism A strongly fatalist position associated with the Manichees, to which Augustine of Hippo attached himself during his early period. A distinction is drawn between two different divinities, one of which is regarded as evil, and the other good. Evil is thus seen as the direct result of the influence of the evil god.

Modalism A Trinitarian heresy, which treats the three persons of the Trinity as different "modes" of the Godhead. A typical modalist approach is to regard God as active as Father in creation, as Son in redemption, and as Spirit in sanctification.

Monophysitism The doctrine that there is only one nature in Christ, which is divine (from the Greek words *monos*, "only one," and *physis*, "nature"). This view differed from the orthodox view, upheld by the Council of Chalcedon (451), that Christ had two natures, one divine and one human.

Neo-orthodoxy A term used to designate the general position of Karl Barth, especially the manner in which he drew upon the theological concerns of the period of Reformed orthodoxy.

Ontological argument A term used to refer to the type of argument for the existence of God especially associated with the scholastic theologian Anselm of Canterbury.

Orthodoxy A term used in a number of senses, of which the following are the most important: orthodoxy in the sense of "right belief," as opposed to heresy; orthodoxy in the sense of the forms of Christianity which are dominant in Russia and Greece; orthodoxy in the sense of a movement within Protestantism, especially in the late sixteenth and early seventeenth century, which laid emphasis upon need for doctrinal definition.

Parousia A Greek term, which literally means "coming" or "arrival," used to refer to the second coming of Christ. The notion of the *parousia* is an important aspect of Christian understandings of the "last things."

Patripassianism A theological heresy, which arose during the third century, associated with writers such as Noetus, Praxeas, and Sabellius, focusing on the belief that the Father suffered as the Son. In other words, the suffering of Christ on the cross is to be regarded as the suffering of the Father. According to these writers, the only distinction within the Godhead was a succession of modes or operations, so that Father, Son, and Spirit were just different modes of being, or expressions, of the same basic divine entity.

Patristic An adjective used to refer to the first centuries in the history of the church, following the writing of the New Testament (the "patristic period"), or thinkers writing during this period (the "patristic writers"). For many writers, the period thus designated seems to be ca. 100–451 (in other words, the period between the completion of the last of the New Testament writings and the landmark Council of Chalcedon).

Pelagianism An understanding of how humans are able to merit their salvation which is diametrically opposed to that of Augustine of Hippo, placing considerable emphasis upon the role of human works and playing down the idea of divine grace.

Perichoresis A term relating to the doctrine of the Trinity, often also referred to by the Latin term *circumincessio*. The basic notion is that all three persons of the Trinity mutually share in the life of the others, so that none is isolated or detached from the actions of the others.

Pietism An approach to Christianity, especially associated with German writers in the seventeenth century, which places an emphasis upon the personal appropriation of faith, and the need for holiness in Christian living. The movement is perhaps best known within the English-language world in the form of Methodism.

Post-liberalism A theological movement, especially associated with Duke University and Yale Divinity School in the 1980s, which criticized the liberal reliance upon human experience, and reclaimed the notion of community tradition as a controlling influence in theology.

Postmodernism A general cultural development, especially in North America, which resulted from the general collapse in confidence of the universal rational principles of the Enlightenment.

Praxis A Greek term, literally meaning "action," adopted by Karl Marx to emphasize the importance of action in relation to thinking. This emphasis on "praxis" has had considerable impact within Latin American liberation theology.

Protestantism A term used in the aftermath of the Diet of Speyer (1529) to designate those who "protested" against the practices and beliefs of the Roman Catholic church. Prior to 1529, such individuals and groups had referred to themselves as "evangelicals."

Quadriga The Latin term used to refer to the "fourfold" interpretation of Scripture according to its literal, allegorical, tropological (moral), and anagogical senses.

Radical Reformation A term used with increasing frequency to refer to the Anabaptist movement – in other words, the wing of the Reformation which went beyond what Luther and Zwingli envisaged, particularly in relation to the doctrine of the church.

Reformed A term used to refer to a tradition of theology which draws inspiration from the writings of John Calvin and his successors. The term is now generally used in preference to "Calvinist."

Sabellianism An early Trinitarian heresy, which treated the three persons of the Trinity as different historical manifestations of the one God. It is generally regarded as a form of modalism.

Sacrament In purely historical terms, a church service or rite which was held to have been instituted by Jesus Christ himself. Although Roman Catholic theology and church practice recognize seven such sacraments (baptism, confirmation, eucharist, marriage, ordination, penance, and unction), Protestant theologians generally argue that only two (baptism and eucharist) were to be found in the New Testament itself.

Schism A deliberate break with the unity of the church, condemned vigorously by influential writers of the early church, such as Cyprian and Augustine.

Scholasticism A particular approach to Christian theology, associated especially with the Middle Ages, which lays emphasis upon the rational justification and systematic presentation of Christian theology.

Scripture principle The theory, especially associated with Reformed theologians, that the practices and beliefs of the church should be grounded in Scripture. Nothing that could not be demonstrated to be grounded in Scripture could be regarded as binding upon the believer. The phrase *sola scriptura*, "by Scripture alone," summarizes this principle.

Soteriology The section of Christian theology dealing with the doctrine of salvation (Greek: *soteria*).

Synoptic gospels A term used to refer to the first three gospels (Matthew, Mark, and Luke). The term (derived from the Greek word *synopsis*, "summary") refers to the way in which the three gospels can be seen as providing similar "summaries" of the life, death, and resurrection of Jesus Christ.

Synoptic problem The scholarly question of how the three synoptic gospels relate to each other. Perhaps the most common approach to the relation of the three synoptic gospels is the "two-source" theory, which claims that Matthew and Luke used Mark as a source, while also drawing upon a second source (usually known as "Q"). Other possibilities exist: for example, the Grisebach hypothesis, which treats Matthew as having been written first, followed by Luke and then Mark.

Theodicy A term coined by Leibniz to refer to a theoretical justification of the goodness of God in the face of the presence of evil in the world.

Theopaschitism A disputed teaching, regarded by some as a heresy, which arose during the sixth century, associated with writers such as John Maxentius and the slogan "one of the Trinity was crucified." The formula can be interpreted in a perfectly orthodox sense and was defended as such by Leontius of Byzantium. However, it was regarded as potentially misleading and confusing by more cautious writers, including Pope Hormisdas (d. 523), and the formula gradually fell into disuse.

Theotokos Literally, "the bearer of God." A Greek term used to refer to Mary, the mother of Jesus Christ, with the intention of reinforcing the central insight of the doctrine of the incarnation – that is, that Jesus Christ is none other than God. The term was extensively used by writers of the eastern church, especially around the time of the Nestorian controversy, to articulate both the divinity of Christ and the reality of the incarnation.

Transubstantiation The doctrine according to which the bread and the wine are transformed into the body and blood of Christ in the eucharist, while retaining their outward appearance.

Trinity The distinctively Christian doctrine of God, which reflects the complexity of the Christian experience of God. The doctrine is usually summarized in maxims such as "three persons, one God."

Two natures, doctrine of A term generally used to refer to the doctrine of the two natures, human and divine, of Jesus Christ. Related terms include "Chalcedonian definition" and "hypostatic union."

Vulgate The Latin translation of the Bible, largely deriving from Jerome, upon which medieval theology was largely based.

Zwinglianism The term is used generally to refer to the thought of Huldrych Zwingli (1484–1531), but is often used to refer specifically to his views on the sacraments, especially on the "real presence" (which for Zwingli was more of a "real absence").

Further Reading

The present work has introduced a wide range of historical, theological, and practical issues relating to Christianity. What follows is a brief listing of some books for further reading which will allow you to follow up these introductory sections in much greater depth. They are arranged topically, in the order in which material is presented in this work.

For more extensive reading, you are recommended to use the Internet as a source for primary and secondary texts. For example, using any good Internet search engine, you might like to enter the following phrase: "Bibliography ecclesiology." This will immediately lead you to some highly relevant websites concerning books dealing with the doctrine of the church. Again, try entering "bibliography early church history." This will give you immediate access to a series of bibliographies focusing on the life and thought of the early church.

Jesus of Nazareth

Barclay, William, *Jesus as They Saw Him* (London: SCM Press, 1962).

Bauckham, R., R. T. France, M. Maggay, J. Stamoolis, and C. P. Thiede, *Jesus 2000: A Major Investigation into History's Most Intriguing Figure* (Oxford: Lion, 1989).

Brown, R. E., *Jesus, God and Man: Modern Biblical Reflections* (Milwaukee: Bruce, 1967).

Cullmann, Oscar, *The Christology of the New Testament* (Philadelphia: Westminster Press, 1959).

Davis, Stephen T., *Risen Indeed: Making Sense of the Resurrection* (Grand Rapids: Eerdmans, 1993).

Drane, John, *Jesus and the Four Gospels* (Oxford: Lion, 1984).

Dunn, James D. G., *Christology in the Making* (London: SCM Press, 1980).

——, *The Evidence for Jesus* (London: SCM Press, 1986).

France, R. T., *The Evidence for Jesus* (London: Hodder and Stoughton, and Downers Grove, Ill: InterVarsity Press, 1987).

——, *Jesus and the Old Testament* (Downers Grove, Ill: InterVarsity Press, 1971).

Green, Michael, *Who is this Jesus?* (London: Hodder and Stoughton, 1990).

Grillmeier, Aloys, *Christ in Christian Tradition*, 2nd edn (London: Mowbrays, 1976).

Harris, Murray T., *Jesus as God: The New Testament Use of Theos in Reference to Jesus* (Grand Rapids: Baker, 1992).

Hooker, Morna D., "Interchange in Christ," *Journal of Theological Studies* 22 (1971), pp. 349–361.

Käsemann, Ernst, "The Saving Significance of the Death of Jesus in Paul," in *Perspectives on Paul* (Philadelphia: Fortress Press, 1971), pp. 32–59.

Macquarrie, John, *Jesus Christ in Modern Thought* (London: SCM Press, 1990).

Marshall, I. Howard, *The Origins of New Testament Christology* (Downers Grove, Ill: InterVarsity Press, 1976).

Morris, Leon, *The Apostolic Preaching of the Cross*, 3rd edn (Leicester: InterVarsity Press, 1975).

Moule, C. F. D., *The Origin of Christology* (Cambridge: Cambridge University Press, 1977).

O'Collins, Gerald, *Jesus Risen* (London: Darton, Longman, and Todd, 1987).

Pannenberg, Wolfhart, *Jesus – God and Man* (London: SCM Press, and Westminster: Philadelphia, 1968).

Saldarini, A. J., *Pharisees, Scribes and Sadducees in Palestinian Society* (Edinburgh: Clark, 1989).

Stott, J. R. W., *The Cross of Christ* (Leicester: InterVarsity Press, 1986).

Theissen, Gerd, *The Shadow of the Galilean* (London: SCM Press, 1987).

Thiede, C. P., *Jesus – Life or Legend* (Oxford: Lion, 1990).

Wright, N. T., *Who was Jesus?* (London: SPCK and Grand Rapids: Eerdmans, 1992).

The Bible

Anderson, Bernhard W., *The Living World of the Old Testament*, 4th edn (London: Longman, 1988).

Barton, John, *Reading the Old Testament: Method in Biblical Study*, 2nd edn (London: Darton, Longman, and Todd, 1996).

Brown, Raymond E., *An Introduction to the New Testament* (New York: Doubleday, 1997).

Buttrick, George A., *The Interpreter's Dictionary of the Bible: An Illustrated Encyclopedia*, 5 vols. (Nashville, TN: Abingdon Press, 1962).

Carson, D. A., Douglas J. Moo, and Leon Morris, *An Introduction to the New Testament* (Grand Rapids: Zondervan, 1994).

Chilton, Bruce, *Beginning New Testament Study* (London: SPCK, 1986).

Clements, R. E., *The World of Ancient Israel* (Cambridge: Cambridge University Press, 1995).

Dunn, James D. G., *Unity and Diversity in the New Testament*, 2nd edn (London: SCM Press, 1990).

Ehrman, Bart D., *The New Testament: A Historical Introduction to the Early Christian Writings*, 2nd edn (Oxford: Oxford University Press, 2000).

Greenslade, S. L., ed., *The Cambridge History of the Bible*, 3 vols. (Cambridge: Cambridge University Press, 1963).

Gundry, Robert H., *A Survey of the New Testament* (Grand Rapids: Zondervan, 1994).

Johnson, Luke T., *The Writings of the New Testament: An Interpretation* (Philadelphia: Fortress Press, 1986).

Kaiser, Otto, *Introduction to the Old Testament* (Oxford: Blackwell, 1975).

Metzger, Bruce M., *The New Testament: Its Background, Growth and Content* (Nashville, TN: Abingdon, 1983).

—— , and Michael D. Coogan, *The Oxford Companion to the Bible* (Oxford: Oxford University Press, 1994).

Perkins, Pheme, *Reading the New Testament: An Introduction*, 2nd edn (New York: Paulist Press, 1988).

Porter, J. R., *The Illustrated Guide to the Bible* (Oxford: Oxford University Press, 1995).

The Teachings of Christianity

The most widely used introduction to Christian theology is:

McGrath, Alister E., *Christian Theology: An Introduction*, 3rd edn (Oxford and Cambridge, MA: Blackwell, 2001).

This can be used in conjunction with a collection of nearly 300 primary texts, gathered together in:

McGrath, Alister E. (ed.), *The Christian Theology Reader* (Oxford and Cambridge, MA: Blackwell, 1995).

The following are also useful as introductions to this general field, and are all worth exploring.

Braaten, Carl E., and R. W. Jenson (eds.), *Christian Dogmatics*, 2 vols. (Philadelphia: Fortress Press, 1984).

Erickson, Millard J., *Christian Theology* (Grand Rapids: Baker, 1992).

Fiorenza, Francis F., and John P. Galvin, *Systematic Theology: Roman Catholic Perspectives*, 2 vols. (Minneapolis: Fortress Press, 1991); also published as a single-volume edition (Dublin: Gill and Macmillan, 1992).

Grenz, Stanley J., *Theology for the Community of God* (Nashville, TN: Broadman and Holman, 1994).

Gunton, Colin E., *The Cambridge Companion to Christian Doctrine* (Cambridge: Cambridge University Press, 1997).

Hodgson, Peter C., and Robert H. King (eds.), *Christian Theology: An Introduction to its Traditions and Tasks*, 2nd edn (Philadelphia: Fortress, 1985).

Migliore, Daniel E., *Faith Seeking Understanding*, 2nd edn (Grand Rapids: Eerdmans, 2004).

Tanner, Kathryn, *Jesus, Humanity and the Trinity: A Brief Systematic Theology* (Edinburgh: T&T Clark, 2001).

The History of Christianity

There are many overviews of Christian history as a whole, as well as specific studies of individual periods or issues. The following are recommended as general overall surveys.

Bainton, Roland H., *Christendom: A Short History of Christianity and its Impact on Western Civilization*, 2 vols. (New York: Harper and Row, 1966).

Dowley, Tim, and David F. Wright, *Introduction to the History of Christianity* (Minneapolis: Fortress Press, 1995).

González, Justo L., *The Story of Christianity* (San Francisco: Harper and Row, 1984).

Livingstone, Elizabeth A., and F. L. Cross, *The Oxford Dictionary of the Christian Church*, 3rd edn (Oxford: Oxford University Press, 1997).

Noll, Mark A., *Turning Points: Decisive Moments in the History of Christianity*, 2nd edn (Grand Rapids: Baker Books, 2000).

Petry, Ray C., and Manschreck, Clyde L., *A History of Christianity: Readings in the History of the Early and Medieval Church*, 2 vols. (London: Prentice-Hall, 1962).

The patristic period

Bettenson, Henry, *Documents of the Christian Church*, 2nd edn (Oxford: Oxford University Press, 1963).

Brown, Peter, *The Rise of Western Christendom*, 2nd edn (Oxford: Blackwell, 2003).

Chadwick, Henry, *The Early Church* (London and New York: Pelican, 1964).

Comby, Jean, *How to Read Church History*, vol. 1 (London: SCM Press, 1985).

Daniélou, Jean, and Henri Marrou, *The Christian Centuries*, vol. 1 (London: Darton, Longman, and Todd, 1964).

Frend, W. H. C., *The Rise of Christianity* (Philadelphia: Fortress Press, 1984).

Hazlett, Ian (ed.), *Early Christianity: Origins and Evolution to A.D. 600* (London: SPCK, 1991).

Kelly, J. N. D., *Early Christian Doctrines*, 4th edn (London: A. and C. Black, 1968).

Stevenson, J., *Creeds, Councils and Controversies: Documents Illustrating the History of the Church, 337–461*, rev. edn (London: SPCK, 1987).

——, *A New Eusebius: Documents Illustrating the History of the Church to A.D. 337*, rev. edn (London: SPCK, 1987).

van der Meer, F., and Christine Mohrmann, *Atlas of the Early Christian World* (London: Nelson, 1959).

Young, Frances M., *From Nicea to Chalcedon* (London: SCM Press, 1983).

Women in early Christianity

Arlandson, James Malcolm, *Women, Class, and Society in Early Christianity: Models from Luke–Acts* (Peabody, MA: Hendrickson Publishers, 1997).

Eisen, Ute E., *Women Officeholders in Early Christianity: Epigraphical and Literary Studies* (Collegeville, MN: Liturgical Press, 2000).

Hooker, Morna, "Authority on Her Head: An Examination of 1 Corinthians 11:10," *New Testament Studies* 10 (1964), pp. 410–416.

Jensen, Anne, *God's Self-Confident Daughters: Early Christianity and the Liberation of Women* (Kampen: Kok Pharos, 1996).

Laporte, Jean, *The Role of Women in Early Christianity* (New York: Edwin Mellen Press, 1982).

Matthews, Shelly, *First Converts: Rich Pagan Women and the Rhetoric of Mission in Early Judaism and Christianity* (Stanford, CA: Stanford University Press, 2001).

Scholer, David M., *Women in Early Christianity* (New York: Garland, 1993).

Thomas, W. D., "The Place of Women in the Church at Philippi," *Expository Times* 83 (1971), pp. 117–120.

Witherington III, Ben, *Women in the Earliest Churches* (Cambridge: Cambridge University Press, 1988).

——, *Women in the Ministry of Jesus* (Cambridge: Cambridge University Press, 1984).

Celtic Christianity

Gougaud, Louis, *Christianity in Celtic Lands* (London: Batsford, 1981).

Hanson, Richard T., *Saint Patrick: His Origins and Career* (Oxford: Oxford University Press, 1968).

Mackey, James P. (ed.), *An Introduction to Celtic Christianity* (Edinburgh: T. and T. Clarke, 1989).

Simpson, Douglas, *The Celtic Church in Scotland* (Aberdeen: Aberdeen University Press, 1935).

The Middle Ages and Renaissance

Burke, Peter, *The Italian Renaissance: Culture and Society in Italy*, rev. edn (Oxford: Polity Press, 1986).

Coplestone, Frederick, *A History of Christian Philosophy in the Middle Ages* (London: Sheed and Ward, 1978).

Crummey, Robert O., *The Formation of Muscovy, 1304–1613* (London: Longman, 1987), pp. 116–142.

Fleischer, Manfred P. (ed.), *The Harvest of Humanism in Central Europe* (St. Louis, MO: Concordia Publishing House, 1992).

Herrin, Judith, *The Formation of Christendom* (Princeton: Princeton University Press, 1987).

Hussey, J. M., *The Orthodox Church in the Byzantine Empire* (Oxford: Clarendon Press, 1986).

McGrath, Alister E., *The Intellectual Foundations of the European Reformation*, 2nd edn (Oxford: Blackwell, 2003).

Magoulias, Harry J., *Byzantine Christianity: Emperor, Church, and the West* (Chicago: Rand McNally, 1970).

Meyendorff, John, *Byzantine Theology: Historical Trends and Doctrinal Themes*, 2nd edn (New York: Fordham University Press, 1983).

Oberman, Heiko A., *Masters of the Reformation* (Cambridge: Cambridge University Press, 1981).

O'Malley, John W., Thomas M. Izbicki, and Gerald Christianson (eds.), *Humanity and Divinity in the Renaissance and Reformation* (Leiden: Brill, 1993).

Overfeld, J. H., *Humanism and Scholasticism in Late Medieval Germany* (Princeton, NJ: Princeton University Press, 1984).

Ozment, Steven E., *The Age of Reform 1250–1550: An Intellectual and Religious History of Late Medieval and Reformation Europe* (New Haven: Yale University Press, 1973).

Pieper, Josef, *Scholasticism: Personalities and Problems of Medieval Philosophy* (London: Faber and Faber, 1961).

Porter, Roy, and Mikulbais Teich (eds.), *The Renaissance in National Context* (Cambridge: Cambridge University Press, 1992).

Price, B. B., *Medieval Thought: An Introduction* (Oxford and Cambridge, MA: Blackwell, 1992).

Spitz, Lewis W., *The Religious Renaissance of the German Humanists* (Cambridge, MA: Harvard University Press, 1963).

The Reformation and post-Reformation periods

Bossy, John, *Christianity in the West* (Oxford: Oxford University Press, 1985).

Cameron, Euan, *The European Reformation* (Oxford: Oxford University Press, 1991).

Chadwick, Owen, *The Reformation* (London and New York: Pelican, 1976).

Elton, G. R. (ed.), *The Reformation 1520–1559*, 2nd edn (Cambridge: Cambridge University Press, 1990).

Iserloh, Erwin, Joseph Glazik, Hubert Jedin, Anselm Biggs, and Peter W. Becker, *Reformation and Counter-Reformation* (London: Burns and Oates, 1980).

Jones, Martin D. W., *The Counter-Reformation: Religion and Society in Early Modern Europe* (Cambridge: Cambridge University Press, 1995).

McGrath, Alister E., *Reformation Thought: An Introduction*, 3rd edn (Oxford and Cambridge, MA: Blackwell, 1999).

Noll, Mark A., *Confessions and Catechisms of the Reformation* (Grand Rapids: Eerdmans, 1991).

Reardon, B. M. G., *Religious Thought in the Reformation* (London: Longman, 1981).

Spitz, Lewis W., *The Protestant Reformation 1517–1559* (New York: Scribner's, 1986).

Stoeffler, Fred E., *German Pietism During the Eighteenth Century* (Leiden: E. J. Brill, 1973).

White, Carol, *Reformation and Counter-Reformation* (Harlow: Longman, 1995).

Wright, A. D., *The Early Modern Papacy: From the Council of Trent to the French Revolution, 1564–1789* (Harlow: Longman, 2000).

Yeide, Harry, *Studies in Classical Pietism: The Flowering of the Ecclesiola* (New York: Peter Lang, 1997).

The modern period

Ahlstrom, Sydney E., *A Religious History of the American People* (New Haven, CT: Yale University Press, 1972).

Aston, Nigel, *Christianity and Revolutionary Europe, c.1750–1830* (Cambridge: Cambridge University Press, 2002).

Chadwick, Owen, *The Victorian Church*, 2 vols. (London: Black, 1966–1970).

Edwards, David F., *The Futures of Christianity* (London: Hodder and Stoughton, 1987).

Emilsen, Susan E., and William W. Emilsen, *Mapping the Landscape: Essays in Australian and New Zealand Christianity* (New York: Peter Lang, 2000).

Gaustad, Edwin S., *A Documentary History of Religion in America*, 2 vols. (Grand Rapids: Eerdmans, 1993).

Hastings, Adrian, *A History of English Christianity 1920–1985* (London: Collins, 1986).

Jedin, Hubert, *The Church in the Modern World* (New York: Crossroad, 1993).

Latourette, Kenneth S., *Christianity in a Revolutionary Age*, 5 vols. (New York: Harper, 1958–1962).

McManners, John, *Church and State in France 1870–1914* (London: SPCK, 1972).

Mead, Sydney E., *The Lively Experiment: The Shaping of Christianity in America* (New York: Harper and Row, 1963).

Norman, Edward R., *Church and Society in England, 1770–1970* (Oxford: Clarendon Press, 1976).

Christianity in the Developing World

Appiah-Kubi, Kofi, and Sergio Torres (eds.), *African Theology En Route* (Maryknoll, NY: Orbis Books, 1979).

Boyd, Robin S. H., *Introduction to Indian Christian Theology*, 2nd edn (Madras: CLT, 1974).

Dryness, William A. (ed.), *Emerging Voices in Global Theology* (Grand Rapids: Zondervan, 1995).

——, *Learning about Theology from the Third World* (Grand Rapids: Zondervan, 1992).

Elphick, Richard, and T. R. H. Davenport, *Christianity in South Africa: A Political, Social, and Cultural History* (Los Angeles: University of California Press, 1997).

Gispert-Sauch, SJ, George, "Asian Theology," in D. F. Ford (ed.), *The Modern Theologians*, 2nd edn (Oxford and Cambridge, MA: Blackwell, 2005), pp. 455–476.

Goodpasture, H. McKennie, *Cross and Sword: An Eyewitness History of Christianity in Latin America* (Maryknoll, NY: Orbis Books, 1989).

Isichei, Elizabeth, *A History of Christianity in Africa* (London: SPCK, 1995).

Kalu, O. U., *The History of Christianity in West Africa* (London: Longman, 1980).

Lande, Aasulv, *Meiji Protestantism in History and Historiography: A Comparative Study of Japanese* and Western Interpretation of Early Protestantism in Japan (Frankfurt am Main: Peter Lang, 1989).

Latourette, Kenneth Scott, A History of the Expansion of Christianity (London: Eyre and Spottiswoode, 1941).

Lee, Joseph Tse-Hei, The Bible and the Gun: Christianity in South China, 1860–1900. East Asia: History, Politics, Sociology, Culture (New York: Routledge, 2003).

Lee, Jung Young, "Korean Christian Thought," in A. E. McGrath (ed.), The Blackwell Encyclopaedia of Modern Christian Thought (Oxford and Cambridge, MA: Blackwell, 1993), pp. 308–313.

Moffett, Samuel Hugh, A History of Christianity in Asia (San Francisco: HarperSanFrancisco, 1992).

Neill, Stephen Charles, A History of Christianity in India, 2 vols. (Cambridge: Cambridge University Press, 1984–1985).

Parratt, John (ed.), A Reader in African Christian Theology (London: SPCK, 1987).

Song, C. S., Third-Eye Theology: Theology in Formation in Asian Settings, rev. edn (Maryknoll, NY: Orbis, 1990).

Sugirtharajah, R. S., and C. Hargreaves (eds.), Readings in Indian Christian Theology (London: SPCK, 1993).

Takayanagi, Shunici, "Japanese Christian Thought," in A. E. McGrath (ed.), The Blackwell Encyclopaedia of Modern Christian Thought (Oxford and Cambridge, MA: Blackwell, 1993), pp. 280–284.

Ustorf, Werner, and Toshiko Murayama, Identity and Marginality: Rethinking Christianity in North East Asia (Frankfurt am Main: Peter Lang, 2000).

Yu, Carver T., "Chinese Christian Thought," in A. E. McGrath (ed.), The Blackwell Encyclopaedia of Modern Christian Thought (Oxford and Cambridge, MA: Blackwell, 1993), pp. 71–77.

Modern Forms of Christianity

Anderson, Robert M., Vision of the Disinherited: The Making of American Pentecostalism (New York: Oxford University Press, 1979).

Baker, Robert A. (ed.), A Baptist Source Book (Nashville, TN: Broadman, 1966).

Bett, Henry, The Spirit of Methodism (London: Epworth Press, 1937).

Blumhofer, Edith Waldvogel, Restoring the Faith: The Assemblies of God, Pentecostalism, and American Culture (Urbana: University of Illinois Press, 1993).

Bucke, Emory S., The History of American Methodism (New York: Abingdon Press, 1964).

Bunting, Ian (ed.), Celebrating the Anglican Way (London: Hodder and Stoughton, 1996).

Corten, André, Pentecostalism in Brazil: Emotion of the Poor and Theological Romanticism (New York: St. Martin's Press, 1999).

Davies, Rupert E., Methodism (London: Epworth Press, 1976).

Elert, Werner, The Structure of Lutheranism (St. Louis, MO: Concordia, 1962).

George, Timothy, and David S. Dockery, Baptist Theologians (Nashville, TN: Broadman, 1990).

Hollenweger, Walter J., Pentecostalism: Origins and Developments Worldwide (Peabody, MA: Hendrickson, 1997).

Leith, John H., Introduction to the Reformed Tradition (Atlanta, GA: John Knox Press, 1981).

McBeth, H. Leon, The Baptist Heritage (Nashville, TN: Broadman, 1987).

McGrath, Alister E., Evangelicalism and the Future of Christianity (Downers Grove, IL: InterVarsity Press, 1995).

McKee, Elsie Anne, and Brian G. Armstrong, Probing the Reformed Tradition (Louisville, KY: Westminster/John Knox Press, 1989).

McKim, Donald K. (ed.), Major Themes in the Reformed Tradition (Grand Rapids: Eerdmans, 1992).

Martin, David, Tongues of Fire: The Explosion of Protestantism in Latin America (Oxford: Blackwell, 1990).

Meyendorff, John, The Orthodox Church, 3rd edn (Crestwood, NY: St. Vladimir's Seminary Press, 1981).

Quebedeaux, Richard, The New Charismatics: The Origins, Developments and Significance of Neo-Pentecostalism (New York: Doubleday, 1976).

Roof, Wade Clark, and William McKinney, American Mainline Religion: Its Changing Shape and

Future (Princeton: Rutgers University Press, 1987).

Samuel, Vinay, and Christopher Sugden, *Lambeth: A View from the Two Thirds World* (London: SPCK, 1989).

Stoll, David, *Is Latin America Turning Protestant?* (Berkeley: University of California Press, 1991).

Sykes, Stephen W., and John Booty (eds.), *The Study of Anglicanism* (London: SPCK, 1988).

Wagner, C. Peter, *The Third Wave of the Holy Spirit: Encountering the Power of Signs and Wonders Today* (Ann Arbor: Servant, 1988).

Christian living

Adam, Adolf, *The Liturgical Year: Its History and its Meaning After the Reform of the Liturgy* (Collegeville, MN: Liturgical Press, 1981).

Bartholomew, Craig G., and Fred Hughes, *Explorations in a Christian Theology of Pilgrimage* (Aldershot: Ashgate, 2004).

Bony, Jean, *The English Decorated Style: Gothic Architecture Transformed 1250–1350* (Oxford: Phaidon Press, 1979).

Cowie, Leonard W., and John Selwyn Gummer, *The Christian Calendar: A Complete Guide to the Seasons of the Christian Year, Telling the Story of Christ and the Saints from Advent to Pentecost* (London: Weidenfeld and Nicolson, 1974).

Dillenberger, Jane, *Style and Content in Christian Art* (London: SCM Press, 1986).

Dowell, Graham, *The Heart Has Seasons: Travelling through the Christian Year* (Worthing: Churchman, 1989).

Duchesne, Louis, *Christian Worship: Its Origins and Evolution* (London: SPCK, 1949).

Foley, Edward, *From Age to Age* (Chicago: Liturgy Training Publications, 1991).

Garrett, Thomas S., *Christian Worship: An Introductory Outline* (Oxford: Oxford University Press, 1963).

Giakalis, Ambrosios, and Henry Chadwick, *Images of the Divine in the Eastern Orthodox Church: The Theology of Icons at the Seventh Ecumenical Council* (Leiden: E. J. Brill, 1994).

Guéron, René, *The Symbolism of the Cross* (London: Luzac, 1958).

Jasper, David, *The Study of Literature and Religion: An Introduction* (Basingstoke: Macmillan, 1989).

Jefferson, H. A. L., *Hymns in Christian Worship* (London: Rockliff, 1950).

Kemp, Wolfgang, *The Narratives of Gothic Stained Glass* (Cambridge: Cambridge University Press, 1997).

Ladner, Gerhart B., *God, Cosmos, and Humankind: The World of Early Christian Symbolism* (Berkeley, CA: University of California Press, 1995).

Laliberté, Norman, and Edward N. West, *The History of the Cross* (New York: Macmillan, 1960).

LaVerdiere, Eugene, *The Breaking of the Bread: The Development of the Eucharist According to Acts* (Chicago: Liturgy Training Publications, 1998).

Lillich, Meredith P., *The Armor of Light: Stained Glass in Western France, 1250–1325* (Berkeley: University of California Press, 1993).

McArthur, Allen A., *The Evolution of the Christian Year* (London: SCM Press, 1953).

Nocent, Adrian, *The Liturgical Year*, 4 vols. (Collegeville: Liturgical Press, 1986–1988).

Nolan, Mary Lee, and Sidney Nolan, *Christian Pilgrimage in Modern Western Europe* (Chapel Hill: University of North Carolina Press, 1989).

Nye, Thelma M., *An Introduction to Parish Church Architecture, AD 600–1965* (London: Batsford, 1965).

Panofsky, E., *Gothic Architecture and Scholasticism* (London: Thames and Hudson, 1948).

Raguin, Virginia Chieffo, and Mary Clerkin Higgins, *The History of Stained Glass: The Art of Light Medieval to Contemporary* (London: Thames and Hudson, 2003).

Routley, Erik, *The Church and Music: An Enquiry into the History, the Nature, and the Scope of Christian Judgement on Music* (London: Duckworth, 1978).

Rubin, Miri, *Corpus Christi: The Eucharist in Late Medieval Culture* (New York: Cambridge University Press, 1991).

Schiller, Gertrud, *Iconography of Christian Art*, 2 vols. (London: Lund Humphries, 1971).

Self, David, *High Days and Holidays: Celebrating the Christian Year* (Oxford: Lion, 1993).

Takenaka, Masao, *The Place Where God Dwells: An Introduction to Church Architecture in Asia* (Hong Kong: Christian Conference of Asia, 1995).

Taylor, Richard, *How to Read a Church: An Illustrated Guide to Images, Symbols and Meanings in Churches and Cathedrals* (London: Rider, 2004).

Turner, Victor, and Edith Turner, *Image and Pilgrimage in Christian Culture: Anthropological Perspectives* (Oxford: Blackwell, 1978).

White, James F., *A Brief History of Christian Worship* (Nashville: Abingdon Press, 1993).

Wilson-Dickson, Andrew, *A Brief History of Christian Music: From Biblical Times to the Present* (Oxford: Lion, 1997).

Wright, T. R., *Theology and Literature* (Oxford: Blackwell, 1988).

Index

Page references in *italic* are to illustrations.